UNRECONCILED

UN RECONCILED

From Racial Reconciliation
to Racial Justice in
Christian Evangelicalism

Andrea Smith

DUKE UNIVERSITY PRESS
Durham and London   2019

© 2019 Duke University Press
All rights reserved
Designed and typeset in Minion and Fira Sans
by Julie Allred, BW&A Books

Library of Congress Cataloging-in-Publication Data
Names: Smith, Andrea, [date] author.
Title: Unreconciled : from racial reconciliation to racial justice in Christian Evangelicalism / Andrea Smith.
Description: Durham : Duke University Press, 2019. | Includes bibliographical references and index.
Identifiers:
LCCN 2019013457 (print)
LCCN 2019016273 (ebook)
ISBN 9781478007036 (ebook)
ISBN 9781478005360 (hardcover : alk. paper)
ISBN 9781478006404 (pbk. : alk. paper)
Subjects: LCSH: Racism—Religious aspects—Christianity. | Reconciliation—Religious aspects—Christianity. | Race relations—Religious aspects—Christianity. | Evangelicalism. Classification: LCC BT734.2 (ebook) | LCC BT 734.2 .S658 2019 (print) | DDC 277.3/083089—dc23
LC record available at https://lccn.loc.gov/2019013457

Cover art: Design and illustration by Drew Sisk

To
Sunjay and Tsali Smith,

everyone involved in Evangelicals 4 Justice, NAIITS,
Liberating Evangelicalism, and Killjoy Prophets,

and the memory of James Hal Cone, Richard Leo Twiss,
and Wendy Beauchemin Peterson

CONTENTS

Abbreviations   ix

INTRODUCTION   1

1   FROM CHIT'LINS TO CAVIAR
    Evangelical Multiculturalism   30

2   "WE DON'T HAVE A SKIN PROBLEM, WE HAVE A SIN PROBLEM"
    Racial Reconciliation and the Permanency of Racism   53

3   MULTIPLE LOGICS OF WHITE SUPREMACY   90

4   THE BIOPOLITICS OF CHRISTIAN PERSECUTION   116

5   THE RACIALIZATION OF RELIGION
    Islamophobia and Christian Zionism   142

6   DECOLONIZATION IN UNEXPECTED PLACES   192

7   NO PERMANENT FRIENDS AND ENEMIES   211

8   WOMEN OF COLOR EVANGELICAL THEOLOGIES   250

    CONCLUSION   Between Black Lives Matter
    and Donald Trump   269

Notes   287
A Note on Sources   305
Bibliography   307
Index   377

ABBREVIATIONS

AIM	American Indian Movement
AIPAC	American Israel Public Affairs Committee
BDS	Boycott, Divestment, and Sanctions
BLM	Black Lives Matter
CBA	Christian Booksellers Association
CCDA	Christian Community Development Association
CIA	Central Intelligence Agency
CUFI	Christians United for Israel
CUIC	Churches Uniting in Christ
DOMA	Defense of Marriage Act
ERLC	Ethics and Religious Liberty Commission
ICEJ	International Christian Embassy Jerusalem
IJM	International Justice Mission
IRD	Institute of Religion and Democracy
IRS	Internal Revenue Service
KKK	Ku Klux Klan
LCJE	Lausanne Consultation on Jewish Evangelism
LGBT	Lesbian, Gay, Bisexual, and Transgender
NAE	National Association of Evangelicals
NAIITS	North American Institute for Indigenous Theological Studies
NARAL	National Abortion and Reproductive Rights Action League
NBEA	National Black Evangelical Association
NGO	nongovernmental organization
NPIC	nonprofit industrial complex
NRB	National Religious Broadcasters
PCCNA	Pentecostal/Charismatic Churches of North America
PCUSA	Presbyterian Church USA
PIC	Prison industrial complex
PICO	People Improving Communities through Organizing
PK	Promise Keepers

PUSH	People United to Serve Humanity
RCA	Reformed Church of America
SBC	Southern Baptist Convention
SIM	Serving in Mission
USDA	U.S. Department of Agriculture
VBS	Vacation Bible School
WCC	World Council of Churches
WCGIP	World Christian Gathering of Indigenous Peoples

INTRODUCTION

Under the gospel, [slavery] has brought within the range of gospel influence, millions of Ham's descendants among ourselves, who, but for this institution, would have sunk down to eternal ruin; knowing not God, and strangers to the Gospel. In their bondage here on earth, they have been much better provided for, and great multitudes of them have been made the freemen of the Lord Jesus Christ and left this world rejoicing in hope of the glory of God.—Pastor Thornton Stringfellow, 1860 (E. N. Elliott & J. H. Hammond, 1968, 491)

I mean, there is no excuse that I can think of for choking a man to death for selling illegal cigarettes. This is about cigarettes. This isn't a violent confrontation. This isn't a threat that anybody has reported, a threat of someone being killed. This is someone being choked to death. We have it on video with the man pleading for his life. There is no excuse for that I can even contemplate or imagine right now. . . . Romans 13 says that the sword of justice is to be wielded against evildoers. Now, what we too often see still is a situation where our African-American brothers and sisters, especially brothers, are more likely to be arrested, more likely to be executed, more likely to be killed. And this is a situation in which we have to say, I wonder what the defenders of this would possibly say. I just don't know. But I think we have to acknowledge that something is wrong with the system at this point and that something has to be done. . . . When we've got police officers killing a man on video with a chokehold, can we not say there are still some problems in American society when it comes to race?—Russell Moore (2014), president of the Ethics and Religious Liberty Commission of the Southern Baptist Convention

A Tale of Two Southern Baptist Conventions

It would not be an exaggeration to say that the Southern Baptist Convention (SBC) organized in 1845 on the foundation of slavery, anti-Blackness, and white supremacy. The SBC broke away from Northern Baptists when the larger Baptist association prevented an elder from a slaveholding church from becoming a missionary. Slaveholding Baptists organized the SBC, which supported slavery, in Augusta, Georgia. The SBC eventually apologized for slavery in 1995. But it was not until Russell Moore became president of the Ethics and Religious Liberty Commission in 2013 that we began to see the SBC explicitly address institutionalized racism in a sustained way. Moore spoke out against racism in policing, anti-immigration organizing, and the Trump campaign.

What explains this shift? This book is focused less on Moore, who has received considerable attention for his position, and more on lesser-known organizers for racial justice (particularly women of color) within Christian evangelicalism,[1] which has enabled prominent figures to begin to shift their position. As discussed in chapter 8, organizers and thought leaders such as Zakiya Jackson, Christena Cleveland, AnaYelsi Velasco-Sanchez, Austin Channing Brown, Brenda Salter McNeil, Angela Parker, Elizabeth Conde-Frazier, Jenny Yang, Lenore Three Stars, Cheryl Bear, Shari Russell, Micky ScottBey Jones, Alexia Salvatierra, Nikki Toyama-Szeto, Lisa Sharon Harper, Chanequa Walker-Barnes, Kathy Khang, Mayra Macedo-Nolan, Erna Kim Hackett, Emily Rice, Evelmyn Ivens, Sandra Van Opstal, and countless others demonstrate that radical racial justice organizing through a critical ethnic studies lens is happening across diverse communities and has the potential to shift racial politics in the future.

Evangelicalism and Critical Ethnic Studies

> Theoretical formulations by white European thinkers are granted general applicability while those uttered from the purview of minority discourse that speak to the same questions are almost exclusively relegated to the jurisdiction of ethnographic locality.—Alexander G. Weheliye (2014, 6)

> I contend that Christian theology and scholarship will remain "provincial" as long as some major challenges continue unaddressed [such as] the perception of indigenous Christian scholars as purveyors of exotic

> raw intellectual material. . . . Indigenous theologians are . . . relegated to the museums of theological curiosity just like their cultures. We are then left with this: the West claiming to produce universal theology and the rest writing to articulate fundamental theology that will make [them] equal partners in the theological circles that determine what is theologically normative.—Tite Tiénou (2005, 16–17)

Alexander Weheliye speaks of the need to develop a critical ethnic studies approach to intellectual inquiry in which ethnic studies goes beyond the positioning of communities of color as ethnographic objects of study. Rather, the theoretical analysis emerging out of critical ethnic studies is one that fundamentally challenges the epistemological frameworks of Western scholarship itself. As ethnic studies has generally developed along identity lines (Asian American studies, Native American studies, etc.), it has done critical work that provides the foundation for looking at intersections of racism, colonialism, immigration, and slavery in the U.S. context. However, this identity-based approach also has its limits, necessitating the development of a critical ethnic studies, which is poised to interrogate the structures in which it can find itself. Ethnic studies often becomes mired in an identity politics that advances what Elizabeth Povinelli describes as "social difference without social significance" (Povinelli, 2002, 16). In this context, critical ethnic studies has emerged to build intellectual and political projects that do not dismiss identity but instead are structured around the *logics* of white supremacy, colonialism, capitalism, heteropatriarchy, and so forth in order to expand its scope. Such a shift in focus is significant in providing a space for all scholars to be part of an engagement with critical ethnic studies, because these logics structure all of society, not just those who are "racialized." As Denise Da Silva points out in her defining text on raciality, the entire Western epistemological system is governed through logics of raciality that fundamentally shape what we even consider to be human (Silva, 2007).

Yet, as Tite Tiénou (professor at Trinity Evangelical Divinity School) suggests in the epigraph at the beginning of this section, critical ethnic studies analyses are not confined to the academy or even to groups that we would see as necessarily being on the "left." He makes a critical ethnic studies claim about Christian evangelicalism: that evangelicalism is only willing to tolerate evangelicals of color to the extent that they can be safely incorporated within white evangelicalism—or, as Povinelli might say, they add theological difference without theological consequence. While evangelical critiques may not use the same terminology as those speaking in more secular critical ethnic studies venues, they are in fact critiquing settler colonialism, white supremacy, and capitalism as well as engaging in movements to challenge them and reconstruct alternative versions of Christian evangelicalism. And in many cases the intellectual trends within Christian evangelicalism and more secular critical ethnic studies circles are not simply similar or parallel but actually intersecting. The continuity of ideas from critical ethnic studies to Christian evangelicalism troubles the notion that critical ethnic studies is a marginal intellectual project that only informs academic elites; in fact, these ideas are actually informing the attempts to create new forms of Christian evangelicalism. Thus, the project of critical ethnic studies is an expansive one capable of informing movements across political, religious, and academic divides.

In that spirit, this book focuses on what possibilities emerge when Christian evangelicalism is positioned within a critical ethnic studies framework through a study of racial justice organizing within Christian evangelicalism. In particular, it focuses on the racial reconciliation movement that developed within Christian evangelicalism beginning in the 1990s. The racial reconciliation movement within conservative evangelicalism began with the aim of promoting racial harmony within evangelical churches in general and within Christian evangelical political activism in particular. The goals of this movement were articulated by Ralph Reed, then head of the Christian Coalition:

> There's no question that white evangelical Protestants, especially in the South, were not only on the sidelines but were on the wrong side of the most central struggle for civil justice of the twentieth century, namely the struggle for civil rights. . . . Until the pro-family, religious conservative movement becomes a truly biracial or multi-racial movement, it will not have moral resonance with the American people, because we were so wrong at that time. I want the Christian Coalition to be a truly rainbow coalition. I want it to be black, brown, yellow, white. I want it to bring Christians of all faith traditions, all denominations, and all races and colors together. I don't think that's going to happen overnight. It's going to take years, but we're committed to it. (quoted in Martin, 1996, 365–66)

Since the early 1990s numerous books on the topic of racial reconciliation have appeared as well as an increasing number of articles in conservative Christian periodicals that have focused on racism and the role of people of color in conservative Christian communities. Most prominent white evangelical organizations have issued statements advocating racial reconciliation. The purpose of racial reconciliation, as racial reconciliationist Tony Evans puts it, was to "establish a church where everyone of any race or status who walks through the door is loved and respected as part of God's creation and family" (T. Evans, 1990, 157).

The impact of this movement has been far-reaching, shaping everything from electoral politics to the formations of new evangelical churches. Because of the presumption within the secular academy that evangelicals, particularly evangelicals of color, are necessarily and singularly politically conservative, there is often not much engagement between these critical ethnic studies projects across religious divides. And yet people of color have not just been involved in this racial reconciliation movement but have developed analysis and critique about this movement as well as larger critiques of the white supremacist, colonial, and imperial nature of evangelical Christianity.

The Christian Right, or Christian evangelicalism more generally, is often portrayed as the "permanent enemy" of liberal democracy. By this I mean that some constituencies can be marked as politically intractable and necessarily antagonistic to social justice struggles. Consequently, liberal democracy's investment in a white supremacist, capitalist status quo goes unremarked. In addition, secularism is presumed necessarily to be the site of political and social tolerance rather than itself also being equally mired in the logics of white supremacy and colonialism, as Vine Deloria Jr. pointed out many years ago (Deloria, 1992).

Liberal democracy's investment in creating permanent enemies so that some sectors are presumed to be on the side of righteousness and others necessarily on the side of injustice also coincides with the development of the nonprofit industrial complex's model of activism. Dylan Rodriguez defines the nonprofit industrial complex as the set of symbiotic relationships that link together political and financial technologies of state and owning class control and surveillance over public political ideology, including and especially emergent progressive and leftist social movements (D. Rodriguez, 2009a, 22–23). He and Ruth Wilson Gilmore argue that the nonprofit industrial complex (NPIC) is the natural corollary to the prison industrial complex (PIC): while the PIC overtly represses dissent, the NPIC manages and controls dissent through incorporating it into the state apparatus. Gilmore explains that NPIC is a shadow state in that it is constituted by a network of institutions doing much of the work that the state used to do through taxation, such as providing education and social services (Gilmore, 2017). The NPIC functions as an alibi for the state, allowing it to make war, expand punishment, and proliferate market economies under the veil of public/private partnerships.

The NPIC impacts how activists organize for social change. In particular, the logic of funder-driven nonprofits diverts activists' attention from grassroots organizing to grant administration—short-term activist or advocacy projects that are funder-friendly—rather than to the slow process of building mass movements of change (Incite, 2007). To end global oppression, it would be necessary to engage in broad-based building work that engages mass numbers of people to topple the system. To accomplish this goal, it becomes necessary to find ways to engage people who do not think as you do, but who, through a politics of rearticulation, may begin to see a long-term interest in struggling for social change. The strategies often employed by the NPIC, however, organize around a "permanent" enemy, such as the "Tea Party," "Christian Right," or "Pro-Life Movement." If these huge sectors of the population remain permanent enemies, it can be guaranteed that progressive movements will never actually build large enough movements to change the system. Creating these permanent enemies provides a space to vent righteous anger but ensures that the system causing this anger will stay in place permanently.

This logic of organizing around a permanent enemy continues even within more radical groups that critique the NPIC. Soon the enemy is not only the Tea Party but other progressives who do not toe the correct party line. The NPIC soon becomes replaced by revolutionary chic, where progressives content themselves with having the most racial political analysis without any concern for actually building movements that can dismantle white supremacy. Unfortunately, progressive movements tend to present two equally unsatisfactory alternatives: either silence around racism within political groups in order to maintain a "united front" for justice or endless witch hunts to root out counterrevolutionaries. This situation suggests not that we should avoid internal critique but that there may be a different way to do critique. This book proposes that some of these possibilities may exist in unexpected places, specifically, Christian evangelicalism.

Given, then, that the logics of domination also structure the way we think to resist and how we even critique how we resist, there is not a clear "correct" alternative way forward. Rather, this context suggests a "revolution by trial and error" approach. It also suggests that we may look to unexpected places for guidance. In particular, this book suggests that Christian evangelicalism, and the Christian Right in particular, should not only be the object of racial critique but perhaps may also be a site and source for new possibilities for engaging racial critique and racial justice work. In doing so, I hope to question what we presume ethnic studies to be. In these times of ethnic studies bans and cutbacks in Arizona and elsewhere, it is easy to panic about the future of ethnic studies. However, this panic often presumes that the state and/or the academic industrial complex owns and controls ethnic studies—and hence is actually in a position to ban it. But if we open our minds to intellectual projects wherever they may be, we may find that critical ethnic studies is alive and well in places that we may not have expected.

This book emerges from the research that I did for *Native Americans and the Christian Right: The Gendered Politics of Unlikely Alliances*. In that book I examined religious and political configurations of Christian Right and American Indian activism as a way of talking about the larger project of rethinking the nature of political strategy and alliance-building for progressive purposes. Large-scale transformation cannot happen without mass movements. In turn, building mass movements requires that we do not organize around the premise of a permanent enemy (the Christian Right), since these "enemies" are people who need to be recruited for movements for social change. If we understand that current configurations of religious and political identity within Native American and Christian Right communities are not givens, then it is possible for them to be rearticulated into new configurations that favor progressive politics. *Native Americans and the Christian Right* explored these possibilities by focusing on sites of political and religious practice that do not neatly fit into categories of "progressive" or "conservative." Borrowing from the analysis of Native American activists as well as Stuart Hall, I argued for a politics of rearticulation whereby political alliances (or antagonisms) were not presumed. Instead, I called for an exploration of the possibilities of rearticulating identities and political formations for more liberatory ends. After all, the Christian Right itself is a result of a political rearticulation in which previously apolitical fundamentalists were rearticulated into right-wing voting blocs. As Stuart Hall argued in *Hard Road to Renewal*, Thatcherism (and Reaganism) was successful because it rearticulated working-class concerns into reactionary political agendas. Thus, it seems appropriate that the Left should return the favor and develop its own politics of rearticulation rather than presume that entire communities of people could never be interested in liberatory politics.

In the course of writing that book, however, I was not able to include many important sites where the politics of rearticulation have the potential to have a major impact on how political coalitions have been formed or might be formed in the future. Thus, this book focuses on racial justice politics in general as they intersect with the Christian Right. While my previous work focused on how Native American evangelicals were rearticulating evangelical rhetoric to support Native sovereignty and self-determination, this work looks at how evangelicals of color are engaged in similar politics of rearticulation. Because these sites of racial contestation and rearticulation within the Christian Right are so dispersed, I am focusing on the racial reconciliation movement that began in the 1990s as a way to distill this study. But, as will become clear, the impact of racial reconciliation reverberates far beyond the confines of its movement to impact how evangelicalism itself is articulated.

In addition, the racial reconciliation movement within Christian evangelicalism perhaps has had the unintended consequence of challenging what we even define as evangelicalism.

As Peter Heltzel argues in his groundbreaking work *Jesus and Justice: Evangelicals, Race, and American Politics*, the manner in which evangelicalism is marked as white requires deconstruction. He contends that this framing of evangelicalism disavows the extent to which U.S. evangelicalism is fundamentally constituted through African American Christianity (Heltzel, 2009, 11). And, as *Christianity Today* notes, surveys on evangelical political thought generally include only white evangelicals. Thus, even though 40 percent of Assemblies of God members are people of color, they will not be included in evangelical surveys (Moon, 2014). Social science research surveys replicate the idea that evangelicalism is white. Similarly, Jonathan Walton critiques how scholarly accounts of evangelical religious broadcasting excise the participation of African Americans with no intellectual justification. He argues that this excision rests on two dual assumptions: (1) conservative evangelicalism is defined as white; and (2) African American Christianity is romanticized as inherently liberal or progressive. Consequently, the role of theologically and politically conservative African American Christians in constituting evangelicalism disappears from view (Walton, 2009, 1–26). While we must problematize the manner in which evangelicalism is marked as white, this book turns to a moment in which white evangelical organizations and churches self-critically began to mark themselves as white and seek incorporation of evangelicals of color in the 1990s. One of the ironies of this move is that by attempting to be "inclusive" of people of color within Christian evangelicalism, this inclusion began to challenge ideas about who can define evangelicalism. The discourse of racial reconciliation illuminates the extent to which evangelicalism has historically equated Christianity with whiteness. And, as discussed later, racial reconciliation has also promoted the racialization of religion in myriad ways, particularly within Christian Zionism. Since evangelicalism is fundamentally constituted through the logics of white supremacy, the racial reconciliation movement cannot help but fundamentally challenge the construction of evangelicalism itself. That is to say, while the project of racial reconciliation might have been a project to rehabilitate the whiteness of evangelicalism within the context of racial justice critique (as discussed more fully in chapter 1), the unintended consequences of it simultaneously destabilized it.

As in *Native Americans and the Christian Right*, my narrative of racial reconciliation and the politics of rearticulation does not tell a simple story of racial progress. Because rearticulation does not presume fixed or stable categories of political identification, it is necessarily the case that even when new political formations are created, they continue to be sites of contestation. Forging new alliances is difficult. As Stuart Hall argues, while there is no fixed relationship between classes and ideologies, these relationships are not free-floating either. Consequently, reconstituting political positions is a Gramscian "war of position," requiring political actors to articulate a platform in light of the political and social forces that shape this war. Thus, racial reconciliation has had varied political effects, many of which reinstantiate reactionary political agendas. On one hand, racial reconciliation may have provided a critical foundation that enabled the mobilization of evangelicals of color to support Barack Obama's candidacy. As a result, even traditionally more conservative organizations (such as the Southern Baptist Convention) have gone beyond calls for racial "color blindness" to support struggles against white supremacy, such as the Movement for Black Lives and immigrant justice. Yet, at the same time, the rhetoric of racial reconciliation is often premised on Christian and U.S. imperialist presuppositions that have fueled both the demonization of Obama and the racial backlash seen in Tea Party politics, culminating in white evangelical support for Donald Trump's candidacy despite his lack of support for traditional Christian Right political positions relative to the other Republican candidates running at that time.[2] The racial logics of Christian evangelicalism impact society as a whole. Thus, this moment in history is perhaps a particularly important time for further analysis of the dynamics of race and religion within the United States.

Of course, the broad-based white evangelical support for Donald Trump's candidacy is arguably overwhelming evidence that evangelicalism cannot be redeemed. Is not evangelicalism itself an inherently colonial and white supremacist project? But here it is important to note that many evangelicals of color are asking the very same question and organizing based on this as an open question. An example can be found in the conference statement for the upcoming Liberating Evangelicalism: Decentering Whiteness conference (Chicago, September 2019):

> Christian evangelicalism, particularly of late, has often been equated with partisan politics and the faulty assumption that all evangelicals are white. Liberating Evangelicalism seeks to challenge this assumption by creating a space for a biblically-based, people of color centered movement that is open to all who seek to build a Jesus-centered vision for social justice.
>
> We imagine a space where people of color are at the center rather than the margins of the conversation, a place to build visions of liberation and inclusion, and a place for belonging and community-building with peoples across diverse political and theological perspectives.
>
> By "liberating evangelicalism," however, this conference does not presume a particular attachment to Christian evangelicalism.
>
> Some may seek to reclaim the term "evangelical" while others, suspicious of its history and contemporary expression, intend to jettison it from their faith identity altogether. We seek to create a space that allows for diverse engagements with biblically-rooted faith traditions. In building this space, this gathering also does not presume any particular theological or political perspectives. (Liberating Evangelicalism, 2019)

Thus, what is at stake is not so much the rehabilitation of the term "evangelical" but an engagement with organizing centered on people of color in support of an anti–white supremacist, patriarchal, and colonial Christianity among conservative constituents, who are not generally being reached by traditional left-wing organizations. This organizing is in many ways distinct from the histories of more white-dominated progressive evangelical organizing because it does not claim to replace a "bad" conservative evangelicalism with a "good" progressive evangelicalism but instead calls for a theological and political enterprise based on uncertainty. It suggests that the process of decolonizing Christianity may result in something that we might not even be able to recognize currently. And as many in this movement have suggested, some of these terms like "evangelical" may or may not survive the process of decolonization. It coalesces around a commitment to an open-ended theological praxis and process rather than a commitment to a bounded-set of theological and political principles. Or, to quote Daniel J. Camacho, it resists the politics of theological stop-and-frisk.

By evangelical theology centered on people of color, I mean a certain political and theological project that is not simply identity-based but signifies what Chanequa Walker-Barnes describes as a commitment to an intersectional theological and political engagement across sites of racialization and oppression. Just as critical ethnic studies emerges out of the field of African American/Black studies, Native American studies, Chicano/Latino studies, Asian American studies, and Arab American studies but is not reducible to the sum of them, evangelicalism centered on people of color emerges out of and overlaps with Black evangelicalism, Latino/Hispanic evangelicalism, Indigenous evangelicalism, and Asian American evangelicalism without being reducible to them. Certainly, many evangelicals of color do not have such theological or political commitments. Yet evangelicalism centered on people of color, would not exist without the work of more conservative evangelicals of color who might not identify with this movement, that is done in organizations like the National Black Evangelical Association, CHIEF (Christian Hope Indian Eskimo Fellowship), the National Hispanic Leadership Conference, and many others, as well as work done through independent ministries and racially or ethnically based denominations and churches. In addition, many people who are part of this movement might not completely identify with the term "evangelical." Currently, for instance, many adopt the term "evangelical adjacent." However, as noted, I am using the term "evangelical" to signify a discursive community rather than a bounded community based on clear doctrinal principles or sociological characteristics. Essentially, then, this project invites a shift from a (presumed white) definitional understanding of "evangelicalism" to an ethical (a.k.a. centered on people of color) understanding of "evangelicalism." "Ethical" means something quite specific. It means "people of color" as theoreticians qua practitioners of "evangelicalism." "People of color" indexes an ethical swerve "in the break" of something that has gone under the name "evangelicalism."[3]

The theologizing and organizing done through evangelicalism centered on people of color is important, this book contends, not just because it demonstrates the possibilities of mobilizing through a critical ethnic studies lens in an unexpected place, but also because it is instructive for racial justice mobilizing among ethnic studies scholars in the academy. That is, as elaborated further in chapter 6, the presence of people of color within the academy or the presence of ethnic studies in the academy is often presumed to be an unquestioned good, because the colonial, capitalist, and white supremacist structure of the academy goes unremarked. However, organizing of evangelicals of color is necessarily forced to reckon with the colonial and racist structure of Christianity itself even as it tries to center the voices of people of color within evangelicalism. It must necessarily go beyond arguing for "inclusion" within evangelicalism to calling for the transformation of evangelicalism itself. Such organizing efforts are instructive to all racial justice organizing that seeks to go beyond inclusion to transformation.

In that sense, like *Native Americans and the Christian Right*, this project is thus ultimately an anticolonial project that seeks to unsettle the presumptions behind the whiteness of evangelicalism by asking what is left of evangelicalism if it is divested from whiteness. Just as Native feminist theorists have asked for American studies without the presumption of something called "America" (A. Smith and J. K. Kauanui, 2008), so too this project does not presume the end goal of evangelical organizing centered on people of color because it recognizes that whiteness has constructed what is conceived to be religion, theology, and politics (P. Metzger, 2013). In not presuming an endpoint, this project also presumes that "secularism" is equally invested in whiteness and is not the default framework from which radical politics should emerge (Mahmood, 2011). If, as Frederick Moten, Denise Da Silva, and Alexander Weheliye have observed, whiteness has constructed the human, whiteness has also constructed theologies, discourses, and political frameworks for explaining the human: hence nothing can be taken for granted.

It is a mistake to dismiss movements such as racial reconciliation under the premise that anything seeming to support progressive politics within evangelicalism is necessarily an evil plot to co-opt progressive movements. First, the changes within evangelicalism to support racial justice struggles were the result of hard-fought battles by evangelicals of color in particular. Their often invisible organizing behind the scenes as well as their willingness to engage the work of critical ethnic studies scholars/organizers outside of evangelicalism provided an entry point for white evangelicals to become informed by critical ethnic studies analyses. Their work has dramatically changed the parameters of evangelical discussions on race, gender, imperialism, and colonialism within a relatively short period. In fact, many evangelicals are also interested in supporting global justice movements. It does not help our movements if we politically isolate entire communities of people through a refusal to engage with those who either are interested in social justice or might be interested if they had the opportunity to be engaged with different conversation partners. Ultimately, mass movements for social change cannot be built if we are unwilling to talk with people with whom we disagree. The point, however, is not to express disagreement but to consider whether there are different possibilities for wrestling with political differences that can assist in building mass movements rather than in foreclosing possible alliances in the future. In progressive movements, splits often arise between those who claim that it is not "practical" to fully address white supremacy, settler colonialism, and so forth in campaigns for justice because it will alienate potential campaign partners. Consequently, certain groups get sacrificed in the name of political expediency. Meanwhile, those who refuse to compromise on these issues often remain content with the critique without then developing a plan for dismantling white supremacy. In some ways, it seems as though both groups agree that it is not possible to build a mass movement for radical change. Thus, the only alternatives are to build mass movements for liberal reform or to engage in sectarian advocacy for radical change. While not holding any answers, this book explores how peoples across religious divides are trying to rethink the way we do organizing and racial critique in order not just to have the correct opinion but actually to try to dismantle white supremacy. In doing so, it attempts to situate evangelicalism centered on people of color as a site for critical ethnic studies theory that has something to add to the project of critical ethnic studies.

The Historical Context for Racial Reconciliation in Christian Evangelicalism

Christian evangelicalism has often claimed to be a discourse based on biblical truth unimpeded by social and political context. Yet the history of evangelicalism demonstrates that white supremacy fundamentally shapes its discursive field such that whiteness becomes constitutive of evangelicalism. Consequently, as discussed later, antiracist organizing in Christian evangelicalism can pose a constitutive crisis for evangelicalism. Before analyzing this crisis, it is useful to detail how white supremacy has shaped Christian evangelicalism.

The history of evangelical complicity in white supremacy, be it slavery, racial segregation, or American Indian genocide, is well documented (Heltzel, 2009; Tinker, 1993; Tise, 1987). Indeed, part of the genesis of the racial reconciliation movement entailed evangelicals coming to terms with the fact that, as Ralph Reed, the former head of the Christian Coalition, admitted, "[the] white evangelical church carries a shameful legacy of racism" (R. Reed, 1996, 65). Of course, Christian evangelicals also engaged in antislavery and racial justice struggles, but this was a minority compared to those who used religion to defend racial hierarchies. In addition, revival movements within Christian evangelicalism often began racially integrated. However, these movements often eventually went the way of racial segregation. For instance, although Azusa Street, considered to be a birthplace of modern Pentecostalism, was racially integrated when it began in 1906, it became segregated within a decade. Charles Parham, called by some "the father of American Pentecostalism," endorsed the Ku Klux Klan in the early 1900s (J. L. Grady, 1994).

More recently, the rise of the Christian Right generally highlighted not only changing gender and sexual politics as one of the movement's rallying points but also racial politics as a major, if often unacknowledged, organizing principle.[4] For instance, commentators often look to the rise of the Moral Majority and the new Christian Right as a reaction against feminism. But when asked why the New Religious Political Right was gaining in popularity at this point in time (1982), Jerry Falwell stated *three* reasons: the *Brown v. Board* decision (1954), the decision banning school prayer (1962), and *Roe v. Wade* (1973) (Rosenberg, 1984, 84). Similarly, the Christian homeschooling movement was as much a reaction against school desegregation as it was a reaction against permissive sexual mores being taught in public schools.

Some evangelicals did speak out against racial segregation. As Peter Heltzel notes, Carl F. H. Henry, a central figure in the rise of neo-evangelicalism, spoke out against racial injustice (although he was not particularly politically active in this arena). At the same time, his ability to speak out on this issue while he was editor of *Christianity Today* (the flagship magazine emerging out of the neo-evangelical movement) was hindered by J. Howard Pew, who financed the magazine, and L. Nelson Bell, Billy Graham's father-in-law and a member of the editorial board, both of whom supported segregation (Heltzel, 2009, 83).

Billy Graham, perhaps the father of neo-evangelicalism, exemplifies this complex relationship between the movement and race. On the one hand, he spoke out against racial segregation in the church two years before the *Brown* case was handed down. However, the manner in which he spoke out gave tacit support for legal segregation: "There is no scriptural basis for segregation. It may be there are places where such is desirable to both races, but certainly not in the church" (Myra and Shelley, 2005, 58). Eventually, Graham did stop segregation in his services by cutting the dividing ropes at a Crusade in Chattanooga, Tennessee, in 1953, but he was hesitant about being too vocal because he did not want to offend his white audiences (Carnes, 2005e; Heltzel, 2009, 82–83). Graham then began to recruit Black preachers to encourage African American participation at his events: Howard Jones became the first Black preacher to join Graham's Crusade in 1957 (Gilbreath, 1998b).

While Graham was not the strongest racial justice advocate, other Christian evangelical leaders were more blatantly racist. Jerry Falwell, for instance, was an admitted racist (M. Olasky, 2007c, 12) who denounced Martin Luther King Jr. in a 1965 sermon (T. George, 2007). He later apologized for this racism (although, as discussed later, he implicitly continued to support racial apartheid in South Africa). Similarly, W. A. Criswell, one of the architects of the fundamentalist takeover of the Southern Baptist Convention, similarly supported racial segregation until 1968, when he preached a sermon on "The Church of the Opened Door," in which he declared: "I have come to the profound conclusion that to separate the body of Christ on the basis of skin pigmentation is unthinkable, unchristian, and unacceptable to God" (T. George, 2002b).

Throughout the 1970s, race continued to be a rallying point for the religious Right. When the Internal Revenue Service (IRS) revoked Bob Jones University's tax-exempt status because it did not admit Black people, the university received widespread support from conservative Christians (and many liberal Christians as well) who felt that the IRS action was an infringement upon religious freedom. In deference to the Christian Right, Ronald Reagan promised to change IRS rules early in his presidency but later retreated. Although the Supreme Court finally heard the case and ruled against Bob Jones in 1983 (Capps, 1994), the IRS dropped its plans to revoke the tax-exempt status of other private schools that did not meet federal standards of racial integration.[5] Curiously, when Ralph Reed discusses the Bob Jones fracas in *After the Revolution*, he omits the fact that the struggle was over racial segregation (R. Reed, 1990).

During the 1980s, the Moral Majority effectively mobilized its constituents to oppose legislation that would have reversed a number of Supreme Court decisions eroding civil rights. The Christian Right was also very active in supporting the South African government, arguing on many occasions that apartheid was an acceptable or even agreeable state of affairs. John Eidsmoe expressed his unconditional support of South African apartheid by claiming that "America must consider its own national security. Whatever its sins, South Africa has no designs of aggression against the United States. The Communist powers do" (Lienesch, 1993, 219). Pat Robertson, Jimmy Swaggart, and Jerry Falwell also strongly supported the white South African government (S. Diamond, 1989; Stafford, 1996). As Jerry Falwell stated: "It is despicable that President Reagan should be forced by a spineless Congress and a biased media into slapping the wrist of such a good friend as South Africa" (Spring, 1985a, 53).

It is perhaps not a surprise that, with such politics, evangelical organizations found themselves very racially segregated with high rates of segregation in evangelical journals, parachurch organizations, and colleges (Spring, 1985b; see also Lehmann, 1991, 54; June, 1996; Maxwell, 1993b; Reynolds, 1988; Sidey, 1990b; Tapia, 1997a, 55). In addition, the National Black Evangelical Association (NBEA), formed in 1963 (originally named the National Negro Evangelical Association), sharply critiqued the racism of white evangelicalism (Rah, 2016, 183). However, as Soong-Chan Rah's germinal study on the NBEA notes, the more NBEA leaders such as Tom Skinner explicitly addressed racism within white evangelicalism, the more they were marginalized within white evangelical venues (Rah, 2016).

The Emergence of Racial Reconciliation
It is within this history of complicity in white supremacy that the evangelical racial reconciliation movement emerged in the 1990s. When Bill McCartney organized the first Promise Keepers (PK, an evangelical men's organization) rally in 1991, he was troubled by the fact that the attendees were all white: "The Spirit of God clearly said to my spirit, 'You can fill that stadium, but if men of other races aren't here, I won't be there, either.'" McCartney decided to make racial reconciliation one of the *top* priorities of Promise Keepers. During its prime, about one-third to one-half of the speakers at Promise Keepers rallies were men of color, and racial themes sounded throughout most if not all speeches. The journal *New Man*, which originally began as a Promise Keepers publication in 1994 but then went independent in 1997 (News Briefs, 1997), also focused on racial reconciliation and prominently featured articles by and about men of color. Over a dozen books on racial reconciliation were published in 1996 by evangelical publishers. Bill Anderson, president of the Christian Booksellers Association (CBA), directly attributes the increased visibility of African American au-

thors in CBA stores to Promise Keepers (Rabey, 1996, 60). Men of color were central to the group's organizational structure as well: R. Leslie Jr. looked into the Promise Keepers' Colorado headquarters and found that not only its board president but also 38 percent of its executive staff were men of color (Leslie, 1996). Promise Keepers then intensified its efforts by forming a "reconciliation division" with national strategic managers for each major racial group (Olsen 1997b, 67; Tapia, 1997b, 58–59). This sparked planning meetings for Latinx, Native American, and Asian American leaders in order to build toward its largest event, the national 1997 Stand in the Gap rally in Washington, D.C. (W. T. Whalin, 1997). These efforts increased the participation of men of color in Promise Keepers. For instance, while in general about 84 percent of the attendees at PK rallies were white, at the 1996 rally in New York City, one-third to one-half of the attendees were men of color (S. King, 1997).

In addition to Promise Keepers, the Los Angeles uprising in 1992 seems to have sparked an interest in racial reconciliation among white evangelicals. Articles contemplating the causes of racial strife and the need for reconciliation proliferated during the crisis and have persisted into the present. William Pannell's *The Coming Race Wars* was one of the first books of the racial reconciliation movement. Written in direct response to the L.A. riots, the book called on evangelicals to admit to their complicity in white racism and address the societal power imbalance between white and Black people. "There is brewing in the nation a full-scale war of people's groups against one another, and the issue is power. Powerless groups are beginning to realize that marginality in America is not about being *dumb*—it is about being *denied*" (Pannell, 1993, 87). Pannell stressed that multicultural evangelism was insufficient; rather, evangelical churches must address their abandonment of urban areas in pursuit of the suburban. He sarcastically noted that *Christianity Today* should change its name to *Suburban Christianity Today* (Pannell, 1993, 137). "The issue is not how Christian congregations might cooperate in an evangelistic strategy or church-growth crusade . . . when a whole city is up for grabs" (Pannell, 1993, 138). Later Pannell essentially criticized racial reconciliation for promoting multiculturalism instead of addressing white supremacy (Gilbreath, 1998a).

Another factor in the rising interest in racial reconciliation may have been the increased visibility, and acceptance, of white supremacist militia groups and the far-right Christian identity movement during this period. *Christianity Today* noted at the time that evangelical groups have traditionally been slow to denounce white supremacists (Stimson, 1986). But with the increased incidents of militia violence and violence against abortion clinics in the 1990s, Joe Maxwell and Andrés Tapia argued that "evangelicals will be challenged in defining why they should not be confused with the militia movement" (Maxwell and Tapia, 1995, 45). Racial reconciliation became one strategy to separate "good" white evangelicals from "bad" white extremists.

In any case, evangelical Christian organizations everywhere began jumping onto the racial reconciliation bandwagon in the early 1990s. In 1995 the Southern Baptist Convention issued an apology for slavery and racism (T. Morgan, 1995b). The mostly white Pentecostal Fellowship of North America dissolved and reformed into the Pentecostal/Charismatic Churches of North America, with a 50-50 Black-white board (S. Strang, 1995, 110). The Dake Bible issued a revision and apology for suggesting that racial segregation was the law of the land in the commentaries (B. Bruce, 1998a). White conservative evangelical events came in the wake of the Promise Keepers' organizing. Increasingly these events featured religiously conservative African Americans like Wellington Boone, Tony Evans, John Perkins, Star Parker, and Kay Cole James. Billy Graham began intensive recruitment of people of color for his Washington Crusade in 1986, his Atlanta Crusade in 1994, and his Minneapolis Crusade in 1996 (J. W. Kennedy, 1994; Olsen, 1996; Spring, 1986). The National Association of Evangelicals (NAE) in its 1994 reorganization announced that it would prioritize combating racism in the church and would initiate discussions with the National Black Evangelical Association to cultivate closer relationships (T. Morgan, 1994b).[6] *Christianity Today* even went so far as to run a cover story supportive of evangelical Black nationalism (Zoba, 1996). A variety of reconciliation efforts developed to allow Christians to repent for sins such as slavery, American Indian genocide, racial exclusion acts that targeted Asian Americans, and so forth (Blair-Mitchell, 1997; Lawson, 1999; Little, 1997; News Briefs, 2008c). Interestingly, at a time when the larger society was retreating from the rhetoric of racial justice through rollbacks in affirmative action, backlash against multicultural education, and other factors, Christian evangelical leaders seemingly wholeheartedly embraced the imperative to address racism within their own ranks. Of course, the *way* they chose to address racism did not necessarily mirror the strategies or analyses employed by more radical racial justice movements. Yet, as discussed later, these attempts to address racism among a constituency that not only had not concerned itself with racism but often wholeheartedly supported it have had significant, and often unexpected, impacts not only on evangelicalism but on society as a whole.

Disillusionment Sets In

> We do not want to down play the genuine conversion that has taken place among religious conservatives over the last few decades with regard to issues of race. Many have acknowledged and repented of their views of white racial superiority. Because of that, conscious racism has largely diminished in the conservative Christian community. However, we challenge conservatives to move beyond a simplistic definition of racism in order better to understand its insidious nature and the varied forms it takes. . . . Those who attempt to call attention to subtle expressions of racism are typically dismissed by conservatives as being "politically correct." . . . We suspect that these same conservatives, who now hail Martin Luther King as a hero, three decades ago would have considered him "politically correct," too, had the term been in vogue. (R. Frame and E. Tharpe, 1996, 160–61)

Many people *within* evangelicalism (as reflected in this quotation) were critical of racial reconciliation. At a meeting of the National Black Evangelical Association, for example, one participant asked Bill McCartney, "What is the Promise Keepers going to say about the anti-affirmative action atmosphere in this country? . . . What are the men in the stadiums this summer going to hear about that?" (Mortimer, n.d.). When asked how African Americans feel about Promise Keepers, Bennie Simmons replied that Blacks would join when Promise Keepers demonstrated willingness to invest money in inner-city businesses (Mortimer, n.d.). Simmons's response was typical of the pragmatic attitude with which evangelicals of color (and white evangelicals as well) regarded racial reconciliation. Andy Crouch criticized racial reconciliation ministries for continuing to maintain leadership in white hands (Crouch, 2002; Wadsworth, 2014, loc. 3138). "Discussion of racial reconciliation is now in vogue," states Ronald Potter of the Center for Urban Theological Studies, "but most discussions tend to be superficial and trite, reduced to 'can't we get along?'" (H. Lee, 1995). In *Christianity Today*'s institute on "The Myth of Racial Progress," many African Americans expressed the belief that white evangelicals were concerned with racial reconciliation only in order to mobilize forces for their conservative agenda and were attempting to substitute personal transformation for a social response to racism (Tapia, 1993, 17). As one Latino pastor commented, racial reconciliation "is helping whites more than it is helping me right now" (Tapia, 1997a, 55).

Indeed, after the initial fervor behind the racial reconciliation movement, the difficulty in effecting true reconciliation became apparent. Michael Emerson and Christian Smith's study on evangelical race relations in *Divided by Faith* concluded that racial reconciliation was largely unsuccessful, a conclusion that proved to be very disturbing to those involved in these programs. According to Emerson and Smith (2000), these failures have three causes:

(1) White evangelicals see racism on an individual rather than structural level. Consequently, they assume that legal equality provides true equal opportunity. If people of color do not measure up to white people on the political or economic level, it must be because they did not work hard enough.[7]

(2) White evangelicals have sporadic contact with people of color. According to Emerson and Smith (2000), having sporadic contact with people of color results in more racism than having no contact with people of color at all. The reason is that white evangelicals feel that their casual relationship with a person of color entitles them to their racist beliefs. Only sustained contact with people of color, particularly people of color who are in a position of authority, results in decreased racism among white evangelicals.

(3) Evangelical theology holds that simple conversion to Christianity is sufficient to address all problems related to race relations.

Emerson and Smith also found that only 60 percent of evangelicals had even heard of racial reconciliation (Emerson and Smith, 2000). At that point in history, even after racial reconciliation, only 8 percent of employees in large evangelical organizations were not white (Aikman, 2003). Of the participants in the 1996 Promise Keepers rallies (which focused specifically on racial reconciliation) who had complaints, 40 percent complained about the reconciliation theme (Emerson and Smith, 2000). Some typical complaints about Promise Keepers' efforts were published in *Christianity Today*: "Why should we all repent for racism as if the guilt of some were imputed to all. That can't be right, since clearly not all men (including both whites and blacks) who attend a PK rally are racists ... PK should not be PC" (Letters to the Editor, 1998, 8).

Evangelical magazines began to document the stumbling blocks faced by Christians interested in reconciliation. *Christianity Today* held a forum in response to *Divided by Faith*. In general, the forum participants noted the importance of evangelicals going beyond individual reconciliation efforts to support efforts to end structural racism. Charles Lyons made an implicit critique of the Promise Keepers approach to racial reconciliation by complaining that white evangelical churches like to do very short-term programs in urban areas and then leave without building ongoing relationships. Eugene Rivers criticized Promise Keepers for substituting "fundamentalist hugfests for the kind of deep, substantive dialogue that has a genuine impact on institutional decisions and public policy" (Gilbreath, 1998a). One of the responses to this forum corroborates the central problem identified by Emerson and Smith: that sporadic contact with people of color entrenches rather than diminishes racism among white evangelicals.

> Like Fred Price, my favorite TV pastor, I really believe that the black community needs to take it upon itself to improve its own conditions. If that makes me a racist and means I'm hindering the healing, so be it. There comes a time in the life of well-meaning individual whites when we realize that whatever we do for the black condition, it really is not our problem and we cannot solve it. Therefore, the best and healthiest thing for us to do is to mind our own business. For myself, my business includes being friend and sister to the blacks, orientals, and Mideasterners in my church. I can't even tell you what the ratio of races is in our church. We don't pay attention. Sometimes I have to stop and think about it before I can remember if a certain friend is black or white. (Letters, 2000, 14)

Other articles spoke to the continuing difficulties in local racial reconciliation efforts (Andrescik, 2000a; A. Gaines, 1997; T. Morgan, 1996, 87; Zylstra, 2008). For instance, in 1994 a Pentecostal convocation known as the "Memphis Miracle" was designed to stir the spirit of repentance and reconciliation between Black and white churches. It was led by the Pentecostal Fellowship of North America, a historically all-white organization. At the climax of the event, Black and white pastors tearfully washed one another's feet. Since then the Pentecostal/Charismatic Churches of North America (PCCNA) has been co-chaired by various Black and white leaders. On September 11, 2003, the organization adopted a position statement condemning racism in all its forms. In addition, leaders from ten denominations in Memphis formed a national organization called Churches Uniting in Christ (CUIC) to commit to worship together. This new organization, however, was accused of fostering worshiping together as a "token gesture" toward addressing racism. Despite these accusations, CUIC thinks worshiping together is not just a "token gesture," but pastors in Memphis concede that their efforts to integrate their churches have largely failed. One African American pastor, Brandon Porter, traces his failure to integrate his church to the fact that "whites are less willing to engage in cross-cultural relationships. The whites who attend our ministry are either in an interracial marriage, are in our drug-and-alcohol ministry or are running for office" (Schweikert, 2004). The one "success story" is John Siebeling's Life Church, which is still 80 percent white (Schweikert, 2004).

The Southern Baptist Convention became embroiled in controversy when it published a Vacation Bible School curriculum called *Far-Out Far East Rickshaw: Racing to the Son* in 2004. The curriculum centered on a children's race through Japan and was replete with stereotypical imagery such as kimonos and chopsticks. Soong-Chan Rah, a prominent evangelical author on racial reconciliation issues, condemned it for its perpetuation of Asian stereotypes and published a website, "Reconsidering Rickshaw Rally," to oppose it.[8] He gathered 1,100 signatures in support of his cause within a month of publishing the website. The response of LifeWay (the Southern Baptist agency that published the curriculum) was that the director was "offended" by the charges because he is not racist. Southern Baptist ethicist Ben Mitchell at Trinity International University said that, while he did not think it was realistic for LifeWay to withdraw the curriculum, it should apologize. "For many people, it will either confirm their view of Southern Baptists as parochial and culturally naive at best, or it will make them suspicious of our commitment to racial justice and ethnic sensitivity" (Walker, 2004b). In the end, the Southern Baptist Convention ignored its complicity in anti-Asian racism. Not until 2013 (as discussed in greater detail later) did LifeWay acknowledge or apologize for Rickshaw Rally. And even when it apologized, it never acknowledged Rah's contribution in bringing attention to the issue in the first place.

The Persistence of Racial Reconciliation
Despite these challenges, racial reconciliation continues, albeit in different forms. Promise Keepers, one of the leading organizations to spark this movement, has not maintained the same focus on addressing racism. The organization has gone through many ups and downs in its history, from bringing close to 100,000 men together at the 1997 Stand in the Gap rally to laying off its entire staff in 1998, to rebirthing itself and rehiring most of its staff soon thereafter, resulting in much less public prominence (Andrescik, 2003). Judging from my participation in the 2004 and 2005 Promise Keepers conferences, racial reconciliation, particularly racial reconciliation among non–African American men of color, figures significantly less prominently than it did in the late 1990s. And, as discussed later in this book, the issue

of racial reconciliation disappeared completely at the 2010 Colorado conference (the only one held that year), replaced by a focus on reconciliation with women, poor people, and Messianic Jews. In fact, McCartney even went so far as to suggest that Promise Keepers has already accomplished racial reconciliation (Horner, 2002).

However, other organizations, such as InterVarsity Christian Fellowship, a national campus-based evangelical parachurch organization, have filled this vacuum. As can be seen in InterVarsity's huge Urbana conferences, both race and gender reconciliation are major program emphases in terms of plenary speakers and issues discussed, workshop topics, and literature sold at the conference. *Christianity Today* interviewed staff members from InterVarsity to discuss how they managed to succeed in maintaining a focus on racial reconciliation when organizations such as Promise Keepers gave up. According to Jim Lundgren: "One thing that keeps predominantly white Christian organizations from continuing in this process is that when they start succeeding, they take a lot of flak. For a two- or three-year period it's really intense" (Neff, 2004a, 54). Other staff members agreed that organizing within InterVarsity was not a simple task. However, according to Jeanette Yep, the groundwork was laid even before the racial reconciliation movement began (Neff, 2004a). In June 1948 the organization resolved not to hold events at facilities discriminating against people of color. In the 1980s Yep chaired a taskforce that called on InterVarsity to make achieving racial diversity an explicit mandate, to create a new staff position for a vice-president of multiethnicity, and to tithe a portion of every dollar raised by staff workers to support multiethnic staff. To Yep's surprise, president Gordon MacDonald approved the proposal. Thirty-seven years ago, 4 percent of its staff and students were ethnic minorities. Today those percentages have grown to 16 percent (for staff) and 35 percent (for students), which compares favorably with the national average of 27 percent of all college students who identify themselves as people of color (Neff, 2004a). As discussed in fuller detail in the conclusion, InterVarsity ran into controversy during its 2015 conference when the speakers declared their support for Black Lives Matter.

Another importance arena for racial justice work is the Justice Conference. Originally headed by Ken Wytsma, this annual conference, which started in 2010, focuses on mobilizing evangelicals for social justice. In 2012 it was critiqued by a number of evangelicals of color for featuring almost exclusively white speakers. But in response to this critique Wytsma changed the agenda and more strongly incorporated by speakers of color as well as workshops that specifically addressed racial justice. As of 2015 Wytsma no longer leads the Justice Conference, but the conferences continue to center on concerns about racial justice.

Of the various evangelical periodicals, *Charisma* has highlighted racial reconciliation the most consistently over time (S. Strang, 2015). Strang Publications (the publisher of *Charisma*) increased its employment of people of color from 5 percent to 25 percent in a Florida county where people of color represent only 9 percent of the population (Neff, 1997a). Passages such as the following are typical of its regular op-ed pieces supporting reconciliation:

> We can no longer cluster in cliques surrounded only by those who happen to be like us. God never intended for His church to be divided into color quadrants. A homogen[e]ous church is an incomplete church, and no pastor or people should be satisfied with it. Will it be uncomfortable to embrace brothers and sisters of different backgrounds and ethnicities? Absolutely. But since when is the kingdom of God comfortable. (Doyley, 2009, 63)

Even *World* magazine (an evangelical magazine explicitly committed to conservative politics), which has generally avoided engagement with racial reconciliation, finally ran a special issue on race in 2001. Joel Belz admitted that prior to writing this forum he had never thought to talk to people about racism (J. Belz, 2001b). Focusing entirely on white-Black relationships, various conservative commentators were asked what they would like to see happen in 2063, a hundred years after Martin Luther King's "I Have a Dream" speech (M. Olasky, 2001d). The forum did acknowledge some continuing structural forms of racism, such as racism in law enforcement, even though it concluded that the United States is a great country if Black people such as Colin Powell are able to rise to power (Race in America: A Historical Timeline, 2001). Its predictions for the future were that capitalism would solve the problem of racism because "corporations [have] no choice but to hire the best and the brightest, whatever their ethnicity" (Taulbert, 2001). One article even implicitly supported some kind of program of national apologies and reparations (W. Plummer, 2001). Ironically, some commentators said that they hoped for an African American president (although Richard Land of the Southern Baptist Convention specified that he wanted only a Republican one) (Land, 2001; W. Plummer, 2001). As discussed later, this wish came true sooner than expected, putting these writers in the position of demonstrating that their interest in a Black president was genuine only insofar as it remained an abstract ideal.

In addition, local efforts that received momentary national visibility through Promise Keepers and other similar organizations continue to persist in their attempts to address racism in Christian communities (E. Belz, 2009a; see also Bonham, 2003; A. Gaines, 2009a; P. Johnson, 2004; J. Kennedy, 2005; Moring, 2011). The Southern Baptist Convention has reported a significant increase in the number of its members that are African American churches since its apology for slavery in 1995 (Dean, 2012b). The SBC added 1,600 churches from the 1990s to total more than 2,700 by 2002. This total is more than the 1,800 congregations of the Progressive National Baptist Convention. After the apology, the SBC instituted an annual Racial Reconciliation Sunday, and made race relations the emphasis of its Ethics and Religious Liberty Commission (ERLC). Albert Mohler of Southern Baptist Seminary received the highest honor given by the Black Southern Baptist Denominational Network for his support of Black studies at the seminary. Finally, the SBC elected its first Black president on June 19, 2012 (A. Green, 2004). In June 2016 the SBC passed a resolution urging Christians to discontinue displays of the Confederate flag (J. Bruce, 2016).

As discussed in later chapters, a newer generation of evangelical thinkers and activists is taking racial reconciliation to a new level, focusing on racial justice as it intersects with all other forms of oppression. In doing so, evangelicals are increasingly integrating into broader social movements for racial justice that are in turn unsettling the constraints of evangelicalism itself.

Chapter Outline

This introduction provides a historical context for the history of the racial reconciliation movement within Christian evangelicalism. Chapter 1 examines the logics of evangelical "multiculturalism" promoted within racial reconciliation. That is, racial reconciliation tends to focus on multicultural representation rather than structural forms of white supremacy. The goal of racial reconciliation is generally framed as making white evangelical institutions more inclusive of people of color without actually fundamentally changing these institutions. Such approaches have been heavily critiqued within critical ethnic studies. At the same time, the efforts within Christian evangelicalism may also provide some important critiques of dismissals of multiculturalism. That is, racial reconciliation efforts dispute the notion that white supremacy can easily accommodate multiculturalism. In fact, evangelicalism's efforts to incorporate multicultural voices has had the unintended consequence of challenging what defines Christian evangelicalism itself. Hence, after promoting racial reconciliation, many white evangelicals complain that inclusion has gone "too far." Thus, even seemingly innocuous attempts to incorporate the voices of people of color can have unintended radical implications.

Chapter 2 explores how the ramifications of the manner in which white evangelicals tend to frame race as a problem of "sin." On one hand, this paradigm generally individualizes race and obscures white supremacy as both an institutional and epistemological structuring system. At the same time, this paradigm implicitly recognizes what many critical race theorists have noted: that racism is a permanent part of the social fabric. The response to the recognition of the permanency of racism is to disengage from social movement struggles while remaining overly optimistic about the ability of evangelicalism to carve a space safe from racism. In addition, most racial reconciliation efforts tend to center white evangelicals as the subjects of reconciliation, with evangelicals of color as their objects. At the same time, some evangelicals of color in particular have been able to analyze white supremacy both as a system and as a personal sin that could be potentially helpful for all those seeking to address social and personal transformation simultaneously.

Decentering whiteness within the evangelical racial reconciliation movement allows us to explain the multiple logics of racialization as they appear within evangelicalism more carefully. Chapter 3 examines how white evangelicalism engages in multiple logics of race: anti-Blackness, people of color as mission field, indigenous disappearance, and so forth, in the service of Christian empire. In doing so, this chapter offers possibilities for how racial justice organizers within Christian evangelicalism might build different kinds of alliances among communities of color.

Chapter 4 examines the racial and biopolitical logic of the "persecuted Christians" movement. Arguably, Christian evangelicalism is a theological system that is fundamentally shaped by biopolitics. That is, through the doctrine of substitutory atonement, Jesus (or other populations put in the place of Jesus) must die so that Christians can live. In this chapter I examine how the Christian persecution movement racially differentiates which Christians should live and which should die. In particular, the persecution movement organizes in support of Third World Christians suffering persecution in the interest of purifying the Western church. At the same time, I explore evangelical theologians who question the logics of this movement by rearticulating Christianity as a faith that does not treat death instrumentally. Echoing the work of Black studies scholars in particular, these evangelical theologians locate the moment of genocide as a place that questions the evangelical world order.

Within the rhetoric of "global persecution," Islam looms particularly large. The perceived threat of Islam predates the events of September 11, 2001. Islam is particularly threatening to the Christian Right because it represents a direct challenge to both Christianization and Westernization. However, Islamophobia within the Christian Right has reached new heights since 9/11. Chapter 5 examines how Arabs and Muslims are racialized within white evangelical discourse, focusing particularly on how this racialization intersects with Christian Zionism. Evangelical ideologies also racialize Jewish people in complex ways in order to support Christian Zionist projects. On the one hand, Christian Zionism often becomes the structural limit to racial reconciliation. On the other hand, racial reconciliation has also paved the way for reformist impulses within Christian evangelicalism regarding Christian Zionism and evangelical-Arab and Muslim relations. At the same time, some of evangelical organizing efforts against Islamophobia question the presumption that the antidote to it is secularism. Because religion is racialized, Islamophobia is present in secular society. Meanwhile, many evangelicals have found a theological base for contesting both Islamophobia and Christian Zionism.

In Native studies, many scholars propose "decolonization" as a guiding principle for Native American scholarship and activism. This work generally presumes a non-Christian framework for decolonization, because the imposition of Christianity within Native communities is understood as part of the colonial process. But interestingly, some Native American evangelicals are reading the same works cited above and are also applying decolonization as a guiding principle for biblical faith. Chapter 6 focuses on one unexpected place for indigenous decolonization: Native evangelical leaders and organizations that circulate through the North American Institute for Indigenous Theological Studies (NAIITS). This chapter further explores how this model of education can be informative for all scholars in considering how they may dismantle the educational system.

As mentioned previously, Emerson and Smith's germinal study (2000) of racial reconciliation concluded that it was largely unsuccessful in changing evangelicalism. Chapter 7 explores a site that would seem to contradict that claim: the 2008 elections. On the one hand, these elections confirmed the entrenched attitudes toward race described in Emerson and Smith's book. At the same time, they show how white evangelical efforts to court Black and Latinx evangelicals though racial reconciliation had the unintended consequence of white evangelical organizations being forced to shift their politics in order to effect racial unity, particularly on the issues of immigration and prison reform. This chapter further examines how this election cycle provided an opportunity for insurgent voices within evangelicalism to challenge more traditional Christian Right politics.

Chapter 8 examines the emergence of a women-of-color consciousness within Christian evangelicalism. Racial reconciliation and evangelical feminism have been two movements within Christian evangelicalism that have often had an orthogonal relationship with each other. Racial reconciliation has generally been male-dominated, and evangelical feminism has generally been white-dominated. Yet race and gender are inextricably linked in Christian Right discourse such that both racial reconciliation efforts and conservative evangelical women's organizing habitually target women of color as scapegoats for social, religious, and political problems. Within this context, women of color have increasingly begun to articulate an intersectional politic within Christian evangelicalism that calls not only for the inclusion of the voices of women of color within evangelicalism but for a broader framework for political and theological transformation altogether. By centering women of color evangelicals, a very different picture of the racial reconciliation movement emerges.

Finally, this book concludes with two pivotal moments in the racial reconciliation movement, the rise of the Black Lives Matter movement and the 2016 presidential election of Donald Trump. While previously white evangelicals could claim to be "color-blind" in response to racial reconciliation, this claim lost credibility in 2016. Even conservative evangelical organizations could no longer ignore institutionalized racism or white evangelicalism's investment in whiteness. The fact that Donald Trump was elected in no small part because four out of five white evangelicals voted for him despite his having virtually none of the credentials that white evangelicals previously claimed to be important for any presidential candidate would suggest that the racial reconciliation movement has been a complete failure. At the same time, this moment has both enraged and emboldened many justice-centered evangelicals, particularly evangelicals of color, to wrest evangelicalism from its white captivity and change it to something that we have yet to imagine.

Conclusion

According to Emerson and Smith's *Divided by Faith*, racial reconciliation has had virtually no impact on race relations within evangelical circles (Emerson and Smith, 2000). They make compelling arguments that the nature of evangelical discourse tends to promote an individualistic approach to racial justice issues—an approach that hinders real reconciliation. However, they fail to consider that racial reconciliation is also a relatively new phenomenon within the Christian Right. Many people of color might argue that actual racial equality comes very slowly, even in progressive organizations that have been working on racial justice for decades.[9] Meanwhile, racial reconciliation in white evangelical circles faces the challenges of working with constituencies that often overtly support racial segregation, slavery, and genocide (A. Smith, 2008; Worthen, 2009). Therefore, it is not clear why we would expect racial reconciliation to alter racial attitudes among white evangelicals dramatically in such a short period. In fact, Emerson and Smith's book itself influenced many racial reconciliation activists to begin to emphasize structural racism in their analysis and reshape the way they approach politics (G. Yancey, 2006).

In addition, the impact of racial reconciliation has had ramifications beyond the personal attitudes about race held by evangelicals at any moment in time. Some of these attitudes may shift generationally and will not necessarily be apparent in a ten-year period. Furthermore, as this book discusses, race cannot be separated from a host of theological, political, and social issues. Consequently, racial reconciliation may have an impact on discourses that do not appear at first glance to be directly related to race. Because evangelicalism has been constituted through whiteness, racial reconciliation does more than engage racial attitudes: it puts questions on the table about the fundamental nature of evangelicalism itself. These questions in turn have shaped evangelical discourse around everything from Christian Zionism to global politics to gender/sexuality politics. The destabilization of the category of "evangelical" itself provides possible spaces for intervention for those who are interested in building new coalitions for progressive politics. This book, then, builds on the work of Emerson and Smith by focusing not so much on individual attitudes about race within evangelical communities but on the political ramifications and possibilities that are emerging and might emerge as a result of this movement.

1 FROM CHIT'LINS TO CAVIAR
Evangelical Multiculturalism

Mission Mississippi's "Chit'lins to Caviar" Cookbook—A 5.5 × 8.5 creatively designed and ethnically diverse cookbook, with plastic comb binding, will definitely become a cherished keepsake on kitchen shelves all over the state of MS and perhaps even all around the world! Each recipe in the cookbook includes the name of the person who submitted it, his/her ethnic origin and affiliate church as given. Great gift idea! To order, send us your check or money order for $15.00.

The proceeds from all sales of the cookbook will contribute greatly toward continuing our great commission of bringing Christians together across racial and denominational lines promoting unity for Kingdom building.—"Chit'lins to Caviar" Cookbook (Mission Mississippi, n.d.)

If you have a relationship with Christ, it should make you less of an ass.—Ray Aldred, North American Institute for Indigenous Theological Studies (interview)

Dolphus Weary began Mission Mississippi in 1993, after plans for a city crusade in Jackson evolved into a racial reconciliation rally that drew 25,000 people. Mission Mississippi includes Thursday prayer meetings held in Black and white churches, annual rallies, governors' luncheons, and monthly pastors' gatherings to promote interracial friendship. It has eight chapters, five affiliates, and seventy-five support churches. According to Weary, "I'm not so interested in putting together black and white churches. I'm more interested in black and white Christians seeing themselves differently" (Herndon, 2005a, 66).[1] One project was a cookbook called "Chit'lins to Caviar," which included recipes from white and Black "cultures." Mission Mississippi's presuppositions about race can be found on its website:

> We could learn a lot from crayons:
> some are sharp, some are pretty,
> some are dull, some have weird names,
> and all are different colors . . .
> but they all exist very nicely in the same box.
> (Mississippi Mission, n.d.)

Essentially, this organization seeks to address racism through the promotion of multiculturalism and interracial relationships. This project is not particularly identified with dismantling structures of white supremacy. Rather it is intent on promoting racial unity "one relationship at a time."

In this regard, Mission Mississippi's approach typifies the racial reconciliation movement, which has depended on a multicultural politics of recognition (Van Opstal, 2016a). Of course, a plethora of scholars, particularly in ethnic studies, have critiqued the politics of multiculturalism as an approach that actually reifies rather than erodes white supremacy (L. Lowe, 1996; D. Rodriguez, 2009b; Sexton, 2008). As Elizabeth Povinelli and Rey Chow argue, liberal multiculturalism often relies on a politics of identity representation that is domesticated by nation-state and capitalist imperatives (Povinelli, 2002, 29; Chow, 2002). Similarly, racial reconciliation tends to focus on recognition of racial and cultural differences rather than on dismantling the structures of white supremacy, particularly the capitalist ideologies that undergird white supremacy.

Chow complains that multiculturalism traps "ethnics" into performing their prescribed role of representing their communities, without allowing any challenge to the analytics of power that constructs society as a whole. Within this system, people of color in particular fall into the Foucauldian trap of thinking that liberation is not structural but requires demonstrating the worth of one's culture (Chow, 2002). Since the goal then becomes representing the "truth" of one's community, the categories of "Asian American," "African American," "Hispanic/Latinx," and "American Indian" are not questioned and are generally described in culturally essentialist terms. Within this discursive economy, as Rey Chow and Matthew Stiffler note, people of color are then positioned to engage in self-orientalizing and self-mimicry in order to be legible within racial reconciliation (Stiffler, 2010). Furthermore, as ethnic studies scholars have argued, multiculturalism tends to disappear the structures of white supremacy. If our attention is turned to self-representation rather than structures of white supremacy, the issue of power disappears. Thus, analysis of the political economy and its intersections with white supremacy also disappears, allowing racial logics to reappear as in other hierarchies such as class, gender, and/or sexuality. And as has been critiqued in critical ethnic studies, an emphasis on multiculturalism has tended to limit our analysis of politics to that based solely on an identity politics. Many have argued that identity politics is necessarily a conservative project that trades in social transformation for identity representation. Certainly, evangelical racial reconciliation generally utilizes an identity-based approach.

Given the manner in which racial reconciliation seems to be preoccupied with multiculturalism instead of racial justice, it would be easy to dismiss this movement. However, the racial reconciliation movement also demonstrates that multiculturalist politics may sometimes have more radical unintended consequences. The inclusion of racial "others" in evangelicalism destabilizes the category of evangelicalism itself. Racial identity politics cannot be separated from evangelical identity politics as a whole. In regard to those previously excluded from the category of "human," or in this particular case the category of "Christian," multiculturalist inclusion necessarily troubles these categories. However problematic the terms of this inclusion are, it may be worthwhile not to summarily dismiss these projects but to consider what possibilities may open up within the categorical ruptures that result. As Ray Aldred suggests, many evangelicals of color became dissatisfied with inclusion and wanted to see white evangelicals actually become "less of an ass." What began as racial reconciliation began to give way to racial justice.

Racial Reconciliation and U.S. Exceptionalism

Dylan Rodriguez contends that the project of multiculturalism is fundamentally opposed to antiracism: the "(non)meeting of these two, proximate mobilizations of racial communion—one antiracist, insurgent, and counterhegemonic, the other multiculturalist, narcissistic, and ahistorically 'culturalist'" (D. Rodriguez, 2009b, 12). While this is an essential critique, a question arises from this critique of multiculturalism: if multiculturalism is so antithetical to the project of antiracism and is so ineffective as a means for critiquing race, then why does it continue to meet with so much resistance? Could it be the case that multiculturalism still continues to trouble the racial order, despite the manner in which white supremacy attempts to domesticate antiracist projects through multiculturalism?

Within Christian evangelicalism, multiculturalism—despite its limitations—troubles both the boundaries of (white) evangelicalism and the U.S. exceptionalism on which it is based. For this reason, there continues to be mass resistance even to seemingly insignificant attempts to promote multiculturalism within evangelicalism (Mouw, 2001; M. Olasky, 2001c), even multiculturalism has been becoming more popular in recent years (J. Belz, 2005d; Board, 1999; Hollywood's Race Problem, 2014). Within many strands of evangelical discourse, true Christianity is predicated on whiteness (A. Smith, 2008). The Christian Right often assumes that to be American is to be Christian and to be Christian is to be American. James Guth describes this theology as part of a "civil gospel," which is a Christian Right rationale for political involvement. "This theology argues that the U.S. was founded as a Christian nation but has fallen from that status, and Christian citizens must take action to protect their own rights and restore the American constitutional system and buttress morality" (Guth, 1996a).[2]

Yet, despite this critique, Christianity becomes equated with U.S. patriotism. Even the relatively progressive evangelical David Gushee argues that those "who do not know how to demonstrate an appropriate fealty to their nation are not well positioned to learn to transcend that loyalty for a higher one" (Gushee, 2006). *Focus on the Family* magazine featured an article on how to raise patriotic children, which included having them pray for the government, write to military personnel, visit patriotic sites, discuss U.S. heroes, take treats to the Veterans' Hospital, teach them how to treat the flag, and observe national holidays. "Children who are thankful for America love America. Our country has its problems, but America needs Christians who love God and their country" (Brooks, 2005, 13). Any history that challenges the idea of a Christian America, particularly from an oppressed group that rejects U.S. claims to religio-moral superiority, threatens Christendom itself. As Harold Brown states, "We cannot repudiate Western civilization and dissociate ourselves from it without at the same time moving ourselves away from Christianity, and potentially from Christ himself" (H. O. J. Brown, 1992, 47).

Because the maintenance of "Christian American" history is so important to Christian hegemony, many evangelicals will eschew multicultural interpretations of American history, even while paying lip service to racial reconciliation (Leggett, 2003; Stafford, 1992; Vincent, 1999c). According to Dennis McCallum, multiculturalism represents the "death of truth," the truth being Christianity (McCallum, 1996). *Christianity Today* implores us to get beyond our politically correct identity labels and just call ourselves "Christian" (Willimon, 1990). The Institute of Religion and Democracy ran two articles that claimed that Christianity *is* the "true" multiculturalism; the lefty kind is a sham (Maudlin, 1992). One writer for *World* complains about multiculturalism: "Now I'm a racist again because I don't believe in black theology and I don't think Toni Morrison's novels (or Danielle Steel's) are as good as Jane Austen's. I believe in the superiority of the Western tradition. I believe in blending the best of other cultures into the Western tradition, and I believe it's possible to identify the best. I believe that we all ought to be assimilated to the best of this blended, but predominantly Western Christianized culture" (W. Smith, 2005).

Similarly, *Christianity Today* ran an article critiquing fears of western imperialism. In its defense of the cultural imperialism of Christian missionaries, it argued: "Americans should focus less on 'western guilt' and more on sharing the gospel" (Yung, 2011, 42). It noted that Western imperialism exists but in the end argued that the West is superior because it feels guilty about imperialism. "But I am not aware of a society that has self-critically developed a guilt complex as deep and extensive over past mistakes as today's West" (Yung, 2011, 46).

Thus, what these thinkers correctly perceive is that the embrace of multiculturalism necessarily challenges the Christian Right's narrative of the United States as exceptionally humane because of its Christian foundation. As an example, Randy Frame and Edgar Tharpe provide an evangelical dissent against Ralph Reed's *After the Revolution*:

> [Reed] calls the sixteenth century the "'age of discovery,' a time when the sails of European explorers dotted the oceans in pursuit of the New World, where they discovered gold, silver, and wealth beyond the wildest imagination." . . . No doubt, neither Reed nor his editors realized how this capsule history might hurt and offend African-American and Native American readers. From a Native American perspective, the sixteenth century was the age of annihilation. From a black perspective, the seventeenth through the nineteenth centuries constituted the age of dehumanization. Reed's account typifies the approach of the overwhelming majority of white scholars and historians, who view past and present only from the perspective of white Europeans. As Hispanic

historian Justo González puts it, "History is written by the winners." (R. Frame and E. Tharpe, 1996, 161)

Thus, a challenge for the racial reconciliation movement has been how to reconcile racial reconciliation with white Christian American triumphalism. Many involved in racial reconciliation follow the logics of multiculturalism to their logical conclusion and do in fact challenge this triumphalism. At the same time, this U.S. exceptionalism becomes challenged by the fact that evangelical Christianity is growing much faster in the Global South than it is in the Global North. Within the U.S. context, white evangelicals note that it is difficult to evangelize people of color globally if they cannot work successfully with people of color in the United States (Hawkins, 1995, 24). As Edward Ellis articulates, God "won't come back until the gospel is preached in all the earth. But that won't happen as long as racism continues to exist" (E. Ellis, 1989, 21). If evangelicalism cannot incorporate people of color within U.S. borders, it cannot expect to incorporate those within countries in the Global South (Marshall, 1995).

While the globalization of the economy continued to expand throughout the world, evangelical commissions became involved in the AD2000 Movement to "reach" all people with the gospel by the year 2000 (Coote, 1991; Reapsome, 1988; Toalston, 1989, 50; Winter, 1991). As Patrick Johnston notes, while probably very few have never heard about Jesus at all, this project entailed a larger political movement of surmounting "the high geographical, cultural, religious and political barriers that keep them isolated from the Good News" (What Does "Reached" Mean? An EMQ Survey, 1990). Thus, evangelization is part of a larger Westernization project to make conditions conducive toward accepting the gospel (Gribben, 1996). U.S. evangelical missionaries offer what they perceive to be a transnational message that transcends cultural or national boundaries, employing such diverse strategies as illegally taking children from Haiti and buying access to churches in Cuba to make illegal radio transmissions into countries closed to missionary activity (Mumper, 1986a). Some groups are now teaching English abroad using Christian material as a way to evangelize (although they claim they attempt to be nonimperialist by also learning the language of the country they are in) (Tennant, 2002). Resistance to Christianization is often dismissed as "mind control efforts" (Guthrie, 1993, 23). The goal is to transcend "racial, cultural, and class barriers" with one message (T. Morgan, 1995a, 36).

As Doug McAdam and others have noted, part of the impetus for the

U.S. federal government passing civil rights legislation was that its ability to "spread democracy" around the world was hampered by its internal practice of racial apartheid (D. McAdam, 1982). Similarly, white evangelicals are challenged with spreading Christianity to the Global South when they practice racially exclusive missionary strategies. Reflecting this problem was *World*'s critique of mainstream media coverage of the Hurricane Katrina crisis: "Harmed by CNN blowhards who politicized hurricane reporting and largely neglected the work of Christian volunteers and others, the American image around the world took a post-Katrina nosedive" (M. Olasky, 2005a). Furthermore, "the gulf coast region was portrayed for several days as if it were something less than a Third World country" (J. Belz, 2005c). How can U.S.-based evangelicals save "Third World" countries if regions of the United States look like "Third World" countries? Implicit in this critique is that it is okay to have racial and economic disparity in the United States as long as the rest of the world does not know about it. Thus, according to *Missiology*, racial reconciliation is necessary so as not to impede the ability to evangelize the gospel. For evangelical missionaries to have credibility, they must "redress the injustices of the past and present" (Guider, 2004). Evangelicals believe that it is necessary, as C. Stuart Lightbody proclaims, to make disciples of "all ethnic groups. When the last chapter is written, people from every corner of the earth will meet in the throne room of the universe" (Lightbody, 1992). Addressing racism within evangelicalism is thus critical to the task of making disciples of "all ethnic groups." And increasing attention is devoted to recruiting people of color as missionaries abroad (A. Gaines, 2007; Loren, 2007).

People of color are often perceived by white evangelicals as being able to do foreign mission work without being labeled as American imperialists (A. Smith, 2008). One missionary who was bent on recruiting Black missionaries to do mission work in Africa stated that "they are the only ones who can reach certain peoples" (Brady, 2000; Zylstra, 2013b). *Charisma* ran an article complaining that fewer than 1 percent of missionaries in the foreign field are African American. "If any ethnic groups should feel compelled to free oppressed people, it should be those who are the descendants of people who were once oppressed. In other words, free black people should be moved with compassion to free other people simply because we remember our history" (Bailey-Jones, 2008, 20). Of course, the reason for the lack of people of color missionaries has not always been lack of interest on the part of people of color but racism within mission organizations. The U.S. branch of Serving in Mission (SIM) issued a formal apology for excluding Black people from service in the past. The director washed the feet of three Black church leaders (News Briefs, 2008b).

Conservative Christians stress the importance of ensuring that "non-Western" people do not convert to non-Christian (and hence non-Western) religions—particularly Islam (Mumper, 1985). The result of Christianizing the world, however, is that "whites comprise only about 40 percent of all Christians, and... the center of Christianity... has shifted to the Southern World, to Asia, Africa and Latin America... the third millennium will be shaped largely by the Southern Church" (Greenway, 1989, 4; see also Mark Hutchinson, 1998). As one ad for Christian Aid Mission suggests, we must now embark on neocolonial mission work in which Indigenous missionaries can reach "hidden peoples" and penetrate "the most difficult barriers of all—political, cultural, religious, language and locale" and travel "behind doors closed to North Americans" (Greenway, 1989, 4; see also Mark Hutchinson, 1998). Evangelical mission journals claim that one-fourth of cross-cultural mission work is done by people from non-Western countries (Schipper, 1988, 198). *Charisma* notes that the fastest growing churches in the United States are non-English-speaking immigrant churches (P. Johnson, 2006a).

The inclusion of people of color and the erasure of racial oppression within the category of Christian is not untroubled, however. As Dorinne Kondo notes, assimilation is always unfinished business. "Even when colonized peoples imitate the colonizer, the mimesis is never complete, for the specter of the 'not quite, not white' haunts the colonizer, a dis-ease that always contains an implicit threat to the colonizer's hegemony" (Kondo, 1997). In other words, not only do groups that attempt to replicate the dominant culture never fully do so, but the very act of mimesis challenges the hegemonic claims of colonizers. The increasing number of non-European Christians threatens to reshape the character of Christianity itself fundamentally. Threatened by these possible shifts, evangelicals argue that it is imperative that Western missionaries train indigenous missionaries; otherwise, they leave open "the doors to syncretism, cults, and false teaching" (Padilla, 1991, 4). A particular "false" teaching seems to arise in churches when more people of color are included in a concern for racial justice (Burns, 2016). As an article in *Charisma* contends; these shifts are contributing to the development of "the new Christian left [which] is twisting the gospel" by confusing "caring for the poor with advancing socialist or big government systems and demonizing the United States for its free market system" (Vicari, 2015, 54).

To illustrate anxieties that develop around racial inclusion, Richard Land of the Southern Baptist Convention was asked what he would like to see in terms of race relations in 2045 in a 2001 *World* forum. He replied that he would like to see "the first African-American president" (little did he know how soon his wish would be granted) but specified that it must be a Republican. He then said he would like a continental Baptist convention that would be a merger of the American, Southern, and National Baptist Conventions (but then he specified that only the "evangelical" elements of these conventions must join). Implicit in these comments is that when the doors to evangelicalism are opened to African Americans they may bring agendas with them that may not coincide with those of white evangelicalism—hence their admission must be strictly regulated (Land, 2001).

Yet not all evangelicals display such levels of anxiety. For instance, *Christianity Today* argued that Western churches must stop thinking of themselves as the theological center. "The theology of the future is the theology of where the Christians are" (Lawton, 1997, 43). At the 2006 Urbana Conference, plenary speaker Oscar Muriu, the senior pastor of Nairobi Chapel in Kenya, explicitly stated that with the growth of Christianity in the Global South white evangelicals will no longer control the direction of Christianity. Although evangelicalism from Africa was perhaps even more socially conservative than in the United States, he contended that it would not remain silent on issues of economic neoliberalism between Africa and Western countries. He rather directly challenged U.S. imperialism within Christian evangelicalism. However, when I spoke to some participants at this conference, they complained that those anti-imperialist challenges were not in the videos produced from his talk.

Similarly, *Christianity Today* ran an article calling on evangelicals to go beyond "multicultural" representation because this form of representational politic becomes divorced from its social, political, and historical context. "While the message behind such images is positive, the images can become unhelpful and even dangerous if they are divorced from a story" (R. Chapman, 2011, 28). Native evangelicals have also contested notions of religious inferiority by arguing that Native peoples should be doing the missionary work rather than being objects of mission (C. Smith, 1997). When the Southern Baptist Convention developed a program with an International Mission Board to use Native peoples in the U.S. to evangelize in other Indigenous missions globally, Native evangelical Randy Woodley contended: "I don't think we should allow ourselves to be exploited for a Western approach to the gospel. . . . If we're going to leverage the fact that we're Native, we have to make sure that it actually is the Good News" (K. Tracy, 2014, 16).

Rethinking Multiculturalism

Many critical ethnic studies and other progressive scholars dismiss multiculturalism as simply a tool of neoliberalism and white supremacy. But then the question remains: if multiculturalism is so unimportant in the context of racial justice struggle, why is it so strongly resisted? For instance, when Barack Obama was elected president, many derided the notion that this election has any significance for antiracist movements. But then the same scholars point to the racial backlash that happened in the wake of his election. If his election meant nothing, then why was there such a backlash against him, culminating in the election of Donald Trump?

The goal and effect of multiculturalism is to domesticate the radical impulse within racial justice struggle. But to dismiss multiculturalism completely is perhaps ironically to minimize simultaneously the importance of white supremacy. That is, if we follow the lead of scholars such as Sylvia Wynter, Denise Da Silva, Alexander Weheliye, and other critical race theorists, racism is not simply a result of unfortunate stereotypes but the fundamental logic by which certain peoples are categorized outside the category of the human (Silva, 2007; Weheliye, 2008). To quote Ruth Wilson Gilmore: "Racism, specifically, is the state-sanctioned or extralegal production and exploitation of group-differentiated vulnerability to premature death" (Gilmore, 2007, 28). Thus, when those categorically defined as nonhuman (or as non-Christian) become included within that category, no matter how provisionally, the category becomes fundamentally destabilized. And in the case of evangelicalism in particular, where the world's majority of evangelicals are now not white, the presumed boundaries of evangelicalism itself become unstable because these boundaries are formulated through a disavowed whiteness.

While racial reconciliation emerged as a politics of inclusion—let us "include" people of color within evangelicalism—the inclusion of people of color served to destabilize the category itself by revealing evangelicalism's disavowed whiteness. In turn, this destabilization has enabled the proliferation of new kinds of evangelicalism, although these evangelicalisms may not necessarily center race either.

This relationship between racial reconciliation and seemingly white-dominated new evangelicalisms can be likened to some Marxist and women of color critiques of postmodernism and poststructuralist analyses of identity. These critiques note that both women of color and Marxist feminists have called into question the unitary category of "woman" that is supposed to be the object and subject of feminist analysis. For instance, Paula Moya discusses how women of color have consistently demonstrated that "women's" liberation in mainstream feminist politics and analysis has actually been a disavowed white women's liberation insensitive to racial differentiation (Moya, 1997). Nancy Hartsock similarly explores class differentiation among "women" (Hartsock, 1990). Both complain, however, that postmodern thinkers, relying on this insight from women of color or Marxist feminists, then use this work to destabilize the category of "women" altogether in order to delegitimize women of color and/or Marxist critique. As Moya protests, after the postmodern turn, "the feminist scholar who persists in using categories such as 'race' or 'gender' can be presumptively charged with essentialism" (Moya, 1997, 126). Similarly, Nancy Hartsock asks: "Why is it that just at the moment when so many of us who have been silenced begin to demand the right to name ourselves, to act as subjects rather than objects of history, that just then the concept of subjecthood becomes problematic?" (Hartsock, 1990, 162).

What is significant about their arguments is not so much that postmodern analysis disenables Marxist or race critiques. The plethora of work by scholars who do address capitalism, white supremacy, and heteropatriarchy from a nonessentialist perspective demonstrates the limits of this critique (Crenshaw, 1996; Joseph, 2004; Kazanjian, 2003; Kim, 2010; Puar, 2007; D. Rodriguez, 2009b; Silva, 2007; Weheliye, 2005). But it is certainly the case that many (white) postmodern scholars whose intellectual possibilities have been enabled by women of color or Marxist thinkers often then do not center the analytics of capitalism or white supremacy in their work. Because they do not do so, it would be easy then to place these strands of thought within an orthogonal relationship with each other rather than recognize their imbrication. One work that makes a critical intervention in this regard is Roderick Ferguson's *Aberrations in Black*. Here he addresses the disavowed whiteness of queer theory, not by arguing that queer theory has nothing to offer people of color but by demonstrating that women of color feminism in fact represents the intellectual genealogy of (white) queer theory. He does not argue that these intellectual strands are identical but demonstrates that even as (white) theory fails to address the logics of white supremacy adequately, its very being could not have existed without the work of women of color scholars and activists (Ferguson, 2003; Muñoz, 1999).

Similarly, various new evangelicalisms have proliferated that are often as white-dominated as mainstream evangelicalism. Consequently, it would be easy to see no analytical relationship between racial reconciliation and the proliferation of these new evangelicalisms. By not making these connections and by narrowly confining our analysis, we can then miss the larger import and impact of racial reconciliation. The inclusion of people of color within evangelicalism does not simply add them to a preexisting category of identification—it challenges that very category itself. Once this category is challenged, the space is created to redefine or transform what evangelicalism means for all peoples, not just people of color. Assessing the impact of racial reconciliation therefore requires us to go beyond projects or people who address race directly and to include the diversity of intellectual, spiritual, and political projects that have been enabled by racial reconciliation, even if they may seem to address race only peripherally. This is important because it challenges dominant modes of intellectual and political genealogy. As Alexander Weheliye notes, poststructuralist analysis is completely indebted to the work emerging out of anticolonial struggle, yet these thinkers disappear in the genealogy of poststructuralism. Whereas people of color are the add-on to the intellectual trends emerging out of Europe, in fact these European trends are actually the product of antiracist work often centered in colonized and racialized communities. As Weheliye cynically states about the disappearance of people of color theorists in critical theory: "If I didn't know any better, I would suppose that scholars not working in minority discourse seem thrilled that they no longer have to consult the scholarship of nonwhite thinkers now that European master subjects have deigned to weigh in on these topics" (Weheliye, 2014, 6).

Peter Heltzel's analysis has similarly critiqued the very notion that evangelicalism should be equated with white evangelicalism. The racial reconciliation movement itself is premised on the notion that white evangelicalism developed uninfluenced by Black evangelicalism. However, as Heltzel contends, white evangelicalism was fundamentally shaped by Black evangelicalism even as it disavows this influence. Perhaps, then, the problem with multiculturalism is that it does not take seriously how these racial inclusions have shaped theory and discourse at the broader level, even in sites that do not appear at first to be marked by race. Thus, ironically, dismissing the impact of multiculturalism can have the unintended consequence of relegating people of color to what Weheliye describes as "ethnographic locality" (Weheliye, 2014, 6), which dismisses their broader impacts and, in doing so, inadvertently reconsolidates the purported intellectual hegemony of whiteness. Thus, to address this concern, the next section explores some of the new evangelicalisms that can be at least partially traced to racial reconciliation.

New Evangelicalisms

Evangelical scholar Soong-Chan Rah's *The Next Evangelicalism* provides a helpful starting point to see the enabling connections between racial reconciliation and the proliferation of new evangelicalisms. In his book Rah goes beyond calling for multicultural inclusion within evangelicalism and challenges the disavowed whiteness of evangelicalism itself. In doing so, his critique fundamentally challenges not just how white evangelicals do or do not discuss race but how evangelicalism understands itself and its work. In particular, he examines how many of the church models seen as fundamental to evangelicalism are in fact based on logics of white supremacy.

Rah tackles the seeker-megachurch model that became prevalent in evangelicalism in the 1980s. The goal of this model was to become attractive to those "seekers" by shaping church life in a manner that would not be alienating to those interested in Christianity. Willow Creek Church in Barrington, Illinois, is often held up as an exemplar utilizing this model. This model often led to the development of huge, widely successful churches at least from an economic perspective. However, as Rah argues, this model was fundamentally based on a white supremacist framework by which church growth was predicated on homogeneity and comfort. This model holds that churches grow faster when they are racially homogeneous. "The homogen[e]ous unit principle allowed the white church to further propagate a system of white privilege by creating a system of de facto segregation. Segregation justified by a desire for church growth allows affluent white churches to remain separate" (Rah, 2009, 36). Theologically, Jesus was marketed as attractive and comforting to seekers rather than as a challenge to the status quo. Since racial integration and discussion of social justice issues frequently cause discomfort, they are projects to be avoided.

Along with the development of racial reconciliation emerges an implicit critique of the seeker model. Is Jesus meant to ratify the status quo or challenge it? Is a capitalist model of growth the best model for worshiping communities? Indeed, Bill Hybels, one of the leaders of the seeker-church model, later declared it a failure. He concurred with Rah that it promoted racial homogeneity because church growth was based on working with socially homogeneous communities that would be comfortable worshiping together (Gilbreath and Galli, 2005). While it attracted seekers, it did not provide a process for seekers to develop into mature believers (W. C. Smith, 2007c; Van Loon, 2008). Hybels was not alone—many began to weary of the megachurch model as well. The megachurch was critiqued for promoting capitalist growth at the expense of spiritually based communities (Veith, 2002, 2005g). The prosperity gospel that undergirds many of these churches was similarly critiqued for promoting materialism, disingenuous spiritual theatricality, and financial corruption rather than discipleship and concern for the poor and the vulnerable (J. L. Grady, 2009c; M. Green, 2005; Horrobin, 2008; Ross, 2009). Some prosperity gospel proponents themselves have begun to shy away (or least apologize for) their displays of financial excess (Briefs, 2007b).

Thus began the Gen-X models of churches that emphasized engaging the world in a manner that was believer-centered rather than seeker-centered. In some ways, these churches do not necessarily look markedly different from some seeker churches. But this trend in turn allowed other models to emerge that did shift possibilities for new kinds of formations. These new models are often as white-dominated as the older seeker-church models. And, in fact, some of them are reactionary. Yet racial reconciliation provided a pivotal intervention into the older model that enabled these newer models to develop.

Emergent Church

One such model is the Emergent or Emerging Church model. The Emergent Church more fundamentally questions some of the basic theological and ecclesiological premises of evangelicalism. Many of its intellectual progenitors, such as postmodern evangelical Stanley Grenz, questioned evangelicalism's investment in foundationalism and boundary-setting. Grenz challenged the "fundamentalist quest for the delineation of the one, timeless, systematization of the doctrine that supposedly lies waiting to be discovered in the pages of the bible" (Grenz, 2000, 159). Unlike postmodern analysis, which might claim no ultimate "truth," evangelical postmodernism did not reject all foundationalist claims to truth but defined these foundations eschatologically. That is, the ultimate truth is not knowable until the next eschaton. In the meantime, this ultimate truth is mediated through social and linguistic context and, hence, humility on the part of faith believers who claim to know it is necessary, Grenz writes with John Franke that there is "'objectivity' to the world. But this objectivity is not that of a static reality existing outside of, and contemporarily with, our socially and linguistically constructed reality . . . [rather, it] is an objectivity of a *future*, eschatological world" (Grenz and Franke, 2000, 53).

As Stanley Fish notes, postmodern analysis does not preclude the making of truth claims:

> While relativism is a position one can entertain, it is not a position one can occupy. No one can be a relativist, because no one can achieve the distance from his [sic] own beliefs and assumptions which would result in their being no more authoritative *for him* than the beliefs and assumptions held by others. When his beliefs change, the norms and values to which he once had unthinking assent will have been demoted to the status of opinions and become the objects of an analytical and critical attention; but that attention will itself be enabled by a new set of norms and values that are, for the time being, as unexamined and undoubted as those they displace. The point is that there is never a moment when one believes nothing. (Fish, 2005, 309)

Similarly, postmodern evangelicals do not avoid truth claims but make them with the knowledge that context shapes our understanding of "truth."

Postmodern evangelical theological method then shifts from boundary setting to theological conversation. According to Grenz, we must question the notion that "theology—or more particularly, a definitive list of doctrinal formulations—can function as the final arbiter as to who is 'in' and who is 'out'" (Grenz and Franke, 2000, 176). Grenz's work is in conversation with other evangelicals who were calling for increased boundary-setting (Olson et al., 1998, 44). Grenz argues in response to boundary-setters for a "generous orthodoxy" in which various theological conversations could constellate around an evangelical center that does not necessarily need to exclude those positions that might be on the evangelical periphery (Grenz and Franke, 2000, 326). Similarly, evangelical theologian Paul Metzger borrows from missiologist Paul Hiebert's work to differentiate between bounded and centered sets as models for defining evangelicalism. A bounded set focuses on static boundaries to define who is in and who is out. A centered set centers on core evangelical beliefs but is less concerned with excluding everyone who falls outside of a certain boundary (P. Metzger, 2012, 33). This methodology advocated by Metzger is generally used by *Relevant Magazine*, which features non-Christian and otherwise controversial people. Editor Cameron Strang explained this approach: "We don't have to agree with everything someone says to learn from them. God has given us all discernment. Don't be afraid to be challenged. God can use a wide variety of people and ideas to draw us closer to Him. . . . We need to have that conversation" (C. Strang, 2011). And in 2002 some evangelical scholars published the "Word Made Fresh," calling for evangelicals to spend less time boundary-setting and more time promoting more open-ended theological conversations (R. Mohler, 2002; T. Morgan, 2002).

Grenz does not engage issues of race substantively or cite the works of evangelicals of color extensively. Yet he notes that the development of postmodern evangelicalism was enabled by the growing visibility of non-Western Christians who demonstrated that (white) evangelicalism's claims to objective doctrinal purity were foundationally based on Eurocentric frameworks (Grenz and Franke, 2000, 176).

Emergent churches developed that then began to operationalize this approach (Crouch, 2004; Gibbs and Bolger, 2005; McLaren and Litfin, 2004). The center of the Emergent Movement is often ascribed to Emergent Village, which formed out of the Leadership Network headed by Doug Pagitt (Emergent Village, n.d.). The Emergent Village was created to help facilitate the emerging conversation, with Tony Jones serving as coordinator. Eventually, however, this position was eliminated to foster more decentralization (O'Brien, 2009b). A prominent emergent writer is Brian McLaren, who adopts Grenz's call for a "generous orthodoxy" (McLaren, 2007b). His work focuses on calling Christians to be actively engaged with social justice in the world. McLaren speaks out against a number of injustices: racism, war, Israeli occupation, imperialism, environmental degradation, and sexism. He rejects the quest for theological certainty in favor of actually doing the work of Jesus in the world. The activity of Jesus is concerned more with people outside the church. "Because Jesus moves toward all people in love and kindness and grace, *we do the same*. . . . Our Christian identity must not make us afraid of, superior to, isolated from, defensive or aggressive toward, or otherwise hostile to people of other religions" (McLaren, 2007b, 281). McLaren in turn is often accused of being insufficiently orthodox on doctrinal issues and social issues such as homosexuality (DeYoung and Gluck, 2008; McKnight, 2010) and is generally portrayed as being on the most radical end of the Emergent Movement (McKnight, 2008).

In general, Emergent theologies, while they are not against propositional truth, often follow Grenz's mandate to assert truth with humility (Friesen, 2007, 209). Of course, because Emerging churches are not primarily concerned with doctrinal boundaries, they can be difficult to define. They do not cluster around a specific set of beliefs or worship practice (Conder, 2007; T. Jones, 2007). However, Eddie Gibbs and Ryan Bolger outline some commonalities among these churches: "Emerging churches (1) identify with the life of Jesus; (2) transform the secular realm, and (3) live highly communal lives. Because of these three activities, they (4) welcome the stranger, (5) serve with generosity; (6) participate as producers, (7) create as created beings, (8) lead as a body, and (9) take part in spiritual activities" (Gibbs and Bolger, 2005, 43). The goal becomes less about telling the gospel of Jesus and more about living the gospel in communities oriented to justice. Services may be conversations rather than one-way sermons. Arts and ritual may be emphasized in addition to intellectual exchange. Worship may be conducted more informally with believers who commit to a more ongoing relationship with each other beyond attending Sunday services (McKnight, 2007).

Brian McLaren traces the shifts in his theological perspective to the challenges made by antiracist and anticolonial critiques that help "us in the West to understand and undermine our own colonial culture's confidence-mania and uncertainty-phobia" (McLaren, 2007a, 44). These antiracist critiques further reveal how the modern missionary movement has adopted "the spirit of colonialism, white supremacy, Eurocentrism, jingoism and chauvinism" (McLaren, 2007a, 285).

Of course, the antiracist critique that emerged from evangelical racial reconciliation is not the only stream that helped produce the Emergent Movement, but many Emerging writers trace the development of their thinking to exposure to antiracist critique. Nevertheless, the Emergent Movement is generally white-dominated. Rah makes a critique of Emergent churches similar to Moya's and Harstock's critique of postmodernism. He contends that the destabilization of the metanarrative in evangelicalism has led to a focus on local instantiations of evangelical faith—but that these local instantiations are also white. The Emergent church has created "a new metanarrative out of the local narrative of younger white evangelicals" (Rah, 2009, 117), which leads to "authenticity expressed exclusively through a white, Western perspective" (Rah, 2009, 116). To illustrate his point, Rah tells the following story of his interaction in an Emergent workshop. "So there I was, sitting in yet another workshop led by yet another blonde-haired, perpetually twenty-nine, white male with a goatee" (Rah, 2009, 108), who was giving examples of model Emergent churches, all of which were white. Rah asked the speaker about churches in Asian, Latinx, and African American communities. The response: "We have found that there are no Black, Asian, or Hispanic . . . churches of any significance" (Rah, 2009, 109). Rah jokes that a book written by someone in the Emergent Movement "was written by a Protestant male under the age of 40. He probably has a goatee. He definitely wears eyeglasses that are much cooler than yours" (Rah, 2009, 109). He further notes that there are about 150 Emergent churches today but more than 50 books written by people in that movement. Meanwhile, there are 700 churches ministering to second-generation Asian Americans but fewer than 5 books written that address Asian American ministry. Thus, Rah's analysis demonstrates the complicated relationship between racial reconciliation and the Emergent Movement. On the one hand, racial reconciliation has certainly enabled the "death of the metanarrative" that provided a foundation for the Emergent Movement. As Emergent leader Tony Jones stated: "Any time you can dethrone an overeducated, loud, brash, white man, people just feel more openness for their own voice to be heard" (O'Brien, 2009a, 14). Yet this movement disavowed this political and theological genealogy and once again recenters whiteness in its articulation of a new church. But the whiteness of the Emergent Movement should not prevent us from seeing the role of racial reconciliation in enabling this movement to develop. And to be fair, at least some sectors of this movement have heard these critiques and have taken them seriously (Pagitt and Jones, 2007).

Meanwhile, the Emergent Movement has had its own divisions and debates, with some key figures such as Scot McKnight, Dan Kimball, and Mark Driscoll eventually disassociating from it (O'Brien, 2009a). However, as Rah argues, the Emergent Church often becomes seen as synonymous with all new evangelical churches that are challenging entrenched theologies and ecclesiologies. While it is a vital strand, it is one of many strands, which include hip-hop churches, hipster churches, Indigenous churches, and others (O'Brien, 2009b, 63; E. Smith and P. Jackson, 2005). In addition, this principle of challenging theological boundedness is not solely located within Emergent churches either. For instance, Efrem Smith and Phil Jackson argue in *The Hip-Hop Church* that Christian Rap is essentially appealing to white suburban audiences, as is holy hip-hop, which they argue is promoted primarily in white venues or Black megachurches rather than in urban areas. Their foundation for the hip-hop church is more grounded in secular hip-hop and liberation theology and does not completely denounce the Nation of Islam as other sectors of evangelicalism do. They call for a Christian hip-hop church that actually speaks to the urban poor who are not churched. "The gospel according to hip-hop is justice" (E. Smith and P. Jackson, 2005, 214). And Indigenous churches are rejecting the evangelical policing of the boundaries between Christianity and Indigenous spiritual traditions and calling for an end to settler colonialism (see chapter 6).

Of course, the conversations and conscientization that emerged from racial reconciliation would not be the only foundation for the emergence of these new movements. But it certainly seems to be the case that many evangelicals were not able to engage seriously with communities of color without questioning some of their presuppositions about evangelical faith. This questioning then produced new conversations that provided an opportunity for new evangelicalisms to emerge even among those not directly involved in racial reconciliation.

New Monasticism

If the Emergent Movement focuses its attention on living the gospel rather than espousing the gospel, New Monasticism takes that focus very literally. One of the most prominent communities of this movement, A Simple Way, began in 1996 when Eastern University students protested the eviction of homeless families from an abandoned St. Edward Church in Kensington, Pennsylvania. They decided to live with the homeless families in the church and posted the sign: "How can you worship a homeless man on Sunday and ignore him on Monday?" (Moll, 2005, 39). This experience inspired these students to rethink what the relationship should be between Christians and the poor. They formed an intentional community (A Simple Way) two years later in that same neighborhood. Shane Claiborne, one of the most prominent spokespersons of this movement, describes the philosophy behind his participation in this movement in *The Irresistible Revolution*. Like Soong-Chan Rah, Claiborne explicitly critiques the seeker model, albeit from a more anticapitalist rather than racial justice perspective:

> In our culture of "seeker sensitivity," . . . the great temptation is to compromise the cost of discipleship in order to draw a larger crowd. With the most sincere hearts, we do not want to see anyone walk away from Jesus because of the discomfort of the cross. I think this is why the disciples [in the gospels] react as they do. They protest in awe. . . . ("Why must you make it so hard? We need some rich folks here, Jesus, we're trying to build a movement"). And yet Jesus lets them walk away. (Claiborne, 2006, loc. 874–90)

While Claiborne focuses on addressing poverty, his work is embedded in a larger global analysis that critiques U.S. imperialism in Latin America and in Iraq, multinational capitalism, and racial injustice. For Claiborne, it is not sufficient to simply "help the poor"; Christians must actually become the poor and organize against the conditions that create poverty and injustice. His work takes Jesus' admonition "Again I tell you, it is easier for a camel to go through the eye of a needle than for someone who is rich to enter the kingdom of God" (Matthew 19:24, NIV) quite literally.

In 2004 a conference in Durham, North Carolina, brought together many of these communities who adopted the name New Monasticism, borrowed from Jonathan R. Wilson's *Living Faithfully in a Fragmented World* (Moll, 2005). The characteristics that the participants in this conference articulated that would define this movement include "submission to the larger church, living with the poor and outcast, living near community members, hospitality, nurturing a common community life and a shared economy, peacemaking, reconciliation, care for creation, celibacy or monogamous marriage, formation of new members along the lines of the old novitiate, and contemplation" (Moll, 2005, 41). As with the Emergent Church, this conference was not necessarily dominated by people of color, but racial reconciliation was a central theme of the conference, with racial reconciliationist Chris Rice in attendance (Moll, 2005).

Like the Emergent Movement, New Monasticism attempts to decenter orthodoxy in order to highlight orthopraxy. This does not mean that doctrine is unimportant, but, to quote Claiborne, "For us belief is only the beginning. What really matters is how we live, how what we believe gets fleshed out, so we also have a statement of orthopraxis (meaning 'right living, right practices')" (Claiborne, 2006, loc. 296–310). Frequently, members of these communities hold outside jobs and then donate a portion (often half or more) of their income to the common household. These communities are often engaged in direct social advocacy. A Simple Way organizes against local antihomelessness legislation. Camden House focuses on organizing against environmental racism in Camden, New Jersey. Rutba House fosters racial reconciliation in Durham, North Carolina. Thus, many of these communities do not focus just on promoting harmonious interpersonal relationships but on addressing social and political inequities.

This movement implicitly critiques the capitalist underpinnings of the evangelical megachurch growth model by calling on Christians to take seriously Jesus' command to bless the poor. Quoting Tony Campolo, Claiborne argues: "Jesus never says to the poor, 'Come find the church,' but he says to those of us in the church, 'Go into the world and find the poor, hungry, homeless, imprisoned'" (Claiborne, 2006, loc. 852–68). Further, argues Claiborne: "Jesus doesn't exclude rich people; he just lets them know their rebirth will cost them everything they have. . . . The kingdom of God . . . has an ethic and economy diametrically opposed to those of the world"

(Claiborne, 2006, loc. 874–90). However, they do so by not simply feeding the poor but attempting to transform the social structures that create poverty in the first place.

Interestingly, this movement in many ways resembles the model of organizing becoming more prevalent in radical social movements that call on activists to take power by "making power" (A. Smith, 2005b). That is, rather than simply attempting to seize state power directly, the movements attempt to create autonomous zones in which they model the world that they would like to live in. They attempt to organize beyond the "nonprofit industrial complex" as well as to reject revolutionary vanguard elite politics.

In fact, radical critiques of the nonprofit industrial complex (Incite, 2007) sound very similar to Claiborne's critique: "With new government funds and faith-based initiatives, the social-work model can easily entangle the church in the efficiency of brokering services and resources. . . . Faith-based nonprofits can too easily be the mirror image of secular organizations, maintaining the same hierarchies of power and separation between rich and poor. They can too easily merely facilitate the exchange of goods and services, putting plenty of professionals in the middle to guarantee that the rich do not have to face the poor and that power does not shift" (Claiborne, 2006, loc. 874–90, 1379–95). However, the more radical movements do not just create separate communities but attempt to proliferate these zones so that they can eventually squeeze out the current system. These movements are in fact reaching critical mass, particularly in Latin America (A. Smith, 2005b). New Monasticism also faces the same challenges as other movements in terms of building long-term sustainability as well as addressing charges of being a "new legalism" or being devoid of biblical principles (Mayfield, 2016).

The New Reformed Movement

While the destabilization of evangelical metanarratives that have resulted from racial reconciliation has provided a space for the proliferation of new evangelicalisms, these new evangelicalisms are not singularly progressive. One such regressive strand can be seen in the evolution of Mark Driscoll's ministry. Originally identifying with the Emergent Movement, he eventually left because he did not deem it sufficiently orthodox. He later became more identified with the growing resurgence of the New Reformed Movement. He retained some aspects of Emergent sensibilities, such as engaging with culture, being open to spiritual gifts, cursing, preaching in an informal style, and so forth. However, the New Reformed Movement is generally theologically conservative and more doctrinally systematic. Eventually, however, allegations of plagiarism and his abuse of authority led to his church being disaffiliated in 2014 from the Acts 29 Network that he cofounded. Driscoll then resigned from his Mars Hill Church, and Mars Hill churches dissolved and formed into independent congregations in 2015.[3]

Many debates have ensued between New Reformed and Emergent pastors. For instance, John Piper (Council on Biblical Manhood and Womanhood), who is a pastor of Bethlehem Baptist Church in Minnesota, told Doug Pagitt of the Emergent Solomon's Porch in Minnesota that "he should never preach" (Hansen, 2008b). Like the Emergent gatherings, groups such as the Gospel Coalition host conferences to foster the Reformed resurgence and marry orthodox biblical interpretation with cultural engagement (Hansen, 2007b). This movement is particularly marked by reactionary gender politics and an almost complete lack of engagement with racial justice issues. Driscoll in particular became a vocal proponent for the evangelical he-man, women hater's club. According to Driscoll, the church has become "a bunch of nice, soft, tender, chickified church boys. Sixty percent of Christians are chicks . . . and the forty percent that are dudes are still sort of chicks" (O'Brien, 2008, 49). He complains that the church images a "Richard Simmons, hippie, queer Christ" that "is no one to love and is no one to die for" (O'Brien, 2008, 49). Jesus is a "heterosexual, win-a-fight, punch-you-in-the-nose dude"—Jesus is not a "limp-wristed, dress-wearing hippie" (O'Brien, 2008, 50). We need an "ultimate fighting Jesus" (O'Brien, 2008, 49). He once implied that Ted Haggard's infidelities were the result of his wife letting herself go (Hansen, 2007a).

The rise of the evangelical he-man women hater's club has been strongly critiqued by many, including an extensive article in *Christianity Today* (O'Brien, 2008). That article argued that this model of Jesus and the church necessarily excludes women and essentially demonizes them for being faithful Christians. According to this logic, "When the church adopts the supposedly male psyche it fulfills its purpose, but when it conforms to the supposedly female psyche, it becomes aberrant" (O'Brien, 2008, 50). It also deifies masculinity. "A man's urge for battle may well be natural, but that doesn't automatically make it godly. In other words, conversion does not sanctify our instincts; rather, it demands that we submit all our instincts to the lordship of Christ" (O'Brien, 2008, 50). In the end, Jesus did not become the "perfect male; he is the perfect human being. . . . If Adam and Eve illustrate the essential differences between men and women, Christ highlights their essential unity" (O'Brien, 2008, 50). Rachel Held Evans called on evangelicals to call out Mark Driscoll for his sexist and homophobic remarks in her blog: "Mark Driscoll is a bully. Stand up to him." She argued, "What we have on our hands is a bully. And this bully is teaching the young men at his church and under his influence that bullying is an acceptable expression of 'biblical manhood.' This has to stop. As followers of Jesus, we are obligated to stick up for the least of these, especially when they are being publicly bullied in the name of Christ" (R. H. Evans, 2011). And to be fair, the Gospel Coalition has published blogs recently critiquing racism and sexism among evangelicals (Anyabwile, 2016, 2018).

The point here, of course, is not to blame racial reconciliation for the misogyny of the New Reformed Movement. Rather, as Stuart Hall notes, it is important to realize that there are no guarantees with liberatory politics. In this case, the effects of racial reconciliation (or any other movement for that matter) can have far-reaching unintended impacts that may be both liberatory and regressive. Those interested in rearticulating evangelical politics must always keep engaging in rearticulation because political formations are not stable or static.

Conclusion

It can be easy to dismiss programs like "From Chit'lins to Caviar" for their multiculturalist politics of racial reconciliation. Like its secular counterparts, much racial reconciliation rhetoric seems intent on effecting racial inclusion within an essentially white evangelical framework. At the same time, when one assesses the profound changes in how evangelicalism is practiced, even in formations that do not center race relations, it seems clear that within this multiculturalist politic (as well as the backlash against it) it is not actually so easy simply to include people of color within Christian evangelicalism without more fundamentally challenging the categories of evangelicalism itself. As will be discussed in the next chapter, some of what seem to be ineffectual multiculturalist responses to race within Christian evangelicalism actually point to the disavowed multiculturalist assumptions within progressive critiques of multiculturalism.

2 "WE DON'T HAVE A SKIN PROBLEM, WE HAVE A SIN PROBLEM"
Racial Reconciliation and the Permanency of Racism

> Black people will never gain full equality in this country. Even those herculean efforts we hail as successful will produce no more than temporary "peaks of progress," short-lived victories that slide into irrelevance as racial patterns adapt in ways that maintain white dominance.—Derrick Bell (1995, 306)

> We don't have a skin problem, we have a sin problem.
> —Wellington Boone (1996, 85)

Wellington Boone's articulation of racism might seem to be diametrically opposed to that of Derrick Bell. However, they are both wrestling with what appears to be the permanent nature of white supremacy. That is, if we understand society to be inherently racial, then the question arises: what can be done to eliminate it? Or even can it be eliminated? A plethora of scholars, such as Bell, have argued that it cannot. He calls on Black people to "acknowledge the permanence of our subordinate status" (Bell, 1995, 306). He disavows any possibility of "transcendent change" (308). To the contrary, he argues, "It is time we concede that a commitment to racial equality merely perpetuates our disempowerment" (307). The alternative that he advocates is resistance for its own sake—living "to harass white folks" (308) or short-term pragmatic strategies that focus less on eliminating racism and more on simply ensuring that we do not "worsen conditions for those we are trying to help" (308).

In many respects, we can understand much evangelical discourse around race following a similar logic. That is, the notion that we don't have a "skin problem, we have a sin problem" suggests a deep pessimism about the role of social change. Earl Jackson essentially argues that racism is caused not so much by structures or institutions, but rather by immorality and sinfulness. Like Bell, racial reconciliationists have noted the limited effects of legislative change. Unlike Bell, however, their pessimism toward social change is accompanied by an optimistic view about the ability of spiritual transformation to end racism as well as the ability of evangelical Christians to create a "safe space" without racism. In this chapter I explore the problems as well as the possibilities inherent in spiritual optimism.

"I had to stop doing those racial reconciliation events. Every time white Christians wanted to repent for their racism against Native Americans, they insisted on washing my feet—and I was having to spend too much money on pedicures."[1] This joke by Native evangelical Richard Twiss speaks to the growing frustration with racial reconciliation among many evangelicals of color. Racial reconciliation tends to focus on symbolic performances of reconciliation without any political commitment to dismantling white supremacy. Particularly during the inception of racial reconciliation, the rhetoric generally equated racism and racial prejudice, leaving out any analysis of social power (Crespo, 2006; Randy Frame, 1988; Geisler, 1994; C. George, 2001; J. L. Grady, 2007a; Hull, 1997; Keener, 2003; G. Lewis, 1995; Lutes, 1988; Mathewes-Green, 1995; J. Moore, 1987; Paulson, 2002; Skinner, 1989; Wiens, 1988). As a result, racism was described primarily as a personal or "spiritual" problem (Randy Frame, 1990; A. Gaines, 2000; V. Lowe, 2001; Stetson, 1997), possibly resulting from faulty biblical analysis (W. Baker, 1987; Loving People Who Are Different, 1986; Mains, 1994). Its remedy lay in the changing of individual attitudes and behaviors rather than in a fundamental reweaving of the social fabric. "Racial diversity brightens and enriches God's mural of humanity" (Weary, 1993), one conservative evangelical asserted; "love—not laws" (Sidey, 1993, 4), intoned another.[2] In fact, *Christianity Today* ran an article that basically espoused Bell's thesis on the permanency of racism. "We cannot rid ourselves of racism. . . . Yet this seeming cause for despair actually prevents despair" (Galli, 2015b, 26). However, the response to the permanency of racism is "bringing blacks and whites together to hear each other out" (Galli, 2015b, 25).

While racial reconciliation through personal relationships is encouraged, racial reconciliation through social action is often depicted as counterproductive (Banks, 2002; No-Comment Zone, 1999). For instance, Cleveland-based minister Damon Lynch III called for a boycott of downtown Cleveland in 2001 in reaction to the lack of city response to riots that resulted from a police officer being acquitted after shooting an unarmed nineteen-year-old Black man. A white Cleveland minister, Phil Heimlich, cited Martin Luther King Jr. as his role model for racial reconciliation while simultaneously criticizing Lynch for having a "political agenda" because he engaged in civil disobedience. Apparently, Heimlich was not aware that King's primary strategy for racial reconciliation was civil disobedience (Carnes, 2001).

Because racism is constructed as a spiritual or personal problem, the solution to racism generally takes the form of "aggressive evangelism" (Bird, 1990, 17; Geisler, 1995; Lawton, 1998; Wooding, 1994) or intense prayer without social action (Daigle, 1999; Richardson, 2007). As former Ku Klux Klan (KKK) member cum racial reconciliationist Tom Tarrants states, "[Racism] is an issue of the lordship of Jesus Christ; it is not a sociological issue" (Maxwell, 1994, 26).³ And *Charisma* helpfully suggests that white people should get their hair cut at African American salons to break down social barriers (J. L. Grady, 2006a).

This failure to acknowledge any sweeping material or ideological basis for racism enables periodicals to print articles on the evils of racial prejudice and then follow them up with calls to repeal affirmative action, support immigration moratoriums, and oppose multicultural curriculums in schools (Neff, 1997a; M. Olasky, 2001c; J. Wilson, 1999). In the "Racism" issue of the NAE's *United Evangelical Action*, for example, Henry Soles offered the following reasonable observation: "The rise of a perceived 'Moral Majority' mentality in evangelical circles has offended many blacks and makes it difficult to have meaningful dialogue. The black community views . . . right-wing religio-political pressure groups as weak in their application of biblical principles to the needs of oppressed people, in general, and blacks in particular" (Soles, 1985, 5). In the same issue, however, the NAE Office of Public Affairs announced that it opposed a Civil Rights Bill up for debate at that time (Dugan, 1985). *World Magazine* and the Christian reconstructionist *Rutherford* argued without a trace of irony that opposing affirmative action was in keeping with the spirit of Martin Luther King Jr. (Hymowitz, 1995; The Year in Review, 1996/1997). Predictably, the more overtly political Christian Right organizations like Concerned Women for America and the Christian Coalition during the inception of the racial reconciliation movement also failed to suggest structural changes for addressing racism, opposed affirmative action, and supported immigration restrictions, the eradication of treaty rights, and rollbacks in civil rights legislation (Field, 1996; Gage, 1996; Jones, 1996b; New Bytes, 1996).

On occasion, conservative Christians did analyze the structural aspects of racism. As discussed previously, William Pannell's work focused on structural racism. Lyn Cryderman in *Christianity Today* wrote about the importance of antidiscrimination legislation and affirmative action within the context of poverty and segregation (Cryderman, 1987). In the wake of the L.A. riots, a few articles addressed racial disparities in the criminal justice system and supported policies like affirmative action (The Church after Rodney King, 1992; Jan Johnson, 1992; McDonald, 1992; Tapia, 1993; J. Wilson, 1993). These articles, however, were typically followed by angry letters of denunciation to the editor (Spickard, 1986). Don Argue, former president of the National Association of Evangelicals (NAE), acknowledged at a 1994 meeting with the National Black Evangelical Association (NBEA) that "racism is prejudice with power. [We] have been the slow ones here. We do not have to deal with the problems of racism day to day" (T. Morgan, 1994a, 51). The NAE and NBEA issued a joint statement maintaining that "although prejudice is a universal sin infecting all peoples, racism in America is basically a white problem," with "practices, systems, and laws which entrench racism ... and perpetuate [it]." The statement calls for a removal of "the institutional barriers" that oppress people of color (NAE NBEA Groups Join to Condemn Racism, 1990). In general, however, even when writers addressed structural issues, their solutions entailed changing personal behavior. The exhortation to develop cross-racial relationships is especially common.[4] For instance, one article in *Charisma* addressed racism in the criminal justice system, particularly sentencing disparities with crack and cocaine convictions. But in the end the problem is not white racism but "the prince of darkness" (K. Daniels, 2005).

The white evangelical response to the disasters in New Orleans demonstrates this tendency to address racism interpersonally rather than structurally. *World* magazine portrayed the discussions about racism and Katrina as mere liberal political ploys designed to appeal to African American constituencies (Vincent, 2006a). "Politics also played a role with liberals framing the story as one of rich people not caring about poor people and whites not caring about blacks. ... The international image of America, crucial to the war on terror, took an enormous hit, as journalists described rampant heartlessness. [It was] an opportunity to campaign overtly for higher taxes and bigger government" (M. Olasky, 2005d).

World did write an article critiquing racism in some of the media coverage and reversing some of its previous articles that depicted evacuees as "repaying kindness with retribution over imagined slights" (Cheaney, 2005b), as well as claims that "all the people requesting aid have last names like 'Ramirez' and 'Garcia' who just want to buy drugs" (Rainey, 2006b). Now, *World* asserted, "the picture that emerged was one of African-American masses of flood victims resorting to utter depravity, randomly attacking each other as well as the police trying to protect them and rescue workers trying to save them. In reality, almost all were law-abiding.... [The narrative was that] 'crazy black people with automatic weapons are out hunting white people'" (Dawson and Olasky, 2005; M. Olasky, 2005d). However, this racism was blamed on "liberal bias" in the media (Lightbody, 1992)![5]

At the inception of racial reconciliation, there appears to have been an inverse relationship between the political focus of writers and organizations and the depth of their race analysis. That is, the more involved an individual or organization was in the political process, the less likely it was to call for sweeping social responses to racism. For instance, the overtly political Christian Coalition, particularly under the guidance of its first executive director, Ralph Reed, hired workers to network with primarily African American communities, but not for the purpose of mobilizing them to fight for racial justice. From the Christian Coalition's point of view, racial justice does not seem to require any legislative change at all. As noted previously, the Reverend Earl Jackson, its director of rural development, explained: "We do not have a race problem in America, we have a sin problem" (Christian Coalition Official Says Ending Sin Will End Racism, 1996). The coalition's inconsistency is apparent in the completely different approach that it took to its true core issues such as abortion. It never argued: "We don't have a problem with abortion; we have a problem with sin. Passing laws against abortion won't work. We must change the hearts of men and women in this society." For *these* issues, the Christian Coalition developed an extensive array of citizen training manuals and videos offering detailed "how-to" information on influencing the legislative process at the local, state, and federal levels. Apparently, the coalition does not trust the persuasive power of the Bible to win over the hearts and minds of America on the issues that it really considers important.

The Christian Coalition's foray into racial reconciliation seemed to end when Ralph Reed stepped down from the position of executive director in 1997 (Christian Coalition's Ralph Reed Steps Down, 1997). The one racial reconciliation program, the Samaritan Project, went independent because "it had difficulty being perceived as genuinely interested in minorities while under the Christian Coalition umbrella" (Christian Coalition Retrenches, 1998). In 2006 it appeared that the Christian Coalition might go in a new direction when Joel Hunter was selected to head it. He had planned to work against political polarization by collaborating with liberal organizations such as MoveOn.org to promote internet accessibility and to broaden the agenda of the Christian Coalition to include "social justice and creation care" (Gaines, 2006c, 19). However, the chapters in Ohio, Iowa, Alabama, and Georgia defected in reaction to this announced broader agenda. When the board then decided that Hunter would only be allowed to work on abortion and same-sex marriage, he resigned (News Briefs, 2007a).

Conservative Christian organizations like the Promise Keepers were a more complex case. At the height of its popularity, Promise Keepers speakers did discuss racism on the institutional level, covering such diverse issues as treaty rights, English-Only laws, busing, and affirmative action. For instance, frequent Promise Keepers speaker A. R. Bernard argued that while people of color should not blame "the system, we cannot judge an individual for his actions solely by his own will without considering the socioeconomic conditions that influenced some of the choices he makes" (Gaines, 2002b, 63). However, the solution to these problems in Promise Keepers was always a personal response: white evangelicals should get to know people of color and befriend them (R. Cooper, 1995; Dawson, 1994; Washington and Kehrein, 1993; G. Yancey, 1996). Unlike the Christian Coalition, Promise Keepers was explicitly apolitical, although its commitment to refraining from electoral politics has shifted considerably since its inception. At the 1996 New York City rally at Shea Stadium, no political literature of any kind was distributed. While Bill McCartney himself campaigned for the anti-gay Amendment 2 in Colorado (Conason et al., 1996), Promise Keepers took no stand on the issue and appears to have made a concerted effort to refrain from overtly anti-gay rhetoric at its rallies—an impressive feat, given the probable anti-gay bias of most of its participants. Promise Keepers' lack of legislative activity on behalf of racial reconciliation therefore does not necessarily connote insincerity. Within the constraints of its mission, Promise Keepers has tried to live up to its rhetoric through program development, staff hiring, and membership recruitment. As discussed in the introduction, after the 1997 Stand in the Gap Rally, attendance at Promise Keepers events peaked. In 1998 Promise Keepers attempted to increase its base by not charging for attendance at its rallies. This strategy failed to attract non-Christians and instead resulted in Promise Keepers having to lay off its staff. As a result, the Promise Keepers began to fall out of mainstream public view. When it was trying to appeal to a broader base, the Promise Keepers seemed to temper its more politically conservative rhetoric. But when its evangelistic efforts failed to gain traction and it was under less public scrutiny, Promise Keepers speakers adopted more explicitly political positions that appealed to its conservative base. Most of the speakers at the 2004 Seattle Rally were white, and virtually no speaker addressed race relations directly. They did, however, promote books that advocated against same-sex marriage, held prayers to support the U.S. war in Iraq, and featured politically conservative comic Brad Stine, who criticized France for failing to support the U.S. "War on Terror."

This comparative analysis of Promise Keepers and the Christian Coalition illustrates that virtually no prominent conservative evangelical organizations were calling for structural changes to eradicate racism at the inception of racial reconciliation. However, this tendency to depoliticize race within evangelical organizations began to shift post-Ferguson (see the conclusion).

Class as Race

The racial reconciliation movement has often minimized any material basis for racism: racism is simply a reflection of stereotypes that can be easily unlearned. Because racial reconciliation activists generally avoid any materialist analysis of racism, racial politics often emerge through class. The Christian Coalition, for example, packaged its racial politics through an appeal to middle-class solidarity. Ralph Reed unequivocally described the coalition as a "middle class, highly educated suburban phenomenon" (Cromartie, 1996b, 35). He asserted that (white) evangelical voters are now of the same class background as mainline Protestants (Guth, 1996b)—although most evangelicals in general are Black and lower-income—and also appealed to the African American middle class to side with him against the inner-city poor, whom he describes as devoid of spiritual and moral values. "What distinguishes the underclass from those who rise out of the ghettos," he opined, "is not their poverty alone but their behavior—crime, lawlessness, illegitimacy, and delinquency" (R. Reed, 1990, 89). Similarly, *World* suggests that sexual deviance and drug use among suburban white youth can be traced to the "blackening" of their culture through hip-hop (Bradley, 2006). Consequently, it is not a surprise that much evangelical rhetoric around poverty is punitive or at least unsympathetic (J. Belz, 2009).[6] As one letter writer to *Charisma* complained: "I really have grown weary of you 'do-gooders.'... You'd be astounded at how quickly all of the poor bums in America would be able to find employment if their alternative were to work in a forced labor camp!" (Letters, 1999, 8).

This rhetoric clearly equates "poor underclass" with "Black." As Christian Reconstructionist R. J. Rushdoony articulates: "Today, millions of Negroes ... are demanding that the federal government become their slavemaster and provide them with security and care" (quoted in Lienesch, 1993, 132). Concerned Women for America's *Family Voice* article "Is the Church Ready for Welfare Reform?" offers a similar portrait of Black dependence and white patronage. In the pictures that accompany the article, welfare recipients are all Black and their benefactors are all white. One fairly typical story describes a church minister who requires that the people who come to him for aid perform some manual labor and be a member of a home church. The minister is surprised that many ungrateful folks balk at these requirements, and nobody takes up the other side of the story: the minister is taking advantage of the poor by paying them subminimum wages and compelling religious affiliation by threatening to withhold even that meager assistance (Hutchens, 1995, 11). This article is emblematic of Christian Right literature: the face of poverty is almost invariably of color,[7] while the face of those who "save" people from poverty is generally white.[8]

Christian Right ideologies trace the roots of poverty among people of color to their "welfare mentality" and ignore the effects of corporate downsizing and the relocation of jobs to the Global South. The reasoning goes: if there are no structural reasons for poverty, then poverty must be the fault of the poor who lack "self-control and personal responsibility" (Vincent, 1999a, 19). George McKinney of American Urban University similarly argues that the cause of urban poverty is spiritual malaise. "If we can develop an educational system that has spiritual values those who graduate from our programs will be able to attack some of these social situations in a much different way.... You'd probably see less folks walking down the street homeless and suffering because there'd be a change mentally" (A. Gaines, 2002a, 16). *World* opines that "a poor teenager can escape the welfare trap by following a simple three-part strategy: Graduate from high school; avoid drugs; don't get pregnant" (M. Olasky, 2006e, 36). Conservative articles on poverty, "illicit sex and drugs," and urban unrest always locate these "vices" in and identify them with communities of African Americans or people of color.[9] As Gary North states, there is a "right relationship between wickedness and poverty" (quoted in Lienesch, 1993, 134), which de facto means between wickedness and skin color. For example, one *Charisma* article analyzed the economic deprivation of people living in New York's Chinatown. However, the suffering of Chinatown residents is not the result of economic or political structures but because they are "idol worshippers" and "don't know God" (Liew, 2003). Similarly, another article traces the causes of urban poverty to youth defiance. The salvation for the urban poor, according to Kenneth Sullivan, founder of the urban-based North Star Christian Academy, is to teach young people to comply with authority unquestioningly. Says one student: "I'll just respect the teachers and not talk back. Just do what they say no matter what they say, even if I don't like it, because it's the right thing" (Shepard, 2002, 47). Similarly, an article on the gang ministry called New Hope for Youth contends that the plight of gang members can be traced to the fact that they need to learn the "alien" world of appointments, steady jobs, and responsibilities (Lukins, 2003). In fact, urban areas are described as "frontier" areas, presumably full of savages in need of civilization (E. Reed, 1999).

Many conservatives of color similarly engage in rhetoric that demonizes poor people and their communities (Hermann, 1995; Parker, 2003). They take up what Cathy Cohen calls a politics of secondary marginalization by arguing that the middle-class of communities of color should define the norms of those communities (Cohen, 1999). For example, *World* quotes Mildred Jefferson, a founder of the National Right to Life Committee: "The stabilizing core of our country is the middle class. They present that great middle ground . . . that has sustained us as a nation through wars, through famines, through the Depression. And that will be the sustaining core that will lead us into the 21st century" (Maynard, 1994, 12). Not surprisingly, then, the great sin of Obama among conservatives (his campaign is discussed later) is that he was secretly a Marxist whose policies would allow people of color to continue in this degraded state (Dean, 2009f; M. Olasky, 2008g; Veith, 2009).

Increasingly, this rhetoric has also been subject to critique. One letter to the editor of *Charisma* complained of an article that described a church in Harlem, New York, as a "lighthouse in Hell." "You should apologize to this community," argued the letter. "It may have problems, but it is as far from hell as the suburbs are from heaven" (Letters, 1997, 12). According to prominent evangelist Luis Palau, "The national majority in America, the Anglo-Saxons, must overcome its fear of the city, where minorities . . . are the majority" (Palau, 1998, 75).

As class is racialized, the solution to racism becomes free market capitalism.[10] *World* blamed race riots in France on the fact that "France is a welfare state" (Veith, 2005f, 28). Apparently, businesses cannot afford to hire people. France gives welfare to the poor, so immigrants have nothing to do but buy drugs, whereas "our immigrants" in the United States are forced to work hard by the demands of a competitive labor market and relatively fewer forms of public assistance. The article goes on to assert that "the tenets of the French welfare state are a breeding ground for radical Islam" (Veith, 2005f, 28). Then, in a stunning twist of logic, *World* calls on President Obama to follow the model of racial reconciliation in South Africa by ending his "class warfare [against] Wall Street" (M. Belz, 2010b, 34). Apparently, the "oppression" of Wall Street can be likened to the oppression of Black people under South African apartheid!

Since class and race are equated in these discourses, it is perhaps not a surprise that their approaches to poverty-reduction are similar to their approaches for racial reconciliation: befriend poor people and offer charity to the deserving rather than advocate for structural change (Aikman, 2005a; Donaldson, 1998; A. Gaines, 1998; S. Strang, 1998b; Vincent, 2006f).[11] Even relatively more progressive Ron Sider emphasized reducing personal materialism and praying for the poor rather than changing the economic system (Sider, 1998). According to Sider, "free-market economics are more compatible with human freedom and dignity and are more efficient in the production of wealth.... I am no longer as concerned as I was earlier with the ratio of money between the rich and poor" (K. Miller, 1997b, 69). Problematizing this approach, Clive Calver of World Relief states, "When people ask me, 'What's more important, social action or the gospel?' I don't hesitate to tell them, 'It's hard to preach the gospel to someone who's dead!'" (Calver, 1998, 61).

In fact, demonstrating the extent to which capitalism can sometimes be almost a tenet of faith within evangelicalism, William Armstrong, the president of Colorado Christian University fired teacher-of-the-year Andrew Paquin for assigning "liberal" books like Jim Wallis's *God's Politics* (which by no means repudiates capitalism). But according to Armstrong, the biblical mandate of the college requires a "preference for limited government rather than expansive government, which we see as a threat to freedom" (Bergin, 2007a, 21). Paquin received a letter from Armstrong, which said it is "deeply troubling to hear you say that capitalism is inconsistent with the teachings of Jesus" (Scharold, 2007, 19).[12] In response Paquin said he did not repudiate capitalism but did not think that Jesus actually espoused capitalism because, of course, Jesus predated capitalism. Armstrong replied

"There is no connection between free markets and Christianity . . . but we teach other things that aren't rooted in Scripture, like that H₂O is water" (Scharold, 2007, 19).¹³

Some of this work that presumes capitalism is the solution does actually echo more radical critiques of statist solutions for economic poverty. Stuart Hall, for instance, argued that one of the reasons why poor and working-class people were supporting conservative economic programs was because they correctly surmised that the welfare state was punitive and policing without actually getting people out of the poverty class. Other groups have argued against the nonprofit industrial complex, which utilizes state and private foundation funding to create a managerial class to monitor and police the poor and derails efforts to organize the poor for social change. For instance, in an interview with *World*, Juan Williams argues that liberal policy makers and advocates "rejoice in your hopelessness because they have jobs mismanaging you. Their goal is not to advance people into good schools and the American middle class but to maintain a large group of poor, undereducated people who are depending on them" (J. Williams, 2007, 37). He argues that government programs produce patronage jobs for their cronies but have few results that actually move people out of poverty by strengthening families and schools: "We cannot allow the poor, who are disproportionately black and Hispanic, to fall into a permanent underclass filled with hopelessness and despair" (J. Williams 2007, 33, 35).¹⁴ Star Parker argues not just against welfare policies but also against faith-based programs that have been championed by many evangelicals, because she contends that they will reinforce the idea of state intervention in the lives of poor people (Parker, 2003, 194–98). In some ways, her call to end government intervention in issues of racial justice is implicitly based on an acknowledgment of the inherent racism in government systems themselves. But the difference between Juan Williams and Stuart Hall, of course, is that Williams, like Parker, reverts back to privatization as a solution that allows the poor to be victimized by capitalism rather than by the state more directly.

There have been some internal critiques of this capitalist orthodoxy (K. Brown, 2014, 64; Dalrymple, 2011a, 70; Moll, 2014; Woodiwiss, 2005, 55). Interestingly, one interview in *Christianity Today* does make a more Stuart Hall–like argument: Raymond Bakke, who works in urban ministries, critiques the welfare system not because he thinks people on welfare are undeserving but because the welfare system is punitive and demeaning. He advocates national health insurance for the poor. He criticizes the hypocrisy of members of his family who are beneficiaries of agricultural welfare in the form of dairy subsidies yet criticize people in the city for going on welfare. He points out the double standard: middle-class women are told to stay home and raise children, while poor mothers are told to work at minimum wage and not see their children. Bakke concludes: "We're resegregating on a class basis. What's happening is a growing gap between the haves and have-nots" (quoted in Kauffman, 1997, 39).[15] *World* ran some articles on the Occupy Wall Street movement. While complaining that it has devolved into "a circus of envy and anti-capitalist sloganeering" (Dalrymple, 2011b, 72), he did say that evangelicals should not dismiss it out of hand and should consider business regulation (M. Olasky, 2011a; Skeel, 2011). An article in *Christianity Today* stated that the idea that the church can end poverty was a myth. Contrary to many capitalist evangelicals who argue that churches are better suited to address poverty, this article stated that churches cannot match the sweep of government initiatives, so better for the government to take the lead on antipoverty initiatives and for churches to help with what is left over (Galli, 2012). It also called on evangelicals actually to assess the effectiveness of Christian charities, noting that many were not effective at all (Wydick, 2012). *Relevant* went one step further to contend that a Christian perspective could engage capitalism and socialism (Bettis, 2017).

More recently, conservative evangelicals have become active on issues involving predatory lending. The Southern Baptist Convention's ERLC joined the Faith for Justice Lending Coalition, which also includes the National Association of Evangelicals, the more liberal PICO (Peoples Improving Commuities through Organizing) National Network (now known as Faith in Action), and the National Latino Evangelical Coalition, to organize against predatory lending and to campaign for more government regulation in this area (Gleanings, 2015a; Skeel, 2016). Another notable example is the work of Keith Stewart, pastor of the conservative evangelical Springcreek Church in Garland, Texas. Stewart first become conscious about poverty through his involvement with World Vision, which supports economic initiatives globally through child sponsorships. This experience led Stewart and his congregation to question the priorities of evangelical churches. After much soul-searching the church ran a full-age ad in the *Dallas Morning News*:

We Were Wrong
We followed trends when we should have followed Jesus.
We told others how to live but did not listen ourselves.

> We live in a land of plenty, denying ourselves nothing.
> While ignoring our neighbors who actually have nothing.
> We sat on the sidelines while AIDS ravaged Africa.
> We were wrong; we're sorry. Please forgive us.
> (K. Stewart, 2015, loc. 211)

In turn, Stewart began to question some of the logics of capitalism more generally. "Someone once said, 'We don't really live in a democracy. We live in a meritocracy.' In other words, we believe people always get what they deserve, so when it comes to poverty, we assume the poor must have brought this condition on themselves" (K. Stewart, 2015, loc. 819). Springcreek Church then began organizing around economic justice issues, particularly predatory lending in the Texas area.

A. R. Bernard, Promise Keepers speaker and head of the Christian Cultural Center in Brooklyn, stated: "Racism today is economic. It speaks to a hangover from a time when blacks were valued only as cheap labor. This sort of racism is potentially more dangerous, because although we brush against it, we can't always see it" (Bernard, 2004, 66). Finally, another article critiqued the assumption that church-based charity was not an effective means to address economic inequity. "Charity is not a substitute for systematic justice. . . . Children cannot be protected by the whim of charity. They must be protected by some basic systematic justice" (Winner, 2000; see also Crouch, 2007b).

Interestingly, the critique of government and nonprofit bureaucracies that administer funds does not seem to apply to churches. In fact, church-based self-help programs are offered as the solution. Welfare programs create dependency, but church programs apparently do not (Loconte, 1998, 37; Sherman, 1994). *World* promotes an antipoverty organization called Youth-Reach that says: "Our top goal is not to meet the physical needs of the poor or oppressed. Our philosophy is that for a man to die with a full stomach and enter hell is a great waste and a moral tragedy" (M. Olasky, 1999, 34). Interestingly, John Dilulio, the first person appointed by George W. Bush to head his White House Office of Faith-Based and Community Initiatives, took a different approach in his critique of Bill Clinton's welfare reform:

> I strongly opposed the welfare bill because I viewed that de-entitlement as tantamount to depriving citizenship. It said, in effect, we will make it now theoretically possible that kids can grow up without sufficient

food, medicine, and shelter—basic life necessities. We simply cannot withdraw government from urban America, from our most distressed populations. While it would be wonderful if we had corporate, private, philanthropic, and church-based efforts that could solve that problem, we absolutely have to have public-private partnerships, and government must play a role. (Wallis and Dilulio, 1997, 20)

Rudy Carrasco, who works with the Harambe Center, synthesizes economic and racial justice with personal development and corporate responsibility:

The poor themselves must realize their capacity to overcome poverty. In saying this, I'm not blaming the victim and letting powerful people and systemic powers off the hook. I mean nothing of the sort. . . . The protest-oriented injustice fighter may discover that some matters are best settled by a personal intervention, not a new law. The personal-responsibility injustice-fighter may discover that impersonal systems often devastate the lives of the poor, and that these systems must indeed be protested. In either case, the best way to get closer to doing justice for the poor is, quite simply, to get closer. (Carrasco, 2006, 48–49)

In *World*, of all places, Anthony Bradley wrote an incisive critique of the intersections of race and class in his predictions about what the state of race would be in 2063. "Racism as we knew it is gone. But government preferences over the years created a new kind of antagonism—based not upon race but instead upon class" (Bradley, 2001, 56). While he is making the familiar criticism of affirmative action policies within the Christian Right, his critique is based not so much on creating a sense of entitlement within communities of color as on creating a class division within them. "Racism was a convenient way of putting in their place those who were not members of the ruling economic class. Today we have racially integrated discrimination. People of all races judge each other not by the color of their skin but by the content of their resumes. Racially integrated discrimination is based on achievement and merit—a meritocracy where one's educational and professional achievements establish social status" (Bradley, 2001, 56). He continued, "Middle-class whites, blacks, and latinos now live together peacefully, but only because they have a common cause, perpetuating the middle-class ethos and working together to keep the lower classes of any race from invading their communities" (Bradley, 2001, 58). This article implicitly critiques capitalism's assumptions behind its "colorblind" philosophy: "A colorblind society is not necessarily a just society" (Bradley, 2001, 58).

(White) Evangelicals as Victims

Because white evangelicals often disavow power within the rhetoric of racial reconciliation, they would utilize the category of "oppression" to describe the social status of evangelicalism itself. It is interesting that the rhetoric of racial reconciliation came to the fore around the same time *Newsweek* and other mainstream journals began sending the alarm that people of color would soon be in the majority in the United States by the year 2000. Conservative evangelicals have sought to realign racial politics by stressing the commonalities between white and nonwhite evangelicals. One way this has been done is by transferring the label "oppressed" from people of color within the United States and globally to the Christian Right itself.[16]

Evangelicals often equate abortion with slavery and then essentially place themselves in the position of the unborn child, whom they call "enslaved" (K. James, 1987, 66; Lockett, 2014). Randall Terry claims the mantle of the civil rights struggle in the formation of his Operation Rescue. He states, "While the injustice blacks faced was intolerable, can segregation be as bad as murder? Isn't this slaughter of the innocent a far darker [*sic*] evil than segregation ever could be? Isn't the decapitation of millions of defenseless children more barbaric than the sufferings blacks endured?" (Terry, 1988, 197). Lauren Berlant describes this strategy as a politics of infantile citizenship whereby U.S. politics is often directed toward protecting the future incipient citizen, such as the child or the fetus. By directing our energies toward the future citizen, the U.S. political imaginary feels justified in instituting repressive policies that oppress today's citizens because they will protect the innocent citizens of the future (Berlant, 1997). While this may be the case, this rhetoric suggests that evangelicals are also putting themselves in the position of the fetus. That is, by assuming the "voice of the voiceless," the unborn child who cannot talk back, the pro-life activist assumes the position of the unborn child who faces "enslavement" and hence displaces the claims of those who have suffered a history of actual chattel slavery.

However, this equation between evangelicals and Blackness and/or racial slavery does not necessarily have to be mediated through abortion. Thomas Oden and others claim that in academia "those most maligned and humiliated and demeaned are believers who bear the unfair epithet of 'fundy,' like Jews who wore the star of David on their clothes in Germany in the 1930s.

Those who have the least voice... far less than ethnic minorities or officially designated oppressed groups—are evangelical students" (Oden, 1995, 402; see also Stafford, 1992; Veith, 2005b; Walker, 2005a). Pat Robertson terms the Christian Right today's "niggers" (Robertson, 1994, 145). A *World* article describing Christian authors' increasing popularity in secular bookstores was titled "Out of the Ghetto" (Veith and Vincent, 2005). *World* complains that atheists write about "evangelical Christians in much the same way and in much the same tone as white supremacists used to talk about blacks" (M. Olasky, 2009f, 33). Ralph Reed is particularly adept at appropriating oppression language, with chapter heads such as "To the Back of the Bus: The Marginalization of Religion" in *After the Revolution* (R. Reed, 1990, 41). He argues that "the curse of Ham has now fallen on us; evangelical whites are the new marginalized community, those most likely to be reviled for our political activism" (R. Reed, 1990, 247). A Pew poll found that 50 percent of white evangelical Christians say they face "a lot" of persecution in the United States, while only 36 percent of white evangelicals think African Americans face discrimination (Slices, 2015). *Christianity Today* asks: "Are US Christians Really 'Persecuted'?" and answers "yes" (K. A. Ellis, 2016).

This language of persecution is becoming especially clear around the issues of homosexuality. While mainstream narratives depict evangelicals discriminating against those who are LGBT, evangelicals argue that it is actually they who face discrimination because of their opposition to homosexuality (Dean, 2007a; T. Dixon, 2002a; A. Gaines, 2008c; Mintle, 2004; S. Strang, 2013b; Vincent, 2005b). They contend that hate-crimes legislation that covers LGBT communities will be used against them if they espouse views critical of homosexuality, although there is no record of federal or local prosecutors interpreting these statutes in this way (Hemingway, 2009; Vuoto, 2000). *Charisma* puts notice of pro-gay legislation being passed under the section "Liberty Watch" (Dean, 2007a). *World's* take on Matthew Shepard's murder was not that this was an incident of gay-bashing but that evangelicals who did not support homosexuality were suffering from Christian bashing (Jones, 1998b; Who's Bashing Whom?, 1998). Louis Sheldon of Traditional Values Coalition complains that gays are "victimizers," intentionally making evangelicals "look bad" by showing "images of ranting homophobes" (Sheldon, 2011, 34). A recent *Charisma* article says that Christians must oppose gay marriage as they should have opposed slavery in the 1800s (as if white evangelicals actually opposed slavery) (M. Brown, 2014a, 24). When *Newsweek* ran an article on "The Religious Case for Same-Sex Marriage," which made the argument that "history and demographics are on the side of those who favor inclusion over exclusion, *Christianity Today* responded: "The Nazis were sure history and demographics were on their side, as were Lenin and Stalin" (Let's Talk—Seriously, 2009, 18). This has heightened since gay marriage is now legal, of course, with *Charisma* explaining that this discrimination against Christians "goes beyond media attacks and smear campaigns and involves spiritual principalities and powers" (Walker, 2015). Similarly, *Christianity Today* reappropriates social justice language on the side of heterosexism by arguing that "the commitment of a man to a woman with whom he has a sexual relationship is not prudery; it is social justice" (Wydick, 2016, 74–75).

While this appropriation of oppression language is increasingly popular, many even within the Christian Right are critical of it. In terms of homosexuality, the prominence of figures like Fred Phelps, the preacher most known for his "God Hates Fags" pronouncements, tends to put a limit on how much evangelicals can claim that they are simply victims who do not engage in victimizing behavior. Phelps's Westboro Baptist Church famously began protesting funerals of dead soldiers, saying that they "rejoice in the deaths of American soldiers who fight to protect a nation that promotes homosexuality" (Dawson, 2006a). Phelps's signs at these protests said: "Thank God for Dead Soldiers," "Thank God for AIDS," and "God Hates You" (Dawson, 2006a). At Matthew Shepard's funeral, Phelps showed up with the sign "Matt is in hell" (Veenker, 1999, 89). *Christianity Today* ran an article strongly critiquing Phelps. Interestingly, it notes that Phelps was involved in the civil rights movement to strike down segregation in Topeka, Kansas. But by the end of his life (he died in 2014), Phelps asserted: "The Bible preaches hate. For every one verse about God's love, mercy, and compassion, there are two verses about his vengeance, hatred, and wrath. What you need to hear is that God hates people, and that your chances of going to heaven are nonexistent unless you repent" (Veenker, 1999, 91). *World* strongly critiqued him, noting that there are limits to how much Christians can claim to be oppressed by homosexuality when evangelicals have done little to counter the hatred of people like Fred Phelps (Veith, 2006c; Vincent, 1999b, 19). *Christianity Today* published an article uncritically quoting George W. Bush from a secretly recorded conversation that he had with the liaison to evangelical and profamily groups after reading Christian Coalition materials. "I'm not going to kick gays, because I'm a sinner. How can I differentiate sin? . . . This crowd uses gays as the enemy. It's hard to distinguish between fear of the homosexual political agenda and fear of homosexuality" (Olsen, 2005e, 23). In the wake of Matthew Shepard's murder, *Christianity Today* declared: "We must find ways to communicate that our motives arise from love, not hate, that our vision is not fear, but hope. We must discern if we harbor any hatred toward those who have a same-sex orientation" (Christianity Today, 1998d). As is often the case, the language structures around intolerance often conflict with evangelistic goals. When former Moral Majoritarian Ed Dobson started his AIDS ministry, he received complaints that his church would be overrun by gays. His response was, "If our church gets overrun with homosexuals, that will be terrific. They can take their place in the pews right next to the liars, gossips, materialists, and the rest of us who entertain sin in our lives" (Merrill, 1997, 30).

Evangelicals have also critiqued the argument that they are somehow "persecuted" in general. *Christianity Today* featured a survey to study how revealing people's religious affiliation impacts how their resumes are perceived. It noted that evangelicals were less likely to get a job than a control group. But it also noted that Muslims were much less likely to get a job than anyone else. The article then noted the importance of addressing "Islamophobia" (Wright, 2014). *Relevant* featured an article critiquing France's ban on burqas as a threat to all religious freedom (Slices, 2011). Even Carl Henry notes: "[While] belatedly, the Religious Right has taken up the cause of freedom . . . the religious Right often fails the freedom test on two scores. . . . It tends to be interested primarily in Christian freedom. . . . It is much less interested in religious freedom 'across the board.' It little realizes that evangelical Christianity blossoms in a context of universal religious freedom" (Henry, 1987, 31).

Christianity Today analyzed a study on the attitudes that nonevangelicals have toward evangelicals and found the problem was not that nonevangelicals have a negative attitude toward evangelicals but that "if American evangelicals do have an image problem, it's not our neighbors' image of us; it's our image of them. . . . Now . . . this seems to be a problem. We Christians are called to love people . . . how [can we] love atheists if we don't like them" (Wright, 2011, 25). This internal critique of the appropriation of oppression language seems to be based on a number of insights. First, as mentioned previously, the Christian Right has not historically or presently been on the side of the struggles of other oppressed groups. Even Reed is forced to admit that "it would be a clear distortion to compare the recent political involvement of the white evangelical church with the black church as a political force. . . . We quote Martin Luther King to great effect, but how many of us marched with him? . . . Sadly, the answer is few" (R. Reed, 1996, 68).

In addition, this appropriation neutralizes the meaning of the term "oppression," implying that it refers to the experience of being forced to live in a society where not everyone agrees with you. The Christian Right cannot make any convincing argument that evangelicals are victimized by hate crimes, are forced to live near toxic waste dumps and uranium mines, or are systematically denied occupational and educational opportunities. As Russell Moore has stated: "We must remember that religious freedom isn't freedom from ridicule" (R. Moore, 2016b, 3). At the 2016 ERLC conference, he phrased it as a difference between being persecuted and being offended. And Nikki Toyama-Szeto of Evangelicals for Social Action states unequivocally that Western Christians are not persecuted: "In America and in western contexts, Christians have been too much at the center of society to truly understand what it means to be despised" (Toyama-Szeto, 2017).

In any case, the implication of this popular oppression language is that evangelicals of color face oppression not because they are people of color but because they are Christian. This reversal was put into practice with the controversy of the Black church burnings of the late 1990s. While the Christian Coalition, and many other Christian Right organizations, garnered much publicity for raising money for burned churches in order to demonstrate a commitment to racial reconciliation (Christianity Today, 1997; Firebombed Churches Thank Re-building Donors, 1997; Walker, 1998a), at the same time it denied that racism had anything to do with these burnings (C. Curtis, 1996, 27). Rather, the coalition argued, these churches were burned because of anti-Christian sentiment rather than because of anti-Black racism. The Institute of Religion and Democracy and *World Magazine* further argued that the National Council of Churches manufactured this crisis in an effort to raise funds for their "radical leftist" programs (Tooley, 1996, 4). Of course, if race had nothing to do with the burnings, then why were all the programs to raise money for these burned churches located in these various organizations' racial reconciliation programs? The Christian Coalition seemed to want to play the issue both ways—deny racism was a factor in the burnings but at the same time get credit for tackling issues of racism through its charitable efforts for burned churches.

Thus, if the real oppression faced by evangelicals of color is religious rather than racial oppression, it is imperative that they unite with white evangelicals against non-Christian enemies. Post-9/11 in particular, there was increasing rhetoric that communities of color must unite with white Christians against terrorism. Ironically, Civil War reenactments have been used by some sectors to unify African Americans and white Christians.

Clifford Pierce, an African American participant in these reenactments, says that they provide an opportunity to unify the country, which is particularly important since 9/11. At these events, he declares, people come together to "speak the joy of the Lord" (Butcher, 2002, 68). The Christian Coalition advocated for a "reconciliation" resolution in 2001, which called for a National Day of Reconciliation on which the U.S. House of Representatives and the U.S. Senate would convene "to humbly seek the blessings of Providence for forgiveness, reconciliation, unity, and charity for all people of the United States, thereby assisting the Nation to realize its potential as the champion of hope, the vindicator of the defenseless, and the guardian of freedom" (Christian Coalition, 2001c). Race became totally occluded in this call for reconciliation in the interests of supporting the War on Terror. According to the Christian Coalition, "In light of the terrorist attacks of September 11 and the subsequent threats to our citizenry which occur daily, the designation of a day for Members of Congress to gather to fast and pray for God's blessings on our nation is needed now more than ever" (Christian Coalition, 2001a). Thus, these calls for reconciliation *within* Christian evangelicalism often rely upon the ongoing racialization of non-Christian others who, as Jasbir Puar notes, are permanently cast outside the category of those who can be enfolded into Christian life (Puar, 2007).

The Power of Repentance: Centering Whiteness

The rituals of racial reconciliation, besides requiring the ongoing racialization of those who will ever remain unreconciled, also reinstate whiteness at the center of evangelicalism. Antiracist politics in general often rely upon the "confession" of the white subjects, who in confessing their racism recenter their subjectivity at the center of antiracist discourse (A. Smith, 2013). Similarly, the rituals of repentance within Christian evangelicalism often center the white evangelicals who repent while disappearing the evangelicals of color who led them to repentance. As evangelical blogger Daniel Fan notes, the structure of "the apology" within racial reconciliation creates the appearance that the critique is being heard while simultaneously erasing the prophetic voices of those who called for the critique (Fan, 2013).

As mentioned in chapter 1, Soong-Chan Rah instigated a campaign against LifeWay, the publishing arm of the Southern Baptist Convention, for its employment of anti-Asian stereotypes in its Vacation Bible School curriculum, Rickshaw Rally, only to be completely dismissed by the SBC. Ten years later, a coalition of Asian American evangelicals and other Christian leaders published an open letter against anti-Asian racism in evangelicalism, in response to several anti-Asian social media postings by prominent evangelicals.[17] Soon thereafter, Ed Stetzer unexpectedly apologized for the Rickshaw Rally at the 2013 Mosaix conference. LifeWay also released a video apology.[18] What was noteworthy about LifeWay apologies is that they did not acknowledge the work of Rah in bringing this issue to its attention. Fan states:

> The story of Rickshaw Rally cannot be told in its entirety without recounting the prominent activism of people like Soong-Chan Rah. This is the story of a small band of Asian American Christians that dared to challenge the juggernaut of Christian publishing and won: it was their risk-filled ten-year struggle that precipitated the apology delivered on November 7th, 2013, at the Mosaix Conference by LifeWay president Thom Rainer. Or is it? . . .
>
> LifeWay's November 7th apology made no mention of the heroic activism by members of any ethnicity who opposed their original Rickshaw Rally curriculum. When specific members of the Asian American community, including Soong-Chan Rah and others challenged the curriculum, LifeWay plodded forward as an uncaring, impersonal, unknowable, faceless, amorphous and unaccountable force of nature. But in LifeWay's November 7th "apology" Thom Rainer is the focal point, and those who dared act as speed-bumps before the steamroller of evangelistic racial stereotyping that was Rickshaw Rally are reduced to the mere mention of "some."
>
> By replacing Asian American activists with a white CEO in the role of protagonist, LifeWay has fundamentally altered the structure of this narrative. In effect, the tale has gone from David v. Goliath, a story of under-dog protest, activism, suffering, and risk, to one of self-realized/actualized repentance. . . . Doesn't the erasure of Asian American activism from this story form a second offense: further reinforcing Asian invisibility and insignificance? (Fan, 2013)

Similarly, before the previously described fall of Mark Driscoll, evangelical feminists such as Rachel Held Evans were calling out his sexism before it became popular to attack him: "What we have on our hands is a bully. And this bully is teaching the young men at his church and under his influence that bullying is an acceptable expression of 'biblical manhood.' . . . This has to stop. As followers of Jesus, we are obligated to stick up for the least of these, especially when they are being publicly bullied in the name of Christ" (R. H. Evans, 2011).

Evans then became the target of attack as a result. Anthony Bradley in *World* complained:

> There is nothing loving about calling a pastor a "bully"—that is, "a blustering, quarrelsome, overbearing person who habitually badgers and intimidates smaller or weaker people.". . . Evans' way of responding cannot and should not be encouraged. What was even more disturbing was the way in which many other believers jumped on the slander bandwagon to feed on the carnage once it went viral. . . . Evans' slanderous post also represents one of the things that God finds detestable, "a false witness who pours out lies and a person who stirs up conflict in the community" (Proverbs 6:19). (Bradley, 2011)

But when the controversies around Mark Driscoll eventually gained traction culminating in Driscoll's resignation from Mars Hill Church, the media sources recounted Driscoll's infractions and generally agreed that he needed to be accountable while simultaneously rendering invisible the prophetic voices of those such as Rachel Held Evans who first called for accountability.

Evans herself spoke to this dynamic when she was called to account by many evangelicals of color for the racially insensitive manner in which she wrote about the Ferguson uprising. Her first response to her critics was that "bullying is wrong" (R. H. Evans, 2014a). But Evans later published an article that implicitly discussed these dynamics within accountability in her account of the Christian prophetic tradition. She noted that while evangelicals love to claim the mantle of "prophet," the real prophets of the world are politically and socially marginalized:

> Prophets disrupt. Prophets offend. Prophets make "big-ole-scenes" and push the edge of the envelope. Prophets are almost always rejected—by conservatives and liberals, by the pious and the rebellious, by their faithful critics and by the ones who once followed them. Prophets get themselves killed. So when you're wondering to yourself who the modern-day prophets might be, the question isn't, who am I following? The question is, who am I rejecting? I don't know about you, but I've made a habit out of rejecting the people who challenge my privilege. (R. H. Evans, 2014b)

Meanwhile, some of Evans's critics did their own internal critique of using social media as an accountability strategy. They questioned whether or not calling out individuals (particularly on social media) should be equated with accountability and instead suggested that accountability requires us to "recognize and challenge horizontal violence, coalition building, learning to trust one another, and the healing that we need to do from centuries of both external and internalized racisms" (Park, 2014).

Reconciliation to Racial Justice

> If you want to be committed to racial justice, you must do more than read a book at home alone. You must do more than add poc [people of color] to your social media lists. You must do more than attend an MLK service or a Ferguson vigil. These are good things. You will benefit from them. But buying our books and reading our blogs and sharing our posts were never intended to BE your journey. These things are to aid you in a much larger commitment to justice and reconciliation in the world. Reclaim your soul. Risk death to your comfort. Place yourself under the authority of a person of color. Connect history to the present.—Austin Channing Brown (Channing, 2014)

Increasingly more evangelicals, such as Austin Channing Brown, are calling for racial justice rather than racial reconciliation. Or, as Erna Kim Hackett put it, they stopped talking about racial reconciliation and started talking about white supremacy (Hackett, 2017). These evangelicals are arguing that Christians actually need to be involved in dismantling structures of white supremacy. This critique has increased in recent years, particularly since the uprising in Ferguson. As evangelical pastor Dominique Gilliard remarked, "Ferguson awakened America [and, I would suggest, evangelicalism as well] of its colorblind stupor . . . many are realizing that Ferguson isn't an anomaly. It's a microcosm of our country" (Gilliard, 2015, 38). However, it has been present since the beginnings of the racial reconciliation movement, even when it may not seem visible.

It is important not to overlook the more diffuse ways in which racial reconciliation has impacted evangelicalism. First, the actual work of social justice is not always obvious. People of color strategically negotiate white evangelical spaces and hence do not always express their positions in the strongest terms. The extent to which the radicalness of writings by evangelicals of color is often more muted when reported within primarily white publications is interesting. Until more recently in the post-Ferguson era, statements by people of color that often were the most challenging of the status quo either were not reported within white journals or were reported without any context. In a *Christianity Today* interview, for instance, Glenn Loury states that "this call for [Black] self-reliance is in danger of being hijacked by 'those who are looking for an excuse to abandon the black poor'" (Cromartie, 1996a, 17). However, this statement was printed without a context and was not developed within the article. John Perkins, a favorite among the Christian Right as proof that Black self-help works, is not quoted in white periodicals when he says that "the roots of poverty were in the system itself, growing out of the very culture and traditions and history...of America" (Perkins, 1995b, 52). The articles praising Malcolm X in John Perkins's *Urban Family* are not found in white evangelical periodicals (C. Ellis, 1993). But Perkins (along with Jim Wallis) was arrested for protesting the budget in December 2005 (Stricherz, 2006). He has also taken a stance against the anti-immigration hysteria, particularly after Senate Bill 1070. The Christian Community Development Association, founded by Perkins, brings together Christian groups whose work centers in poor communities. Their 2010 conference featured film festivals and workshops that addressed a variety of political and social justice issues, including immigration, Native sovereignty, economic development, and others.[19]

Clarence Shuler, who works with Focus on the Family, articulates a much more radical approach toward addressing racism in his *Winning the Race to Unity* (1998) than one typically sees in Focus on the Family materials. In fact, he disputes the premise of reconciliation itself, which he says is based on the idea that we should restore relationships that have been damaged. "In the context of American history, blacks and whites in this country have not had a previously good, consistent relationship to which most blacks would want to be restored" (Shuler, 1998, 117). He also critiques the church integration approach espoused in *United by Faith* (DeYoung et al., 2004) (a follow-up book to the previously described *Divided by Faith* that advocated for racial integration in the churches as the solution for ending racism), saying it sounds like the failed integration strategies of the 1960s that essentially forced Black peoples to lose their one independent source of power: Black churches. As much racial separation exists outside the church as inside, so why dismantle the one institution that provides a base to address racial segregation outside the church (Shuler, 1998, 127)? In my informal conversations, many evangelicals support more radical political agendas, but the full scope of their views is not always portrayed in white-dominated evangelical forums. Many evangelicals of color frequently have complained to me that white evangelicals often monitor their talks for potential radicalness. For instance, one individual reported that he was on a popular evangelical TV show when he made a comment that evangelicals need to rethink their uncritical support for Israel. He found out later that this comment was deleted from the television broadcast. Others complain that white evangelical venues have asked them to send texts of presentations in advance to monitor them for unseemly radical material.

This strategy perhaps also speaks to the importance of racial reconciliation interventions. While calls for multiculturalism and apologies may seem mild, they are made to audiences who do not have a problem with white supremacy. So, if this movement convinces someone from the KKK to stop terrorizing people of color, even if that former KKK member still opposes affirmative action, it may be an improvement on the status quo. To illustrate these dynamics, Anthony Bradley wrote a favorable review of Soong-Chan Rah's *The Next Evangelicalism* in *World* (Bradley, 2010), which at the time made one of the strongest internal critiques of white evangelicalism's complicity with white supremacy (Rah, 2009). Perhaps because the review was published in *World* magazine, which is generally hostile to questions of race, Bradley's description of the book is fairly mild. He describes the book as calling for churches and denominations to become "Rah-certified" by becoming multiethnic. In actuality, the book focuses less on calling for integration and more on dismantling structures of white supremacy within the church. Nevertheless, even this milder rendition of Rah was apparently too much for *World*'s readers. A representative letter to the editor objected:

> Rah certified. Wasn't Rah an Egyptian God? I thought God brought us out of Egypt with a mighty Hand and an outstretched Arm.
>
> The very fact that I am white means that I am racist according to these types of definitions. The facts that I would be fine with one of my children marrying a person of color, or that I would be fine working with or for a person of color (and have), or that I would be friends with a person of color . . . none of it means anything. The very fact of my European ethnicity supposedly makes me a racist who simply can't see beyond my own nose despite my actions and despite what I think I believe. (Apparently, being white means that I just generally lie to myself.) (Bradley, 2010)

Thus, we cannot completely dismiss what may seem to be baby steps toward addressing racism in communities that do not want to have this discussion at all.

In addition, as noted previously, Emerson and Smith's (2000) conclusion that racial reconciliation was largely a failure in evangelicalism itself impacted the direction of evangelical racial justice organizing. Many evangelicals have changed their strategies to address precisely their concerns. George Yancey, while still emphasizing the need for white people and people of color to work together, does cite *Divided by Faith* and speak to structural white supremacy at length (G. Yancey, 2006). Brenda Salter McNeil and Rick Richardson's *The Heart of Racial Justice* also cites this work in calling for a racial reconciliation model that incorporates interpersonal work with institutional change (McNeil and Richardson, 2004). *Being White*, another post–*Divided by Faith* book, specifically speaks to white privilege and white supremacy rather than framing the issue of racism as one in which people of color and white people are represented as similarly impacted by race (P. Harris and D. Schaupp, 2004). And Rah calls for a shift from racial inclusion to racial justice:

> Why are American evangelicals so willing to overlook corporate sin, such as the torturing of political prisoners, an unjust economic system leading to structures of poverty, or structural racism? Is it because we may personally benefit via cheaper gas prices, an improved economy and economic privilege? Is it because our favored political candidate will benefit when we overlook certain social and political injustices? . . . Evangelicals focus on abortion and sexual immorality while downplaying the issues of poverty, racism, and social injustice. And when they address such problems, they believe that they can be solved primarily through individual, church, or local efforts. . . . Rather than confront sin, we begin to look for ways to categorize it as a theologically liberal agenda—thereby stripping corporate confession and repentance of its prophetic power. (Rah, 2009, 41)

Others are focusing on racial justice rather than on racial reconciliation as well. Lisa Sharon Harper of Freedom Road is one example; she worked in racial reconciliation for several years with InterVarsity Christian Fellowship before deciding this work needed to focus on political organizing. She later worked with New York Faith and Justice and then Sojourners to coordinate evangelical constituencies to support a number of social justice issues, such as immigration reform. Moss Ntlha, head of Evangelical Alliance of South Africa, criticized racial reconciliation programs for benefiting the powerful who need amnesty at the expense of the poor and the vulnerable. He declared that reconciliation without reparations is "cheap grace" (Okite, 1999b) and that reconciliation must also address inequities "among social and economic classes" (Maclean, 2004; Okite, 1999b). Mae Cannon calls on evangelicals to get involved in a wide range of social justice issues that include everything from criminal justice reform to Native land rights struggles to environmental justice in her *Social Justice Handbook* (Cannon, 2009). Amos Yong stated that the false teaching that evangelical Christians are most likely to believe is that "racism is gone" (Yong, 2015). Scott Roley, a former contemporary Christian artist who later decided to focus full-time on racial reconciliation ministry, similarly focuses on interpersonal relationships in his autobiographical *God's Neighborhood*. At the same time, however, he cites Emerson and Smith's definition of racism to argue that racial reconciliation requires institutional intervention:

> Racism is not mere individual overt prejudice or the free-floating irrational driver of race problems but the collective misuse of power that results in diminished life opportunities for some racial groups. Racism is a changing ideology with the constant and rational purpose of perpetuating and justifying a social system that is racialized. . . . Because racialization is embedded within the normal, everyday operations of institutions, this framework understands that people need not intend their actions to contribute to racial division and inequality for their actions to do so. (Roley, 2004, 156–57)

With the rise of Black Lives Matter, increasingly more evangelicals began to critique the limits of racial reconciliation (J. R. Butler, 2016, 66–67). For instance, Fuller Seminary held an event in 2015, "Do Black Lives Really Matter?" At the event, the moderator Love Sechrest argued that "evangelicalism is ground zero for racial segregation": consequently, "We should not leap too quickly to the idea of reconciliation" (Reconciling Race, 2015, 42–43). She further argues that "discourse about racial reconciliation tends to diminish the notion by focusing only on overcoming personal prejudice while turning a sometimes deliberately blind eye to structural matters of inequality" (Sechrest, 2015, 65). Similarly, Willie James Jennings argued that Christians must "confront the principality of whiteness" (Jennings, 2015, 50). This approach puts a twist on race being a "sin problem." Here sin is a problem of whiteness. Jennings, borrowing from Edward Said's *Orientalism*, concurs that whiteness fundamentally structures the evangelical worldview. And Reggie Williams, in the same *Fuller Magazine* special issue, specifically names "white supremacy as a social organizing principle," rather than racial prejudice, as the key issue facing Christians (R. Williams, 2015, 55).

AnaYelsi Velasco-Sanchez, founder of the En Conjunto Collective, similarly reinterprets "reconciliation" to argue that addressing racism interpersonally must be simultaneous with ending structures of oppression. Rather than position interpersonal dynamics in isolation, she argues that they reflect larger structures of domination.

> Our world is run by systems that sanction racism and those systems favor white people over people of color. Rather than being a prophetic voice for the redemption or dismantling of such systems, the Church is often guilty of participating in them. There are the overt acts—genocide, displacement and colonization of the "other" in Christ's name. More common, and more insidious, are the unintentional microaggressions—the brief verbal and behavioral indignities to which marginalized people are regularly subjected. Intentional or not, they communicate the internalized biases of those in power, and Christians, including advocates for social justice, are often the perpetrators. (Velasco-Sanchez, 2016)

As discussed in chapter 8, many evangelical women of color in particular have organized against "heteropatriarchal white supremacy." As Emily Rice, a cofounder of the more radical evangelical organization Killjoy Prophets, described its mission: "We refuse to settle for a 'racial reconciliation' that envisions the goal as representation and recognition by whiteness because our aim is to dismantle white supremacy altogether" (Killjoy Prophets, 2014b).

The Sin of White Supremacy

While not diminishing the importance of understanding racism as a structural relationship, there may be an important element to the idea of racism as a "sin." As Denise Da Silva, Alexander Weheliye, Sylvia Wynter, Frederick Moten, and many others have noted, white supremacy fundamentally shapes subjectivity. As Moten articulated in a class lecture at University of

California, Riverside, in 2014, "White supremacy is not simply the belief in white superiority; it structures belief itself." The concept of sin, then, echoes this notion that we cannot simply "do" good because our subjectivity is fundamentally shaped by sin. Of course, the typical evangelical articulations of sin differ from these critical Black studies analyses of race because they often presume that we can escape our sinful grid of intelligibility by being "born again." That is, the notion of "born again, free of sin" tends to presuppose that we can escape our grid of intelligibility through a faith decision. Thus, what approach would synergize an ideological/epistemological approach with a structural analysis?

Mark Galli speaks to this in his articulation of a "fully biblical liberation theology" (Galli, 2011b, 51). On the one hand, he does not really address the larger structural issues. He does say that political liberation is important, but he focuses on what he calls moral and spiritual liberation. Building on this analysis, it could be possible to synergize the concept of being "born again" with the mandate to end structural forms of oppression if we think of the early church practices as a form of structural change designed to enable a change in subjectivity. That is, these early church practices implicitly recognize that we cannot simply will ourselves into a sin-free existence. Rather, we must live under different structures that enable us to be different people. Thus, early church practices of baptism, which were designed to initiate the less hierarchical and more egalitarian worship and living praxes necessary to enable Christians to be in fact born again, as identified by Elisabeth Schüssler Fiorenza (Fiorenza, 1985). Furthermore, these practices had to be ongoing, because being born again is an ongoing commitment to total transformation.

Many movements for social justice today are deeply informed by indigenous peoples' movements, which utilize similar principles of creating different community structures that in turn enable participants to become different people (A. Smith, 2005b). The principle undergirding these models is to challenge capital and state power by actually creating the world we want to live in now. These groups develop alternative governance systems based on principles of horizontality, mutuality, and interrelatedness rather than hierarchy, domination, and control. In beginning to create this new world, subjects are transformed. These "autonomous zones" can be differentiated from the projects of many groups in the United States that create separatist communities based on egalitarian ideals in that people in these "making power" movements do not just create autonomous zones but *proliferate* them. A lesson learned from these organizing models is that less hierarchy does not equal less structure. In fact, the opposite is the case. Informal hierarchies develop when there are no clear structures, because people who have grown up under structures of white supremacy and capitalism will tend to act in conformity with those structures. As Jo Freeman famously argued in the 1970s, we end up with the tyranny of structurelessness (Freeman, 1972–1973). Thus, these organizations have discovered the need to develop new structures of accountability that force them to act in ways that are not natural to them. Yet they have found that the longer they live in structures that are committed to nonhierarchy, the more they start acting differently. To end our "sinful" orientation to oppression, it is not sufficient to profess belief or to think ourselves into a new liberated subject position but to live this change through the creation of collective structures that dismantle the systems of sinful oppression. To quote Judy Vaughn, former co-ordinator of the National Assembly of Religious Women, "You don't think your way into a different way of acting; you act your way into a different way of thinking."[20]

Love Not Laws

The articulation of oppression as sin potentially intersects with the racial justice movements led primarily by women and trans people of color demanding that movements address not only violence directed at communities of color but violence *within* communities of color. In addition, the focus on white supremacy as sin actually provides a vantage point to assess some of the multiculturalist assumptions behind antiracist critique that focuses on structural change. The notion that "love not laws" can address racism does actually speak to the limitations of the legal system as the most effective strategy for addressing racism. Dean Spade, for instance, notes that the assumption that the legal system can actually address white supremacy serves to obscure the white supremacist foundation of the legal system. In *Normal Life*, Spade argues:

> The critical analysis built by many resistant social movements illuminates the limitations of a theory of law reform that aims to punish the "few bad apples" supposedly responsible for racism, sexism, ableism, xenophobia, or transphobia. It also helps us understand why, since U.S. law has been structured from its inception to create a racialized-gendered distribution of life chances that perpetuates violence, genocide, land theft, and exploitation, we will not resolve those issues solely

by appealing to law. We must also be cautious not to believe what the law says about itself since time and again the law has changed, been declared newly neutral or fair or protective, and then once more failed to transform the conditions of disparity and violence that people were resisting. . . . Law reform tactics can have a role in mobilization-focused strategies, but law reform must never constitute the sole demand of trans politics. If we seek transformation that is more than symbolic and that reaches those facing the most violent manifestations of transphobia, we must move beyond the politics of recognition and inclusion. (Spade, 2010, 27–28)

Interestingly, Ed Dobson, who was formerly with the Moral Majority but later became disenchanted with Christian political organizing, made similar critiques of the overemphasis on legal reform, but from the position of the Christian Right. "Legislation must reflect the consensus of the people governed, or they will just disregard the law. . . . While we work toward legislation, we must also do the more difficult task of changing people's minds and beliefs on the matter. The most effective laws *follow* moral consensus" (E. Dobson and C. Thomas, 1999, 70). Essentially, he makes a Gramscian argument that struggle to change the ruling power system requires not only a battle over control of the state and capital but is also an ideological battle to reshape the common sense. Thus, the insight that emerges from the call for "love not laws" is the recognition that the legal reform is not the solution to ending white supremacy, especially since the legal system itself is created through the logics of white supremacy.

And as Glen Coulthard notes, this "structural" approach to addressing racism actually depends upon a logic of multicultural recognition whereby the state (rather than being recognized as white supremacist of itself) becomes the arbiter of completing claims. Thus, the racial reconciliation movement suggests the possibility that perhaps communities can address white supremacy without depending on the state. As one example, Nelson Johnson of the Truth and Community Reconciliation Project recounted at a New York-based "This Is How We Do It" conference (2012) how his organization developed an alternative response to white supremacist violence that was not mediated by the state. Within white supremacy the far Right is generally imagined as constituting the "real" racism that makes the everyday racism of society seem normal. The state is then needed to protect people of color from these hard-core racists, thus disappearing the racism of the state itself. Beyond the claim to focus on structural racism, these more liberal antiracist approaches actually do not address the constitutive white supremacy of these institutions and instead mark them as outside the system that can provide multicultural recognition for competing racial claims. However, Nelson Johnson of the Beloved Community Center in North Carolina recounted how local activists, instead of going to the state to act as the arbiter, began to talk directly with the KKK in order to successfully deescalate racial tensions in the area.[21] And many Native activists have developed successful coalitions with peoples on the "far right" when it became clear that the state was not going to do anything to stop racial attacks from these groups (A. Smith, 2008). Thus, it may be instructive that many of these organizations take on the charge of actually talking to people on the right. They do not presume that an antiracist politic can only emerge from the left.

A session on transformative justice and white supremacist violence at a Los Angeles summit in 2014 brainstormed strategies for developing noncarceral approaches to address police brutality or hate crimes. The problem, as discussed by participants, was that police officers or those who commit hate crimes are imagined by the Left as wholly outside society. Prison abolitionism is a strong strand within radical organizing. It is based on the idea that people are not expendable and should not be cast into civil death as the means by which to hold them accountable. However, most radical social justice organizations tend to operate from a similar logic in their organizing. That is, certain individuals, such as those on the Right, are seen as socially and politically disposable. What would accountability look like if such individuals were not seen as outside prison abolitionist politics? Mariame Kaba similarly explained why she was not invested in a particular outcome when a grand jury refused to indict Darren Wilson over the killing of Mike Brown:

> It feels blasphemous to suggest that one is disinvested from the outcome of the grand jury deliberations. "Don't you care about accountability for harm caused?" some will ask. "What about justice?" others will accuse.... I just know that indictments won't and can't end oppressive policing which is rooted in anti-blackness, social control and containment. (Kaba, 2014)

Essentially, abolitionism could be framed as articulating a "love not laws" approach toward justice—or perhaps more appropriately, "nondisposability not laws" approach.

The problem with both "love" and "laws" as the appropriate response for dismantling white supremacy can be seen in some of the evangelical responses across the political spectrum to killing of Trayvon Martin. Stephen Strang of *Charisma* responded to the outcry by organizing a meeting of pastors to put forth a Sanford proclamation on racism:

> We believe that God has gifted us and millions yet to be called to minister for Him in this regard. We believe that God works in the lives of chosen men and women. Further, we believe that the Lord uses His appointed leaders to transform history. We believe that the key to ending racism in the United States and in other nations lies in Christians developing and promoting genuine relationships among each other—just as it is being done in Sanford, Florida, since the spring of 2012. As a result, Sanford did not experience the rioting, looting, and violence that other regions did after the July 2013 George Zimmerman not guilty verdict. Additionally, Christians should develop intentional relationships that will result from "living life together," thereby manifesting in some of the following:
>
> 1. Pulpit exchanges between Church families.
> 2. Joint leadership and family retreats.
> 3. Cross-cultural evangelism of other races.
> 4. Multi-racial church planting and development.
> 5. Cross-cultural home mission projects in the local metropolitan areas to assist in
>   - Lifting families out of generational poverty.
>   - Motivating at risk black, white, Asian, and Hispanic youths (especially males) in developing a sense of personal respect, destiny and worthwhile goals.
>   - Developing minority, university scholarship programs and entrepreneurial opportunities
> 6. Other creative local programs that will be developed locally.
> 7. Lay a foundation for change with prayer and intercession.
>
> (S. Strang, 2013a)

Now, it is not that Strang ignores the institutional reality of racism altogether. He states that it is important to "end injustice and institutional racism wherever it exists" (S. Strang, 2013a). But the primary goal articulated here was not to end anti-Black violence and other forms of institutional racism but to stop any reaction to this violence and racism. The solutions put forth (mentoring people of color so that they have worthwhile goals) indicate that the problem entailed in this violence was not the perpetrators of it but the victims of it who lack "entrepreneurial opportunities." Nothing here actually indicates any analysis that this anti-Black violence is itself a problem that needs addressing. According to Strang: "That's because this problem is not a political problem. It's a sin problem. It's spiritual in nature and must be dealt with in the spiritual realm" (S. Strang, 2013a). Similarly, *World* magazine argued that anti-Black racism cannot end until Black people become Christian. In response to the work of Ta-Nehisi Coates, it contended that reparations are not needed for Black people because the cross has already provided the reparations. "If there were some way to make real reparations for slavery and bigotry, we should not hesitate to pay the cost . . . [but] there's no material compensation for spiritual harm. The greatest reparation was made on a cross. If he [Black people] could meet me here, I would gladly ask his forgiveness for any perceived harm on my part, because that's the only place he could forgive me. Otherwise, resolution seems forever out of reach" (Cheaney, 2016c, 18). This same author contended that organizing for racial equality seems like a noble goal but eventually gives way to "bitterness over inequality, with indiscriminate looting and murder . . . thrown in" (Cheaney, 2016b,16). Hence it is better to seek freedom in Jesus instead. At the same time, some of the "solutions" offered by more progressive evangelicals for addressing racism in the wake of the Zimmerman verdict tended to rely upon simple policy recommendations like ending "Stand Your Ground" laws (Wallis, 2014). Given the larger problems of how the self-defense law is racially constructed, Zimmerman might well have been acquitted on general self-defense grounds even if Stand Your Ground laws had not existed in Florida (Markovitz, 2015). In both cases, neither love nor laws may be sufficient to end white supremacy.

Thus, while many progressive evangelicals correctly critique conservative evangelicals for their quick-fix approaches to ending racism, they also frequently fail to address the fact that liberal political and legal approaches to race often suffer from the same quick-fix approach. As Spade notes, white supremacy is not the result of a "bad" law but structures the legal system itself. Thus, how can the insights of the more conservative end of the racial reconciliation movement that recognize the limitations of legal reform be synthesized with the more progressive components that recognize that white supremacy is institutional and structural?

The Jesus Approach to Social Justice Organizing

Some evangelicals do attempt to organize around the nexus of individual and corporate sin. One such person is Alexia Salvatierra, who has been engaged in evangelical faith-based organizing for over twenty years. As discussed later, she was one of the key organizers behind many Christian Right organizations shifting their position on immigration in the past few years. In a book she coauthored with Peter Heltzel, she suggests a possible way to rethink the relationship between organizing and healing. On the one hand, this book tends to limit its organizing focus to legislative change. On the other hand, the philosophy in this book mirrors the "making power" organizing models described earlier in this chapter. She distinguishes between "dream based" and "issue based organizing." Rather than organizing to change one law, she states that organizing should be based on the question "How do we want the world to be different because of our efforts?" (Salvatierra and Heltzel, 2014, 28). Her philosophy also mirrors much of the strategy behind antiviolence organizing by radical women of color that tries to organize around violence directed at communities (such as state and economic violence) while simultaneously organizing around violence *within* communities (such as interpersonal gender violence). Salvatierra similarly contends with the problem with traditional modes of organizing:

> [This] assumes that giving a particular community power will result in the best use of that power. The Christian doctrine of sin throws this assumption in question. Sin, the form of human attraction to deny others human dignity and work power for selfish ambition, is a perennial problem. Sin also has an institutional dimension when the institutions of society, like banks, schools, and government, become oppressive "powers and principalities" that must be prophetically confronted. (Salvatierra and Heltzel, 2014, 29–30)

Salvatierra notes that faith-based organizing respects the humanity of those that we seek to organize as well to challenge. In addition, the goal is not simply a redistribution of political power, but a transformation in the way we interact with each other. "Faith-rooted organizing aspires beyond democracy to establish the beloved community" (Salvatierra and Heltzel, 2014, 32). At the same time, this effort to create a "beloved" community must be done in a manner that is cognizant of how systems of domination operate. "Jesus did not call us to be only innocent as doves, he also called us to be wise as serpents" (Salvatierra and Heltzel, 2014, 182), which requires us not only to act faithfully but to "act strategically" (Salvatierra and Heltzel, 2014, 184), cognizant of the conditions under which we organize. "The saying is well known: Give a man a fish and he will eat for a day; teach him to fish and he will eat for a lifetime. . . . Knowing how to fish, however, is not much use if there is a wall around the fish, and fisherman are not allowed access to the water" (Salvatierra and Heltzel, 2014, 8). At same time, she advocates the use of dove power because "we take seriously the best in people, and reality of the image of God in each of us and the transforming work of the Holy Spirit" (Salvatierra and Heltzel, 2014, 75).

In the end, similar to the way many Native feminists have argued, the goal that Salvatierra advocates is not to gain greater power in the current system but to decolonize the system altogether. As Salvatierra puts it: "We are not concerned with merely winning short-term political victories but . . . we pursue a new social order" (Salvatierra and Heltzel, 2014, 32).

The organizing strategies thus focus on addressing individual and corporate sin simultaneously. For instance, she details how part of the organizing practice in one campaign that she coordinated was the practice of storytelling in addition to other strategies where those involved in the campaign addressed the "lies that justify injustice" and "hold us back internally" (Salvatierra and Heltzel, 2014, 160). For instance, Salvatierra notes that organizing movements often disintegrate because feelings of low self-worth can create jealousy and competition among members of a movement. Through this praxis, people learn to identify when their own tendencies toward "sin" are undermining the collective organizing and get support to address these concerns in an open, honest, and accepting manner. The praxes take on the sense of a "laboratory" because it is also understood that many mistakes will be made along the way as movements deal with internalized oppression. Thus, groups that seem to be engaged in self-sabotage experiment with different approaches for how the organizing culture can be transformed (Salvatierra and Heltzel, 2014, 160).

Certainly, one of the insights of the radical antiviolence movement has been that social transformation necessarily results in individual transformation: if global oppression were to end tomorrow, none of us who grew up under structures of white supremacy, settler colonialism, and heteropatriarchy would even understand how to operate in such a world. However, particularly with the development of the nonprofit industrial complex, social and individual transformation often split into organizing and social services spheres, respectively. Organizing movements are supposed to be led by bad-ass organizers who have their acts together. Healing becomes privatized through the social services arena. The result is that we create a gendered and capitalist split in how we organize. Healing is relegated to the "private" sphere and becomes unacknowledged labor that we have to do on our own with a therapist or a few friends. Once we are healed, then we are allowed to enter the public sphere of organizing. Of course, since we continue to have problems, we continue to destroy our own organizing efforts internally with no space even to talk about what is going on.

A focus on sin alone is obviously not sufficient to end structures of oppression. But the reality of sin is important to integrate into our organizing strategies. Of course, the word "sin" itself may be too loaded a term for non-Christians. Nonetheless, the insight that comes from this analysis is that organizing strategies must consciously create a space for individual transformation in order to be sustainable.

3 MULTIPLE LOGICS OF WHITE SUPREMACY

> While we agree it is absolutely critical that the evangelical church be confronted with anti-Asian racism, stereotyping and the overall lack of concern around issues raised by Asians/Asian Americans, we feel it is unhelpful—even harmful—when the framing of the problem serves to minimize anti-black racism. For example, the line "efforts have been reduced to black-white relations" implies that because blackness is *visible* it has been more seriously addressed than anti-Asian racism. This couldn't be less true. Black hypervisibility causes increased violence against black bodies on both an interpersonal and state level.—Killjoy Prophets (Park, Rice, and Kim-Kort, 2014)

A coalition of Asian American evangelicals and other Christian leaders published an open letter against anti-Asian racism in evangelicalism in response to several anti-Asian social media postings by prominent evangelicals (Asian American Christians United on Cultural Insensitivity and Reconciliation in the Church, 2013). One such posting included an evangelical conference that used a Karate Kid skit and Rick Warren making a "Red Army" joke on his Facebook page. What sparked this letter was the refusal of the individuals involved to apologize, although they did apologize later (Gleanings, 2013, 19).

This letter had an important impact in mainstream evangelicalism that contributed to LifeWay's previously described apology for its anti-Asian Vacation Bible School curriculum. It also contributed to a cover article in *Christianity Today* on Asian American evangelical leaders that addressed anti–Asian American racism within evangelical communities (H. Lee, 2014). At the same time, while recognizing the importance of this letter, some Asian American evangelicals expressed concern that it was addressing anti-Asian racism by engaging in anti-Black racism when it complained that racial reconciliation "efforts have largely been reduced to black-white relations," implying that addressing anti-Asian racism was in competition with addressing anti-Black racism. Upon self-reflection, many signatories of this letter have become very involved in addressing anti-Black racism specifically. This critique perhaps thus signaled a new direction in racial reconciliation: what would it look like if racial reconciliation did not center on white Christians? What would racial reconciliation look like if it was focused on developing relationships between communities of color?

As discussed in the introduction, critical ethnic studies has emerged to build intellectual and political projects that do not necessarily dismiss identity but structure their work around *logics* of white supremacy, colonialism, capitalism, heteropatriarchy, and so forth, in order to expand its scope. In applying a critical ethnic studies framework to evangelical multiculturalism, we can discern how these logics become evident in regard to the manner in which disparate racial groups are imagined within the Christian Right. Racial reconciliation efforts have not been uniform across diverse communities of color. The precondition of racial reconciliation within Christian evangelicalism is, of course, Christianity. Evangelical theology has impacted which communities of color are to be included in the "call to unity" and under what conditions they have been included. As many evangelical scholars have noted, religion and theology are co-constitutive with the multiple logics of white supremacy. An examination of the specificity of the distinct ways in which white supremacy operates in different contexts opens up different possibilities for dismantling white supremacy.

Anti-Blackness and U.S./Christian Exceptionalism

At the inception of the racial reconciliation movement, conservative Christian groups, with the possible exception of Promise Keepers, tended to work almost exclusively with African Americans in their racial reconciliation programs for many reasons. Many people (Christian and non-Christian) see Black-white or Black-non-Black relations as paradigmatic of race relations as a whole. Mark Noll, for instance, argues that "Black and white divisions are probably the deepest divisions in American religious life" (J. L. Grady, 1994, 58). Some groups (such as the Christian Coalition) are specifically focused on electoral politics, so they may be primarily concerned with those constituencies able to muster a voting bloc. As the importance of the Latino voting bloc has risen in importance, so too have efforts to develop relations with them.

Because of this focus on African Americans within racial reconciliation, it can be tempting to critique evangelicalism for articulating race in a "black-white" paradigm. As Jared Sexton, Angela Harris, and others have pointed out, however, this complaint about "Black-white" paradigms fails to account for the specificity of anti-Blackness within white supremacy. Thus, it is more helpful to analyze what the centrality of African Americans within the Christian Right says about how anti-Blackness operates specifically within an evangelical context. In particular, this centrality is dependent on the presumed propertied relationship between African Americans and white evangelicalism.

As Saidiya Hartman notes in *Scenes of Subjection*, Black people, while property, were still bound by the law—but only as potential transgressors of it. They were owed no protection under the law but owed complete allegiance to it. Even after Black people are no longer formally recognized as property, Black people's ontological status as property governs their being granted citizenship. While Black people may not be formal property, their ontological status of property guarantees their presumed natural relationship to the United States. For instance, unlike Native peoples, who were not recognized as "natural" citizens without congressional intervention, Black people were deemed to belong naturally to the United States after the 14th Amendment passed. As Cheryl Harris and Addie Rolnick argue, Black people are imagined as necessarily belonging to the state and are subject to it as property but are deprived of any ability to claim rights as citizens (C. Harris, 2011; Rolnick, 2011).

Similarly, African Americans are imagined as naturally belonging to (white) evangelicalism. Particularly in the early days of racial reconciliation, non–African American people of color were regarded primarily as objects of mission work rather than as partners in reconciliation within the church. African American Christian Right activist Harry Jackson Jr. of Hope Christian Church says: "White, Hispanic and Asian churches desperately need to be exposed to the best practices of their African-American counterparts" (H. Jackson, 2004, 94). There is a presumption that the practices of Black evangelical churches have something to offer evangelicalism as a whole.

Thus, Black evangelicals featured prominently (and sometimes almost exclusively) within racial reconciliation efforts at the inception of the movement because of this presumed relationship of belongingness. *Christianity Today*'s first Institute on Racism addressed only African Americans, as did *United Evangelical Action*'s issue on race (Christianity Today, 2001, 39; Tapia, 1993). Tellingly, in the 1985 National Convocation on Evangelizing Ethnic America, African Americans were the only people of color *excluded* from the effort—presumably because they have all been safely Christianized. Indeed, African Americans complained that the organizers did not seem to realize that the Christian gospel needs to be contextualized for Black people, just as it does for other people of color (Randy Frame, 1985). In general, conservative Christian articles rarely mentioned non–African American people of color apropos of racial reconciliation (Porter, 1996); they did, however, discuss other people of color as "the mission field around us" (Doucet, 1996; Pease, 1985; Plowman, 1996) under headings like "Foreign Missions: Next Door and Down the Street" (Bjork, 1985; For Koreans in America—Grown and Growing Pains, 1989). When *Christianity Today* finally brought in non-Black people of color for one of its institutes—Listening to America's Ethnic Churches—the editors gave scant attention to their discussions about racism, even though racism seemed to concern them as much as it concerns African Americans. Essentially, non–African American Christians do not belong to evangelicalism—they are perpetually outside of it.

Corroborating the thesis that white evangelicals tend to see evangelicals of color, particularly those who are not Black, as mission fields was *Christianity Today*'s cover article on implicit bias. Bradley Wright, sociologist at the University of Connecticut, sent emails using names that sounded "white," "Hispanic," "African American," and "Asian" to thousands of churches asking for information about joining. Wright noted that evangelicals mostly treated all names the same. However, mainline denominations were less likely to respond to people of color, especially those with "Asian-sounding" names, and also gave less information to people of color. The study suggested that the reason evangelical churches were more responsive was not because they were less racist but because they saw people of color as a mission field (Wright, 2015).

In any case, while African Americans may also be treated as a mission field, particularly in urban church ministries, they are also often represented as having finally been "reached" and therefore as being able to participate in the Christian American dream of missionizing others (V. Becker, 1989; Boone, 2008; Pelt, 1989; C. Williams, 1996). Evangelicalism advocates that Black people should be missionaries, particularly to Africa, because they will arouse less suspicion than white people because people understand their prior (not present) history of oppression. Emphasizing mission work in Black churches will help contradict liberalizing tendencies within these churches (Sutherland, 2004). Pursuing mission work is, in fact, the sign that a group "has arrived" (Listening to America's Ethnic Churches, 1989, 32, 37; Maust, 1993). Testifying about the "successful" conversion of Blacks to Christianity, *Christianity Today* reported on one Black church in Oakland, California, that set up a mission in Castro Valley to reach white people (Man Bites Dog, 1990).

This natural belongingness is the critical strategy by which the history of white evangelicalism in slavery and Jim Crow ceases to be a problem for Christian evangelicalism. As Sylvester Johnson argues in *The Myth of Ham* (2004), white supremacy cannot be separated from Christianity in the United States. Given Christianity's complicity in slavery and white supremacy, Christian identity is necessarily in tension with any antiracist politic. However, white evangelicalism resolves this tension by articulating Black people as naturally belonging to Christianity—consequently dissipating the tensions posed by Christian complicity in white supremacy.

As mentioned in the introduction, many racial reconciliation events and articles focus on repentance for slavery and racial segregation (Cheaney, 2016b; Hamilton, 2016; Herndon, 2005b; R. Pulliam, 2005). There is debate, however, as to whether slavery requires apology and redress or whether it can be safely relegated to the past with no ongoing implications for society today (M. Olasky, 2005h). Many contend that redress for slavery is unnecessary. A *Charisma* article on 'The History America Chose to Forget" was criticized for asserting that "Americans cannot fully repent for the sins of racism and injustice if we do not face the fact that horrendous atrocities were committed against blacks in our recent history" (V. Lowe, 2000, 164). Mark Pollard's call for repentance and restitution for slavery and Native genocide in this article provoked many negative responses: "I would strongly encourage any American who has been owned as a slave, injured in a lynching or discriminated against to seek restitution through the civil court system immediately. However, Pollard's demand for racial restitution for all African Americans by all white Americans is the highest order of racism" (Letters, 2001a, 11). However, there has been some advocacy for restitution in some form. A *Christianity Today* article argued that white people "bear a moral connection to actions that we did not ourselves commit" (Marino, 1998, 82). "White people have profited from our racist past, and thus, relative to slavery, we are more like receivers of stolen goods than innocent bystanders who just happen to bear a physical likeness to slave owners.... If ignorance of being privileged is an ignorance we ourselves are responsible for producing, then we become morally reproachable" (Marino, 1998, 83; see also Chen, 1998; Marino, 1998, 83; Potter, 2000).

Evangelicals were also involved in the 1997 class action suit filed by Black farmers against the U.S. Department of Agriculture. The USDA agreed to pay $58,000 and forgive federal debts because these farmers had previously been refused loans. Explaining evangelical involvement, Mark Pollard says, "When whites say reconciliation, they mean prayer and repentance.... Blacks, on the other hand, because they are hurting... they want to know what you're going to do. For them, reconciliation starts at social action" (A. Gaines, 1999, 32). As Pollard explains in another article: "Confession is worthless, and forgiveness invalid, where restitution has not been made,... Is the cancer of slavery and native genocide inoperable? I think not" (Pollard, 2000, 69; see also J. Gaines, 2000, 70).

At the same time, even Black evangelicals tend to view slavery as part of God's providence. "God sent some Africans to North America to suffer human indignation, to be prepared in a special way for a special ministry" (Soaries, 1986, 26). Jefferson Edwards argues that Blacks must "dewesternize" history and "develop our own educational system, with our own books, our own history" (Edwards, 1996, 153). However, to accomplish this goal, Black people must "de-Africanize some of our teaching" so as to avoid the "animism and ancestral worship" that is part of Black African history (Edwards, 1996, 154). The Reverend Earl Carter goes so far as to state that the United States was realizing God's will by enslaving African Americans because God desired that Africans be punished for idolatry. God wants everybody to know that He sent the ships (E. Carter, 1988). He contends that African American slaves were the descendants of Egypt and were enslaved in the United States as punishment for Egypt's enslavement of Israel for 3,000 years. He declares: "Slavery is over; the sentence has been served. And there is no apology necessary" (R. E. Carter, 1997, 67). Another article contends that Christianity in Africa is not the product of colonialism but the product of freed slaves who went to Africa. These freed slaves then introduced freedom to Africans (Stafford, 2000).

Not surprisingly, then, contemporary Africa is demonized within this rhetoric as the site of "idol worship and black magic" (R. Lee, 1986, 43). According to *World*, "From Africa comes word of reversion to witchcraft and daily pagan practice. If these practices come wrapped with superstition and even violence, so be it" (J. Belz, 2008g, 6). *Christianity Today* warns that practitioners of African religions are regularly conducting human sacrifices (Minchakpu, 2004c). Afro-Caribbean traditions are similarly seen as "demonic religions" (Harmon, 2000). Ethiopia is portrayed as savage, with child sacrifices (LaPlante, 2011). According to the Reverend Carter, "When I look at the tribal warfare that is going on in Africa and the multiplicity of problems there—drought, dissension and political wars—I'm glad that the ships came. God used drastic means to bring us out of a life of idol worship, darkness and ignorance, but He did bring us out into the knowledge of the one true God" (R. E. Carter, 1997, 45).[1] Of course, this suggests that God has no interest in Africans currently living in Africa.[2]

Some sectors of evangelicalism are even reluctant to admit to a Christian role in slavery. Writers tend to focus on uplifting those evangelicals who opposed slavery rather than the majority who did not (Colson, 1985; Leggett, 2003; M. Olasky, 2015b; Olsen, 2010). David Barton of Wallbuilders even went so far as to argue that the Constitution's designation of Black people as three-fifths of a person was actually pro-Black (Barton, 1995)! David Chilton also argues that slavery was beneficial to Black people: "Granted that some Negroes were mistreated as slaves, the fact still remains that nowhere in all history in the world today has the Negro been better off. . . . He was not taken from freedom into slavery, but from a vicious slavery to degenerate chiefs to a generally benevolent slavery in the United States" (quoted in Lienesch, 1993, 150). Some Christian organizations are now involved in Civil War reenactments in which they argue that the Civil War actually had nothing to do with slavery. One participant in these reenactments, Alan Farley, was asked if he believed in slavery. His response: "I do believe in slavery. Every person is enslaved to their own sin until they are set free by the blood of Jesus" (quoted in Butcher, 2002, 68).

Even in recent history, Christian periodicals describe evangelicals as standing at the forefront in the struggle against apartheid (Burke, 2006) or segregation (E. Owens, 2003). They seem to have experienced some form of historical amnesia; they forget that the Christian Right supported the white South African government, was opposed to sanctions against South Africa, and often claimed that Nelson Mandela was a menace and that apartheid was not that bad (Letters, 1985b; Patterson, 1990; South African Churches Win at Polls, 1994).[3] As a not particularly progressive South African white evangelist stated about American evangelicals during the time of apartheid:

> In South Africa we feel that some North American evangelicals are too gullible. North American leaders are too ready to accept the line offered by many South African whites, which says the only problem with South

Africa is that we're misunderstood, and we're really trying very hard to fix our problems. We're a Christian country; we are against communism; and there we just need a bit more encouragement and everything will come right. [They believe the line] that apartheid is not quite as bad as it's made out to be. (Cassidy, 1989, 55–56)

Nowadays, however, Christian periodicals describe evangelical Christians as being at the forefront of this struggle toward racial justice in South Africa. The actual programs for change, however, seem to entail such revolutionary programs as white women setting up dressmaking schools for their Black domestics (Van Leeuwen, 1989) and forming interracial music groups (Can Music Be the Instrument of Racial Reconciliation?, 1987; Van Leeuwen, 1989). If apartheid and slavery were not so bad and Black people were relatively happy in these systems, the obvious question is: why is racial reconciliation necessary now?

The rhetoric of evangelical racial reconciliation depends on the presumed belongingness of Black people to the United States. Black evangelicals, as they are represented in white evangelical forums, tie their Christian faith to U.S. patriotism. As John Perkins asserts: "I am not an African; I am an American. Any black American who puts his allegiance to Africa above his allegiance to America is only hurting himself . . . [the] United States is my country. I love her" (Perkins, 1995a, 40, 42; see also Black Magazines Stress Strong Families and Spiritual Values, 1986). This enforced belongingness, however, betrays the anxiety that Black people may in fact not actually belong to the United States. Borrowing from Alexander Weheliye's work, despite the efforts to spiritualize white supremacy, a fleshly surplus apparently remains in the wake of social death. "Racializing assemblages of subjection that can never annihilate the lines of flight, freedom dreams, practices of liberation, and possibilities of other worlds" (Weheliye, 2014, 1). In the 1990s the evangelical anxiety over this remainder seemed to crystallize in preoccupation with the influence of Louis Farrakhan and the Nation of Islam in African American communities. Especially during this period, both evangelical progressives and conservatives typically depicted Farrakhan as one of the biggest threats to the United States (K. Daniels, 2005; Maxwell, 1995; Tapia, 1994; C. Thomas, 1995). Even the relatively more progressive Tony Campolo said that "our biggest concern about African-Americans is that their greatest linkage right now is to the Nation of Islam. When Farrakhan emerges instead of an evangelical black pastor as the prime spokesperson for the black community, we are concerned" (quoted in

Cromartie, 1996b, 38). Charles Colson argued in the same article that Farrakhan is "one of the most dangerous men who has come along in American life. And we should be much more concerned about that than whether 'blacks' are Republicans or Democrats" (quoted in Cromartie, 1996b, 38). A *Charisma* article asserted that the Nation of Islam "promotes racism and is against American interests" (K. Daniels, 2004, 16). It lambasted Christians who participated in the Million Man March because Farrakhan is an infidel. "Millions of deceived souls . . . are sucked into hell from his teachings" (K. Daniels, 2004, 16). They don't offer much explanation for how Farrakhan, no matter what one may think of him, can be this much of an actual threat other than the fact that he is not Christian and hence represents the threat that Blacks may choose not to join Christian America—and hence may have never "belonged" to Christian America in the first place. Thus, racial reconciliation became a way for Black peoples to do antiracist work properly, since the Nation of Islam does not understand the importance of forgiving white people (H. Jackson Jr., 2005a).

This concern over Farrakhan then spills over to a concern about Islam as a whole. Noting that the majority of converts to Islam in the United States are black (Zoba, 2000a, 42), Islam becomes racialized as a religion of blackness. Consequently, ministries such as Project Joseph have formed to keep African Americans from Islam. Carl Ellis, its head, says that to reach Black Muslims "we need to look at the social and cultural issues that are affecting the black community—the need for justice" (C. Ellis, 2000, 52–53). Prison ministries are often focused on saving Black people from Islam (D. Olasky, 2010). However, this project relies on a demonized understanding of Islam whereby its adherents are struggling for world domination.

It may have also been because of Farrakhan's perceived popularity that a growing acceptance of "Afrocentric Christianity" emerged (Bray, 1992, 42–44; June, 1996, 259–71). Proponents include Clarence Hilliard (NBEA), who argued that African cultures provide a model for how to live together in community because they do not separate the sacred and the profane (T. Morgan, 1994a, 51). Tony Evans is reluctant to embrace Afrocentricism wholeheartedly. Yet he uses it to critique whites by arguing that "pagan" African religions had more in common with biblical Christianity than did the "Christian" religion of white slavemasters (T. Evans, 1995, 52). Glenn Usry and Craig Keener articulate the basis of what they call an Afrocentric Christianity in *Black Man's Religion* in direct response to the Nation of Islam (Usry and Keener, 1996, 10). Other writers advocate for a Black Jesus (Carney, 1990).

On the one hand, this evangelical "Afrocentrism" appears to domesticate the radical impulses within Afrocentricism by reinstantiating Christian imperialism. For instance, *Christianity Today* prominently featured evangelical Black Nationalist Eugene Rivers, who argued that true Black Nationalism is Christian, not Muslim. He claims that Black people who reject Christianity are "acting white." Thus, even Black Nationalism, not particularly desirable but necessary to counter the Nation of Islam, can still fit within the Christian empire. Ultimately, under his framework, Black Christians still have more in common with white Christians than with Black non-Christians, especially since the "church is *the only* true hope for reform" (Zoba, 1996, 2). On the other hand, it potentially challenges the presumed whiteness of evangelicalism itself. Is the Christianity affirmed by Eugene Rivers actually the same Christianity affirmed by Pat Robertson? Building on the work of Peter Heltzel, white evangelicalism is already constructed on a disavowed Blackness. Racial reconciliation, then, while perhaps intent on domesticating Blackness within evangelicalism, foregrounds the fact that "because the master does not possess exclusively, and *naturally*, what he calls his language, because, whatever he wants or does, he cannot maintain any relations of property or identity that are natural, national, congenital, or ontological . . . , he can . . . pretend historically . . . to appropriate it in order to impose it as 'his own'" (Derrida, 1998, 23). The evangelical discourse around anti-Blackness shifted dramatically however, with the rise of the Movement for Black Lives. This shift is discussed in greater detail in the conclusion.

Evangelical Orientalism: The Outsiders Within

In addition to operating through a logic of anti-Blackness in which Blackness is construed as the property of whiteness, white supremacy also operates through Orientalist logics by which some populations are constructed as the permanent foreign threats to the well-being of empire. This logic is particularly evident with respect to Arab and Muslim peoples—two categories seen as mutually interchangeable within Christian evangelicalism. Prior to 9/11 Arab and Muslim Americans were generally not featured either as potential partners in racial reconciliation or even as objects of mission. After 9/11 they have received more attention, either as objects of mission or as internal terrorist enemies, but have not been featured in racial reconciliation programs. This absence is significant: as *Charisma* reports, 70 percent of Arab Americans are Christians (A. Gaines, 2003). Arabs and Muslims are so frequently conflated in evangelical literature because religion is racialized both in evangelical discourses and in the broader post-9/11 U.S. political climate (see chapter 5). Consequently, this section addresses both Arabs and Muslims simultaneously.

Trey Hancock, a white missionary who does mission work to Arab people in Dearborn, Michigan, despairs that he has only been able to convert one Arab to Christianity each year, and most of those converts eventually reconvert to Islam. But he decided to continue his work after he had a dream about a vampire. "The Lord let me know this was the Spirit of Islam. It was here to scare and intimidate people so they will leave the Muslims alone" (Walker, 2002, 54). *Christianity Today* featured a more extended article on Arab Americans, which did note that racism against Arab Americans is severe in the United States and that the situation for Christians in Arab countries is not as bleak as usually depicted in the Christian press. The article also noted that many Arab people are in fact Christian: "Arab for some Americans means Muslim and potential terrorist." This article notes that not all Arab people are Muslim but does not question the connection between Muslim and "potential terrorist" (Coffman, 2004, 41). Another article describes Muslims as manipulating U.S. democratic principles for nefarious purposes: "While Muslims gain religious rights in the West, persecution of religious minorities by extreme Islamic elements in some Muslim countries in Asia and the Middle East continues unabated" (Zoba, 2000a, 42). Muslims are accused of using Christian principles of democracy to attack Christianity by calling it "anti-Muslim propaganda" (42). Apparently, Muslims have also infiltrated YouTube and the internet (Bergin, 2007e; Richardson, 2005). A *World* magazine article blames multicultural ideology for hindering people from criticizing Islam, which Muslims insidiously use as cover to turn the United States and other Western countries into Islamic states. "Multicultural freedom puts an end to freedom. Multiculturalism commits suicide" (Veith, 2008b, 33; see also M. Belz, 2007a). *World* further complained that we should be quick to blame all acts of terror on Islam even before we know the facts, recommending that we be more belligerent in our opposition to Islam and consciously engage in acts that "offend and antagonize the Muslim community" (J. Belz, 2015, 8). It further critiqued Muslims who think of "Islam as a religion of peace, tolerance, and equality—even as past and present demonstrate otherwise" (S. Lee, 2015b, 65–66). As one article headline anxiously announced, "The Muslims Are Coming Here!" (R. Bailey, 1990).

World suggests that evangelicals should not just center their anti-immigrant fervor on Mexico: "Canada's generous welfare program, lax immigration policies, and high Muslim immigrant population provide an ideal nesting ground for terrorist cells" (Bergin, 2006a, 30; see also L. McAdam, 2004). The proposed solution: fences at the Canadian border. Europe is also invoked as another negative case study of Muslims run amok. "Europe could become predominantly Muslim in our children's lifetime" (L. McAdam, 2004, 418–19). Riots in France demonstrate the violence of Islam (J. Belz, 2005a; M. Belz, 2005c). *World* featured a book by Bay Ye'or called *Eurabia* (2005), which "chronicles Arab determination to subdue Europe as a cultural appendage to the Muslim world—and Europe's willingness to be subjugated" (C. Thomas, 2007, 4). Marvin Olasky of *World* contends: "It is clear: we must fight Islam wholesale or Europe will become 'Eurabia'" (M. Olasky, 2008b, 56). The proposed solution: end immigration and reestablish European identity. Furthermore, *World* reports that a new study has found that British schools are not teaching about the Jewish Holocaust anymore in order to not offend Muslims. "All of this . . . comes from the flawed Western point of view that others will be nice to us if we are nice to them. . . . Europeans are going out of their way to make nice with those who would destroy them" (C. Thomas, 2007, 4). An article in *Charisma* similarly contended that the anti-Christ was about to control the United States through Islamic terrorism, thus advocating strict immigration control. It blamed environmentalists for playing into Muslim hands by trying to stop oil drilling in Alaska, thus allowing terrorists to control the U.S. economy (Stone, 2011, 47).

Of course, not all evangelicals share these rigid anti–Arab/Muslim American positions. Thirty-three leaders (including eleven Muslim Americans) signed a new document called "Changing Course: A New Direction for US Relations with the Muslim World." It emphasized the need for diplomacy and the need to improve civil participation in Muslim countries. Richard Land of the Southern Baptist Convention was one of the participants in efforts to improve Muslim-evangelical relations (Galli, 2011c; M. Olasky, 2008b). And even *World* sometimes argues for an alternative approach to the Muslim threat:

> Some Christians call for restrictions on free speech when they're bothered by atheistic attacks on religion or secularist critiques of fundamentalism. The challenge of Islam shows us that we need exactly the opposite. We need more free speech, even if we find some utterances obnoxious. Let Christians and Muslims have a peaceful but vigorous debate, no verbal holds barred. The gospel will hold its own in this country and soar in Muslim lands. That's what defenders of Islam fear. (M. Olasky, 2007a, 56)

Christianity Today ran an article critical of the state of Oklahoma's attempt to ban Shari'ah law. Its defense for allowing Shari'ah law was that it would help Westernize Islam (Witte, 2012).

In addition, another exception to this exclusion of Arab peoples in reconciliation work was the 1993–1996 Reconciliation Walk in which 1,150 Christians retraced the path of the First Crusade (1095–1099 CE) to offer apologies for the atrocities committed during these wars (Butcher, 1997; T. Dixon, 1999b). The walk, purportedly well received by Israel, ended on July 15, 1999 (T. Dixon, 1999c). This effort did not pertain to Arab Americans and also did not take an explicitly political stand against current Western imperialism in the Arab world (T. Dixon, 1998, 1999a). The text of the apology was as follows:

> Nine hundred years ago, our forefathers carried the name of Jesus Christ in battle across the Middle East. Fueled by fear, greed and hatred, they betrayed the name of Christ by conducting themselves in a manner contrary to His wishes and character. The Crusaders lifted the banner of the Cross above your people. By this act, they corrupted its true meaning of reconciliation, forgiveness and selfless love.
>
> On the anniversary of the first Crusade, we also carry the name of Christ. We wish to retrace the footsteps of the Crusaders in apology for their deeds and in demonstration of the true meaning of the Cross. We deeply regret the atrocities committed in the name of Christ by our predecessors. We renounce greed, hatred and fear, and condemn all violence done in the name of Jesus Christ.
>
> Where they were motivated by hatred and prejudice, we offer love and brotherhood. Jesus the Messiah came to give life. Forgive us for allowing His name to be associated with death. Please accept again the true meaning of the Messiah's words:
>
> "The Spirit of the Lord is upon me, because He has anointed me to bring good news to the poor. He has sent me to proclaim release to the captives and recovery of sight to the blind, to let the oppressed go free, to proclaim the year of the Lord's favour." As we go, we bless you in the name of the Lord Jesus Christ. (The Reconciliation Walk, 2000)

Some Muslim critics argued that this march was simply a benign form of mission work, especially because it did not offer any practical assistance (Jankowski, 1999). However, the rhetoric of this walk and the follow-up assembly held in Beirut and Damascus in April 2002 does make an intervention in the anti-Islam fervor within evangelicalism. One participant stated that Christians "come to the East with the attitude that we are superior, both spiritually and culturally, and that we have all the right answers" (T. Dixon, 1997, 76). Lynn Green of Youth with a Mission International argued that Christians must not treat Muslims as "if they were all hostile and dangerous and potential terrorists" (quoted in T. Dixon, 2002c, 26). He further argued that the United States cannot condemn Muslim terrorism without looking at its own complicity in terrorism. We must look at "governments and organizations claiming biblical support for unjust or even terroristic violence, such as the Crusades, the Inquisition, apartheid, slavery or white supremacy in America" (T. Dixon, 2002c, 26). While the march did not take an explicit stance on the colonization of Palestine, his remarks implicitly critique the presuppositions of Christian Zionism (discussed in more detail in chapter 5): "Our call is to remember, but while remembering, to consider carefully our own current views. Do we allow our zeal for the eternal fate of a soul to obscure that soul's present value to God? Do we harbor a millennarian vision that is willing to sacrifice Jewish, Muslim or Eastern Christian lives for the sake of an eschatological timetable?" (E. R. Fletcher, 1999).

Lynn Green concludes: "Is the anti-Christian spirit at work in parts of the Muslim world stronger than the anti-Christian spirit of Western materialism? I personally do not think so" (T. Dixon, 2002c, 26).[4] As another possible example of evangelical-Muslim dialogue, the Houston Baptist University, a member of the Council for Christian Colleges and Universities, has a 3 percent Muslim community. The university is one of the most diverse evangelical schools with equal numbers of Latinx, white, and Black people. The university does not require students to sign a Christian faith statement (although faculty and staff do). Muslims enroll because they want a socially conservative atmosphere, and the university leaders see their presence as an opportunity to evangelize. They also have hired a formerly Muslim evangelical as support staff for this population (Chenoweth and Benoit, 2009). *Christianity Today* also covered from a generally favorable perspective the Marrakesh Declaration that came out in support of religious liberty and condemned terrorism. It was reported that Arab evangelicals particularly supported it (Casper, 2016).

Since 9/11 Arab and Muslim Americans have been particularly portrayed as permanent threats, but this logic has also informed the manner in which Asian Americans and Latinos have been constructed within the racial reconciliation movement.[5] According to some authors, Asian Americans have only recently emigrated from "the Heart of Darkness" where the "unseen powers of the demonic realm are noticeably more evident" (South Asia: Into the Heart of Darkness, 1993, 27).[6] Another warns of the "dark netherworld of the Hindus involvement with tantric sex" (J. Belz, 2008g, 6). In addition, Hindus apparently cannot distinguish trees from human beings: "For some Indians, their wooden idols happen to be actual trees. Disturbed by an outbreak of robberies, murders, and other crimes, natives of Malda, India, decided to conduct a wedding ceremony for a pair of conjoined trees in order to ward off evil spirits. . . . Spectators brought wedding gifts, including some scarves for the newlywed trees" (The Buzz Quicktakes, 2006, 7). The item was entitled "A Bunch of Saps," indicating its contempt for spiritual practices in India. *World* implies that Cho Seung-Hui may have become the gunman in the Virginia Tech massacre because his family was not affiliated with a church. Fortunately, *World* assures us, most Korean Americans are Christians (Dean, 2008d). Asian Americans are often associated with Buddhism, which "is overtly a power religion with real demonic power displays. It is a 'do it yourself' religion, which often suits Westerners seeking freedom to live outside structures of morality" (Tiansay, 2003, 44).[7] *Christianity Today* did note, however, that this equation between Asian Americans and Asian religions is problematic, given that 85 percent of Yale's Campus Crusade for Christ chapter are Asian; meanwhile, Yale's Buddhist meditation meetings are almost exclusively attended by whites (Olsen, 2003a). As previously discussed, only recently have Asian Americans been featured as evangelical leaders and has anti–Asian American racism within evangelicalism been addressed (H. Lee, 2014). Asian Americans were discussed more frequently, however, during the height of Jeremy Lin's fame (Lu, 2011).

Somewhat surprisingly, Latinos were only rarely discussed as potential racial reconciliation partners during the emergence of the movement (Cizik, 1988). Latinos are sometimes still regarded as insufficiently "Christian" because they are primarily Catholic. Despite the efforts of the Christian Right to develop coalitions, anti-Catholic sentiment remains strong among a constituency that views Catholicism as the "whore church" (Letters, n.d., 4).[8] Protestant inroads into Latin America were considered one of *Christianity Today*'s top ten stories of 1991 (Campbell, 1991; Tapia, 1992), and evangelicals still write about the great need to evangelize there (How Can North Americans Help Evangelize Mexico?, 1986; D. Miller, 1996; Witt, 1996; Woehr, 1992). Evangelizing U.S. Latinos is also a top priority: "If the Hispanics are not reached," says Raimundo Jimenez, "they will be influenced by occultism and by the leftist militants in the universities." The very survival of

Los Angeles, he claims, depends upon successful Hispanic mission work (quoted in Wooding, 1994, 29). Why? For an answer we turn to David Neff, who tells us that when evangelical Latinos "no longer participate easily in Latin America's culturally sanctioned corruption; they become honest, industrious, and thrifty; and they resist the tradition of drunkenness" (Neff, 1990a, 15). According to Neff, evangelical Latinos are more likely to seek employment and settle happily into U.S. society. A similar article claims that, upon embracing the "Protestant ethic," Latinos work harder, make more money, and pursue the American dream (Tapia, 1991, 20). These articles reflect a deep-seated belief of the Christian Right: Protestantism equals capitalism equals America (Neff, 1990a).

The characterization of Latinos as a permanent foreign threat is especially prevalent in conservative evangelical discourse around immigration, and was particularly evident at the beginning of the racial reconciliation movement. In a 1986 issue of *United Evangelical Action* devoted to immigration issues, most articles were anti-immigration (Bjork, 1986; Piecuch, 1986; Rudolph, 1986). The issue did, however, feature two brief articles sympathetic to immigrant concerns. One mentioned a forum for evangelical leaders, cosponsored in part by the National Association of Evangelicals (NAE), where Latinos vigorously denounced anti-immigration sentiments. Another article discussed the abusive behavior of the border patrol (Forum Examines Immigration, 1986; Reporter at the Border, 1986). (As discussed later, the NAE began to shift its position as the Latinx voting bloc grew in strength and numbers.) *World*, in particular, tended to run solidly anti-immigrant articles until recently, and even ran an ad by the Minuteman Civil Defense Corps calling for a border fence (M. Olasky, 2006c).[9] (Apparently the Minutemen are saving the United States from terrorists, as evidenced by the fact that one person crossing the border had a Sudanese coin in his pocket [Dawson 2005a].)[10] One article describes immigrants as evil bandits who rape women and then ask the Border Patrol to pay for their medical expenses after they get shot (Dawson, 2005b). Another *World* article complained that "Hispanics have a lack of respect for our law and culture which contributes to unwed mothers, trash in the streets, unpaid bills, drugs, forgery, and other crimes" (M. Olasky, 2006a, 37; see also Dawson, 2006c).

Anti-immigrant letters also frequently appear in *Charisma*:

> It is time to close the borders.... It is not just drugs and the mafia that come from Mexico. Illegals take jobs from American citizens. Illegals

have ripped off our hospitals and schools. Quality health care and education programs have been replaced by bilingual classes that don't teach English well. It is your grandchildren who will not have an education or job choices because of this foreign invasion. (Feedback, 2007c, 10)

The real issue is not immigration. The real problem is rooted in drugs, gangs, terrorists and other criminals. Fox News reports that there are 80,000 illegal immigrants in the United States right now who have active warrants out for their arrests. Their crimes range from murder to rape to shoplifting. (Feedback, 2007c, 12)[11]

Borrowing from Jasbir Puar, this rhetoric of immigration rests on a logic of biopower, whereby immigrants are portrayed as populations inherently threatening to the social order (Foucault, 1980; Puar, 2007). Anti-immigration rhetoric is not even seen as anti–human rights; rather, the very survival of the United States supposedly rests on the constant elimination of immigrant populations. And the United States is a settler state, so anti-immigration rhetoric helps resolve the colonial dis-ease arising from European immigrants' unjust occupation of the Americas.

Ironically, however, evangelical imagining of Latinos as a mission field has served to complicate their positions on immigration.[12] For one thing, the National Association of Evangelicals reports that undocumented immigrants "make up a significant portion of the membership of hundreds of NAE member churches. Even the pastors of some NAE churches are undocumented" (Randy Frame, 1987, 34). Also, it is often underfunded urban churches that are forced to make up for the cutbacks in immigrants' benefits. Even during the immigrant-bashing debate over California's Proposition 187, *Christianity Today* ran a fairly even-handed article on immigration, arguing that "if evangelicals don't get involved [in immigrant rights] . . . this could result in another blemish on the church's social witness much like when conservative Christians avoided early involvement in the civil rights movement" (Maxwell, 1993a, 51). Consequently, anti-immigrant bashing can run counter to the missionizing imperatives of evangelical churches. *Christianity Today* has also raised a surprising challenge to anti-immigration stances in the church: "Ninety-five percent of missionaries in [Mexico] are there illegally because Mexico does not give visas to missionaries. If the evangelical church can justify breaking the law in order to stay [in Mexico] . . . why can't Mexicans break the law in order to stay here?" (Tapia, 1991, 22).[13] An op-ed argued that "creating criminal penalties for those who aid illegal immigrants falls short of solving our problems" and argued for an approach that does not demonize immigrants (Blessed Are the Courageous, 2006, 26–27). One writer to *Charisma* asserts: "In God's kingdom there are no borders. Where are the conservatives? The church is keeping silent while our immigrant nation turns into a nation of hatred" (Feedback, 2007c, 10).

This logic of exclusion is in tension with the evangelical impulse to missionize to the world. Some writers argue that global instability is good because unstable conditions are more conducive to people being open to the gospel (Foreman, 1999). The impact of globalization in creating the conditions of forced migration are also beneficial for missionary work because immigrants are also more receptive to the gospel. "There are vastly more winnable people in the world now than ever before" (Mumper, 1986b, 21; see also Divino, 2003). *Charisma* opines: "Immigrants represent the greatest missionary opportunity America has ever had" (Farrell, 1997, 56; see also Dean, 2013a; S. Lee, 2015a). Richard Pease talks about these patterns of migration as great opportunities for Christians. When people are uprooted from their countries and their traditions, when "they have lost everything," they are more likely to "come to faith in Christ." This forced dislocation is not a tragedy but a cause for celebration. Pease asks: "Is it possible that the sovereign Lord of history is at work in a special way in this situation?" (Pease, 1985, 22; see also R. Bailey, 1990; Lotte, 1989). Or, as Raymond Bakke of International Urban Associates claims, "Since God owns the whole world, he's bringing the whole world to the U.S. for a wonderful purpose—evangelism" (quoted in Guthrie, 1991, 40; see also Bjork, 1985; Carnes, 2003; P. Johnson, 2003a; Lu, 2010). Some articles explicitly talk about taking advantage of economic instability globally in order to provide "humanitarian" aid in conjunction with evangelistic efforts (Guthrie, 1993, 25).[14] These trends of destabilization are no longer caused by governmental and economic institutions (which are often supported by the Christian Right); rather, they are caused by God in order to create circumstances conducive to evangelism. The tragedy of the 2006 Indonesian tsunami, for instance, was portrayed as an opportunity to further mission work into Muslim communities through relief work (Carnes, 2006c).

As a result, evangelicals are sometimes more supportive of immigration and helping refugees than non-Christian conservatives, even amid the War on Terror. "Of course we want to keep terrorists out of our country, but let's not punish the victims of ISIS [the Islamic State of Iraq and the Levant] for the sins of ISIS," said Leith Anderson, president of the National Association of Evangelicals in response to U.S. governors saying that they would not accept refugees from Syria. "Our system is designed to keep terrorists out and to help desperate families with little children. We want to help the victims of terrorism in the Middle East, not punish them" (quoted in Zylstra, 2015a). *World* opined on the subject of Syrian refugees, "Sheltering homeless war victims isn't a mission strike, but it could signify strategic engagement of a higher order" (M. Belz, 2013b, 32). *Christianity Today* also ran a cover article expressing the importance of accepting refugees, which it describes as an "Arab spring from above," and featuring an Iraqi pastor who argues, "Why are you Christian brothers in the West afraid? We are here on the front line" (J. Weber, 2016a, 33). In a similar cover article, *World* raises security concerns regarding Syrian refugees but ultimately seems to focus on the question of "who is my neighbor?" (Dean, 2015c). *Relevant* notes that 80 percent of Republicans don't want to accept Syrian refugees (Slices, 2016, 14). But Christian organizations have been defying this trend. In June 2016 the Southern Baptist Convention broke with the Republican Party position to pass a resolution to "encourage Southern Baptist churches and families to welcome and adopt refugees into their churches and homes as a means to demonstrate to the nations that our God longs for every tribe, tongue and nation to be welcomed at his throne" (J. Bruce, 2016, 59; see also Fausset and Blinder, 2016). The SBC has been a key organization in support of Syrian refugees. Russell Moore of the SBC's ERLC says "Christians should be the ones calling the rest of the world to remember the image of God and inalienable human dignity of persecuted people whether Christian, Jewish, Muslim or Yazidi" (Slices, 2016, 14). Similarly, Matthew Soerens of World Relief declared: "Jesus was a refugee himself. . . . The journey Jesus took when fleeing to Egypt as a boy looks a lot like what little Syrian boys and girls have done in the past five years" (Zylstra, 2015a). World Relief released a statement calling for support rather than rejection of Syrian refugees from a biblical perspective.

It should be noted, however, that in general white evangelicals are much less likely than Black evangelicals to support allowing refugees in the United States.[15] And many prominent evangelicals certainly supported Donald Trump's candidacy because they supported his proposed ban of Muslims entering the country. For instance, Franklin Graham stated: "We must reform our immigration policies in the United States. We cannot allow Muslim immigrants to come across our borders unchecked while we are fighting this war on terror" (Zylstra, 2015a). Advocating an end to Muslim immigration, Graham further contended: "If we continue to allow Muslim immigration, we'll see much more of what happened in Paris—it's on our doorstep. France and Europe are being overrun by young Muslim men from the Middle East, and they do not know their backgrounds or their motives and intentions" (Zylstra, 2015a).

In addition, though the assumption behind missionization is that "the biblical message is classless and colorless" (Henry and Mouw, 1991, 37), the growing popularity of various forms of cultural nationalism is forcing some evangelicals to argue that an inability to embrace any form of cultural pride will prevent evangelicals from accomplishing mass conversions. They are thus willing to make some token efforts just so long as those who are the objects of mission join on the Christian bandwagon (J. Anderson, 1988; C. Chapman, 1990; Kraft, 1991). David Teeter, for instance, reports a Muslims for Jesus project, similar to the widely criticized Jews for Jesus project, where Muslims are taught that they can be most truly Muslim by becoming Christian (Teeter, 1990). Hence missionary groups such as the Jesus for Muslims Network have emerged (C. Lewis, 2008). This has led to a concern about a "Chrislam" movement that, according to *World*, blends Islam with Christianity. This movement has been accused of converting Christians to Islam (Schartel, 2011).[16] *Charisma* featured an article completely attacking this movement, asserting that contextualization is not really necessary because Islam is "not a culture": it is a "religion with a false god" (Walker, 2013, 46). The InterVarsity Urbana 1996 convention, which attracted close to 20,000 young evangelicals, called for the "de-Westernization of the gospel" (Olsen, 1997a, 86). Essentially, as the growing numbers of evangelicals in both the United States and the world are not white, white evangelicalism finds itself potentially standing outside the global majority of evangelicalism. Hence communities once viewed as permanent threats have become increasingly more incorporated through this evangelical approach toward multiculturalism. To exemplify, *Charisma* featured an article on Che Ahn with Harvest Rock Church, who seeks to break through the "bamboo curtain." Instead of portraying Asian Americans as a mission field, Ahn describes the United States as a mission field for Asians. "God is raising up a generation of Asians in this country who will take authority over demonic powers" (J. Kilpatrick, 1999, 54). At the same time, he reminds Christians that racism against Asians is alive and well (J. L. Grady, 1998). The notion that Asians are somehow inherently not Christian is called into question as *Charisma* notes that some of the largest Christian groups in many cities are all-Asian chapters of Campus Crusade for Christ or other such groups. At the same time, Asian Americans are separated from the full benefits of Christendom by the "bamboo curtain."

Disappearing Natives: The Genocidal Logics of Evangelicalism

A fundamental problem with evangelicalism is how it can proclaim itself the good news for Native peoples when Christianity itself is responsible for Indigenous genocide. Genocide is another fundamental logic of white supremacy: the presumption that Native peoples have disappeared and must always be disappearing is what enables colonial entitlement to Indigenous lands. The role of Native Americans in racial reconciliation is more thoroughly assessed in my earlier work (A. Smith, 2008). To summarize briefly here, however, except as the object of mission work, Native America has historically been almost completely invisible to the Christian Right. Native cultures are seen as having nothing of value. Sophia Lee of *World*, who regularly publishes blatantly racist articles on Native peoples, states: "With a history of injustice and a present full of extreme social pathologies, Native Alaskans are a broken people. Are they ready for gospel solutions?" (S. Lee, 2016b, 49). Apparently, Native Alaskans suffer from no contemporary injustices. As it turns out, they did not suffer from much historical injustice either, because "much of the anti-missionary rhetoric comes from the revisionist history of liberal scholars and is grossly skewed" (S. Lee, 2016b, 51).

Evangelicals have never fully regarded Indians as Christians because, as tribal peoples, Indians "continue to be influenced to some degree by the animistic world view" (Mumper, 1986b, 21; see also Ankerberg and Welson, 1996, 532–52; Larson, 1989, 106–9). In other words, Christian one day, primitive the next (Maust, 1985; 1992, 38). Sophia Lee from *World* asks in another article: "Would Navajos distinguish positive aspects of their cultural history from blatant idolatry?" (S. Lee, 2014, 45). Indeed, what looks like anti-Catholic prejudice against Latino Christians is really anti-Indigenous prejudice in disguise. Latino Catholics are seen as incomplete Christians because they have only partly cast off Indigenous traditions and remain "christo-pagans" (Woehr, 1992, 68; see also Crouch, 2007a). They are also influenced by the "ancestral roots" of the Aztecs, who "worshiped pagan deities by performing human sacrifices" (Teixeira, 2001, 94). Actual Indians tend to be regarded as inassimilable pagans. Native Hawaiians are similarly depicted as demonic. James Marocco started a Christian ministry in Maui, because Maui has no "Christian presence in the local culture" and because Hawaii is "very demonized" (quoted in J. Kilpatrick, 2002, 61). Now, he has 3,000 people per week in his church. "Some even said there were demons controlling the islands from the top of the volcano. They didn't understand that when God creates an anchor church in a given locale, He changes the spiritual temperature" (J. Kilpatrick, 2002, 61–62). Thus, this anti-Catholic prejudice essentially revolves around the anxiety of the Native peoples who refuse to disappear.

White Christian triumphalism seems to have impacted the way in which Native peoples were generally ignored in the beginning of racial reconciliation: it seemed as if any validation of Native society, culture, or religion would call into question the legitimacy of Christian ownership of the land. In fact, racial reconciliationist Scott Roley would later make this critique in *Charisma*: "Native North Americans were perhaps denied assimilation to the same degree as Africans because of the threat of their claim to land. A case could also be made that these original landowners of the Americas wanted no part of assimilation. The white settlers who came to America from Europe eventually settled the land belonging to the Indians. Instead of assimilation, our founding fathers practiced annihilation" (Roley, 2004, 178).

The logics of annihilation are prevalent in evangelical discourse. Paul Marshall and David Manuel, for instance, argue that "in the virgin wilderness of America, God was making His most significant attempt since ancient Israel to create a new Israel living in obedience to the laws of God, through faith in Jesus Christ" (Lienesch, 1993, 141). How could Marshall and Manuel acknowledge that Europeans stumbled upon an already populated land and tried to depopulate it by force without mussing up their pretty story of God's people in a "virgin wilderness"? Nevertheless, the inconvenient fact of a Native presence must be dealt with somehow. Most writers try to make a virtue of necessity by describing the massacre and forced missionization of Indians as a sign of European moral superiority: white Christians, after all, were the only people willing to bring Jesus to the savages (Lienesch, 1993, 141). With few exceptions, conservative Christian writers are staunch supporters of Christopher Columbus, whom they view as a "man of God" (Colson, 1993, 36).[17] While John Eidsmoe admits that Columbus did convert the Native peoples by force, he asserts that "millions of people are in heaven today as a result" (Eidsmoe, 1992, 140). Kay Brigham concedes that Columbus may have had "a dark [sic] side" in that he decimated the tribes he "discovered" (although these tribes were cannibalistic after all) but she nevertheless "admire[s] his devotion and faith to God"[18] (Brigham, 1991, 27; see also Oke, 1996). "I believe God raised up this man to extend the gospel to those religions that had never heard" (Brigham, 1991, 28). (For the record, Brigham also approves of the expulsion of Jews from

Spain.) David Neff, too, believes that Columbus "was motivated by a love for God" and so must be excused for his genocidal actions (Neff, 1991, 29).

John Dawson is one of the few writers to criticize the genocide of Indian people in the United States. Perhaps because he is from New Zealand, Dawson is capable of distancing himself somewhat from the idea of a Christian America, but even he incorrectly asserts that the earliest British colonizers did not oppress the Native peoples—only the later colonizers on the frontier slaughtered Indians: thus the founding of the United States is beyond moral reproach (Dawson, 1994, 177). Interestingly, *Charisma* featured an article on David Pott, who led a walk of healing to apologize for the "African Holocaust" and for the slave trade (Price, 2007b). It was placed next to another article that highlighted One Nation under God, a prayer ministry of Rock Church, whose members sponsored a dedication to commemorate colonists landing in the Americas so that they would rededicate "themselves and the nation to God." Featuring Pat Robertson and Kenneth Copeland, this event included "repentance for sins and for the nation, reconciliation with people groups, [and] rededicating the land to God," with no mention of Native peoples (Ghiringhelli, 2007a). As I have argued in my previous work, some of this discourse has shifted as a result of Native evangelicals arguing that Native traditions are not antithetical to evangelicalism (A. Smith, 2008; Persaud, 2011). However, to the extent that Native peoples are allowed to reappear within evangelicalism, it is always within the logics of ethnographic entrapment. At Promise Keepers and other similar events, Native peoples are always expected to wear regalia, whether from that person's Native nation or not.

Interestingly, the situation is much different in Canada, where periodicals highlight First Nations people. *Faith Today*, a Canadian evangelical magazine, has probably printed more articles on contemporary Native American issues than all of the U.S. magazines listed in the evangelical-based Christian Periodical Index combined. Its articles express much less suspicion of Native spirituality. *Faith Today* also tackles contemporary issues such as the Oka Crisis in Mohawk territory and the James Bay project (Barnes, 1989; Cowan, 1991; B. Diamond, 1991; Dorsch, 1991; Maracle, 1991; Oevering, 1989). It regularly features a section on "Native concerns." However, the thrust of these articles is often to suggest that "militant resistance" in support of Native land rights is not "Christian." Billy Diamond and Ross Maracle, for instance, while understanding the basis of militant action against Hydro-Québec, contended that instead of supporting such actions churches should do things like "sponsor native students for study in

Bible colleges" (B. Diamond, 1991, 28; Maracle, 1991, 29). Most recently in the United States, *Relevant* finally featured an article on a contemporary issue facing Native peoples, NoDAPL (protests against the Dakota Access Pipeline). It defended the NoDAPL struggle on the basis of "creation care" rather than Native land rights, however (What's So Important about the Dakota Pipeline?, 2017). In addition, while evangelicals in the United States focus their racializing discourse on Native peoples there, some groups pathologize Indigenous organizing on a global scale, particularly the World Christian Gathering of Indigenous Peoples (WCGIP), which brings together evangelical Native peoples around the world. A member of the anti-Indigenous organization Deception in the Church, for instance, complains that it is "my unpleasant duty to write this article in order to warn the churches of some 'indigenous people movements' that are not biblical. The World Christian Gathering on Indigenous People (WCGIP) is a front for the Third Wave and will not only divide the churches but is fostering bigotry and animosity against their partnerships with historical Western mission organizations" (Sampson, 2002). Despite the silence among non-Native evangelicals about the contemporary issues facing Native peoples in the United States, growing numbers of Native Christians are refusing an evangelical future of genocide. In chapter 6, I explore in greater detail how Native evangelicals are engaging in a politics of decolonization from a Christian perspective.

Decentering Whiteness

One of the impacts of the manner in which racial reconciliation tends to homogenize communities of color is that reconciliation with white people becomes the central project rather than the development of relationships between communities of color within evangelicalism. As Emily Rice argues, the goal of racial reconciliation is then for communities of color to become included within white evangelicalism rather than dismantling the distinct and differing logics of white supremacy (Killjoy Prophets, 2014b). As seen in the previously described controversy around the Asian American letter to evangelicals, the manner in which communities of color can engage in oppressive behaviors often goes unremarked. As discussed later in detail, much of the work done by the Evangelical Immigration Roundtable has not critiqued and has even supported increased border enforcement without an analysis of how border enforcement militarizes Indigenous lands (K. Kilpatrick, 2014) and relies upon an anti-Black ideology of criminalization to differentiate "good" from "bad" immigrants (Escobar, 2008). Similarly, the

World Indigenous Conference was once sited in Israel with no participation of people from Palestine. Of course, such conflicts among communities of color are not unique to Christian evangelicalism.

However, efforts have begun that focus on people or women of color organizing to decenter whiteness within racial justice organizing. Leroy and Donna Barber founded the Voices Project, which holds several gatherings each year to foster dialogue between evangelical leaders of color. These dialogues address tensions between communities of color and the differentiated ways in which people of color are racialized.

Two gatherings of women of color were held in 2015 and 2016 as part of the Christian Community Development Association Conferences that specifically focused on developing what co-organizer Chanequa Walker-Barnes described as a "woman of color consciousness" (Plenary Address at the 2015 conference). Other evangelical racial justice thinkers and activists have also spoken out about racial conflict among communities of color. Kathy Khang wrote in her blog "#Ferguson Is More Than a Hashtag":

> So to my non-black Christian brothers and sisters—maybe the point of honest confession and repentance is where we need to start. What's the point of pretending to be better than we are. We are far more broken, yet far more loved by the God of Justice, than we know.
>
> So, here are my thoughts for my Asian American Christian community. There is so much that needs to be addressed to correct for the sinful and broken ways in which we have essentially adopted a broken White evangelical view of race and justice. But these are a few starting points. (Khang, 2014)

AnaYelsi Velasco-Sanchez similarly called on Latinx people to support the Black Lives Matter (BLM) movement and address anti-Black racism (Velasco-Sanchez, 2016). InterVarsity worship leader Erna Kim Hackett, who is Korean American, helped bring InterVarsity to national prominence at the 2016 Urbana conference by centering BLM throughout the worship. She similarly centered BLM in the 2015 Christian Community Development Association (CCDA) conference, wearing a BLM T-shirt while moderating a plenary session on Israel and Palestine to send the message that anti-Blackness is a global phenomenon. Dominique Gilliard, a CCDA board member, has linked struggles against mass incarceration and police actions against Black communities to struggles against anti-Asian racism and Native genocide. He outlines his comprehensive vision for racial justice:

> Christianity [has played] a paramount role in legitimating and exacerbating racial injustice from our nation's origin—colonizing Native Americans, enslaving Diasporic Africans—to our present-day crises of immigration and mass incarceration. Throughout history, Christians have been guilty of a multitude of racialized sins ranging from apathy to complicity and genocide. Furthermore, Christians' silence and inaction regarding racism's overt and covert manifestations have caused Christianity to appear irrelevant, if not oppressive, to many. Consequently, the church has lost much of its moral platform and legitimacy within the broader racial reconciliation dialogue. (A. J. Becker, 2014)

And Alexia Salvatierra partnered with Black Lives Matter–Los Angeles (BLM-L.A.) in organizing El Camino de Immigrante in which 170 evangelicals walked from Tijuana to Los Angeles for immigrant justice. This walk made the connection between mass incarceration as it impacts Black people with immigrant detention centers.[18] These are a few examples of increasing work being done among evangelicals of color to address racial oppression between communities of color. As Killjoy Prophets articulated, this emerging politic is premised on "centering voices of most marginalized rather than seeking acceptance from whiteness" (Park et al., 2014) and hence allows people of color to redefine evangelicalism rather than primarily seek acceptance from white evangelicalism.

4 THE BIOPOLITICS OF CHRISTIAN PERSECUTION

Islam is a religion in which God requires you to send your son to die for him. Christianity is a faith in which God sends his son to die for you.—John Ashcroft (quoted in L. McAdam, 2004, 418)

Evangelicals like to skip the cross and go right to the resurrection.
—Soong-Chan Rah, Plenary Address, NAIITS Conference, Wheaton, Illinois (June 9, 2012)

Why in this period of so-called liberal democracy are so many wars of genocide committed, yet these wars are *not* seen as contradictions to democracy? While we often articulate racism as an aberration to democracy or as a result of scapegoating in times of social crisis, Michel Foucault argues that racism is endemic and permanent in the modern state. He contends that the rise of the carceral system entails a shift from punishment to normalization. This shift is effected through a policing of the body via a technology of the soul. That is, the person who fails to follow the norms of society becomes less a criminal and more a "deviant" who must undergo processes of normalization. However, society simultaneously polices collective bodies and manages them as populations. In the service of life, others are allowed to die. "One might say that the ancient right to take life or let live was replaced by a power to foster life or disallow it to the point of death. . . . One had the right to kill those who represent a kind of biological danger to others" (Foucault, 1980, 138). Consequently, entire populations get marked as expendable because they are viewed as threats to the colonial world order.

Wars are no longer waged in the name of a sovereign who must be defended; they are waged on behalf of the existence of everyone; entire populations are mobilized for the purpose of wholesale slaughter in the name of life necessity; massacres have become vital. It is as managers of life and survival, of bodies and the race, that so many regimes have been able to wage so many wars, causing so many men to be killed. (Foucault, 1980, 137)

Racism is the necessary precondition that marks certain people for death in a society based on normalization. Modes of death may not be direct physical extermination but can include creating social conditions that mark communities of color suitable for death. Racial logics are manifest through population politics in which racism essentially becomes normalized. The "life" of society simply requires the deaths of those populations that threaten it. "In a normalizing society, race or racism is the precondition that makes killing acceptable" (Foucault, 1997, 256).

As these quotations demonstrate, the theology of evangelical Christianity is fundamentally shaped through a logic of biopower. That is, through the doctrine of substitutory atonement, Jesus (or other populations put in the place of Jesus) must die so that Christians can live. As Rita Nakashima Brock and Rebecca Parker have demonstrated, the centrality of death is not fundamental to Christianity—the centrality of the cross in Christian theology coincides with the rise of Christian conquest and imperialism. In particular, as Christianity embarked on the crusades, the spread of Christianity became increasingly tied to the death of others that enabled the life of Christendom (Brock and Parker, 2008). The "life" of Christendom thrived through the mass extermination of Indigenous peoples, crusades against Muslim peoples, and the enslavement of Africans. Thus, while the rise of biopolitics is often situated in the rise of the modern biopolitical state, Brock's and Parker's work suggests a different temporality: biopolitics is integral to Christian conquest of the Americas, in which the resurrection of Christ symbolizes the life of European Christianity at the expense of religious/racial Others left at the cross.

Ironically, however, one of the consequences of European Christian expansionism is that now the majority of Christians in the world are people of color and people from the Global South. Consequently, biopolitics structures not only the relationship between "saved" Christians and an "unsaved" world, but relationships within Christianity. Thus, racial Others who become incorporated within Christendom do not leave their place at the cross. As Soong-Chan Rah notes in his analysis of Lamentations, white evangelicalism is in some ways theologically structured around the centrality of the cross, but ultimately the suffering and death of Jesus on the cross represents a brief layover on the trip toward the triumphalism of the resurrection. Building on Rah's analysis, it would seem that evangelicalism does not avoid the cross but racially differentiates who gets the cross versus who gets the resurrection. It is this biopolitical relationship between people of color and the cross that led William Jones to ponder his famous question: "Is God a White Racist?" (W. Jones, 1973).

While Christian evangelicalism has been and continues to be involved in U.S. imperialistic ventures around the world, it simultaneously disavows this involvement by claiming that it is championing "persecuted" Christians. Christians are no longer complicit in imperialism; instead, Christians are the people most likely to suffer religious persecution. Thus, within the United States and globally, religion itself becomes racialized. On the global stage, the Christian persecution movement positions (white) evangelical Christians in the United States in the place of the oppressed Third World Christians, allowing white evangelicalism to disavow its complicity in creating conditions of oppression through the export of U.S. capitalist exceptionalism. Theologically, the Christian persecution movement also positions the well-being of white evangelicalism on the death and torture of Christians in the Global South, which "purify" and strengthen the faith.

Dylan Rodriguez argues in his critique of multiculturalist forms of ethnic studies that these versions arise as a result of communities of color wishing to remember a colonial history that circumvents the genocide of the colonial moment. In the efforts to recover the "agency" of the oppressed, multiculturalism creates an agency that forgets that the genocide ever occurred in the first place (D. Rodriguez, 2009b). Many years ago, William Jones argued that liberation theology suffered from a similar problem. In its hopes to find redemption and argue that God was on the side of the oppressed, it basically had to forget the historical suffering of the oppressed (W. Jones, 1973). At the same time, however, this movement has sown some of the seeds of its own deconstruction. The work of Rodriguez and Jones provokes a question: what kinds of hope and articulations of "agency" are possible when we take suffering and genocide seriously? These issues are implicitly forming some strands of the Christian persecution movement who are rethinking their biopolitical relationship to the persecuted Christians.

History of the Christian Persecution Movement

Allen Hertzke's *Freeing God's Children* documents the rise of the Christian persecution movement. He traces it to the Russian Revolution in 1917, when Christian missionary groups began to support Christians that they felt were being persecuted behind the Iron Curtain. One such organization was Voice of the Martyrs, formed by Pastor Richard Wurmbrand, who spent four years in a Romanian prison for his ministry with the underground church. He left Romania in 1956 and founded Voice of the Martyrs,[1] with the following goals:

1) Give Christian Bibles, literature and broadcasts in their own language in Communist countries and other restricted areas of the world;
2) Give relief to families of Christian martyrs;
3) Undertake projects of encouragement to help believers rebuild their lives where there is "Communist oppression";
4) Win to Christ those opposed to the gospel;
5) Inform the world about atrocities committed against Christians. (Voice of the Martyrs, 2000)

Another prominent organization, Brother Andrew's Open Doors, was founded in 1955 to smuggle Christian materials into Eastern Europe and the Soviet Union. It now has offices in seventeen countries (Hertzke, 2004, 111). Open Doors USA organizes the International Day of Prayer for the persecuted church every November 14 (Guthrie, 2004c). It also sponsors Compass Direct News, which sends monthly reports on incidents of Christian persecution that are routinely published in *Christianity Today* and *Charisma*. Other such groups include Christian Solidarity International, which engages in religious liberty advocacy and disaster relief (Hertzke, 2004, 111), and Christian Solidarity Worldwide (Baroness Caroline Cox), which focuses on Sudan, Burma, and Armenia (Hertzke, 2004, 113–14). In addition, Nina Shea (former human rights lawyer) of Freedom House wrote *In the Lion's Den*, a documentation of human-rights violations committed against Christians globally (Shea, 1997). Paul Marshall, a political theorist and former chair of religious studies at the University of Toronto, similarly conducted a project on the scope of persecution of Christians, which he documented in *Their Blood Cries Out* (Marshall, 1997). These books collectively sold over 100,000 copies and helped promote interest in Christian persecution among evangelicals (Hertzke, 2004, 120–26). Nina Shea also collaborated with Michael Horowitz (a Jewish advocate on the issue of Christian persecution) to organize a conference for Christian leaders on Christian persecution in 1996 (Hertzke, 2004, 125).

All of these groups and individuals provided a groundswell of legislative pressure that resulted in Congress passing the International Religious Freedom Act in 1998. Horowitz authored the first version of this bill, called the Wolf-Specter Bill on Persecution, in 1997, which relied exclusively on denunciations and automatic sanctions (Carnes, 2002b). The competing International Religious Freedom Act, which focused on diplomacy, was introduced to replace the bill. In addition, the Wolf-Specter bill was criticized for making it too easy for victims of religious persecution to receive asylum (Cagney, 1998b). In October 9, 1998, the Senate passed the International Religious Freedom Act. It removed a provision in an earlier version that required mandatory economic sanctions, which free-trade Republicans argued would hurt U.S. business. This bill allows the president to select from a broad menu of options, including public condemnation, withdrawal of aid, and a variety of sanctions (Gardner, 1998). This act created the bipartisan ten-member Commission on International Religious Freedom, appointed an ambassador-at-large who works with the Democracy, Human Rights, and Labor Bureau but reports directly to the secretary of state, and mandates that the commission publish an annual report that looks at religious freedom in 194 countries (the United States is not included in this list, although it has a continuing history of infringing on the religious freedom of Native peoples) (Seiple, 2001). It was passed with bipartisan support, including from the Anti-Defamation League, Joseph Lieberman, the National Jewish Coalition, and Michael Horowitz of the Hudson Foundation as well as New York Times columnist A. M. Rosenthal (Aikman, 1999).[2]

In 1996 a U.S. State Department advisory committee on religious freedom was formed, including representatives from the National Association of Evangelicals (NAE) and the Southern Baptist Convention (SBC). The United States announced its first sanctions under the International Religious Freedom Act against Eritrea in 2005, which included the denial of commercial export of defense articles and services as well as technical data and services (Stricherz, 2005). Don Argue, who had spearheaded the National Association of Evangelicals' efforts at racial reconciliation, was appointed to serve on the United States Commission on International Religious Freedom on the recommendation of Hillary Clinton in 2007 (News Briefs, 2007d; Passages, 2007). While this act was widely celebrated, evangelicals complained that it was "too ideologically diverse" with Muslim, Baháʼí, Jewish, and Mormon representatives (Persecution Panel Appointed, 1997). Today many (such as *Christianity Today*) complain that the International Religious Freedom Act has been ineffective and has not created a successful way to do advocacy or reform. Countries take minimal steps and are no longer scrutinized (Christianity Today, 2008b; Derrick, 2015b).

Whatever the perceived shortcomings of this act, however, the issue of Christian persecution has become so prevalent within evangelicalism that *Christianity Today*, *Charisma*, and *World* feature articles on Christian persecution in almost every issue.[3] *Christianity Today* listed the global persecution of Christians as the top religion story of the year in 1996 and of the decade in 2000 (Christianity Today, 1997, 2000c). Global persecution has become such a Christian industry that there is now a dating website for persecuted Christians that provides "a romantic pathway to escape from persecution, bringing hope and love to a dire situation" (Gleanings, 2016b, 19).

The Logics of Christian Persecution: Christian and U.S. Exceptionalism

The Christian persecution movement is premised on both U.S. and Christian exceptionalism. This movement holds that Christians are systematically persecuted throughout the world simply because they are Christian. It is they—not people of color, poor people, or people from the Global South—who are targeted for "premature death." Richard Land of the Southern Baptist Convention notes: "Too often people in the West, peering through the selective prism of Christian history in the West, reflexively think of Christians as persecutors, rather than the persecuted" (quoted in Steinfeld, 1996, 26). An NAE statement on religious persecution maintains that there are "reigns of terror now being plotted and waged against Christians" (Freedom House, 1996, 11). As Elizabeth Castelli notes, the myth of Christian martyrdom has a long history. In her germinal text *Martyrdom and Memory* she contends that Christians have fundamentally shaped their collective identities around martyrdom, remembering the history of early Christianity as marked by persecution and martyrdom even when the historical record suggests that persecution was in fact not prevalent. She argues that early Christian writers "did not simply *preserve* the story of persecution and martyrdom but, in fact, *created* it" (Castelli, 2004, 25). Regardless of its historicity, however, this framing of early Christianity through martyrdom provides the lens through which evangelical Christians understand themselves as persecuted today (Castelli, 2004). *Charisma* even says that persecution plays an important role in encouraging church growth among nonpersecuted Christians. "In the West our blessings have let us be content without revival. If a man can live without revival, then he will be content without it. But when he is desperate for a touch from heaven, then God will bring brokenness—and he will no longer trust in the arm of the flesh" (Turner, 2005, 59). It further stated that "history proves that the church thrives amid persecution" (Yoars, 2013, 6). "Even here in America, we can't forget that persecution was the bedrock of our nation's very existence" (Yoars, 2013, 6; but this persecution does not include the persecution of Black and Native peoples). Open Doors promotional material says that "Suffering Christians Can Help Your Church Grow" (2001). Voice of the Martyrs says:

> Every day Christians in Bangladesh deal with the poverty that comes from the natural disasters and political hardships but endure even more than the average Bangladeshi: persecution by those opposed to the gospel. Materially, they have nothing. But spiritually, they have everything—Jesus Christ. And Christians in Bangladesh are doing more than dealing with, or surviving, the poverty and oppression. They are turning them into opportunities to witness of the eternal riches of Christ. (Nettleton, 2005b, 3)

Voice of the Martyrs literature follows the narrative of the persecuted Third World Christian who overcomes adversity to witness to God. Using the logic of substitutionary atonement, the Third World Christian is brave on behalf of more privileged Christians, so they do not have to be. Resting on the dynamics of biopower (which we will see again in terms of how Jewish people are situated within Christian Zionist narratives), the Third World Christian must die so First World Christians can live. This dynamic then presumes that Christianity from the Global South is not "real" Christianity. Otherwise, the death of those Christians would be seen as killing Christianity rather than allowing it to thrive and prosper. Because of the disavowed whiteness of evangelical Christianity, the fate of persecuted Third World Christians is not seen as negatively impacting Christianity as a whole because "real" Christianity is white Christianity, which benefits from this persecution. This logic of Christian persecution then serves a purifying function for white evangelicalism. For instance, in *Faith Today* persecution is used to critique liberalizing tendencies within the church. According to this article, persecution arises when stories of gay practices being sanctioned in Christian U.S. churches reach overseas. "When Muslims hear about the liberal attitudes of North American Christians, it confirms their suspicion . . . that all Christians are immoral" (Fieguth, 2004, 20).

This logic bears a striking similarity to many colonialist narratives about Indigenous peoples when the so-called "New World" became the place that would allow corrupted European society to remake itself. As many historians have noted, colonizers expected to find "Eden" in the Americas, "a place of simplicity, innocence, harmony, love, and happiness, where the climate is balmy and fruits of nature's bounty are found on the trees year round" (Stannard, 1992, 166). Free from corruption, the New World and its innocent indigenes would facilitate the reinvigoration of an enfeebled European society. However, as Kirkpatrick Sale argues, colonizers approached "paradise" through their colonial and patriarchal lens. Consequently, they viewed the land and Indigenous peoples as something to be used for their own purposes; colonizers could not respect the integrity of either the land or Indigenous peoples (Sale, 1990, 203). Within this colonial imaginary, the Native is an empty signifier that provides the occasion for the European to remake its corrupt civilization. Once the European is remade, the Native is rendered permanently infantile (or as most commonly understood, an innocent savage).

Similarly, narratives of Christian persecution often situate persecuted Christians in the Global South as empty signifiers that will reinvigorate (white) evangelicalism. The narratives of Christian persecution often rest on a simplistic notion that "forces of darkness" are out to destroy Christianity simply because it is a beacon of light in a fallen world. As *Charisma*'s J. Lee Grady states: "Christians in other countries are displaying apostolic courage in the face of resistance. Risking jail, torture and martyrdom, they are proclaiming Christ, planting churches, and overthrowing demonic powers" (J. L. Grady, 2003, 35). *World* also combines persecution with a masculinist analysis: "We American Christians have become so prosperous, so successful, so optimistic that we have become spiritually soft and thus ineffective. The Chinese churchman sees that we could use the bitter medicine of persecution" (Veith, 2005d, 24).

To maintain this narrative, evangelical discourse must often ignore the broader context in which "persecution" takes place. That is, conflicts between Christians and other groups are often the result of larger political, social, and economic forces, not mere religious intolerance. In addition, this narrative minimizes the other religious groups that are also persecuted along with Christians. Finally, it erases the complicity of evangelicalism in supporting Western economic and political interests that may contribute to other countries not desiring an evangelical presence in their lands. In many cases, Christians face persecution not as a special category of people but as part of a larger policy of religious intolerance that impacts other religions as much as Christians, if not more so. To acknowledge the persecution of other religions, however, would contradict the evangelical narrative that Christianity is particularly targeted for persecution by "demonic" forces because of its salvific power. Consequently, articles on Christian persecution often present the misleading picture that *only* Christians are the victims of significant persecution. These articles often do not mention other religious minorities that are also facing persecution. Or they mention other minorities so briefly that Christians appear to be particularly targeted in areas where it may be other groups that are facing persecution to the same or an even greater degree (Christian Coalition, 2001b; Flinchbaugh, 2002; P. Johnson, 2002a).

In addition, by framing persecution on a purely religious basis, evangelical discourse often ignores broader regional or political differences that provide the context for persecution.[4] For instance, *Christianity Today* asserted that in Nigeria "Muslim leaders are deliberately using fanatics in the name of Islam to engage in periodic attacks on Christians with the sole aim to intimidate, terrorize, and force Christians into submission and into renouncing their faith" (Minchakpu, 2004b, 17; see also M. Belz, 2012b; Dean, 2010b). Similarly, *Charisma* asserts that Nigeria is heading a "Muslim-led holy war" against Christians (D. Mundy, 2004b, 19). As evangelicals who live in Nigeria note, however, this persecution is often the result of conflict that is primarily regional rather than religious in nature, and the Nigerian state often violates the human rights of everyone in Nigeria, not just Christians (Agang, 2012; Gbonigi, 2000; Kure and Idowu-Fearon, 2000). Similarly, India, particularly with a Hindu nationalist government in power, is often presented as persecuting only or primarily Christians.[5] The massacres in Gujarat, according to these reports, primarily impacted Christians, when in fact Muslims have been the primary target of the Hindu Right.

This Christian exceptionalism in turn depends on U.S. exceptionalism, which assumes the United States should be the guarantor of religious liberty around the world. Consequently, evangelicals often remain unaccountable for their complicity in Western imperial interests that might spark antievangelical sentiment in other countries. When even the Institute of

Religion and Democracy admits that the Central Intelligence Agency (CIA) is using missionaries as intelligence sources, it would stand to reason that there might be some basis for Christian persecution (CIA and Missionaries: More Confusion, 1996). For example, the CIA lied to Congress about a tragic drug war shooting that killed Baptist missionary Veronica Bowers and her seven-month-old daughter. The Peruvian Air Force shot down the Bowers plane after receiving a CIA tip that it could be carrying narcotics. It was owned by the Association of Baptists for World Evangelicalism. This scandal prompted the suspension of the CIA-aided drug interdiction program, even though the CIA said that shooting the plane was a one-time mistake in an otherwise good program (Vincent, 2008c). The NAE testified before Congress about "the need to keep pastors, missionaries and Christian workers free from recruitment by the Central Intelligence Agency" (Safety of Christian Workers Cannot Be Compromised, 1996). Nevertheless, when critics of the Christian Right point to missionary complicity in U.S. military interests, their criticism is dismissed as Christian "scapegoating" (Freedom House, 1996, 43). *Christianity Today* called it the "CIA Myth," saying there was no basis to think the Summer Institute for Linguistics was ever involved in promoting U.S. interests (Alford, 2006a, 58).

In addition, the Christian Right does not focus on progressive Christians who are persecuted in U.S.-supported right-wing regimes (M. Belz, 1998e),[6] instead focusing on Muslim or Communist groups and socialist or Communist countries.[7] Muslims are trying to "wipe out Christian communities" (M. Belz, 2013a, 50; see also Justice, 2015; J. Nelson, 2009a). In one op-ed Charles Colson discusses how the famous story of a nine-year-old South Vietnamese girl running down the street covered in napalm after a bomb attack made him question his support for policies that supported her agony. But she later became a Christian and defected to Christianity. At a talk at the Vietnam War Memorial, she said: "I thought I could not live, but God saved my life and gave me faith and hope." He concludes: "The world will always be full of wars and rumors of war, but Christ's resurrection brings peace—supernatural peace—to those who give their lives to him" (C. Colson and N. Pearcey, 1997).

U.S. exceptionalism is alive and well in the global persecution movement, in which most of the world's problems, even those that seem to be result of U.S. policy, are always another country's fault (Coffin, 2005; Loconte, 2007; M. Olasky, 2004b). Consequently, U.S. allies, regardless of their actual treatment of Christians, are supported and nonallies are not. For example, the groups singled out for criticism by Voice of the Martyrs include China, Iran,

Pakistan, Indonesia, Sudan, the Comoros Islands, Equatorial Guinea, Nigeria, Somalia, Cuba, Cyprus, Nepal, Bhutan, Burma, Sri Lanka, Tibet, Laos, North Korea, Vietnam, Afghanistan, Bangladesh, Brunei, Malaysia, Maldives, Algeria, Egypt, Libya, Mauritania, Morocco, Sudan, Turkey, Tunisia, Iraq, Saudi Arabia, Kuwait, Oman, Qatar, Syria, Yemen, United Arab Emirates, Azerbaijan, Tajikistan, Turkmenistan, Uzbekistan, India, Chechnya, and Chiapas. According to Voice of the Martyrs, radical Catholics are persecuting evangelicals in Chiapas and Chechens are persecuting Christians (the violence being perpetrated against Chechens and the Indigenous peoples of Chiapas goes unremarked) (Voice of the Martyrs, 2000).[8] *Rutherford* blames the Mexican government for "persecution" but states that Indigenous peoples are oppressed not because they are Indigenous but because they are Christian (Mexico, 1994). *World* states that it is the Zapatistas who are mindlessly massacring evangelicals (Alford, 1999b).

From the perspective of the Christian Right, being "anti-Western" often becomes equated with being anti-Christian. Or, as *World* describes it, U.S. imperialist policies are "God's redemptive work": forces that oppose U.S. imperialism (such as Cuba) represent "Satan's response" (M. Belz, 1996). Kim Lawton in *Christianity Today* echoes this: "Whenever communism, Islam, or nationalism is struggling for dominance [that is, any force that opposes Westernization or U.S. imperialism], there is a new surge of anti-Christian violence and repression" (Lawton, 1996, 3). Dean Curry goes so far as to argue that imperialism and colonialism have had *no* negative impact on Third World countries. Instead Third World poverty is merely the result of "indigenous tyranny." In fact, *without* colonialism, Third World countries would be much worse off than they are today. He dismisses any complaints from the Third World as simply part of an anti-Western and socialistic agenda (Curry, 1990, 243). Curry does not answer the question: if colonialism is so benevolent, then why would anyone in the Third World be interested in embracing an anti-Western agenda? This disavowal of Christian imperialism is particularly apparent in Marvin Olasky's analysis of Christianity versus Islam in *World*: "Christianity grew by the blood of its martyrs, but Islam grew by killing those who opposed it" (M. Olasky, 2004a, 56). This history is obviously incomplete: the Crusades, the Inquisition, and the genocide of Indigenous peoples certainly expanded Christendom, which Olasky either disavows or treats as aberrations.

Similarly, Olasky opines that the cause of poverty and other social ills in India is not "capitalism" but Hinduism. He contends that racism has virtually disappeared in the United States, while it continues unabated in

India. "Why does such bigotry remain in India at a time when it is largely gone from the United States? One reason may be the difference between the biblical sense of equality and a common Hindu theology of inequality" (M. Olasky, 2004d, 48). Similarly, analyses of Christian persecution in India conflate Dalits with Christians. That is, when Dalits face discrimination, it is because they are Christians facing religious discrimination rather than because they are Dalits facing caste discrimination.[9] This approach, it appears, has actually undermined evangelistic efforts in India. According to *Christianity Today*, Indian Christians became involved in a mass Dalit rally to oppose the caste system, which was hyped by overseas Christian mission organizations as an event where millions of Dalits would convert to Christianity. This hype then led to local groups in India calling the event a "Christian conspiracy" (M. Singh, 2002a, 26). Only *Christianity Today* had a more nuanced article, noting that anti-Christian sentiment is tied to a history of Western imperialism. It also criticized Indian Christians for not making common cause with Muslims: "'Please don't rape a nun, or murder a pastor, but please feel free to murder a Muslim.' The church is very naive ... the church cannot seek its own protection, but rather must pursue a just and free society" (Stafford, 2004, 33). It also noted that Christians make themselves vulnerable to persecution by displaying cultural insensitivity. Consequently, 50,000 Dalits converted to Buddhism instead (Stafford, 2004, 33). Similarly, articles on North Korea and other countries negatively impacted by Western imperialism neglect any analysis of empire in their assessments of Christian persecution (Carnes, 2004c; Chenoweth, 2004; Christianity Today, 2004c; Compass Direct, 2001; Guthrie, 2004a; Hyeok, 2004; D. Miller, 2002b; T. Morgan and D. Neff, 2004; Morse, 2002; Sellers, 2001a, 2001e, 2003a, 2004b).

Some articles do note that evangelicals are also victimized by the Colombian army (a U.S. ally) but neglect to mention that this is allied with U.S. interests (Alford, 1999a, 2001a, 2004a; M. Belz, 1998d; MacHarg, 1999; D. Miller, 1998).[10] Or they complain that "Marxist" (Fidler, 2005) groups or "satanists" (Flinchbaugh, 1999b) are the sole problem in Colombia. Another article talks about Fuerzas Armadas Revolucionarias de Colombia (FARC) interactions with Christian groups but mentions that they do not attack those who "genuinely serve the people without taking a political stance" (MacHarg, 2000a, 31). Similarly, during President Alberto Fujimori's tenure in Peru, *Indian Life* complained that Maoist guerrillas were persecuting Incan Christians, conveniently forgetting the Peruvian government's repression of Indigenous peoples, such as its sterilization policies.

The brutal repressions of Christian liberation theologians and base communities by U.S.-backed regimes are justified because they did not employ biblical teaching (J. W. Carter, 2000). One article tells the story of a Christian named "Pablo" who escaped assassination to serve God while working under Salvador Allende but gives no context indicating why Allende was under attack (he was just "unpopular") (Matthews, 2003).

Thus, the rhetoric of Christian "persecution" is inextricably linked to Christian empire-building. Because it is Christians who are "oppressed" and "persecuted," the Christian Right can justifiably support genocidal policies in Latin America and elsewhere, destructive economic policies, right-wing repressive regimes throughout the world, or anything else that makes the world "safe" for Christianity (right-wing Protestant Christianity, that is). The relationship between evangelicalism and U.S. empire-building is clear when we differentiate between the way evangelicals often uphold the previously discussed "civil gospel" that supports Christian America on one hand but then trace persecution of Christians to the fact that other religions, such as Islam and Hinduism, do not separate religion from the state (Abraham, 2004e; Mitri, 2000). Apparently, only Christianity can be legitimately tied to state power.

Evangelical Critiques of the Christian Persecution Movement

As the global persecution movement has developed, so too have internal critiques of some its presuppositions. Mark Galli (*Christianity Today*) questions the romanticized notion that martyrdom strengthens and purifies the church, arguing that sometimes it contributes to the destruction of the Christian presence in an area (Galli, 1997). James Reapsome in *Evangelical Missions Quarterly* also notes that "Western cultural imperialism—our movies, books, music, TV shows, fashions—is a horrendous obstacle for world evangelization" (Reapsome, 1989, 22). Gustavo Parajon in *Christianity Today* challenges the anti-Sandinista efforts of the Christian Right: "I find it very hard to understand how Christians in the U.S. who believe in the Almighty God . . . would be so concerned about some supposed threat [the 'Communist' threat] that they would allow their tax dollars to support violence that devastates so many people, many of them believers" (Parajon, 1989, 48).

These alternative voices were few and far between in evangelical literature as the Christian persecution movement first gained popularity. However, as the movement has developed, splits and tensions within this movement have increased. These tensions were evident in a debate between Michael

Horowitz of the Hudson Institute's Project for International Liberty and Jeremy Gunn, senior fellow for Religion and Human Rights at Emory University, featured in *Christianity Today*. Horowitz's approach represents the more simplistic analysis of Christian persecution, which emphasizes punitive sanctions in the efforts to destabilize countries viewed as Christian persecutors. Even though he is Jewish, Horowitz tends to separate Christian persecution from its larger political and economic context. "The reality is this: the well-being of Christian communities in the developing world now increasingly signals and determines whether entire populations and cultures remain in the dark ages or enter a world of modernity [and] tolerance . . . a particular contribution of Judeo-Christian culture-democracy" (Horowitz and Gunn, 2003a, 49). He further argues that Christians are the "worst victims" because "American elites are often blind to the contributions of Christianity to Western art, music, and culture, to what Christianity has meant to our economic productivity, democracy, and freedom" (Cromartie, 1999, 53). Horowitz contends that State Department–centered diplomacy is largely a failure and instead advocates a sanction-driven approach to addressing Christian persecution (Horowitz and Gunn, 2003b).

Gunn, by contrast, argues that while it is important for the United States to intervene in cases of religious persecution, the United States is not in a position to hold itself to be the guarantor of human rights globally. It cannot hold other countries accountable when it is not accountable for its own human-rights violations.

> We should candidly acknowledge that American governments have often supported regimes that have brutally suppressed a wide range of human rights, including religious freedom. The United States was one of the strongest supporters of many of the world's worst regimes after World War II, including those of Augusto Pinochet, Efrain Rios Montt, Ferdinand Marcos, the apartheid regime in South Africa, and others. Just as we wish others to recognize what they have done, we also must be willing to acknowledge what we have done. We will be more convincing and effective when we speak the truth about others' failings when we are known for speaking the truth about our own. (Horowitz and Gunn, 2003a, 54)

Gunn further contends that the punitive approach is excessively narrow. Sometimes sanctions work and sometimes they do not. Particularly with increased anti-U.S. sentiment, punitive sanctions may only increase persecution and resistance. "Americans sometimes believe that foreigners and their governments will naturally trust American criticism of their countries and believe that our motivations are good. Anyone who has traveled abroad and spoken to others will quickly learn that others do not see us as we see ourselves" (Horowitz and Gunn, 2003a, 53). He also takes issue with the traditional framing of Christian persecution as the result of countries that target people simply because they are Christian. In actuality, Christians are persecuted in countries where all human rights are suppressed. To say, for example, that Uzbekistan (a country highlighted in the Christian persecution lists) persecutes Christians solely because they are Christian disregards that fact that Uzbekistan has also incarcerated thousands of Muslims. He concludes: "I also believe, however, that the United States will be most effective when it speaks clearly not only about religious persecution, but clearly, consistently, and accurately about all major human-rights abuses committed by friends and foes alike" (Horowitz and Gunn, 2003a, 51).[11]

Gunn's more sophisticated analysis of "Christian" persecution is reflected in some sectors of evangelicalism (Galli, 2008). For instance, in a letter to the editor of *Christianity Today* a writer working in Laos complains:

> A hard-line stance and threats/sanctions only evoke the response, "Go to hell." The people here have seen enough of poverty and hardship, and those in positions of authority are not the ones who suffer from sanctions. It is always the common man, usually quite far away from these issues, who will suffer. The response of Western Christendom should be very sensitive and careful, because it is the local people of the Way who will bear the fallout of militant and hardline reactions in the West. (Letters, 2001b, 12–13)

Some articles now note that Christians may be persecuted in a country as the result of other political factors rather than a simple desire to stomp out Christianity (Fawzy, 2000; John, 2000; Marshall, 2000; Mombo and Mwaluda, 2000; Mugyenzi, 2000; Nyberg, 1999; Ponniah, 2000; Rogers, 2004; Sellers, 2001e, 2003b). *World* and *Christianity Today* ran articles that contended that Vietnam is often targeted as engaging in religious persecution when its policies are actually directed at political dissidents (Abraham, 2007b; Galli, 2007). The China Aid Association sent out a notice that it had been supporting Pastor Gong Shengliang, founder of the underground South China Church, after he was arrested in 2001 and sentenced to death for "organizing and utilizing a cult organization to undermine law enforcement, to intentionally cause bodily injury and to commit rape." The Chinese Aid Association at first assumed he was innocent but later conducted an independent investigation and concluded that he was guilty of sexually molesting women in his church. Gong also admitted to being guilty of some of the charges for which he was convicted (Imprisoned Chinese House-Church Leader Admits Guilt, 2007). A story in Egypt reported that a woman got fifteen years in prison for converting to Christianity. But she was actually convicted of fraud. This article stated that many individuals converted to Christianity claim to be persecuted for the Christian beliefs for fraudulent purposes (Casper, 2013).

One article in *Christianity Today* on the murder of SBC missionaries in Iraq noted that they were not specifically attacked for being Christians: "another car full of Westerners would have met the same fate" (Moll, 2004a, 18). An article on Christian persecution in Turkey frames the issue in political rather than religious terms: Christianity is associated with the interests of Western imperialism. It then goes on to say that this association applies to "evangelical and charismatic churches in particular because of their Western-style worship and close ties with (and often financial dependence on) U.S. and western European churches and missionaries" (T. Dixon, 2002b, 58). However, the article stops short of validating the analysis that evangelicalism supports the interests of Western imperialism.

A *Charisma* article admits the complicity of colonialism in fomenting anti-Christian sentiment. It even implicitly criticizes the "War on Terror" as an imperialist venture (which is surprising, since *Charisma* generally supported the war in Iraq). "Colonialism proved to be a great deterrent to the cause of Christian missions, even as the war on terrorism is proving to be today. The Christian message becomes blurred by association with Western politics and military objectives, raising a formidable psychological barrier for the Saudi Muslims to eventually want to consider who Jesus really is" (B. Baker, 2003b, 92).

Christianity Today also reports that gunrunners in African countries are posing as missionaries. Three men claiming to be missionaries—John Dixon, Gary Blanchard, and Joseph Petty John of Indianapolis—were caught with a cache of sophisticated weapons in Harare, Zimbabwe (Okite, 1999a). It notes that Davis and Fiona Fulton, who were ostensibly sentenced to hard labor because of missionary work in Gambia, were actually engaged in antigovernment activity (Wunderink, 2009).

Open Doors ran an article in its newsletter that asked the question: "When do Christians deserve persecution?" (What Defines "Real" Persecution?, 2001). When conflict arises between Christians and other groups, Christians are not always blameless. Hence, according to Open Doors, real persecution happens "if opposition comes *after* Christians have tried every way to be friends" (What Defines "Real" Persecution?, 2001, 4). Open Doors called on its supporters to be sophisticated in their understanding of persecution: "Defining persecution is increasingly more complicated. It can be bound up in politics, sensationalized, or denied because it is not a welcome message. Regardless, we must learn to live with these complications so we can serve persecuted Christians" (What Defines "Real" Persecution?, 2001, 4).

Mark Noll points out in his review of the book series Evangelical Christianity and Democracy in the Global South that the "persecuted" evangelicals in the Global South often do not see themselves in political solidarity with U.S. evangelicals because of U.S. support for right-wing regimes. "To say that some group is 'evangelical' tells us almost nothing about its approach to politics" (Noll, 2008, 54). *Christianity Today* also notes the exaggeration of the number of Christian martyrs: anyone who gets killed in warfare is often listed (Zylstra, 2013a). David Neff in *Christianity Today* argues that State Department reports "on human-rights violations have tended to minimize the seriousness of violations by America's historical allies and key trading partners" (Neff, 1997b, 19). As Charles Taber notes in *Transformation*, "In exchange for relatively minor privileges, some Protestant bodies have given despotic governments fulsome praise and expressions of total support, and have become apologists for those governments among bodies related to them in the United States" (Taber, 1991, 2). A powerful counterexample of evangelical discourse critiquing the notion of Christians always being victims is Jeanette Hardage's review of the video *Precarious Peace: God and Guatemala*, which documents the CIA overthrow of a democratically elected government and the suppression and massacres of Indigenous peoples.[12] She notes how evangelicals either supported these massacres or refused to take a stand against them (Hardage, 2004). *Christianity Today* has critiqued its own support for Efraín Ríos Montt's 1982 military coup that enabled him to gain the presidency, noting that Luis Palau, Jerry Falwell, and Pat Robertson also supported him and reflecting that his rule was "probably the most violent period of the 36 year internal conflict, resulting in about 200,000 deaths of mostly unarmed indigenous civilians" (Alford, 2006e, 20–21). It also ran an article criticizing the evangelical support of dictator Alberto Fujimori in Peru (D. Miller, 2001).[13] *World* further argued that Christians were actually being falsely accused of being part of the Shining Path and facing persecution under Fujimori's regime (Alford, 1999c). It also noted that the genocide in Rwanda took place in a predominantly Christian country (Lawton, 1997). *Christianity Today* reported that the Orthodox Church in Ethiopia was calling for accountability for British leaders who plundered hundreds of sacred items in 1868 and demanded the return of a 400-year-old tabor, a sacred replica of the Ark of the Covenant. The replica was returned, which it is hoped will lead to the return of other sacred objects (many of which are not even on display), despite objections by the British Museum (Okite, 2002). And an article in *Christianity Today* noted that evangelicals were instrumental in bringing leftist president Luiz Inácio Lula da Silva to power in Brazil as well as supporting left-wing movements in El Salvador (Alford, 2009; Guilherme, 2002). Finally, delegates from the World Evangelical Alliance, the Pentecostal World Fellowship, the World Council of Churches, and the Vatican gathered to apologize for the persecution of Christians by other Christians (Gleanings, 2016a, 18).

Christianity Today has published several articles calling on Christians to recognize and organize around the persecution of all religious minorities. An article on persecution in Pakistan asserted that "it is also important to convey concern not just for Christians, but for all religious minorities, as well as advocate human rights for Muslims. Diffusing the perception of evangelicals as just another narrow special interest group helps to disarm anti-West, anti-Christian bias" (Sellers, 2004c, 102). *Christianity Today* also published several articles and debates that highlighted the need for a more sophisticated approach toward addressing religious persecution (Horowitz and Gunn, 2003a, 2003b; Neff, 2004b; Seiple, 2001). One such article was that by Robert Seiple, who served as ambassador-at-large for the Commission on International Religious Freedom. He advocated that Christians become involved in combating the persecution of all religious minorities, not just Christians. He further contended that evangelicals must look at religious freedom in a larger context of illiteracy, poverty, and border wars. He criticized the arrogance of the United States for not including itself in the report when it has not achieved religious freedom and then attempting to impose five-year-plans on other countries to eliminate religious persecution. Seiple concluded that the United States needs to take a comprehensive approach to religious freedom within the broader context of human rights as a whole (Seiple, 2001).

Sometimes commitment to religious persecution does cause evangelicals to be critical of U.S. policies when it appears to them that the United States is ignoring Christian persecution in countries where it has vested political interests (M. Belz, 1999c; Commission Urges Economic Sanctions, 2000; J. C. Johnson, 2006a; Sellers, 2002b). Such has been the case with the U.S. alliance with Saudi Arabia, marked as a great persecutor of Christians (Abraham, 2005j, 2005m; A. Moore, 2001; Sellers, 2002d, 2002h), and with the reluctance of the United States to sanction Sudan in order to take advantage of its oil reserves. Some sectors of the Christian persecution movement have no problem with these compromises. "If politics is the art of compromise, international relations is the art of getting along with thugs. . . . Our prophetic calling—to seek real liberty for the oppressed—is sometimes best advanced by dealing with unsavory oppressive states. . . . And when this chapter of the war on terrorism is over, we should strongly lobby our government to make another repressive state tomorrow's target in the fight for liberty and justice for all" (Shaking Hands with Thugs, 2001, 30; see also Blunt, 2009).

Interestingly, many sectors of the Christian Right often uphold a U.S.-centric foreign policy and argue that the United States should not be involved in the United Nations. However, the rhetoric of "persecuted Christians" is often couched in "human rights" language that is based on international human-rights standards passed by the United Nations (B. Baker, 2001b; Doyle, 1999; P. Johnson, 2002a; Price, 2004b). Thus, this rhetoric has sometimes contributed to Christians having to recognize international legal standards beyond those of the United States, even as some Christians remain anxious that these international standards represent a threat to U.S. sovereignty. In addition, the use of "human-rights" rhetoric has put some sectors into contact with other human-rights advocates who are not Christian-centered. This dialogue in turn encourages Christians to think about human rights on a broader scale. *Christianity Today* also opined that Christians need to show concern for those of all faiths who are persecuted.[14] "Care should extend to aiding persecuted Jews and Muslims, Hindus and animists, not just our own Christian brothers and sisters" (Christianity Today, 1999b, 17).

As an example, evangelical Christians were involved in a campaign to stop the persecutions of Christians specifically in Sudan (Aikman, 1997; Carnes, 2000c; Christianity Today, 2000a; Cox, 1999; Gardner, 1999; Kisuke, 1998; Sellers, 2001d; J. Stewart, 1999; Zurowski, 2004). For instance, one Voice of the Martyrs ad (found in the June 12, 2000, issue of *Christianity Today*) pictures a young Sudanese boy on the cover, with the text: "They killed his entire family. They threw him on a burning fire, and they left him to die. Why would a young boy be subjected to such cruelty? . . . [H]e is a Christian." However, when the ethnic cleansing practices became focused on Darfur, in which primarily Muslims rather than Christians were being victimized, evangelical groups did not respond, because this narrative did not easily play into the narrative of Muslims persecuting Christians. Wilfred Mlay of World Vision complained that evangelicals were focusing on tension in southern Sudan, which is primarily Christian, while almost no Christian groups were providing relief in Darfur (Guthrie, 2004b). Articles on Darfur often framed the conflict in terms of Christian persecution, even though those being attacked were Muslims (Abraham, 2004c; Aikman, 2005c; Nyberg, 2004). Eventually, however, the National Association of Evangelicals, the International Pentecostal Holiness Church, and the Assemblies of God signed a letter to President George W. Bush on August 1, 2004, advocating action against genocide in Darfur. "We view this as an opportunity to reach out to Muslims in the name of Jesus," stated NAE president Ted Haggard (News Briefs, 2004a, 32). The articles on Darfur eventually began to acknowledge that Muslims, rather than Christians, were under attack (Abraham, 2004a; Alford, 2005c; D. Anderson, 2005; M. Belz, 2004a, 2008c; Christianity Today, 2004b; J. C. Johnson, 2006b). However, this crisis is still frequently (although not always) framed as an example of the evils of Arab governments,[15] as in *World*'s analysis that "the Khartoum regime's motive in Darfur soon became clear. Its leaders are not only Islamists but Arabists, who believe blacks—even Muslims—are 'slaves.' Witnesses say it is why Arabs rape women; to impregnate them and so water down the African races" (Abraham, 2005i, 25). This discourse is explored in greater detail in the next chapter.

Persecuted Christians and the "War on Terror"

Interestingly, the rhetoric of "persecuted Christians" translated into complicated positions during the inception of George W. Bush's "War on Terror." According to some in this area of activism, "There are times when you see such evil and such terror that there's no nice and easy way of finding solutions" (Price, 2004b, 24). However, as already mentioned, evangelical missions often see global unrest as creating an opportunity for mission work because missions can provide needed food, hospital care, and other aid for people who are in war zones. For instance, Voice of the Martyrs says in one of its pamphlets: "With the recent war in Iraq, a tremendous opportunity exists. No one knows for sure how the new government will take shape and how much 'freedom' Christians will have to be a witness. But we do know that the current upheaval has opened a tremendous door of opportunity."[16] Countries are more likely to accept Christian missions under these conditions, which provides more opportunity to share the gospel. Consequently, some missionaries are saying the Muslim world is more responsive to the gospel after 9/11 as a result of the "War on Terror" (Guthrie, 2002b).

For others however, U.S. militarism puts Christians in greater danger of persecution. Before 9/11 *Christianity Today* ran articles strongly critiquing the U.S. sanctions for their devastating impact on Iraqi Christians, particularly children (Lehman, 2000; Veenker, 2000). It contended that "when broadly and harshly imposed, sanctions are 'weapons of mass destruction'" (A Silent Holocaust, 1999, 29). Ajith Fernando of Youth for Christ in Sri Lanka criticized the impact of Western militarism on evangelism efforts in the Global South after the Persian Gulf War.

> The bombings of Iraq and Yugoslavia remind many here of the attempts of Western nations to dominate poorer nations during the colonial era. Our concerted efforts to get people to separate Western political powers from the Christian enterprise do not have much success.... Christians are associated with the West and with colonialism. (Fernando, 1999, 77)

Some of the biggest critics of the war in Iraq were foreign missionaries who contended that Saddam Hussein generally allowed the practice of Christianity in relative peace but that instability in the country might contribute to a backlash against Christians. Their predictions proved to be correct (Guthrie, 2002c; C. A. White, 2003). *Christianity Today* contended that Christians in the Middle East are often safer under autocracies that allow some measures of discrimination while generally protecting Christians. They often intervene if radical Islamists start persecuting Christians. Democratic countries may elect Islamist regimes that make things worse. Iraqi Christians are more vulnerable to political and criminal violence now that Hussein has been deposed (M. Belz, 2007b). Arab Christians are then blamed for Western values even though "many Arab Christians oppose U.S. intervention in Iraq as well as the West's decadent values" (Hoffman, 2005, 86). Iraqi Christians have been subjected to "religicide" since the Iraq war (Gavlak, 2011). *Christianity Today* featured a story on one Iraqi Christian who was forced to leave because "although I aided my Muslim colleagues, they identified me as a crusader because of the American presence" (Gavlak, 2005b, 88).

Missionaries often find that aggressive anti-Arab U.S. foreign policies make their missionizing work more difficult (Channing, 2015; Sellers, 2002a). For instance, Sat-7, a Christian satellite TV service, is broadcasting shows via satellite in Arabic and on the internet. The shows do Christian witnessing, but they are not openly critical of Islam. They also do not make political statements or say anything to embarrass governments. This strategy runs directly counter to the more virulently anti-Arab and anti-Muslim rhetoric of evangelical leaders who are not engaged in mission work (Arabs outside Middle East to Hear Webcasts, 2001). Such sectors argue that the aggressive evangelism popular in Western countries is counterproductive in non-Western countries (J. Smith, 2002).[17]

Another article noted that persecution has increased because "the current U.S. involvement in Iraq is adding to the anti-Western and anti-Christian sentiments" (T. Dixon, 2007, 28). In fact, nearly a hundred retired Southern Baptist missionaries signed a plea in June 2003 asking Christian leaders to refrain from making inflammatory public statements about Muslims. They said that it harms missionary work in Muslim lands. Fuller Seminary received a $1 million grant from the Justice Department to fund a project to calm relations between Christians and Muslims. It features a proposed code of ethics that rejects offensive statements about each other's faiths, affirms a mutual belief in one God, and pledges not to proselytize. Some evangelical leaders say it goes against the grain of the church's mission to evangelize the world (News of the Year, 2004). A *Charisma* article on Brother Andrew, an evangelical who smuggles Bibles into "closed" countries, says that "he doesn't think it's smart to fight fire with fire. . . . The more you fight [radical Muslims] militarily, the more they will fight. Almost all the actions the West takes are creating more fundamentalists and terrorists . . . Bibles are better than bombs" (J. L. Grady, 2005c, 42). Similarly, Philip Yancey asserted: "Most of the Westerners who come here [to the Middle East] represent something other than Jesus. Some bring in military equipment. Some come to exploit the resources and invest their dollars. But you have a different calling: to make known the spirit of Jesus and to join the stream of liberation that broke free, 2000 years ago" (P. Yancey, 2010, 35).

Unsettling Christian Persecution

As evangelicals have engaged in strategic alliances with others to promote the Christian persecution movement, this political and intellectual exchange has ironically destabilized the Christian and U.S. exceptionalism that is the very foundation of this movement. For instance, *Christianity Today* ran an op-ed using the persecution rhetoric to complain about how evangelicals claim to be oppressed within the United States. "How soft we in the West have become. How could we possibly tell a fellow Christian hanging from a cross in Sudan that the American Civil Liberties Union is 'persecuting' us? How would the story of our church's zoning woes sound to a Christian sister in Pakistan who has been raped and forcibly married to a Muslim neighbor?" (Persecution Is a Holy Word, 2003, 32). Ironically, while the rhetoric of evangelicals as victims in the United States described in the previous chapter as well as the rhetoric of the global persecution movement rest on the assumption that evangelical faith itself is a marker of oppression, this article's engagement with global persecution undermines this assumption because it applies to white evangelicals in the United States.

As these assumptions get questioned, so too does the presumed efficacy of Christian persecution. *Christianity Today* also ran an article critiquing the glamorization of Christian persecution as a means to revitalize the Western church. In an interview Philip Jenkins calls for a theology of church extinction. He contends that persecution is not just a "seed of the church" but can actually kill the church. He argues, for instance, that Christianity will probably die in Iraq within the next generation. Implicitly employing Achille Mbembe's necropolitics, this analysis turns our attention to the deaths that are the foundation of Christian life. According to the article, the death of Christian peoples is just that—death (Guthrie, 2009).[18] Churches in South Korea were also strongly critiqued for sending missionaries to Afghanistan in 2007, who were then kidnapped. Rather than herald their actions or frame them as signs of Christian persecution, these churches were accused of being "self-centered" for not considering social and political issues (Abraham, 2007d; S. Pulliam, 2007a). Critical of the necropolitics embedded in Christian persecution that require Christians in the Global South to die so that white Christianity can live, these thinkers suggest that the fate of Third World Christianity should not be demarcated from the fate of Christianity as a whole. When Third World Christianity dies, Christianity as a whole also dies. In doing so, these critics more fundamentally question the racialization of religion that is embedded in the Christian persecution movement that would sacrifice some Christians for the benefit of others.

In fact, some evangelicals have gone so far as to call for a disengagement from this movement altogether. One missionary argued in *Evangelical Missions Quarterly* (from the Billy Graham Center), that "I see no biblical precedent for using political means to fight persecution on others' behalf" (Ramstad, 2004, 474). He contends that as long as the church is faithful, believers will be persecuted. This should be addressed through prayer but should not blur distinctions between the church and any government. Again, the contradictions emerge between seeking state power that favors select populations and desiring to share the gospel with all peoples. On the one hand, it is evangelicalism's relationship with state power that enables it to spread its message so forcefully. On the other hand, missionaries who want to share the gospel find that evangelical complicity in U.S. imperialism dampens their ability to gain a receptive audience. These experiences then enable a space for evangelicals to hear the other side of "Christian persecution." Ironically, many evangelicals have found the best way to protect Christians in the Global South who face persecution is to challenge the U.S. and Christian exceptionalist assumptions behind the Christian persecution movement itself.

Soong-Chan Rah further suggests that the problem with how Christian persecution is articulated within evangelicalism is that it ultimately frames persecution within a narrative of triumphalism rather than suffering. Consequently, the actual suffering of those who face persecution becomes erased in order to serve the triumphalist visions of Christians who are not suffering. Rah calls on all Christians to stay at the point of suffering through lament. In his recent text *Prophetic Lament* Rah argues:

> The American church avoids lament. The power of lament is minimized and the underlying narrative of suffering that requires lament is lost. But absence doesn't make the heart grow fonder. Absence makes the heart forget. The absence of lament in the liturgy of the American church results in the loss of memory. We forget the necessity of lamenting over suffering and pain. We forget the reality of suffering and pain. . . .
>
> Those who live in celebration "are concerned with questions of proper management and joyous celebration." Instead of deliverance, they seek constancy and sustainability. "The well-off do not expect their faith to begin in a cry, but rather, in a song. They do not expect or need intrusion, but they rejoice in stability [and the] durability of a world and social order that have been beneficial to them. . . ."
>
> Lament recognizes the struggles of life and cries out for justice against existing injustices. The status quo is not to be celebrated but instead must be challenged. (Rah, 2015a, loc. 185–202)

In many ways, Rah's analysis echoes those of Frank Wilderson and Dylan Rodriguez. As previously discussed, Rodriguez suggests that groups seeking racial justice frame narratives of liberation and survival as if the originary moment of colonialism, slavery, or conquest never happened. Going even further than Rodriguez, Wilderson contends that the willingness to stay at the moment of genocide enables an antagonistic relationship with the social order that provides the possibility of the creation of a relationality not marked through whiteness. "Genocide, however, has no speaking subject; as such it has no narrative. It can only be apprehended by way of a narrative about something that it is not" (Wilderson, 2010, loc. 2668). In occupying this position of nonrelationality to whiteness (that is, Blackness) one gives up attempting to strive for humanity, which is ultimately defined by whiteness: "From the coherence of civil society, the Black subject beckons with the incoherence of civil war, a war that reclaims Blackness not as a positive value, but as a politically enabling site. . . . One would have to lose one's Human coordinates and become Black. Which is to say one would have to die" (Wilderson, 2010, loc. 341). Alexander Weheliye departs from Wilderson in identifying Blackness not simply as a negation; he also argues that Black suffering via Black flesh can be the source of a different humanity that is not White Western Man. This is not a hope that acts as if the moment of slavery/colonization did not happen, but the hope that emerges in that context. Or, as Weheliye articulates, this is not a hope to stop you from slitting your writs, it is the hope that emerges after you have slit your wrists (or after your wrists have been slit).

Bringing Rah into conversation with critical ethnic studies and Black studies scholars reveals how these questions are ultimately theological questions—what is the source of hope amid death? Rah is similarly asking the question, where does hope emerge in a Christian context in which God is not articulated through whiteness? A *Charisma* magazine article asked the question: "Could it be that God is more than a Santa Claus–type figure, more than a two-hour weekend commitment, more than a mascot for a voting bloc?" (Schatzline, 2013). Rah extends this analysis to say that a God that is a Santa Claus figure who always answers people's prayers favorably if they have enough faith is ultimately a God of white supremacy. But if white supremacy structures belief itself, Christian belief is thus ultimately structured by white supremacy. Evangelical scholar Paul Metzger similarly states: "When I speak of Evangelical theology as racialized, I am not thinking primarily of what we say and write about race, but of what we don't articulate and possibly assume. In other words, it is not always the black print, but the white backdrop on the page that makes a theology white" (P. Metzger, 2013). Evangelical racial reconciliation organizer Brenda Salter McNeil notes that evangelicals lack a theology of atrocity within the context of white evangelicalism (McNeil, 2013). Atrocity becomes domesticated within white evangelicals' demand for a triumphalist narrative. In this context Rah suggests that the response to the suffering wrought by Christian persecution is lament, which can be understood as occupying the place of unintelligibility within Christian and United States exceptionalism.

5 THE RACIALIZATION OF RELIGION
Islamophobia and Christian Zionism

Bitter hatred and animus are the very heartbeat of Islam. The Muslim approach is to scream "foul" anytime something negative is said, but I'm here to say Islam is the most horrifying, dangerous thing on the horizon facing America. Islam will dominate America. You can go around the globe, there's not a nation that Islam has ever started in that it did not ultimately control. Ignorant, anemic, immature Christians don't understand the threat because they haven't studied the Word of God.—Gene Youngblood (B. Jones III, 2003a, 17)

Things are calm at our family gatherings because we're so good at pretending to get along. But we Christians also have our own toxic relatives.... [W]e need to talk about one of them: Christians United For Israel (CUFI), an extremely powerful and influential pro-Israel lobby that condones the displacement of Palestinians....

It may seem easy for us to cast off those who have been influenced by CUFI's messages, but these are not just some people who we can simply ignore.... [By] refusing to challenge those (like CUFI) who promote injustice, we become a party to that very injustice.—Killjoy Prophets (2014a)

As Amaney Jamal and Nadine Naber note in *Arab Americans and Race before and after 9/11* (2008), Arabs and Arab Americans are often racialized through religious discourse. Against those who would argue that Arab people are not racialized because they are categorized as "white" in the United States census, Jamal and Naber contend that racializing logics as they apply to Arab peoples take the form of cultural and religious determinacy. First, Islam is typically articulated as a religious/cultural system that is intent on the destruction of Western/Christian civilization (the two are generally conflated). Then Arab and Muslim peoples are also conflated, such that Arabs are marked as inherently threatening regardless of their actual religious affiliation. In addition, because Islam becomes the marker of inherent difference, the geopolitical relationships between the United States and Arab and/or Muslim countries is never understood in terms of Western colonialism or imperialism. In fact, this discourse marks the Arabs as imperial, whereas the West is simply protecting itself from Arab efforts to colonize the world. As the quotation above from the Reverend Gene Youngblood of Conservative Theological Seminary indicates, Islam is bent on the destruction of America. Consequently, in Foucauldian terms, Muslims must die so that America can live.

Junaid Rana further contends that the racialization of Islam casts light on the fact that racialization and religious othering are fundamentally connected. He notes that for European Christianity "religion was defined not only in terms of broad ideologies of belief, but also as states of being in relation to cultural notions of civilization and barbarity—as the terms of inclusion and exclusion within the 'family of man'" (Rana, 2011, loc. 435). He argues that Islam as a racial project provides the foundation upon which anti-Indigenous racism and chattel slavery in the United States developed. "Phenotype was never really everything; rather, it represented a number of discursive logics that connected culture to appearance, skin color, and all of the features that normally were presumed to stand in for race" (Rana, 2011, loc. 495). As such, Jews and Muslims were early categories of racial/religious others that enabled the legibility of other racializations (Rana, 2011, loc. 455).

At the same time, it is difficult to assess the racialization of Islam without simultaneously assessing the racialization of Judaism, because these racial projects converge within Christian Zionism. Christian Zionism holds that God has an unconditional covenant with the modern state of Israel and hence that Christians are obliged to protect Israel's interests against its perceived enemies. This movement ironically puts evangelicals, who generally hold that people must be Christian in order to be saved, in the position of defending Jewish people in Israel against Palestinian Christians. By exploring the inherent contradictions within this movement, this chapter sheds further light on the fluid logics of race and racialization as they impact evangelicalism's relationship to other religious movements. In addition, as argued in chapter 1, racial reconciliation is frequently deployed within the U.S. context to consolidate a multiculturalist evangelicalism against perceived non-Christian religious and political threats within the United States and the world. This movement espouses a U.S. Christian nationalism against the threat of Islam in particular. At the same time, however, I explore how the rhetoric of multiculturalism destabilizes the logics of Islamophobia and Christian Zionism. This destabilization has enabled a growing movement within evangelicalism to challenge Christian evangelicalism's unwavering support for the state of Israel, as exemplified in the quotation from Killjoy Prophets in the epigraph.

The Islamic Threat

Within the previously described rhetoric of "global persecution," Islam looms particularly large as responsible for the persecution of evangelicals. The perceived threat of Islam predates 9/11. For instance, in 1991 evangelical groups such as the National Association of Evangelicals (NAE) and the Institute of Religion and Democracy (IRD) held a forum to explore the threat that Islam poses to Christianity. Participants raised concerns that Muslims are closed-minded (A. Harris, 2008c) and often suppress groups that are considered apostates, and that "a Muslim may not choose to embrace another faith" (as if evangelical Christians are free to embrace other faiths) (Does Islam Have Room for Religious Liberty, 1991).[1] Even before 9/11 Pat Robertson described Saddam Hussein as "satanic" (Leaders Wrestle with Faith and War, 1991, 50). Evangelical "experts" on Islam frequently describe it as a menace. According to one such expert, Steve Johnson, it is impossible to do interfaith work with Muslims, because they will try to convert people (it is not clear from his analysis why non-Christians could ever work with evangelicals) (M. Belz, 2010d, 44; Leaders Wrestle with Faith and War, 1991, 50). In addition, unlike Christians who "love" their enemies, Muslims "hate" their enemies (Cheaney, 2010; Leaders Wrestle with Faith and War, 1991, 50). *World* profiles a Black prisoner whose incarceration for murder is described as the result of being a "militant Muslim." "When I was a Muslim, I was angry and bitter and full of vengeance and wrath, because Islam tells you it's OK" (D. Olasky, 2010, 81). But through Christianity, he learned to be nonviolent. Muslims are also perceived to have an irrational hatred of Jews (S. Johnson, 1989). This anti-Muslim fervor was even echoed in the works of relatively more progressive evangelicals such as Ron Sider (1988, 12). Articles note a mysterious "anti-Western" sentiment among many Muslim countries but never mention resentment of Western imperialism as a valid source of these sentiments (T. Morton, 1991). One exception to this anti-Arab hysteria is a *Christianity Today* article that addressed anti-Arab stereotypes (Neff, 1990b). As I discuss later, some strands of evangelical analysis of Islam have become increasingly more self-critical and self-reflective in recent years.

Generally speaking, after 9/11 the rhetoric around the Islamic threat has become particularly fervent among conservative evangelicals (Outpaced by Islam?, 2002). Jonathan Bernis wrote in *Charisma*, "This terrorist act should wake up Christians to the diabolical spirit of fanatical Islam. Israelis live constantly with these horrors" (Bernis, 2001, 38).² Articles on Christian persecution after 9/11 have tended to focus on the evils of Arab and/or Muslim countries or groups.³ Alarmists contend that Islam's goal is "to conquer America" (New York Post, 2003). "Radical Islam [is] the biggest threat to Christians," especially since "communism is not a force for the future" (Fieguth, 2004, 20). According to *Christianity Today*, the top news story of 2002 was "Martyrs' Brigade: Militant Muslims Murder Christians in Pakistan, Indonesia, Philippines, Vietnam, Sudan, and Nigeria" (Top Ten News Stories of 2003, 2003). In an article on Christian persecution, activist Maria Sliwa argues that the mind-set of radical Muslims is clear. They hate Christians and Jews. "She believes the attack [of 9/11] is a forerunner to a movement bent on world domination. She openly criticizes the Bush administration for 'schmoozing' with Arab nations" (P. Johnson, 2002a, 85).

While anti-Arab/Muslim rhetoric is prevalent within conservative evangelical discourse, this rhetoric is not necessarily consistent. As discussed later, not all of the critiques of Islam are equally virulent. And the more extreme critiques of Islam themselves are often contradictory. It is these contradictions that have allowed a space for some sectors within evangelicalism to call for a tempering of anti-Arab/Muslim rhetoric. But before I explore these spaces of reform, I first focus on the logics of evangelicalism's articulation of the Islamic threat.

Islam/Muslims as Inherently Evil

One tension within anti-Islamic rhetoric is the extent to which the problem is identified with Islam as a religious system or with the followers themselves. A prevalent narrative is that Muslims are evil because Islam is an evil system (Claydon, 2000; Seu, 2001). It is not "reformable" because the core of Islam is violent and oppressive (Durie, 2010).⁴ Ted Haggard described his travels to Muslim countries as journeys to the "Kingdom of darkness," where he intended to "discover the demonic power points of the region and disarm them" (Haggard, 1999, 52). According to Concerned Women for America, "Islam cannot be peaceful because conquest is inherent in its nature. Muslims desire to conquer Christians. That is what they believe. The [Muslim] leaders ... are trying to push their agenda, which is that Islam is a religion of peace. [The attacks are] a public relations nightmare for them" (T. Green, 2002, 17). Much of this rhetoric rests on a "clash of civilizations" presumption in which Islam is compared unfavorably to Christianity (M. Olasky, 2009f; Shibley, 2009; Veith, 2006b). According to *World*, the reason why Muslims become irrational when Islam is insulted is that "a religion with no insulted Savior will not endure insults to win the scoffers" (Piper, 2006). This is just one of the many flaws of Islam outlined in *World Magazine*: (1) "Christians and Muslims do not worship the same god" (M. Olasky, 2001a, 14). (2) Islam does not recognize original sin and hence Muslims have a "tendency to revere strong leaders" (unlike evangelical Christians, apparently) (M. Olasky, 2001a, 14). (3) Muslims do not believe in the Trinity; as a result, they do not respect diversity and are much less tolerant than evangelicals (who, apparently, greatly respect religious diversity) (M. Olasky, 2001a, 19). (4) Muslims like dictators, and hence Islamic societies have much in common with "Marxist countries" (M. Olasky, 2001a, 19). (5) Islam does "not understand compassion" or "suffering with the poor" (M. Olasky, 2001a, 19). (6) Muslim "men can beat their wives" (a proposition that ignores the high rate of domestic violence in evangelical homes) (M. Olasky, 2001a, 20). (7) Penalties for crime under Islam are cruel. "Christianity is the religion of the second chance. With Islam, it's often one strike and you're out" (M. Olasky, 2001a, 20). (8) "Jesus was a man of peace, Muhammad at times a man of war" (M. Olasky, 2001a, 22; see also J. Belz, 2001a, 5). *Charisma* assures readers that "Not All Muslims Want to Kill You" (Alam, 2011, 42). But still "Islam is not a religion of peace because Muhammed was a man of violence" (J. Morton, 2011, 44).

From the perspective of many evangelicals, Islam is so corrupt that Christians should not even converse with Muslims. Bill Hybels of the famous Willow Creek Church in Illinois came under sharp attack when he invited Fisal Hammouda, a Muslim imam, to speak to the church so that parishioners could learn "how a Christian can dialogue with someone who has radically different views." Hybels was accused of promoting Christian persecution and promoting false belief (Bill Hybels Says Christians Distorted Facts about Visit from Muslim Cleric, 2002, 19). David Claydon in *Transformation* argues that we cannot dialogue with Muslims because they make demands on the basis of a claim to authoritative truth (Claydon, 2000). Furthermore, Islam is premised on legalism, whereas Christianity is premised on freedom (Veith, 2001b). Another *World* article critiqued the Christian Crusades but then argued: "Today's crusaders are the Muslim extremists," allowing for Christianity's disavowal of its own history while simultaneously positioning Islam as the inheritor not only of its own history of oppression but of Christianity's history of oppression as well (Veith, 2001c, 14; see also Stark, 2014). An *Evangelical Missions Quarterly* article further asserts: "Islam is a religion in which God requires you to send your son to die for him. Christianity is a faith in which God sends his son to die for you" (L. McAdam, 2004, 418). Some even advocate complete obliteration of Islam: "Can anyone cite a literal reference to any nation God destroys in the end times that is not today Muslim?" (Shoebat, 2009, 74). Robert Morey, author of *The Islamic Invasion* (1992), announced a spiritual crusade against Islam and invited Christians to sign this pledge:

> In response to the Muslim Holy War now being waged against us, We, the undersigned, following the example of the Christian Church since the 7th century, do commit ourselves, our wealth, and our families to join in a Holy Crusade to fight against Islam and its false god, false prophet, and false book. We, the undersigned, believe that Islam is the root of all Muslim terrorism, which is the fruit of Islam. (quoted in Beverley, 2002, 34)

Perry Stone in *Charisma* further explains that the Antichrist will be Muslim: "I became convinced that the Antichrist will claim the Islamic religion as his religion" (Stone, 2016, 56). With this type of rhetoric, it is not a surprise that 42 percent of people in the United States who are not religious perceive Islam to be inherently violent, while 65 percent of those who define themselves as highly religious do (Olsen, 2005b). Another study conducted by the Ethics and Public Policy Center found that 79 percent of evangelical leaders believe Muslims do not "pray to the same God" as Christians, while 17 percent think they do; 52 percent of evangelical leaders say that Islam "preaches justice and moral values" while 32 percent of evangelical leaders disagree (Olsen, 2003c).

In another *World* analysis, "Christianity grew by the blood of its martyrs, but Islam grew by killing those who opposed it. . . . Christianity looked at slavery critically over the centuries and often fought for its abolition, but Muslims began the practice of enslaving Africans, and some Islamic countries today still allow slavery" (M. Olasky, 2004a, 56). Also, these articles often assert that beheading is a traditional Islamic practice, marking Muslims as inherently savage (M. Olasky, 2004a). Muslims riot when their sacred scriptures are desecrated, whereas Christians are more civilized and, based on their spiritual evolution, realize that a book is not commensurate with actually being a divine object (Olsen, 2005a). This logic follows Anne McClintock's previously described analysis of racism, in which colonized subjects are imagined as evolutionarily anterior to Christians (McClintock, 1995, 38). For example, Focus on the Family's Mark Hartwig argues that not all Muslims are terrorists. However, the extent to which they are not terrorists reflects the degree to which they have been influenced by Western Christian ideas (Hartwig, 2002). Pat Robertson explains that Allah is the moon God Hubal, a Babylonian god in pre-Islamic times (Spector, 2009, 77). Richard Land of the Southern Baptist Convention (SBC) similarly explains: "The biggest problem with Islam . . . is that it never went through a Reformation, which led in the West to modernity and the conviction that you don't kill people with whom you disagree. As a result, Islam includes violent elements, as Christianity has in the past. Islam is a very normal religious expression for the twelfth century" (Spector, 2009, 82).

Islam is demonized so much that some evangelicals do not even concern themselves with evangelizing to Muslims. This tendency toward total demonization somewhat contradicts the missionary impulse to convert Muslims. That is, if there is such a radical incommensurability between Muslims and Christians, then how is evangelism even possible? And yet many articles stress how, under correct conditions, Muslims can be receptive to the gospel (Compass Direct, 2005b; J. Nelson, 2006a; Walker, 2008c; Woodberry et al., 2007).

This tension is reflected in debates on the proper techniques by which one can evangelize to Muslims. For instance, the Southern Baptist Convention has been criticized for the "camel method" of evangelization. It uses the acronym CAMEL to explore a Qur'an passage to describe the virgin birth and resurrection of Jesus as a bridge to the New Testament. Critics decry this method as heretical for providing any sort of validation of Islam (Walker, 2010c). After all, "The type of prayer Muhammad modeled was of a slave trying to please a distant master." Consequently, Muslims prayers are "empty prayers to Allah" (Gabriel, 2004, 18).[5] *World* declared Coptic priest Zakaria Botros a Daniel of the Year for starting an internet chat room that engages Muslims. "My program is to attack Islam, not to attack Muslims but to save them because they are deceived. . . . Muslims are victims. Muhammad deceived them as he himself was deceived by Satan. ... As I love Muslims, I hate Islam" (quoted in M. Belz, 2008a, 39–40). The purpose for this award was to challenge Christian engagements with Islam: "For his fearless determination in the face of his enemies, for his willingness to label Islam a false religion in a year when many Christian leaders have overreached in their quest for common ground with its worshipers" (M. Belz, 2008a, 39). Similarly, a debate has arisen as to whether or not Muslims who convert need to call themselves Christian. That is, it is generally considered acceptable for Jewish people who convert to Christianity to call themselves Messianic Jews rather than Christians. The question arises: is it similarly acceptable to be a Messianic Muslim? Some argue that, unlike Judaism, Islam is too radically different from Christianity to support this practice. Others say that it allows Muslims to engage in deceitful syncretism. Defenders argue that it helps Muslims escape persecution in Muslim countries if they convert (Cumming, 2009; Tiansay, 2005a).

While Islam is often depicted as inherently evil, sometimes critics juxtapose Islam as a more ethical religious system in relation to its barbaric adherents. That is, Muslims are often described as not really knowing the real dictates of the Qur'an (Russell, 2004). In these narratives, Christian writers frame themselves as those who know the Qur'an better than do Muslims. *Christianity Today* opines that "the most effective way to address the human-rights disaster in Saudi Arabia may be to let Muhammed do the talking" (Sellers, 2002h, 35). And *Charisma* informs us that Muslims are having dreams of Jesus all around the world and converting to Christianity (A. Lee, 2011).

Evangelical Critiques of Islamophobia

On the one hand, the attacks of 9/11 seem to have intensified the virulence of evangelical anti-Islamic rhetoric. At the same time, this virulence seems to have also encouraged some sectors of evangelicalism to become more critical of Islamophobia.[6] One such example was the scandal that erupted when Franklin Graham, son of Billy Graham, preached a sermon at the Pentagon where he said Islam was a "wicked" and "very evil" religion (Jesus Freak, 2002). His stance was supported by *World* (M. Olasky, 2001b) and Sandy Rios of Concerned Women for America, who said that "a religion that teaches killing the infidels is wicked" (A Convenient Scapegoat: The Right's Demonization of Muslims, 2002). *New Man* ran an interview with Marvin Yakos, author of *Jesus vs. Jihad* (1990), who asserted: "America needs to understand that the Quran is a terribly evil spiritual device. It was concocted by Satan to kill, steal and destroy, not only the body, but also the soul. . . . The media declares Islam a religion of peace. In truth, Islam is a religion of the Antichrist" (Yakos, 2002, 19). Other prominent evangelists such as Jerry Falwell, Pat Robertson, and former SBC president Jerry Vines have also made similar derogatory remarks about Islam. Falwell, for instance, declared the Prophet Muhammad a terrorist on *60 Minutes* (M. Olasky, 2007c, 14). As a result the National Association of Evangelicals and Institute of Religion and Democracy (IRD) convened a meeting to issue guidelines on dialogues between the evangelicals and Muslim communities (Wisdom, 2003). On the one hand, it calls on Christian leaders to tone down their language and to acknowledge some of the validity of Muslim complaints about Western imperialism. It calls on Christians to become more educated about Islam and to assume that, while Christians may have critiques of Islam, Muslims also have valid critiques of Western Christianity. On the other hand, it stresses that Christians should not overemphasize the role of Western empires in creating social ills within Muslim and Arab countries. It also cautions not to equate Christianity with Islam and emphasizes respect for the boundaries of Christianity. The statement concludes by arguing that some sectors of Islam are so violent that there is no place to dialogue with these groups (Wisdom, 2003). All participants in the forum stated that they disagreed with Franklin Graham's statement. The forum was critiqued for not inviting Falwell, Graham, or Robertson.[7] Broader response to the statement was mixed. Dudley Woodberry, professor of Islamic studies at Fuller Seminary, supported the statement. Roy Oksnevad, director of Ministries to the Muslim Department of the Billy Graham Center at Wheaton College, stated by contrast that dialogue is good but limited. "There is a dark side in Islam" (Strichers, 2003, 21).

In addition, Mahathir bin Mohamad, Muslim prime minister of Malaysia, addressed the 11th General Assembly of the World Evangelical Fellowship in the Malaysian capital in May 2001 and received a standing ovation from 800 Christian leaders. He called on evangelicals to promote dialogue and tolerance. Propagation of faith is necessary for both Christians and Muslims but must be done without violence (Stephen, 2001). Hal Lindsey was pulled from the Trinity Broadcast network in 2006 over a message that was "too pro-Israel and too anti-Muslim" (News Briefs, 2007b).

Controversy within evangelicalism erupted when plans to build an Islamic Cultural Center near the World Trade Center became publicized in 2010. Many evangelicals spoke out against this proposal, while some churches even went so far as to propose burning copies of the Qur'an on September 11. The National Association of Evangelicals issued this statement against religious intolerance in 1996: "If people are to fulfill the obligations of conscience, history teaches the urgent need to foster respect and protection for the right of all persons to practice their faith." In the same resolution, the NAE pledged to "address religious persecution carried out by our Christian brothers and sisters whenever this occurs around the world":

> The National Association of Evangelicals encourages increased understanding and reconciliation between those of different faiths and backgrounds, and it laments efforts that work against a just and peaceful society. The plans recently announced by a Florida group to burn copies of the Qur'an on September 11 show disrespect for our Muslim neighbors and would exacerbate tensions between Christians and Muslims throughout the world. The NAE urges the cancellation of the burning.
> NAE President Leith Anderson said, . . . "The most powerful statement by the organizers of the planned September 11th bonfire would be to call it off in the name and love of Jesus Christ." (National Association of Evangelicals Denounces Church's Quran Burning Event, 2010)

Similarly, *Christianity Today* spoke out in support of the center. It advocated religious tolerance, argued that Islamophobia in the United States would increase the repression of Christians in Muslim countries, and contended that "treating all Muslims as potential jihadists does not open opportunities for sharing the Good News" (Mosques in Middle America, 2010, 53). It further complained that the mainstream media was misrepresenting the pastor who was threatening to burn the Qur'an as representative of Christian evangelicalism, a reasonable complaint given that even Sarah Palin denounced him (Burned by the Qur'an Burning, 2010). Another article noted that evangelicals often make assumptions about Islam based on problematic readings of the Qur'an resulting from language translation issues and the inability to read it contextually. It advocated that evangelicals engage Muslims directly to gain a better understanding of the complexity of Islam (Qureshi et al., 2012).

Christianity Today ran an article critiquing Islamophobia. When asked in an interview if Muslims and Christians worship the same God, Miroslav Volf responded: "First, all Christians don't worship the same God, and all Muslims don't worship the same God" (Galli, 2011a, 29). "We've come up with this idea that Muslims are our enemy, and that Muslim terrorism and extremism are the most important enemies we should be combating. I think this is bogus" (Galli, 2011a, 30). Instead, "to have Muslims as allies in combating de facto hedonism is a very important thing" (30).

An increasing number of articles have been published that question the demonization of Muslims and Arabs and the oversimplification of geopolitics in the Arab/Muslim world.[8] *World*, one of the most consistently anti-Arab evangelical magazines, has argued that Islam has positive aspects: (1) "Islam moved Arabs and many other people from polytheism." (2) "Islam is strongly creationist." (3) "Muslims developed a civilization that made great advances in science, medicine, and mathematics." (4) "Islam stands with Christianity on many social issues"—including homosexuality and abortion. And (5) Islam welcomes "adherents of every skin color and ethnicity" (M. Olasky, 2001a, 12; see also Veith, 2005g). It also published an article that emphasized the number of Muslims who oppose terrorism (Abraham, 2007a). Bob Jones III (who, while very conservative, seems to be the most sympathetic *World* writer on issues relating to Arab peoples and Islam) criticized the aforementioned statement of Gene Youngblood: "Simplistic, broad-brush portrayals rarely do justice to a complex faith" (B. Jones III, 2003a, 17). And it published this response from Wendy Merdian in a set of individual reflections on 9/11: "Arabs are more often targets of terrorism than the West and bear media-imposed culpability when they can be its victims, too.... In the 10 years since, I have been dismayed when I see fear and pain morph into hate in Christian hearts" (Merdian, 2016, 69).

Charisma ran an article in response to the secularist laws being passed in Europe that are targeting Muslim religious practices. "As Bible-believing Christians we have lots of common ground with Muslims. We have got more in common with them than with our secularist neighbors. If, on the other hand, we isolate the Muslims, we only create room for fundamentalist Islam" (T. Dixon, 2005, 101). Furthermore, if European nations pass restrictions on Muslim practices, they will eventually be used against Christian practices (T. Dixon, 2005, 2010). After Obama's election, however, *Charisma* seemed to lose its charitable spirit toward Muslims.

Fides et Historia, published by Calvin College, ran several articles critiquing Samuel Huntington's "clash of civilization" thesis (Huntington, 2000), which the authors argued is the governing logic of much evangelical anti-Islam rhetoric. This logic stereotypes Islam, fails to consider the impact of Christian imperialism on Islamic countries, and creates a self-fulfilling prophecy (Benson, 2004; Hoffmann, 2004; Markovic, 2004; G. Miller, 2004;

Waalkes, 2004). One contributor states: "Muslims have invoked jihad more in conflict with other Muslims than in conflict with outsiders. For the last two or three centuries, the aggressor in Islam's clashes with the West has been the latter more often than not. Overall Islamic history has not been any bloodier than European history" (Hoffmann, 2004, 117). He argues that this civilization thesis has an "orientalist bias" (Hoffmann, 2004, 117). And Philip Yancey states that Christians are guilty of many of the same things of which they accuse Muslims:

> The very things we resist in Islam, some Christians find tempting. We, too, seek political power and a legal code that reflects revealed morality.... We, too, tend to see others (including Muslims) as a stereotyped community, rather than individuals. Will we turn toward our own version of the harsh fundamentalism sweeping Islam today? (P. Yancey, 2006, 64)

Christianity Today has run several articles that counter the demonization of Islam and Arabs (Beverley, 2002; Cartoon Chaos, 2006; Christianity Today, 2007b; J. White, 2007). It has featured Arabs and Muslims who advocate religious dialogue and attempt to counter misinformation about Arab peoples and Muslims (C. Hulsman, 2008). *Christianity Today* also ran an op-ed criticizing Muslim "phobia" (Muslim Phobic No More, 2002). Brother Andrew of Open Doors Ministry, which champions the persecuted church, similarly calls for a nonantagonistic approach to Islam: "Today many of us have created an enemy image of the Muslims. They are all terrorists who hijack our planes, blow up our embassies, and take innocent people hostage. Not only is this untrue, but the very minute we view them this way we make it impossible to reach them with the gospel. God cannot use us" (Brother Andrew, 1998, 57).[9] For these critics of Islamophobia, it is important to avoid double standards in doing evangelism. Paul Marshall, an activist on Christian persecution, states: "When we talk with Muslims about punitive passages in the Qur'an, we should remember the Bible commands Israel to stone followers of Molech (Lev 20:2)" (Marshall, 2006, 91; see also Guthrie, 2006). "We need to be careful to not have a double standard" (Guthrie, 2006, 65).

In *Focus on the Family Citizen*, Mark Hartwig notes that the demonization of Islam can contribute to increased anti-Christian sentiment in the Muslim world. When Muslims are oppressed, this oppression puts Muslims on the path to extremism. "We can keep it [9/11] from happening again by remembering that loving our neighbors—Muslim or otherwise—isn't just our Christian duty. It also might change the world" (Hartwig, 2001, 25). So, while 9/11 has certainly amplified anti-Muslim rhetoric in evangelical communities, there has also been an increase in attention to evangelical-Muslim dialogue that is geared toward coexistence, not condemnation (Beaumont, 2005; Carey, 2005; Rice, 2010; D. E. Singh, 2005; D. Thomas, 2005; Tivassoli and Howarth, 2005).

An implicit sustained critique of Islamophobia can be found in Colin Chapman's book *Cross and Crescent*. As discussed later, Chapman has also written extensive critiques of Christian Zionism. In this work, he attempts to give an accurate summary of Muslim cultural practices and beliefs without negative commentary. He also contests prevalent evangelical assumptions that "if Christianity is true, then Islam is false" (C. Chapman, 2003, 41) and that "Islam needs to be strongly resisted in the west. Muslims are aiming to conquer the world" (43). He critiques evangelicals who hold Muslims to a double standard and describes Zionism as "another manifestation of Western domination" (152). He challenges the notion of the "oppressed" Muslim woman: "We need to resist the temptation, however, to . . . compare the best in our own tradition with the worst in the other. . . . We need to admit that the Christian church has not always had a very good record in its attitudes to women" (176). He further calls on those concerned about Christian persecution to organize with Muslims who face persecution and to oppose Western colonialism, especially in Palestine.

An example of these conflicting trends within evangelicalism concerning Islamophobia is the controversy that arose around Larycia Hawkins, who was the first female African American tenured professor at Wheaton College. She wore a hijab to demonstrate solidarity with Muslims who were being subjected to Islamophobia and commented that Muslims and Christians worshipped the same God. As a result, she was suspended and essentially forced out of Wheaton. Her dismissal sparked a tremendous movement in support of her. Her supporters organized a Twitter intervention on her behalf under the hashtag #DocHawk. In this intervention, Hawkins's evangelical supporters noted that her theological comments were not sharply different from those of many white male evangelicals, such as Billy Graham, who have also held that Muslims and Christians worship the same God. They argued that this dismissal was a reflection of the precarious professional position of women of color in evangelical seminaries in particular and academia in general: their analyses are always seen as inherently threatening to disciplinary and theological boundaries. They also critiqued the Islamophobia that led to her suspension and eventual dismissal. Hawkins's colleagues supported her too: Wheaton's faculty council unanimously voted to ask the administration to reinstate Hawkins (M. Lee, 2016b). Hawkins thus became simultaneously an evangelical symbol of heresy for some and of courage for others.

At the same time, the white evangelical backlash against Obama, who was perceived as "soft" on the terrorist threat, also ignited an anti-Muslim trend that significantly reversed efforts toward evangelical-Muslim dialogue. *World*'s post-Obama coverage, for instance, focuses on how Obama was unable to recognize Muslim countries for the threat that they are (E. Belz, 2010b; M. Belz, 2009b).[10] Overt Islamophobia seems to have significantly increased with Donald Trump's presidential candidacy. In fact, it seems to have been a major factor in why so many white evangelical leaders galvanized around him despite Trump's complete lack of credentials that Christian Right leaders claimed to have previously supported. Thus, for instance, Southern Baptist leader Russell Moore became vocal against Islamophobia and signed on to an amicus brief supporting the right of a Muslim group in New Jersey to build a mosque, which became one of the reasons some Southern Baptist pastors called for his resignation after Trump was elected (Crookston, 2017).

Christian Zionism

Islamophobia is inextricably linked to Christian Zionism, which racializes both Arab and Jewish peoples in complex ways. The emergence of Christian Zionism developed along intersecting theological and political fronts. Evangelical scholar Stephen Sizer defines Christian Zionism:

> Christian Zionism is born out of the conviction that God has a continuing special relationship with, and covenantal purpose for, the Jewish people, apart from the church, and that the Jewish people have a divine right to possess the land of Palestine. This is based on a literal and futurist interpretation of the Bible and the conviction that Old Testament prophecies concerning the Jewish people are being fulfilled in the contemporary State of Israel. (Sizer, 2005, 20)[11]

Sizer notes that a variety of theological movements within Christian Protestantism helped seed the later development of Christian Zionism.

While pro-Zionist impulses existed within Puritan theology as early as the seventeenth century, in which some predicted Palestine would be restored after the conversion of Jewish peoples to Christianity, a premillennial movement developed in the late eighteenth and early nineteenth centuries that eventually began to emphasize God's separate covenant with Jews. Premillennialists argued that Christ's kingdom, far from being realized in this age or in the natural development of humanity, lay wholly in the future and was totally supernatural in origin. They stood in contrast to postmillennialists, who believed that the defeat of the Antichrist was taking place in the present age through a gradual process (Marsden, 1980, 49).

Dispensationalism, a movement founded by John N. Darby of the Plymouth Brethren, arose from premillennialism. Darby divided history into three periods or dispensations. God's rules for one dispensation would not necessarily be applicable to another. C. I. Scofield systematized these dispensations into the scheme followed by most U.S. dispensationalists: innocence (before the fall), conscience (the fall to the flood), human government, promise (Abraham to Moses), law (Moses to Christ), grace (the church age), and the kingdom (millennium) (T. Weber, 2004, 20). Premillennial dispensationalism involved a complex rendering of history in which Christians would be "raptured" into heaven after the current church age comes to an end.[12] The Rapture would be followed by the Antichrist's reign on earth. Then Christ would come to the earth, defeat the Antichrist, and rule for 1,000 years (Marsden, 1980, 48–50). Darby, through a reading of Daniel 7–9, concluded that in the "times of the Gentiles" Israel would suffer in the hands of four Gentile powers, until Jesus returned. The return would occur seventy weeks after a Gentile ruler allowed exiled Jews to return to Jerusalem. During the first seven weeks after the decree, the city would be rebuilt. Sixty-two weeks later, the Messiah would be repudiated by his people. In the seventieth week, an evil ruler would gain power. At the end of the seventieth week, the Messiah would return and restore David's throne. Because the Hebrew word translated as "week" actually means "a seven," dispensationalists concluded that a week actually means seven years. However, since the second coming of Jesus did not occur seven years later, Darby concluded that God has postponed the seventieth week because the Jews rejected Jesus and is now turning to the Gentiles (T. Weber, 2004, 21–22). Eventually the church will be raptured right before the seventieth week continues, however, and the prophetic timetable will continue its relationship with the Jewish people. Essentially, the Christian church is a parenthetical period between God's original covenant with Israel and the Rapture, when

Christians will be transported into heaven (T. Weber, 1998). According to Weber: "God would not deal with the two peoples or operate the two plans concurrently. Consequently, God had to remove the church before proceeding with the final plans for Israel" (T. Weber, 2004, 23). Many dispensationalists hold that the church age ends after the Rapture; history will then continue through God's relationship to Israel (Sizer, 2005, 146–47).

After the Rapture, the Antichrist will ascend. He will promise peace and the protection of Israel. This leader will come from the west (some opine that it will be a leader from Europe). For a short time, Jews will resume their sacrificial system in a restored temple and will experience peace and prosperity. However, 3.5 years later, an alliance will be created from the north (generally understood to be Russia) and the south (generally understood to be an Arab/African alliance) to launch an attack on Israel (Daniel 11). However, God will supernaturally destroy five-sixths of the invaders. In the wake of this destruction, the Antichrist's force will then protect Israel from an invasion from the east (often assumed to be China). One-third of the human race will be destroyed, but the Antichrist and Israel will win. But now that all these nations have been eliminated, the Antichrist will reveal his true colors. He will demand that he be worshiped in the temple and that all people must receive the "mark of the beast" on their hands or foreheads in order to buy and sell. In response, 144,000 Jews will become missionaries and preach the gospel of Jesus. The Antichrist will then begin killing all Jews, not just those who have converted to Jesus. All 144,000 will die, and the persecution will be much worse than that of Adolf Hitler (T. Weber, 2004, 150–51). Some sectors of dispensationalist thought, such as those popularized by Hal Lindsey, hold that two-thirds of Jewish people will die during the Tribulation, with the rest converting to Christianity. Those who do not convert are often represented as operating in league with Satan before they are destroyed (Sizer, 2005, 173). Other Christian Zionist groups, particularly those that work directly with the state of Israel, eschew the belief that the End Times necessitates the devastation of the world's Jewish population (Sizer, 2005, 198).

Finally, at the end of the seventieth week, all forces from the north, south, east, and west will converge on Israel to destroy God's people. At this point, Christ and all the raptured saints will destroy everyone at the battle of Armageddon. The Antichrist and his followers will be cast into the lake of fire, all the world will be judged, and Satan will be thrown into a bottomless pit. Thus begins the Millennium when Jesus restores the throne of David. The Millennium will be a Jewish kingdom, with a restored temple, animal sacrifices, and King Jesus reigning from Jerusalem. After the Millennium, Satan will be freed for one last rebellion. It will be squelched, and the resurrection of the dead and the last judgment will occur. A new heaven and earth will be created for the redeemed, and time will come to an end (T. Weber, 2004, 25).

In addition, many hold that before the Rapture can occur the Muslim Dome of the Rock must be destroyed and a third Jewish temple must be built in Jerusalem. While some evangelicals espouse replacement theology, which holds that God's covenant with Jewish people ended when they failed to accept Jesus as their Messiah, dispensationalists often hold that God has a dual covenant with both Jews and Christians (Hinn, 2009). This thought was later systematized in the Scofield Bible, published in 1909. It gained such prominence that by the 1920s many Christian fundamentalists accepted the Scofield Bible and dispensationalist thought as part of Christian orthodoxy (T. Weber, 1998). What is noteworthy is that dispensationalist thought no longer rested on the conversion of Jews to Christianity before the restoration of Jews to Israel would take place. This conversion would happen afterward (Sizer, 2005, 70). Consequently, as discussed later, some Christian Zionist organizations eschew evangelism directed toward Jews because their conversion is not supposed to take place until Jesus returns (Sizer, 2005, 146–47).

Initially, Christian Zionists did not necessarily support of the state of Israel. Some were ambivalent about the secular basis of Zionism, and many rejected the idea that Israel was the formation foretold in prophecy or that the state of Israel should be supported unconditionally. For instance, another prominent early Christian Zionist, Paul Allen, contended that "God does not need to use questionable methods in bringing about the fulfillment of prophecy. . . . The Israel of today must justify its acts, not in terms of its ultimate destiny (which is not universally recognized or accepted) but in terms of the moral conscience of the nations of today" (T. Weber, 2004, 178–79). In addition, as evangelical scholar Mae Cannon demonstrates, most leading Christian voices for Zionism were actually liberal Protestants rather than evangelicals:

> American liberal Christians integrated their theological beliefs with internalized assumptions of imperialism as a means of justifying and supporting the settlement of Palestine by Jewish immigrants. The practices of Christian Zionism were informed by Orientalism and imperialist ideologies which manifested themselves in three primary ways: the

assumed right of Jewish possession and rule over the land of Palestine; assumption of Arab inferiority; and belief that progress and prosperity were only possible under British occupation or subsequent Jewish Zionist enterprise. Protestant liberal support of Zionism prior to 1948 was inspired and informed by the integration of theology and imperialist ideologies or theological imperialism. (Cannon, 2014, 92)

However, after the founding of Israel in 1948, and particularly after the war of 1967 when Israel occupied Jerusalem, evangelical Christian Zionists consolidated around support for Israel and became the more vocal Christian supporters. Hal Lindsey's wildly popular books based on Christian dispensationalism were instrumental in fueling evangelical support for Israel. After the Six-Day War, evangelicals organized Christians Concerned for Israel (which later became the National Christian Leadership Conference for Israel) and defended Israel's invasion of Lebanon with a pro-Israel rally in the White House.

Stephen Spector traces the political alliance-building between evangelicals and Israel in *Evangelicals and Israel*. He suggests that scholars overemphasize the popularization of premillennial dispensationalism, particularly through Hal Lindsey's popular books on the role of Israel in the End Times, in the development of alliances between evangelicals and Israel. He contends that evangelicals have varied beliefs on what is the modern state of Israel's role (if it even has one) in the End Times. He also notes that these tendencies to judge geopolitical situations through biblical prophecy are becoming less popular. In addition, many evangelicals who are Zionists do not necessarily tie their support to dispensationalism but rather to their belief in accordance with Genesis 12:3 that God blesses those who bless the Jews (Spector, 2009, 1–35, 158–85).

Spector emphasizes instead the role of the state of Israel specifically in furthering this movement. W. A. Criswell, former president of the Southern Baptist Convention, traveled to meet with prime minister David Ben-Gurion in the early 1950s and became a staunch supporter of Israel. Ben-Gurion also convinced the World Conference of Pentecostal Churches to hold its event in Jerusalem in 1961 and spoke at the conference. In 1969 Israel opened a Department of Christian Affairs to develop evangelical support for Israel. This ministry commissioned a study by Yona Malachy to assess evangelical support in the United States. While doing his study, Malachy convinced Biola College to issue a statement of support for Israel. His study was published in 1978, after his death, under the title *American Fundamen-*

talism and Israel: The Relation of Fundamentalist Churches to Zionism and the State of Israel. Ben-Gurion also participated in the Jerusalem Conference on Biblical Prophecy, held June 15–17, 1971, which became the largest Christian gathering in Israel since 1948. It sparked the beginning of evangelical tourism to Israel (T. Weber, 2004, 213–14). Menachem Begin aggressively solicited Christian Zionist support. He convinced Assemblies of God evangelist Davis Lewis to establish a travel agency to promote evangelical tourism (T. Weber, 2004, 215). Upon Begin's death, the Evangelical Christian Zionist Congress of America issued a letter stating that his friendship "forged the first visible bonding of the people of Israel with their Biblical allies" (Spector, 2009, 144). Begin developed particularly close ties with Jerry Falwell, whose organization the Moral Majority quickly became active in supporting Israel (Spector, 2009, 147). Begin gave Falwell the prestigious Jabotinsky Award for his continued support, and Falwell received a Windstream jet from the Israeli government to facilitate his travels to Israel (T. Weber, 2004, 218). Begin called on Falwell's support when he launched a preemptive strike against an Iraqi nuclear reactor. Falwell similarly supported the Israeli invasion of Lebanon in 1982 (T. Weber, 2004, 219). He later developed close ties with every Israeli leader after Begin (Spector, 2009, 148). When President Bill Clinton was pushing Benjamin Netanyahu to fulfill the terms of the Oslo agreement, Netanyahu contacted Falwell to arrange a welcome by 1,500 evangelicals, including Ralph Reed of the Christian Coalition and Jane Hansen of Women's Aglow through Voices United for Israel as an affront to Clinton (Spector, 2009, 148).[13] In 2001 Ariel Sharon gave Pat Robertson an award in recognition of his service, and the Zionist Organization of America gave him the State of Israel Friendship Award in 2002 (Spector, 2009, 148). Many Israeli officials attended Robertson's birthday party in Israel. In 2004 the Knesset Christian Allies Caucus was formed to enhance relations with Israel and Christian supporters (Christian Allies Caucus, 2004) but also condemned efforts to convert Jews. This caucus organized a Women's Summit in Jerusalem in 2007. But prominent Christian Zionist radio personality Janet Parshall withdrew because it condemned efforts to convert Jewish people (Spector, 2009, 119).

Benny Elon, who became a leader of the political far Right in Israel, was also instrumental in the development of alliances between evangelicals and Israel. He became minister of tourism in 2001 and developed a strategy for courting evangelicals as tourists. An example of the kinds of relationships that he helped form was through his friendship with Ronn Torossian, a public relations executive that, in turn, represented the Christian Coalition and the government of Israel. Its clients include John Hagee, Christians United for Israel, Benny Hinn, the American Jewish Congress, and the Zionist Organization of America. Elon makes these connections possible. He forged alliances with many evangelical leaders and helped them develop lobbying infrastructures on Israel. And in 2003 he launched a major campaign to attract evangelical tourists (Spector, 2009, 218).

The Israeli Ministry of Tourism recruited evangelical leaders for free familiarization tours. Tourists can fly only on the Israeli airline El Al, employ only tour guides licensed by the Israeli Ministry of Tourism, and use only Israeli ground transportation companies. Even when they request it, tourists are not allowed to meet Palestinian Christians (T. Weber, 2004, 219). The ministry also tapped a Colorado Springs–based marketing firm to attract tourists. The solution is to "create spiritual SWAT teams of Christian Zionists to experience a peaceful Israel free of conflict" (Robert Smith, 2004, 839). It collaborated with Christian Friends of Israel to place scriptural verses on landmark stones in any town in Israel that figures in the biblical narrative.[14] Chuck Smith, founder of Calvary Chapel, became a prominent tour leader, whose tours featured mass baptisms of Christians in the Jordan River. His tours are given infrastructural support by the state of Israel (T. Weber, 2004, 215). Israel's Ministry of Tourism put a forty-page ad in conservative evangelical Christian magazines called *The Holy Land* to recruit evangelicals to tour Israel. The slogan of the magazine directed to evangelicals is "No one belongs here more than you."[15] Furthermore, it now hosts a museum in Jerusalem devoted to celebrating "friends of Zionism" (Rutland, 2015). It also sponsored a four-day solidarity tour for Christian Right organizations, in which the Christian Coalition and other groups participated (Christian Coalition, 2002a). At the Feast of the Tabernacles, Ariel Sharon stated: "Your [evangelical] friendship is important to us. With your support, we can realize the hopes and dreams for peace, security and prosperity in the whole land" (Fisher and Gaines, 2004, 18; see also Wagner, 2001). One church, Faith Bible Chapel of Arvada, Colorado, has an Israeli flag flying by a Christian one. It also has an Israeli Outreach director, Cheryl Morrison, who has an office with "framed posters of Israeli military tanks, Apache attack helicopters, and Israeli Defense Forces" (Robert Smith, 2004, 839). After 9/11 visits to Israel fell 45 percent. In response, the Israeli Ministry of Tourism intensified its marketing efforts toward American Christians. "For many years, American Christians have been among our best friends and greatest supporters of the State of Israel and of tourism to Israel. We really appreciate it. We are calling upon all of those who have encouraged tourism in the past to work with us to bring as many American Christians to Israel as possible, despite the headlines" (M. Smith, 2002, 32).

The most prominent Christian Zionist lobbying group today is probably Christians United for Israel, headed by John Hagee, along with many others, including the National Christian Leadership Conference for Israel, the Unity Coalition for Israel, Christian Friends of Israeli Communities, Christians' Israel Public Action Committee, and the International Christian Embassy Jerusalem. In addition, Christian Zionists are active in the International Fellowship of Christians and Jews, an organization headed by Rabbi Yechiel Eckstein in order to develop broad-based Christian and Jewish support for Israel. This group worked with former Christian Coalition director Ralph Reed to organize Stand for Israel, which hosts an annual day of solidarity with Israel.[16] The campaign mobilized 100,000 churches and 1 million Christians to be in solidarity with Israel and to receive alerts on pressing issues (T. Weber, 2004, 229).

According to John Mearsheimer and Stephen Walt, Christian Zionists, despite their fervency, are a relatively small part of the overall Israel lobby. The reason is that these groups organize around a number of domestic issues, such as abortion and same-sex marriage, which compete for time and resources. Consequently, they contribute a relatively small amount of financial resources and lobbying power relative to the Jewish Zionist lobbying groups that focus more solely on Israel (Mearsheimer and Walt, 2007, 138–39). However, with Obama's presidency and the manner in which he was racialized as a Muslim threat, Christian Zionism overlapped with the general Islamophobic support for the war on terror that helped fuel the evangelical movement in support of Trump's presidency. At the same time, Obama's presidency complicated the consolidation of Christian Zionism across evangelical communities. The International Fellowship of Christians and Jews noted that its effort to diversify by spreading Christian Zionism among African Americans was stalled by its harsh stances against Obama (Gleanings, 2015b, 23). *World* proclaimed: "Through U.S. front groups, Muslim radicals overtaking the Middle East have found support in the Obama Administration" (M. Belz, 2012a).

Probably the most prominent and hardline spokesperson for Christian Zionism is John Hagee. According to Hagee, "all other nations were created by an act of men, but Israel was created by an act of God" (J. Hagee, 2007b, 10). He contends that if you do not support Israel, you "are under the curse of God and headed for eternal, everlasting fire with the devil and his angels" (J. Hagee, 2005, 71).[17] Hagee announced that he would give $1 million toward Israel's effort to resettle Jews from the USSR in the Occupied Territories. When confronted with the fact that this act would be illegal, he said, "I am a Bible scholar and theologian and from my perspective, the law of God transcends the law of the United States government" (Robert Smith, 2004, 855). In 2006 John Hagee along with George Morrison, Stephen Strang, Gary Bauer, and Jerry Falwell formed Christians United for Israel (CUFI), whose purpose is to "provide a national organization through which every pro-Israel organization and ministry can speak and act with one voice in support of Israel in matters of biblical issues" (M. Green, 2006). Hagee began his public advocacy of Israel in 1981 and has organized "A Night to Honor Israel" events every year since then. At the 2007 event alone Hagee raised $8 million for Israel. He envisioned CUFI as a Christian version of the American Israel Public Affairs Committee (AIPAC). He has a dozen regional directors and a network of evangelical activists who can be reached within twenty-four hours to lobby. The board of directors includes Benny Hinn and Jack Hayford. It also organizes nights to celebrate Israel in major cities. It started 150 campus groups, because supposedly Christian colleges are now espousing "replacement theology" (discussed later) and are attacking Israel (A. Gaines, 2009b; Roth, 2015). In July 2006 it brought together 3,400 Christian Zionists for a conference and lobbying effort that entailed 2,880 meetings with members of Congress (Ghiringhelli, 2007b; Mundy, 2006). The 2007 meeting drew 4,000 delegates and featured presidential candidate John McCain. At this meeting, Senator Joe Lieberman described Hagee as a "man of God" (Spector, 2009, 169–70) and compared him to Moses: "I see God's hand in this" (D. Hagee, 2007, 12). John McCain and Benjamin Netanyahu attended. The CUFI mantra is "The Bible Belt Is Israel's Safety Belt" (D. Hagee, 2007, 22). According to CUFI, all nations, including Arab ones, are required to pray for Israel (Morrison, 2007). Their platform is as follows: (1) Palestinians have no claims to land; (2) Israel should not be pressured to give land for peace; (3) Jerusalem belongs to Israel; (4) move the U.S. embassy from Tel Aviv to Jerusalem; (5) annihilate Hezbollah; (6) stop Iran's nuclear pursuits; and (7) do not withdraw from Iraq prematurely (D. Hagee, 2007). "War isn't totally off the table for CUFI," but "we are not warmongers" (Kehnemui Liss, 2007). At the 2008 CUFI meeting, members lobbied Congress to support the Iran Counter-Proliferation Act and the Iran Sanctions Enabling Act and to provide $2.5 billion in aid for Israel. It launched a movement to call for South Africa–like sanctions against Iran, Syria, Sudan, and North Korea.[18]

As Stephen Strang, one of the co-founders of CUFI, is also the publisher of *Charisma*, which has become a mouthpiece for the organization (S. Strang,

2009a). Strang routinely calls on *Charisma* readers to join CUFI (S. Strang, 2006a). Interestingly, while *Charisma* is probably the evangelical magazine that focuses most on issues of racial reconciliation, it is also the magazine that is the most uniformly pro-Zionist. Its critique of racism within evangelicalism does not extend to Arab or Palestinian Christians. The state of Israel regularly funds magazine inserts or even 100-page ads in *Charisma*. Many of these ads are targeted at encouraging evangelical tourism in Israel. One of them includes a magazine entitled *Charisma Israel* that appears simply to be part of the magazine. It features op-eds formatted to resemble *Charisma* op-eds, which focus on the importance of supporting Israel. In May 2009 *Charisma* ran a 250-page ad entitled "Will Israel Survive?" These inserts include a mix of proposed travel itineraries to Israel, the theological basis of Christian Zionism, and stories about the horrors of Hamas and Hezbollah (Bernis, 2008; Hickey, 2007; LeClaire, 2016a; V. Lowe, 2009a; Scimone, 2007, 2008).[19] In fact, the June 2010 issue of *Charisma* was split in two: one half was the regular issue and the other half was designed as a separate magazine dedicated to ads and articles supporting the Israeli Board of Tourism. *Charisma* regularly features John Hagee and virtually never includes any critique of Israeli policies. Especially since the election of Obama, almost every issue has a pro-Israel article in it (A. Gaines, 2006a). Indeed, the 2008 election issue of *Charisma*, which endorsed John McCain, included a special section on Israel. Entire issues are regularly devoted to Israel (Troy Anderson, 2015a; S. Strang, 2014). *Charisma* recently did a special "Standing with Israel" issue. The key focus remains a spiritual requirement to support Israel with the caveat: "To stand with Israel is not to oppose the Arab people as an entity nor to oppose the rights of Arabs living in Israel" (Hayford, 2013, 26).

At the same time, these pro-Zionist arguments intersect with the discourse of racial reconciliation. Glenn Plummer started the Fellowship of Israel and Black America to revive a relationship between Blacks and Jews. He describes Martin Luther King Jr. as a "black Zionist" and started a Martin Luther King Jr. Israel award to individuals who advance relationships between Black and Jewish people. Israel and the U.S. Embassy in Israel officially recognize this awards event, which is held in Israel. Plummer says, "I do believe that if we bless Jews openly, unapologetically and clearly, God is obligated to bless us. If I can get black Americans to bless Israel, God is obligated to bless my people" (G. Plummer, 2008, 17). His group has seventeen chapters in cities such as Detroit, Los Angeles, New York, Tampa, and Columbus, with an office in Israel. Similarly, the Hispanic Israel Leadership Coalition was formed to court Hispanic support for Israel (Akers, 2016).

As Ella Shohat has argued, Zionism relies on the logic of European racism that not only privileges Israelis over Palestinians but also Ashkenazi Jews over Sephardim. This logic is clear in the culturally racist argument made in a *Charisma* magazine article:

> Studies have shown that Ashkenazi Jews (those from Northern Europe) are highly intelligent.... Historically, the Jewish people have been both the most successful and the most persecuted of any ethnic group. Their business expertise has exalted them to the highest position in the global business community, producing top lawyers, skilled doctors and surgeons, and successful civil leaders.... Many books explaining why many Jewish people are gifted with high IQs, creative genius, financial skills and the ability to survive against the odds omit the one feature that has separated the devout Jews from all other nations—their belief that they have a special covenant with God. (Stone, 2009, 53–54)

The article does not explain why, if all Jews have a special covenant with God, only European Jews are "highly intelligent."

As mentioned, contemporary geopolitics often become predetermined within a Christian Zionist narrative that seems to foreclose possibilities for different kinds of political agendas. As stated in *Charisma*, Jerusalem is important "for only one possible reason: It is important to God and to His plans for the last days" (Bernis, 2009, 20). It published another article uncritical of Gershon Salomon of the Temple Mount Faithful Movement, who is trying to rebuild the third temple at the Temple Mount in Israel in order to usher in the Messiah who will defeat Israel's enemies. Some evangelicals think that this action will bring in the second coming, but others think it means that the Antichrist will inhabit this temple (Daigle, 2002b).

Not surprisingly, these kinds of stances have been critiqued even within evangelicalism for creating a self-fulfilling prophecy that ensures continued conflict in the area. This critique seems to be making some impact within these circles. It would seem that there has been some tempering of the rhetoric. Generally, the critiques have not been greeted positively. Jimmy Carter's book *Palestine: Peace Not Apartheid* (2007) was sharply denounced in *Christianity Today* (Aikman, 2007) (although Evangelicals for Middle East Understanding rebutted this critique in the letters to the editor).[20] *World* intimated that Carter is subsidized by Arab countries (J. Nelson, 2007d). The efforts of some mainline Christian denominations to critique or divest from Israel have also received sharp criticism.[21] For instance, the highest legislative body of the Presbyterian Church USA (PCUSA) voted 531–62 to begin a phased, selective divestment from multinational firms contributing to the Israeli occupation of Palestine. Two months later, it studied a similar stock-selling plan to protest the "ongoing occupation, home demolitions, settlement building, and the separation wall," which was critiqued by Jewish leaders as "an assault on the Jewish people" (K. Rutledge, 2004, 18). The Institute of Religion and Democracy sided with the Jewish critics. On September 27, 2004, it released a report that claimed that more than a third of church criticisms of human rights abuses focus on Israel but that there are no criticisms of countries such as China, North Korea, and Saudi Arabia (K. Rutledge, 2004). *World* also complained that PCUSA was meeting with Palestinian "terrorists" (Plowman, 2004b). And *Christianity Today* concurred that Israel was being unfairly singled out (Leveling the Investment Fund, 2006).

Despite these reactions to evangelical criticism of Zionism, it seems that the critique may be tempering some of the rhetoric of those who unconditionally support Israel. For instance, John Hagee, who previously has argued that those who do not support Israel will burn in hell, felt forced to temper some of his comments:

> I've read that CUFI is anti-peace, that we oppose any compromise with Israel's Arab neighbors, and that we really just want to start a war. As ridiculous as these allegations are, they demand a response. We must not permit our opponents to define us. . . . I want to be clear about this: We in CUFI want peace for the Jews and Arabs of the region every bit as much as we do for our own nation. We daily pray for such a peace. But until our prayers are answered with some fundamental changes on the ground, we cannot and will not ignore some disturbing realities. There is no evidence that giving more land to the Palestinians will bring peace any closer. (J. Hagee, 2007a, 6–7)

Benny Hinn (who is Palestinian) organized a lunch with fourteen evangelical leaders (including Ralph Reed, Richard Cizik, and Jonathan Falwell). His rationale: "We've had our arm around Israel for years. . . . It is time for us to put our other arm around you" (Spector, 2009, 107). *Charisma* ran article on Zionism's new face, though it is not clear what is new other than counterpropaganda about "Palestinian Christians," and saying that it allows religious freedom for Palestinians. The article is pro-justice and pro–religious freedom and a relationship between Christians and Jews, without mentioning the plight of Palestinians (J. Fletcher, 2012). And *Sojourners* noted that

40 percent of U.S. evangelical leaders have changed their thinking about Israel and Palestine over the past fifteen years, with the change being "a greater awareness of the struggles faced by the Palestinian people" (Beiler, 2015, 18). Thus, the tempering of this rhetoric suggests that the growing criticism of unconditional Zionism is having an impact. This critique includes a strand of conditional Zionists who are not prepared to defend Israel unconditionally.

Evangelical Critiques of Christian Zionism

Some sectors of evangelicalism espouse Christian Zionism, but with varying degrees of restraint. Some evangelicals more explicitly engage political considerations in their stances toward Palestine and hence oppose the complete liquidation of Palestine for security concerns because they believe that liquidating Palestine would destabilize the region. *World* news coverage seems to take the stance that a militant approach is just increasing Palestinian terrorism and devastating Israel's economy (M. Belz, 2001a, 2004d).[22] Particularly after Obama became president, *World*'s slant seemed to become less sympathetic to Palestine—arguing that easing the blockade of Gaza, for instance, will lead to the liquidation of Israel and suggesting that it is only Hamas and not Israel that has stood in the way of peace. It also ran an article that equated critiques of Israel with anti-Semitism and suggested that antioccupation organizing on college campuses is pro-Hitler (J. Nelson, 2010). Yet it still contends that "*World* has consistently supported Israel's right to exist while also reporting sympathetically on the plight of Palestinians in Gaza" (M. Olasky, 2010d). It has represented Palestinian perspectives sympathetically on the Israeli withdrawal from Gaza (J. Nelson, 2005). It also critiqued John Hagee's position on Israel: "Rather than give a blank check to even the most morally bankrupt governmental policy that might emerge from a present or future Knesset—whether it restricts Christian missions or oppresses Palestinians—the better way to aid Jews, it seems to me, would be to tell one the Good News" (Maynard, 1998). In an op-ed on Jerusalem, a *World* article rejected the idea that Palestinians should not be considered in the final deposition of Jerusalem. It should be a place for peace rather than extreme nationalism. In addition, cautioned *World*, let us not forget Arab Christians (C. Shenk, 1998). Mindy Belz asked, "What do Palestinians want?" in terms of issues of checkpoints, borders, and impacts on peoples from Palestine as well as the uprootedness of families that have lived there for generations (M. Belz, 2010f). Andrée Seu gave an even sharper critique of Zionism in a *World* op-ed:

The Palestinians have given us suicide bombers and the 1972 Munich Olympics massacre. The Israelis have given us the . . . Sabra and Shatilla massacres. If you have two political entities, both with their hands steeped in blood up to the elbows, would you confuse either party's cause with the cause of God? . . . As for jumping on the Zionist bandwagon, however, should we "help" God hasten His agenda by abetting the political ambitions of a secular nation that continues to this day in rebellion and unbelief? . . . How must Christian Palestinian students at the Bethlehem Bible College feel—who study through the tumult of tanks, choppers, water shortages, power outages, travel restrictions, and millions in property damage—when American Christians ignore them and give their hearts and dollars only to Israel? (Seu, 2005a)

Part of the difference between *World*'s and *Charisma*'s coverage of Israel, as *World* notes, is that it generally writes from a Reformed perspective that does not distinguish between the old and new covenants. Thus, it is not theologically tied to any presumptions of Israel's role in the end times, even as it may support Israel for geopolitical reasons (Abraham, 2005e).

Others contend that God's covenant with Israel is conditional upon its consistency with social justice principles or on its relationship with God (The Buzz, 2004; How Far Is Too Far?, 2002). For instance, Gerald McDermott expresses general support for Israel but also argues that there is not a one-to-one correspondence between the modern state of Israel and the Israel of biblical prophecy. While he suggests that God has a covenant relationship with Jewish people, and perhaps Israel by extension, this covenant is valid to the extent that Israel upholds its end of the covenant through a just relationship with Palestinians. He also questions the extent to which Israel can lay a religious claim to the land when its state is secular (McDermott, 2003). Interestingly, an editorial by John Piper in *World* states that, while God promised the descendants of Abraham the land of Israel and Israel was blessed by God, "neither of these facts leads necessarily to the endorsement of present-day Israel as the rightful possessor of all the disputed land. Israel may have such a right. And she may not. But that decision is not based on divine privilege" (Piper, 2002, 51).

Mark Harlan similarly argues that the covenant relationship between God and Israel is both conditional and unconditional: it is unconditionally open to all generations of Jewish people, but they will be cursed if they violate the terms of the covenant. He holds that the Law of Moses forbids "murder, theft, and coveting" (sins that he thinks the state of Israel is guilty of). "Possession of the land must bring blessing to non-Israelites and ultimately to the world" (Harlan, 2003, 85). He criticizes the racialized manner in which strict Christian Zionists liken Palestinians to irredeemable biblical Canaanites who simply need to be exterminated from the face of the earth.[23] To quote David Stern (a Messianic Jew who otherwise calls for unconditional support of Israel): "It cannot be stated rationally that the Palestinian Arabs today are in the category of the Canaanites.... Such an ethnic comparison expresses an unbiblical attitude of racism, nationalism, and hate which cannot be disguised by calling it 'faithfulness to God's promise'" (quoted in Harlan, 2003, 85).

Christianity Today took a similar position in outlining its official stance on Israel and Palestine: We "strongly support Israel's right to exist and defend itself. We also support the right of Arabs to fair treatment and to opportunity to live with dignity. It is not anti-Semitic to hold the Jewish state to biblical standards of righteousness ... and justice is in the best interest of Israel" (The Longest Hatred, 2004, 30). *Christianity Today* also ran an article distinguishing "biblical" versus "political" Zionists. It quoted Malcolm Hedding of the International Christian Embassy Jerusalem, a Christian Zionist group, as remaining neutral on "political" issues, particularly the withdrawal of Jewish settlers from Gaza Strip that began in 2005. Its position is that Israel will inherit all the land promised to the Jewish people "when the Messiah comes [again]. Not before. We can't be more interested in land recovery than in spiritual restoration" (Alford, 2005b, 46). It has also run articles critiquing evangelicals for uncritically supporting U.S. and Israeli policies in the name of prophecy fulfillment (Marshall, 2006).

Evangelicals must address the theological contradiction of supporting the claims of a Jewish-only state against the claims of Christian Palestinians. J. Lee Grady writes in *Charisma:* "It is my duty to defend Israel ... [but] has anybody noticed that there are Arab Christians in Israel who also need our support?" (J. L. Grady, 2008, 8). Grady complains that anyone who calls attention to the plight of Palestinian Christians is branded a heretic. "But Christian solidarity with the Jewish people should not deprive another group of God's love and acceptance. God does not show favoritism. He loves Jews and Arabs alike" (J. L. Grady, 2008, 8). Consequently, an increasing number of articles feature Palestinian or Arab Christians (Gavlak, 2005b; Gill, 2000; Letters, 2002b; T. Morgan, 2010; Neff, 2010; Walker, 2010d). It appears that evangelical venues have had tremendous difficulty finding Arab or Palestinian Christians who will offer the unqualified support for the state of Israel that would help them to resolve this contradiction.²⁴ Consequently, by featuring Palestinian Christians at all, they must address at least some critiques of the state of Israel.²⁵

A *Charisma* article interviewed evangelical Palestinians who largely framed Israel as the problem rather than Palestinian Muslims. "Many traditional and some evangelical Christians consider being Palestinian a unifying force for Christians and Muslims in the territories, with their common enemy being the 'occupier' Israel" (Schiavi, 2008b, 32). Furthermore, "Christian Palestinians, almost without exception, say they are neglected by the church at large, especially by Christian Zionists who come to Israel to support the Jewish state" (Schiavi, 2008b, 62). Pastor Abu Saada stated in an interview: "Yes, we have to stand for the right of Israel to exist, but that is not on the expense of the Palestinian people" (Schiavi, 2008b, 62). In fact, "Arab Christian leaders have stated their loyalty to the Palestinian cause" (E. R. Fletcher, 2000, 67). For instance, Habib Khoury of Shepherds Tours & Travel Company is quoted in an article showcasing evangelical tourism to Israel: "Christians of the Holy Land can be Palestinians, and we are suffering the same as our Palestinian Muslim brothers. Occupation does not differentiate between Christian and Muslim, and a pilgrimage to the Holy Land at this time is very important" (M. Smith, 2002, 34). One article in *Charisma* (which generally tends to have an extremely pro-Christian Zionist perspective) featured the views of Salim Munayer, an Arab Christian in Israel. He argued that U.S. Christians have a superficial understanding of the Middle East, promote anti-Arab sentiment, and should stop expressing love for Israel at the expense of other groups. "To love the Jewish people doesn't mean to hate the Arab people. Jesus died for all" (Daigle, 2002a, 42). He called on Christians to stop supporting right-wing Israeli leaders who do not act according to biblical principles and concluded: "The land belongs to God at the end of the day. We don't worship the land; we worship the Lord" (Daigle, 2002a, 42).

Charisma ran another article entitled "Arab Christians Take a Hard Line on Israel." Interestingly, none of the Arab Christians interviewed actually took a hard line on Israel, suggesting that any critique of Israel is hardline from *Charisma*'s perspective. Rather, their perspectives were similar to those of Ehab El Kharrat, an Egyptian Christian in Cairo, who says: "Nobody has any right to kill civilians, even in occupied land. However, Israel does occupy a land that belongs to Palestinians [referring to Gaza and the West Bank]" (quoted in B. Bruce, 2002, 16). Even archconservative *World* ran an article critiquing Israel from the perspective of Palestinian Christians (M. Belz, 2002a). Bob Jones III (the writer most sympathetic to Palestinians at that time), while not necessarily sympathetic to the Palestinian Authority, argued that Israel has turned the West Bank into a prison through check points and other oppressive measures. He asks: "To what extent do the Israeli government and the Palestinian Authority allow, protect, and guarantee the religious rights of persons of different faiths?" (B. Jones III, 2003b, 18).

The unconditional support by evangelical Christians in America has encouraged Israeli policy for the past fifty years. In this process, the church has supported oppression, occupation, demolition of houses, strangulation of the Palestinian economy, and the denial of basic human rights (B. Jones III, 2003b, 19).

Christianity Today asserts: "For these [Palestinian] Christians, today's Palestinian struggle against Israel is the struggle of Jesus against an unjust Rome" (E. R. Fletcher, 2000, 67).

Gary Burge further asserts that, ironically, Christians are being driven away from the Holy Land in the interests of Zionism. "The situation among the Palestinian Christians is becoming so critical that a virtual exodus of people is leaving the country" (Burge, 2003, 220). He notes that Bethlehem was historically 75 percent Christian and is now 30 percent Christian or less. Because of Zionism "we may witness the 'emptying' of Christianity from the Holy Land for the first time in two thousand years" (Burge, 2003, 221).

Christianity Today published a study, conducted by University of Akron's John Green, to determine whether evangelical leaders are monolithically pro-Israel. According to Green, 60 percent of them back Israel over Palestine, but 52 percent favor a Palestinian state. The majority thought that Palestinians do have legitimate claims but want to be assured that the fulfillment of their claims does not threaten Israel. For instance, Richard Land, president of the Southern Baptist Ethics and Religious Liberty Commission, said that he "would argue that nothing could be more secure for Israel than creating a viable, self-sustaining Palestinian state that agrees to live in peace and agrees to suppress terrorism" (Road Blocks and Voting Blocs, 2003). In his book, Land outlines a biblically based approach for political involvement, arguing that evangelicals who do not support the idea that Israel has a special relationship with God have a legitimate perspective. He calls for all evangelicals to support "an independent, democratic Palestinian state in the West Bank and Gaza" (Land, 2007, 208). He reported a statement posted on the Knox Theological Seminary website signed by 100 mostly Presbyterian and Reformed leaders that compared the "bad Christian theology" that "contributed to the tragic cruelty of the Crusades" to the "bad Christian theology" that "is today attributing to Israel a divine mandate to conquer and hold Palestine, with the consequence that the Palestinian people are marginalized and regarded as virtual 'Canaanites'" (Road Blocks and Voting Blocs, 2003, 32–33). *Christianity Today* also reviewed two movies that critique Christian Zionism, including one by a Christian pastor, *With God on Our Side* (Avery, 2010). Moss Ntlha of the general secretariat of Evangelical Alliance in South Africa said, "Between you and me—I am black, and you are white South African Jews—who do you think has more credibility in deciding whether or not this is apartheid?" (Beiler, 2015, 18).

World Vision, one of the most prominent evangelical charities in the world with a budget of over $1 billion, is involved in thousands of relief projects globally and has become active in advocating for human rights in Israel through its Jerusalem office. World Vision works with Palestinian and Israeli human-rights organizations. The organization previously felt constrained from taking a political stance, but, after working in Israel and confronting its record of human-rights violations, concluded that it needed to challenge this injustice. This led to it being attacked by some evangelicals for "contributing to a growing pro-Palestinian, anti-Israel bias among some Christians," in keeping with its tendency to be "always pro-Palestinian, pro-abortion, and pro-homosexuality" (Troy Anderson, 2015b, 40).[26] North Coast Calvary Chapel hosted World Vision's "Hope for the Holy Land" tour aimed, according to its critics, to "present the Palestinian narrative." In actuality, this tour always features Palestinian and Israeli speakers and reaches thousands of evangelicals each year. Mae Cannon previously coordinated these tours as well as trips to Israel and Palestine to provide more balanced tours about conditions in the area. Chuck Smith, the founder of Calvary Chapel, said that he was shocked to see them have "an anti-Israel speaker" (Calvary Chapel Founder Rebukes Arab-Israeli Church Event, 2013, 27). In fact, the Hope for the Holy Land Tour was well received by the churches that hosted it, which came from across the theological and political perspective. Mae Cannon later left World Vision but continues the same work through Churches for Middle East Peace.

Other evangelicals take even a more critical stance of Christian Zionism. Some evangelicals support supercessionist theology, which holds that God no longer has a covenant with the Jewish people and hence has no particular relationship with the state of Israel. Some members of the Reformed tradition, particularly Reconstructionist, Peterist, and some sectors of militant fundamentalist thought, hold that the church has taken the place of Israel in the covenant relationship with God. Thus, the state of Israel no longer figures in the eschatological drama. Some dispensationalists have criticized this as "theological anti-Semitism" or "nazism," which "manifests itself in both contempt for the Jewish people and the idea of replacement (the church takes the place of National Israel). God has no further use for Israel as a nation or people" (Juster, 2008, 137; see also Rausch, 1988, 59). In response Richard Mouw contends that dispensationalism rests on a logic of anti-Semitism. That is, dispensationalists often direct their affection toward an idealized Judaism. They support an abstract version of what they believe to be a divine plan for the Jews more than they support individual Jewish people. At the very least, their theology of Judaism has not regularly manifested itself in active efforts to eradicate anti-Semitism (Mouw, 2001, 75).

Certainly, it is the case that some strands of anti-Zionism are based largely on anti-Semitism and a rejection of Judaism. One example is the work of Charles Provan, who writes in *The Church Is Israel Now*:

> During this century, Christians have been told over and over that "God has an unconditional love for Old Testament Israel," by which it is meant that God's love is directed toward persons racially descended from Abraham, regardless of faith or obedience. Membership in Israel, therefore, is viewed as a matter of race, not faith.
>
> *The Church Is Israel Now* demonstrates that the Bible totally repudiates this racialist viewpoint. Being a member of Israel in the Old Testament was dependent upon faith and obedience to God. When the Israelites obeyed God, God loved them. But when the Israelites turned from him, He hated them, stripping them of their Israelite status. After centuries of Israelite rebellion against God, culminating in their rejection of Jesus the Messiah, the titles, attributes and blessings of Israel were transferred to all who accept Jesus Christ as Lord and Savior, and to no one else, regardless of Abrahamic descent. The Church is Israel Now. (Provan, 1987, back cover)

Provan, in addition to his theological anti-Judaism, was involved in Holocaust revisionism, although he was sharply critiqued within these circles because he did not deny that the Holocaust happened even though he thought the death numbers were exaggerated (Roddy, 2000). Anti-Semitism can be seen in this letter to *World*: "Israel has no tolerance for Christians, so why should we support them? The Judaism today has little to do with the fulfillment of prophecy, as so many things, it is, in fact, the very Judaism that Jesus condemned" (Mailbag, 2007a, 49).

Other supercessionists, however, center the plight of Palestinians in their rhetoric. Their concern is less with demonizing Judaism than it is with challenging the Zionist theology that justifies the oppression of Palestinian peoples. Strait Gate Ministries, for instance, argues that Christians and Muslims coexisted peacefully until the growth of Zionism. They argue that evangelical Zionism is contributing to the genocide of Palestinians. For instance, Spotlight, a Peterist website, featured an interview with Grace Halsell, one of the earliest evangelicals to oppose Zionism. She describes how she became involved in this work:

> One day I started living with the Jewish settlers who were taking land illegally from the Palestinians and many of these Jews were Americans who had moved over there from Brooklyn, N.Y. One of these was Bobby Brown, a third generation American who had moved to the Middle East. Sitting in this illegal colony outside Bethlehem, I heard Brown say, "You know God gave us all this land and the Palestinians all have to leave."
>
> That hit me very hard because I had to ask myself what I believed as a Christian. Was God in the real estate business? Was he really giving land and taking it away from the people who had been living there for about 2,000 years?
>
> So that question in my mind stayed with me and then later I began to take these tours with Jerry Falwell and meet Christians who condoned what Bobby Brown was doing, which was taking guns and illegally confiscating land from the owners who lived there. This led to this latest book, which is called *Forcing God's Hand: Why Millions Pray for a Quick Rapture*. . . .
>
> I did document the fact that Israel had given Jerry Falwell a jet airplane, which is a nice gift. He uses it to go around and he uses that jet, politically, I would say. I personally heard Jerry Falwell thank Israeli leader Moshe Arens when I was traveling with Falwell. He didn't know I was writing a book, but I traveled with two of his delegations that went to Israel. (Valentine, 2000)

Prominent evangelical leader Richard Mouw uses a combination of supercessionist and conditional covenant logic to make similar critiques. On the one hand, he contends that Israel's covenant with God is conditional:

> I am especially disturbed by what I see as a refusal on the part of many dispensationalists to criticize the policies of Israeli governments. . . .

Christians in Arab countries have some good reasons to resent the policies of Israeli governments. Unfortunately, dispensationalists often obscure these issues. They are often so caught up in an enthusiasm for bible prophecy scenarios that they take it as obligatory to support the Israeli cause no matter what.... Suppose that the establishment of the modern state of Israel is indeed a fulfillment of prophecy.... None of this exempts us from assessing and criticizing when necessary, the details of Israeli policies. The Old Testament prophets make it clear that the nation of Israel will never be truly blessed by God unless she pursues justice. (Mouw, 2001, 74)

At the same time, he seems influenced to some degree by supercessionism:

This ethnocentric redemptive economy of the old covenant was never viewed—contrary to what I was taught by dispensationalists—as the final arrangement.... I must quickly add that this does not rule out the acknowledgment that God still honors a continuing commitment to the specific ethnic people who served as special agents under the old covenant. But this commitment is to a people who, already in ancient times, were encouraged to anticipate a day when God's Spirit would be poured out on all flesh.... There was never a time when the Israel of God had a right to think the covenant blessings were her exclusive property. (Mouw, 2001, 76)

It should be noted that Mouw makes a similar critique of Christian ideas of a "Christian America" that would hold that the United States has a special relationship with God (Mouw, 2001, 72–73).

Other evangelicals, such as Colin Chapman, reject supercessionism but still hold that Christian Zionism is not biblically sound. While making the biblical argument for rejecting Christian Zionism, his stance is based more on the framework of social justice. Chapman's *Whose Promised Land?* uses quite sophisticated rhetoric to challenge Christian Zionism. He does try to appeal to evangelicals who unquestioningly support the state of Israel. He is also careful to avoid rhetoric that could contribute to anti Judaism and anti-Semitism. But then in the end he is arguing that the state of Israel is a colonial project. While *Jewish* people may have some theological justification to support Zionism, there is no biblical justification for Christian Zionism. He demonstrates the colonial nature of the Zionist movement through use of historical documents by those involved in it. While anti-Semitism is an issue of great importance, particularly to Christians who have perpetuated it, he contends that Zionism, rather than representing the *cure* for anti-Semitism, is actually the natural corollary to it (C. Chapman, 2002).

Stephen Sizer critiques Christian Zionism on both theological and political grounds. He articulates covenant theology as an alternative to replacement and dispensationalist theology (although covenant theology sounds similar to replacement theology). Elsewhere, he suggests that replacement theology is a caricature of covenant theology proffered by Christian Zionists. In any case he contends that God has only had one group of people: those who recognize Jesus as their Messiah. He states that Jewish people have a unique role in history and prays that all Jews will come to follow Jesus. Since God loves all people, it is the role of Christians to work for peace for both Jewish and Palestinian peoples (Sizer, 2005, 261–62). Politically, he argues that Christian Zionists' belief in Jews as chosen people causes them to unconditionally support Israel despite its "racist and apartheid policies" (Sizer, 2005, 252). He charges that Zionist ideology promotes the demonization of Arabs, including Arab Christians. Because Zionist ideology is funded on the presupposition of apocalypse, Zionist activists refuse to work for peace and may consequently bring about an apocalypse as a self-fulfilling prophecy (Sizer, 2005, 206–53).[27]

Timothy Weber, president of Memphis Theological Seminary, has also extensively critiqued Christian Zionism. He does not directly challenge its theology but does note that Christian Zionism and dispensationalist theology contribute to a lack of concern for the well-being of Arab and Palestinian peoples, including Palestinian Christians. He further asserts that Christian Zionism also coexists with an anti-Judaism/anti-Semitism in which Jews are positioned as those who should eternally suffer in order to fulfill God's prophecies. In addition, because relatively few numbers of Jews will actually survive the End Times, this ideology frequently divides good from bad Jews, who are then blamed for the rise of the Antichrist (T. Weber, 2004).

Donald Wagner, one of the founders of Evangelicals for Middle East Understanding, has been very involved in trying to counter Christian Zionism within evangelical Christianity, encouraging magazines to reconsider their editorial policies on Israel. He also directed the Center for Middle East Studies at North Park Seminary until he was fired (possibly for his non-Zionist convictions). Gary Burge of Wheaton College also works with Evangelicals for Middle East Understanding and wrote *Whose Land? Whose Promise?* His work centers on the unjust treatment of Palestinians by Israel's "apartheid state" (Burge, 2003, 263) and the oppression created by Israeli occupation of Palestine. He notes that the very constitution of the Israeli state is fundamentally premised on the expulsion of Palestinians from their lands (Burge, 2003, 136). He explores the various aspects of occupation, including home demolitions, security checkpoints, arrests and detention, and thefts of land and water resources. He questions the idea that anyone, including Jews, has a claim to any lands. Rather, he argues, all land is God's land. People's ability to remain on any land must depend on how they treat the other inhabitants of that land (Burge, 2003, 75–79). He similarly argues that the covenant with Israel is conditional:

> The Bible is not ambiguous when it describes how God's people must live when they reside in his land. They must pursue justice and integrity at all costs.... To abuse the non-Israelites is to neglect God's commitment to the underprivileged and the alien.... And to mistreat the alien by taking his land places Israel's inheritance in jeopardy. While the covenant promises to Abraham are forever, those who inherit and enjoy these blessings must live righteously in order to keep them. (Burge, 2003, 92)

Burge contends that "unbelieving Israel still holds a place of honor" (Burge, 2003, 188). However, Israel has no exclusive claim to the land because the promises of God now go to all Christians. "God's people are called to infiltrate the empires of the world, bringing the gospel of Jesus Christ to all, regardless of history, race, or religious persuasion" (Burge, 2003, 189). In *Perspectives*, a reformed journal, John Hubers of the Reformed Church in America provides an extensive critique of Christian Zionism, which he says trades on the myth of America as a brave pioneering people defeating "savage" Natives. This ideology holds that "any attack on America is an attack on freedom." He critiques this ideology as "ethnic cleansing" (Hubers, 2004, 13) and argues that dispensationalism combined with the myth of American exceptionalism is the foundation for Christian Zionism. According to Hubers, Christian Zionism disavows the oppression of Palestinian Christians to the point that many American Christians are unaware that they exist. He notes, however, that Dr. Riad Jarjour, general secretary of the Middle East Council of Churches, visited the General Synod of the Reformed Church of America (RCA) in 2002. After this visit, the synod voted to support a resolution calling for Israel to return to its pre-1967 border, which was remarkable because the RCA does not generally pass such political resolutions. He calls for more exchange between evangelical (not just mainline) Christians and Palestinian Christians. He also recommends that people engage in alternative tours to visit with Palestinians in particular.

Some Christian Right groups also do not take a specifically pro-Zionist perspective. For instance, the Fellowship led by Douglas Coe, which received much liberal coverage in 2010 as a "stealth" Christian organization of public officials shaping U.S. policy, has not adopted a pro-Zionist stance. It was involved in the Camp David Accords and has sponsored events with Yasser Arafat (Spector, 2009, 106).[28] And in 2002 fifty-eight evangelical leaders wrote a letter to then President George W. Bush to challenge his policy regarding Israel and the notion that evangelicals necessarily support Zionism. Part of the text of the letter reads:

> We . . . encourage you to move boldly forward so that the legitimate aspirations of the Palestinian people for their own state may be realized. . . . We urge you to provide the leadership necessary for peacemaking in the Middle East by vigorously opposing injustice, including the continued unlawful and degrading Israeli settlement movement. The theft of Palestinian land, the destruction of Palestinian homes and fields is surely one of the major causes of the strife that has resulted in terrorism and the loss of so many Israeli and Palestinian lives. The continued Israeli military occupation that daily humiliates ordinary Palestinians is also having disastrous effects on the Israeli soul. Mr. President, the American evangelical community is not a monolithic bloc in full and firm support of present Israeli policy. (Burge, 2003, 256)

While John Hagee and Gary Bauer attempted to frame the leaders as marginal to evangelicalism, in fact they included many prominent people (Bauer, 2007), such as John Perkins, Eugene Rivers, several representatives of the National Association of Evangelicals, Richard Mouw and Glen Stassen of Fuller Seminary, Ronald Nikkel, president of Prison Fellowship, John Ortberg of the famous Willow Creek Community Church, and Philip Yancey. In 2007 thirty-four evangelical leaders urged the president to promote peace in Palestine and critiqued the notion that Israel had carte blanche to pursue its interests. Blessing Israel can mean rejecting "the notion of a Greater Israel that encompasses the occupied territories" (Spector, 2009, 108). Signees included David Neff (*Christianity Today*) and Joel Hunter and Don Argue (formerly of National Association of Evangelicals).

There has been less support for the Boycott, Divestment, and Sanctions

(BDS) campaign gaining traction in the general movement for Palestinian liberation (Beiler, 2015, 18). However, some, such as Killjoy Prophets both supported BDS and challenged CUFI directly:

> Let's give Bethlehem, the land of Jesus' birth, a gift this year. Let's resolve in 2015 to speak truth to power. Standing on the sideline and shaking our heads as CUFI supports the destruction of Palestinian communities is unacceptable, and for that we must repent. Palestinian Christians have discerned it is time for change and asked for our help. We as Christians who love justice and seek shalom owe this to ALL Palestinians regardless of their faith. Let's begin a movement to speak strongly to CUFI. This stand will take courage, but the world, especially the Christians in Bethlehem: ask if you have faith in the face of empire. (Killjoy Prophets, 2014a)

Racialization of Judaism

Christian Zionism obviously rests upon the racialization of Islam. However, it equally rests on the racialization of Judaism, even as it is ostensibly supportive of Jewish peoples. On the one hand, Christian Zionism holds that Israel must remain a Jewish-only state. On the other hand, evangelicals generally also hold that Jewish people must convert to Christianity to attain salvation. As Timothy Weber notes, many dispensationalist groups also founded missions to Jewish organizations that specifically targeted Jewish people for conversion between the 1880s and 1910s (T. Weber, 2004, 118). Evangelicals often still hold to the need to evangelize to Jewish people, including those in Israel.[29] The Lausanne Consultation on Jewish Evangelism (LCJE) reaffirmed the necessity of faith in Jesus as God incarnate at a meeting in Helsinki on August 7–12, 2003. According to Kai Kjaer-Hansen, international coordinator of the LCJE, "If Jesus is not the Messiah of the Jewish people, how can he possibly be the Messiah for the rest of us?" (Consultation Reaffirms Jewish Evangelism, 2003, 36). The World Evangelical Alliance released a statement in March that called on all evangelicals to share the love of Jesus Christ with Jewish people (interestingly, a news notice for this appeared in *Charisma* in the same paragraph that says "80 percent of American Christians still believe they have a 'moral and biblical obligation' to support the state of Israel") (News Briefs, 2008b).[30] The Southern Baptist Convention, the Presbyterian Church in America, and the Lutheran Church–Missouri Synod have adopted statements of conviction on the necessity of Jewish evangelism (Mohler, 1999). The Southern Baptist Convention also published a booklet called *Days of Awe: Prayer for Jews*, which calls churches to do special prayers for Jewish people during the first ten days of the Jewish calendar, from Rosh Hashanah to Yom Kippur. In 1999 the SBC organized against both "two-covenant theology" (which holds that Jewish people have a separate covenant with God and therefore do not need to accept Christ) and replacement theology (which, as described previously, defines the church as the New Israel that replaces old Israel) (Wagner, 2003). And Southern Baptist Bailey Smith at a 1980 Religious Roundtable national affairs briefing in Dallas issued the infamous comment: "God Almighty does not hear the prayer of a Jew."[31]

If we understand racism through Ruth Wilson Gilmore's definition as subjecting peoples to premature death, we can understand this theological anti-Judaism as a form of racism that frames the historic oppression of Jewish peoples as a result of their unwillingness to accept Jesus as their messiah. "If the Sanhedrin had accepted Jesus as the Messiah, then Israel would have been 'saved,' or rescued, from 2,000 years of earthly judgments, calamities, and persecutions. The temple would not have been destroyed in AD 70. There would have been no Crusades in the Holy Land, no pogroms in Russia, and no Holocaust in Nazi-dominated Europe. None of these events would ever have happened" (Israeli, 2001, 6). *World* featured a review of David Klinghoffer's *Why the Jews Rejected Jesus* (2006). This book argues that if Jews had embraced Jesus, the Jesus movement would have remained a Jewish sect. There would be no Christian Europe, and Islam would have taken over their countries, so we "should thank the Jews for their decision to cleave to their ancestral religion instead of embracing the rival teachings of Jesus and his followers" (M. Olasky, 2005e, 48). Olasky does not concur with that, but says it shows "God's providence does work out in surprising ways" (M. Olasky, 2005e, 48). It is the death of Jewish people, both historically and predicted to occur in the End Times, which enables Christian life.

Timothy Weber argues that this complicated attitude about Judaism and Jewish peoples follows from dispensationalist thought. On one hand, Jews are God's chosen people. On the other hand, only a relatively small number of Jewish people will actually accept Christ at the end. The majority will collaborate with the Antichrist. Thus, dispensationalist thought often differentiates good Jews from bad Jews. Weber traces how many of the key figures in the development of Christian Zionism within the United States—such as Arno Gaebelein, James Gray of Moody Bible Institute, Gerald Winrod, and Baptist leader William Bell Riley—actually believed in the veracity of the

Protocols of the Elders of Zion (the infamous manuscript that supposedly detailed Jewish attempts to take over the world) and promoted it (T. Weber, 2004, 130–37). While a fragment of the Jewish population would be saved, the rest were involved in supporting Bolshevism and other Satan-inspired conspiracies that would give rise to the Antichrist. Consequently, many of these figures such as Gaebelein and Gray initially supported Hitler because they saw him taking necessary steps to stop Bolshevism. Eventually, when Hitler's genocidal actions became apparent, Christian Zionists articulated the persecution as part of God's prophecy, even as they condemned Hitler. "God intended the Jews to suffer, but God would also deal with those through whom the suffering came" (T. Weber, 2004, 147). Through the suffering and death of Jewish peoples, Christian peoples can be saved.

In some sectors, evangelicals have tempered their insistence on Jewish evangelism while still maintaining this commitment to maintain alliances with Jewish groups. For instance, Roberta Combs, executive director of the Christian Coalition, couches Christian support for Israel in terms of appreciation for Judaism's contribution to Christianity: "Christian support for Israel signifies an appreciation for the influence of the Jewish people in the foundation of Christianity, and stands in opposition to the terrorism against Israel" (Christian Coalition, 2002b). Similarly *World* devoted an issue to promoting Jewish-Christian relations because "Jews and Christians face a common threat in radical Islam" (M. Olasky, 2002a, 8). This article, unlike those on Christian-Muslim relations, stresses the commonalities rather than the differences between Judaism and Christianity. It critiques Christianity for its role in the Inquisition and seems to applaud Jewish people for maintaining their separate religious identity in the face of Christian persecution (M. Olasky, 2002a, 18). However, the bulk of the issue is devoted to highlighting Jewish people throughout history who have converted to Christianity through a twenty-page timeline (M. Olasky, 2002a, 33–55). The issue ends with an editorial by John Piper, who defends Jewish evangelism: "There is no doubt that many people in Christendom have treated Jews badly over the centuries and often fostered a horrible attitude of anti-Semitism. That we repudiate, for the same reason we repudiate the call to abandon efforts to win Jewish faith in Jesus Christ. . . Jesus Christ is so central to Judaism that there is no salvation without Him" (M. Olasky, 2002a, 55). A reader response concurs: "If Jesus is the only way, but our liberal friends don't want to offend our Jewish friends with the gospel, how will they be saved? Being offended is not as bad as ending up in hell" (Mailbox, 2002, 30). Richard Mouw argues that evangelism to Jewish people is an evangelical requirement. Yet he also encourages Christians to appreciate the spiritual contributions of Judaism and be sensitive to thinking about how to "evangelize Jews after the Holocaust" (Mouw, 1997, 12). He further notes: "I am indeed firmly committed to Jewish evangelism . . . I do also have a deep respect for the Jewish people. And there is indeed a kind of 'irreconcilable tension' in trying to hold this all together. . . . I have chosen to live with the tension" (Mouw, 2001, 70). He did hold a conference on religion and politics with the American Jewish Committee (which opposes evangelistic outreach to Jewish people) in January 1997, which was criticized by Messianic Jewish peoples (who accept evangelical Christianity but maintain a commitment to "cultural" Judaism) (Carnes, 1997).

In addition, some prominent evangelical leaders and organizations contend that Jewish peoples do not need to convert to Christianity. Prominent Charismatic leader John Hagee argues that Christians have no duty to evangelize Jews, but they do have a responsibility to support them. He says that Jewish people have a special place in God's plan and that "all of Israel will be saved" (quoted in Douglas, 2004, 51). "Gentiles are commanded to treat Jewish people lovingly until the revelation of Jesus to them. . . . It is not possible to say, 'I am a Christian,' and not love the Jewish people. . . . God has an eternal covenant with the land of Israel, and Israel needs no one's permission to do what's best for the Jewish people" (Douglas, 2004, 51). At the 2007 CUFI Summit, Hagee emphasized that he was "not interested in converting Jews." "I can assure you that eschatology has nothing to do with our support for Israel" (D. Hagee, 2007, 20). This dual covenant theology holds that the status of Israel is actually superior to the status of the church, and the primary purpose of the church is to support Israel (Sizer, 2005, 136; Spector, 2009, 177). But this perspective is becoming more prevalent in evangelicalism today. According to *Christianity Today*, 64 percent of white evangelicals say that Judaism can lead to eternal life (Olsen, 2009a).

Stephen Spector asserts that Hagee later disavowed this "dual covenant" position in 2006, claiming that Hagee's position today is as follows: "When we're standing in Jerusalem and the messiah is coming down the street, one of us is going to have a very major theological adjustment to make. But until that time, let's walk together in support of Israel and in defense of the Jewish people, because Israel needs our help" (Spector, 2009, 177).

Interestingly, John McCain was pressured to drop Hagee's endorsement because he was charged with anti-Semitism. Hagee was accused of saying that God had used Hitler as an instrument (even though Hagee is probably one of the most vociferous advocates against anti-Semitism within evangelical circles). But, as Timothy Weber notes, this position has been fairly representative of dispensationalist thought. "Dispensationalists could condemn anti-Semites such as Adolf Hitler yet still argue that they fit into God's plan for Israel as punishment for their past sins and a catalyst for their desire for a home of their own" (T. Weber, 2004, 17).

At the same time, the state of Israel has often found it politically expedient to appeal to the interests of Christian evangelicalism to promote tourism and generate political support, even at the expense of defending Jewish people from Christian anti-Judaism. Many Jewish Zionists have also taken up the charge to defend evangelicalism. Donald Feder, *Boston Herald* writer and columnist, started Jews against Anti-Christian Defamation in April 2005. The major point of cooperation was identified as same-sex marriage and Israel.

> As American Jews, we view attacks on Christians basically as attacks on biblical morality. . . . By and large, Israel today is getting more support from Christians than from the Jewish community. Now, I want to make it clear that this is not our way of thanking Christians for supporting Israel, although we do appreciate Christian support. If evangelical Christians weren't pro-Israel, then the Jewish state would really be in a perilous position. . . . I hope it will raise the level of awareness of what seem to be growing attacks on Christians in a country that was founded by Christians and the tenets of Christianity. We're saying that if Christians fail, America will fail. So we all have a stake in this. (quoted in Guthrie, 2005, 17)

Michael Medved similarly states:

> The truth remains that the greatest Jew-haters of our time—Hitler, Stalin, and Islamo-Fascist terrorists—have been either pagans or Muslims. Today's devout Christians—particularly Christian evangelicals—are far more likely to bless Jews and Israel than to threaten us. In part, this Jewish-Christian coalition continues to grow because we face common enemies in the Islamic world, and in part it thrives because we share common deliverers—the United States of America and the God of Abraham who has blessed this magnificent nation beyond all measure. (Medved, 2005, 32)

As mentioned previously, religious persecution activist Michael Horowitz frequently contends that Christians are the most persecuted group in the world. The American Israel Public Affairs Committee has established a liaison office to work with evangelical organizations. Leaders from the Anti-Defamation League and the American Jewish Committee, while often critical of evangelical domestic policies, generally welcome evangelical support on Israel. For instance, David Harris of the American Jewish Committee stated that "the end of times may come tomorrow, but Israel hangs in the balance today" (quoted in Mearsheimer and Walt, 2007, 137). Nathan Perlmutter, formerly of the Anti-Defamation League, similarly argued: "Jews can live with all the domestic priorities of the Christian Right, on which liberal Jews differ so radically, because none of these concerns is as important as Israel" (quoted in Mearsheimer and Walt, 2007, 137).

Meanwhile evangelical groups also have put political interests over religious interests. Fifty Christian organizations and churches working in Israel made a joint statement promising not to carry out missionary activity in Israel. "We believe that the covenant God concluded with the people of Israel was never revoked. We deeply respect the Jewish people in their identity and integrity and will therefore not engage in activities which have as their intention to alienate them from their tradition and community." It praised Israel's "enlightened, democratic" policies (The White Flag, 1998, 10). The International Fellowship of Jews and Christians was formed by Rabbi Yechiel Eckstein, who "wants Jews to trust evangelicals, and evangelicals to love Israel" (J. Kennedy, 2009, 32). The organization contends that "it's imperative that Jews in Israel recognize evangelicals as their most reliable ally in fighting radical Islam and terrorism" (J. Kennedy, 2009, 35). After Bailey Smith made his previously cited comment that God does not hear the prayers of a Jew, Eckstein brought him to Israel; Smith later apologized. This group works with the Israel Ministry of Tourism. Of its seventy employees, 90 percent are Christian. The organization opposes Christian evangelism efforts that target Jews specifically. Jack Hayford withdrew his endorsement of the organization when it made remarks critical of Messianic Judaism. Eagles' Wings disavows evangelism all together. Bridges for Peace and International Christian Embassy Jerusalem (ICEJ) similarly does not engage in evangelism but will share faith if people ask. Christian Friends of Israel says it does not try to convert Jews: "We believe that Jesus is the promised Messiah for the Jewish People . . . but redemption is God's responsibility" (Spector, 2009, 123).

According to evangelical scholar Stephen Sizer, groups such as the International Christian Embassy and Bridges for Peace are indistinguishable from other right-wing Israeli lobbying groups. Bridges for Peace produces the *Dispatch from Jerusalem* magazine as well as a monthly *Israeli Teaching Letter* on Christianity's Hebraic roots and disseminates weekly email updates. It focuses on building political support for Israel within evangelical Christian communities. It also has a practical ministry, involving foodbanks, adoption programs, and rescue programs for Jews from the Soviet Union. Its material says: "Don't just read about prophecy when you can be part of it" (T. Weber, 2004, 225). Bridges for Peace, which also eschews Jewish evangelism, was founded in the early 1970s by Dr. G. Douglas Young in order to facilitate Jewish immigration and bridge evangelical support for Israel (Burge, 2003, 245). In fact, ICEJ has diplomatic status in Honduras and Guatemala and has been implicated in facilitating the funding of U.S.-backed Contras during the 1980s (Sizer, 2005, 22fn.21). The organization was founded in Jerusalem by a group of Christian Zionists when many nations moved their embassies from Jerusalem to Tel Aviv after Israel annexed East Jerusalem in 1980. It provides social services to Jerusalem, refers to the occupied territories by the biblical names of Judea and Samaria, and hosts annual Feast of Tabernacles conferences, regularly attended by 5,000 Christians, to focus on the prophetic role of Israel. Its overall goal is to provide conditional support to Israel against any pressures to return lands to Palestinians and to promote evangelical tourism, but it does not engage in Jewish evangelism. It also has sponsored four International Christian Zionist Congresses, held in 1985, 1988, 1996, and 2001 (T. Weber, 2004, 216–17). Of course, these groups provide theological justifications for their politically convenient policies on evangelism. According to ICEJ, Jewish people "remain elect of God, and without the Jewish nation His redemptive purposes for the world will not be completed" (Sizer, 2005, 146). Others essentially argue that Christian Zionism will necessarily lead to conversion of Jews without evangelism, which will then usher in the coming of Jesus (Troy Anderson, 2010; Roth, 2015). Essentially then, anti-Arab racism helps mediate theological racism within Christian evangelicalism.

Messianic Judaism

The manner in which some sectors of evangelicalism address the contradictions of supporting Israel and supporting Jewish evangelism is to center their support on Messianic Judaism. Jamie Cowen is the rabbi of Tikvat Israel, a Messianic Jewish congregation based in Richmond, Virginia, and explains Messianic Judaism this way: "The whole thrust of Messianic Judaism is to restore the roots of the faith as a belief in Jesus as a Jewish Messiah. We see our mission as being two primary things—to help Jews understand Jesus as their Messiah, and to help the Christian church understand her Jewish roots" (G. Thomas, 1998, 63). Within Messianic congregations, worship services are offered on Friday night and Saturday morning. Visitors are offered a prayer shawl and keppa. They do not use the term "Christian" (A Jewish Awakening?, 2010). Essentially, they are evangelical Christians.

Promise Keepers has featured Messianic Judaism prominently within its work. In 1997 Promise Keepers incorporated "Messianic Jews" into its racial reconciliation program, thus grouping Messianic Jews in the same category as people of color. Messianic Jewish organizations very actively participate in PK rallies as speakers and distribute their literature. Bill McCartney launched a new ministry aimed at forging a strong relationship between Christians and Messianic Jews called the Road to Jerusalem (News Briefs, 2004b).

Evangelical support for Messianic Judaism results in evangelicals portraying non-Messianic Jews as the problem. For instance, in a 1994 photo essay on the Summer Witnesses Campaign conducted by Jews for Jesus each summer, Jews are portrayed as unreasonably hostile to Jews for Jesus. Two captions illustrate this point:

> In the Diamond District, which has many Jews, a man draws his hand back in anger, while Steve Sinar turns away to avoid being struck. Another pedestrian is looking on in apparent shock.
>
> A Jewish man in the Diamond District angrily confronts campaigner David Mishkin, a missionary in New York City. David tried to respond, but the man left without listening. (Post, 1990, 44)

Similarly, in a Jews for Jesus newsletter, evangelists tell how "We Dared to Tell Them His Gospel." They likened their experience of evangelizing to Jews at George Washington University to the persecution of Christians globally. "We face our share of opposition from the Jewish student body.... Many of us will never be beaten for our faith or placed in chains [but we] received a taste of that opposition recently at GWU."[32] Jewish peoples who resist evangelism are depicted as inexplicably hostile (M. Jones, 1999).

Messianic Jews are often depicted as the "real" Jews, thus supplanting any political, religious, or moral claims of Jewish people at large. In fact, one of the slogans for Jews for Jesus is "Be More Jewish; Accept Christ."

Messianic Jews position themselves in a complicated relationship to the state of Israel, which had some 6,000 Messianic Jews in 1999 (although one

Jewish group put the number at 20,000). There are at least 4,000 missionaries, and Messianic Judaism is perhaps the fastest growing religious movement in the country (Spector, 2009, 116). On the one hand, they are among the fiercest defenders of Christian Zionism and the most virulently anti-Arab and anti-Muslim (B. Bruce, 2002; Guthrie, 2002a). They call for unequivocal support for the state of Israel, arguing that lack of Christian support is based on a replacement theology that fails to see the role of Israel (and hence Jewish people) in God's divine plan (Bernis, 1997).

On the other hand, they present themselves as marginalized by "other Jews" in Israel. According to Weber, Israel has passed antimissionary laws, but they are written in such a way so as to have virtually no effect on current missionizing efforts (T. Weber, 2004, 245). As mentioned, many Christian Zionist groups do not evangelize in order to maintain friendly relationships with the government of Israel, but Messianic Jewish groups are an exception. In particular, although not exclusively prior to 9/11, evangelical magazines have sometimes argued that Israel was persecuting Messianic Jews (Alford, 2000b; B. Bruce, 1998b; Muller, 2000; J. Nelson, 2008a; Schiavi, 2008a, 2010; S. Strang, 2007b). For instance, Paul Lieberman of the Messianic Action Committee in Israel compares the situation of Messianic Jews in Israel to that of "Jews in the Middle Ages, when false reports that Jews kidnapped Christian children to use their blood in religious ceremonies were repeated so often that the Christian majority believed them to be true" (Miles, 1999, 36). The fervently pro-Zionist Stephen Strang even took issue with Israel on its stance on evangelism. He contended that if Israel passed a proposed law to make it illegal to possess proselytizing materials, then Israel will "face being viewed as no different than Iran, Saudi Arabia and other intolerant neighbors who persecute converted Muslims. This proposal strikes me as one of the most frightening threats to religious freedom in the world—all the more so because it is taking place in a nation that is supposedly a vibrant democracy" (S. Strang, 1998a, 114). In a strange turn of events, *Charisma* ran an uncharacteristic exposé on Christian Zionist groups, CUFI in particular. It complained that no money given to CUFI benefits Christians; these organizations do not proselytize; and they are not part of Evangelical Council for Financial Accountability. The article further targeted Eckstein and his International Fellowship of Christians and Jews for being an organization that does not serve Christians and for Eckstein's $1 million a year salary (Troy Anderson, 2013).

Following Christ is almost imagined as a neutral practice that would not reflect on the religious integrity of either Judaism or Islam. That is, one can follow Jesus under evangelical prescriptions but still be Muslim or Jewish. Consequently, an advertisement from Jews for Jesus recommends the solution to conflict in Palestine: "Only when Palestinians and Jews can say to one another, 'I love you in Jesus' name' will the whole world take note and see the power of the gospel." Further, "Now is the time for Christians to share the love of Messiah with Jews and Arabs alike" and "seek justice on both sides."[33]

Case Study: Promise Keepers

The complicated racializing logics of religion are evident in the Promise Keepers' movement. As mentioned previously, Promise Keepers was a key organization that helped spark the racial reconciliation movement within evangelicalism. Eventually, Promise Keepers actually incorporated Messianic Jews (not Jews in general) as a group within its reconciliation movement. Issues of religious tolerance are difficult for members of PK as well as other evangelicals to resolve. I asked one staffer about the impact that PK could have on non-Christians, particularly Jews.

I asked: "Some of the greatest concerns about PK I have heard expressed have been from Jewish individuals who feel that a Christian organization, even if it is not political, could help fan the flames of Christian intolerance of which they have been victims. What is your response?"

He stumbled and became very emotional and choked up over this question in an interview before replying:

> Jews are God's chosen people, and Messianic Jews are coming in record numbers. God is love. We are not to be judges. We need to love Jews and be in relationship with them, and perhaps they will see Christ. In Christ, there is no room for intolerance. I have been to Dachau personally. Jews should be concerned, because they've been incredibly damaged by Christianity. They have every right to feel strongly and defend their position strongly. I finally watched *Schindler's List*. My heart goes out to Jews and Native Americans, and our Asian Brothers, and our Hispanic brothers. They think we're here to take over. I'm just waiting for heaven when all this pain will go away. I don't know who will be there, but it will be fantastic.

At Stand in the Gap, PK president Randy Phillips declared, "We have not come to impose our religious beliefs on others. We celebrate a land of religious freedom for all. We gather not to denigrate other faiths." But then he concluded by saying, "but [we gather] to affirm our belief and life message that salvation comes through faith in the death and resurrection of Jesus Christ alone." For evangelicals, reconciling exclusivist religious claims with pluralistic political ideals clearly is not easily achieved.

In 1997 Promise Keepers incorporated Messianic Jews into its racial reconciliation program, thus categorizing Messianic Jews in the same category as people of color. This strategy allows Promise Keepers to address Christian intolerance of Judaism without renouncing Christian exclusivism. The group calls for racial reconciliation because white evangelicals have sinned by excluding people of color from the body of Christ. The question arises: who has sinned against Messianic Jews? At Stand in the Gap and the Minneapolis rally, there was talk that white evangelicals have displayed some prejudice toward Messianic Jews. However, the real sinner in this relationship appears to be not the evangelical church but the Jews. Marty Waldman prayed at Stand in the Gap that the Jews be forgiven for their pride because they "have forsaken their position to follow the Messiah. We must take our place in the body of Christ. We have forsaken the blood of the Messiah." Reconciliation efforts by PK include no attempts to reconcile with Jewish people. The sole emphasis is on reconciling with Messianic Jews, who are in fact Christians. It is difficult to comprehend what reconciliation is really necessary on these grounds, given that (1) these Messianic Jewish organizations are largely funded by conservative Christian organizations/denominations; and (2) the major rift between Jews and Christians has been the constant attempt of Christians to force Jews to accept Christian beliefs. Since "Messianic Jews" have conceded to this demand, reconciliation has already occurred. The tension between Jews and Christians over religious evangelism remains intact.

At the 2009 Promise Keepers rally held in Colorado, interestingly, the logic of racial reconciliation shifted from Messianic Jews being likened to people of color to supplanting them. Promise Keepers held only one rally, which was the first specifically to invite women (Promise Keepers, 2009). The three principal divides that PK addressed during this event were those between men and women, haves and have nots, and Jews and Gentiles. Explicit discussions of racism were reframed as class issues (which included poor white people). The one group remaining within the racial reconciliation program was Messianic Jews. Again, while the divide to be healed in this rally was between Jews and Gentiles, the only Jews referenced were Christian Jews.

The supplanting of people of color by Messianic Jews as racial reconciliation's primary concern was clear in Raleigh Washington's talk. He admonished people of color specifically to reconcile with Jewish believers, arguing that Jewish people are a righteous remnant chosen by God. Those who don't believe this to be the case will be destroyed. He then argued that such reconciliation between Christians and (Christian) Jews was the important site of racial reconciliation because if it occurs all other racial reconciliation will naturally follow. Furthermore, the evidence of this reconciliation is manifest in support for the state of Israel.

A summary of the slideshow presented during the rally illustrates how reconciliation was framed in this manner:

> Did you know Jesus was Jewish? About 200 years after Jesus' death, the church was Jewish. In 385 AD, the church severed tied with Jews, including Jewish believers. Since that time, there has been anti-Semitism throughout Jewish history. Jews were forced to convert and burnt at the stake. The Reformers, even Martin Luther, were anti-Semitic. Nazism emerges from Martin Luther's writings "on the Jews and their lies." Now a replacement theology is being espoused that is also anti-Semitic. In 1948 Israel was miraculously born. In 1967 Jerusalem came back to Jewish hands, and a revival swept the Jewish people. Jews are coming to faith in unprecedented numbers even though less than 1 percent in Israel are saved. Jewish believers are fathers of the faith. Scriptures have declared that Jews are entrusted with oracles of God. But the church has not opened its arms to Jewish brothers. Is there nothing we can gain from each other? During the tragedy of the Holocaust, the church kept silent. Forty percent of Jewish believers in Israel are beneath the poverty line. Very few Messianic congregations have their own building. God has declared that whoever blesses Israel will be blessed. The time has come for us to lay down our lives for them and bless [those] whom God has blessed. It is time for us; "never again will we shut out Jews and Jewish believers." Never again.

Then non-Jewish participants were asked to make a pledge to Messianic Jews to lay down their lives for them. They were told that Jews are being persecuted around the world. All the nations will rise up against the Jewish people (in other words, Israel) and are standing in the way of Israel's rise. In light of the "persecution" of Israel, participants were commanded to say "Never again." At this point Messianic Jews in the audience pinned yellow stars of David on themselves. Thus, the politics of racial reconciliation has transformed itself from addressing racism against people of color in the United States to supporting the state of Israel. Nevertheless, at the same time, Jewish people are still imagined as one of the primary perpetrators of "racism" against Messianic Jews, who are essentially positioned as the "real" Jews and representatives of Israel. The unspoken enemies of Judaism (Muslims) who form the foundation of reconciliation between Jews and Gentiles are so perverse as to be unincorporable into a movement of racial reconciliation (Puar, 2007).

Thus, we can see logics of racial exclusion and engulfment operating simultaneously within Christian evangelicalism. Muslims become the permanent enemy of Christianity. Jews, by contrast, can escape terror and exclusion as long as they are engulfed within the Christian narrative in order to be redeemed. But, as this chapter indicates, many strands within evangelicalism work against these logics, particularly within the emerging critique of Zionism within Christian evangelicalism.

6   DECOLONIZATION IN UNEXPECTED PLACES

Decolonization is intelligent, calculated, and active resistance to the forces of colonialism that perpetuate the subjugation and/or exploitation of your minds, bodies, and lands, and it is engaged for the ultimate purpose of overturning the colonial structure and realizing Indigenous liberation. . . . But make no mistake: Decolonization ultimately requires the overturning of the colonial structure. It is not about tweaking the existing colonial system to make it more Indigenous-friendly or a little less oppressive. The existing system is fundamentally and irreparably flawed.
—Waziyatawin Angela Wilson and Michael Yellow Bird (2005, 5)

Colonization is violence and violation of the most extreme sort. Colonization is theft and rape and murder and cannibalism on the grandest scale. Colonization is genocide. We should understand that there are indeed people with a heart for decolonization in the churches, in business, even in the military as well as in schools, colleges and seminaries, even if . . . the systems themselves are . . . malignant, delivered over to the enemy as tools or weapons of colonization. Even so, it is not for us to somehow share power with the colonizers.—Robert Francis, Keynote Address, NAIITS Conference, Rapid City, South Dakota (November 29, 2007)

In Native studies, many scholars propose "decolonization" as a guiding principle for Native scholarship and activism. In the first epigraph above, from *For Indigenous Eyes Only: A Decolonization Handbook*, Waziyatawin Angela Wilson and Michael Yellow Bird outline their understanding of decolonization. They call on community members and scholars to go beyond a politics of inclusion in order to build a world in which Native peoples are not governed under a settler colonial state. They further call on Native peoples to deconstruct the manner in which their own political and social imaginaries are shaped by the processes of colonization. Many other scholars similarly argue that Native communities live in a colonial relationship with the United States government: hence the fundamental challenge these communities face is to dismantle this relationship.

This work generally presumes a non-Christian framework for decolonization because the imposition of Christianity within Native communities is understood as part of the colonial process. Interestingly, however, some Native evangelicals are reading the same works cited above and also applying decolonization as a guiding principle for biblical faith. At the 2007 North American Institute for Indigenous Theological Studies (NAIITS) conference, Robert Francis gave a keynote address centering on the need for decolonization. According to Francis, colonization can be defined as "what happens when one people invades the territory of another people, appropriating the territory as their own, asserting control over and actually or essentially destroying the original inhabitants through outright murder, hegemonic subjugation, enslavement, removal, or absorption into the society and culture of the colonizers" (Keynote Address, 2007). Ironically, the shared history of missionization that Native peoples have endured with other Indigenous peoples and communities in the Global South has inspired a politics of global anticolonial solidarity as well as a politics of decolonization with U.S. and Canadian settler states.

This chapter focuses on one "unexpected place" for Indigenous decolonization: Native evangelical leaders and organizations that circulate through NAIITS. Philip Deloria notes in *Indians in Unexpected Places* that part of the legacy of colonialism is to mark the presence of Indigenous peoples within contemporary society as inherently anomalous (Deloria, 2004). As Anne McClintock argues, Native peoples exist in anachronistic space and thus always in an anterior relationship to post/modernity (McClintock, 1995). Consequently, according to Deloria, "expectations" are formed in terms of "the colonial and imperial relations of power and domination existing between Indian people and the United States": Native peoples are simply not supposed to exist in any meaningful way within U.S. society because the United States' colonial imaginary depends on their perpetual absence (Deloria, 2004, 11). In looking at Native evangelicals in particular, we are then left with a double anomaly. First, Native peoples, marked as "primitive," are not supposed to be Christian in the first place without becoming less Native. Second, Native Christians, because they are deemed less Native by virtue of supporting the colonizer's religion, are constructed as less interested in decolonization. In taking up Deloria's analysis, I am focused less on his project of articulating Native peoples within the context of modernity (although we can certainly understand Christian mission as an aspect of modernity). Rather, I am interested in how "expectation" within the context of colonialism always places Native peoples within an anterior relationship to humanity itself, such that they can exist only as ethnographic objects, assimilated by discourses presumed to be owned by those in the dominant culture rather than being figured as actual producers, shapers, and theorizers of those discourses.

Building on Deloria's work, this chapter is another "secret history of the unexpected"—a project that indicates "the complex lineaments of personal and cultural identity that can never be captured by dichotomies built around crude notions of difference and assimilation, white and Indian, primitive and advanced" (Deloria, 2004, 14).

Furthermore, I wish to explore how the contribution of NAIITS engagement with decolonization actually has much to offer scholars of Indigenous and critical ethnic studies who are engaging in decolonization. Within Indigenous/critical ethnic studies, the call for decolonization is extended to the academy as well—we must "indigenize the academy" (Mihesuah and Wilson, 2004) and "decolonize methodologies" (L. T. Smith, 1999). However, as Scott Lyons notes, these calls are often not accompanied by any corresponding political project actually to dismantle colonial structures, including the colonialist apparatus that is the academic industrial complex. Instead, these calls often become an appeal for better representation of Indigenous and/or critical ethnic studies *within* the academic industrial complex, rather than fundamentally questioning its structure. In this regard, the project of NAIITS suggests different avenues for decolonizing the academy that more fundamentally redistribute power.

In *Native Americans and the Christian Right* I focused more specifically on Native peoples within Christian evangelicalism in greater detail. Three individuals involved in the North American Institution for Indigenous Theological Studies—Richard Twiss, Randy Woodley, and Terry LeBlanc—read and critiqued this work. While my first book argued that many Native peoples within evangelicalism use evangelical rhetoric to support Indigenous self-determination, these individuals showed me that their work has even more radical implications. This chapter is a follow-up to that work, assessing the next direction being explored by Native evangelicals.

Missionization, Globalization, and Decolonization

The North American Institute for Indigenous Theological Studies was launched to provide master's and doctoral degrees for Native leaders in the area of contextualized evangelical missions. In addition, NAIITS creates forums for dialogue and engagement with other emerging Indigenous theological streams, including the variety emerging in Native North America. The organization has developed partnerships with several denominational and nondenominational organizations, colleges, and seminaries. In her genealogy of NAIITS, Janine LeBlanc situates it within the larger call within Native studies to decolonize/indigenize the academy. Citing the work of Taiaiake Alfred, she calls on the importance of the academy fundamentally changing its structures and policies in light of the colonial realities faced by Native peoples. She further notes that NAIITS positions itself in dialogue within a larger global context with Indigenous peoples who are similarly interested in academic decolonization (J. LeBlanc, 2005). The conferences sponsored by NAIITS bring together Native peoples within the United States into conversation with Native peoples globally as well as Christians from the Global South. This global framework in turn has inspired a varied discourse on decolonization and how it might impact Native evangelicals in particular and Native communities in general.

Native peoples have become more visible within white-dominated evangelical circles through their participation in the racial reconciliation movement in conservative evangelicalism (A. Smith, 2008). This movement began in the early 1990s with the goal of fostering racial unity among evangelical Christians. One of the rationales for fostering racial reconciliation is to involve people of color in general and Native peoples in particular in Christian missionization programs (A. Smith, 2008). For instance, Native evangelical Craig Smith suggests that Native peoples in the United States and Canada need to be incorporated into Christianity in order to facilitate the missionization of Indigenous peoples in other parts of the world. Native peoples, he contends, more easily evade the "imperialist American" label and thus more successfully convert other Indigenous peoples (C. Smith, 1997, 106). Ironically however, the inclusion of Native peoples within missionization programs also has the consequence of bringing Native peoples into conversation with other colonized peoples and vice versa. At the NAIITS conferences, these conversations between Native peoples in North America and Indigenous peoples globally as well as peoples from the Global South have promoted cross-national dialogues on the impact of colonization and strategies for decolonization.

An example can be found in the keynote address from the 2007 NAIITS conference held in Sioux Falls, South Dakota, given by Charles Amjad-Ali (a Lutheran Seminary professor and presbyter of the Church of Pakistan). Amjad-Ali likened colonialism in South Asia with the colonialism experienced by Native Americans and explained that the survival of Native Americans is an inspiration to all colonized peoples. "Truly in all humility and awe I say that in that sense you have been our salvation. Because of what happened to you not only have we survived, but we have learned how to survive under the current global hegemony" (Amjad-Ali, 2007, 6). He then critiqued the United States' claim to be a multicultural nation: "America has made claims of multiculturalism and plurality of identities for a long time.... In this metaphoric melting pot, the Native Americans, whose land was stolen, were never to be incorporated, nor were African Americans whose labor was stolen, ever to be a part of it" (Amjad-Ali, 2007, 12). He unapologetically criticized the complicity of Christendom in genocide and slavery, which has "allowed the whites to go on pretending that no wrong was committed in the theft of the land and even of labor since this was the way God had planned the matter.... If people were killed, maimed, decimated, oppressed, dislocated, etc., this was part of the predestined reality and not because some wrongs were committed.... We forget that the cross was an instrument of torture, murder and political oppression." He concluded with a mandate for all Christians to divest from the interest of empire (Amjad-Ali, 2007, 5).

At the 2004 NAIITS conference, Tite Tiénou (professor at Trinity Evangelical Divinity School and former dean of the Faculté de Théologie Evangélique de l'Alliance in Abidjan, Côte d'Ivoire) contended that the consequence of Christian mission is that Christianity is becoming "de-westernized" (Tiénou, 2005, 14). Consequently, "Christians in Africa, Asia, and Latin America, indeed indigenous Christians everywhere, are able to defend themselves when accused of being agents of westernization and puppets in the hands of foreigners whose intention is the destruction of local cultures and religions" (Tiénou, 2005, 14). However, while the church is becoming less Western, Tiénou argues, the theological and intellectual production of the church is still centered in the West.

> I contend that Christian theology and scholarship will remain "provincial" as long as some major challenges continue unaddressed [such as] the perception of indigenous Christian scholars as purveyors of exotic raw intellectual material.... Indigenous theologians are ... relegated

to the museums of theological curiosity just like their cultures. We are then left with this: the West claiming to produce universal theology and the rest writing to articulate fundamental theology that will make [them] equal partners in the theological circles that determine what is theologically normative. (Tiénou, 2005, 16–17)

In this regard, we can see Tiénou's words as a call to "decolonize methodology" within evangelicalism as well as to resist "ethnographic entrapment" (A. Smith, 2014, 207). Similarly, NAIITS has been involved in such calls, questioning the tendency within many evangelical churches to condemn all Native spiritual and cultural practices as heretical and pagan. Anita Keith of NAIITS states:

> So the traditional people, that's just another way that Creator is teaching us how to relate to him—here is my story and here is how you can love me. You can smudge, you can Sundance, and in that process I will communion with you. And some people can do the Sundance without integrity and God will not meet them. And others can do it with a very pure heart and God will meet them there. Some people study the Bible without integrity, and slam people with it, and try to have other people live it out, and God will not meet them. But if they read the word with integrity, God will meet them there.
>
> I have no problem with moving from traditional way of worshiping, sweat, Sundance, or any of those ceremonies. There is no demonic in it, it's all about creator, and us connecting to him.

Thus, ironically, while evangelicals have been missionizing the worlds' Indigenous peoples, these peoples are simultaneously redefining what it means to be an evangelical.

In this respect, the approach of NAIITS contrasts with some strands of decolonization that tend to equate it with intellectual purity. That is, to decolonize tends to mean that we should not engage the work of those not from our community because this engagement would indicate that our thoughts have been colonized. Kirisitina Sailiata has critiqued the term "decolonization" for its tendency to be understood as an "extractive" process.

> The term decolonization suggests we can undo the process of colonization as if it never happened. Decolonization becomes then an extractive process whereby we remove all the "colonial" impulses that shape us

today, as if this is even possible. Such moves quickly lead to a politics of purity whereby we must remove any colonial impure thoughts that we have in order to regain a prelapsarian sense of innocence. This is problematic because our sense of what we were before colonization is inevitably shaped by the way we think now, which is inextricably shaped by colonialism. It is also not possible to remove the effect of colonization on our lives and communities. Indigenous people cannot erase the last 500 years of colonialism, but select philosophies and practices from 500 years ago can shape a vision of the future we would like 500 years from now. (Sailiata, 2015, 302)

Klee Benally has further contended that the preferred term for Indigenous struggles should be "anticolonialism" rather than "decolonization," as it indicates the needs for Indigenous peoples to link their struggles to the broader movements against colonialism. As Sailiata further argues:

In addition, the term decolonization tends to separate indigenous peoples from others engaged in anticolonial struggle. We tend to focus solely on our unique position such that we aim to return to before colonization rather than join with others in a more global struggle against colonialism. Consequently, decolonization often lapses into a more individualized lifestyle politic—"I will now decolonize by not eating turkey tail or fry bread" instead of "I will engage in mass-based organizing and resistance against colonial struggles." (Sailiata, 2015, 302)

Thus, to end global oppression, it is important to build sufficient political power necessary to dismantle these structures. The activities of NAIITS have been strategic in carving intellectual and political alliances in order to challenge the white supremacist and colonialist assumptions within Christian evangelicalism.

Disidentification with Evangelical Mission

Of course, one can argue: is not Christian evangelicalism itself colonialist? While this is a reasonable argument to make, it is helpful to look at the engagement of NAIITS with evangelicalism through the lens of disidentification—a model for political engagement proffered by José Esteban Muñoz. According to Muñoz, whereas assimilationism seems to identify with the dominant society, and counteridentification seeks to reject it completely, disidentification "is the third mode of dealing with dominant ideology, one that neither opts to assimilate within such a structure nor strictly opposes it; rather, disidentification is a strategy that works on and against dominant ideology" (Muñoz, 1999, 11–12). Muñoz explains that disidentification neither fully accepts nor rejects dominant cultural logics but internally subverts them, using the logic against itself. He clarifies that disidentification is not a middle ground between assimilationist and contestatory politics; rather, it is a strategy that recognizes the shifting terrain of resistance (Muñoz, 1999, 18). Within the discursive economy of NAIITS, we can see a strategy of disidentification with evangelical mission. As previously mentioned, Robert Francis (Mid American Indian Fellowships) gave a keynote address at the 2007 NAIITS conference centering on the need for decolonization. He began his talk with an adaption of Mark 5:1–20:

> One day Jesus got into a fishing boat with his twelve disciples, and they all sailed out onto Lake Gennesaret, intending to picnic on the opposite shore. As they were about halfway across the lake, a sudden storm swept in. In keeping with his usual behavior during inclement weather, Jesus was fast asleep in the stern of the boat when a huge twister or whirlwind swept up the little craft, transporting the boat, along with all 13 passengers through space and time to 21st Century North America. When the wind abated, Jesus and his disciples found themselves on dry land, somewhere in the midst of an Indian reservation. Jumping down from the boat, John and Peter looked around, shrugged their shoulders, and spread a cloth on the ground for the picnic.
> Just then an automobile came roaring down the paved road not far from where the group sat eating. Having no prior experience with any such machine, the disciples were astonished and more than a bit frightened. The car slowed but did not stop, the passenger door flew open, and a woman, pushed by a hairy, masculine hand, tumbled out into the roadside ditch. She lay there for a moment, a seemingly lifeless heap of rags and flesh. Then leaping to her feet, the woman began to scream and cry in an alarming manner. She watched the automobile disappear over a distant hill; then turning, she suddenly noticed the disciples and Jesus at their picnic. Shaking her head with fury the woman ran shrieking up to where they were, only to stop short, a look of shocked recognition in her eyes.
> The woman stood there, hesitating, a hideously twisted expression on her face, but her astonished silence did not last long. "Jesus! What

are you doing here?" screamed a voice from within the woman. "You're the last person I'd expect to see here!" This statement was followed with maniacal laughter.

Looking deeply into the woman's eyes, Jesus asked, "What is your name?"

"My name?" asked the voice. "What is my name? My name is . . . Cavalry . . . Infantry . . . Military Mega-Complex. My name is Trading-Company . . . Border-Town Liquor Store . . . Multi-National Corporation. My name is Proselytizing Missionary . . . Religious Order . . . Denominational Mission Board. My name is White Man's School . . . Historical Misrepresentation . . . Hollywood Stereotype. We are many. We are organized. We are in control. Our intentions are always and only for the very best."

"Get out of here," Jesus said. . . . "There remains no place for you in any land. Get out! Get the Hell out!"

With one last shriek, the evil spirits left the woman. The disciples and Jesus took her to a nearby house, where she bathed, shampooed her hair and put on clean clothes. . . . Finally, Jesus stood up and said, "I appreciate your hospitality, but we have to be going now if we're to catch the next twister back to Galilee."

The woman who had been healed also stood. "Jesus," she said, "may I go with you? I want to become a Christian."

With a weary smile and a shake of his head, Jesus replied, "No child; this is not my intent for you. Stay here, with your own people, and tell them what Creator has done." (Keynote Address, 2007)

This parable contains an implicit critique not only of past acts of colonization but also of the current colonial world order. In addition, the last paragraph seems to suggest that Native peoples can best follow Jesus not by becoming Christian but by following their traditional ways.

In this parable Francis specifically names the many facets of colonization: capitalism, militarism, and racism. However, he situates the Christian church as a colonizing institution on a par with the military. Consequently, he ends the parable with a call to divest not only from the settler state but from the Christian church as well.

> We should understand that there are indeed people with a heart for
> decolonization in the churches, in business, even in the military
> as well as in schools, colleges and seminaries, even if most of these

organizations, the systems themselves are broken or even malignant, delivered over to the enemy as tools or weapons of colonization.

Even so, it is not for us to somehow share power with the colonizers. Can you imagine Jesus saying this to his disciples? "Here's good news: I had a positive meeting with Lucifer in the wilderness. He shed light on several issues. Afterward, the two of us met with Caesar, Pilate, Herod and Caiaphas. They are expressing a willingness to share some of their power with us. All we have to do is, ahem, submit to their superior authority. What do you say, guys? 'If you can't beat 'em, join 'em! Right?'"

If we are called into church, into the economic system, into the military, into school, college or seminary, it is proper that we go in the way of a warrior entering the camp of the enemy, knowing the dangers that are there, knowing that we risk captivity and death at the hands of cannibals, knowing that at the very least we will sustain grievous wounds, the scars of which we will bear all our lives.

I am not saying the Spirit of Creator cannot be encountered in church. The Spirit of Creator is everywhere and may reach out to anyone anywhere—even in the most unlikely of settings.

What I am saying is inasmuch as churches theologically inspire, empower, encourage and drive all aspects of colonization while directly participating and occupying themselves in colonizing activities, churches are dancing to the devil's tune. There is no healing or wholeness to be found in that dance. Damage and death are found in that dance. Beware!

Jesus entered the seat of the colonizing power. He rode into Jerusalem. He stormed into the temple. He walked into the governor's own mansion and out of the city to the place of the skull. He will forever bear the scars. That is what Jesus did, and as surely as we choose to call ourselves Jesus' followers, we may do no less. We must live our lives and give our lives for the purpose of decolonization, that the People may live.[1]

Francis seems to suggest that evangelicals may even need to leave the church to follow a truly decolonized Christianity. Others argue for decolonization while not calling for a complete abandonment of Christianity. My People International (a collaborating organization that recently merged with NAIITS) created a Vacation Bible School (VBS) curriculum that addresses one of the tensions that Native evangelicals address: "For many Native people nothing good came of colonization. For others, only one good thing came—the news about God's son Jesus which came to us with the

Bible. . . . We realized we are part of this plan of God from the beginning as all people everywhere" (My People International, 2000, 35).

Native evangelicals address the entanglement of colonization and Christianization in a number of complex ways. Adrian Jacobs, a former board member of NAIITS, argues that God uses nations to judge other nations. So he suggests that colonization may have been a judgment against Native nations. For instance, he considers the possibility that the colonization of the Iroquois may be a judgment for their role in the destruction of the Huron. He also postulates that the destruction of the Aztec was a judgment against their human sacrifices (Jacobs, 1998, 64). He does not think that all Native nations are equally "guilty" but believes that Native nations that were less sinful may have escaped more harsh forms of genocide.

However, Jacobs does not place colonizers on the side of God. Rather, he contends that they too may face the same judgment. He evokes Saul's broken treaty with the Gibeonites in the Bible to say that "God really does care about broken treaties and will bring judgment eventually" (Jacobs, 1998, 64). He suggests that the billion-dollar damage to Hydro-Québec during an ice storm in January 1998 was perhaps a consequence of its destroying Cree lands through a dam that was constructed that flooded their territory. Jacobs states that he is not a prophet and thus cannot "declare the state of affairs in the North America to be His judgment on broken treaties," but concludes that "when there is a recounting concerning broken treaties, I do not want to be on the side of the violators" (Jacobs, 1998, 66).

Another approach to addressing these tensions is found in a leaflet for a "Memorial Prayer for Reconciliation" developed by the Healing for the Native Ministry handed out at one of the NAIITS events. It says in part:

> For the policy of genocide and for the ongoing unjust policies of the United States government, we ask your forgiveness. . . .
> For the destruction of the Native family structure through the demoralization of Native American men, for placing your children in foster homes and boarding schools, and for the subservient positions forced on your women, we ask for your forgiveness.
> For over three-hundred broken treaties, for the myth of "Manifest Destiny," and for the notion that Native people stood in the way of progress, we ask your forgiveness.
> For the sins of the church, for withholding the true gospel, for misrepresenting Jesus Christ, and for using religion in an attempt to "civilize the Natives," we ask your forgiveness . . .

We ask for . . .
Forgiveness for taking your land at gunpoint and for forcing you on to barren reservations . . .
Forgiveness for the policy of our government of genocide toward the Native Americans . . .
Forgiveness for the broken treaties . . .
Forgiveness for the ongoing policies of the government . . .
Forgiveness for misrepresenting the gospel to our Native American forefathers. When your fathers asked us for truth we gave them white man's religions. When your fathers asked for God we withheld the true gospel of Jesus Christ.

This prayer seems to address the relationship between Christianization and colonization by suggesting that the Christianity that came with colonization is not "true" Christianity. Randy Woodley, formerly of NAIITS, in turn separates Christianity from Christ. He argues that he is not a "Christian" and hence carries no allegiance to the Christian Church but is a follower of Jesus. Hence, true Christianity is not actually complicit in colonization. Similarly, Anita Keith separates the Bible from colonization:

Well, I think it's unfortunate in North America, we've had our head in the sand and we think we are a "Christian" country and really, the country has been based on the oppression, slavery, of marginalization of aboriginal people. It has been about the economy and unfortunately that means the church too because they've been in bed together—business, government, and the church. So I think that the Bible, for me, has to be separated out of that equation because the way that God has told the story in the Bible is pure and true.

Evangelicalism and Political Praxis

Within the racial reconciliation movement, struggles against racism are frequently spiritualized. Certainly, this tendency exists among some participants at NAIITS conferences. According to one participant:

Yes, the Bible I believe does inform my view of colonization. And it's interesting to me that Jesus himself was under the dominant Roman society, and the people who were part of his group desperately wanted out from under that oppressive government, and they thought he might be king and take them out of that. And they were looking for a revolution, and it's interesting to me that Jesus was more interested in a revolution of their hearts than society, and I think that's what he's on about today as well. Although I appreciate our chiefs and all of the hard work that they do, and in Canada we have grand chiefs that go to Ottawa and speak on our behalf and I appreciate all of their work, but I know Jesus is more interested in our hearts than in politics.

Richard Twiss, NAIITS speaker and founder of Wiconi International, also addressed the problems of radical political activism when it becomes spiritually unmoored:

And during that time AIM was going strong and I joined the American Indian Movement and went to Washington, DC, to participate in the takeover of the Bureau of Indian Affairs office building with that whole eight days of occupation and all that. And during that time, I began to hate white people and hate Christianity, hearing all the stories of Catholic Boarding School and abuse. Although [boarding school was] positive for my mom, it was a horrible experience for my other five aunties and uncles. And so after AIM, I spent some time in jail, involved in drugs and alcohol. And I just felt that my life as a 19-year-old was not going in a good direction. I did not know what else to do. I ended up in jail in Washington State on some drug and alcohol charges. The judge wanted me to go into this treatment program because of my blood alcohol content, but I didn't want to go. So, I talked this friend into going to Hawaii with me, her brother was in the army, in Honolulu. So, we left and went to Hawaii and by that time, after my time at AIM, there would be times when I would watch our highly respected spiritual leaders, our medicine men, who were very much espousing a kind of lifestyle, a set of values—respect and honor and all of that. And yet, there would be times during the height of the whole focus on spirituality, whether it be Lakota or First Nation, that these men would come out of the bar drunk as a skunk with a woman under each arm. And there was this whole phenomena of this stud complex and so many of those guys have children all over the country today. Some guys have a couple dozen babies. But there was this sort of hypocrisy, they would be espousing these values and holding us young guys to it, but meanwhile it was about drugs, it was about promiscuity, it was about drinking and carousing. So it created a bit of a disillusionment.

At the same time, many participants critique the tendency to spiritualize responses to colonization. Ray Aldred, board chair of My People International, said:

> If you have a relationship with Christ, it should make you less of an ass. I just think you can't take people's land and somehow justify that. That's just wrong. I try not to spiritualize stuff too much. There are specific land claims dealing with this land right here. They need to give it back. When it comes to those reconciliation gatherings, the ones that have really been effective in helping the relationship move forward are talking about specific things. They aren't just talking airy fairy, it's about specific things.

Randy Woodley similarly ties a belief in Jesus with a political commitment to social justice:

> God has a preference for the poor and justice and so anything that reeks of corporate greed or anti-environmentalism, I would use the Bible to support and say, you can't say you follow Creator and follow the policies of George Bush, like war. I wouldn't say I'm a pacifist, I guess I'm a wannabe passivist, but I really do believe in peace. The evangelical church has used the Bible to make it into the opposite of what it says and that's very sick.

Besides these critiques of colonization, some evangelicals proffer visions of sovereignty based on biblical principles that echo some feminist and other more radical perspectives. Terry LeBlanc, the director of NAIITS, ties Native nationalism to an implicit critique of capitalism:

> The gap between rich and poor still exists. In fact, it is widening at an increasing rate—despite the assurances of the World Bank and the G7 that there is overall improvement in the human condition worldwide. Sadly, those of us in the indigenous community seem to be buying it hook, line, and sinker! MBA's are being churned out in Indian country faster than the social work and legal degrees. . . . The battle against assimilation is being conceded on a selective front. We are buying into an economic world-view so foreign that it didn't even register as a remote possibility to our ancestors. . . . When, under the rubric of development, we disguise unchecked greed for bigger and better and

more of Western free enterprise and big business we do a grave disservice to our fellow human beings. (T. LeBlanc, 2000, 21)

Shari Russell, NAIITS board member and employee of the Salvation Army, explicitly employed Frantz Fanon's model of decolonization at the 2017 NAIITS conference to argue that seemingly reformist strategies such as the Truth and Reconciliation Commissions could be used for more revolutionary long-term goals of decolonization. Thus, evangelical commitments do not necessarily deradicalize Native peoples' political commitments to decolonization.

Decolonizing the Academic Industrial Complex

As mentioned previously, many scholars discuss decolonizing the academy, yet their recommendations for decolonization tend to presume the continuation of the academic industrial complex itself. The issue gets framed as a problem of racism and colonialism *within* the academy rather than a problem of the academy as a white supremacist, capitalist, and colonialist institution. In this regard, the work done by evangelicals perhaps provides a productive alternative to this approach.

One of the interesting approaches of NAIITS is that many of the Native peoples attached to it do not operate through traditional church denominational structures. In fact, NAIITS organizers have noted that many Native peoples complain about their exclusion within those structures. However, the approach from NAIITS has been to leave those structures and begin ones that they can lead. Of course, this practice is widespread within evangelicalism, as can be seen by the growth of new Charismatic movements. Evangelicals have often not presumed the continuation of structures that they do not support and have created the ones that they did support. However, this impulse has not necessarily been adopted by critical ethnic studies scholars. Much of the rallying cry for, instead of against, Senate Bill 1070 was to oppose the banning of ethnic studies, as if the state of Arizona somehow owns ethnic studies. By contrast, evangelical groups respond to exclusions by creating their own models. This impulse is not absent within progressive movements, of course. For instance, the prison abolitionist movement has argued not simply for a critique of the current prison system but for the development of alternatives based on principles of justice. Yet the same development of an academic abolitionist perspective has not (yet) occurred. When we consider the level of dissatisfaction expressed about the current system, the responses (even by radicals) always seems geared toward reform rather than toward creating the system they would like.

Of course, one hindrance is that the academy is often tied to current capitalist system. It is perceived that to be necessary to receive a college education to get a job (even if, increasingly, a college education does not lead to a job and a PhD certainly does not to lead to jobs). Thus, to create alternatives to the academic industrial complex, we must create the alternative economies and then develop appropriate learning practices that can enable the development of these economies. This has been a key insight of NAIITS. Seminary education becomes a pathway to ministry only if we presume that it is necessary to do ministry through the current denominational structures. Someone who develops a different method of ministry does not have to attend seminaries dictated by denominational or other standards. We can create the standards. Thus, by creating the alternative ministry, NAIITS is in the position to develop new forms of ministry education that are not based on the presumption that people must leave their community to get an education but that take place within the context of community.

Of course, as mentioned, an academic abolitionist stance does not require all teachers to drop their positions immediately and all graduate students to drop out of school. It is a positive project about creating alternative liberatory models for education. But there is no pure space to work. One can certainly hold positions that might enable resources to help develop the alternatives. Similarly, NAIITS has continued to partner with seminaries as a means to make its presence known. However, it maintains an independence so that it can sever relationships as they become unproductive.

Decolonizing Methodology

Despite the controversies and disagreements that exist within NAIITS, it is clear that NAIITS articulates "decolonization" not simply as theological or political content but as a methodology by which to do theological work. First, NAIITS has been in critical conversation with the Emergent Movement within evangelicalism (discussed in greater detail in chapter 1). Stated briefly, this reformist movement within evangelicalism tries to articulate itself around a method of theological conversation rather than boundary-setting. That is, rather that articulate a set of boundaries that defines who is and who is not an evangelical, the Emergent Movement, undergirded by postmodern thought, understands that while there may or may not be an inerrant scripture, there is certainly no inerrant reader of it. Consequently, while this movement may see a theological center around which to organize, its goal is not to exclude those who do not fit within the evangelical boundary but to engage in theological conversations with all who are willing to engage. Brian McLaren, one of the leaders of this movement, headlined the 2009 NAIITS conference. He called on evangelicals to move from a position of certainty to being comfortable with not knowing all the answers in advance. Terry LeBlanc, one of the primary organizers of NAIITS, similarly states that one cannot have a true dialogue if one presumes an outcome before the conversation is started.

In that spirit, NAIITS conferences are primarily organized around conversations rather than through lectures. It is the goal of NAIITS to have everyone be able to engage in discussion regardless of educational training or professional standing. In addition, those who speak at conferences or who write in the NAIITS journal are not identified by professional title.

Adrian Jacobs explains how these approaches within NAIITS suggest an alternate model of both Indigenous and church governance that echoes some of the visions for Indigenous nationhood found in anarchist and feminist Indigenous scholars and activists. Mohawk scholar Taiaiake Alfred contends that while the term "sovereignty" is popular among Native scholars/activists it is inappropriate to describe the political, spiritual, and cultural aspirations of Native peoples. He contends that sovereignty is premised on the ability to exercise power through the state by means of coercion and domination. Traditional forms of Indigenous governance, by contrast, are based on different understandings of power:

> The Native concept of governance is based on . . . the "primacy of conscience." There is no central or coercive authority and decision-making is collective. Leaders rely on their persuasive abilities to achieve a consensus that respects the autonomy of individuals, each of whom is free to dissent from and remain unaffected by the collective decision. . . .
>
> A crucial feature of the indigenous concept of governance is its respect for individual autonomy. This respect precludes the notion of "sovereignty"—the idea that there can be a permanent transference of power or authority from the individual to an abstraction of the collective called "government."
>
> In the indigenous tradition, . . . there is no coercion, only the compelling force of conscience based on those inherited and collectively refined principles that structure the society. (Alfred, 1999, 25)

As long as Indigenous peoples frame their struggles in terms of sovereignty, Alfred argues, they inevitably find themselves co-opted by the state-reproducing forms of governance based on oppressive Western forms of governance. In addition, the concept of sovereignty continues to affirm the legitimacy of the state: "To frame the struggle to achieve justice in terms of indigenous 'claims' against the state is implicitly to accept the fiction of state sovereignty" (Alfred, 1999, 570). He generally juxtaposes "nationhood" and "nationalism" as terms preferable to "sovereignty." "Sovereignty is an exclusionary concept rooted in an adversarial and coercive Western notion of power" (Alfred, 1999, 59). Through Indigenous notions of power such as these, contemporary Native nationalism seeks to replace the dividing, alienating, and exploitative notions, based on fear, that drive politics inside and outside Native communities today (Alfred, 1999, 53).

Similarly Adrian Jacob argues that both churches and society at large can model themselves through the principles of consensus and egalitarianism that Alfred outlines. He concurs that Iroquois leaders "derived their power from the people" (Jacobs, 1998, 69). Jacobs contends that this model is one that can be informative to all Christians:

> I am suggesting that one of the greatest contributions that Iroquoian people can make toward reformation among Aboriginal people is assisting the return to the value of consensus decision-making and the inherent respect of that process. Abusive people find it very hard to work in an environment of open heartedness, respect, trust, and group sharing. Hierarchical systems maintain their structures through the careful control of information. Closed-door meetings and in-camera sessions abound in this system emphasizing privileged information. Dictators know the value of propaganda. (Jacobs, 1999, 25)

These principles articulated by Jacobs resonate with Native feminist calls to envision nationhood based on principles of horizontal authority, interconnectedness with a larger global world, and mutual respect and responsibility. These visions contrast sharply with nation-state forms of governance that are based on principles of domination, violence, and social hierarchy (A. Smith, 2008). They also echo many of the calls made by Indigenous activists in Latin America, who argue against statist forms of governance in favor of nonhierarchical models of organizing. Thus, even more important than the specific positions that various NAIITS members may hold regarding the politics of decolonization is the process by which NAIITS attempts to decolonize the process of theologizing itself.

Conclusion

Decolonization as a political project within Native studies and Native activism does not emerge out of a vacuum. While Native decolonization within the United States often centers on the colonial relationship between the U.S. settler state and Native nations, this political agenda is informed by decolonization struggles on a global scale. Some key sites for such global solidarity include the involvement of Native peoples in the United Nations Permanent Forum on Indigenous Issues and the Working Group on Indigenous Affairs, both of which provide a space for Native peoples in the United States to coalesce with Indigenous groups from around the world. Other nonstatist global sites include the World Social Fora that have provided an opportunity for Indigenous peoples to strategize with each other and with peoples from radical social movements around the world. At the 2008 World Social Forum, an entire day was dedicated to highlighting the struggles of Indigenous peoples, who called on *all* peoples to resist the nation-state form of governance in favor of Indigenous models of radical participatory democracy. However, as this chapter has demonstrated, sites for global dialogue and exchange between Native peoples in North America, Indigenous peoples around the world, and other Third World decolonization movements can exist in unexpected places. One such place is the Christian mission field, which has brought Native evangelicals into conversation with evangelicals from colonized nations around the world. In what would seem to be purely a site of religious and cultural imperialism, a politics of decolonization has emerged that threatens to reshape the boundaries of Christianity itself. How decolonization discourse within Native evangelicalism will develop and to what effect remains to be seen. But the emergence of decolonization within what would appear to be an intrinsically colonial evangelical discourse perhaps speaks to the inherent instability of colonization itself. To quote African theologian Emmanuel Martey: "Unlike Audre Lorde, who might be wondering whether the master's tools could indeed be used to dismantle the master's house, African theologians are fully convinced that the gun, in efficient hands, could well kill its owner" (Martey, 1994, 46).

7   NO PERMANENT FRIENDS AND ENEMIES

Large-scale transformation cannot happen without mass movements. In turn, building mass movements requires that we do not organize around the premise of a permanent enemy (such as the Christian Right), since these "enemies" are people that need to be recruited for movements for social change. If we understand that current configurations of religious and political identity within Christian Right communities are not givens, then it is possible for them to be rearticulated into new configurations that favor progressive politics.

Since the advent of racial reconciliation, the possibilities for evangelical rearticulations have become manifest, particularly in the areas of prison and immigration reform. The story of rearticulation, however, is not a simple story of movement toward racial progress. It has been accompanied by extreme racial backlash, the marriage between racial justice and heteronormativity, and politically dubious compromises. Yet the stunning racial justice politics within Christian evangelicalism should not only not be ignored but might actually be instructive for racial justice politics in general. This chapter traces the genealogy of these shifts, beginning with the 2008 election of Barack Obama as president. Racial reconciliation may well have paved the way for Obama's victory in 2008. Evangelicals of color have been able to utilize the cultural capital that they gained with white evangelicals through the racial reconciliation movement to make significant shifts in the traditional politics of the Christian Right. Yet, at the same time, the previously described imperial and U.S.-centric logics as well as the racialization of religion within racial reconciliation also provided a foundation for the Tea Party backlash politics that emerged after the elections. This backlash was also enabled by the "Left"'s failure to build on the momentum of the 2008 elections to forge a more solid movement for social change. Thus, the 2008 elections demonstrate both the possibilities for rearticulation and the failures to take advantage of these possibilities.

While it seems the secular Left has largely disregarded and dismissed the possibilities of rearticulation created by the 2008 elections, evangelical progressives did not adopt the "gloom and doom" approach of secular progressives and began seizing on the opportunities of this historical moment to shift the political paradigms of the Christian Right. The effect of their organizing became most apparent within immigration reform and organizing against police violence and mass incarceration. But before I trace this genealogy, let me begin with some background on the Christian Right's involvement in electoral politics that help set the stage for Obama's presidential election.

Obama and the Rearticulation of Christian Right Politics

The rise of Obama can be situated in the growing discontent, even among evangelicals, with George W. Bush's presidency. Bush's approval rating among white evangelicals in 2002 was at 77 percent. In October it was at 64 percent (by comparison, 61 percent of Americans in general supported Bush in 2002 and 37 percent approved in 2005) (Carnes, 2006b). *Christianity Today*, in its assessment of Bush's presidency, approved of his work to stop AIDS and malaria as well as his federal court appointments. But it was critical of the war in Iraq and the administration's support of torture. It also condemned the handling of Hurricane Katrina and the collapse of the economy (Carnes, 2009). In another article *Christianity Today* expressed disappointment that Bush seemed to have misled the public with the charge that Iraq had weapons of mass destruction. It also criticized Karl Rove's involvement with the scandal involving Valerie Plame and Jack Abramoff's financial dealings. Black evangelicals in general said that they could no longer defend Bush in light of his handling of Katrina (Carnes, 2006b). The Pew Forum on Religion and Public Life found that evangelicals were more likely to vote based on the Iraq war than on abortion or gay marriage (J. Green, 2007).

The increasing reports about corruption in the Republican Party also began to take their toll, such as Ralph Reed's role in the Jack Abramoff scandal as well as the scandals involving the various evangelical public officials found guilty of adultery who were part of the Fellowship, including former

South Carolina governor Mark Sanford and former Nevada senator John Ensign (Dean, 2009c). *World* began to demand that the Republican Party clean up its act (Vincent and Dawson, 2006). Similarly, David Kuo, former deputy director of the White House Office of Faith-Based and Community Initiatives, wrote a book, *Tempting Faith* (2006), accusing the president of essentially manipulating evangelical voters while doing nothing behind the scenes to further a faith-based agenda (Kuo, 2007).

When President Bush was picked to be commencement speaker for Calvin College of Grand Rapids, 130 professors (one-third of Calvin's faculty) took a half-page ad in the Grand Rapids Press, saying, "No single political position should be identified with God's will." It criticized his policies on war, politics, and the environment. Eight hundred Calvin College alumni, faculty, and friends also took out a full-page ad protesting the visit. When one of the faculty members was offered a seat on the platform with Bush, he replied that "he would rather weed his garden" (Dean, 2005a, 23). The talk, however, was largely nonpolitical and was well received (Hansen, 2005).

Even during the 2004 elections, *Charisma* began to note a surprising number of anti-Bush letters as well as critiques of *Charisma*'s one-sided support of the Republican Party (Letters, 2004c):

You have turned Charisma into a political mouthpiece. Did you give Jimmy Carter the same write-up as you did Bush? Bush is just another politician who puts re-election above all else. Intelligent people know he has been a disaster for the country. (Letters, 2004b, 8)

Many have died, and are still dying, in Iraq just so that the United States could take power from one small man, Saddam Hussein. Weapons of mass destruction have yet to be found there, but we see the devastation of genocide. Yet we offer only humanitarian aid. How do we ignore our national debt of more than $7 trillion? There is more to the election than same-sex marriage. (Letters, 2004d, 74)

Greed is just as sinful as homosexuality. . . . Your blindness is upper-middle class bias. (Letters, 2004d, 10)

I am confused about why [we should vote for Bush]—when we are killing innocent human beings in Iraq. Bush's views are helping the rich and not the poor or the middle-class. I couldn't live with myself if I voted for someone who believes in not helping the helpless. (Letters, 2004d, 10)

Bush needed to divert America's focus from terrorists to defenseless Iraq. At the same time, Dick Cheney's company, Halliburton, lost billions in drilling operations and was on the verge of bankruptcy. So they came up with an idea: Why not kill two birds with one stone—invade Iraq and give all the rebuilding and oil contracts to Halliburton. The Democrats would have been impeached had they done what Bush and Cheney had done. (Letters, 2004d, 11)

President Bush is a big liar. He is no man of God. (Letters, 2004a, 9)

Until President Bush and members of Congress send their Ivy League children to the war in Iraq, I'd rather not hear how important the war is to national security. Tragically, as in so many wars before, middle- and lower-class Americans are fighting and dying while the rich get richer through war and reconstruction enterprises. (Letters, 2005, 9, 74)

I do not know when you decided to become a political magazine, but I feel that you crossed the line when you published a book about our president's faith. You pretty much had a financial interest in him becoming re-elected and it showed. Because of your political stance, I have lost faith in your ability to cover anything impartially. (Letters, 2005, 74)

In the 2006 midterm elections, evangelical voters crossed party lines. One Beliefnet survey said that 770 "conservative only" voters thought Iraq was a more important voting issue than homosexuality or abortion (News Briefs, 2007a).

Amid this growing discontent Barack Obama decided actively to court the evangelical vote. His strategy actually preceded his run for presidency: he engaged evangelicals in a variety of high-profile events while he was in the Senate. In particular, he attended Rick Warren's 2006 Global Summit on AIDS. This event was indicative of a double-shift. On the one hand, Obama, a Democrat, was not ceding the evangelical vote to the Republican Party. On the other hand, Warren, a prominent evangelical spokesperson, was shifting away from a politics almost solely tied to the Republican Party or connected to fixed issues. He was engaging all candidates on the issue of AIDS. He was heavily critiqued for this move, but his decision has continued to have effects on younger generations of evangelical voters (Vincent, 2006d). Obama then hired a Pentecostal pastor, Joshua DuBois, to coordinate outreach with Christian communities (Conant, 2008). Obama continued to engage evangelicals after he became president. Joshua DuBois became the director of the Office of Faith-Based and Neighborhood Partnerships. A faith-based counsel was appointed to advise this office, which included Frank Page, former president of the Southern Baptist Convention (SBC) (along with Joel Hunter, Jim Wallis, and Richard Stearns of World Vision) (Pitts, 2009a; S. Pulliam, 2009c).[1]

Evangelical magazines began to pick up on Obama's outreach. *Christianity Today* noted that Obama might have a chance to woo over white evangelicals who wanted to prioritize different issues, such as the war or the environment. Mara Vanderslice, who had previously worked for John Kerry, formed an organization that coordinated direct outreach for Democrats with evangelical venues. Instead of publishing statements in the *New York Times*, which the evangelical "Left" had a tendency to do in the past, these new strategists were advertising on Christian radio and directly engaging evangelical audiences (S. Pulliam, 2008d; Zylstra, 2007). Evangelicals working for Democratic candidates became increasingly featured in evangelical venues (Bergin, 2007d).

Notable evangelicals also affiliated with Barack Obama, even if they did not directly endorse him (Dean, 2008h). Frank Schaeffer, son of Francis Schaeffer—one of the most respected evangelical intellectuals and a key person who helped galvanize the evangelical pro-life movement—supported Obama and wrote regular items on the *Huffington Post* to support his candidacy (W. C. Smith, 2007a). Kirbyjon Caldwell, the pastor who gave the benediction at George W. Bush's presidential inauguration, supported Obama (J. Kennedy, 2008): "I am pro-life both before birth and after birth. It's shameful and sinful to abandon the baby before it's born, and it's equally sinful to abandon the baby after birth. . . . During the administrations of pro-life presidents, you did not see a decrease in abortions, so—why not give Obama's policies a chance?" (quoted in Conant, 2008, 38).

Richard Cizik, then of the National Association of Evangelicals (NAE), noted that Obama was the first Democratic candidate to request a meeting with an NAE official in twenty-eight years (J. Kennedy, 2008). After the election, he stated: "I have strong confidence that evangelicals will find a willing ear from their new president. We need to respond" (S. Pulliam, 2008a, 15).

Obama also prayed with Joel Hunter before his acceptance speech (S. Pulliam, 2008a). Evangelicals across the political spectrum began to speculate as to whether there might be a notable political shift among evangelicals (Blunt, 2007c; How America Decides, 2008; S. Pulliam, 2008b; Vincent, 2007c, 20).

George Barna reported that in February 2008 evangelicals could well end up voting Democrat rather than Republican (and that evangelicals were more likely to vote for Hillary Clinton or Barack Obama than the next highest Republican candidate, Mike Huckabee) (News Briefs, 2008a). More conservative evangelicals began to fear that some evangelicals, particularly Black evangelicals, might be fooled by Obama and vote for him without realizing that he was not pro-life (Dean, 2007e). At the same time, evangelicals became discontented with the lack of attention to religious faith or evangelical outreach on the part of Republican Party candidates (Zylstra, 2007).

For instance, in June, after the primary election season had ended, Obama held an off-the-record meeting with several influential evangelical leaders, including T. D. Jakes, Ron Sider, Franklin Graham, Stephen Strang, Richard Cizik, and many others. He also launched the Joshua Generation Project to target young evangelical and Catholic voters. Meanwhile, McCain had resisted any efforts to court the evangelical vote (News Briefs, 2008f). Stephen Strang blogged about the meeting. While Strang did not feel Obama had anything to offer conservative evangelicals, he "returned from the meeting very concerned. Here is a liberal—Obama—reaching out to the Christian community at a time the conservative—Sen. John McCain—seems to be distancing himself from the so-called 'Christian Right'" (New Republic, 2008). While Obama did not win over Strang, "he seemed to have the support of at least half of the 43 leaders who attended the Chicago meeting. And in my opinion, he 'made points' with the rest" (S. Strang, 2008e). In Obama's favor, Strang did say, "He came across as thoughtful and much more of a 'centrist' than what I would have expected. He did not appear to be the crazy leftist that is being supported by George Soros and his radical leftist friends" (S. Strang, 2008e). Strang concludes by ringing the alarm:

> I urge Sen. John McCain to have a similar meeting—or several such meetings. There is a lot of latent support for him in the Christian community. But after being "stiff armed" by the McCain camp, while being wooed by the Obama camp, this may be the first time a majority of evangelicals will vote for a Democrat for president since Jimmy Carter, who talked of being "born again" and got many evangelical votes in 1976. (S. Strang, 2008e)

Stephen Strang's son, Cameron Strang (founder of *Relevant* magazine, which is geared toward young evangelical adults), attended that same meeting. Unlike his father, Cameron Strang reported being undecided rather than being a solid supporter of McCain. This difference between father and son is perhaps indicative of the generational shift evidenced within evangelical communities. Cameron Strang reported: "I've never seen this before in the Christian community. . . . They're staunchly morally conservative still, but they're saying maybe there's a different paradigm" (Lakshmanan, 2008). He noted that his readers are "broadening the definition of pro-life" to include the fight against poverty, war, disease, global warming, and genocide as well as abortion. "What I'm hearing is that out of the two candidates, one of them is pro-life on five of the six" issues, he said of Obama. "And one is pro-life on one of the six" (Lakshmanan, 2008). Similarly, Robert Andrescik and former editor of *New Man* started ProLifeForObama.com (Lakshmanan, 2008). An Obama for America chapter formed at Liberty University, founded by Jerry Falwell (Lakshmanan, 2008). And Katelyn Steaffans, a church worker in Vienna, Virginia, who had voted for Bush in 2004, reported: "The difference between 2004 and 2008 is that young evangelicals no longer feel we have to be Republicans to be Christian" (quoted in Lakshmanan, 2008; see also Conant, 2008).

In addition, more liberal and progressive evangelicals took this opportunity to promote the visibility of pro-life Democrats (Dean, 2008g) and promote an "abortion-reduction" platform within the Democratic Party (S. Pulliam, 2008e). In particular, evangelicals in the Democratic Party touted a revised platform aimed at "reducing abortions while keeping the procedure legal." Joel Hunter, Jim Wallis, and Tony Campolo endorsed it (Dean, 2009b).

At the beginning of his campaign Obama was aided by the inability of evangelicals to coalesce around a single candidate. At a 2007 meeting of conservative Christian leaders, James Dobson asserted that if the Republican Party did not nominate a pro-life president he would support a third-party candidate. "The Republican party simply must get the message that if they nominate a pro-abortion candidate, we won't be with them" (quoted in W. C. Smith, 2007d, 26). McCain was also not well supported by many evangelical leaders. As mentioned, he was the target of a smear campaign in which he was accused of being gay, mentally unstable, and the father of a Black child out of wedlock. He thought that the Christian Coalition was behind it and called the religious Right an "evil influence" (Carnes, 2008, 34). He also did not make public declarations about his faith. He solicited John Hagee and Rod Parsley (Parsley was often credited with Bush's victory in Ohio in 2004) (N. Anderson, 2006), but later disavowed them when these endorsements came under fire (Carnes, 2008). Black evangelicals had even less interest in McCain, and he started to lose traction with Hispanic evangelicals when he began to shift his position on immigration (Carnes, 2008).

The argument that the evangelical vote was now up for grabs did encounter pushback, however, including from *Christianity Today*:

> Evangelicalism doesn't function like an AFL-CIO, granting endorsements and delivering votes on Election Day. There isn't an evangelical vote. We are not some prior voting bloc up for grabs. Regardless of how pollsters might pigeonhole us, evangelicals come from across a broad spectrum of society—pragmatic, purist and in-between. We should press the candidates to answer questions such as these: What is your plan for Iraq? For the Middle East? What would you do to stop the genocide in Darfur? How would you expand religious freedom worldwide? What would you do to reduce abortion and to protect innocent life in general? How would you secure our border against terrorists, reform our immigration laws, and permit more refugees to resettle here? How would you promote equal economic opportunity for all while protecting the environment? (What We Really Want, 2008, 23)[2]

Indeed, the seeming potential for Obama to capture the evangelical vote was eventually hindered by two major events: (1) his lackluster performance at Saddleback Church; and (2) the nomination of Sarah Palin as the vice-presidential candidate. Rick Warren sponsored a candidates' forum for McCain and Obama at Saddleback Church. McCain was praised for giving direct answers on the issues of gay marriage and abortion, whereas Obama rather obliquely answered the question "When does life begin?" with "That's above my pay scale." Evangelical commentators thought that it might assist Obama's candidacy, but it ended up benefiting McCain (J. Belz, 2008d; Conant, 2008; Dean, 2009b). Evangelical enthusiasm for Obama seemed to dampen considerably in evangelical media after that.

Sarah Palin garnered significant enthusiasm from the Christian Right.[3] Gary Bauer and Richard Land were ecstatic when Sarah Palin was picked as vice president. It was an indication that the Republican Party in fact had not dispensed with evangelicals as an important voting bloc. James Dobson and Tony Perkins thought her pick would spell the end of Obama's chances of winning because he would now no longer be able to pick up any Republican states (Carnes, 2008). Dobson, who had previously said that he would never support McCain, declared that he would reverse his position based on

Palin being on the ticket (Gaines, 2008b). Some strong evangelical gender hierarchicalists opposed Palin's candidacy:

> Sarah Palin's candidacy is a sure sign of God's judgment on the nation. We must continue to uphold the biblical, traditional roles of women who are wives and mothers. Unless we do this we will proceed into darkness and apostasy. I believe God has been trying to chasten His daughter Palin. Her greatest hour is ahead—when she returns to her family sphere, honors her husband, and publicly renounces her despising of her place as a wife and mother. I will not join with the wicked who think they are in control by casting their votes for John McCain. (Feedback, 2008e, 8)

In general, however, Palin received strong support even from those who support gender hierarchy: hierarchicalists generally make a distinction between the importance of men being the head of a household and in church versus political and business leadership, which can be asserted by women and men (Misunderstanding Sarah, 2008). The attacks against Palin's charismatic faith practices in mainstream media outlets particularly riled evangelicals, who argued that these critiques were based on misinformation and stereotype (Bergin, 2008a, 2008c; Dean, 2008e; Lukins, 2009).[4]

In the end *Charisma* endorsed first Huckabee (S. Strang, 2007a, 2007d, 2008b) then McCain (S. Strang, 2008c, 2008g).[5] *World* did not endorse but frequently espoused the "anything but a Democrat" perspective. *Christianity Today* also did not endorse any candidate (Readers Write, 2008) and was often equally critical and praising of both McCain and Obama (D. Taylor and M. McCloskey, 2008). After the election, for a brief moment, there was some awareness of the importance of electing the first Black president as well as the need to pray for him and support him (A. Gaines et al., 2009; A. Harris, 2008a; M. Olasky, 2008d; S. Strang, 2009b). Stephen Strang mused: "I don't believe the election of Barack Obama signals an end to racism, but it is a significant step toward healing America's racist past" (S. Strang, 2009c, 66). This did not last long, as *Charisma* and *World* sharply attacked Obama on everything from health care to the "War on Terror" (M. Olasky, 2015c). *Christianity Today* complained that Obama talked to evangelicals but that they did not actually influence his policies (Can We Come to the Party?, 2008). Obama did not see major gains in the white evangelical vote, except with younger evangelicals (Top News Stories of 2008, 2009). However, the fact that he did make gains with younger evangelicals is indicative of a more long-term strategy to rearticulate evangelical politics. In terms of actually influencing the presidential elections, Obama did shift the vote for Black and Hispanic evangelicals (News Briefs, 2008d). The reverberations of these shifts are continuing to be felt.

From James Dobson to Rick Warren

One of the major reverberations has been the shift from the politics of James Dobson to the politics of Rick Warren. James Dobson had characterized much of the religious Right politics, as inherited by the Christian Coalition, Moral Majority, and others throughout the 1980s and 1990s and through the George W. Bush administration. This politics was largely identified with the Republican Party, which held up certain issues as the litmus tests for identification. However, the reign of Dobson and old-school Christian Right leadership was starting to decline during the election of 2008. As mentioned, evangelicals had difficulty coalescing around a Republican candidate (Dean, 2007b; A. Green, 2008; House Divided, 2007). Commentators frequently held Dobson and the old-school Christian Right responsible for this predicament. Pat Robertson endorsed Rudy Giuliani, even though most considered him unacceptable because of his pro-choice politics (Blunt, 2007b; Dean, 2007c, 2008f). Drew McKissick, secretary of the Christian Coalition, Jay Sekulow, and Charles Colson joined Mitt Romney's campaign, although, again, many evangelicals were suspicious of his prior pro-choice record and his Mormon beliefs (J. Belz, 2007a; Dean, 2007g; News Briefs, 2007d). While it did not argue that presidential candidates should have to pass a religious litmus test, *World* in particular thought that Romney's Mormon beliefs were responsible for his flipflopping on abortion and other issues: "I want a president who tells the truth. And I worry deeply when people are overly ready to believe a man whose religious upbringing, of all things, suggests that the truth is a negotiable commodity" (J. Belz, 2007d, 5).[6] *Christianity Today* agreed that it was acceptable to vote for a Mormon, especially in light of the Obama alternative (Is There Anything Wrong with Voting for a Mormon for President?, 2012).

A split developed between the evangelical elite and the grassroots over Mike Huckabee: most of the elite refused to support him until it was too late because they perceived him to be unelectable (M. Belz and M. Olasky, 2007; Hansen, 2008c; M. Olasky, 2009d). *Charisma*, which supported Huckabee, ran a number of scathing attacks on the Christian Right leadership for their lack of support. One article quotes Brannon Howse, president of the American Family Policy Institute: "I want to thank Bauer, Sekulow, Perkins, Dobson and Robertson for their service to our country and the pro-family, pro-life movement. You have accomplished many good things. . . . However, your time has now passed and you have failed a huge test. Thus I must no longer follow your lead or trust your instinct. If others can still follow you, then I believe they may do so at the peril of our cause" (quoted in Dyck, 2008, 40; Mailbag, 2007c). *World* was less enthusiastic about Huckabee, expressing concern that he might not be sufficiently conservative on government spending or immigration (M. Olasky, 2007g, 2008c). But in the end, it remarked on the split between Christian Right leaders and their constituents: "Religious right leaders who thus far have emphasized poll standings over potential may then be willing to follow their followers" (M. Olasky, 2007e, 11; see also J. Belz, 2008c). "Followers are leading and the leaders are playing catch-up" (M. Belz and M. Olasky, 2007, 16). *World* also criticized James Dobson's threats to leave the Republican Party if McCain was the Republican nominee: "We shouldn't imagine we've got political clout we don't have. When we engage in such pretense, we run the risk of hearing God laugh—not at the bewildered unbelievers, but at us as well" (J. Belz, 2008b, 6). Paul Weyrich also later declared that Christian Right leaders had made a mistake by not endorsing Huckabee from the beginning (W. C. Smith, 2008). Dobson came under further attack when he denounced Obama and questioned his claims to be Christian. Kirbyjon Caldwell started a website and petition, "James Dobson Doesn't Speak for Me" (Caldwell, 2008).[7]

Meanwhile, Rick Warren, while certainly not politically progressive, signaled a new approach to politics that was not identified with a single political party. He refused to say who he would vote for during the 2008 elections, although he had supported Bush in previous elections (J. Belz, 2008d). Just as importantly, his political involvement began to shift from a single-issue to a more multi-issue focus, including AIDS, poverty, and other concerns (Van Biema, 2008). Rick Warren has never claimed to shift his position on abortion and homosexuality (S. Pulliam, 2009b) but has asserted that many issues must be of concern to evangelicals (J. Belz, 2008e). His model of mission work is also less hierarchical and is based on grassroots participation and the development of networks, which implicitly critiques the nongovernmental organization (NGO) model based on professional service providers or missionaries (T. Morgan, 2008). In his efforts to build these networks in different countries, Warren has also come under attack for not necessarily toeing a Republican Party line on who should be in the conversation, be it in Arab or Communist countries (Plowman, 2006).[8]

This ascendancy is providing more space to broaden political choices and options, even if in the end Warren himself may still vote Republican. A number of leaders during Obama's presidential campaign became more vocal about resisting the Dobson bandwagon. Most notable was Richard Cizik, then with the National Association of Evangelicals. He was a key player in the expansion of the political agenda of the NAE, particularly around creation care (terminology generally used by evangelicals to signal commitment to protecting the environment). In fact, James Dobson, Harry Jackson Jr., and others (who were generally not affiliated with the NAE) led an unsuccessful move to have Cizik fired (Walker, 2007).[9] While the NAE affirmed both Cizik and creation care, it later forced Cizik's resignation when he publicly supported gay civil unions—thus showing the current limits on expanding evangelical political agendas (News Briefs, 2007c). Cizik later formed the New Evangelical Partnership for the Common Good in conjunction with David Gushee, an organization that works on a number of issues, including religious tolerance, immigration, and torture.[10]

The NAE, despite Cizik's departure, has not given up its more expanded political agenda. It also announced that it would work "across ideological lines" to reduce abortions through support policies that would expand health-care services, contraceptive availability, and adoption services (Gleanings, 2010). And the NAE has become active in the immigration debate, as discussed later. It has also continued to support creation care.

In addition, those on the evangelical "Left," who had often been marginalized within mainstream evangelical discourse, gained a new hearing (Campolo, 2008; Olsen, 2003c). Jim Wallis of Sojourners commented that he was getting more evangelical attention now than ever before (Olsen, 2008). Ron Sider, founder of Evangelicals for Social Action, who is often portrayed as the "good" evangelical progressive versus Jim Wallis, who is just too "left" (Hansen, 2008a; Olsen, 2007; Veith, 2005i), also seemed to gain new credibility (Carpenter, 2003; Saint, 1998). Even *World* magazine featured an interview with Sider without any negative commentary (Veith, 2005e).

The value of broadening the evangelical political agenda continues to be debated. For instance, in the wake of the elections, Liberty University stripped the College Democrats of their official recognition status, giving the following explanation: "While the students in the college Democrat club are pro-life and support traditional marriage, the constitution of the club pledged support to advance the Democratic platform and candidates. The 2008 Democratic platform has taken an extreme turn to the left on social issues" (Olsen, 2009b, 15). The president of the club later resigned to transfer to another school. School officials started a new policy: all political clubs will only be recognized as unofficial clubs (Human Race, 2009).

Evangelicals have debated whether it is possible to develop bipartisan coalitions around abortion (Dean, 2007f), with many expressing concern that the net result of a "broader agenda" was to water down opposition to abortion (Guthrie, 2008b; R. Miller, 2008; C. Thomas, 2008). In its defense of single-issue politics, *World* asserts: "Abortion is the single issue that tells us about all the others" (Veith, 2007b, 26). According to *World*, the Bible requires that Christians engage in divisive politics (Seu, 2009). Others framed the 2008 elections as a beginning of a "wilderness" period in which the Christian Right needed to assess its shortcomings and plan a new future (Colson, 2009; The Editors, 2008; M. Olasky, 2007h; S. Pulliam, 2008g; Woodlief, 2009). Generally more right-wing (except on prison issues), Charles Colson framed this possible shift positively: "Many commentators are now saying evangelicals, who they still mistakenly assume are all Republicans, are headed for a political crack-up." "Every evangelical leader I know—Rick Warren, Jim Dobson, Bill Hybels, Jim Wallis, and Ron Sider—all of us, right and left, in our own ways, are battling for traditional values. We're defending life, pursuing justice, and caring for the poor" (Colson, 2008b, 124). And a *Christianity Today* article stated that a Christian politician might vote for the state to call same-sex unions "marriages," while preserving the rights of religious groups to reserve their own marriage ceremonies only for those unions that they can conscientiously bless. Or the politician might want to take the word "marriage" out of the state's vocabulary entirely and endorse "civil unions" or "registered domestic partnerships" instead. Or he or she might well decide instead that traditional Christian teaching about marriage is exactly what is needed and vote that way. We need to go "beyond the easy categories of 'all or nothing' and 'red or blue'" (Stackhouse, 2008, 57).[11] In 2009 nine prominent evangelicals, including the board chair of *Christianity Today*, along with eighty others, signed onto an evangelical manifesto declaring that "our identity is centered not in political activism . . . but in our faith in Jesus" (Gospel Independence, 2008, 20; see also Sandvig, 2008a). An interesting cross-section of evangelicals signed on, from Stephen Strang to Jim Wallis (News Briefs, 2008c).

This broadening of the evangelical agenda, however, does not always lead to progressive political shifts. As discussed in the conclusion, it also enabled the evangelical support for the candidacy of Donald Trump, demonstrating that rearticulation can be effected for diverse political ends.

Obama and Race

Needless to say, both Obama's presidential run and his presidency were fraught with the politics of race. These politics played out in evangelical discourse in very complicated ways. On the one hand, evangelicals often portrayed Obama in racist terms. On the other hand, his campaign afforded Black and Latinx evangelicals an opportunity to force white evangelical leaders to change some of their positions on issues of concern, particularly prison reform and immigration.

White evangelicals often portrayed Obama as secretly Muslim, a supporter of terrorists, and a supporter of unpatriotic Black liberation theology. His affiliation with Trinity Church received widespread criticism because the church espouses Black theology, and "the goal of black theology is the destruction of everything white" (Devine, 2008; 43; see also Dean and Olasky, 2008). Obama was often accused of being either a Muslim or a terrorist sympathizer (or both) (Dean, 2008i). Stephen Strang echoed these charges:

> It's been rumored that Obama is a Muslim because his father was a Muslim from Kenya. . . . Obama's political handlers are playing down any connection to Islam. . . . Who would have thought that a man raised as a Muslim would become the darling of the liberal media and be put forward as a possible presidential candidate. . . . I think you can sense that we are engaged in serious spiritual warfare. (S. Strang, 2007c, 82)[12]

While *Charisma* tends be the most supportive of racial reconciliation, a clear limit to addressing racism is its unconditional commitment to Zionism. Others complained that Obama's presidential campaign was contributing to more violence against Christians in Muslim countries (J. Nelson, 2008b). Since, as discussed in chapter 5, Christian Zionists often hold that the reign of the Antichrist will involve massive war between Israel and Arab nations, it is not a surprise that Obama is routinely suspected of being the Antichrist: the "missing" birth certificate not only testifies to his foreignness but also purportedly has a 666 on it (J. L. Grady, 2009a). Philip Yancey complained in *Christianity Today* that he received regular emails from evangelicals regarding Obama,

> pointing out that he was a child of Africa ("the dark continent where worship of demonic spirits, bloodshed, and violence have been the

rule"); a child of Islam ("a religion based upon absolute submission to the god of forces of violence for all infidels"); and a "well-documented deceiver/liar who's [sic] tongue is set on fire with the flames of hell." How far have we come, after all? (P. Yancey, 2009, 96)

Yet, despite this hysteria during the elections, the majority of evangelicals still thought Obama was a Christian. After the election, the perception changed. Now more evangelicals think Obama is Muslim than think he is a Christian (Spotlight: Getting Obama's Faith Wrong, 2010). White evangelicals' hesitancy to critique Obama in general soon evaporated after his election (Cheaney, 2009; M. Olasky, 2015c).

Along with racial panic, the Obama administration's later support of Lesbian, Gay, Bisexual, and Transgender (LGBT) issues—such as the repeal of "Don't Ask, Don't Tell" policies in the military, support of trans-inclusive bathrooms, and gay marriage—has evoked sexual/gender panic. *Charisma* sent out alert with "Obama Now Officially Forcing Girls to Share Showers with Boys" (Thomas More Society, 2015).

This backlash has also manifested itself in anti-Indigenous discourse. When Obama declared his intent to sign the nonbinding UN Declaration on the Rights of Indigenous Peoples (the United States was the last country to sign), Christian Right groups complained that he was engaged in a nefarious plot to return all of the United States to Indigenous peoples. Referring to Obama's adoption by the Crow tribe during the 2008 elections, Brian Fischer declared: "Perhaps he [Obama] figures that, as an adopted Crow Indian, he will be the new chief over this revived Indian empire. . . . But for the other 312 million of us, I think we'll settle for our constitutional 'We the people' form of government, thank you very much" (quoted in Rayfield, 2010). The settler-colonial logic in this statement almost requires no comment. Miraculously, Native peoples become equated with an "empire" that is unjustly usurping lands from "the people." This equation positions Indigenous peoples (along with the perpetually foreign Obama) as somehow foreign to their own lands.

The racial ideologies evident during the 2008 elections continued after Obama's election, especially with the rise of Tea Party politics. While the Tea Partiers and evangelicals overlap, they are not identical. The libertarian tendencies within the Tea Party movement overlap with *World*'s general economic philosophy, for instance, but there is also much evangelical critique of this movement (Sandvig, 2008b). Charles Colson, while sympathetic to complaints about big government, says, "The tea party movement ... makes no attempt to present a governing philosophy. It simply seeks an outlet—an understandable one—for the brooding frustrations of many Americans. But anti-government attitudes are not the substitute for good government" (Colson, 2010, 60). *World* has expressed skepticism that the Tea Party is actually a bottom-up movement (Pitts, 2010a), arguing that bad government is better than no government and that Tea Partiers should be channeled into "fixing government, not throwing the baby out with the bath water" (Colson, 2010, 60). The Tea Party's involvement in the 2010 elections seems to have addressed many of *World*'s concerns (Pitts, 2010b). *Christianity Today* published a debate on the Tea Party in which David Brody (Christian Broadcasting Network) and Wendy Wright (Concerned Women for America) advocated evangelical involvement in the Tea Party.

But David Gushee contended that, while there may be some minimal points of engagement, "to the extent that it is a veil for white reaction to Barack Obama and our increasingly heterogeneous and multiracial society, the movement must be roundly condemned by any who follow Jesus Christ" (Brody et al., 2010, 55). Similarly, *Christianity Today* published an interview with Michael Gerson, who critiqued Tea Party politics for being overly antigovernment: "Instead of adopting a broad, essentially anti-government attitude, essentially libertarian[,] the mainstream Christian reflection has concluded that government has an important role in pursing the common good. It plays an important role in defending the weak and the vulnerable" (quoted in S. P. Bailey, 2010b, 39). Jonathan Merritt warns: "We should be slow to enlist ourselves in any organization whose message could usurp the Gospel's and cautious about any agenda other than Christ's" (Merritt, 2011, 52). Others have critiqued the extremist language on the Right as unbiblical (Perry and Olasky, 2007). *Christianity Today* ran an article that may provide a framework for understanding the relationship between Tea Partiers and evangelicals. It describes what he calls "flea market Christians." These people do not go to church or like church, are biblical literalists, do not use the terminology "born again," and believe in the Bible without reading it or knowing what it says. They are patriotic and support capitalism but do not necessarily ally with the rich and the powerful (Farnsley II, 2006). To borrow from Martin Marty, the Bible serves more as an icon for this constituency than as something that serves as a basis for any sustained political or theological reflection. It is not clear, then, how well biblically based racial reconciliation efforts can intervene here. This racial backlash, what Dylan Rodriguez terms "white reconstruction," has only intensified, as seen with the 2016 election of Donald Trump: white evangelicals constituted his most solid voting base. The rise of Trumpism is discussed in greater detail in the conclusion.

Unintended Consequences of Racial Reconciliation for Party Politics

Obama's presidency frequently put the Christian Right on the defensive over issues of race. The Republican Party was already lacking Black representation in the U.S. Congress (B. Jones III, 2004b). Before Obama's candidacy, evangelical periodicals often focused on the increase in relationships between Black evangelicals and the Republican Party (Daigle, 2005b; A. Gaines, 2005a, 2005b; V. Lowe, 2006a; News Briefs, 2005; Olsen, 2002; S. Strang, 2006b). Black evangelicals were often credited with Bush's victory in Ohio and Florida in 2004. However, any gains made in recruiting Black evangelicals to the Republican Party seemed to erode. Evangelicals frequently accused Black Obama supporters of betraying evangelical principles for identity politics. *Charisma* and *World* often highlighted Black evangelicals who did not support Obama (A. Harris, 2008a; H. Jackson, 2008b). "Regardless of political opinions, the Bible makes it clear; those who support the homosexual agenda and the murder of unborn babies will be judged" (K. Daniels, 2008, 78). Harry Jackson Jr. rather optimistically and incorrectly guessed that Black people would be more supportive of a Republican agenda for 2008 because of social issues like abortion and homosexuality (H. Jackson, 2008a). And *World* consistently asserted that what would appear to be racist attacks against Obama were in fact justified (J. Belz, 2008a; Dean, 2008a; Dream vs. Reality, 2008). In addition, many complained that Black evangelicals had become distracted from these important issues to support Obama (Feedback, 2008a, 2008b, 2008e, 2009a; Rabey, 2010). Evangelical magazines increasingly began to stress the need to address the concerns of voters of color (E. Belz, 2012a, 2012c; J. Belz, 2012; Dean, 2012a, 35; Lu, 2013; M. Olasky, 2012c). They stressed to evangelicals of color that "race can never be used to trump the bible" (E. Belz, 2012e, 45) and "don't celebrate your race over grace" (Dean, 2012a, 36).

At issue, of course, is that a Christian Right agenda, despite the rhetoric of racial reconciliation, is a disavowed white agenda, which has become particularly clear during the 2016 presidential elections. In one article, however, *World* did concede this point. It complained that there was no way for the Christian Right to attract people of color without becoming more leftist—implicitly acknowledging that right-wing politics are white. A politics of inclusion is dangerous because "issues may get watered down in an attempt to attract more minority voters" (B. Jones III, 1998c, 17; Lee, 2009b). Similarly, *Christianity Today*, which normally provides a space for racial critique, was clearly suffering from racial reconciliation burnout in an article by Mark Galli. He complained that evangelicals were focusing too much on social justice and not enough on God (thus presuming that God is not concerned about social justice). He then criticized Soong-Chan Rah's previously described book, *The Next Evangelicalism*, for calling on the evangelical church to renounce its investment in individualism, consumerism, materialism, racism, and imperialism. According to Galli, this call wrongly presumes that racism in the church negatively impacts it in any significant way. Of all the writers Galli cited in his article, Rah was the only person that he did not name (just an "Asian" theologian) (Galli, 2009a). Again, the presumption behind this analysis is that the evangelical church is white and should add "diversity" when it is convenient (this presumption, ironically, is the heart of Rah's critique of white evangelicalism).

Perhaps one of the unintended consequences of *Charisma*'s consistent advocacy of racial reconciliation is that it seemed to receive much criticism from its constituency for its endorsement of McCain and Huckabee over Obama (Feedback, 2008c, 2008d, 2009a, 2009b). One reader asked: "Why is it difficult for some Christians to accept the fact that Barack Obama just may be God's choice? . . . How else can anyone explain—especially with our racist history—that a black man was overwhelmingly elected president?" (Feedback, 2009c, 8). Many of the Black charismatic leaders regularly featured in *Charisma*, such as Juanita Bynum and Donnie McClurkin, expressed their support for Obama rather than McCain (Feedback, 2008a, 2008b). For instance, Derrick Hutchins, chair of the General Council of Pastors and Elders for the Church of God in Christ, declared that he supported Obama, even though he did not share Obama's positions on abortion and same-sex marriage. He opposed McCain because McCain did not support making Martin Luther King's birthday a national holiday or show concern for education, poverty, and racial profiling in law enforcement (Hutchins, 2008). Stephen Strang seemed to be consistently put in the position of having to moderate his critique of Obama ("On a personal level, I found Obama very likeable. . . . But for me, the pro-life issue trumps all the other important issues in the election" [S. Strang, 2008d, 74]). After the elections, he was forced to concede that it was white evangelicals' inability to address racism that contributed to evangelicals of color supporting Obama.

Though conservative white Christians are vigilant to stand against the evils of abortion and oppose making same-sex marriage legal, they have not focused on the other great evil of our day—racism. . . . Now we must make it one of our evangelical priorities. . . . In the same way that some evangelicals say the "religious right" must care about protecting the environment, helping the poor and eradicating AIDS, I propose that we add ending racism to our list of top priorities, along with supporting life, upholding traditional marriage and backing Israel. (S. Strang, 2009c, 66)

Race and Heteronormativity

Besides forcing conservative evangelicals to address race, the 2008 elections also forced conservatives increasingly to rely on evangelicals of color to wage their battle against gay rights. Evangelicals began to see that they were losing the war on homosexuality and same-sex marriage.[13] According to *Christianity Today*, "But seemingly out of nowhere, gay marriage advocates have won stunning judicial, legislative, and social victories" (Galli, 2009b, 31). In fact, *Charisma* argued that the Supreme Court's decision that restrictions on gay marriage were unconstitutional was going to usher in the complete destruction of the United States (Cahn, 2016). It referred to the statistic that 63 percent of evangelicals say that they would have sex before marriage as "rising sexual atheism" (Luck, 2014, 44).

Concern was growing that the anti-gay movement was becoming counterproductive. For instance, Andrew Marin complained that the passage of Proposition 8, which banned same-sex marriage in California, was not a victory for evangelicals, contending that this activism has "yielded few concrete political results while alienating gays and lesbians from the love of Christ. . . . Tell me who really won, then? I don't think anybody did, especially not Christ" (Rabey, 2010, 12). *World* complained that an anti-gay protest demonstrated that "Christianity equals hatred. . . . Wouldn't it be better to have an alternative chorus that shows God's grace?" (M. Olasky, 2007l, 30). These trends have inspired some to temper their anti-gay rhetoric (Christianity Today, 2004a; Stanton, 2009). After restrictions on gay marriage were ruled unconstitutional, *Christianity Today* ran an article arguing that evangelicals should avoid "apocalyptic and hysterical rhetoric" in favor of showing compassion as a "faithful minority" (Gerson and Wehner, 2015, 46). An article in *World*, for instance, opposed gay marriage but nonetheless stated that "reducing homophobia is in fact a worthy and important goal" (World, 2007, 34).[14] *Christianity Today* ran one article suggesting that, rather than trying to end gay marriage, evangelicals should focus on religious exceptions for same-sex marriage (Gleanings, 2014).

Interestingly, the responses to trans politics have been more mixed. A fair amount of hysteria has arisen around the issue of trans-inclusive bathrooms, which some evangelicals argue is being promoted by "transgender activists [who are] deliberately rebelling against God's order" (M. Olasky, 2016d, 6).[15] But *Christianity Today* published an article on trans identity that articulated it as a "Disability" to be managed. It noted that many Christians don't see trans identity as an issue of immorality as they do homosexuality (J. L. Grady, 2016; Yarhouse, 2015). For instance, Pat Robertson was reported as saying with regard to trans identity, "I don't think there's any sin associated with that."[16]

In addition, many prominent evangelical pastors have been caught engaging in homosexual activity (Briefs, 2006; J. L. Grady, 2005b). Members of the LGBT community are also becoming increasingly prominent within evangelical circles (Gushee, 2015). Of course, one of the most prominent cases was Ted Haggard, formerly president of the National Association of Evangelicals, who admitted to soliciting a male sex worker. More recently accusations of sexual abuse have been made by men against Bishop Eddie Long. Although these scandals do not necessarily change evangelicals' theological outlook on homosexuality, they do make it more difficult for them to advance anti-gay rhetoric publicly without being accused of hypocrisy.

Of even greater concern is the fear that the consensus over seeing homosexuality as a sin may be breaking down even within the evangelical church.[17] According to John Stackhouse, professor of theology at Regent College, the decade's biggest change is "the collapse of Christian consensus against homosexual marriage in North America" (Briefing, 2010b). Some indication of this shift is exemplified by a group of organizers called Soulforce, which organized an "Equality Ride"—an eight-week bus tour to Christian college campuses in order to speak to the issue of homophobia (J. Belz, 2006b). What this emerging collapse in consensus reflects is that there is not simply a divide between Christians and gays but that Christianity is actually changing: many think "Moses and Jesus and Paul would affirm same-sex marriage" (M. Brown, 2014a, 24). In addition, Richard Cizik created a stir when he said on a December 2, 2008, interview with National Public Radio that "I'm shifting, I have to admit. In other words, I would willingly say that I believe in civil unions" (NAE Ouster, 2009, 12; see also S. Pulliam, 2009a). As a result of outcry, he was forced to resign from his position. But his shift is not isolated; increasingly, evangelicals are shifting their position in favor of civil unions and some for gay marriage (Galli, 2009b, 31; Veith, 2008a).[18] Jay Bakker, son of Jim and Tammy Faye Bakker, created a stir when he said, "I felt like God spoke to my heart and said homosexuality is not a sin" (quoted in J. L. Grady, 2007b, 6).[19] This statement came in response to an invitation that he received to speak at an Exodus International event (an ex-gay ministry) in which he was asked to sign a form affirming that homosexuality was a sin, which he refused to do. David Gushee, a prominent Southern Baptist scholar, also publicly reversed his position on gays and lesbians in the church and has offered biblical defenses in support of affirming LGBT evangelicals (Gushee, 2015). And *Christianity Today* was shocked when one of its former editors, David Neff, reversed his position and came out in support of same-sex marriage, which the magazine immediately denounced (Galli, 2015a). What was noteworthy, as David Gushee stated in a speech at the American Academy of Religion conference in 2015, was that now the critique of homophobia was becoming internal to evangelicalism. Evangelical organizations such as the Reformation Project have developed specifically to organize against homophobia and heterosexism within evangelical communities. Now LGBT evangelicals have begun to appear at justice-based conferences, such as the Justice Conference, the Sojourners Summit, and Why Christian, to demand inclusion and have sometimes even been invited to speak at such events. As a result, evangelical magazines are now running articles explaining why homosexuality is not biblical (M. Brown, 2014b). What is noteworthy is that these articles generally did not exist until very recently, as same-sex marriage was generally presumed to be nonbiblical. We are currently at a stage similar to what happened during the emergence of the evangelical feminist movement, where conservatives would write articles explaining that feminism simply is not "biblical" (A. Smith, 2008).

In addition, there has been a shift within evangelicalism over the assumption that homosexuality is easily "cured" or "changed." Evangelical discourse has tended to focus on homosexuality as a set of behaviors that people can easily stop doing rather than as an orientation that cannot be changed. They have advocated that people strive to resist temptation and change their behaviors, especially with the help of ex-gay ministries. Now more articles are suggesting that ex-gay ministries are not particularly effective and that homosexuality may in fact be an orientation after all (Ensley, 2008; Lyons, 2007). For instance, a split occurred within Exodus Ministry when President Alan Chambers disavowed reparative ministry (Gentry, 2012). Exodus eventually shut down, and Chambers said that he would start a more welcoming ministry (Dean, 2013c).

Within this context, people of color are becoming increasingly positioned within evangelical discourse as the saviors of heteronormativity. That it is, white evangelicals have begun to regard people of color as more likely to oppose same-sex marriage and the legalization of abortion (Vincent, 2006b). Some credited Black evangelical turnout in Ohio and Florida with George W. Bush's victory in 2004 (Dean, 2008a; B. Jones III, 2004a, 2004c).[20] *Charisma* reported a 6 percent increase in African American Christians who voted Republican in the 2006 election, with Black support increasing by 5 percent in Ohio (Gaines, 2006b). When the City Council of Washington, D.C., voted 12–1 to recognize same-sex marriages from other states, Harry Jackson Jr. attributed it to white people moving to the city and infiltrating it with liberal ways (E. Belz, 2008). According to *Christianity Today*, while 65 percent of Black Protestants in 1996 thought that homosexuals should have the same rights as other Americans, only 40 percent agreed with this statement in 2004 (Olsen, 2004a). And while many evangelicals expressed distress about evangelicals of color supporting Obama, they attributed the passage of anti–gay marriage bills to this same constituency (Gaines et al., 2009). When Michael Irvin came out in support of gay marriage despite his conservative Christian background, *World* blamed this on ESPN trying to find gay people in sports (Bergin, 2011).

Consequently, *World* and *Charisma* began frequently featuring people of color attacking same-sex marriage and homosexuality. One such person is Charlene Cothran, a former publisher of *Venus*, a magazine for Black gays and lesbians. She became a Christian and published an article in *Venus* saying that she had changed her mind and that God does not support homosexuality. "I was suddenly rescued from a sinking ship, but my family is still on that ship" (A. Tracy, 2007, 19).[21] The Family Research Council sent a letter to Washington, D.C., dated Tuesday morning (no year), which said: "Do you think two men should be able to get 'married' just because they like to sodomize each other?"[22] It contained a note from Alan Keyes (who ran against Barack Obama for the U.S. Senate). *Charisma* describes how Harry Jackson Jr. invited 100 church leaders to a national marriage summit in Washington, D.C., to lobby for the Defense of Marriage Act (DOMA). In this case, Jackson is being articulated as leader for the anti-gay movement in general, not just for communities of color (Rabey, 2010). And *Christianity Today* ran two articles that described Black and Hispanic evangelical coalitions being forged to defend traditional marriage. Again, people of color are heralded as leaders of the anti–gay marriage movement. The article notes that Hispanic Christians organized the largest rally against gay marriage at the time in the Bronx, in July 2004 (Carnes, 2004a, 2004b). *World* similarly notes that while the number of people identifying as Christian is declining (including conservative Christians), Asian and Hispanic churches are growing (M. Olasky, 2009g). *World* was so confident in the ability of Black evangelicals to save "traditional" marriage that it predicted that Obama would lose the Black vote when he supported gay marriage (E. Belz, 2012d; News, 2012), and then complained that Democrats were able to exploit "guilt over segregation" to elect an African American president (M. Olasky, 2011b, 72).

Some challenges to this strategy of sharply separating LGBT justice from racial justice emerged after the Pulse Nightclub shooting in Orlando, Florida, in 2016. Some prominent evangelicals called on other evangelicals to repent for their homophobia, which provided a foundation for the attack in Orlando. *World* sharply disputed this and stated that homophobia had nothing to do with the attack, which was simply an act of Islamic terrorism (M. Olasky, 2016b). The response of the Southern Baptist Convention was to adopt a resolution to pray, donate blood, and otherwise give assistance to those in Orlando, while reaffirming that "marriage is between one man one woman" (J. Bruce, 2016, 59). Russell Moore in particular stated:

> Let's call our congregations to pray together. Let's realize that, in this case, our gay and lesbian neighbors are likely quite scared. Who wouldn't be? Demonstrate the sacrificial love of Jesus to them. We don't have to agree on the meaning of marriage and sexuality to love one another and to see the murderous sin of terrorism. Let's also pray for our leaders who have challenging decisions to make in the midst of crisis. Let's mobilize our congregations and others to give blood for the victims. Let's call for governing authorities to do their primary duty of keeping its people safe from evildoers. (R. Moore, 2016a)

This tone was considerably more conciliatory than his address to the 2016 Justice Conference given right before the Orlando massacre, where he referred to members of the LGBT community and their supporters as "cowards who do not love the Word." Popular evangelical blogger Jen Hatmaker created a major stir when she posted on her Facebook page: "I've been listening to my gay friends and leaders the last two days . . . and this is what

I am hearing: It is very difficult to accept the Christian lament for LGBTQ folks in their deaths when we've done such a brutal job of honoring them in their lives. Anti-LGBTQ sentiment has paved a long runway to hate crimes. ... We are complicit" (quoted in D. Green, 2016).

Hatmaker later publicly affirmed same-sex relationships. As a result, LifeWay Publishers of the SBC refused to sell her books anymore (Shellnutt, 2016). And AnaYelsi Velasco-Sanchez organized a memorial for the victims of Orlando at the 2016 Reformation Conference that framed it as reflective of both homophobia and racism in U.S. society.

This discourse also impacts Christian Right views on Islam. That is, Arab and Muslim countries are credited with having a valid critique of the West, not against Western imperialism but rather against the West's immoral acceptance of homosexuality, commercialized sex, and "family breakdown" (broadly construed). For instance, *World* magazine engaged in a debate with Dinesh D'Souza in which he argued against *World*'s position that it is impossible for the United States to engage politically with moderate Muslims because they are inherently intolerant and hence will only engage in political alliances as a cover to persecute Christians. D'Souza contended that Muslims have been much more religiously tolerant than Christians have been historically. But, he further contends: "Let's say you are right about the extent to which Christians are persecuted today in Muslim countries. What is the solution? To attack Islam and drive the traditional Muslims into the arms of the radical Muslims? To declare a 'clash of civilizations' which will only make Christians more vulnerable as perceived stand-ins for the enemy?" (quoted in M. Olasky, 2007i, 28). While critiquing the tendency to caricature Islam within evangelicalism, D'Souza identifies the issue between Muslims and the United States as the U.S. embrace of homosexuality rather than U.S. imperialism: "Some Muslims complain about U.S. activities in the Middle East or support for Israel, but an even more widespread concern is cultural: What Muslims see is an American descent into homosexual marriage, family breakdown, and a popular culture that is often morally repulsive" (D'Souza, 2007, 26). His solution is to support heteronormative family values on a global scale as a bulwark against Islamic terrorism:

> We should recognize how our domestic culture war and the war on terror are linked. The restoration of American culture will not only be better for our children, but will help America's image abroad. . . . [The] Bush administration should do more to highlight the presence, and

values, of conservative and religious America. Moreover, we should do what we can to export this America, which is good America, to the rest of the world.... By proclaiming our allegiance to the traditional values of Judeo-Christian society, we can reduce the currents of anti-Americanism among the Muslims, and thus undercut the appeal of radical Islam to traditional Muslims around the world. (D'Souza, 2007, 27)

New Man similarly contends that the reason Muslims hate America has nothing to do with foreign policy but is Muslims' "desire for domination" and because America "has embraced immoral ways of living such as homosexuality, pornography, drug addiction, alcoholism, divorce, and prostitution" (Penemaker, 2005, 51). "Why do they hate us?" asks Philip Yancey. It is the *Baywatch* factor: "How differently would the world view us if it associated the U.S. with Jesus rather than Baywatch?" (P. Yancey, 2002, 80). In *Christianity Today*, Timothy George further asserts the possibility of cooperating with Muslims on conservative family values, although he notes that their refusal to believe in the Trinity may make cooperation difficult (T. George, 2002a).

It should be noted however, that while people of color are often positioned as the saviors of heteronormativity, they are also often "queered" within Christian evangelical organizations across the political spectrum. As Gabe Veas contended in his address at the 2018 Voices conference, people of color are seldom hired in evangelical organizations because they are not deemed sufficiently orthodox. Many evangelicals of color have informally complained to me they have either not been hired at an institution or had their programs defunded because they were neither deemed sufficiently orthodox nor sufficiently progressive on LGBT issues. In that sense, the position of people of color mirrors Jasbir Puar's analysis of the queering of Muslims, who are always simultaneously too sexually perverse and sexually repressed to be enfolded into the whiteness of heternormativity (Puar, 2007). Thus, LGBT litmus tests in Christian institutions across the political spectrum often function as veiled racial litmus tests.

Race and Abortion

Articles on abortion also often highlight the role of people of color within this movement and frame the pro-life movement as an antiracist movement (J. L. Grady, 2015; M. Olasky, 2012e, 2015d). *World* ran an article in which abortion is articulated as a form of anti-Black racism (Bradley, 2005). It recounts Margaret Sanger's involvement in eugenics and that 3,445 Black people were lynched from 1882 to 1960, but then notes that this number dwarfs in comparison to the 12 million Black children aborted since 1973 (Bradley, 2005). The article advertises the website maintained by Clenard Childress, president of Life Education and Research Network, the largest African American evangelical pro-life group (Bradley, 2005). The website, www.blackgenocide.org, lists Black deaths since 1973 due to AIDS, violent crimes, accidents, cancer, heart disease, and abortion. Another article in *World* accuses Planned Parenthood of targeting Hispanic women for abortion services. While *World* generally does not show much concern for undocumented women, this article reverses that position and charges that abortion-rights groups are victimizing undocumented women (Vincent, 2009). It also focuses on Earl Walker Jackson, who was running for office under the slogan "Planned Parenthood has been far more lethal to black lives than the KKK" (Pitts, 2013, 43).

In reporting the pro-life march that happened January 22, 2009, after Obama's inauguration, *World* admitted: "Minorities joined in, too, though they were few" (E. Belz, 2009e). This did not stop *World* from quoting people of color in disproportion to their attendance. Interestingly, the article cited one African American who made implicit critiques of the pro-life movement and its racism. Marcia Lane-McGee, who attended this march but described herself as an Obama supporter, said, "Pro-lifers need to focus more on providing support for children after they're born, through better health care and helping moms get off welfare" (quoted in E. Belz, 2009e). Alveda King, niece of Martin Luther King Jr., spoke in front of White House to oppose the Mexico City policy and said, "While he is living his dreams, those babies will be dying horrible deaths because of the policies he supports" (quoted in E. Belz, 2009e).

Utilizing the sexist and racist rhetorical stance that African American women are the cause of all problems in African American communities, *Christianity Today* asserts: "The most dangerous place for an African American to be is in the womb of his or her African American mother" (Delahoyde et al., 2009, 56). *World* explained that the pro-life movement is the arena that brings people of color together. "The pro-life movement also has ethnic diversity" (Veith, 2004a, 33). An example of this diversity is Indians for Life, headed by Little Hawk Hernandez, who says that Native Americans have a principle "of not killing our unborn babies, elders, and people that are handicapped or sick" (Veith, 2004a, 33). Day Gardner of Black Americans for Life asserts, "Abortion has become the new form of black genocide which is systematically destroying about 400,000 black babies each year" (Veith, 2004a, 33). *World* concludes: "Like no other domestic problem, abortion is an exercise of raw power against the weakest" (Veith, 2004a, 33). It ran another cover article on the connection between abortion and the eugenics movement (Dean, 2015b). Similarly, *Charisma* reported on a march in Selma, modeled after Martin Luther King Jr.'s march, that was intended to drive out abortion centers in the city and apparently was successful in making Selma "abortion free" (Brumfield, 2016, 18).

Pro-life activist Alveda King is featured prominently within white evangelical venues. After having two abortions and three divorces, Alveda King became a Christian and had six children. In 2004 she became a pro-life activist. *Charisma* stresses that she did not support Obama's presidency because of his pro-choice politics (apparently the only person in the King family not to do so) (V. Lowe, 2009b). In response to a Department of Homeland Security report that discussed terrorist activities committed by pro-life groups she stated, "To say, as the Department of Homeland Security does, that white supremacists have exercised a 'longstanding exploitation of social issues such as abortion' tells me that either the government, the supremacists, or both are clueless about abortion's grave impact on the black community. Abortion is the white supremacists' best friend" (Quotables, 2009, 16).

Alveda King led an abortion "freedom ride" in 2010, based on the civil rights Freedom Rides of the 1960s. The reason: "Another precious class of human beings is now suffering discrimination . . . and the threat to them is abortion. . . . Black children are an endangered species" (Freedom Ride for Life, 2010, 26). In a similar vein, *World* conducted an interview with E. W. Jackson, who was asked, "Does it bother you when folk equate the gay rights movement with the civil rights movement" (M. Olasky, 2013d, 29). Jackson replied that he is bothered because Black people suffered from Jim Crow, but "nobody is interested in persecuting homosexuals. Most Americans don't care. It's none of our business" (M. Olasky, 2013d, 29).[23]

While reproductive justice groups based on women of color would concur that there is rampant racism within the white-dominated pro-choice groups, it is also the case that the pro-life groups often trade on the same racial ideologies (A. Smith, 2005a, 2008). Of course, to maintain this argument that reproductive justice is "white," only white-dominated groups are featured, such as Planned Parenthood or the National Abortion and Reproductive Rights Action League (NARAL). Groups based on women of color that may adopt a reproductive justice rather than a "pro-choice" framework (the Native Youth Sexual Health Network, SisterSong, the National Latina Institute for Reproductive Health, etc.) disappear from the analysis because then evangelicals would have to address racism within the pro-life movement.

Although conservative evangelicals' desire to stop gay marriage and abortion has increased the visibility of conservative evangelicals of color, this spotlight can have unintended consequences. First, these evangelicals of color are often not single-issue oriented and couch their heteronormative stances within critiques of racism, including white evangelical racism. For instance, *Christianity Today* ran an article on James Meeks, a pastor of Chicago-based Salem Baptist and a state representative from the south side of Chicago. He works with Operation PUSH (People United to Serve Humanity), and his candidacy for state representative was supported by Jesse Jackson. On the one hand, he says that he would support a constitutional amendment to oppose gay marriage (although he supports other gay civil rights legislation). On the other, he critiques evangelical preoccupation with issues like homosexuality.

> Evangelicals must be very careful not to be irrelevant. . . . Evangelicals will grab . . . one issue—like abortion—and they think that because they take a tough stand on abortion then they have addressed a societal ill. I don't hear the same outcry from any evangelical pulpit about the unequal funding for education among the haves and the have-nots. I don't hear from the evangelical pulpit about the disparity in the prison population between blacks and whites, between the test scores of African American kids and white kids. If white kids couldn't read and black kids could . . . the evangelical church would address it. If white kids were in jail and not going to college, the evangelical church would address it. So if you live in a society and you only address the things that face your ethnicity, you are not really concerned about social ills. (Smietana, 2004, 35)

Similarly, *World* notes that a trade-off in garnering support from people of color against gay marriage is being pressured to take a stronger stance against discrimination against people of color. *World* explains the strategy for increasing Black opposition to gay marriage in an article on the city council of Columbus, Ohio, which repealed a domestic partners benefits package for city employees in 1998. "The secret to securing the support of black churches . . . is to keep the rhetoric from being mean-spirited" (Maynard,

1999). Eric Seabrook, an African American attorney who was a spokesperson for the repeal, was quoted as saying, "The gay movement has capitalized on and tried to piggyback itself on the civil-rights movement, and that trivializes the black experience. The Stonewall incident was ugly, yes, but it does not compare to the Middle Passage.... [However,] African-Americans are very sensitive to any kind of discrimination as everyone should be. At the same time you're doing this, you must be in the forefront of condemning any act of violence or discrimination against gays" (Maynard, 1999, 21). *Charisma* ran an article on political involvement by Black evangelical pastors. It noted that this generation of Black evangelicals held conservative family values, supported capitalism, and opposed homosexuality but was also politically independent. For instance, Eugene Rivers hosted Bill Clinton at a fundraiser in 2005. Rivers declared that Black evangelicals should form their own "moral majority" to influence elections that would be independent of both parties as well as independent from the white dominated Christian Right (A. Gaines, 2006b). Yvonne Miller, of the Church of God in Christ, was quoted in the article as saying that "exploitation of the poor is sin. Paying low wages to people just because you can is sin" (A. Gaines, 2006b, 34). Similarly, when *Christianity Today* ran a cover article on the proper response to the legalization of gay marriage now that Christian Right politics "has largely failed" and "evangelicals have lost influence," Gabriel Salguero of the National Latino Evangelical Coalition noted that Christianity was implicitly talking about white evangelicalism. Many Hispanic, Asian, and African American evangelicals are not having what he called a "Chicken Little moment." He continued:

> Our sky is not falling, because we have lived under fallen skies for years. Conservative Christians have been disproportionally affected by racism, immigration, poverty, and denial of voting rights (to name a few issues) for decades and centuries. Why did lack of progress on these issues not arouse similar concerns long ago? (Salguero, 2015, 47)

Salguero then quotes Lisa Sharon Harper, "While it is true that white males have enjoyed the sinfully partial U.S. law and cultural dominance since our nation's founding, the same is not true for all evangelicals" (Salguero, 2015, 40).

And at the same time, evangelicals often do not find it so easy to separate racial and gender justice. For instance, Mark Labberton, president of Fuller Seminary, discusses these tensions in a special issue that *Fuller Mag-*

azine did on Reconciling Race. Just after the 2015 Charleston shootings and the Supreme Court decision recognizing the right for same-sex couples to marry, Labberton asserted that Fuller continued to "affirm marriage as the union of one man and one woman" (Labberton, 2015, 7). But he then notes that Christian stances against same-sex marriage can further "religious hatred, rejection, or separatism," and ultimately racism. He concludes. "The church is divided by so many things—race and sexuality among them—but the road ahead will show how the people of God will express the love of God for their family, friends, and neighbors" (Labberton, 2015, 8).

An unintended consequence of white evangelicals courting the support of evangelicals of color to support pro-life and anti-gay politics, however, was that Black and Latinx evangelicals began to demand reciprocity. As a result, white evangelical politics began to shift significantly on these issues in unexpected ways. The recruitment of people of color into the evangelical pro-life movement has shifted what that movement represents. One of the most startling examples of this shift in the pro-life paradigm was evidenced in the 2017 Evangelicals for Life conference organized by the Southern Baptist Convention. While abortion was certainly discussed at this conference, it was situated as one of many pro-life issues that were all equally addressed: in particular, racial justice, immigration reform, and disability. There was as much criticism of the Muslim ban that had just been enacted by President Trump as of pro-choice politics. Keynote speaker Eugene Cho in particular articulated a very expansive pro-life politic. If we are pro-life, then we must be concerned about not only American lives but Syrian lives. We must be concerned about not only Christian lives but Muslim lives. If we are pro-life, we must unapologetically state that Black lives matter. And, Cho stated dramatically, no matter how uncomfortable it makes us feel, we must care about the high suicide rate among LGBT youth. A pro-life politic must advocate for expanded birth control. And, in a serious challenge to the assumption that a pro-life politic must support the criminalization of abortion, Cho stated that Korea has outlawed abortion and yet has a higher abortion rate than in the United States. A pro-life politic, he concluded, must concern itself with not only the unborn child but with the mother seeking an abortion.

In addition, Black and Latinx evangelicals in particular began to respond that if they were going to support white evangelicals on gay marriage and abortion then white evangelicals were going to have to support them on the issues of policing/mass incarceration and immigration reform, thus signaling major shifts in policy focus from white evangelical organizations.

Policing and Prison Reform

Even predating Obama's candidacy, the courting of Black evangelicals seems to have increasingly put prison reform and other social justice issues on the radar screen for white evangelical groups. For instance, *Charisma* noted that some of the various coalitional efforts between Black charismatics and Black civil rights groups address not only the issue of same-sex marriage but also the issues of prison reform, health care, and ending the war in Iraq. As I have argued in previous work, evangelicals have worked on prison reform for many years, particularly through Prison Fellowship. However, the political stances taken by Prison Fellowship and Charles Colson were often not taken up by other white-dominated evangelical groups. This preexisting work began to coalesce with conservative Black evangelicals' consistent critique of the prison industrial complex. As mentioned, Harry Jackson Jr.'s High Impact Leadership Coalition advocates a federal marriage amendment and prison reform (Daigle, 2005b). This message's conjunction with the preexisting evangelical organizing on prison issues through groups such as Prison Fellowship is spurring even more conservative authors to start tackling this issue.[24] Even *World*, which heretofore generally published "get tough on crime" articles, printed an editorial denouncing the prison industrial complex: "Our nation's prison industrial complex has unbiblical roots." It notes that prisons are a multibillion-dollar industry, which creates an economic incentive to maintain high crime rates. It discussed a securities report for the private prison industry that listed "risks" for that industry: "A falling crime rate, shorter prison sentences, a move toward alternative sentences, and changes in the nations' drug laws" (Seu, 2008, 75). It concluded: "I do not believe that any reform could be adequate for the system that is wrongheaded from the beginning."[25] One of the key editors of *World*, Marvin Olasky, eventually also came out against the death penalty.[26] Shane Claiborne has become particularly active in organizing against the death penalty. He wrote the book *Executing Grace* (2016), and calls on Christians to incorporate anti–death penalty work into pro-life politics. He further calls on evangelicals to "think and speak of Christ as one who was executed" (Michel, 2016, 75).

The public policy manifesto of Harry Jackson Jr. and Tony Perkins, which generally espouses fairly conservative positions on most issues, strongly supports prison reform and denounces the racism of the prison system: "We could go on about violation of rights, excessive use of force, violent prison terms, insufficient prison aftercare, and the generational impact of prison-induced fatherlessness. It is little wonder that so many blacks are against the death penalty. After all, false imprisonment, lynching, and torture were all perpetrated on blacks in the name of 'justice'" (Jackson and Perkins, 2008, 147). And evangelicals became involved in challenging the sentencing disparity between crack and cocaine use. Rod Parsley argued: "Current sentences disproportionately impact African Americans and force law enforcement agencies to spend their time and effort on low-level drug users rather than the distributors that cause most of the damage" (Grant, 2010). Even Pat Robertson weighed in on this issue by proposing that marijuana should be decriminalized.

> It got to be a big deal in campaigns: "He's tough on crime," and "lock 'em up!" ... That's the way these guys ran and, uh, they got elected. But, that wasn't the answer.... We're locking up people that have taken a couple puffs of marijuana and next thing you know they've got 10 years with mandatory sentences.... These judges just say, they throw up their hands and say nothing we can do with these mandatory sentences. We've got to take a look at what we're considering crimes and that's one of 'em. (LeClaire, 2010)

With the rise of the Black Lives Matter movement, evangelicals became increasingly involved in policing and prison reform. *Christianity Today* ran a cover issue on mass incarceration, critically analyzing it as a system of the "new Jim Crow," to use Michelle Alexander's terminology, and called on churches to engage not just in prison ministry, but in prison reform (quoted in M. Lee, 2016a, 41).[27] The Ethics and Religious Liberty Commission (ERLC) of the Southern Baptist Convention included criminal justice reform on its 2016 legislative agenda for the first time (M. Lee, 2016a, 46). Meanwhile, more progressive evangelicals have called for more radical critiques of incarceration, including abolition (Gilliard, 2018).

Immigration

In addition to Black evangelicals successfully garnering support from white evangelicals for prison reform, the Latinx evangelical leadership successfully pressured white evangelicals to shift their position on immigration (Carnes, 2005d; Plowman, 2007). In fact, *Christianity Today* ranked the growing split within evangelicalism over immigration as one of the top ten stories of the year (Top Ten Stories of 2006, 2007). As discussed, some strands within evangelicalism have been sympathetic to immigration reform, as immigrants are seen as a rich mission field. Immigration became a particularly divisive issue in 2006 amid the massive immigration organizing against federal anti-immigration bills. Latinx evangelical groups began to serve notice that immigration reform was a nonnegotiable demand. *Charisma* reported that on February 2, 2006, a coalition representing more than 20 million Latinx evangelicals announced its opposition to immigrant reform proposals that they viewed as anti-immigrant. Their major opposition focused on House of Representatives bill 4437, which would subject anyone assisting undocumented workers to arrest. The Hispanic Coalition for Comprehensive Immigration Reform outlined four goals, including humanitarian border policies and expanded opportunities for immigrants already in the United States to become citizens (News Briefs, 2006a). The coalition is headed by Samuel Rodriguez, head of the National Hispanic Leadership Conference—the largest Hispanic evangelical organization, which represents 15 million Hispanics. He declared: "This legislation is anti-Hispanic, anti-immigrant, and anti-Christian" (Richardson, 2006, 24).[28] Rodriguez warned white evangelicals that the Hispanic evangelical community could lose 40 percent of its members if the legislation passed (Richardson, 2006). While he supports pro-life and anti–gay-marriage positions, he noted that his support has a price:

> We need to know from white evangelical leaders, why did they not support comprehensive immigration reform, why did they come down in favor exclusively of enforcement without any mention of the compassionate side? . . . So down the road, when the white evangelical community calls us and says, "We want to partner with you on marriage, we want to partner on family issues," my question will be, "where were you when 12 million of our brothers and sisters were about to be deported and 12 million families disenfranchised?" (Stafford, 2006, 82)

Rodriguez does not oppose increased border enforcement in order to "protect our citizenry from possible terrorists and drug trafficking" (Scheller, 2006, 48). At the same time, "we have a moral, biblical, God-given obligation to take care of the disenfranchised, the alienated, and the foreigner. How they got here is not our issue" (Scheller, 2006, 48). The previously anti-immigrant *World* listed Samuel Rodriguez's *The Lamb's Agenda* (2013) as one of top ten books of year: "It will help some anti-immigration conservatives understand why the increased number of Latinos in the

United States is likely to benefit evangelical churches rather than weaken them" (M. Olasky, 2013c, 48–49).

The growing pressure has been so effective that many white evangelicals who were not sympathetic began to see the writing on the wall. If they did not change their policies on immigration, they could lose their political power in the long term (E. Belz, 2009e). *Christianity Today* noted that four out of ten Hispanics (two out of three Hispanic evangelicals) voted for Bush. After the immigration debate was sparked in 2006, only 30 percent were voting Republican. Richard Cizik commented that evangelicals saying "throw them out of the country, declare them illegal . . . is not the best way to court Hispanic evangelicals. Moreover, it's not the slightest bit realistic. If that's your method of courting Latino voters, I'd suggest you start over" (quoted in Hughes, 2008, 15; see also Rainey, 2006a, 2008).

World has consistently espoused anti-immigration positions. But after the 2006 elections, its positions began to shift. While the anti-immigrant strand continued, it also espoused policies that support "the free flow of labor and robust homeland-security measures. President Bush would be best served by a program that offers major incentives for both" (Hewitt, 2005a, 9).[29] At the same time, *World* ran an interview with Victor Davis Hanson charging that there should be stricter quotas for Mexican versus Asian immigrants because Asians prefer private enterprise whereas Mexicans want entitlement programs. In addition, Hanson complained that America should be a melting pot not a salad bowl, through total assimilation and the end to bicultural/bilingual educational programs. Hanson further contended that progressive support for immigration reform was just a liberal plot to get a stronger leftist voting bloc (M. Olasky, 2005g, 2005i; see also J. Kilpatrick, 2007). As it turns out, *World* later began to realize that anti-immigration positions were actually dividing a potential right-wing voting bloc (Bergin, 2007b; Dean, 2008c).[30] *World* has not been particularly sympathetic to the immigrant boycotts and protests, contending that they were largely unsuccessful because they were not "pro-American" (Dawson, 2006f, 19). Another article claimed that the massive protests created a backlash that deepened anti-immigrant sentiment, particularly in response to images of immigrants carrying Mexican flags. The number of Americans thinking that illegal immigration is a serious problem increased by 11 percent after the protests. However, this article did point out that anti-immigrant laws are victimizing people (Dawson, 2006d). It also ran a more sympathetic op-ed saying that Christians should remember that they were immigrants once. "God does not want us to be partners in oppression, and someone who has illegal status can be readily oppressed" (J. Belz, 2006c, 6). Its more comprehensive article on the proposed 2006 legislation was more balanced, giving voice to those who complained particularly about the HR 4437 provision that made illegal immigration a felony and penalized those who assisted or harbored illegal immigrants (Dawson, 2006e).[31] *World* commented on the debate about immigration, particularly Bush's proposed immigration reforms in regard to Mexico. "The vision of the future held by anti-immigrant Republicans contends that an ingrafting of millions of Mexicans will nudge America to the left. Pro-immigration forces, though, suggest that immigrants committed to family and work will help to save America from cultural decay" (T. Graham, 2001a, 23). While *World* has continued to feature articles that describe immigration as "an invasion" (Dean, 2011a, 36),[32] overall its approach has become more nuanced (Lu and Smith, 2011).

Christianity Today featured ministers supporting immigration reform. According to Art Lucero of Sunrise Church: "Immigrants are hungry, and they need a place to work, to move ahead to the American dream. Is it illegal to want that? These are not wicked evil people" (quoted in Callahan, 2004b, 20). Another article asserted: "Terrorists don't come through the desert with a jug of water. Terrorists do not come through tunnels. It's not practical. They come with legal papers" (D. Nelson, 2006, 85). In one forum on how Christians should address illegal immigrants, two participants, M. Daniel Carroll and Matthew Soerens, said that ministering to them should take precedence over following the law. Soerens stated that in this case following the Bible would sometimes mean engaging in "civil disobedience" (What Should Churches Do about Illegal Immigrants in Their State?, 2011, 53).

Charisma has generally been supportive of immigration reform. For instance, J. Lee Grady opined: "We cannot be truly pro-life if we don't love immigrants. It is the height of hypocrisy to defend unborn babies and then mistreat foreigners; it's also shamefully two-faced for us to defend traditional marriage on one hand and then split up families on the other" (J. L. Grady, 2012, 96). *Charisma* ran an op-ed sympathetic to immigrant rights organizing, noting that many Latina Pentecostals were organizing against HR 4437 and calling the bill "anti-Hispanic, anti-immigrant, and anti-Christian" (J. L. Grady, 2006h, 8). It quoted Jim Backlin of the Christian Coalition, who supported the bill: "The Bible says national borders are to be respected, and we need to respect the rule of law" (J. L. Grady, 2006b, 8). However, it recommended that before white evangelicals join the anti-immigrant backlash "we go out to spend a few minutes listening to our Hispanic Christian brothers—some of whom have fresh memories of what it is like to live under dictatorship. We might discover that God's perspective isn't based on right-wing or left-wing rhetoric but on a higher law of love that transcends divisive politics" (J. L. Grady, 2006b, 8). In 2006 the Family Research Council hosted a discussion on immigration, a move away from its previous negative position that immigrants were having an undesirable effect on U.S culture (Carnes, 2005d; Richardson, 2006). World Relief and the World Evangelical Alliance called for immigration reform. Focus on the Family, Family Research Council, the National Association of Evangelicals, and Concerned Women for America refused to take positions at that time. Meanwhile, Richard Land of the Southern Baptist Convention said that he supported stronger border security but also wanted a guest worker program: "We believe that God ordained government to punish those who break the law and to reward those who will keep the law" (Richardson, 2006, 26).

Similarly, as noted, a book jointly written by Harry Jackson Jr. and Tony Perkins of the Family Research Council outlines what they perceive to be biblically based positions on a number of issues, all of which are generally conservative. However, the chapter on immigration contains a decidedly more moderate turn, even as its policy reform suggestions still support such things as increased border enforcement. It describes the plight of undocumented workers in the United States as "the new slavery" (H. Jackson and T. Perkins, 2008, 86; see also Seu, 2008). It opposes efforts to require charities to ask for documentation before providing services. We "must never forget that we are often dealing with needy people whose foremost need is to receive Jesus Christ as their Savior. Any Christian approach to immigration that does not acknowledge our need to preach the gospel to these diverse communities will fall short" (H. Jackson T. Perkins, 2008, 94).

In the 2008 election cycle, the rhetoric shifted even further. Latinx evangelical leaders (although not Samuel Rodriguez, who supported McCain) started to assert that they would switch parties on the issue of immigration (Dean, 2008b, 2008c). Wilfredo De Jesus, senior pastor of New Covenant (an Assemblies of God church), reported that Obama was going to be his first vote for a Democrat because of this issue (J. Kennedy, 2008). *World* reported that Hispanic Protestants supported Obama by a 50 percent to 33 percent margin (with 80 percent describing themselves as born again or evangelical). Bush had gotten 63 percent of this vote (Dean, 2008b). The Christian Right noted that anti-immigration positions were alienating their potential allies in the fight against gay marriage (Carrasco, 2001). Samuel

Rodriguez admonished the Christian Right, saying that if it wanted Hispanics to support its issues, it would have to side with them on immigration. Concurring, Matt Daniel of Alliance for Marriage said that "it has been a mistake for some evangelical leaders, operating under the banner of marriage and family, to take hard-line positions on immigration and alienate their most natural ally. . . . [Marriage] is not the private property of Americans" (Vincent, 2007a, 25).

Charisma ran a cover page article on Samuel Rodriguez, which critiqued Arizona SB 1070 and included a section on the need for Christians not to oppress immigrants (Schweikert, 2010). *Charisma* did not take a stand itself, but the article was largely favorable to immigrant rights (Yoars, 2010). Richard Land argued that anti-immigration stances among evangelicals were not about racism. It is just that "Americans overall don't want to be a bilingual nation" (Schweikert, 2010, 72).

In a stunning reversal of its previously espoused perspectives, *World* argued that evangelicals need to be less anti-immigrant because "you too were once immigrants. . . . Arrogance, especially on the subject of immigration, has no place among God's people" (J. Belz, 2008f, 6).[33] *World* noted that white evangelicals were losing constituents who could be political allies. Furthermore, U.S. states with the most immigrants (even illegal immigrants) had the best statistics on poverty, crime, and unemployment. "The conservative scare is just plain wrong" (J. Belz, 2008f, 6). *World* also condemned the Alabama anti-immigration bill that criminalized anyone who harbored, transported, or entered into contracts with undocumented immigrants and allowed checks on immigration status on any suspicion. "Alabama church leaders say the state's tough new immigration law is hostile to all Hispanics and creates obstacles to ministry" (E. Belz, 2012b, 50). Some churches had lost half their parishioners (E. Belz, 2012b, 52). The Southern Baptist Convention passed a resolution in 2011 with 80 percent of the vote calling for a path to citizenship for undocumented immigrants. It advocated securing borders, but churches should be for all persons regardless of immigrant status and no bigotry or harassment. (E. Belz, 2012b, 53).

Thus, within the anti-immigration hysteria that has been accentuated in the recent debates around the passage of SB 1070 in Arizona, it is noteworthy that so many mainstream evangelical groups have departed from traditional Republican Party politics to support immigration reform. Hispanic evangelical groups contemplated boycotting the 2010 census over the issue of immigration (Briefing, 2010a; Walker, 2009a). *Christianity Today* ran a forum on the best way to reform immigration (What's the Best Way to Reform U.S. Immigration Now?, 2010). The positions it supported on immigration included improve border security with humane enforcement methods; facilitating the ability of employers to check workers' status; facilitating pathways to citizenship; having stronger family reunification programs; increasing guest worker programs; improving refugee resettlement; teaching respect for the law; and allowing for provision of social services to all peoples regardless of citizenship (Aliens in Our Midst, 2005; The Soul of the Border Crisis, 2009). It also ran a cover story on the plight of immigrants, particularly immigrant women who are domestic survivors as well as those who came to United States at a young age. It criticized Arizona SB 1070 and noted that it was leading to churches losing members (Beaty and Jethani, 2012). *Christianity Today* also featured a nurse who provides free medical care to those who are undocumented in Arizona and well as a high school teacher who focuses on organizing high school Latinos (Moring, 2012a, 2012b). InterVarsity, World Relief, and NAE sent an open letter to Congress opposing more restrictive language in the Violence against Women Act for U-Visas (Concerned Women for America, by contrast, complained this was "obscuring real violence in order to promote a feminist agenda") (Beaty and Jethani, 2012, 28). In 2009 the National Association of Evangelicals endorsed immigration reform that reflects "biblical grace to the stranger" (Banks, 2009). It supports safeguarding national borders, family reunification, and equitable processes to enable citizenship for currently undocumented immigrants (Banks, 2009; S. Pulliam, 2008f).

Charisma has been providing greater visibility for this issue, even hosting a conference call with Samuel Rodriguez in October 2010 so that its readers could learn his perspectives on biblically based responses to immigration. He continued to galvanize evangelical support for pro-immigration reform rallies and events (Walker, 2010b). The Southern Baptist Ethics and Religious Liberty Commission under Richard Land and the National Association of Evangelicals criticized SB 1070. Rod Parsley, president of the Center for Moral Clarity, said that arguments in favor of the Arizona SB 1070 "betray a selfish, arrogant and, at times, racist attitude that is incompatible with the Christian's command to love one's fellow man and to serve the poor among us" (Grant, 2010).[34] *World* ran an article that covered both proponents and opponents of the bill, noting it would erode Latinx support for the Republican Party (Basham, 2010b). The shift crystallized in the formation of the Evangelical Immigration Roundtable, which brought together evangelicals across the theological and political spectrum to advocate for immigration reform (Blanton, 2014).

Of course, the shifts in evangelical leadership are not necessarily reflected at the grassroots level. A Pew Research Center survey found that 64 percent of evangelicals chose the statement that "immigrants today are a burden because they take jobs, housing, and health care" over that statement that "immigrants today strengthen our country with their hard work and talents," compared to 52 percent of all Americans. In a survey on the Family Research Council's website, 80 percent of respondents advocated a border fence and deploying U.S. armed forces to the border (S. Pulliam, 2006). *Christianity Today* featured a poll with different results: 82 percent say Bible verses on welcoming the stranger apply to the U.S. immigration debate; 54 percent think the U.S. government should establish a path to citizenship; 31 percent think it should offer blanket amnesty; and 15 percent said that current law should be enforced (I Was a Stranger, 2007). In addition, many Christian Right leaders are also anti-immigrant: Mark Tooley of the Institute for Religion and Democracy, for instance, argues that the church should not support pastors who are undocumented: "Breaking the civil law is a sin." "To acclaim them as victims meriting redress is dishonest and points them away from the obedience . . . that is central to following Jesus" (K. Metzger et al., 2013, 77).

Conclusion

The Obama presidency began to spark a greater interest in racial justice beyond racial reconciliation among evangelicals, particularly around the issues of mass incarceration and immigration reform. At the same time, however, racial reconciliation began to reach its limits. On one hand, some sectors of Christian evangelicalism began to extend beyond the logics of multiculturalism to openly challenging white supremacy. On the other, some sectors began to more openly declare their investments in whiteness. While the election of Obama gave rise to Christians who were interested in voting beyond the single-issue politics of abortion and gay marriage, it also sparked evangelicals who were willing to vote beyond these issues in support of more conservative political ends in the candidacy of Donald Trump. These trends are explored in the conclusion.

8 WOMEN OF COLOR EVANGELICAL THEOLOGIES

> To be a woman of color committed to racial reconciliation and social justice in the Christian church—whether evangelical or mainline—is to be a perpetual outsider. Many of us are culturally and theologically isolated in the spaces where we live, work, and minister. Our existence at the intersection of race and gender invites unique experiences, different from those of our white sisters and our brothers of all races. Sometimes those experiences include struggling to be heard and valued by the very communities and organizations that we serve.—Promotional material for the Women of Color Institute held at the 2016 Christian Community Development Association Conference in Los Angeles

In 2015 a group of organizers—Erna Kim Hackett, Emily Rice, Chanequa Walker-Barnes, Christena Cleveland, Zakiya Jackson, and Mayra Macedo-Nolan—held the first Women of Color Institute for the 2015 Christian Community Development Association (CCDA) conference.[1] This effort arose from the frustration of many evangelical women of color over the marginalization of women of color in male-dominated and white-dominated evangelical conferences. This discontent became apparent during the 2015 Justice Conference in which many women of color tweeted about their dissatisfaction with the marginalization of women of color at Christian conferences. At that particular conference a panel of women of color was held at the preconference event, but women of color were virtually absent from the main stage unless they were on a panel, where they would only have a few minutes to speak. In addition, while the conference spoke about racial and gender justice, they were not discussed simultaneously. Thus, the speakers on gender justice would talk about "saving" women in the Congo from gender violence, while the male speakers on racial justice would speak about prisons and policing with no reference to the gendered forms of this policing. Chanequa Walker-Barnes reflects on how this experience helped give rise to the Women of Color Institutes:

> But many of the names of the women of color had been omitted from the conference brochure and website. My name was included in a few obscure places, but incorrectly. As the conference unfolded, it became clear that women of color were almost exclusively featured as panelists, their wisdom reduced to soundbites. It became even clearer that we were not the audience that many of the speakers—including both the White women and the men of color—had in mind. On multiple occasions, we bristled at offensive comments and jokes made from the main stage, while the White brothers and sisters surrounding us cheered. At one point, even the call to prayer left us stumped about how we could participate. In a room filled with over two thousand Christians who cared about justice, we were not only a minority, we were culturally and theologically isolated.
>
> To be a woman of color committed to racial reconciliation and social justice in the Christian church—whether evangelical or mainline—is to be a perpetual outsider. While we share many of the same concerns and experiences as our white sisters and our brothers of color, our existence at the intersection of race and gender brings unique experiences. Those experiences provide a unique vantage point from which to view the complex dynamics through which race, gender, class, power, privilege, and oppression operate. But they also predispose us to unique hardships in the struggle for justice in Christian community, hardships that make us want to quit, to walk away, and to give up on the hope for beloved community.
>
> If any of us were looking for a cultural safe space, we didn't find it in that auditorium. We found it instead on Twitter, as we began to carry on a separate, online conversation in reaction to what we were hearing. We found it in the lobby as we shared glances of recognition with women of color whom we didn't know and hugs with those whom we did. We found it over shared meals, as we vented and processed and laughed and prayed together. By the end of the weekend, we were like the women in Gay's painting, standing together in defiance and in

hope, knowing that our ability to sustain the journey is born not only of our baptism, but also of our sisterhood. (Walker-Barnes, 2015)

The emergence of a specific "women of color" consciousness within evangelicalism is relatively recent. I mean not just women who are racialized but, as Walker-Barnes described at the 2015 event, a political consciousness that seeks to build a coalition across varied forms or gendered racial oppression. This intersectional consciousness thus has the potential to do more than increase the visibility of women of color within the racial reconciliation movement.

Saving Brown Women from Brown Men

Evangelical feminism and the racial reconciliation movement tended to operate rather independently, with women of color being relatively absent as prominent spokespeople in both (A. Smith, 2008). Instead, women of color in particular have often been the targets of evangelical savior projects rather than treated as subjects capable of analysis. The racial/gender politics behind this can be seen in this one woman's explanation for why she supports male headship:

> In America, we get it really good as women. I can't believe that women sit around and cry about it. There are so many places that women are still considered about as good as a dog.... One time it really hit me was when I went on one ministry tour with my husband to Egypt. Women had to walk around with scarves over their faces.... They were like nonpeople.... Here, women can do anything they want. (Brasher, 1998, 145)

Diane Knippers (who was the head of the Institute for Religion and Democracy before she passed away) complained at the December 1998 World Council of Churches (WCC) Assembly in Harare, Zimbabwe, that antiviolence activism among liberal feminists and liberation theologians

> demeans and diminishes the plight of women who truly suffer the worst kinds of physical abuse.... It disgusted me to see women who enjoy Western privileges and comforts claim a victim status along with women who suffer far more terrible abuses. Also there was no mention of the most serious abuses against women today—female genital

mutilation in parts of Africa, bridal dowry burnings in India, or the enslavement of girls in Sudan. Of course, these are problems whose sources lie mainly outside the Christian faith. But, by ignoring these problems, the WCC festival created the impression that the Church is the major source of violence against women and that Christian teaching needs to be radically changed to address this problem. A more honest look at the world would produce a different conclusion—that biblical faith, in spite of its imperfect implementation, has been a force of protection and elevation of women in human history. (Knippers, 1998–1999, 8)

Evangelicals cannot agree whether women are oppressed in the United States, but they can all agree that they are oppressed in the Global South, particularly in the Arab world (A. Smith, 2008).[2]

Trafficking, in particular, has become the form of gender oppression in the Global South that evangelicals are fixated upon. Attention to trafficking is becoming almost as popular as the topic of Christian persecution (E. Belz, 2009b; Bergin, 2009b; Chesser, 2007; E. Cooper, 2010; Hoang and Johnson, 2016; Mary Hutchinson, 2011; Justice, 2016; Scimone, 2009; Walker, 2009b). This discourse trades on an anti-Black racism in which trafficking supplants the legacy of chattel slavery, as in this assertion: "During the last two decades worldwide human trafficking totals surpasses that of 400 years of colonial slavery by a million" (C. Powell, 2009, 40; see also Justice, 2016; M. Olasky, 2010c). In fact, trafficking is often described in a manner that erases the importance of chattel slavery: "Today 27 million people live on in captivity, their lives worth far less than any colonial era slave" (Abraham, 2007c, 16). Antitrafficking is described as the "new abolition movement" (Alford, 2007, 35; see also Beaty, 2011; Blunt, 2007a).

In fact, *Relevant*'s *Reject Apathy* published an article on the "U.S. Slave Traffic" that does not address slavery's connection to anti-Blackness at all (Tracking the Rise of U.S. Slave Traffic, 2011). This rhetorical strategy follows from the fact that those guilty of the "new slavery" are generally people of color and the rescuers of enslaved women are usually white, thus erasing historical connections between white supremacy and slavery as well as contemporary connections between neoliberalism and trafficking (Abraham, 2006a; Jewell, 2007; C. Powell, 2009; Price, 2007a; Scimone, 2009). Within the realm of trafficking, evangelicals often adopt "feminist rhetoric" that would be shunned in other contexts. Vanguard University (Costa Mesa, California), affiliated with the Assemblies of God, started a Center for Women's

Studies, the first program in an Assemblies of God institution. It affirms that "men and women are equal spiritually" (A. Gaines and V. Chandler, 2008). The annual gender and justice conferences held at Vanguard frequently focus on trafficking, because "globally women are at great risk of being trafficked for sex, raped and abused" (A. Gaines and V. Chandler, 2008, 24).

This feminist intersection is not informed in any way by the critiques emerging from sex workers and women of color, who point to the imperialism and racism in the antitrafficking movement. These critiques note that antitrafficking laws are disproportionately focused on those countries with which the United States has political tension, whereas allies who do engage in sex trafficking, such as Israel, are generally not subject to punitive antitrafficking measures. They also note that these laws do not differentiate trafficked women from sex workers, who find that these laws criminalize their attempts to make a living (Kempadoo, 2005). Consequently, evangelical critiques of antitrafficking movements are rare. *World* did publish an interview stating that rescue missions do not work, which notes that trafficked women rarely see themselves as victims, which would indicate that evangelicals tend to put all sex workers in the category of "trafficked." The article says that the approach should be about increasing choices for women who might want to leave voluntarily (T. Owens, 2013, 59). *Relevant* did note that in order to battle trafficking "in an ends-justify-the means stratagem, some activists have resorted to exploiting, even manufacturing, shocking survivor stories to convince the world it should care" (Thompson, 2015, 44). Another *Relevant* article contended that the movement against global slavery and trafficking fails to address the fact that trafficking is part of the same economy that produces iPhones and other commodities that U.S. Christians buy. It called on Christians to address complicity in this exploitative economy (Global Slavery Is Growing, 2014).

Gary Haugen's International Justice Mission (IJM), which engages in legal advocacy for victims of human-rights violations from a Christian perspective, has become particularly prominent within the antitrafficking movement (Haugen, 2005, 2007). While it does not solely focus on trafficking, its work on fighting trafficking and sexual violence in the Global South is most prominently featured within evangelical venues (Mundy, 2007). On the one hand, with its involvement with the criminal justice system, IJM's approach completely occludes state complicity with gender violence. In fact, Haugen has blamed poverty on the lack of law enforcement (T. C. Morgan, 2014). A plethora of feminists, particularly feminists of color, have detailed the destructive impact of the antiviolence movement working uncritically with the state and assuming that the state is the solution to rather than the perpetrator of gender violence. And, just as the discussion of trafficking often rests on the disavowal of the trans-Atlantic slave trade, Haugen's criminal justice work rests on the disavowal of mass incarceration of people of color in the United States. In *Terrify No More* he compares the police in the United States, whom he calls "the good guys," to the police in the Global South, who are "corrupt and unchecked" (Haugen, 2005, 38). The mass number of incidents of police brutality committed, particularly against people of color in the United States, disappears from view (Human Rights Watch, 1998; Ritchie, 2006; K. Williams, 2007). Countries in the Global South are challenged to "establish a sound legal system that actually works, especially one that works for the poor," compared to the U.S. system, which apparently works well for the poor, despite all indications to the contrary (Haugen, 2005, 85).[3]

However, in a context in which conservatives such as Glenn Beck at the time were denouncing churches who proclaim "social justice," Gary Haugen unapologetically called on conservatives to understand justice as a "fundamental biblical calling" and that the Good News means that God is against injustice (M. Olasky, 2008e, 28).[4] "We are talking about protecting the most basic liberties of poor people made in the image of God—the right not to be raped, illegally detained, assaulted, dispossessed, and enslaved" (M. Olasky, 2008e, 28). At an IJM workshop that I attended at the 2007 Urbana conference, the main focus was not on the particular kinds of advocacy work that IJM engages in but on trying to inspire evangelicals to understand social justice as central to evangelical Christianity. Haugen also broke with the Republican Party line and opposed the Bush administration's use of torture. And Nikki Toyama-Szeto, who worked with IJM at the time, routinely wrote on racism and imperialism (R. H. Evans, 2013; Toyama-Szeto, 2017).

If the new evangelical feminism is concerned about the plight of "Third World" women in general, it is particularly concerned about saving Arab and Muslim women. While locked in battles against feminism within the U.S. context, evangelicals often rely on feminist rhetoric to argue that Christianity can end the oppression of women in Arab and Muslim countries.[5] This strategy was similar to the approach of the Bush administration, which used feminist rhetoric to justify the invasions of Afghanistan and Iraq. As Bush stated in a *Charisma* interview: "We are dealing with extreme, radical people who have a deep desire to spread an ideology that is anti-women, anti–free thought, and anti–art and science" (S. Strang, 2004, 54). *World* explains that the primary emphasis within Islam is "on 'subjugating the enemy'—whether a foreign power or your own wife" (J. Belz, 2008g, 6). Consequently, evangelical literature is replete with narratives of oppressed, veiled Muslim women, many of whom become "liberated" by converting to Christianity (T. Green, 2002; M. Olasky, 2007f; S. Olasky, 2010). In fact, an entire ministry, Zennah Ministries, was developed by white evangelical W. L. Cati to reach out to women married to Muslims. The 2001 Global Celebration for Women, designed to be the evangelical counterpart of the Beijing Conference on women, highlighted tales from white Christian missionaries telling of their success of "liberating" Muslim women from the veil by teaching them how to apply makeup. Elisabeth Farrell describes in her "exposé" on Christian women married to Muslim men how these women invariably seem to find themselves "trapped in a nightmare of oppression, abuse, and control" (Farrell, 2000b, 89). While contending that she "is not bashing Muslims," Farrell argues that Muslim men are all wife batterers (Farrell, 2000b, 89). "You might be surprised by what some Muslims believe about wife-beating and male superiority," she says, blithely ignoring the multitude of passages in the Christian Bible that also support male dominance, command unmarried women to marry their rapists, and seem to condone the rape and sexual mutilation of women (Farrell, 2000b, 90).

Ex-Muslim narratives within evangelicalism are frequently gendered. Muslim women tell of their freedom from Islam, albeit often filtered through white evangelicals. Such is the case with *Lifting the Veil*, written by two white missionaries, Phil and Julie Parshall. They dedicate their book to "Amma, Bhabi, and Meye—Three Muslim women who graciously allowed us to peek beneath the veil." The book, while still insisting that Islam is more gender-oppressive than other monotheistic religions, does provide a somewhat more nuanced analysis (Parshall and Parshall, 2002, 45). The Parshalls note the gender oppression in Christianity and point to Paul's dictate that wives should submit to their husbands (Parshall and Parshall, 2002, 45). They also say that some Christian women who have married Muslim men have happy marriages (Parshall and Parshall, 2002, 5, 211). Unlike most other narratives, theirs shows the feminist strands within Islam that can bring about change internally rather than presuming that Christians will save Muslim women (even as they perpetuate the notion of Islam as premodern). "It appears that it will be the 'unruly' women of protest who will one day make a difference in the world of Islam. Until then, entrenched traditionalists will hold modernity at bay" (Parshall and Parshall, 2002, 86).

Arab men are frequently described as sexual predators who prey on

Christian women (Deloriea, 1998; Luke, 2007; Stalcup, 1999). Zennah Ministries ministers to women being oppressed by Muslim men. Its founder, W. L. Cati, tells such a tale in her book *Married to Muhammed*. The cover of the book warns: "As many women have discovered, Middle Eastern men can be charming.... In this eye-opening expose of the often deceptive tactics Muslims use to gain converts, W. Cati warns women of the dangers of dating and marrying Islamic men ... [and] sheds light on the dark side of Islam—especially the teachings and practices that keep women in suffocating bondage" (Cati, 2001). The image on the cover is of a white woman veiled. As Sora Han notes, the image of the veil rhetorically operates within the war on terror to equate liberation with unveiling. This equation requires the disavowal of the "contemporary Warfare state" dependent on the incarceration of mass numbers of people of color in the United States, the genocide of Native peoples, and imperial capitalist relations between the United States and the rest of the world (Han, 2002, 5). Unveiling "liberates" the Muslim woman into the circuits of imperial capital where she can wear a "miniskirt" instead of a veil. The veiled woman is also evidence of the threat posed by the Arab male terrorist, although in the end he primarily threatens white womanhood. The plight of the Arab woman does not stand on its own but functions as evidence of the Arab threat for the West. "Unveiling, as a visual representation of liberation for the postcolonial woman abroad, cannot, then, protest the War on Terrorism in any meaningful way precisely because it is grounded in the dominant imaginary of interracial sexual violation, that is, the historical panic motivating the state's punishment of the perpetual enemy within" (Han, 2002, 11).

Indeed, Cati's book is primarily a narrative of white female victimization. While she does not actually state anywhere that she was physically abused, she contends that all Muslim men beat their wives. In addition, they prey on (white) women. "They wine and dine women into their webs. The sad part of their deceit is that they have the appearance of a man who loves God, holds high moral values and wants a decent home and family" (Cati, 2001, 52). The reason for this deception is that "Allah, their god, will love them more because of the possibility of conversion" (Cati, 2001, 52)! Once married, these good Christian women are then forced to engage in sexually perverse acts with their husbands. Evoking Puar's Muslims as terrorist fags, Cati reveals, "Homosexuality is secretly practiced in Islamic countries. Muhammed pleased his homosexual followers by promising them pre-pubescent boys in 'paradise.' So, after committing plunder, loot, rape, and murder in this life, the followers of Islam were told they would be 'rewarded' with untouched virginal youths, who were fresh like pearls" (Cati, 2001, 83). After a lengthy discussion of how Muslim men oppress their wives, Cati, with no apparent sense of irony, advises Christian women to submit to their husbands (Cati, 2001, 87).

As a counternarrative to this kind of gender imperialistic rhetoric, *Daughters of Islam* actually cites Edward Said's *Orientalism* (1994) to critique evangelical depictions of Muslim women. "Certainly there were abused women in Muslim countries, as elsewhere.... Yet when we focus on the weaknesses of another culture, we miss its strengths and beauties. We also miss the sins in our own culture. For example, Muslims are appalled at Western family life when they hear about disrespect for parents and neglect of the elderly" (Adeney, 2002, 19). Muslim women are not passive and submissive, the book notes. Using the postcolonial analysis of Lila Abu-Lughod, this book contends that the status of women in Islam cannot be separated from a larger political context of imperialism. It also suggests that Muhammad's teachings should be seen as improving the status of women at the time and that many aspects of Islam are liberating for women. However, it is not uncommon for women to become marginalized as religious systems become bureaucratized (Adeney, 2002, 114).

Saving Brown Men from Brown Women

On the flip side of the woman of color who needs "saving" is the woman of color who threatens the well-being of civilization. She is raising terrorists or her "loose" activity is threatening communities of color or her reproductivity is threatening capitalism. Just as disavowed racialization is often reproduced through class in evangelicalism, it is also communicated through gender.

Women of Color as a Terrorist Threat
The other side of the Arab woman who needs saving is the Arab woman whose veil hides her terrorist activity. This ideology was also explicit in the 2003 Interfaith Alliance on Zionism held in Washington, D.C. (May 17–18). There Helen Freedman from Americans for a Safe Israel declared that there will only be peace in Israel when Arabs love their children as much as they hate us. But, she said, Arabs are simply incapable of loving their children. Charles Jacob, who promotes Zionism on college campuses through the Davis Project, offered the following PowerPoint Presentation to explain the difference between Israeli Jews and "Arabs/Palestinians."

Israel	Arab/Palestine
Teach kids songs of peace	Teach kids songs of hate/*Sesame Street* is about being a suicide bomber
Every effort to prevent civilian death	Kill lots of civilians
Anguish when civilians hurt	Dancing when atrocities happen
Mothers don't want kids to fight	Mothers celebrate fighting

He summed up his presentation: "I grieve for Palestinian people who have leaders that succumbed to evil, and have fallen prey because of their 'perceived sense of oppression.' They are filling their children with hate and death."

Another such example is a *World* article on a Palestinian woman who reportedly killed her daughter because she had been gang-raped by two of her brothers and pregnancy ensued. According to *World*, this story shows that we can dismiss complaints that U.S. evangelicals are supporting Western imperialist efforts by supporting Israel. Instead, Muslims "need the true light that alone brings peace," which is Christianity (Seu, 2004, 47). Thus, within conservative evangelical rhetoric, it is the woman of color who continues to inhabit the space of liminality in evangelical discourse about race and gender: she represents the threat of effeminacy for Christian men of color and the racialized bad mother who destroys her children, whom white women must organize against.

Part of this comparison between "oppressed"/"terrorist" Third World women and "liberated" Western women is anxiety about the liberation of Western women. Just as the Muslim woman threatens the safety of Christian America from outside, the "feminist" threatens it internally by challenging heteronormativity. Charles Colson opined that same-sex marriage actually contributes to terrorism and is responsible for the prison scandals in Iraq. Apparently, same-sex marriage also contributes to gender confusion (L. Grady, 1991; Greene, 1973; Norfolk, 1975; Ogle, 1995; Olford, 1982),[6] which in turn contributes to women abusing prisoners in Abu Ghraib (J. Belz, 2004; Olsen, 2004b; Veith, 2004b). This abuse then contributes to more terrorist activity. Not passing the Federal Marriage Amendment "is like handing moral weapons of mass destruction to those who use America's decadence to recruit more snipers and hijackers and suicide bombers" (C. Colson and A. Morse, 2004). We must preserve traditional marriage in order to "protect the United States from those who would use our depravity to destroy us" (C. Colson and A. Morse, 2004, 152).[7] Stephen Strang similarly explains that "our nation faces many threats from without and within. ... Terrorism threatens our way of life, but so does an ultraliberal agenda that wants to legitimize homosexuality" (S. Strang, 2005b, 90).

New Man likens terrorism to feminism: "like terrorism, the new gender wars are made up of little ambushes" (Hunter, 2004, 32). As heteronormativity is understood as the building block of Christian America, feminism and homosexuality are its constitutive threats.[8] Focusing on these threats relieves perhaps even deeper anxiety about evangelical sexuality itself. *World* reports that evangelical teenagers are actually more sexually active than liberal Protestants and more likely to have three or more sexual partners. Of those who take abstinence pledges, 88 percent do not fulfill them (Veith, 2007a). Thus, a focus on external threats relieves anxiety about the fact that evangelical sexuality may already be compromised.

Women of Color as Threats to Communities of Color
If brown children must be saved from terrorist brown mothers in the Global South, evangelicals also aspire to save Black children from Black mothers on the domestic front. Racial reconciliation often reinscribes racism through sexism. As mentioned in chapter 2, poverty is generally racialized within evangelicalism, which equates poverty with wickedness and criminality. The face of this "wickedness," in turn, is gendered and sexualized in the figure of the hypersexualized welfare queen who refuses to live under the auspices of male headship. The sentiment that the primary problem faced in Black communities is family breakdown is widely expressed (A. Gaines, 1998; V. Lowe, 2001; M. Olasky, 2006d; J. Williams, 2007). *World* contends that the report by Daniel Patrick Moynihan, which blamed female-dominated households for social decay in African American communities, was visionary. "A community that allows a large number of men to grow up in broken families, dominated by women, never acquiring any stable relationship to male authority; that community asks for and gets chaos" (quoted in M. Olasky, 2006d, 48; see also Black Family Betrayed, 2001). The problem of poverty, according to *World*, has nothing to do with economic structures. Rather, poverty and family problems "all stem from a lack of marriage" (Black Family Betrayed, 2001, 24). Gary Bauer of the Family Research Center says:

> Millions of inner-city dwellers ... "choose" single motherhood only because government makes it look like a good deal. Government

offers the unmarried mother an attractive contractual arrangement: The equivalent of somewhere between $8,500 and $15,000 per year in combined welfare benefits, on the condition that the young woman *not work for pay, and not marry an employed male*. What the government offers her is a classic contract. In consideration of the government's offer of a package of benefits, the mother agrees not to engage in the activities that are crucial to the formation of a decent society. Government has bargained for social breakdown, and it has gotten it. (Domigues, 1994, 68–69)

Thus, the oversexed nature of Black communities (Gilbreath, 1999) is the cause of poverty because, as it turns out, "men who practice biblical sexuality make more money and experience more success at work than other men. Most of the guys we minister to have doubled their incomes in a year ... sexual immorality drains spiritual authority," says Christian sex therapist Doug Weiss (quoted in Tiansay, 2004b, 22). Apparently, the best way to address poverty, according to Weiss, is to eradicate masturbation (Tiansay, 2004b).

Many Black conservative evangelicals in particular blame the "welfare queen" for the demise of the Black family (Edwards, 1996, 155; Vincent, 1999d, 18) and hold Black female-led households, not the racist criminal justice system, responsible for the large numbers of Black men in prison (Maxwell, 1991, 36). Rodney Cooper argues that feminism, not racism or capitalism, is "the greatest enemy of black progress in America" because it encourages Black women to rob Black men of their jobs and their manhood (R. Cooper, 1995, 41). Similarly, according to the Urban Family Council's Chester Fatherhood Initiative: "When you get good, committed fathers in their homes, their daughters aren't going to be going out getting abortions, and their sons aren't going to be doing drugs and getting arrested" (Jefferson, 2001, 25). In an opinion piece in *Christianity Today*, Stephen Carter critiques both the Democratic and Republican parties for inadequately addressing institutional racism post-9/11. Again, however, his solution is an individual one that targets women of color as the problem. "The sparkling world *Brown* hoped to build is yet in our grasp. But we will have to build it as individuals, with the small decisions of everyday life, rather than through bigger and better government programs. The nation is full of fatherless children to mentor, collapsed families to support, crumbling schools to visit and human hearts to touch" (S. Carter, 2004, 64). Wellington Boone similarly contends that the issue facing Black communities is not primarily racism but Black "self-genocide." "Instead of rejecting the Bible's commandments to value unborn children, sexual purity, and the sanctity of marriage, blacks should be leading the next spiritual awakening" (Boone, 2008, 18). *World* similarly explains that there are "legions of black women who've grown weary of the crime and poverty caused by liberal social programs" (Vincent, 1999d, 17). It then quotes African American conservative Beverly Williams: "the entitlement era made it easy for people on welfare to give themselves over to vices like sex and drugs. But the recent slashing of the welfare rolls, she says, has sparked new ambition among urban black women" (Vincent, 1999d, 18).

Conservative evangelical organizations also rely on gender hierarchies to appeal to men of color by offering them a chance to take control of a fragment of their lives through patriarchy. Christianity is often viewed as feminized, given that the majority of Christian parishioners are women. Hence it becomes necessary to assert a "muscular" Christianity that will enable men to bond with others in a community that stresses relationships without being deemed effeminate. Such a strategy has a long history in evangelicalism, such as the "muscular Christianity" and "Men and Religion Forward" movements at the beginning of the nineteenth century (Bederman, 1995; Bendroth, 1984). Such movements attempted to create a hypermasculine place that allowed men to be Christian and manly. However, both in the nineteenth century and today, these movements have actually failed to change the demographics of church membership significantly. According to prominent evangelical pollster George Barna, despite the popularity of the Promise Keepers movements in the 1990s, church membership of men actually *dropped* (Andrescik, 2000b; Morley, 2000).

The move to masculinize the church has a decidedly racial cast. Much of the rhetoric focuses on how the Black church has become "feminized," and the notion that men of all colors need to assert their headship at home and in church (Hawkins, 1995, 29). The Nation of Islam, many evangelicals claim, appeals to Black male youth because it is more masculine than the "too female," too "male unfriendly" Christian church (A. Gaines, 2002b; Gilbreath, 1998b; Tapia, 1994, 37). Promise Keepers hopes to provide a Christian alternative to the Nation of Islam; women are asked not to participate in Promise Keepers events except as volunteer labor. Latinos, too, apparently suffer from a "feminized" church—the Roman Catholic Church, which "worships Mary as a holy mother" (Brouwer et al., 1996, 71). Latino men complain that Latinas, like Black women, have too much authority in the home. In Latin America, so-called female religious hegemony is thought to have "turned men into groveling worms who believe they are weak, incompetent, and loaded down with sin" (Brouwer et al., 1996, 71). Similarly, Promise Keepers held a five-day event in 2005 in the Bahamas. The rationale for this "Bahamas Awakening," in partnership with the Bahaman government, is that the Bahamas is "a matriarchal society where women are advancing faster than men" (Walker, 2005b, 46). This project illustrates Jacqui Alexander's critique of the logics of heteropatriarchy within postcolonial states in her analysis of Bahamas' anti-gay legislation. She argues that the postcolonial state, in this case the Bahamas, is biologized as incapable of self-governance through the image of the indigenous sodomite. This figure is used to justify the colonial policing of "nonprocreative noncitizens" to legitimate claims to govern. In policing the gender and sexual boundaries of the nation-state for racialized and gendered contaminants, the postcolonial state obfuscates the complete permeability of its boundaries to multinational capital. This permeability is feminized in the heteropatriarchal logics of global capital (Alexander, 2005).

Particularly at the beginning of the racial reconciliation movement, one almost never encountered literature on racial reconciliation written by women or even literature by men linking issues of race and gender. One important exception was Don Argue's statement that the NAE needed to strive for race *and* gender inclusivity at its 1995 convention (H. Lee, 1995, 97). As J. Lee Grady notes, the Pentecostal/Charismatic Churches of North America (PCCNA), which so vigorously "tackled the issue of racism in 1994, are more reluctant to deal with sexism" (J. L. Grady, 1996, 15). Perhaps one reason for this reluctance is the understanding among evangelicals that "most commitments to Christ are made before the age of 18" (J. A. Smith and R. Maracle, 1989, 36). Given the previously discussed fear of evangelicals of color threatening to shift the meaning of evangelical Christianity, evangelical women of color may be perceived as having the potential to reproduce the next generation of potentially unruly evangelicals of color. There are some exceptions. Jonathan Walton calls on Black churches to "pray for and be deeply concerned and saddened about an unhealthy culture of hypermasculinity and a patriarchal savior complex that possibly helps to cultivate sadomasochistic and misogynistic tendencies" (Walton, 2009, 227). The scandal that resulted from the disclosure of the domestic violence suffered by prominent evangelist Juanita Bynum has also highlighted the importance of gender justice (A. Gaines, 2008a; Walker, 2008a). *Charisma* magazine is one discursive arena where race *and* gender justice are both addressed. As discussed, *Charisma* most consistently highlights racial reconciliation its pages. At the same time, it regularly features articles that suggest sympathies toward gender equality and women's ordination (Brookes, 2004; Groothuis and Groothuis, 1999). J. Lee Grady has written several articles that speak against women's subordination in the church. He calls for a simultaneous pursuit of gender and racial justice: "Come on guys, let's get off the macho bandwagon. Real men are not threatened by anointed women of God. Instead, we must pursue a radical, New Testament faith that melts gender prejudice in the same way that it demolishes racial and class divisions" (J. L. Grady, 2007c, 8).

Evangelical Theologies of Women of Color

It is within these constraints and frustrations with evangelical discourses on race and gender that women of color began to call for intersectional race/gender politics. But these women have gone beyond advocating for the inclusion of women of color within evangelicalism and instead employ an intersectional analysis that disrupts evangelicalism in general and its savior tendencies in particular. For instance, the more white-dominated Christians for Biblical Equality organized defensively around the issues of sexuality by making heterosexual marriage part of its values statement (A. Smith, 2008), whereas the second Women of Color Institute hosted workshops for queer women of color. While some have critiqued "people of color" movements for erasing the specificities of distinct racializations (Byrd, 2011; Lawrence and Dua, 2005; Sexton, 2010; Wilderson, 2010), at the same time the coalitional framework inherent in this structure generally encourages people to develop politics that address interlocking logics and oppressions. Thus, many of the prominent women of color activists within evangelicalism generally have the most expansive politics within evangelicalism. I have shared their theoretical insights throughout the book, but here is a brief summary.

Myles (formerly Amelia) Markham of the Reformation Project and Ana-Yelsi Velasco-Sanchez organize for LGBT inclusion in evangelical churches. As indigenous activists, they both organize around the intersections of settler colonialism, racism, and heteropatriarchy. In addition, Velasco-Sanchez founded a blog, Brown-Eyed Amazon, whose slogan is "Love Jesus, Seek Justice, Wear Cute Shoes." She explicitly uses a women of color intersectional analysis to argue that the Bible requires Christians to dismantle all forms of oppression simultaneously. In particular, she argues that racial and queer justice struggles are interlocking. Alexia Salvatierra and Jenny Yang are two of the primary organizers behind the previously described effort to get conservative evangelicals to switch their positions on immigration reform. Salvatierra is responsible for a number of evangelical organizing efforts across the country, many of which she describes in *Faith-Rooted Organizing* (Salvatierra and Heltzel, 2014). Yang's work on evangelical mobilizing for immigrants and refugees is outlined in *Welcoming the Stranger* (Yang and Soerens, 2009).

Kathy Khang with InterVarsity Fellowship organizes around the intersection of racism (particularly anti-Asian racism), gender oppression, and disability. She was one of the central spokespersons behind the previously described influential Open Letter to the Evangelical Church on racism against Asian Americans. Since that she has written extensively on the linkages between racism against Asian Americans and Black Lives Matter, such as one blog that linked the police violence against organizing in Ferguson with global militarism (Khang, 2014, 2015). She also writes extensively on the connections between disability and racism, exploring the connections between "model minority" myths and psychiatric disabilities (Khang, 2016). Her most recent work, *Raise Your Voice*, focuses on how evangelicals from marginalized communities can make interventions in structures of oppression rooted in their community contexts (Khang, 2018).

Sandra Van Opstal is a prominent pastor with Grace and Peace Church in Chicago as well as a community-organizer and worship leader. Her book *The Next Worship* focuses on challenging the disavowed white models of worship services within evangelical communities (Van Opstal, 2016b). In addition, she also organizes against classism *within* communities of color and develops models that center the voices of those most marginalized within particular communities.

Shari Russell, who is a survivor of the 1960s scoop of First Nations children in Canada, focuses on decolonizing indigenous nations within Christian churches. As part of the Salvation Army, she has been very involved in Canada's Truth and Reconciliation Commission and in supporting justice for survivors of residential schools and the 1960s scoop. She also organizes around recognition for the United Nations Declaration on the Rights of Indigenous Peoples (Salvation Army, n.d.). She also serves on the board of the previously described North American Institute for Indigenous Theological Studies (NAIITS). Also affiliated with NAIITS is Lakota organizer Lenore Three Stars. She served as the Women's Ministry chair of the Evangelical Covenant Church and organized evangelical dominations to support Native sovereignty struggles, most recently #NoDAPL, environmental justice, and repeal of the Doctrine of Discovery.[9] Cheryl Bear also works with

NAIITS (discussed in chapter 6). She is a prominent musical artist, community organizer, and speaker whose work articulates a vision of a decolonial Christianity.

Christena Cleveland, whose work on antiracism was featured at the 2016 Southern Baptist Convention's (SBC) Ethics and Religious Liberty Commission (ERLC) conference, speaks to the need to develop an approach that is intersectional and focused on power relationship. She frequently critiques "color-blind" ideologies within white evangelicalism (Cleveland, 2014), arguing that "Jesus is not white" and that this matters. "Jesus didn't simply care about refugees, Jesus was a refugee. Jesus didn't simply care about the poor, he was poor" (Cleveland, 2016b, 36). She was very vocal on Twitter in critiquing InterVarsity's recent decision to fire staff who support gay marriage.[10]

Lisa Sharon Harper of Freedom Road has been involved in organizing from an intersectional perspective on everything from Black Lives Matter to immigration justice to Native rights to gender justice, particularly for women of color. She contends that the "spiritual lie" of white evangelicalism is "white dominion" and explains the theological basis of her work: "In the United States, a ruling class has been established; along with it an assumed underclass. We see it clearly when we observe disparities in schools, healthcare, housing, food access, and justice. This is sin. Images of God are being diminished across our land" (Harper, 2014). She has been particularly vocal in speaking out not only on issues but on the evangelical parameters of proper protest. Having been centrally involved in the organizing around Ferguson, she defends not only the right of Black Lives Matter to protest but its methodology as well. "Many are calling today's protesters 'violent' because they yell, they look angry, and they don't play by the rules" (Harper, 2015). She argues that calling protesters "violent" is intended to disguise the violence of white supremacy.

Chanequa Walker-Barnes employs a Black feminist/womanist intersectional framework to speak out on the marginalization of women of color within evangelical racial reconciliation movements. On the reluctance to address violence against Black women, Walker-Barnes argues:

> You don't know how many legacies Black women have protected and continue to protect. You don't know how many of your heroes' images we could take a hammer to, if we were simply to tell the truth about them.
>
> You don't know because you don't want to know. You don't ask us to share our stories. You don't read, watch, or listen to our stories. You

don't attend the conferences, seminars, or courses about "women's issues." In your "race-first" mentality, you put our "issues" on the back-burner in the name of racial solidarity. Meanwhile, you parade our rapists in your pulpits, lamenting their legacies while we're trying to hold together the pieces of our shattered selves. (Walker-Barnes, 2016)

Walker-Barnes's most recent work develops an intersectional analysis of white supremacy to radically critique the evangelical racial reconciliation movement (Walker-Barnes, 2019).

Emily Rice, who was a co-founder of Killjoy Prophets and served on the board of Christians for Biblical Equality, organizes around the intersections of heteropatriarchy, settler colonialism, imperialism, and anti-Black racism, with a particular focus on centering Indigenous struggle within liberation movements in the Philippines. She writes:

We refuse to settle for a "racial reconciliation" that envisions the goal as representation and recognition by whiteness because our aim is to dismantle white supremacy altogether.

We seek to disrupt the dominant narratives of white Christian feminism by centering women of color feminism and activist politics.

We work to interrogate how Christian institutions and theologies—from conservative to progressive—have remained complicit in perpetuating systems of oppression. (Killjoy Prophets, 2014b)

Erna Kim Hackett, formerly of InterVarsity and now a pastor, has explained that she "stopped talking about racial reconciliation and started talking about white supremacy" because white evangelicals hold a "Disney princess" theology in which "they see themselves as the princess in every story. They are Esther, never Xerxes or Haman. They are Peter, but never Judas. They are the woman anointing Jesus, never the Pharisees. They are the Jews escaping slavery, never Egypt" (Hackett, 2017). Zakiya Jackson currently works at the intersections of race, gender, and educational reform and is one of the leaders of the Women of Color Institute. She explains the need for an intersectional analysis (Z. Jackson, n.d.). Austin Channing Brown writes on the intersections of policing, anti-Black racism, and white supremacy. She has been particularly vocal in critiquing attempts to engage in "reconciliation" without addressing the systemic nature of anti-Black racism in particular. She calls for an "UNbalanced" approach in addressing violence against Black peoples.

> It happens every time there is an unjust and inhumane shooting of an unarmed black person. There are many posts, tweets, and status updates that are committed to giving a "balanced view." This usually means admitting the racial inequities in America's criminal justice system. Then to balance the other end of the teeter totter it becomes necessary to also admit that there are problems in the black community—black on black crime, fatherlessness, poverty, etc. . . . While I understand the desire to be balanced, I need you to know that you won't get that here. . . .
>
> Why? Because I believe it is fine to say, "This is wrong. Unarmed black people should not lose their lives" and leave it right there. That is enough. (Channing, 2015)

These are just a few of the many voices of evangelical women of color who are promoting an intersectional evangelical politic. Of course, naming these specific individuals can exceptionalize their work rather than recognizing it as part of a larger movement for racial/gender justice within evangelicalism. The emergence of a growing queer of color organizing in evangelicalism as seen in the work of Kenji Kuramitsu, Michael Vasquez, Alicia Crosby's Center for Inclusivity, and Myles Markham and Shae Washington through the Reformation Project is also transforming the evangelical landscape. As the racial and gender faultlines within evangelicalism have become clearer to increasingly more evangelicals, as I discuss in the conclusion, these voices point to the possibility of new evangelical futures that are less concerned with being included within white evangelicalism and more concerned with developing women of color-centered evangelical theologies without apology.

CONCLUSION
Between Black Lives Matter and Donald Trump

On the biggest threats to America . . . [Jerry] Falwell Jr. said: "Osama, Obama, and yo mamma," and since Osama bin Laden is dead and President Obama has just six months left in office, the only thing left is "is to tell Chelsea's mama, you're fired. And the only way to do that is to elect Donald Trump and Mike Pence president and vice president of the United States".—Jerry Falwell Jr. (P. Weber, 2016)

The past year is illustration enough. The evangelical movement is filled with younger, multiethnic, gospel-centered Christians. They are defined by a clear theology and a clear mission—not by the doctrinally vacuous resentment over a lost regime of nominal, cultural "Christian America."

The people who have used the gospel to sell us politically cynical voting guides have done damage. But they are not replicating themselves in the next generation.

The old-guard is easier to engage in politics, because they find identity in a "silent majority" of Americans. The next generation knows that our witness is counter to the culture, not just on the sanctity of life and the stability of the family but, most importantly, on the core of the gospel itself: Christ and him crucified.—Russell Moore (2016c)

In the midst of an awakening to racial realities in our nation, a cry to not derail the prophetic call of #blacklivesmatter *with all lives matter.*

It was not ALL lives that were ripped from their homes in Africa.

It was not ALL lives that were separated from families and marched to the West African coast.

It was not ALL lives put into the dank, dark tombs of the slave castles.

It was not ALL lives that were offered as a tithe to the church and accepted by the church.

It was not ALL lives crammed into the European slave ships.

It was not ALL lives laid side by side like cargo in the hull of the ship.

It was not ALL lives that were force fed because they staged hunger strikes.

It was not ALL lives that were casually thrown overboard to be devoured by sharks following the slave ships.

It was not ALL lives that were brought to the New World as slave labor.

It was not ALL lives stripped naked and put on the auction block.

It was not ALL lives for whom the slave auction bell rang, often in rhythm to the church bell.

It was not ALL lives that were bought and sold by God-fearing white American Christians.

It was not ALL lives that were whipped and beaten on the plantations.

It was not ALL lives that were systematically and repeatedly raped by white slave owners.

It was not ALL lives who were daily assaulted in their very identity as those made in the image of God.

It was not ALL lives who were repeatedly told they were less than human.

It was not ALL lives who were diminished by the 3/5 compromise, the Missouri compromise, and the Dred Scott decision.

It was not ALL lives whose communities were wiped out because they sought to build a life for themselves after emancipation.

It was not ALL lives that were told "separate but equal" with equal never being equal.

It was not ALL lives but black lives that hung like strange fruit from Southern trees.

It was not ALL lives, it was Addie Mae Collins, Cynthia Wesley, Carole Roberson, and Carol Denise McNair, four little black lives who were blown up when they bombed a church.

It was not ALL lives that were beset by attack dogs and by fire hoses.

It was not ALL lives but the black lives of Emm[e]tt Till, Medgar Evers, Martin Luther King Jr., and Malcolm X who were systematically assassinated.

It was not ALL lives that have been victims of police violence, but it was the black life of Oscar Grant.

It was not ALL lives, it was the black life of Trayvon Martin.

It was not ALL lives, it was the black life of Michael Brown.

It was not ALL lives, it was the black life of John Crawford, Eric Garner, Tamir Rice, Freddie Gray, Sandra Bland.

It was not ALL lives, it was the black life of Clementa Pinckney, Sharonda Singleton, Tywanza Sanders, Ethel Lance, Susie Jackson, Cynthia Hurd, Myra Thompson, Daniel Simmons Sr., DePayne Middleton Doctor.

It was not ALL lives, it was the black life of Rekia Boyd.

It was not ALL lives, it was the black life of Laquan McDonald.

It is not ALL lives that are targeted for mass incarceration.

It is not ALL lives that the prison industrial complex exploits.

These historical events did not involve the destruction and death of ALL lives, they were black lives that have been systematically targeted and abused by American society.

So next time, white evangelical leaders, you feel the urge to mouth off that 'ALL Lives Matter'—CLOSE your mouth and OPEN your eyes, ears, and minds to get yourself some knowledge.—Soong-Chan Rah (2015b)

With the 2016 presidential elections, it became clear that Christian Right politics as we have known them have sharply changed, largely because of race. On the one hand, white evangelicals supported Donald Trump's candidacy by 80 percent despite his support of Planned Parenthood, his lack of interest in any of the previous Christian litmus tests, and his engagement in behaviors that evangelicals insisted meant that Bill Clinton was unworthy to be president (S. P. Bailey, 2016). Despite these problems, many evangelicals, such as Wayne Grudem, prominently endorsed him as a "morally good choice" (Grudem, 2016). At the same time, however, other sectors of Christian evangelicalism openly began to embrace or engage more radical politics, particularly the Black Lives Matter movement. They began to worry less about "guilt by association" and to work with secular justice struggles regardless of their positions on the traditional evangelical litmus tests. I have previously written that it might be possible to rearticulate Christian Right politics into new formations. This is clearly already happened across the political spectrum. The dividing line seems to largely be based on race.

Black Lives Matter

The deaths of Trayvon Martin, Michael Brown, and Eric Garner, along with the uprisings in Ferguson and the rise of Black Lives Matter (BLM), dramatically impacted the rhetoric around racial reconciliation within Christian evangelicalism. Even more conservative venues found it difficult to reduce racism to racial prejudice and were forced to address institutionalized racism to some degree. After the death of Trayvon Martin, *Charisma* ran a special issue on race. The editor explained: people "have given 101 reasons why this *isn't* about race" and it is "merely a legal matter—period." "I doubt you'll hear that logic from many minority groups" (Yoars, 2012, 6). "Like it or not, racism is still a factor. . . . This is especially true in the church, where we've dealt with the issue as if it were something we 'fix,' only to move on to another problem. But racism isn't something we can apply a Band-Aid to with a conference session" (Yoars, 2012, 7). *Charisma* became particularly invested because Stephen Strang, its former editor, had an office a few miles from where Martin was killed. Strang collaborated with Samuel Rodriguez and Harry Jackson Jr. to dialogue on race. Strang was critical of the outcry against George Zimmerman's acquittal and tended once again to focus on relationship-building rather than on institutionalized racism. But he did quote Frederick K. Price: "Racism isn't about color; it's about money and power. Those with money and power are the only ones who can be racist because they have the resources. The superior can only be racist, not the inferior. But the superior or inferior can be prejudiced" (S. Strang et al., 2012, 53).

Even *World*, which generally never addresses racism, ran an article in which it "urged white evangelicals to listen closely to the concerns of black Americans" in light of the murder of Philando Castile. After the deaths of police officers in Dallas that soon followed the killing of Castile, *World* talked about the "need for racial healing" and ended by stressing the need to listen to Black people in particular (Dean, 2016b, 7).[1] As mentioned previously, BLM also inspired *World* write more articles critical of mass incarceration and its disproportionate impact on Black people in particular (Americans Can't Escape Their Racist Past or Present, 2015; Criminally Broken: Numbers of Inequity in the U.S. Justice System, 2015).

Christianity Today's response to this movement was to declare that we are now having a "God moment" with respect to race:

> We are currently experiencing a new "God moment," when God is shining his burning light on how our nation and our churches are fractured by racial division and injustice. In the past two years, we've seen image after image of injustice perpetrated against Black Americans. We've studied the statistics. And most important, we've heard the anguished cry of a suffering community that is understandably hurting, angry, and demanding progress. Moderate white evangelicals, who made up the bulk for our movement, see more clearly than ever how racism is embedded in many aspects of our society. We have been slow to hear what the black church has been telling us for a while. And in all that, we hear God calling his church to seek justice and reconciliation in concrete ways. (Galli, 2016, 31–32)

Christianity Today featured an interview with Jimmy Carter, who started the New Baptist Covenant to unite Baptist churches to "champion the weak and oppressed" and support racial justice (Clark, 2016a, 68). In response to BLM, Carter states: "I don't have any quarrel with Black Lives Matter" (Clark, 2016a, 69). It also ran an article on the importance of social media in bringing to light issues around police violence (Clark, 2016b).

The Gospel Coalition, not known for its progressive racial politics, ran a blog in response to the Ferguson uprising: "Ferguson is ripping the bandages off the racial wounds we thought were healing but instead are full of infection . . . make no mistake. Privilege is real, and so is oppression. We live in the same country, in different worlds. The town of Ferguson is speaking up; this is the time to listen, and pray for justice" (Wax, 2014). In addition, many evangelical leaders became directly involved in the organizing at Ferguson, which radicalized their politics. For instance, Brenda Salter McNeil, a prominent evangelical preacher on racial reconciliation, noted her in talk at the 2016 Justice Conference how her meeting with leaders at Ferguson challenged her politics with respect to LGBT organizing. Lisa Sharon Harper also organized to make sure that the Urbana 2015 conference, which is held in St. Louis, Missouri, centered on voices of Ferguson organizers. Worship leader Erna Kim Hackett strongly advocated for Black Lives Matter throughout the conference. It also featured a controversial speaker, Michelle Higgins, who spoke very directly not just against racism and police violence but also on transphobia, capitalism, reproductive justice, and other intersecting forms of oppression. She argued that the evangelical church has "committed adultery with white supremacy." InterVarsity came under fire because of her talk, but many prominent evangelicals wrote a letter in support of it (Harper, 2016).[2] In November 2014 evangelicals organized online under the hashtag #evangelicals4justice in support of the Ferguson movement that trended nationally.

The Southern Baptist Convention (SBC) and the Gospel Coalition organized an entire conference on racism at the 2015 Ethics and Religious Liberty Commission (ERLC) Leadership Summit that very pointedly addressed institutionalized racism as well as police violence against people of color. Almost half of the speakers were not white, which is unusual for evangelical conferences (R. Graham, 2015). Russell Moore began the conference with a talk on "why racial reconciliation is a gospel issue." While we know the faces and names of the men who started the SBC, "no one knows the names of the enslaved men and women who were kidnapped to work the fields of some of those men. . . . No one memorializes the names of the women who were raped and the families who were split apart often by people who knew how to preach on family values." This conference was certainly mixed in its analysis. For instance, one of the talks on race and the pro-life movement echoed the Moynihan theme that the major problem facing communities of color is their family structure. However, it closed with a talk by Trip Lee saying that it was not enough for white evangelicals to listen to people of color about racism; they need to take action.[3] Interestingly, Christena Cleveland noted the progress at this conference but also offered this critique: "The way evangelicals look at race, they think racism in interpersonal meanness" (R. Graham,

2015). But the following year ERLC prominently displayed Cleveland's work as a resource for churches to read on race relations.

Evangelical and White Nationalism

As discussed, the election of Barack Obama seemed to spark an explicit white reconstructionism within white evangelicals that became too difficult for even conservative evangelicals to ignore. Four out of five white evangelicals voted for Donald Trump (Shellnutt, 2016b). Given that Trump seemed to support so few of the values supposedly claimed by evangelicals, and given the explicit racism of his campaign, it was difficult to reach any other conclusion than that white evangelical investment in Trump was an explicit investment in whiteness itself. As Christena Cleveland argued in *Christianity Today*, while evangelicals claim to be voting on the basis of faith, race was a bigger determinant of voting patterns than doctrine (Cleveland, 2016a). Racial reconciliation no longer seemed suited to the task of addressing white reconstructionism.

Donald Trump appeared to be an unlikely candidate for Christian evangelicals. He did not have strong positions on the usual evangelical litmus tests. He did not appear to support evangelical social values. He even made statements in support of Planned Parenthood during the primaries. Consequently, he received much criticism in the evangelical press. After he received the nomination, however, many evangelicals began to rally around him under the "lesser of two evils" banner. Yet, even during the primaries, Trump received support from megachurch leaders Paula White and Joel Osteen. But the most stunning endorsement he received was from Jerry Falwell Jr., to the consternation of many even at Liberty University (which Jerry Falwell Jr. took over on the death of his father). His rationale: "All the social issues—traditional family values, abortion—are moot if ISIS blows up some of our cities or if the borders aren't fortified. . . . Rank-and-file evangelicals are smarter than many of the leaders. They are trying to save the country and may vote on the social issues next time" (Dean, 2016c, 38).

Charisma's Stephen Strang endorsed Ted Cruz during the primaries. He argued that too many liberal Republicans were voting in the primaries but that liberal Republicans do not win the general elections. He urged evangelical Republicans to vote for conservatives, particularly Ted Cruz, whom he saw as most likely to win the general election (S. Strang, 2016a). *Charisma* stated that while we never know people's hearts, we can judge their claims by their fruits. "You may plan to vote for him to be president, even though he shows no true signs of being a genuine Christian. . . . But let's not foolishly proclaim him to be a Christian" (M. Brown, 2016a, 76). After Trump won the nomination, *Charisma* began to speculate whether Trump was like the biblical Cyrus—an ungodly man who serves God's purposes— or like Nebuchadnezzar, who will destroy Jerusalem. Only time will tell (M. Brown, 2016b). But during this period of speculation *Charisma* also ran an article by Harry Jackson Jr., who said that, while he did not think Trump was racist, "even if Trump should win the White House, a whites-only campaign strategy would hurt the GOP in the long term" (H. Jackson, 2016). However, in the end, *Charisma* decided that Trump was indeed Cyrus. Strang decided to "enthusiastically endorse Donald Trump" and reversed his previous position, referring to him as a Christian (even if not a "perfect Christian") and emphasizing that he was pro-Israel. The rationale was that "even if you have to hold your nose," vote for Trump for the sake of the Supreme Court (S. Strang, 2016c, 8; see also J. R. Curtis, 2016; LeClaire, 2016b; Sheets, 2016; S. Strang, 2016b). *Charisma* then proclaimed that Trump was indeed the modern-day Cyrus prophesied in the Bible in Isaiah 45 to protect Christians from terrorism, the "inner city," and attacks on religious liberty (Allanau, 2016, 38). *Charisma* featured self-described prophets who explain that God has "chosen Trump to be the next president in what will be part of a global awakening that will lead to a restoration of biblical Israel, a return of the Jewish nation and rebuilding of the Temple" (Eschliman, 2016, 52). One such "prophet," Bill Harmon of Christian International, argued: "In 2012, the church didn't want to vote for Romney because he was a Mormon, which led to the election of Obama, who has been more of a Muslim than a Christian" (quoted in Eschliman, 2016, 52). C. Peter Wagner of Global Harvest Ministries also affirmed: "Many evangelicals voted for Sunday school teacher Jimmy Carter because of his spirituality only to end up with a disaster. God is not limited to using Christians to accomplish his purposes" (quoted in Eschliman, 2016, 54). *Charisma* apparently also implicitly supported fascism when it stated (quoting James Dobson): "Democracy is the worst form of government if the people want evil. In that system, there will be no stopping those who want what is harmful and wicked" (LeClaire, 2016b, 45).

World was generally critical of Trump throughout the cycle, although more because of character issues than because of his racism or immigration policies (Dean, 2016f; M. Olasky, 2016a, 2016f).[4] One article sharply criticized Jerry Falwell Jr.'s support of Trump. Falwell justified his endorsement despite Trump's moral indiscretions: "Jesus said 'Judge not, lest ye be judged.' Let's stop trying to choose the political leaders who we believe are the most godly because, in reality, only God knows people's hearts. You and I don't, and we are all sinners" (quoted in Dean, 2016g, 57). *World* noted that this was "a perplexing argument," given that his father advocated that Bill Clinton should resign based on his sexual indiscretions, and opined that Jerry Falwell Sr. "would be rolling over in his grave" if he knew of this endorsement (Dean, 2016g, 57). The magazine concluded: "The anger of man does not produce the righteousness that God requires" (Dean, 2016g, 57; see also Cheaney, 2016a). *World* ran a very critical exposé of Jerry Falwell Jr., suggesting that he might have taken a financial donation from Donald Trump. Its interviews indicated that most students at Liberty University were not happy with the endorsement and that Falwell would block any student who questioned his endorsement of Trump (Derrick, 2016). The magazine harshly criticized Joel Osteen, who endorsed Trump by describing his faith as "dubbed an evangelical by Huffington Post" (M. Olasky, 2016g, 68). Another article described the view that Trump is evangelical as one of his "wildest recent claims" (Dean, 2015a, 39). Finally, after Trump's sexually predatory comments came to light, *World* called on him to withdraw from the presidential race. It noted that it had called on President Clinton to resign after his sexual harassment came to light, so by the same standard Trump should also resign. While *World* bemoaned the idea of Hillary Clinton potentially winning the presidency, it affirmed the opinion of Albert Mohler, head of Southern Baptist Seminary, when he said that Christians should not "allow a national disgrace to become the Great Evangelical Embarrassment" (M. Olasky, 2016h, 7).[5]

In the end, however, *World*'s complaints about Trump seemed to disappear when he won. *World* saw the Republican victory as vindication of its hatred of the Obama administration and an opportunity to erase Obama's legacy (M. Olasky, 2016c, 2016e). It noted that Christians needed to concern themselves with "vulnerable populations" after the election. While it mentioned race relations briefly, however, "vulnerable populations" seemed to mean Christians who are battling abortion and homosexuality (Dean, 2016e).

Christianity Today ran an election section with three different positions: Ronald Sider endorsed Hillary Clinton, James Dobson endorsed Trump, and Sho Baraka endorsed neither. Sider argued that, while he did not support Clinton's position on abortion, Trump was essentially dangerous and unqualified (Sider, 2016). Dobson did step back from his previous endorsement that Trump was a Christian and said that he was actually concerned about his immorality and that he was not Godly. However, there was no

Godly candidate to vote for. If evangelicals had direct access to Trump then if he "turns out to be an incorrigible demagogue, we can hope he will be reined in by the political process." In the end, "Hillary Clinton, given her lawless behavior and what she has promised to do, would be a disaster" (J. Dobson, 2016, 60). The big issues of concern to Dobson were religious liberty and abortion.

Baraka contended that neither candidate showed concern for Black people, critiquing Trump's obvious racism and the Clinton administration's previous support of the 1994 Crime Bill. He argued that Christians should be willing to engage in "political disruption" (Baraka, 2016, 64).

Unlike *Charisma* and *World*, *Relevant* did not celebrate the Trump election, stating that the large number of white evangelicals voting for Trump had damaged the church's credibility.

> When I see the reaction to the direction of the United States from African Americans, Latinos, whites and those all over the theological spectrum about the church's loss of credibility, I wanted to say that the Church will have credibility when she lives out all the implications of the Gospel when she cares and fights for diversity in her ranks, when she's not happy in hegemony. (Chandler, 2017, 26)

Relevant had also condemned the "idolatry of patriotism": "It's a Kingdom that is no more Israeli than it is Palestinian; no more American than it is Iraqi; and no more socialist than it is democratic" (Boyd, 2010, 30). Of course, this presumed that socialism cannot be democratic.

Although four out of five white evangelicals did vote for Trump, he did get considerable criticism from some white evangelical leaders, based not just on his morality but on his sexism and racism. The Gospel Coalition ran several guest blogs calling on followers not to vote for Trump because of his racism (Anyabwile, 2016). Max Lucado, who generally is not vocal in politics, came out against Trump (Lucado, 2016). But perhaps the most outspoken leader was Russell Moore. He published an op-ed criticizing not only Trump but the racial nostalgia among evangelicals that was the basis of their support for Trump.

> This election has cast light on the darkness of pent-up nativism and bigotry all over the country. There are not-so-coded messages denouncing African-Americans and immigrants; concern about racial justice and national unity is ridiculed as "political correctness." . . .

The Bible calls on Christians to bear one another's burdens. White American Christians who respond to cultural tumult with nostalgia fail to do this. They are blinding themselves to the injustices faced by their black and brown brothers and sisters in the supposedly idyllic Mayberry of white Christian America. That world was murder, sometimes literally, for minority evangelicals.

This has gospel implications not only for minorities and immigrants but for the so-called silent majority. A vast majority of Christians, on earth and in heaven, are not white and have never spoken English. A white American Christian who disregards nativist language is in for a shock. The man on the throne in heaven is a dark-skinned, Aramaic-speaking "foreigner" who is probably not all that impressed by chants of "Make America great again." (R. Moore, 2016d)

In response to this article, Trump responded in a tweet that Moore is "a nasty guy with no heart." Moore responded with: "I am a nasty guy with no heart . . . which is why I need forgiveness of sins and redemption through the gospel of Jesus Christ" (Dean, 2016d, 17). After James Dobson vouched that Trump was now a born-again Christian, evangelical blogger Jonathan Merritt posted, "Many evangelicals who support Trump owe Bill Clinton an apology,"[6] to which Russell Moore replied: "They certainly do. Especially those who built fundraising empires on character in office."[7]

Moore did more than challenge Trump: he has also challenged Christian evangelicalism's investment in "Christian America": "For too long we have assumed that the church is a means to an end to save America. America is important. But the end goal of the gospel is not a Christian America. The end goal of the gospel is redeemed from every tribe and tongue and nation and language. . . . We belong to another kingdom" (S. P. Bailey, 2015, 33).

Against those who argued that evangelicals are losing their influence in society, Moore contended: "On the wrong side of history? We started on the wrong side of history—a Roman Empire and a cross. Rome's dead and Jesus is fine" (S. P. Bailey, 2015, 37). Against the explicit Islamophobia of the Trump campaign, Moore argued: "We have to be arguing for religious freedom for everyone," including Muslims (S. P. Bailey, 2015, 34). Moore also advocated for creation care and immigration. His gender politics, as mentioned, are not progressive. He sits on the board of the Council of Biblical Manhood and Womanhood, which advocates male headship. He does not support same-sex marriage whatsoever. Yet despite these orthodox credentials, he has certainly received much criticism for his outspoken support of racial justice. After the election, Moore received significant criticism within the SBC for his refusal to back Trump, with some SBC pastors calling for his resignation (Shellnutt, 2016a). However, many rallied to Moore's side under the hashtag #IStandWithMoore, and otherwise published articles of support (Merritt, 2016). In particular, it seems that the support of pastors of color in the SBC may have significantly contributed to Moore retaining his position (E. Green, 2017).

Donald Trump, though never specifically named, provided the subtext for the SBC's Ethics and Religious Liberty Commission 2016 National Conference. The ERLC continued to focus on race, with some speakers even coming out in support of Black Lives Matter. Bryan Loritts, the opening speaker, while starting on a more conciliatory note, became increasingly stronger in his critique. He explicitly rejected "color-blind" ethics, which he called an ethic for people of privilege. "Racial reconciliation is not a church growth technique; it is a way of life." He also essentially criticized the ethnographic entrapment of Black theology, which he said is reducible to James Cone and easily knowable. But when asked to explain white theology, he said it could not be done because it is assumed to be the norm. Evangelicals do not see the whiteness of their theology. He concluded by stating that racism makes Jesus angry: hence evangelicals are mandated to act against racial injustice.

Russell Moore continued his critique of appeals to nostalgia. "When we say we need to go back to before everything fell apart, that would mean going back to Genesis 3." The old "America" was not good either. "We can't be the people who are cringing, fearful and anxious." And David French stated that white evangelicals need to repent of their racism that enabled Trump to win the nomination. Moore further questioned the appeals to a Christian America: "Politics has become a transcendent source of identity that must be dethroned by the gospel." Numerous other conservative evangelicals also spoke out against Trump.[8]

As the election grew closer, more organized evangelical efforts against Trump began to coalesce. Students at Liberty University launched a petition drive disagreeing with Falwell's endorsement of Trump (S. Smith, 2016). Alumni and students and others affiliated with Wheaton College took out an anti-Trump advertisement (Anonymous, 2016). And a coalition of prominent evangelicals developed a statement that challenged not only Trump but the assumption that white evangelicals have the right to define evangelicalism, critiquing the equation of evangelicalism with whiteness:

Imperfect elections and flawed candidates often make for complicated and difficult choices for Christians. But sometimes historic moments arise when more is at stake than partisan politics—when the meaning and integrity of our faith hangs in the balance. This is one of those moments.

A significant mistake in American politics is the media's continued identification of "evangelical" with mostly white, politically conservative, older men. We are not those evangelicals. The media's narrow labels of our community perpetuate stereotypes, ignore our diversity, and fail to accurately represent views expressed by the full body of evangelical Christians.

We are Americans of African and European descent, Latino/a, Asian American, and Native American. We are women and men, as well as younger and older evangelical Christians. We come from a wide range of denominations, churches, and political orientations.

We believe in the unity of the body of Christ, but we acknowledge the diverse nature of a community whose faith is biblical and evangelical. And we are growing. Given the rich diversity within our unity, we call upon the political world to hear all our voices, and for the media to acknowledge that the evangelical community is quite diverse.

As evangelical Christians, we believe our hope and allegiance rests in the person of Jesus Christ, Savior of the world, and Lord of our lives. That is why no politician, party, movement, or nation can ever command our ultimate loyalty. As citizens both of the Kingdom of God and [of] this world, we vote with humility, knowing that our favored candidates always fall short of biblical values. We recognize that despite our unity in Christ, we will inevitably disagree about which political stances come closest to the heart of God for our nation.

We believe that the centrality of Christ, the importance of both conversion and discipleship, the authority of the Scriptures, and the "good news" of the gospel, especially for the poor and vulnerable, should prevail over ideological politics, and that we must respond when evangelicalism becomes dangerously identified with one particular candidate whose statements, practice, personal morality, and ideology risk damaging our witness to the gospel before the watching world.

We believe that racism strikes at the heart of the gospel; we believe that racial justice and reconciliation is at the core of the message of Jesus.

We believe the candidacy of Donald J. Trump has given voice to a movement that affirms racist elements in white culture—both explicit and implicit. Regardless of his recent retraction, Mr. Trump has spread racist "birther" falsehoods for five years trying to delegitimize and humiliate our first African-American president, characterizing him as "the other" and not a real American citizen. He uses fear to demonize and degrade immigrants, foreigners, and people from different racial, ethnic, and religious backgrounds. He launched his presidential campaign by demonizing Mexicans, immigrants, and Muslims, and has repeatedly spoken against migrants and refugees coming to this country—those whom Jesus calls "the stranger" in Matthew 25, where he says that how we treat them is how we treat him. Trump has steadily refused to clearly and aggressively confront extremist voices and movements of white supremacy, some of whom now call him their "champion," and has therefore helped to take the dangerous fringes of white nationalism in America to the mainstream of politics.

Mr. Trump has fueled white American nationalism with xenophobic appeals and religious intolerance at the expense of gospel values, democratic principles, and important international relationships. He mocks women and the sanctity of marriage vows, disregards facts and the accountability to truth, and worships wealth and shameful materialism, while taking our weakening culture of civility to nearly unprecedented levels with continuing personal attacks on others, including attacking a federal judge based purely on his Mexican heritage, mocking a disabled reporter, and humiliating a beauty pageant winner for her weight and Latina ethnicity—to give just a few examples.

Because we believe that racial bigotry has been a cornerstone of this campaign, it is a foundational matter of the gospel for us in this election, and not just another issue. This is not just a social problem, but a fundamental wrong. Racism is America's original sin. Its brazen use to win elections threatens to reverse real progress on racial equity and set America back.

Donald Trump's campaign is the most recent and extreme version of a history of racialized politics that has been pursued and about which white evangelicals, in particular, have been silent. The silence in previous times has set the environment for what we now see.

For this reason, we cannot ignore this bigotry, set it aside, just focus on other issues, or forget the things Mr. Trump has consistently said and done. No matter what other issues we also care about, we have to make it publicly clear that Mr. Trump's racial and religious bigotry and treatment of women is morally unacceptable to us as evangelical Christians, as we attempt to model Jesus' command to "love your neighbors as yourself."

Whether we support Mr. Trump's political opponent is not the question here. Hillary Clinton is both supported and distrusted by a variety of Christian voters. We, undersigned evangelicals, simply will not tolerate the racial, religious, and gender bigotry that Donald Trump has consistently and deliberately fueled, no matter how else we choose to vote or not to vote.

We see this election as a significant teachable moment for our churches and our nation to bring about long-needed repentance from our racial sin. Out of this belief we have written this declaration, inviting you to be part of what we have learned from one another and long to see in the churches and the world—a commitment to justice and the dignity of all human lives.

We invite you to stand with us, join in this declaration, and pass it along to your friends, congregants, pastors, students, and the diverse evangelical church. (Rushton, 2017)

Meanwhile, the rise of BLM and Donald Trump have emboldened many evangelicals of color to take stronger stances against white supremacy and other forms of oppression. As mentioned in chapter 8, this evangelical investment in whiteness has also spurred increasing numbers of evangelicals of color to refuse their positioning as Native informant or mission object. As discussed, progressive evangelicalism has still had the tendency to view communities of color or communities in the Global South as the objects of missions for white evangelical saviors. This notion was sharply critiqued by Soong-Chan Rah, who argued at the 2015 Christian Community Development Association (CCDA) conference that a synonym for urban missions is "gentrification." Eugene Cho similarly stated: "God never intended people to be your 'project.' . . . We might be the mountain God wants to move." As Brenda Salter McNeil similarly stated at the 2016 CCDA conference, "Folks don't need us to develop more reconciliation committees, they need us to show up with them and fight for justice." She further contended that reconciliation requires reparations. Even former conservative favorite Kay Cole James stated that the Republican Party and conservatives have completely abandoned the Black community. She said that the Christian Right had used her but does not find her useful anymore. "Evangelicals in general do not care about Black people anymore" (M. Olasky, 2013a, 30–31). What we may be seeing is the inception of a justice-centered evangelicalism that is no longer content to remain at the margins of this movement or seek inclusion from the white evangelical establishment but is intent on the claiming the center.

These interventions raise the question: what exactly is an evangelical? *Christianity Today* ran an article by Leith Anderson and Ed Stetzer, who stated that white Christians are much less likely to have evangelical beliefs than are Black Christians but are also more likely to call themselves evangelicals than are Black Christians. Thus, they argued, Trump might have been voted in by those who called themselves evangelicals but do not necessarily share evangelical beliefs. The question remaining from this study as well as from the election results is: does evangelicalism essentially connote a commitment to whiteness (L. Anderson and E. Stetzer, 2016)? If justice-centered people of color begin to claim the center of evangelicalism, what will evangelicalism look like? As Kathy Khang said to white evangelicals in response to the election of Donald Trump, "We are angry, we are grieving, we are organizing" (E. E. Evans, 2016). And in response to white evangelicals on the issue of who defines what an evangelical is, Khang argues: "Leaving a label is one thing, but changing an understanding of what is Christian or Christ-like is another. Why do I have to leave? Why don't you stick around and fix this mess" (E. E. Evans, 2016)?

Conclusion

Baylor Religion Survey found that reading the Bible more frequently (as compared to just saying you believe in the Bible) increases the chance that you will oppose the death penalty and mass incarceration and support "social justice" and economic justice as being important (Franzen, 2011). Evangelicals who went to church more frequently were also less likely to vote for Trump than those who went less frequently.

Given conservative evangelicalism and the Christian Right's investment in politics that often deify capitalism, support U.S. and Christian imperialism, consolidate gender hierarchy and heteronormativity, and replace racial justice with racial reconciliation, it would be easy to dismiss the importance of social justice movements within evangelicalism. And yet Christian belief often complicates conservative politics in unexpected ways. Many even within evangelicalism argue that racial reconciliation has not fostered effective change within conservative evangelicalism. Certainly, the mass support of Donald Trump by white evangelicals would bolster this argument. However, the effects of this movement cannot be confined to changes in white evangelical attitudes in a short period. Rather, we must also examine the discursive effects of racial reconciliation. What new conversations are enabled? What conversations are disabled? How has racial reconciliation challenged evangelical metanarratives that presuppose complete doctrinal certainty and the centrality of boundary-setting that have in turn created space for other formations that might not even seem to engage race politics directly? Certainly, many sectors of white evangelicals have remained immune to racial critique, yet at the same time racial reconciliation has emboldened many evangelicals, particularly evangelicals of color, to interrogate the disavowed whiteness of evangelicalism and claim it as something other than what has been defined by whiteness. Meanwhile, the white reconstructionist movement within evangelicalism perhaps reflects an evangelical uneasiness with the suspicion that its foundations are in fact based on white supremacy and Eurocentrism rather than on the eternal Word of God.

As the emergence of critical ethnic studies has shifted our focus from racial identity to race as an analytic of power, an analysis of racial reconciliation must address the politics of racialization more broadly. If we borrow from Foucault's analysis of biopower that demonstrates that racialization is ultimately about predisposing some populations to "premature death" so that others might live, then the terrain of who is enfolded in life and who is left to die is constantly shifting. The biopolitics of racial reconciliation then require us to look at the intersections of racial reconciliation and U.S. imperialism, Christian Zionism, heteronormativity, and capitalism. This movement is not a simple story of racial exclusion and inclusion; rather, different sectors within evangelicalism often negotiate for their inclusion at the expense of other groups, who become disposable populations. The demand of Black and Latinx evangelicals that white evangelicals support prison and immigration reform in exchange for political solidarity against same-sex marriage is just one of many examples that illustrate this dynamic. Thus, a fuller story of the effects of racial reconciliation cannot be told outside its intersection with other analytics of power such as gender, sexuality, and U.S. imperialism. This fuller analysis, in turn, demonstrates the extent to which religion itself is a racializing logic that determines who is worthy of life.

Nonetheless, the history of racial reconciliation demonstrates that we cannot presume who can be the subject of a critical ethnic studies politic and analysis that is capable of bringing about social and political transformation. Centering people of color, particular of women of color within Christian evangelicalism, tells us a different story about evangelicalism. Informed by a critical ethnic studies analysis, people of color have been instrumental in shifting the political positions of conservative evangelical organizations on immigration reform, mass incarceration, police violence, racial justice, the death penalty, and other issues, and shifts are continuing. Engaging people across religious, social, geographic, and political divides in critical ethnic studies conversations is essential for a future beyond premature death.

The revolution begins with a conversation.

NOTES

Introduction

1. I use the word "evangelical" to refer to Protestants who generally subscribe to the five fundamentals of faith that have served as a rallying points for evangelicalism: biblical inerrancy, the deity of Christ, substitutionary atonement, bodily resurrection, and the second coming of Christ. This definition centers on the neo-evangelical movement that emerged out of Christian fundamentalism in the 1950s but also includes Pentecostals and groups that do not trace their roots to the fundamentalist/modernist debates of the 1920s. I do not include here the more explicitly racist Christian movements, such as Christian Identity groups. I use the term "evangelical" to signify a discursive community rather than a bounded community based on clear doctrinal principles. Thus, some peoples within this discursive community might not always use the term "evangelical" themselves but nonetheless remain part of the ongoing conversations that emerge from Christian evangelicalism. For a more extensive mapping of how I define "evangelical," see my previous work (A. Smith, 2008).

2. As Robert P. Jones notes, the white evangelical vote for Trump in the general election was not distinguishable from its votes in any other presidential election since 1984. White evangelicals vote for Republicans regardless of the religious affinity of the candidate. But, as he notes, white people in general tend to vote Republican, so race is more significant than religion in terms of voting patterns. However, the question arises, given the critique of Donald Trump by evangelicals for his support of Planned Parenthood, his previous pro-choice positions, and his ambivalent position on gay marriage (Camosy, 2016; Gremore, 2016), why was he favored by evangelicals over other Republican candidates in the primaries who had more solidly traditional Christian Right positions on these issues? Jones contends that white evangelicals are more likely explicitly to support a white racial nostalgia, which Trump explicitly campaigned around (R. P. Jones, 2018).

3. Thank you to J. Kameron Carter for this articulation.

4. Historically, commentators on the Christian Right have often minimized the importance of race as an organizing principle for its genesis. An early exception was Ellen Rosenberg (1984). Almost two decades later after Rosenberg's book, other scholars began to address race in their analysis of the Christian Right (Burlein, 2002; Kintz, 1997; A. Smith, 1999). Newer works are now centering a race analysis. Peter Heltzel's work is a key text in this area (Heltzel, 2009). See also Balmer, 2014.

5. Bob Jones University dropped its ban on interracial dating on May 3, 2000, claiming that it "had become an obstacle" (News Service Briefs, 2002, 34).

6. Talks between the NAE and the NBEA broke down in 1992 because the NBEA felt that the NAE's rhetoric of racial reconciliation was not matched by its deeds. "[The NAE] holds itself as white first and Christian second," stated William Bentley, president of the NBEA. "White supremacy—they would shrink from being called that. But they practice it. They practice it like white people" (Bray, 1992). The NAE continued with its racial reconciliation efforts, however, distributing a seven-point racial reconciliation packet to clergy and inviting the NBEA and the Hispanics to meet in 1996 (J. Kennedy, 1996, 101). In January 2003 leaders from both organizations met to hold have a joint summit for the NAE and NBEA, to emerge with common strategies. Don Argue, former leader of NAE, stated: that "racism and reconciliation are not on the radar screen of most white evangelicals, because we don't deal with it daily. . . . Racism is always on the agenda at black evangelical meetings because they deal with it every day" (J. Kennedy, 2002, 18).

7. This finding was contradicted by the follow-up study of Nancy Wadsworth, who concludes that all evangelicals regardless of race tend to assess race on an individual rather than a structural level (Wadsworth, 2014, loc. 3249). Robert P. Jones, by contrast, found that the exception to the tendency for evangelicals to ignore structural racism is among African American evangelicals (R. P. Jones, 2016).

8. Reconsidering Rickshaw Rally (December 8, 2018), at http://www.geocities.ws/reconsideringrickshawrally/.

9. Nancy Wadsworth in her follow-up study on the racial reconciliation movement documents that at least evangelical elites took Emerson and Smith's arguments to heart. Her focus, however, is on the development of multiethnic ministries as a response to this critique (Wadsworth, 2014).

Chapter 1

1. But Herndon does address power differentials between white and Black churches by arguing that white people need to stop thinking of Black churches as mission churches and understand them as partner churches (Mission Mississippi, n.d.).

2. Much internal critique of Christian America also shapes evangelical discourse (A. Smith, 2008). For further examples since the publication of that book, see K. Miller, 1997a; S. Carter, 2006; Cheaney, 2005a; Olsen, 2005f; C. Thomas, 1999.

3. See "Mars Hill Bible Church," n.d., https://marshill.org/.

Chapter 2

1. Richard Twiss, personal communication, January 4, 2013.

2. See also A. Gaines, 2000; Maxwell, 1997; McKissic, 2008; Stetson, 1997, 34.

3. See also Boone, 1996, 85; Kantzer, 1989; S. Lee, 2014; M. Olasky, 2004d; Veith, 2006a.

4. See, for example, R. Cooper, 1995; Dawson, 1994; Neff, 2002; P. B. Powell, 2000; Rice, 2002; S. Strang, 1998c; Walker, 1998c, 2008b; Washington and Kehrein, 1993; G. Yancey, 1996 This trend is still prevalent within evangelical circles. See Gray, 2015.

5. One *World* article did say that Katrina demonstrates some need for government spending. "Too many [Republicans] act is if poverty doesn't exist" (Abraham, 2005a, 26). Regarding similar responses to Haiti and other disasters, see Alford, 2005a, 2006c, 2006f; S. P. Bailey, 2010a; J. Belz, 2005b, 2005e; Bergin, 2006c; Carnes, 2005b; Carnes and Moll, 2005; Christianity Today, 2005; Courbat, 2011; Cushman, 2005; Daigle, 2005a;

Dawson, 2005c, 2005d, 2005e; Dean, 2005c, 2005d, 2005e, 2006a, 2006d, 2010a, 2010d; J. L. Grady, 2005a; A. Harris, 2010; Hot Sauce for Haiti, 2010; Mary Hutchinson, 2010; Lamer, 2005a, 2005b; News Briefs, 2006b; M. Olasky, 2005b, 2005c, 2005f; S. Olasky and B. Perry, 2005; Olsen, 2005d; Tiansay, 2005b; Vincent, 2005a; Watson, 2005.

6. Interestingly, *World* did criticize the Democratic mayor of Dallas for criminalizing panhandling, which included criminalizing being on the street as well as criminalizing individuals who give food and water to people on the street. because this was not solving the problem of homelessness but pushing it out of sight. It is not clear whether this shift in stance was motivated in part because the person issuing the policy was a Democrat (Dawson, 2007a).

7. See M. Belz, 2009a; Cole, 2007; A. Cook, 2007; Couto, 2002; A. Gaines, 2002a; A. Harris, 2007a, 2007b, 2009a; Liew, 2003; Moeller, 2007; M. Olasky, 2007d; Shepard, 2002; Sherman, 1997, 1999; Vercher, 2007a, 2007b. Exceptions that focus on white people who are victims of poverty include Devine, 2015 and Rieger, 2007a.

8. See M. Belz, 2009a; Bergin, 2009b; Conant, 2009; Daigle, 2002c; Dean, 2005b; B. Elliott and M. Olasky, 2004; Ghezzi, 2003; P. Johnson, 1998, 2002b, 2003b, 2008; Lukins, 2003; M. Olasky, 2008a; Stertzer, 2004; Walker, 2004a. For counterexamples of stories of people of color working with the poor, albeit in a pro-capitalist framework, see Carnes, 2004a; Dean, 2011b; V. Lowe, 2005; Sherman, 1999; Rhonda Smith, 2005; Williford, 1998. *Charisma*, the magazine that most focuses on racial reconciliation and features articles by people of color, increasingly tends to feature people of color who are engaged in "racial uplift."

9. See Bird, 1989; Carrasco, 1993; Curry, 1993; Cushman, 2001; Dawson, 2006b; Denominational Leaders Address Drug Crisis, 1990; Randy Frame, 1997; T. Graham, 2002; P. Johnson, 1998; Lawton, 1991; 1998; S. Lee, 2016a; V. Lowe, 2006b; Lupton, 1989; Maxwell, 1991, 36; D. Miller, 1995; Nash, 1996, 187; C. Owens, 1998; Passantino, 1991; Pearson-Wong, 2000; Rainey, 2007a; Richardson, 2004; Sherman, 1995a, 1995b; 1996; Stertzer, 2001; Teen Sex: Black Youth Leaders for a Solution, 1990; Vincent, 2001a; T. Whalin, 1997; B. Wilson, 1996; Wood, 2003; Wooding, 1994.

10. See Bergin, 2006b; Carlson, 2000; Jackson, 2005b, 2006; B. Jones III, 1998a; Lamer, 2006; V. Lowe, 2008; M. Olasky, 2008h; Palmer, 2005; R. Pulliam, 2004; Reese, 2005; Lee Sillars, 1999; Rhonda Smith, 2005; Svanoe, 2001; Taulbert, 2001, 28; J. Williams, 2007; Williford, 1998; see also Buss, 1994; T. Evans, 1990, 134; K. C. James, 1992, 181; V. Lowe, 2008, 20; Perkins, 1995b; Waters, 1992.

11. While 50 percent of Americans say that government should help more needy people, even if it means more national debt, only 39 percent of committed evangelicals say this (those who attend church at least weekly) (Olsen, 2005c).

12. Interestingly, Paquin was replaced by Phil Mitchell, who was fired from the University of Colorado–Boulder even though he had very high evaluations. The American Association of University Professors determined that this was an "academic hit job" and that he had been fired because of his conservative religious beliefs (Bergin, 2007a, 20).

13. For further examples of this equation between Christianity and capitalism, see Douglas, 2005; Veith, 1998, 30.

14. *World*, a major proponent of free-market capitalism, does make valid critiques of both government and nonprofit models for poverty reduction in which monies go to fund the bureaucracies that

manage the problem rather than actually solve it (M. Olasky, 2010a; Vincent, 2001b). Echoing some of the more radical critiques of the nonprofit industry, Robert Woodson of the Center for Neighborhood Enterprise complains in one profile that nonprofits ask not what is solvable but what is fundable. He does support government intervention in some cases, such as ending racial segregation, and criticizes conservatives for taking a blanket antigovernment approach on all issues. Woodson suggests that programs should be required to show that they are effective (M. Olasky, 2010b). *World* runs similar critiques of aid programs that are supposed to alleviate Third World poverty (M. Belz, 2005d; M. Belz and A. Harris, 2009). They also share more radical critiques of such programs, such as that the funds do not actually go to the poor or break the chains of dependency between Third World and First World countries. But, unlike radical critiques that would point out that these programs maintain rather than challenge neocolonialism, *World* offers church charity, Christian financial institutions that are principled, and individual effort as the solution to economic crises. (M. Belz, 2009a; Bergin, 2008b, 2009a; A. Harris, 2009a, 2009b; M. Olasky, 2007b, 2009b). Of course, some of the critiques of nonprofits are sharply different: while radicals complain that businesses fund progressive groups in order to divert their energies so that their organizing becomes safe for capitalism, *World* complains that businesses "are funding antibusiness propaganda: capitalists are funding socialism . . . funds . . . go to groups whose policies, if put into place, would destroy the very businesses that are funding them" (Veith, 2001a).

15. *Christianity Today*'s articles on Third World debt (Carnes, 2005a; Christianity Today, 1998b) also address more structural causes of poverty. Although it did not discuss how this debt accrued in the first place, one advocated canceling the debt, arguing that this would help the poor and "support free-market policy reforms" (Sellers, 2001c, 66). It did note, however, that World Bank monies often went to support corrupt regimes, such as in Indonesia. Another article noted problems in government corruption but also cited church corruption as equally problematic (Carnes, 2005a). *World*, by contrast, decried debt relief as a "fashion statement" (M. Belz, 1998c, 23). *Christianity Today* ran an article semicritical of Walmart's policies, even though it is a "Christian" company (Sellers, 2005a; see also *Christianity Today*, 2000b). It also ran an article on George Galatis, a Christian who was not supported by his church when he became a whistleblower and contacted the Nuclear Regulatory Commission over suspected safety violations at the Millstone Nuclear Power station. The investigation eventually vindicated him. Hence, in this case Christianity is put in opposition to corporate interests (Bowles, 2000). Charles Colson also made some mild critiques of capitalism after the Enron scandal: "Scripture endorses concepts like private property, contract rights, rule of law, and the discharge of debts—all essential to free markets. The Bible also demands justice, warning of God's judgment against oppressors who withhold wages to take advantage of the needy; it condemns those who manipulate the economy, whether by greed, hoarding, indolence or deception" (Charles Colson, 2002). The assumption that Reagonomics is biblical was questioned in another *Christianity Today* article (Eskridge, 2000; see also F. Rutledge, 2008).

16. *World* complains of Christophobia (M. Olasky, 2002b, 16; see also Adamczyk, Wybraniec, and Finke, 2004; Tony An-

derson, 2007; Troy Anderson, 2009; Armey, 1999; Bacote, 2000; Baer, 1989; M. Belz, 1996, 2006; Bennett, 1994; Charles Colson, 1996; Charles Colson, 1990, 2000; Charles Colson and A. Morse, 2007; A. Harris, 2011a; Hewitt, 2005b, 2006; How the Liberals Are Rewriting History, 1995; B. Jones III, 1998b; D. J. Kennedy, 1996, 190; Lawton, 1995; Neff, 1996; Long, 2000; M. Olasky, 1998a, 2007k, 2009c; A Secularist Jihad, 2002; Seidl, 2009; Sidey, 1990a; Les Sillars and L. Vincent, 1999; Stackhouse, 1992; Veith, 2005b; Vincent, 2006e, 2007b; Whitehead, 1995).

17. Asian American Christians United on Cultural Insensitivity and Reconciliation in the Church, 2013. A copy can be found at http://blog.angryasianman.com/2013/10/an-open-letter-from-asian-american.html. For more on the controversies that gave rise to the open letter, see Ahab, 2013.

18. LifeWay Media, "An Apology from Dr. Thom Rainer on Behalf of Lifeway Christian Resources" (video: 1 minute, 28 seconds, November 6, 2013), https://vimeo.com/78735039.

19. See Christian Community Development Association, https://ccda.org/, for list of speakers and talks at CCDA conferences.

20. Judy Vaughn, Address to National Assembly of Religious Women national conference, October 15, 1992.

21. "This Is How We Do It, Foundry Center, New York, April 20, 2012. For a video of the opening plenary of this conference, at https://www.youtube.com/watch?v=4307X3RBJCE.

Chapter 3

1. For a critique of Carter, see Potter 2000.

2. Expressing a contrary view, *Christianity Today* ran one article in which it stated that Christian missionaries were actually to blame for the rise of witchcraft in Africa: witchcraft is essentially the result of Christian theology's influence on African traditional practices (Moon, 2011).

3. Mick Lantis complained that Christians should not jump on the "anti–South Africa bandwagon" (Letters, 1985b, 10–11). The Southern Baptist Convention would not change its investment policies in South Africa during apartheid (Churches Take Action against Firms Doing Business with South Africa, 1986; Apartheid and American Christians, 1988). For a more critical essay, see Beth Spring (1985b). Even she, however, espoused a relatively conservative position—just supporting the Sullivan principles rather than divestment—that was considered radical in evangelical circles. In a 1986 *Christianity Today* survey, most respondents did not support sanctions against South Africa, and a bare majority (54 percent) even considered apartheid to be an important issue (South Africa: Can the Church Mend the Anguish of a Nation?, 1986, 13/I). The following statement is typical for that time: "If the racism of the South African government is so heinous, why has it produced blacks who are better fed, better clothed, and better educated than their counterparts elsewhere in Africa?" (Letters, 1985a, 7). Even Carl Henry argued that apartheid should not be dealt with through a "program of political engagement" but through speaking "prophetically in terms of the biblical vision of the unity of man" (quoted in Spring, 1985a, 56). *Christianity Today* at least admitted that evangelicals were actually silent on the issues of apartheid, although it claimed that evangelicals were heading the struggle toward race "reconciliation" in South Africa (it describes no program of repentance that goes along with this program other than telling Blacks that

"the Cross also requires the supernatural spirit of forgiveness from blacks for all that has been inflicted upon them," according to South African evangelist Michael Cassidy (The Mandela Moment, 1990, 12; see also Church Leaders Condemn Apartheid, 1990; Nyberg, 1994; Phiri, 1992; U.S. Advisory Committee Cites Church's Role in South African Reconciliation, 1987). By contrast, *World* continued to hold that Mandela was a Communist menace, who was essentially saved by White Afrikaners who showed him how to be nonviolent (News, 2013, 6).

4. See also T. Dixon, 1999d. Cathy Nobles says that she learned after going on the Reconciliation Walk that we need to stop the "western way" of evangelism "which demands immediate and measurable results": "You cannot ask somebody's forgiveness and at the same time ask him or her for something in return" (quoted in T. Dixon, 1999d, 32–33).

5. One article mentioned that racism was a primary concern for Asian churches but did not itself discuss racism (H. Lee, 1996).

6. *Charisma*'s article refers to China as a "heart of darkness," where people "follow ancient superstitions that involve magic and the worship of spirits" (South Asia: Into the Heart of Darkness, 1993, 27). See also Farrell 2000a and *Christianity Today*'s description of India as the "heart of darkness" (Zoba, 1999; see also Lindner, 1997b). The author of a *Charisma* article complains about an "invasion from the dark side" in the Burning Man Festival held annually in Nevada, adding, "I had to remind myself that what I had witnessed [was] not in the temples of India" (Otis, 1997, 56).

7. *World* similarly notes that Cambodian religious culture is "satanic," citing as evidence the proliferation of snakes (the symbol for Satan) in Cambodian temples (M. Olasky, 2004c). *World* attributes the genocide perpetrated by the Khmer Rouge to this satanic spirit.

8. For instance, Cecil Robeck is an Assemblies of God minister and Fuller Theological Seminary professor who has been engaged in the International Roman Catholic–Pentecostal Dialogue since 1985. He has been subject to calls to be disciplined in violation of an Assemblies of God rule that prohibits ministers from "supporting the 'ecumenical movement.'" He has been described as "meeting with the Antichrist" (Rabey, 1998, 23).

9. In an accompanying op-ed, *World* opined that it supported a border fence but not necessarily private anti-immigrant militia groups. Bob Jones IV complained that illegal immigrants were simply criminals. B. Jones IV, 1996a; see also Carrasco, 1993; Dawson, 2006g; Dean, 2007d; Vincent, 2007d. For a more generous article on immigration, see T. Graham, 2001b.

10. Interestingly, some readers of *World* criticized this article for demonizing Mexican immigrants and failing to look at how U.S. economic policy creates the conditions for the immigration "problem" (Mailbag, 2005).

11. For more positive letters, see Feedback, 2006.

12. See, for instance, J. Miller, 1996; Rapp, 1988. *World* noted that evangelicals are realizing "that the growing Hispanic population now represents one of their greatest evangelistic opportunities" (T. King, 2013, 82).

13. Tapia has written sympathetically on immigrant rights, including a fairly positive review of *Sanctuary: A Resource Guide for Understanding and Participating in the Central American Refugees' Struggle*. Another sympathetic article is Maol, 1989.

14. For articles suggesting that poverty, the War on Terror and natural disasters

have been helpful in bringing more Muslims to Christ, see Lukins, 2004a, 2004b; Price, 2004a. *World* notes that "a million migrants have made their way from war-torn countries to Europe, prompting threats to security but also opportunities for Christian service" (M. Belz, 2016, 30).

15. Just 31 percent of white evangelicals said they approve of raising the refugee cap, much lower than the 58 percent of black Protestants (two-thirds of whom identify as evangelicals) and 51 percent of overall Americans who approved (Zylstra, 2015a).

16. See also in-depth coverage of "insider movements" of those who follow Jesus but formally continue to engage in other religious practices. This article debates to what extent contextualization is "too much" but also see insiders as able to convert where other missionaries would be less successful (G. Daniels, 2013, 31). John Piper of the Gospel Coalition is a critic of these movements.

17. One letter to the editor that did not celebrate Columbus also claimed that he was not a real Christian because "Christians" do not commit genocide.

18. For more information, see Scott Overpeck, "El Camino del Inmigrante" (March 12, 2017), https://ccda.org/faqs/el-camino/.

Chapter 4

1. *Voice of the Martyrs* (an undated mailer).

2. This Jewish support is noted by *Charisma*, which frequently stresses that Jewish individuals and organizations are supporting persecuted Christians, so Christians should support the state of Israel (discussed more in chapter 5).

3. In addition to articles cited throughout this book, see also Abraham, 2004d, 2006e; Aikman, 2004; M. Belz, 1998a, 1999d; Carnes, 2000d; Christianity Today, 2007a; Donnally, 2000; Guthrie, 2001c; C. Hulsman, 2004; J. King, 1998; Lombardo, 2005; Meral, 2008; Newman, 2004a; Persecution Watch, 2004c, 2004e, 2005b, 2005d, 2005f, 2005g, 2005h, 2006c, 2006d, 2006e, 2006f, 2007f, 2007a, 2007b, 2007d, 2008, 2010; Price, 1997; Rearing Its Ugly Head, 1999; Religious News Service, 2003; M. Singh, 2002d, 2004a; Stamp, 2001; G. Taylor, 2000; Walker, 2016; J. Weber, 2016b; Wolf, 2000. Despite this prevalence of the issue, those in the movement complain that Christians are apathetic about this issue (Cagney, 1998a).

4. See Doyle, 1999; Ecumenical News International and Religious News Service, 2000; Minchakpu, 2000b, 2001, 2002, 2004a, 2006; News Service Briefs, 2002; Persecution Watch, 2004b; M. Singh, 2002b. By contrast, some *Christianity Today* article on Nigeria have contended that framing the conflict on religious grounds ignores the larger context of political and ethnic strife in the area (Cartoon Chaos, 2006; Chambers, 1999; Keener, 2004). For a similar treatment of anti-Hmong repression being equated with anti-Christian repression in Vietnam, see Littleton, 1999.

5. See Abraham, 2004e, 2005c; Fischer, 1999; J. Newton, 2003b, 2004b; Religious News Service, 1999; M. Singh, 2000a, 2001a, 2001b, 2003, 2004b, D. E. Singh, 2005. Some exceptions did highlight the fact that it was Muslims under attack in Gujarat (including Ankara, 2002; Christianity Today, 1999a; David, 2002; Sellers, 2002g).

6. One book review does briefly mention (one sentence) that Christians are sometimes persecuted by other Christians, such as in Latin America (Knippers, 1997). Another article critiques Zambia for declaring itself a "Christian" nation despite its political and economic problems and widespread corruption. Of course, it may be the case that anti-Black racism in this discourse precludes evan-

gelicals from seeing African countries as Christian (Ecumenical News International, 2000). For instance, a *Christianity Today* article focuses on the Congo, describing it as primarily Christian, but the title of the article is "Hope in the Heart of Darkness" (Phiri, 2006).

7. See Abraham, 2004b, 2005d, 2005f, 2005g; Aikman, 2005b; Alford, 2000a; E. Belz, 2011a; M. Belz, 1998b, 1999a, 1999b, 2005b, 2008b, 2010c, 2011b, 2015; Bjelajac, 2001; Brookes, 2008; F. Brown, 1999, 2000b; B. Bruce, 1999a, 2001; Buchan, 2001; Callahan, 2004a; Carnes, 2000a, 2000b, 2002a, 2002c, 2005c, 2006a; Cheng, 2015, 2016a, 2016b, 2016c; Christianity Today, 2002a, 2011; Cleary, 2004, 2005; Compass Direct, 2000a, 2001, 2003, 2004b; CT Staff, 2005; Dean, 2011c, 2012c, 2013b; Fischer, 2000; Flinchbaugh, 2007; A. Gaines, 2004; Hall of Shame, 2010; Hamilton, 2016; Hickey, 1997; P. Johnson, 2006b; Katz and Cheng, 2016; J. Kennedy, 1998; Lane, 2005; Mathewes-Green, 1999; Mei, 2006; Mundy, 2005a, 2005b; Nettleton, 2004; News Briefs, 2007b; Nickles, 2000a; North Korea: Hopeful for a Better Tomorrow, 2004; M. Olasky, 2004b, 2006f; Osanjo, 2013; Persecution Watch, 2006f, 2007a; Sellers, 2002c, 2004a, 2005b; Tennant, 2006; Veith, 2005h; Voice of the Martyrs, 2006; VOM Staff, 2005; T. White, 2005; Wood, 2001. For some reason, *World* published articles on the persecution of Christians in China in almost every issue of 2016. Anti-Communism also intersects with pro-Zionist rhetoric in stories that feature Russian persecution of Jews and Messianic Jews (F. Brown, 2000a, 2001; J. King, 2000). For a more complex rendering of the position of Christians in China, see Christianity Today, 2010; R. Cook, 2005; Galli, 2004; on Cuba, see Landers, 1999. A letter to *Christianity Today* further complains: "Why is it that CT can only paint China's incredibly complicated religious landscape in black and white? My Christian Chinese friends, most of them evangelicals, would be stunned and hurt to see so many one-sided portrayals of the religious situation in China. . . . The religious trends here are largely positive" (Letters, 2002a, 8). *Christianity Today* also notes tensions with many evangelicals in China who have severed ties with the Southern Baptist Convention because of its support for clandestine missionary activity (Walker, 1998b). Interestingly, Gao Zhan, a Christian human-rights activist, was imprisoned in the United States for selling illegally more than $539,000 worth of militarily sensitive semiconductors to an institute in Nanching, China, which was connected with the country's military. It is not clear whether she is an agent or a double agent or for which government. She had originally been sentenced in China, but President George W. Bush had her released and returned to the United States. It is not clear why Bush had her released because she had also been under investigation there. She claims that her motivation was to finance a women's research center in China (Plowman, 2004a).

8. For the view that Indigenous peoples are oppressing Christians in Mexico, see also Isais, 1998; MacHarg, 2000b. *Christianity Today* has run somewhat more balanced articles on the Indigenous uprising in Chiapas, which are critical of the movement but also suggest that some of their claims are beneficial for Indigenous peoples (Alford, 1998b, 2001b).

9. See Arora, 2008; M. Belz, 2001b; Dean, 2009a; J. L. Grady, 2009d; Lindner, 2000, 2008a, 2008b; J. Nelson, 2006b; News Briefs, 1999; J. Newton, 2003a, 2003c, 2004a; M. Singh, 2000b, 2006; Top Ten News Stories of 2003, 2003; Wunderink, 2008a. An exception is Abraham, 2005h. Other articles do not conflate Dalits with Christians but

do suggest that Christianity saves Dalits from caste discrimination (David, 2007; J. L. Grady, 2009b; M. Singh, 2002c; Sreeprasad, 2007). A *Charisma* article frames the oppression of Dalit Christians as religious persecution, but the Dalit Christian who is interviewed frames it as caste persecution (J. Newton, 2005). Philip Yancey does completely distinguish between the two and focuses on caste discrimination specifically, likening it to contemporary race discrimination in the United States, rather than religious discrimination (P. Yancey, 2009).

10. *World*, however, did briefly mention that some groups say that "human rights violations are more common among Colombian soldiers than the guerrilla fronts. They oppose increased U.S. military aid to Colombia's military, given its past history of abuse" (M. Belz, 1998g, 16), although its stance was to support increased funding for Colombia to stop rebel forces.

11. In the following *Christianity Today* issue, Gunn and Horowitz responded to each other's analysis. Horowitz did not actually address Gunn's substantive arguments, for which Gunn then took him to task (Horowitz and Gunn, 2003b).

12. While problematically critiquing liberation theology, one article does critique evangelicals for not addressing social problems in Guatemala. "Some believe the evangelical community has purposely avoided public criticism or action because it witnessed what happened when Roman Catholics and mainline Protestants fell into liberation theology. That doctrine provided the theoretical basis for a so-called 'preferential option for the poor,' but class warfare is not biblical, and in practice the government viewed the Catholic church as joined with leftist guerrilla groups" (Dabel, 1998, 20). An interview with Ruth Padilla DeBorst,

who works with the International Fellowship of Evangelical Students, quotes her as saying that evangelicals should be "biblically conservative yet socially active." She also calls for trade agreements that address political power between Guatemala and First World countries (Crouch, 2007a, 32).

13. Other articles mention that evangelicals were also persecuted under this regime (Alford, 1998a; D. Miller, 2002a).

14. This concern has some limitations. Christian groups are opposed to an attempt to elevate nonbinding religious defamation resolutions at the United Nations to international treaty status. While these resolutions are intended to speak to xenophobia and racism, some think they will be used to crack down on Christian converts and evangelists (Walker, 2010a).

15. See Abraham, 2005k; M. Belz, 2004c, 2007c, 2007d; Dean, 2006c, 2006e; Hotel Sudan Isn't a Film—Yet, 2005. An alternative framing was offered in *Christianity Today*: "Like most genocide and mass murder, the crimes in Sudan have been driven mostly by powerful people trying to stay in power" (Phiri, 2009, 61).

16. "Ministering in Iraq," undated Voice of the Martyrs pamphlet.

17. At the same time, fear of Christian persecution is used to justify the continuing U.S. presence in Iraq (M. Belz, 2010c; see also Woodberry, 2011 for the political implications of missionary work after 9/11).

18. Jenkins later undermined this argument in a *Christianity Today* article: "But if communities perished, the church endured" (Jenkins, 2014, 41).

Chapter 5

1. Christian apologist Ravi Zacharias argues that the United States is a Christian nation and was "not founded on an Islamic, Hindu or Buddhist worldview" but then says: "Until those who are not

Muslims are free to practice their faith in Muslim countries . . . Islam will never be free from the fear it can engender" (Fowlds, 2002, 18–19). Similarly, *World* argues that evangelicals are simply accepting the lack of religious liberty in the Muslim world. We cannot "embrace democracy without religious liberty" (M. Belz, 2011a).

2. He does also argue: "It would be a profound mistake, however, to blame all Arabs or Muslims for this attack. Many Muslims are sincere, peace-loving people, and many Arabs are actually Christians" (Bernis, 2001, 38).

3. See Abraham, 2005b, 2005j, 2005l, 2006d; Adams, 2003; Aikman, 1999; Al Qaeda Targets Christians in Kingdom, 2004; Alford, 2002, 2006b, 2006d; B. Baker, 1997a, 1997b, 2000, 2001a, 2001c, 2003a, 2003b, 2006; Bandow, 2002; M. Belz, 1998f, 2000, 2001c, 2001e, 2002b, 2004b, 2005a, 2010a; Blunt, 2001; Briefs, 2007a; F. Brown, 2002; B. Bruce, 1999b; Buchan, 1999; Casey, 1997; Christianity Today, 1998a, 1998c; Compass Direct, 2000b, 2002a, 2002b, 2004a, 2005a; Compass Direct and Ecumenical News International, 2000; Compass Direct News, 2009; Dean, 2006b, 2009d; H. Dixon, 2009; T. Dixon, 2010; Duin, 2000, 2002; M. Evans, 2007; Farrell, 1999a; Flinchbaugh, 2000, 2001, 2006; Flinchbaugh, 1999a; Gabriel, 2002; J. L. Grady, 2002; Guthrie, 2001a, 2001b, 2003; Guthrie and Zoba, 2002; K. Hulsman, 2000; Iraq Church Attacks, 2008; Karha, 2002; Karwur, 2009; Keefauver, 2000, 2005; J. Kennedy, 2004; Killing Christians, 2008; J. Kilpatrick, 2008; Lindner, 1997a; MacHarg, 2000b; D. Miller, 2003; Minchakpu, 2000a, 2008; Moll, 2004b; T. Morgan, 1997; Mundy, 2004a; Mundy and Gaines, 2004; J. Nelson, 2007a, 2007d, 2009b; Nettleton, 2005a; Newman, 2005; Nguku, 2008; Okite, 2001; Persecution Watch, 2004a, 2004b, 2005a, 2005c, 2005e, 2006b, 2007c, 2007e; Plowman, 2002; Reaching Out to Muslims, 2004; Sellers, 2001b, 2002e, 2002f, 2003b, 2005c; Sprenkle, 2002; Stamp, 2001; Stephen, 2002; Stritcherz, 2004; Taliban Targets Christian Worker, 2008; J. Taylor, 2001; L. Taylor, 2002; Tiansay, 2004a; Vincent, 2006c; J. Weber, 2009a; T. White, 2004; Wooding, 1998; Worries over Rights in Afghanistan, Iraq, 2004; Wunderink, 2008b. One article mentions that within Kenya there is also "Christian-on-Christian violence" (Blunt, 2008, 24). Another article does focus on Muslims as persecuted (in Chechnya) but also frames the story with Christians saving Muslims from persecution (Nickles, 2000b). A *Christianity Today* article focuses on Baroness Caroline Cox crusading against Muslim persecution of Christians but does note that her organization also works for Muslims who face persecution (Zoba, 1997). Another article on Egypt suggests that U.S. intervention may not be an appropriate response to persecution and that persecution comes from individual Muslims rather than from the government (K. Hulsman, 2001). A *World* article notes that Uzbekistan is persecuting both Muslims and Christians, claiming that the threat of radical Islam in Uzbekistan is that it targets moderate observant Muslims (Abraham, 2006c). *Christianity Today* observes that Muslims headed an investigation that demonstrated that law enforcement was involved in the killing of three Christians in January 2008. Zekai Tenayr, chair of the Association of Protestant Churches in Turkey, states: "These men and women are not Christians, and yet have voluntarily and tirelessly taken on this cause in the face of what they feel is a great injustice and human rights violation. . . . They have carried the injustice, the cover-ups, and the trial into public

awareness . . . much more than we could have dreamed" (Kremida, 2009). An article in *Christianity Today* discusses the persecution of Muslims by Christians (Religious News Service, 2000). Another *Christianity Today* article describes Muslims in Nigeria as trying to build peace rather than war with Christians (Christianity Today, 2002b).

4. See also Wafa Sultan, who argues that there is no such thing as "moderate" Islam. Those following Islam are "brainwashed" (S. Olasky, 2010). In a milder version of this logic, after 9/11 Philip Yancey published a fax that he received from a "Muslim seeker" who said that "violence does have a strong precedent in Islam. . . . The terrible tragedy that happened yesterday in this country seems to be the logical outcome of teachings that tell you it's okay to reply in kind." However, this letter did not let Christianity off the hook—the seeker claimed he was thinking about converting but wanted to know if Christians would accept someone "who has a different color of skin and speaks with an accent" (P. Yancey, 2001).

5. This approach is disputed by James Lewis in *Christianity Today*, who argues that God can hear the prayers of Muslims: hearing prayers does not imply salvation. To contend that the prayers are "empty" implies that God cannot find those who seek Him (J. Lewis, 2002).

6. Kevin Eckstrom, editor of the Religion News service, summarizes what he sees as the shifts in perceptions about Islam in his analysis of "the emergence of and reaction against Islam as a political and religious force" as the most important trend of the decade. "Muslims were welcomed in 2001, demonized for much of the decade, and now we have a more pragmatic philosophical engagement with the Muslim world" (Briefing, 2010b, 11). Pope Benedict XVI quoted a seventeenth-century emperor who said, "Show me what Muhammed brought that was new, and there you will find things only evil and inhuman" (Woodberry, 2007, 108). In response, an assembly of Muslim leaders drafted "A Common Word between Us and You." A Christian group from Yale Divinity School then issued a reply that received endorsements from several evangelicals such as Bill Hybels, John Stott, and David Neff. However, many other evangelicals critiqued it for being overly positive about Islam (Ostling, 2008). Some contended that it ignored major differences between the traditions, did not address Muslim persecutions of Christians, and blamed the state of Muslim-Christian relationships on Christians. Others argued that "if our lives were aligned with God's, would we not love-truly love our Muslim neighbors, including our Muslim enemies? Anything less than that is sub-Christian." They contended that the Muslim response demonstrated that many Muslims do want peace and that Christians should be self-critical of how their support for the war in Iraq seems like another Christian crusade (Woodberry, 2007). Others took a more moderate position: "If we really, truly love Muslims, we must tell them the truth as God has revealed it. . . . Let the dialogue continue, but with the Apostles' Creed in hand" (Guthrie, 2008a, 71). They also felt that the Muslim response was based on taking the pope's words out of context.

7. Diane Knippers, coordinator of the event and head of the IRD, responded that the event was organized so quickly that she did not think these people would be able to attend.

8. When *New Man* featured an article by Marvin Yakos on Islam (January/February 2002), it received many letters from readers stating that they were

canceling their subscriptions because they felt the article was "hate filled." One reader writes: "I found Yakes to be a shallow hate-filled, ignorant man who is no better than the Taliban or the Ku Klux Klan (the Christian version of Taliban)" (In Box, 2002, 10; see also Carnes, 2008; Dyck, 2008; J. Nelson, 2007c).

9. See also T. Dixon, 1999d; Readers Write, 2005; Zoba, 1998. In addition, a brochure from Arab World Ministries, based in Upper Darby, Pennsylvania, provides tips for reaching out to Muslims in the United States: (1) use the word of God; (2) be constantly in prayer; (3) be a genuine friend; (4) ask thought-provoking questions; (5) listen attentively; (6) present your beliefs openly; (7) don't argue; (8) never denigrate Muhammad or the Qur'an; (9) respect their customs and sensitivities; (10) persevere.

10. *World* also criticized Obama for pressuring Israel to end settlements on the West Bank (J. Nelson, 2009c) and for being soft on Darfur (Dean, 2009e). See also CUFI's critique of Obama (W. C. Smith and R. Leonard, 2009). In a pre-Obama article, *World* suggested that anti-Bush sentiment was being secretly organized by terrorists (J. Nelson, 2006c).

11. For an overall history of Christian Zionism, see Robert Smith, 2004.

12. Todd Strandberg founded the Rapture Index, which measures how likely we are to see the rapture. Various categories (earthquakes, Israel, civil rights, etc.) are ranked on a scale of 1 to 5 for level of prophetic activity. Any score over 145 indicates "fasten your seatbelts," we are rapidly approaching the Rapture.

13. Aglow International launched Watchmen on the Wall seminars to educate participants about why Christians should support Israel (Deloreia, 2007, 22).

14. *For Zion's Sake* (newsletter of Christian Friends of Israel, third quarter 2003), Jerusalem, Israel, http://cfijerusalem.org /web/.

15. "Israel: Land of Creation," https:// new.goisrael.com/.

16. For a more extended discussion of Christian Zionist lobbying groups, see Mearsheimer and Walt, 2007.

17. *Charisma* did publish some letters that disagreed with Hagee's approach: "Is there no compassion for the suffering that Israel is causing the Palestinians who are living in their country? The land of Palestine belongs to God, and he gave it to Israel as long as they obeyed His covenant. When they continued to break covenant and crucified God's son, they lost their right to the land" (Feedback, 2005, 8). Another letter states: "When one ties eternal destiny to a minor theological issue and proclaims condemnation for all those who disagree, the message of salvation by faith is compromised" (Feedback, 2005, 8).

18. Information on this movement is found at terrorfreeinvesting.com (S. Strang, 2008f). Interestingly, this is similar to the strategy adopted by the Boycott, Divestment and Sanctions movement launched against Israel for its human-rights abuses perpetrated against Palestinians.

19. See examples of these ads in *Charisma* in October 2007 and May 2009.

20. Leonard Rodgers, educational director of Evangelicals for Middle East Understanding, responded that many seem all too willing to fence Arabs in; Carter has the courage to break down barriers and to recognize that Arabs, too, are created in the image of God (Readers Write, 2007, 14). Aikman defended the wall, arguing that it was only to protect Israel from suicide bombers (Aikman, 2007). Stephen Strang makes a similar defense of the wall (S. Strang, 2008a), arguing that the wall is "saving lives." He critiques

mainline denominations for organizing against Israel when the real problem is Palestinian terrorists. We must "restore the true destiny of the Jewish people" (S. Strang, 2005a, 122).

21. See the paid ad for FLAME (Facts and Logic about the Middle East), *World*, February 25, 2006.

22. Nevertheless, it still strongly advocates a pro-Israeli policy (J. Belz, 2007f).

23. For an example of the Palestinians as Canaanites rhetoric, see *For Zion's Sake* (newsletter of the Christian Friends of Israel, fourth quarter, 2003), in which Palestinians are likened to the Amalekites (Exodus 17:14–16).

24. One exception is the Christian Jew Foundation, which claims that it knows a Palestinian Christian, Anis Shorrosh, who is a supporter of the Jewish state (Hedrick, 2001, 11). Also, *World* reported on three "Muslim terrorists" from Palestine, who now call themselves the "3 Ex-Terrorists," who are now "pro-Israel Christians." Interestingly, the article did not actually cite anything from these three "terrorists" that was pro-Israel, although they certainly were critical of Islam (Abraham, 2006b, 17–18).

25. See Alford, 2004b, 2005d; Awad, 1998; M. Belz, 2001d, 2010e; B. Bruce, 2002; E. R. Fletcher, 2001; Guthrie, 2001d, 2002a; Lawton, 1989; Madison, 2001; McDermott and McDermott, 2010; Miles, 2008; Mitri, 2000; T. Morgan, 2000; Neff, 2003; Seeking Peace But Finding War in the City of Jesus' Birth, 2001; Seu, 2005b; G. Shenk, 2000, 39; M. Smith, 2002; W. C. Smith, 2007b; Strohmer, 2007; J. Weber, 2008, 2009b.

26. World Vision came under fire when it announced that it would permit gay Christians in same-sex marriages to work there, saying that it did not condone same-sex marriage but would defer to the local church. It lost so much money immediately (10,000 child sponsorships) that it reversed its position within forty-eight hours (Troy Anderson, 2015b, 40).

27. While not addressing Israel so specifically, J. Lee Grady critiques those who assume that eschatology can be definitely linked to contemporary events as well as those who say that Obama has a 666 on his birth certificate. Grady describes himself as a "pan-millennialist as in it will all pan out in the end." "What concerns me most about an unhealthy focus on eschatology is that it distracts us from the priority of evangelism" (J. L. Grady, 2009a, 66). David Neff says that eschatology must increase interest in social justice (Neff, 2011).

28. The Fellowship, however, has also been criticized by *World* for indirectly supporting Muslim terrorist organizations, as it was the group that funneled the Islamic American Relief Agency's funding for Mark Siljander's lobbying efforts described in chapter 1 (E. Belz, 2010a).

29. See Gaines, 2010; Garrison, 2007; Guthrie, 2008c; M. Olasky, 1998b; Schiavi, 2009.

30. The World Evangelical Alliance ran an advertisement in *Charisma* that stated: "If Jesus is not the Messiah of the Jewish people, He cannot be the Savior of the World." The advertisement defended special ministries that target Jews for evangelism. "We reject the notion that it is deceptive for followers of Jesus Christ who were born Jewish to continue to identify as Jews." Signers included D. A. Carson, Joel Belz, Charles Colson, Stan Guthrie, and Stephen Strang. The advertisement appeared in *Charisma* (May 2008): 119.

31. "Dabru Emet: a Jewish Statement about Christianity," *Religious Tolerance .org: Ontario Consultant on Religious Tolerance* (March 6, 2006), https://icjs.org/resources/dabru-emet.

32. Jews for Jesus newsletter (San Francisco, CA), March 6, 1998: 4–5.

33. The ad appears on back cover of *Charisma* 27 (June 2002).

Chapter 6

1. A written version of Robert Francis's talk: Francis, 2007.

Chapter 7

1. Many evangelicals expressed reluctance to engage faith-based funding under Obama for fear that he would force Christian organizations to hire homosexuals and non-Christians (E. Belz, 2009c; S. Pulliam, 2008c). Interestingly, Marvin Olasky of *World*, one of the big advocates and coiners of the term "compassionate conservatism," has the view expressed that faith-based programs were a failure even under Bush. He argues that a centralized grants program disadvantages smaller groups. He advocates vouchers instead, so that people can choose the programs that they prefer (M. Olasky, 2006b, 2009a, 2009e).

2. See also J. Belz, 2007e; Yes: Nominal Evangelicals Exist, 2008.

3. For some critiques of Palin, see Feedback, 2008e, 2009c.

4. *World* was generally supportive of Palin, but even in the beginning warned that she may not be the "messiah" that the Christian Right was hoping for (J. Belz, 2008h).

5. For critiques of *Charisma*'s endorsement, see Feedback, 2008a.

6. See also J. Belz, 2007a, 2007c; M. Olasky, 2007j. For more evangelical responses to Romney's Mormonism, see Dawson, 2007b; Dean, 2007g; Latter-Day Politics, 2007; Mailbag, 2007b; News Briefs, 2007c; Rainey, 2007b. Some implicit critique of evangelical anti-Mormonism was contained in *Christianity Today*. Charles Colson quoted Martin Luther that he "would rather be governed by a competent Turk than an incompetent Christian" (Christianity Today, 2008a; Charles Colson, 2008c, 150; see also J. Belz, 2011).

7. Richard Cizik also implicitly critiqued attacks on Obama as race-baiting (J. Kennedy, 2008). James Dobson resigned in February 2009 from his position as board chair of Focus on the Family but was going to continue to host the radio program (Passages, 2009). However, he then left the show in 2010 to start a new radio show with his son, Ryan Dobson. Some speculate that the reason was that Ryan would not be able to succeed James because he was divorced, which would violate board policy (News Briefs, 2010).

8. A letter defended Warren's approach: "He is trying his best to hold to biblical standards while also loving sinners. We will never be able to bring the love of God into our opponent's lives if they think we hate them" (Feedback, 2009d, 10).

9. *Christianity Today* strongly condemned this move to have Cizik fired (Christianity Today, 2007c). A similar controversy developed when Dobson successfully pressured the National Religious Broadcasters (NRB) board to force the resignation of its president, Wayne Pederson, for critiquing NRB's close identification with right-wing politics. Board member Phil Cooke complained about this move: "If we're perceived as a right-wing organization who's only interested in politics, a significant part of that audience will just turn us off and never listen" (Tiansay, 2002, 25). See also J. Belz, 2007b. For more critiques of animal rights and environmentalism, see Charles Colson, 2008a. Controversy arose when NAE received $1 million from the National Campaign for Prevention of Teen and Unmarried Pregnancy to promote contraception. The NAE responded

that it was not applying for another grant and claimed that the grant was just to work toward ending unwanted pregnancies. John Piper contended that unwanted pregnancies are a positive thing because they are the price women should pay for unmarried sex, which is sin. The Institute of Religion and Democracy also complained of NAE's "leftward drift" on climate control, shielding some entitlement programs and unilateral nuclear disarmament (M. Olasky, 2012a, 41).

10. "New Evangelical Partnership," n.d., http://www.newevangelicalpartnership.org/.

11. For another article promoting dialogue between homosexuals and evangelicals, see Stanton, 2009. See also Galli, 2009c, where *Christianity Today* argues that it is trying to create a space for dialogue between evangelicals of diverse political backgrounds.

12. Several letters complained about Strang's attacks on Obama (Feedback, 2007b).

13. *World* at first took solace in the passage of Proposition 8 in light of the depressing (in its perception) presidential results (Vincent, 2008a). But soon thereafter it began to complain that Christians were losing the battle on homosexuality (M. Olasky, 2009f; see also Cheaney, 2011).

14. It also ran an article on the conservative case for gay marriage, featuring Andrew Sullivan, which acknowledged the merits of these arguments but rejected them in the end (Veith, 2005a).

15. See also J. Belz, 2016; Dean, 2016a; Finch, 2016. Olasky also stated that trans people need "love" in the form of "truth" (M. Olasky, 2016d, 7). *Charisma* ran an article on a trans person achieving "deliverance from gender confusion" (Kanafani, 2016, 37).

16. Sieczkowski, 2013.

17. In addition to examples in this section, see Derrick, 2015a; M. Olasky, 2015a; Zylstra, 2015b.

18. Even James Dobson has supported compromise legislation that either leaves space for civil unions or provides some legal protection for gay couples (K. Rutledge, 2005; Stricherz, 2006).

19. *Charisma* critiqued Bakker as well as the gay Pentecostal movement. But some of the letters in response declared that "some of the people you see as sinful are on fire for the Lord and are making a difference in the world" and "Jesus defined sin as lack of love. What is so unloving about homosexuality?" (Feedback, 2007a, 74).

20. Black support for Bush in Ohio is often attributed to a marriage amendment being on the ballot.

21. See also Robinson, 2007. For other "ex-gay" evangelicals of color, see Boynes, 2011; M. Olasky, 2014a; Stegall, 2011.

22. Author's personal collection.

23. See also "Planned Parenthood is killing so many black babies" (Pitts, 2012b) and the accusation that the goal of Planned Parenthood is to eliminate Black children (M. Olasky, 2012e, 2014b).

24. For a more extended discussion on evangelical prison organizing, see A. Smith, 2008.

25. *World* has article critiquing the drug war, mandatory minimums, and three strikes legislation (M. Olasky, 2012d). It ran another article quoting Mike Huckabee, who stated: "We're locking up people we're mad at and not people we're afraid of" in arguing against mandatory minimums (quoted in Pearson, 2011, 57). For another *World* article critiquing prisons, see M. Olasky, 2008f.

26. In referencing Olasky's new stance, David Neff of *Christianity Today* concurs, because "U.S. standards for the death penalty are far below the Old Testament law" (Neff, 2014, 26). First, *World* did a big article on death penalty. It did

not call for a ban but stated that there should be a higher standard for its implementation and noted the class and race disparities in who receives it (M. Olasky, 2013b). Another article positively reviewed *Convicting the Innocent* (2011) by Brandon Garrett, which documents 250 innocent people who went to prison and were later exonerated (M. Olasky, 2012b). It also reported on federal prosecutors who indicted eighteen members of the L.A. Sheriff's Department for torture and stated that the abuse might have been systematic (News, 2013, 13). *World* eventually called for a ban on the death penalty.

27. Note that the author of the *Christianity Today* article did not take a position that mass incarceration is the new Jim Crow but did substantially engage this analysis and feature evangelical activists such as Dominique Gilliard who do hold this position.

28. Representatives from Focus on the Family and the National Association of Evangelicals lent moral support. See also S. Pulliam, 2007b.

29. See also J. Belz, 2006a. *World* later speculated that maybe immigration was not such a problem because fertility rates in Mexico will go down, resulting in less immigration, and eventually the United States will need more workers (Bergin, 2007c).

30. See, for instance, discussion on immigration policy as negatively impacting the Republican Party. At the same time, *World* hoped that Hispanic conservatives would vote Republican and suggested that they might not support Obama in the 2008 elections (Pitts, 2012a).

31. For a similar but more "balanced" analysis of immigration, see Dean, 2010c; Rainey, 2007c.

32. *World* also had a rabid article about a white farmer who was trying to help an "illegal alien" only to be shot and killed.

These aliens have changed Arizona into the "wild west" in a "land without law" (Basham, 2010c, 40). This same author complains about "anchor babies" who are overrunning hospitals and taking over the country. But even this author in the end seems to support some kind of pathway to citizenship rather than ending birthright citizenship (Basham, 2010a).

33. Of course, it also ran another article basically accusing those who observed the boycotts of Arizona and Israel of being Nazi-sympathizers (Orteza, 2010).

34. Evangelical groups that supported SB 1070 included the American Family Association and the American Center for Law and Justice.

Chapter 8

1. CCDA Guest, "Woman of Color Post-Conference Retreat," *Christian Community Development Association* (July 27, 2015), https://ccda.org/women-of-color-ccda-post-conference-retreat/ (no longer available).

2. For articles that explain how oppressed Third World women are, especially in reference to their "liberated" Western counterparts, see M. Belz, 2011c; Christianity Today, 2012; Courtney, 2009; Farrell, 1999b; A. Harris, 2008c; Newman, 2004b; Swerdlow, 2012. See also an article that focuses on concerns about Ghana priests that are really doing dark magic and harboring rapists (Quaicoo, 2011). The "laws had just been brought into the 21st century" in Rwanda, says the Saddleback Church (Zylstra, 2012, 17). Christian marriage helps widows in Rwanda protect their rights (Zylstra, 2012, 19). Another article focuses on the "quiet holocaust" of sex-selection abortions in Asia (Gentry, 2012, 17). J. Lee Grady did begin speaking out on gender oppression and gender violence in general and has noted that

it is prevalent in the First World and in the Third World. He then organized the Mordecai Project to stop gender violence, but its ministry is located only in the Third World (Scimone, 2015).

3. For similar pro–law enforcement approach, see A. Harris, 2011b. For an account of how the court system impacts the poor in the United States, see Bach, 2009.

4. See also C. Crosby, 1999, which says that the Good News is that God is against injustice.

5. One article makes a slight critique of this approach, calling for a gendered-approach to missions as a "shift away from the 'imperialistic' missions model that is more indigenous and relational" (Zoba, 2000b, 48).

6. *World* in particular seems to think that women in the military threaten civilization as we know it (Piper, 2007; Vincent, 2008b).

7. This opinion piece was criticized by Gary Roth of St. Andrew Lutheran Church in the letters section of *Christianity Today*, who stated that "blaming gays for broader social problems is like blaming a lesion for our illness when there is cancer throughout the entire body. 'Gay marriage' needs to be judged on its own merits (or demerits)—not on fear and suspicion, nor as a scapegoat for idolatries we would rather have go unchallenged" (Readers Write, 2004, 16–17).

8. *World* tells the story of Judy Brown, a professor at Central Bible College and an Assemblies of God minister. Ted Smart of World of Life Center invited her to move into his home when he found out that she had a heart condition. She bought a house next door and began having an affair with his wife. On August 25, 2003, she tried to kill Ted so that she could be with his wife. She was sentenced to thirty years. *World* informs us that Brown had contributed a chapter to the anthology *Discovering Biblical Equality* (published by InterVarsity Press in 2004). The book was withdrawn so that her submission could be omitted. "What can we conclude from this lurid mix of feminist theology, homosexuality, and attempted murder? It would be wrong to generalize from this case to make conclusions about all evangelical feminists or all female Pentecostal preachers. But it is more evidence—as if we needed any more—for total depravity and the mystery of iniquity" (Veith, 2005c, 29).

9. Her writings online can be found at "Lenore Three Stars," *Theoloqui*, https://theoloqui.net/category/lenore-three-stars/.

10. Christena Cleveland, Twitter post, October 7, 2016, 11:25 A.M., https://twitter.com/cscleve/status/784414398773272576.

Conclusion

1. *World* had a moderate approach on the lack of indictment for the death of Eric Garner, criticizing broken windows policing but saying there was a problem with the "terror of local gangs" in New York (E. Belz, 2014, 14).

2. A video of Higgins's talk can be found at this site as well.

3. Videos from the talks of this conference can be seen at "Black, White, and Red All Over: Why Racial Reconciliation Is a Gospel Issue," ERLC Leadership Summit 2015, video clip (52 minutes and 37 seconds, March 30, 2015), https://www.youtube.com/watch?v=Ff58OfBgcG4&list=PLB0ivTHLjHTuGeJeMJxI8WoZ3vHFZSCCb&index=1.

4. Similarly, Mark Tooley of the Institute for Religion and Democracy critiqued Trump and his evangelical supporters from a nationalist perspective—essentially that America is already great (Tooley, 2016).

5. *World* did, however, let a guest editor publish an op-ed disagreeing with

its position, which implicitly argued that Trump was "unacceptable" but was less unacceptable than Hillary Clinton (B. Newton, 2016).

6. Jonathan Merritt, Twitter post, June 25, 2016, 12:52 P.M., https://twitter.com/JonathanMerritt/status/746793282760507392.

7. Russell Moore, Twitter post, June 25, 2016, 3:41 P.M., https://twitter.com/drmoore/status/746835625727275008.

8. See, for example, J. Jenkins, 2016.

A NOTE ON SOURCES

This book builds on my work *Native Americans and the Christian Right: The Gendered Politics of Unlikely Alliances* (2008) in its theoretical and methodological assumptions, particularly its employment of intellectual ethnography. Intellectual ethnography, while emerging from Native American studies, is also valuable in analyzing other communities, such as the Christian Right. This book, then, is not primarily concerned with making broad claims about the communities that are its focus; rather, I intend to investigate the possibilities and pitfalls of fostering resistance struggles in conservative evangelical communities through a study of the ideas about racial thinking developing within conservative evangelicalism.

I base my research on Christian evangelical literature as well as attendance at Christian evangelical events in order to ascertain how these ideas are being articulated, debated, and contested on a national basis. My methodology includes an extensive survey of conservative articles drawn from the Christian Periodical Index that are pertinent to understanding racial reconciliation. I have surveyed all issues of *Christianity Today*, *World*, and *Charisma* (Charismatic) from 1991 (when racial reconciliation appeared on the evangelical landscape) through 2016. *Christianity Today* provides the widest coverage of issues in conservative evangelicalism generally, although it is rooted within neo-evangelicalism. *World* provides coverage from an explicitly right-wing political perspective. This survey was supplemented with a survey of periodicals published through the Christian Coalition, Concerned Women for America, and Promise Keepers, as well as evangelical publications indexed through the Christian Periodical Index. *Charisma* provides coverage of issues rooted in Pentecostal/Charismatic Christianity. In addition, I surveyed books, blogs, and websites by conservative Christians on racial reconciliation and related issues. All of the materials surveyed are cited in the endnotes or the text.

I draw primarily from these sources rather than from ethnographic data of particular evangelical communities because I want to focus on national discourses about these issues. My primary focus is not simply on what is true about evangelicals and race now but what could be true in the future. Thus, by looking at national debates at conferences, websites, blogs, and books, we may be able to glean sites of intervention that may shift current evangelical discourses on race.

Because this book covers materials from hundreds of sources, it may be difficult to follow all of the ideological and political "camps" that have emerged in relationship to racial reconciliation. Consequently, I generally cite relatively less well known authors by magazine (generally *World*, *Charisma*, or *Chris-*

tianity Today) to provide a mapping of what ideas are being discussed in which venues. For prominent evangelical figures, I provide brief identifying material when the individual is first cited.

I also attended numerous national and local conferences organized by Promise Keepers, the Christian Coalition, Christians for Biblical Equality, Concerned Women for America, Wiconi International, the National Association of Evangelicals, the North American Institute for Indigenous Theological Studies, the Southern Baptist Convention, the Justice Conference, the Christian Community Development Association, Why Christian, Catalyst, Voices, and Envision. This material is supplemented by data from thirty informal interviews conducted among men and women involved in the Promise Keepers while I staffed the Promise Keepers project for the National Council of Churches in 1997. These interviews were conducted primarily on the basis of convenience, so I make no claims that they are representative. Nevertheless, they do provide some additional insight into evangelical discourse around racial politics. In addition, this project is informed by eighteen interviews conducted through the Institute of Signifying Scripture's research project on Native American communities and scriptural fundamentalism in 2008–2009. Quotations without attribution come either from these interviews or from talks at these conferences I attended.

My analysis is also informed by personal conversations and interactions as well as participation in evangelical organizing. However, given the political complexity in which justice-centered evangelicals must operate within Christian evangelicalism, I did not include information that is not publicly available and relied instead on public statements and writings.

Earlier versions of some of the material in this book have appeared in the following articles: "Decolonization in Unexpected Places: Native Evangelicalism and the Rearticulation of Mission," *American Quarterly* 62 (September 2010), 569–90; "Native Evangelicals and Scriptural Ethnologies," in Vincent Wimbush (ed.), *Misreading America*, pp. 23–85 (Oxford: Oxford University Press, 2013); "The Biopolitics of Christian Persecution," in Suvendrini Perera and Sherene Razack (eds.), *At The Limits of Justice: Women of Colour on Terror*, pp. 107–40 (Toronto: University of Toronto Press); "The Racialization of Religion: Christian Zionism, Islamophobia, and Imperial Peace." *Journal of Race, Ethnicity and Religion* 1 (December 2010), http://www.raceand religion.com; "A Born Again Theology of Liberation" in Mae Cannon and Andrea Smith (eds.), *Evangelical Theologies of Liberation and Justice*, pp. 111–29 (Downer's Grove: InterVarsity Press, 2019).

In order to reduce this book to a manageable size, I had to delete close to 300 pages of material. If you would like additional material and sources in a particular area covered in this book, please email me at asmith@ucr.edu. I can provide the material that was omitted.

BIBLIOGRAPHY

Abanes, Richard. (1996). *American Militias*. Downer's Grove, IL: InterVarsity Press.

Abraham, Priya. (2004a). Deadline on Darfur. *World Magazine, 19* (September 4), 24.

Abraham, Priya. (2004b). Evil Teachings. *Charisma, 30* (December), 25–26.

Abraham, Priya. (2004c). Out of the Shadows. *World, 19* (July 17), 29–30.

Abraham, Priya. (2004d). Remember the Persecuted. *Christianity Today, 19* (November 13), 30–31.

Abraham, Priya. (2004e). Separation of Temple and State. *World, 19* (May 29), 20–21.

Abraham, Priya. (2005a). Battle for Conservatism's Soul. *World, 20* (October 8), 25–26.

Abraham, Priya. (2005b). Beyond Terror. *World, 20* (November 12), 24–25.

Abraham, Priya. (2005c). Crisis Averted. *World, 20* (July 23), 21.

Abraham, Priya. (2005d). Devotion Quotient. *World, 20* (April 9), 26–27.

Abraham, Priya. (2005e). Engaging Israel's Disengagement. *World, 20* (August 20), 20–22.

Abraham, Priya. (2005f). Freedom to Conform. *World, 20* (July 2–9), 24–25.

Abraham, Priya. (2005g). Justice Denied. *World, 20* (November 26), 24.

Abraham, Priya. (2005h). Left Behind. *World, 20* (December 3), 27–28.

Abraham, Priya. (2005i). Slave-to-Slave. *World, 20* (January 29), 24–25.

Abraham, Priya. (2005j). Soft on Saudis. *World, 20* (May 14), 26–27.

Abraham, Priya. (2005k). Spectator to Genocide. *World, 20* (April 2), 24–26.

Abraham, Priya. (2005l). Teaching a Lesson. *World, 20* (September 24), 24–25.

Abraham, Priya. (2005m). Wrist Slap. *World, 20* (November 19), 20–21.

Abraham, Priya. (2006a). The Abolitionist. *World, 21* (November 4), 39–40.

Abraham, Priya. (2006b). Brothers to the End. *World, 21* (July 15), 17–18.

Abraham, Priya. (2006c). Foley Failure. *World, 21* (October 14), 26–27.

Abraham, Priya. (2006d). Operation Rescue. *World, 21* (July 1–8), 28–29.

Abraham, Priya. (2006e). Uncovering Deeds of Darkness. *World, 21* (December 2), 34.

Abraham, Priya. (2007a). Dissident Voices. *World, 22* (June 16), 12–15.

Abraham, Priya. (2007b). Lawyered Over. *World, 22* (May 19), 25–26.

Abraham, Priya. (2007c). Let My People Go! *World, 22* (February 24), 16–19.

Abraham, Priya. (2007d). Zeal for the Lost. *World, 22* (August 4), 30.

Adamczyk, Amy, John Wybraniec, and Roger Finke. (2004). Religious Regulation and the Courts: Documenting the Effects of *Smith* and RFRA. *Journal of Church and State, 46* (Spring), 237–62.

Adams, Stephen. (2003). American Missionary Gunned Down. *Christianity Today, 47* (January), 26.

Adeney, Miriam. (2002). *Daughters of Islam*. Downer's Grove, IL: InterVarsity Press.

Agang, Sunday. (2012). Breaking Nigeria's Fatal Deadlock. *Christianity Today, 56* (April), 48–51.

Ahab. (2013). Asian-American Christians Condemn Racism in Evangelical Culture (October 21). http://republic-of-gilead.blogspot.com/2013/10/asian-american-christians-condemn.html.

Aikman, David. (1997). A Campaign against Cruelty. *Charisma, 22* (April), 94.

Aikman, David. (1998). Persecutors, Beware. *Charisma, 24* (December), 110.

Aikman, David. (1999). Faith under a Death Threat. *Charisma, 24* (February), 78.

Aikman, David. (2003). Racial Reconciliation. *Charisma, 29* (November), 94.

Aikman, David. (2004). Religious Freedom Matters. *Charisma, 30* (November), 78.

Aikman, David. (2005a). Be Kind to the Poor. *Charisma, 30* (July), 78.

Aikman, David. (2005b). China's Crackdown. *Charisma, 30* (February), 79.

Aikman, David. (2005c). The Crisis in Darfur. *Charisma, 30* (January), 76.

Aikman, David. (2007). Throwing Rocks at Israel. *Christianity Today, 51* (April), 82.

Akers, Shawn. (2016). For Zion's Sake. *Charisma, 42* (September), 32–36.

Alam, Christopher. (2011). Not All Muslims Want to Kill You. *Charisma, 37* (September), 42–48.

Alexander, Jacqui. (2005). *Pedagogies of Crossing*. Durham, NC: Duke University Press.

Alford, Deann. (1998a). Imprisoned Evangelicals Dispute Accusations of Terrorism. *Christianity Today, 42* (February 9), 94–95.

Alford, Deann. (1998b). Words against Weapons. *Christianity Today, 42* (March 2), 66–67.

Alford, Deann. (1999a). Caught in the Conflict. *World, 14* (October 2), 45–46.

Alford, Deann. (1999b). Massacre Post-Mortem. *World, 14* (May 15), 31–32.

Alford, Deann. (1999c). Maximum Security. *World, 14* (March 27), 22–23.

Alford, Deann. (2000a). Abducted Pastor Pays His Own Ransom on Installment Plan. *Christianity Today, 44* (October 23), 23.

Alford, Deann. (2000b). How Free Are We? *Christianity Today, 44* (March 6), 31.

Alford, Deann. (2001a). Death Threats Denied. *Christianity Today, 45* (January 8), 32.

Alford, Deann. (2001b). A Peacemaker in Power. *Christianity Today, 45* (May 21), 26–27.

Alford, Deann. (2002). Entrapment Suspected. *Christianity Today, 46* (February 4), 22–23.

Alford, Deann. (2004a). New Life in a Culture of Death. *Christianity Today, 48* (February), 48–53.

Alford, Deann. (2004b). Outreach to Despair. *Christianity Today, 48* (April), 25–26.

Alford, Deann. (2005a). Amid the Survivors. *Christianity Today, 49* (October), 84–85.

Alford, Deann. (2005b). Christian Zionists Split over Gaza Pullout. *Christianity Today, 49* (July), 46.

Alford, Deann. (2005c). Fragile Accord. *Christianity Today, 49* (March), 22.

Alford, Deann. (2005d). Love in the Land of Enmity. *Christianity Today, 49* (July), 44–47.

Alford, Deann. (2006a). The CIA Myth. *Christianity Today, 50* (January), 58–59.

Alford, Deann. (2006b). Malay Melee. *Christianity Today, 50* (November), 21.

Alford, Deann. (2006c). The Saints Go Marching Back. *Christianity Today*, 50 (May), 48–50.

Alford, Deann. (2006d). Targeting Christian Youth. *Christianity Today*, 50 (January), 19–20.

Alford, Deann. (2006e). The Truth Is Somewhere. *Christianity Today*, 50 (September), 20–21.

Alford, Deann. (2006f). Word and Deed, Again and Again. *Christianity Today*, 50 (March), 60–62.

Alford, Deann. (2007). Free at Last. *Christianity Today*, 51 (March), 30–35.

Alford, Deann. (2009). Values Voters. *Christianity Today*, 53 (May), 18.

Alfred, Taiaiake. (1999). *Peace, Power, Righteousness*. Oxford: Oxford University Press.

Aliens in Our Midst. (2005). *Christianity Today*, 49 (April), 31.

Al Qaeda Targets Christians in Kingdom. (2004). *Christianity Today*, 48 (February), 24.

Americans Can't Escape Their Racist Past or Present. (2015). *Relevant* (September–October), 12.

Amjad-Ali, Charles. (2007). Redemption, Reconciliation, Restoration: Journeys toward Wholeness. *Journal of North American Institute for Indigenous Theological Studies*, 5, 5–18.

Anderson, David. (2005). Giving Hope a Chance. *Christianity Today*, 49 (January), 21.

Anderson, Joy. (1988). Reaching Minorities Takes Cultural Acceptance. *Evangelical Missions Quarterly*, 24 (July), 9 12–15.

Anderson, Leith, and Ed Stetzer. (2016). A New Way to Define Evangelism. *Christianity Today*, 60 (April), 52–55.

Anderson, Nate. (2006). Meet the Patriot Pastors. *Christianity Today*, 50 (November), 46–50.

Anderson, Tony. (2007). Group Aims to Oppose Anti-Christian Bias. *Charisma*, 33 (December), 25.

Anderson, Troy. (2009). Attorneys: Christians Face Growing Hostility. *Charisma*, 35 (November), 14.

Anderson, Troy. (2010). A Jewish Awakening? *Charisma*, 36 (October), 50–54.

Anderson, Troy. (2013). Where Your Israel Donation Really Goes. *Charisma*, 39 (October), 20–26, 50–70.

Anderson, Troy. (2015a). Why the Church Must Tell Israel: "Here Am I." *Charisma*, 41 (October), 10.

Anderson, Troy. (2015b). Why World Vision Changed Its Mind on Hiring Gays, and What Now? *Charisma*, 40 (March), 26–42.

Andrescik, Robert. (2000a). A Movement Divided? *New Man*, 7 (November–December), 10.

Andrescik, Robert. (2000b). Welcome to the New Men's Movement. *New Man*, 7 (September–October), 10.

Andrescik, Robert. (2003). "Coach Mac" Resigns. *New Man*, 10 (November–December), 12.

Ankara, Anton. (2002). Hindus Contine to Slaughter Muslims. *Christianity Today*, 46 (June 10), 23.

Ankerberg, John, and John Welson. (1996). *Encyclopedia of New Age Beliefs*. Eugene, OR: Harvest House Publishers.

Anonymous. (2016). No to Trump— A Christian Appeal by and to Wheaton College Stakeholders (September 27). https://fsfasmithblog.wordpress.com/2016/09/27/noto trump_wc-il-2/.

Anyabwile, Thabiti. (2016). On Abortion and Racism: Why There Is a Greater Evil in This Election (June 7). https://blogs.thegospelcoalition.org/thabiti anyabwile/2016/06/07/on-abortion-and-racism-why-there-is-a-greater-evil-in-this-election/.

Anyabwile, Thabiti. (2018). An Apology to Beth Moore and My Sisters (May 3). https://www.thegospel coalition.org/blogs/thabiti-anyabwile /apology-beth-moore-sisters/.

Apartheid and American Christians. (1988). *Christianity Today, 32* (October 21), 44–45.

Arabs outside Middle East to Hear Webcasts. (2001). *Christianity Today, 45* (February 19), 28–29.

Armey, Dick. (1999). American Bigotry. *World, 14* (October 16), 22–23.

Arora, Vishal. (2008). Premeditated Mobs. *Christianity Today, 52* (March), 19.

Asian American Christians United on Cultural Insensitivity and Reconciliation in the Church. (2013). An Open Letter to the Evangelical Church (October). http://nextgenerasianchurch .com/wp-content/uploads/2013/10 /Open-Letter_AAU_PDF1.pdf (no longer available).

Avery, Tim. (2010). Christian Zionism in the Dock. *Christianity Today, 54* (July 10), 56.

Awad, Bishara. (1998). West Bank: Squeezed by Warring Majorities. *Christianity Today, 42* (November 16), 68–69.

Bach, Amy. (2009). *Ordinary Injustice: How America Holds Court.* New York: Metropolitan Books.

Bacote, Vincent. (2000). The New Scarlet Letter. *Christianity Today, 44* (November 13), 98–99.

Baer, Richard. (1989). The High Court's "S" Word. *Christianity Today, 33* (September 8), 20–21.

Bailey, Richard. (1990). The Muslims Are Coming Here! *United Evangelical Action, 49* (July–August), 4–7.

Bailey, Sarah Pulliam. (2010a). A Different Kind of Tent Revival. *Christianity Today, 54* (October), 13–15.

Bailey, Sarah Pulliam. (2010b). Faithfully and Politically Present. *Christianity Today, 54* (November), 36–39.

Bailey, Sarah Pulliam. (2015). Moore on the Margins. *Christianity Today, 59* (September), 30–39.

Bailey, Sarah Pulliam. (2016). White Evangelicals Voted Overwhelmingly for Donald Trump, Exit Polls Show. *Washington Post* (November 9). https://www.washingtonpost.com /news/acts-of-faith/wp/2016/11/09 /exit-polls-show-white-evangelicals -voted-overwhelmingly-for-donald -trump/?utm_term=.e115db39308d.

Bailey-Jones, Patricia. (2008). Fulfilling the Great Commission. *Charisma, 33* (February), 20.

Baker, Barbara. (1997a). In the Shadow of Islam. *Charisma, 23* (October), 44–52, 112.

Baker, Barbara. (1997b). Two Filipino Christians Beheaded. *Christianity Today, 41* (September 1), 86.

Baker, Barbara. (2000). Where the Gospel Is a Secret. *Charisma, 25* (January), 43–49.

Baker, Barbara. (2001a). Christian Principal Accused of Blasphemy. *Christianity Today, 45* (May 21), 31.

Baker, Barbara. (2001b). Christians Cleared of Blasphemy. *Christianity Today, 45* (April), 31.

Baker, Barbara. (2001c). Taliban Threatens Converts. *Christianity Today, 45* (March 5), 34.

Baker, Barbara. (2003a). Court Acquits Christian of Blasphemy. *Christianity Today, 47* (August), 26.

Baker, Barbara. (2003b). Unlocking the Heart of Islam. *Charisma, 28* (January), 37–39, 92.

Baker, Barbara. (2006). Whose Law? *Christianity Today, 50* (May), 22.

Baker, William. (1987). Equal before God. *Moody Monthly, 87* (January), 18–20.

Balmer, Randall. (2014). The Real Origins of the Religious Right. *Politico* (May 27). http://www.politico.com/magazine/story/2014/05/religious-right-real-origins-107133.

Bandow, Doug. (2002). Slave Wages. *World, 17* (May 4), 21–22.

Banks, Adelle. (2002). Graham Calls Bigotry a Sin. *Christianity Today, 46* (August 5), 19.

Banks, Adelle. (2009). Evangelicals Endorse Immigration Reform. *Christianity Today* (October [web version]). https://www.christianitytoday.com/ct/2009/octoberweb-only/evangelicals-endorse-immigration-reform.html.

Baraka, Sho. (2016). Why I'm Voting for Neither Candidate. *Christianity Today, 60* (October), 62–64.

Barnes, Esther. (1989). Native People Need Native Missionaries. *Faith Today, 7* (May–June), 58–59.

Barton, David. (1995). The Race Card. *Wallbuilders* (Fall), 1–7.

Basham, Megan. (2010a). Anchors Away. *World, 25* (September 25), 50–52.

Basham, Megan. (2010b). Immigration Equation. *World, 25* (August 28), 44–45.

Basham, Megan. (2010c). Land without Law. *World, 25* (May 22), 40.

Bauer, Gary. (2007). Turning a Blind Eye. *Torch, 1* (October), 24–25.

Beaty, Katelyn. (2011). Portland's Quiet Abolitionist. *Christianity Today, 55* (November), 26–30.

Beaty, Katelyn, and Skye Jethani. (2012). Meanwhile, Love the Sojourner. *Christianity Today, 56* (September), 14–16.

Beaumont, Mark Ivor. (2005). Early Muslim Interpretations of the Gospel. *Transformation, 22* (January), 20–27.

Becker, Amy Julia. (2014). Multiculturalism beyond Photo Ops and Potlucks: An Interview with Dominique Gilliard (August 20). http://www.christianitytoday.com/amyjuliabecker/2014/august/multiculturalism-beyond-photo-ops-and-potlucks.html.

Becker, Verne. (1989). A New Era for Black Missionaries. *Christianity Today, 33* (October 22), 38–39.

Bederman, Gail. (1995). *Manliness and Civilization*. Chicago: University of Chicago Press.

Beiler, Ryan Rodrick. (2015). Pro-Israeli, Pro-Palestinian, Pro-Jesus. *Sojourners, 44* (March), 16–19.

Bell, Derrick. (1995). Racial Realism. In Kimberle Crenshaw, Neil Gotanda, Gary Peller, and Kendall Thomas (eds.), *Critical Race Theory* (pp. 302–14). New York: New Press.

Belz, Emily. (2008). Gentrification, Gay Marriage, and the Gospel. *World, 24* (August 1), 40–41.

Belz, Emily. (2009a). From the Ashes. *World, 24* (April 11), 50–51.

Belz, Emily. (2009b). Jesus and Strippers. *World, 24* (October 10), 64–66.

Belz, Emily. (2009c). Keeping the Faith? *World, 24* (June 20), 47–49.

Belz, Emily. (2009d). Party of Steele. *World, 24* (February 28), 43–44.

Belz, Emily. (2009e). A Spring in the March. *World, 24* (February 14), 46.

Belz, Emily. (2010a). Bad Connections. *World, 25* (August 14), 44–47.

Belz, Emily. (2010b). The Special Religion. *World, 25* (June 5), 46–48.

Belz, Emily. (2011a). Dangerous Exposure. *World, 26* (October 8), 12.

Belz, Emily. (2011b). Inside Out. *World, 26* (May 7), 44–47.

Belz, Emily. (2012a). Beyond the Base. *World, 27* (September 22), 44–45.

Belz, Emily. (2012b). Law and Orders. *World, 27* (April 7), 50–54.

Belz, Emily. (2012c). Old Reliables. *World, 27* (October 20), 42–43.

Belz, Emily. (2012d). Politics of Marriage. *World, 27* (World), 9.

Belz, Emily. (2012e). Vote Your Priorities. *World, 27* (October 20), 44–45.

Belz, Emily. (2014). Community Crisis. *World, 29* (December 27), 14.

Belz, Joel. (2001a). A Faith of Peace. *World, 16* (October 6), 5.

Belz, Joel. (2001b). Sidewalk Survey. *World, 32* (August 25), 5.

Belz, Joel. (2004). No Preservatives. *World, 19* (May 22), 8.

Belz, Joel. (2005a). Empty Religion. *World, 20* (November 19), 4.

Belz, Joel. (2005b). Getting a Bit Carried Away? *World, 20* (September 24), 4.

Belz, Joel. (2005c). Media Disaster. *World, 40* (October 15), 4.

Belz, Joel. (2005d). Our Social Smoothie. *World, 20* (September 10), 6.

Belz, Joel. (2005e). Unquenchable Appetite. *World, 20* (September 24), 24–25.

Belz, Joel. (2006a). Common-Sense Solution. *World, 21* (November 4), 6.

Belz, Joel. (2006b). Uninvited Guests. *World, 21* (March 4), 6.

Belz, Joel. (2006c). You Used to Be One. *World, 21* (April 15), 6.

Belz, Joel. (2007a). Catching Mitt. *World, 22* (May 19), 17–19.

Belz, Joel. (2007b). Evangelical Steamroller. *World, 22* (February 3), 6.

Belz, Joel. (2007c). The Right Questions. *World, 22* (December 22), 3.

Belz, Joel. (2007d). Trifling with the Truth. *World, 22* (November), 5.

Belz, Joel. (2007e). Two Left Feet. *World, 22* (November 17), 8.

Belz, Joel. (2007f). What about Israel? *World, 22* (June 16), 3.

Belz, Joel. (2008a). Don't Blame Racism. *World, 23* (May 17–24), 5.

Belz, Joel. (2008b). End of an Illusion. *World, 23* (February 23–March 1), 6.

Belz, Joel. (2008c). Gloomy Conservatives. *World, 23* (March 22–29), 6.

Belz, Joel. (2008d). His to Lose. *World, 23* (September 6–13), 38–39.

Belz, Joel. (2008e). Ordinary Man. *World, 23* (September 6–13), 6.

Belz, Joel. (2008f). Pathetic Tradeoff. *World, 23* (April 5–12), 6.

Belz, Joel. (2008g). Spirits of the Age. *World, 23* (February 9–16), 6.

Belz, Joel. (2008h). Unscripted Moment. *World, 23* (September 20–27).

Belz, Joel. (2009). For Good or Ill? *World, 24* (August 15), 5.

Belz, Joel. (2011). Defining the "Test" Clause. *World, 26* (November 5), 3.

Belz, Joel. (2012). Tipping Point? *World, 27* (December 1), 3.

Belz, Joel. (2015). No Concessions. *World, 30* (May 30), 8.

Belz, Joel. (2016). Signage of the Times. *World, 31* (May 38), 10.

Belz, Mindy. (1996). Faces in the Crowd. *World Magazine, 11* (November 30–December 7), 12–15.

Belz, Mindy. (1998a). Count Your Blessings. *World, 13* (November 28), 16–19.

Belz, Mindy. (1998b). Finding Their Voice. *World, 13* (October 3), 23–24.

Belz, Mindy. (1998c). Jubilee Politics. *World, 13* (October 10), 23–24.

Belz, Mindy. (1998d). Let My People Go. *World, 13* (October 3), 12–16.

Belz, Mindy. (1998e). Micromanaging Micronesia. *World, 15* (April 18), 17–19.

Belz, Mindy. (1998f). To Execute or Not? *World, 13* (June 6), 18–20.

Belz, Mindy. (1998g). To the Front Lines. *World, 13* (May 2), 15–17.

Belz, Mindy. (1999a). A Complete Lie. *World, 14* (July 24), 24–25.

Belz, Mindy. (1999b). Laying Down the Law. *World, 14* (March 20), 30–31.

Belz, Mindy. (1999c). A Milestone, with Many Miles to Go. *World, 14* (October 2), 42–44.

Belz, Mindy. (1999d). Taking on the Thugs. *World, 14* (November 6), 16–18.

Belz, Mindy. (2000). Beirut All Over Again. *World, 13* (Jaunuary 29), 24–25.

Belz, Mindy. (2001a). Bethlehem under Siege. *World, 16* (November 3), 26.

Belz, Mindy. (2001b). Opening the Safety Valve. *World, 16* (November 17), 21–22.

Belz, Mindy. (2001c). Sunday-Morning Jihad. *World, 16* (November 10), 22–24.

Belz, Mindy. (2001d). Unfriendly Fire. *World, 16* (September 15), 25–27.

Belz, Mindy. (2001e). An Unholy War of Nerves. *World, 16* (September 1), 25.

Belz, Mindy. (2002a). Martyrs by the Millions. *World, 17* (April 13), 20–23.

Belz, Mindy. (2002b). We Will Be Here. *World, 17* (March 30), 7.

Belz, Mindy. (2004a). Baroness for Battle. *World, 19* (December 11), 34–38.

Belz, Mindy. (2004b). Coffins of Freedom. *World, 19* (Februay 28), 20.

Belz, Mindy. (2004c). Improbable Cause. *World, 19* (July 31), 26.

Belz, Mindy. (2004d). Risking the Roadmap. *World, 19* (February 14), 27.

Belz, Mindy. (2005a). Apostasy Rules. *World, 20* (April 9), 24.

Belz, Mindy. (2005b). Open and Shut. *World, 20* (April 16), 30–32.

Belz, Mindy. (2005c). Suburban Warriors. *World, 20* (November 19), 16–19.

Belz, Mindy. (2005d). Whose Jubilee? *World, 20* (June 25), 18–21.

Belz, Mindy. (2006). Pentagon Attacked. *World, 21* (December 23), 5.

Belz, Mindy. (2007a). Kangaroo Court. *World, 22* (February 10), 20–21.

Belz, Mindy. (2007b). Kidnapped. *World, 22* (May 19), 22–23.

Belz, Mindy. (2007c). Name Change. *World, 22* (August 18), 41.

Belz, Mindy. (2007d). Too Little, Too Late. *World, 22* (August 18), 42–43.

Belz, Mindy. (2008a). Broadcast News. *World, 23* (December 13–20), 36–41.

Belz, Mindy. (2008b). Missed Opportunity. *World, 23* (January 26–February 2), 56.

Belz, Mindy. (2008c). Plane Truth. *World, 23* (October 18–25), 7.

Belz, Mindy. (2009a). Sacrificial Poor. *World, 24* (February 28), 60–61.

Belz, Mindy. (2009b). Stifling the Messengers. *World, 24* (March 28), 66.

Belz, Mindy. (2010a). Capital Crime. *World, 25* (July 3), 14.

Belz, Mindy. (2010b). Eyes on the Prize. *World, 25* (November 6), 34.

Belz, Mindy. (2010c). First Guns, Then Ballots. *World, 25* (March 13), 36–37.

Belz, Mindy. (2010d). Smelting Pot. *World, 25* (July 17), 44–46.

Belz, Mindy. (2010e). Tested by Fire. *World, 25* (May 8), 48–52.

Belz, Mindy. (2010f). What Do Palestinians Want? *World, 25* (April 10), 28–35.

Belz, Mindy. (2011a). A Global Crisis. *World, 26* (March 26). https://world.wng.org/2011/03/a_global_crisis.

Belz, Mindy. (2011b). Remembering Captives. *World, 26* (February 26), 12.

Belz, Mindy. (2011c). What the Veil Reveals. *World, 26* (April 23), 32.

Belz, Mindy. (2012a). The New Authoritarians. *World, 27* (March 10), 34.

Belz, Mindy. (2012b). Nowhere to Run. *World, 27* (March 10), 50–56.

Belz, Mindy. (2013a). An Effective Extinction? *World, 28* (October 19), 50–51.

Belz, Mindy. (2013b). Give Me Your Tired. *World, 28* (November 16), 32.

Belz, Mindy. (2015). Fallen and Forsaken. *World, 30* (October 31), 40–43.

Belz, Mindy. (2016). Tortured Journeys. *World, 31* (September 3), 30–37.

Belz, Mindy, and Alisa Harris. (2009). Minding Africa's Business. *World, 24* (October 10), 34–40.

Belz, Mindy, and Marvin Olasky. (2007). Huckabee's Surge. *World, 22* (December 22), 16.

Bendroth, Margaret. (1984). The Search for "Women's Role" in American Evangelicalism, 1930–1980. In George Marsden (ed.), *Evangelicalism in Modern America* (pp. 122–34). Grand Rapids, MI: Eerdmans Publishing Company.

Bennett, William. (1994). Stop Bashing the Christian Right. *Christianity Today*, 38 (August 15), 10.

Benson, Erik. (2004). A Bleak Prospect. *Fides et Historia*, 36 (Summer/Fall), 99–103.

Bergin, Mark. (2006a). Due North. *World*, 21 (February 11), 30–31.

Bergin, Mark. (2006b). Llama Herder's Leftward Ho. *World*, 21 (February 4), 18–19.

Bergin, Mark. (2006c). Shake, Rattle and Toil. *World*, 21 (February 25), 32–35.

Bergin, Mark. (2007a). Campus Cleansing. *World*, 22 (October 27), 20–21.

Bergin, Mark. (2007b). Not So "Grand" a Bargain. *World*, 22 (June 23), 12–15.

Bergin, Mark. (2007c). Plan B. *World*, 22 (July 14), 35.

Bergin, Mark. (2007d). Prodigal Party. *Charisma*, 22 (January), 18–21.

Bergin, Mark. (2007e). Raw Footage. *World*, 22 (March 3), 35.

Bergin, Mark. (2008a). Sarah Surge. *World*, 23, 32–36.

Bergin, Mark. (2008b). Sublime Lending. *World*, 23 (November 1–8), 51–52.

Bergin, Mark. (2008c). The Weathermen. *World*, 23, 44–45.

Bergin, Mark. (2009a). The Other Stimulus. *World*, 24 (February 28), 41.

Bergin, Mark. (2009b). Shame of the Cities. *World*, 24 (February 28), 54–56.

Bergin, Mark. (2011). Out of the Locker. *World*, 26 (August 13), 70.

Berlant, Lauren. (1997). *The Queen of America Goes to Washington City*. Durham, NC: Duke University Press.

Bernard, A. R. (2004). The Shape of Racism. *New Man*, 11 (January–February), 66.

Bernis, Jonathan. (1997). Have You Hugged a (Messianic) Jew Lately? *Charisma*, 22 (April), 62–69.

Bernis, Jonathan. (2001). Hope amid Crisis. *Charisma*, 27 (November), 36–46.

Bernis, Jonathan. (2008). Stand with Israel. *Charisma*, 34 (October), 79.

Bernis, Jonathan. (2009). Jerusalem's Future. *Charisma*, 34 (May), 20.

Bettis, Kara. (2017). A God's Economy. *Relevant* (January–February), 74–77.

Beverley, James. (2002). Is Islam a Religion of Peace? *Christianity Today*, 41 (January 7), 32–42.

Bill Hybels Says Christians Distorted Facts about Visit from Muslim Cleric. (2002). *Charisma*, 27 (June), 19.

Bird, Brian. (1989). Christians Who Grow Coca. *Christianity Today*, 33 (September 8), 40–43.

Bird, Brian. (1990). Reclaiming the Urban War Zones. *Christianity Today*, 34 (January 15), 16–20.

Bjelajac, Branko. (2001). Evangelical Churches Stoned, Vandalized. *Christianity Today*, 45 (August 6), 28–29.

Bjork, Don. (1985). Foreign Missions: Next Door and Down the Street. *Christianity Today*, 29 (July 12), 17–21.

Bjork, Don. (1986). The Sanctuary Movement: Can Evangelicals Remain Uncommitted? *United Evangelical Action*, 45 (January–February), 8–9.

Black Family Betrayed. (2001). *Focus on the Family Citizen*, 15 (February), 24.

Black Magazines Stress Strong Families and Spiritual Values. (1986). *Christianity Today*, 30 (March 21), 27–28.

Blair-Mitchell, Lynette. (1997). Prayer Targets Civil War-Era Wounds. *Charisma*, 22 (February), 18–19.

Blanton, Matthew. (2014). Can Immigration Be Reformed? *Relevant*, (November–December), 48–50.

Blessed Are the Courageous. (2006). *Christianity Today*, 50 (May), 26–27.

Blunt, Sheryl Henderson. (2001). Caught in the Crossfire. *Christianity Today*, 45 (November 12), 30–31.

Blunt, Sheryl Henderson. (2007a). The Devil's Yoke. *Christianity Today*, 51 (March), 38–39.

Blunt, Sheryl Henderson. (2007b). The Giuliani Choice. *Christianity Today*, 51 (June), 20.

Blunt, Sheryl Henderson. (2007c). Spoils of Victory. *Christianity Today*, 51 (January), 54–55.

Blunt, Sheryl Henderson. (2008). Post-Mayhem Woes. *Christianity Today*, 52 (March), 24.

Blunt, Sheryl Henderson. (2009). Justice before Peace? *Christianity Today*, 53 (May), 16–17.

Board, Russell. (1999). Identity. *World*, 14 (December 18), 33.

Bonham, Chad. (2003). Concert Tour Aims to Promote Unity and Racial Reconciliation. *Charisma*, 29 (November), 32.

Boone, Wellington. (1996). *Breaking Through*. Nashville: Broadman & Holman Publishers.

Boone, Wellington. (2008). Black Genocide. *World*, 33 (May), 18.

Bowles, Adam. (2000). A Cry in the Nuclear Wilderness. *Christianity Today*, 44 (October 2), 66–68.

Boyd, Gregory. (2010). The Idolatry of Patriotism. *Relevant* (July–August), 30.

Boynes, Janet. (2011). A Way Out. *Charisma*, 36 (July), 40–43.

Bradley, Anthony. (2001). A New Division, a New Dream. *World*, 32 (August 25), 56–58.

Bradley, Anthony. (2005). Abortion by Race. *World*, 20 (February 19), 32.

Bradley, Anthony. (2006). Black Man's World. *World*, 21 (May 6), 28–30.

Bradley, Anthony. (2010). Is Your Church Rah-Certified? (May 26). https://world.wng.org/2010/05/is_your_church_rah_certified.

Bradley, Anthony. (2011). Libel Is Not Love (July 13). http://www.worldmag.com/2011/07/libel_is_not_love.

Brady, Deanne. (2000). Christians Repent for Slave Trade at Prayer Vigil in Jamestown, Virginia. *Charisma*, 25 (May), 34–35.

Brasher, Brenda. (1998). *Godly Women: Fundamentalism and Female Power*. New Brunswick, NJ: Rutgers University Press.

Bray, Hiawatha. (1992). Evangelical Racism. *Christianity Today*, 36 (November 23), 42–44.

Briefing. (2010a). *Christianity Today*, 54 (January), 9.

Briefing. (2010b). Quotation Marks. *Christianity Today*, 54 (January), 11.

Briefs. (2006). *Christianity Today*, 50 (March), 23.

Briefs. (2007a). *Christianity Today*, 51 (June), 21.

Briefs. (2007b). *Christianity Today*, 51 (October), 21.

Brigham, Kay. (1991). The Columbus Nobody Knows. *Christianity Today*, 35 (October 7), 26–28.

Brock, Rita Nakashima, and Rebecca Parker. (2008). *Saving Paradise*. Boston: Beacon Press.

Brody, David, Wendy Wright, and David Gushee. (2010). What Place Do Christians Have in the Tea Party Movement? *Christianity Today*, 54 (October), 54–55.

Brookes, Adrian. (2004). Aussie Women Lead the Way. *Charisma*, 29 (May), 54.

Brookes, Adrian. (2008). China's Emerging Church. *Charisma*, 34 (August), 40–45, 73.

Brooks, Rebecca. (2005). Raising a Patriot. *Focus on the Family*, 29 (July), 12–13.

Brother Andrew. (1998). The Muslim

Challenge. *Christianity Today, 42* (October 5), 57.

Brouwer, Steve, Paul Gifford, and Susan Rose. (1996). *Exporting the American Gospel.* London: Routledge.

Brown, Frank. (1999). Christian Lawyer Battles for Rights of Russian Church. *Charisma, 24* (February), 32–35.

Brown, Frank. (2000a). Opposition Is Mounting as Messianic Jewish Groups Grow in Russia. *Charisma, 26* (September), 34–35.

Brown, Frank. (2000b). Pentecostals in Former Soviet Republic Face Persecution. *Charisma, 25* (January), 30–32.

Brown, Frank. (2001). Messianic Jews Face Organized Resistance in Russia and Ukraine. *Charisma, 27* (December), 33–34.

Brown, Frank. (2002). Christians Bullied in Muslim Republics. *Charisma, 27* (March), 14–15.

Brown, Harold O. J. (1992). The Importance of Being Western. *Christianity Today, 36* (October 5), 46–47.

Brown, Kevin. (2014). Capitalism and the Common Good. *Christianity Today, 58* (September), 60–64.

Brown, Michael. (2014a). The Great Gay Deception. *Charisma, 39* (March), 22–26.

Brown, Michael. (2014b). What the Bible Really Says about Being Gay and Christian. *Charisma, 40* (October), 56–60.

Brown, Michael. (2016a). Can We Question Trump's Christianity? *Charisma, 41* (May), 76.

Brown, Michael. (2016b). Is Donald Trump a Modern-Day Cyrus? *Charisma, 42* (August), 68.

Bruce, Billy. (1998a). Dake Publishing Apologizes for Racist Remarks in Bible. *Charisma, 23* (April), 17.

Bruce, Billy. (1998b). Messianic Jews Fight Proposed Law in Israel. *Charisma, 23* (February), 36.

Bruce, Billy. (1999a). Cuban Churches Gain New Freedom. *Charisma, 24* (March), 20–21.

Bruce, Billy. (1999b). Indonesian Believers Multiply under Leadership of Bethel Church of God. *Charisma, 24* (June), 27–28.

Bruce, Billy. (2001). Sharing Jesus in the Land of Lenin. *Charisma, 27* (December), 30–37.

Bruce, Billy. (2002). Arab Christians Take Hard Line on Israel. *Charisma, 27* (April), 16–17.

Bruce, James. (2016). Southern Summit. *World, 31* (July 9), 59.

Brumfield, Natalie. (2016). How Prayers for Life Shuttered an Illegal Abortion Center. *Charisma, 41* (April), 18.

Buchan, Alex. (1999). Christians Killed, Churches Burn. *Christianity Today, 43* (January 11), 24.

Buchan, Alex. (2001). Khmu Christians Arrested. *Christianity Today, 45* (September 3), 34.

Burge, Gary. (2003). *Whose Land? Whose Promise?* Cleveland: Pilgrim Press.

Burke, Kristen. (2006). No Longer Separate. *Decision, 45* (July–August), 16–20.

Burlein, Ann. (2002). *Lift High the Cross.* Durham, NC: Duke University Press.

Burned by the Qur'an Burning. (2010). *Christianity Today, 54* (November), 57.

Burns, Jeremy. (2016). Hijacking Jesus. *Charisma, 41* (April), 32–35.

Buss, Dale D. (1994). Banking on the Inner City. *Christianity Today, 38* (October 24), 94.

Butcher, Andy. (1997). "Prayer Walk" Follows Crusades Roots. *Charisma, 22* (March), 14–15.

Butcher, Andy. (2002). Reaching the Weekend Warriors. *Charisma, 28* (August), 64–73.

Butler, Joshua Ryan. (2016). Black and White in the Red, White, and Blue. *Christianity Today, 60* (January–February), 65–67.

Butler, Judith. (1990). *Gender Trouble.* New York: Routledge Press.

The Buzz. (2004). *World Magazine, 19* (May 29), 10–11.

The Buzz Quicktakes. (2006). *World, 21* (December 23), 7.

Byrd, Jodi. (2011). *Transit of Empire.* Minneapolis: University of Minnesota Press.

Cagney, Mary. (1998a). Evangelicals Warned against Persecution. *Christianity Today, 49* (May 18), 20.

Cagney, Mary. (1998b). Senators Champion Rival Bill on Religious Persecution. *Christianity Today, 49* (May 18), 20–21.

Cahn, Jonathan. (2016). The Tectonic Event. *Charisma, 41* (September), 44–46.

Caldwell, Kirbyjon. (2008). James Dobson Doesn't Speak for Me (June 25). http://ac360.blogs.cnn.com/2008/06/25/james-dobson-doesnt-speak-for-me/.

Callahan, Timothy. (2004a). "Appalling" Persecution. *Christianity Today, 48* (January), 30–31.

Callahan, Timothy. (2004b). Immigration Consternation. *Christianity Today, 48* (March), 20.

Calvary Chapel Founder Rebukes Arab-Israeli Church Event. (2013). *Charisma, 38* (July), 27.

Calver, Clive. (1998). The Gospel and Empty Stomachs. *Charisma, 24* (December), 61.

Camosy, Charles. (2016). What Could Stop Antiabortion Momentum? Trump Winning. *Washington Post*, October 20.

Campbell, Heidi. (1991). Enter the New World Order. *Christianity Today, 35* (December 16), 54–57.

Campolo, Tony. (2008). My Top 5 Books on Social Justice. *Christianity Today, 52* (January), 61.

Can Music Be the Instrument of Racial Reconciliation? (1987). *Christianity Today, 31* (May 15), 47, 49.

Cannon, Mae. (2009). *Social Justice Handbook.* Downer's Grove, IL: InterVarsity Press.

Cannon, Mae. (2014). Mischief Making in Palestine: American Protestant Christian Perspectives of Israel and Palestine, pre-1916 to 1955. PhD dissertation, University of California at Davis.

Can We Come to the Party? (2008). *Christianity Today, 52* (October), 23.

Capps, Walter H. (1994). *The New Religious Right.* Columbia: University of South Carolina Press.

Carey, George. (2005). Islam and the West: The Challenge to the Human Family. *Transformation, 22* (January), 2–10.

Carlson, Ray. (2000). Building Jobs for a Better Future. *Mission Frontiers, 22* (September), 20.

Carnes, Tony. (1997). Is Jewish-Christian a Contradiction in Terms? *Christianity Today, 41* (April 7), 50.

Carnes, Tony. (2000a). Arrests of Pastor Signal Religious Freedom Setback. *Christianity Today, 44* (February 7), 28–29.

Carnes, Tony. (2000b). How to Change China. *Christianity Today, 44* (May 22), 34–35.

Carnes, Tony. (2000c). Mixing Oil and Blood. *Christianity Today, 44* (April 3), 26–27.

Carnes, Tony. (2000d). The Torture Victim Next Door. *Christianity Today, 44* (March 6), 70–72.

Carnes, Tony. (2001). Lost Common Cause. *Christianity Today, 45* (July 9), 15–16.

Carnes, Tony. (2002a). New China: Same Old Tricks. *Christianity Today, 46* (March 11), 38–42.

Carnes, Tony. (2002b). Religious Persecution Bill Drops Trade Sanction Clause. *Christianity Today, 46* (April 22), 25.

Carnes, Tony. (2002c). The Unlikely Activist. *Christianity Today, 46* (March 11), 44–45.

Carnes, Tony. (2003). The Peoples Are Here. *Christianity Today, 47* (February), 76–79.

Carnes, Tony. (2004a). New York's New Hope. *Christianity Today, 48* (December), 32–37.

Carnes, Tony. (2004b). Rainbow Coalitions. *Christianity Today, 48* (May), 22.

Carnes, Tony. (2004c). Termites to National Security. *Christianity Today, 48* (October), 21.

Carnes, Tony. (2005a). Can We Defeat Poverty? *Christianity Today, 49* (October), 38–40.

Carnes, Tony. (2005b). Hurricane Heroes. *Christianity Today, 49* (November), 74–78.

Carnes, Tony. (2005c). A Look of Love. *Christianity Today, 49* (February), 71–72.

Carnes, Tony. (2005d). Opportunities of a Generation. *Christianity Today, 49* (February), 66–68.

Carnes, Tony. (2005e). Victory Lap. *Christianity Today, 49* (August), 60–62.

Carnes, Tony. (2006a). China's New Legal Eagles. *Christianity Today, 50* (September), 106–10.

Carnes, Tony. (2006b). Disappointed but Holding. *Christianity Today, 50* (February), 78–81.

Carnes, Tony. (2006c). Walking the Talk after Tsunami. *Christianity Today, 50* (March), 63–66.

Carnes, Tony. (2008). Talking the Walk. *Christianity Today, 52* (October), 32–36.

Carnes, Tony. (2009). Bush's Faith-Based Legacy. *Christianity Today, 53* (February), 44–47.

Carnes, Tony, and Rob Moll. (2005). The Sunday After. *Christianity Today, 49* (October), 82–83.

Carney, Glandion. (1990). Amen, Brother. *Christianity Today, 34* (March 19), 21–23.

Carpenter, Joel. (2003). Compassionate Evangelicalism. *Christianity Today, 47* (December), 40–42.

Carrasco, Rodolpho. (1993). Good News and Bad News. *World, 8* (April 24), 10–12.

Carrasco, Rodolpho. (2001). Catching Up with Hispanics. *Christianity Today, 45* (November 12), 66–69.

Carrasco, Rodolpho. (2006). Habits of Highly Effective Justice Workers. *Christianity Today, 50* (February), 46–49.

Carter, Earl. (1988). Should America Apologize for Slavery? *Charisma, 23* (April), 76–82.

Carter, Jimmy. (2007). *Palestine: Peace Not Apartheid.* New York: Simon and Schuster.

Carter, Joan Wilson. (2000). Faith Defeats Communism. *Charisma, 25* (January), 72–76.

Carter, Earl. (1997). *No Apology Necessary.* Orlando, FL: Creation House.

Carter, Stephen. (2004). Hope Deferred. *Christianity Today, 48* (July), 64.

Carter, Stephen. (2006). The "Judicial Philosophy" Dodge. *Christianity Today, 50* (January), 66.

Cartoon Chaos. (2006). *Christianity Today, 50* (April), 29.

Casey, Ethan. (1997). Five Imprisoned in Wake of Muslim Mob Violence. *Christianity Today, 41* (September 1), 80, 85.

Casper, Jayson. (2013). Conversion Confusion. *Christianity Today, 57* (April), 50–51.

Casper, Jayson. (2016). Muslims Pledge to Protect Christians. *Christianity Today, 60* (April), 26–27.

Cassidy, Michael. (1989). Hope for a Peaceful End to Apartheid. *Christianity Today, 33* (November 17), 55–56.

Castelli, Elizabeth. (2004). *Martyrdom and Memory*. New York: Columbia University Press.

Cati, W. L. (2001). *Married to Muhammed*. Lake Mary, FL: Creation House Press.

Chambers, Steve. (1999). Can Christianity and Islam Coexist and Prosper. *Christianity Today, 43* (October 25), 22.

Chandler, Matt. (2017). How the Church Can Regain Credibility? *Relevant* (January–February), 26.

Channing, Austin. (2014). Ferguson Racial Tension: White Church Still Doesn't Get the Danger of Being Black (August 19). http://www.christianpost.com/news/ferguson-racial-tension-white-church-still-doesnt-get-the-danger-of-being-black-125037/.

Channing, Austin. (2015). UNbalanced (April 11). http://austinchanning.com/blog/2015/4/unbalanced.

Chapman, Colin. (1990). The Riddle of Religions. *Christianity Today, 34* (May 14), 16–22.

Chapman, Colin. (2002). *Whose Promised Land?* Grand Rapids, MI: Baker.

Chapman, Colin. (2003). *Cross and Crescent*. Downer's Grove, IL: InterVarsity Press.

Chapman, Reynolds. (2011). Worship in Black and White. *Christianity Today, 55* (March), 26–28.

Cheaney, Janie. (2005a). Star-Spangled Symbol. *World, 20* (July 30), 39.

Cheaney, Janie. (2005b). Will It Be Our Finest Hour? *World, 20* (September 24), 24–25.

Cheaney, Janie. (2009). Enemies Within. *Charisma* (October 24), 28.

Cheaney, Janie. (2010). Whose Offense? *World, 25* (June 5), 24.

Cheaney, Janie. (2011). The Real Me. *World, 26* (July 30), 18.

Cheaney, Janie. (2016a). Dead-End Revolutions. *World, 31* (March 19), 22.

Cheaney, Janie. (2016b). Free and Equal? *World, 31* (September 17), 16.

Cheaney, Janie. (2016c). The World between Us. *World, 31* (January), 18.

Chen, Pat. (1998). No Apology Necessary. *Charisma, 23* (April), 79.

Cheng, June. (2015). Off the Grid. *World, 30* (September 5), 38–43.

Cheng, June. (2016a). Author in Exile. *World, 31* (May 28), 70–73.

Cheng, June. (2016b). House Church on a Hill. *World, 31* (April 30), 30–35.

Cheng, June. (2016c). Witness to Persecution. *World, 31* (August 20), 46–49.

Chenoweth, Gregg. (2004). The Heartless Homeland. *Christianity Today, 48* (October), 44–46.

Chenoweth, Gregg, and Caleb Benoit. (2009). Where Jerusalem and Mecca Meet. *Christianity Today, 11* (July), 46–47.

Chesser, Paul. (2007). Business Proposition. *World, 22* (August 25), 26–27.

Chow, Rey. (2002). *The Protestant Ethnic and the Spirit of Capitalism*. New York: Columbia University Press.

Christian Allies Caucus. (2004). For Zion's Sake (second quarter), 15.

Christian Coalition. (2001a). Christian Coalition Action Alert (email).

Christian Coalition. (2001b). Christian Coalition Action Alert (email).

Christian Coalition. (2001c). Christian Coalition Action Alert (email).

Christian Coalition. (2002a). Christian Coalition Action Alert (email).

Christian Coalition. (2002b). Christian Coalition Action Alert (email).

Christian Coalition Official Says Ending Sin Will End Racism. (1996). *Christian American, 8* (November/December), 4.

Christian Coalition Retrenches. (1998). *Christianity Today, 42* (March 2), 74.

Christian Coalition's Ralph Reed Steps Down. (1997). *Charisma, 22* (July), 20–24.

Christianity Today. (1997). Top Religion Stories of 1996. *Christianity Today, 41* (January 6), 58.

Christianity Today. (1998a). Christians Expelled from Maldives. *Christianity Today, 42* (September 7), 27.

Christianity Today. (1998b). Churches Seek Debt Cancellation. *Christianity Today, 42* (October 26), 20.

Christianity Today. (1998c). Pakistani Bishop's Death Sparks Riots. *Christianity Today, 42* (June 15), 18.

Christianity Today. (1998d). Who Killed Matthew Shepard? *Christianity Today, 42* (December 7), 35.

Christianity Today. (1999a). Hindu Radical Fingered in Killing. *Christianity Today, 43* (September 6), 26.

Christianity Today. (1999b). Persecution Is Persecution Is Persecution. *Christianity Today, 43* (August 9), 17.

Christianity Today. (2000a). Confronting Sudan's Evils. *Christianity Today, 44* (April 3), 35.

Christianity Today. (2000b). Crushing Debt. *Christianity Today, 44* (May 22), 39.

Christianity Today. (2000c). Top Ten Religion Stories of the Decade. *Christianity Today, 44* (January 10), 22.

Christianity Today. (2001). Changing Hearts and Laws. *Christianity Today, 45* (March 5), 38–39.

Christianity Today. (2002a). Free China's Church. *Christianity Today, 41* (January 7), 31.

Christianity Today. (2002b). Violence-Weary Muslims, Christians Talk Peace. *Christianity Today, 46* (November 18), 34.

Christianity Today. (2004a). Let No Law Put Asunder. *Christianity Today, 48* (February), 26–27.

Christianity Today. (2004b). Never Again? *Christianity Today, 48* (September), 33.

Christianity Today. (2004c). Nightmares and Miracles. *Christianity Today, 48* (December), 29.

Christianity Today. (2005). Parable of the Good Church. *Christianity Today, 49* (October), 30–31.

Christianity Today. (2007a). Faith Perfected. *Christianity Today, 54* (July), 21.

Christianity Today. (2007b). Love Your Muslim as Yourself. *Christianity Today, 51* (April), 27.

Christianity Today. (2007c). One-Size Politics Doesn't Fit All. *Christianity Today, 51* (May), 22–23.

Christianity Today. (2008a). The Faith Factor. *Christianity Today, 52* (October), 25.

Christianity Today. (2008b). See No Evil. *Christianity Today, 52* (October), 22–23.

Christianity Today. (2010). Should Christians Continue to Smuggle Bibles into China? *Christianity Today, 54* (August), 46–47.

Christianity Today. (2011). The Curse of Blasphemy Laws. *Christianity Today, 55* (March), 39.

Christianity Today. (2012). Subverting the Taliban. *Christianity Today, 56* (December), 57.

Churches Take Action against Firms Doing Business with South Africa. (1986). *Christianity Today, 30* (February 7), 51–52.

Church Leaders Condemn Apartheid. (1990). *Christianity Today, 34* (October 17), 54.

CIA and Missionaries: More Confusion. (1996). *Faith and Freedom, 16* (Spring), 11.

Cizik, Richard. (1988). The New Conquistadors. *United Evangelical Action, 47* (July–August), 16.

Claiborne, Shane. (2006). *The Irresistible Revolution* (Kindle Version). Grand Rapids, MI: Zondervan.

Claiborne, Shane. (2016). *Executing

Grace: How the Death Penalty Killed Jesus and Why It's Killing Us. San Francisco: HarperOne.

Clark, Richard. (2016a). Jimmy Carter: Pursing an Arc of Reconciliation. *Christianity Today, 60* (October), 66–69.

Clark, Richard. (2016b). Slow Down, You Hashtag Too Fast. *Christianity Today, 60* (March), 21–22.

Claydon, David. (2000). Islam in a Western Context: Australia. *Transformation, 17* (January–March), 29–31.

Cleary, Steve. (2004). Over the Wall with the Gospel. *Voice of the Martyrs* (December), 6–8.

Cleary, Steve. (2005). Dare to Speak . . . Dare to Die. *Voice of the Martyrs* (Special Issue), 4–5.

Cleveland, Christena. (2014). 7 Signs That Jesus Reveals Himself Most Clearly to the Oppressed (November 3). http://www.christenacleveland.com/blogarchive/2014/11/7-signs-that-jesus-reveals-himself-most-clearly-to-the-oppressed.

Cleveland, Christena. (2016a). The Bias in Our Votes. *Christianity Today, 60* (January–February), 32.

Cleveland, Christena. (2016b). Why Jesus' Skin Color Matters. *Christianity Today, 60* (April), 36.

Coffin, Andrew. (2005). A Different Kind of Horror Movie. *World, 20* (January 29), 12.

Coffman, Elesha. (2004). Lost in America. *Christianity Today, 48* (April), 37–41.

Cohen, Cathy. (1999). *The Boundaries of Blackness*. Chicago: University of Chicago Press.

Cole, Allie. (2007). All in the Family. *World, 22* (September 1–8), 24–25.

Colson, Charles. (1985). Standing Tough against All Odds. *Christianity Today, 29* (September 6), 26–33.

Colson, Charles. (1990). From Moral Majority to a Persecuted Minority. *Christianity Today, 34* (May 14), 80.

Colson, Charles. (1993). *A Dance with Deception*. Dallas: Word.

Colson, Charles. (1996). Tortured for Christ—and Ignored. *Christianity Today, 40* (March 4), 80.

Colson, Charles. (2000). The Ugly Side of Tolerance. *Christianity Today, 44* (March 6), 136.

Colson, Charles. (2002). The Wages of Secularism. *Christianity Today, 46* (June 10), 64.

Colson, Charles. (2008a). Keeping Pets in Their Place. *Christianity Today, 52* (April), 80.

Colson, Charles. (2008b). No Utter Collapse. *Christianity Today, 52* (February), 124.

Colson, Charles. (2008c). Voting Like It Matters. *Christianity Today, 52* (October), 150.

Colson, Charles. (2009). Political Exile. *Christianity Today, 53* (February), 96.

Colson, Charles. (2010). Channeling the Populist Rage. *Christianity Today, 54* (April), 60.

Colson, Charles, and Anne Morse. (2004). The Moral Home Front. *Christianity Today, 48* (October), 152.

Colson, Charles, and Anne Morse. (2007). Overheated Rhetoric. *Christianity Today, 51* (June), 80.

Colson, Charles, and Nancy Pearcey. (1997). Victory over Napalm. *Christianity Today, 41* (March 3), 96.

Commission Urges Economic Sanctions. (2000). *Christianity Today, 44* (June 12), 26.

Compass Direct. (2000a). 7 Christian Executions Suspected. *Christianity Today, 44* (October 23), 25.

Compass Direct. (2000b). Arrested Priest Denies Violence Charges. *Christianity Today, 44* (April 3), 26.

Compass Direct. (2001). Highlands

Christians Targeted. *Christianity Today, 45* (July 9), 22.

Compass Direct. (2002a). Protestants Face Police Crackdown. *Christianity Today, 47* (June), 26.

Compass Direct. (2002b). Troops Foil Attack on Christians. *Christianity Today, 46* (January 7), 22.

Compass Direct. (2003). Authorities Crack Down on Churches. *Christianity Today, 47* (January), 28.

Compass Direct. (2004a). Ex-Muslims Harassed. *Christianity Today, 48* (January), 48.

Compass Direct. (2004b). House-Church Christian Dies in Custody. *Christianity Today, 48* (February), 22.

Compass Direct. (2005a). Lay Pastor May Face Martyrdom. *Christianity Today, 49* (June), 21.

Compass Direct. (2005b). A Miracle in Babylon. *Charisma, 31* (November), 76–80.

Compass Direct and Ecumenical News International. (2000). Military Leader Backpeddles on Human Rights Decision. *Christianity Today, 44* (June 12), 27.

Compass Direct News. (2009). Fault Line of Faith. *Christianity Today, 53* (February), 11.

Conant, Cameron. (2008). A House Divided. *Charisma, 34* (October), 33–39, 81.

Conant, Cameron. (2009). An Angel of Mercy. *Charisma, 35* (September), 36–39, 65.

Conason, Joe, Alfred Ross, and Lee Cokorinos. (1996). The Promise Keepers Are Coming. *Nation, 263* (October 7), 11–19.

Conder, Tim. (2007). The Existing Church/Emerging Church Matrix: Collision, Credibility, Missional Collabortion, and Generative Friendship. In Doug Pagitt and Tony Jones (eds.), *An Emergent Manifesto of Hope* (pp. 98–107). Grand Rapids, MI: Baker Books.

Consultation Reaffirms Jewish Evangelism. (2003). *Christianity Today, 47* (November), 36.

A Convenient Scapegoat: The Right's Demonization of Muslims. (2002). *Christian Science Monitor*, September 14 (email newsletter).

Cook, Allie. (2007). On the March Again. *World, 22* (September 1–8), 54–55.

Cook, Richard. (2005). Behind China's Closed Doors. *Christianity Today, 49* (February), 70–72.

Cooper, Elissa. (2010). Sexual Slavery on Main Street. *Christianity Today, 54* (May), 17–19.

Cooper, Rodney. (1995). *We Stand Together.* Chicago: Moody Press.

Coote, Robert. (1991). The Numbers Game in Evangelism. *Transformation, 8* (January–March), 1–5.

Courbat, Cindy. (2011). Haiti's Healing Revival. *Charisma, 36* (July), 24.

Courtney, Camerin. (2009). Voiceless Women. *Christianity Today, 11* (July), 60.

Couto, Joe. (2002). Reaching Immigrants from South Asia. *Faith Today, 20* (January–February), 44–46.

Cowan, Len. (1991). An Indigenous Church for Indigenous People. *Faith Today, 9* (July–August), 23–26.

Cox, Baroness Caroline. (1999). The Price of a Slave. *Christianity Today, 43* (February 8), 68–69.

Crenshaw, Kimberle. (1996). Mapping the Margins: Intersectionality, Identity Politics, and Violence against Women of Color. In Kimberle Crenshaw, Neil Gotanda, Gary Peller, and Kendall Thomas (eds.), *Critical Race Theory* (pp. 357–83). New York: New Press.

Crespo, Orlando. (2006). Our Transnational Anthem. *Christianity Today, 50* (August), 32–35.

Criminally Broken: Numbers of Inequity in the U.S. Justice System. (2015). *Relevant* (May–June), 46.

Cromartie, Michael. (1996a). Conquering the Enemy Within. *Christianity Today*, 40 (January 8), 17.

Cromartie, Michael. (1996b). One Lord, One Faith, One Voice? *Christianity Today*, 40 (October 7), 35–43.

Cromartie, Michael. (1999). The Jew Who Is Saving Christians. *Christianity Today*, 43 (March 1), 50–55.

Crookston, Paul. (2017). Religious Freedom for Me but Not for Thee? *National Review* (February 21). http://www.nationalreview.com/corner/445106/russell-moore-muslim-mosques-religious-liberty-universal.

Crosby, Cindy. (1999). The Good News about Injustice. *Charisma*, 24 (July), 88.

Crouch, Andy. (2002). The Future Is P.O.D. *Christianity Today*, 46 (October 7), 104.

Crouch, Andy. (2004). The Emergent Mystique. *Christianity Today*, 48 (November), 36–41.

Crouch, Andy. (2007a). Liberate My People. *Christianity Today*, 51 (August), 30–33.

Crouch, Andy. (2007b). Powering Down. *Christianity Today*, 51 (September), 39–42.

Cryderman, Lyn. (1987). Lingering Racism. *Christianity Today*, 31 (March 6), 15.

CT Staff. (2005). House-Church Leader Arrested. *Christianity Today*, 49 (February), 21.

Cumming, Joseph. (2009). Muslim Followers of Jesus? *Christianity Today*, 53 (December), 32–35.

Curry, Dean. (1990). *A World without Tyranny*. Wheaton, IL: Crossway Books.

Curry, Dean. (1993). Lawlessness and Disorder. *World*, 8 (April 24), 13.

Curtis, Carolyn. (1996). Coming Together. *Christian American*, 7 (September/October), 22–27.

Curtis, Jenny Rose. (2016). America's Revival? *Charisma*, 42 (September), 60–64.

Cushman, Candi. (2001). Leading Young Leaders. *World*, 16 (June 16), 76.

Cushman, Candi. (2005). Filling the Void. *Focus on the Family Citizen*, 19 (November), 24–25.

Dabel, Greg. (1998). Bulldogs, Bodyguards. *World*, 13 (April 25), 19–20.

Daigle, Richard. (1999). Shouting It from the Housetops! *Charisma*, 25 (August), 38–44.

Daigle, Richard. (2002a). Arab Believer in Israel Calls for Equal Support of Palestinians and Jews. *Charisma*, 28 (October), 42.

Daigle, Richard. (2002b). Doomsday Prophet? *New Man*, 9 (November/December), 42–46.

Daigle, Richard. (2002c). Waves of Healing in Peru. *Charisma*, 27 (January), 66–70.

Daigle, Richard. (2005a). 500 Pastors Mobilize to Help Gulf Region. *Charisma*, 31 (December), 22–23.

Daigle, Richard. (2005b). Black Pastors Split on Moral Agenda. *Charisma*, 30 (June), 20–21.

Dalrymple, Timothy. (2011a). Long's Story. *World*, 26 (July 2), 69–70.

Dalrymple, Timothy. (2011b). Unequally Yoked. *World*, 26 (December 17), 72.

Daniels, Gene. (2013). Where's Christian? *Christianity Today*, 57 (January/February), 22–31.

Daniels, Kimberly. (2004). The Farrakhan Factor. *Charisma*, 29 (July), 16.

Daniels, Kimberly. (2005). Don't Be Fooled by Farrakhan. *Charisma*, 31 (November), 86–90, 122–23.

Daniels, Kimberly. (2008). Draw the Line! *Charisma*, 34 (November), 78.

David, S. (2002). Critics Assail Dialogue

with Hindu Radicals. *Christianity Today, 46* (May 21), 33.

David, S. (2007). Caught on Tape. *Christianity Today, 51* (August), 16–17.

Dawson, John. (1994). *Healing America's Wounds*. Ventura, CA: Regal Books.

Dawson, John. (2005a). Illegal Invasion. *World, 20* (November 5), 20–23.

Dawson, John. (2005b). On the Border of Madness. *World, 20* (November 26), 22–23.

Dawson, John. (2005c). Riding Out the Post-Storm. *World, 20* (November 26), 20.

Dawson, John. (2005d). Unnatural Disaster. *World, 20* (September 10), 18–27.

Dawson, John. (2005e). You Can't Go Home Again. *World, 20* (September 24), 16–18.

Dawson, John. (2006a). Banning a Bully. *World, 21* (April 29), 20.

Dawson, John. (2006b). Border War. *World, 21* (April 1), 27.

Dawson, John. (2006c). Counting the Costs. *World, 21* (September 16), 18–21.

Dawson, John. (2006d). Heartland Uprising. *World, 21* (May 6), 20–21.

Dawson, John. (2006e). The New "New Colossus." *World, 21* (April 15), 18–21.

Dawson, John. (2006f). No Way Out. *World, 21* (May 13), 19–20.

Dawson, John. (2006g). Running for the Border. *World, 21* (August 26), 24–25.

Dawson, John. (2007a). Not in My Backyard. *World, 22* (March 24/31), 28–29.

Dawson, John. (2007b). Religion Test. *World, 22* (June 16), 18–19.

Dawson, John, and Marvin Olasky. (2005). Up and Down. *World, 20* (October 8), 18–22.

Dean, Jamie. (2005a). Cold Shoulder. *World, 20* (June 4), 23.

Dean, Jamie. (2005b). Homecoming on Hold. *World, 20* (October 22), 16–19.

Dean, Jamie. (2005c). Home Improvement. *World, 20* (June 18), 31–32.

Dean, Jamie. (2005d). Mississippi Misery. *World, 20* (September 24), 19–21.

Dean, Jamie. (2005e). Trailer Park Blues. *World, 20* (November 26), 16–20.

Dean, Jamie. (2006a). Dark to Daylight. *World, 21* (August 26), 16–21.

Dean, Jamie. (2006b). Home Invasions. *World, 21* (February 11), 22–23.

Dean, Jamie. (2006c). Looming Storms. *World, 21* (May 27), 28.

Dean, Jamie. (2006d). Minding Mississippi. *World, 21* (April 8), 32–33.

Dean, Jamie. (2006e). No Way Out. *World, 21* (May 13), 14–18.

Dean, Jamie. (2007a). Criminal Minds. *World, 22* (May 19), 21.

Dean, Jamie. (2007b). Elephant in the Room. *World, 22* (November 3), 20–23.

Dean, Jamie. (2007c). Evangelical Eggshells. *World, 22* (July 14), 22–23.

Dean, Jamie. (2007d). Hunting for Votes. *World, 22* (February 10), 16–19.

Dean, Jamie. (2007e). Leap of Faith. *World, 22* (October 6), 18–21.

Dean, Jamie. (2007f). Life Decisions. *World, 22* (November), 27.

Dean, Jamie. (2007g). Right Man, Wrong Religion. *World, 22* (October 27), 19.

Dean, Jamie. (2008a). 4th Quarter, 3rd and 10. *World, 23* (November 1/8), 34–39.

Dean, Jamie. (2008b). America Spoke. *World, 23* (November 15/22), 34–39.

Dean, Jamie. (2008c). Borderline Voters. *World, 23* (May 17/24), 30–32.

Dean, Jamie. (2008d). Darkest Moment. *World, 23* (October 18/25), 16–23.

Dean, Jamie. (2008e). Forecast: High Pressure System. *World, 23*, 38–40.

Dean, Jamie. (2008f). Gambling Man. *World, 23* (January 26/February 2), 41–42.

Dean, Jamie. (2008g). His to Win. *World, 23* (September 6/13), 34–37.

Dean, Jamie. (2008h). Morality Plays. *World, 23* (October 18/25), 44–45.

Dean, Jamie. (2008i). What Lies Beneath. *World, 23* (November 1/8), 39–41.

Dean, Jamie. (2009a). Castes Vote. *World, 24* (May 9), 48.

Dean, Jamie. (2009b). Change Most Could Believe In. *World, 23* (December 27/January 3), 26–30.

Dean, Jamie. (2009c). Giving Account. *World, 24* (July 18), 38–39.

Dean, Jamie. (2009d). Islam, or Else. *World, 24* (February 14), 55.

Dean, Jamie. (2009e). Standing Down. *World, 24* (June 20), 68–70.

Dean, Jamie. (2009f). States of Bind. *World, 24* (February 28), 33–35.

Dean, Jamie. (2010a). Aftershock. *World, 25* (February 13), 32–40.

Dean, Jamie. (2010b). Boiling Point. *World, 25* (April 10), 42.

Dean, Jamie. (2010c). Immigration Equation. *World, 25* (May 22), 38–40.

Dean, Jamie. (2010d). Long Night. *World, 25* (January 30), 28–31.

Dean, Jamie. (2011a). Border Bandits. *World, 26* (December 3), 34–41.

Dean, Jamie. (2011b). Things a Dad Would Do. *World, 26* (August 13), 52–55.

Dean, Jamie. (2011c). 'Tis the Season. *World, 26* (Janurary 29), 56–58.

Dean, Jamie. (2012a). Demographic Hope. *World, 27* (December 1), 34–40.

Dean, Jamie. (2012b). Milestone. *World, 27* (June 16), 60–62.

Dean, Jamie. (2012c). Not Forsaken. *World, 27* (November 3), 64–68.

Dean, Jamie. (2013a). Cities of Refuge. *World, 28* (April 6), 36–42.

Dean, Jamie. (2013b). Finding Freedom. *World, 28* (April 20), 44–47.

Dean, Jamie. (2013c). Leaving Exodus. *World, 28* (July 13), 40–41.

Dean, Jamie. (2015a). Leaps of Faith. *World, 30* (July 25), 36–43.

Dean, Jamie. (2015b). Unwanted. *World, 30* (September 19), 36–41.

Dean, Jamie. (2015c). Who Is My Neighbor? *World, 30* (November 14), 34–40.

Dean, Jamie. (2016a). False Profits. *World, 31* (May 14), 46–49.

Dean, Jamie. (2016b). House in Mourning. *World, 31* (August 6), 6–7.

Dean, Jamie. (2016c). Just as I Am. *World, 31* (April 2), 34–40.

Dean, Jamie. (2016d). No and Maybe. *World, 31* (May 28), 16–17.

Dean, Jamie. (2016e). Postelection Opportunities. *World, 31* (November 26), 30–34.

Dean, Jamie. (2016f). Race to the Bottom? *World, 31* (June 25), 12–13.

Dean, Jamie. (2016g). Winter of Discontent. *World, 31* (February 20), 52–57.

Dean, Jamie, and Marvin Olasky. (2008). Obama's Challenge. *World, 23* (April 5/12), 38–39.

Delahoyde, Melinda, Clenard Childress, and Charmaine Yoest. (2009). Pro-Life's Next Moment. *Christianity Today, 53* (October), 56–57.

Deloreia, Renee. (1998). Indonesian Muslims Thank Christians for Food and Prayers. *Charisma, 24* (December), 35–38.

Deloreia, Renee. (2007). Aglow International Marks 40th Anniversary. *Charisma, 33* (September), 22–23.

Deloria, Philip. (2004). *Indians in Unexpected Places*. Lawrence: University of Kansas Press.

Deloria, Vine, Jr. (1992). *God Is Red*. Golden, CO: North American Press.

Denominational Leaders Address Drug Crisis. (1990). *Christianity Today, 34* (November 19), 58–59.

Derrick, J. C. (2015a). Christian Crossroads. *World, 30* (September 5), 13.

Derrick, J. C. (2015b). Sins of Commission. *World, 30* (July 25), 40–43.

Derrick, J. C. (2016). Trumping Liberty. *World, 31* (March 19), 44–47.

Derrida, Jacques. (1998). *Monolingualism*

of the Other. Redwood City, CA: Stanford University Press.

Devine, Daniel James. (2008). Obama's Church. World, 23 (March 22/29), 43.

Devine, Daniel James. (2015). Michigan's Homeless Makeover. World, 30 (August 8), 54–56.

DeYoung, Curtiss Paul, Michael Merson, George Yancey, and Karen Chai Kim. (2004). United by Faith: The Multiracial Congregation as an Answer to the Problem of Race. New York: Oxford University Press.

DeYoung, Kevin, and Ted Gluck. (2008). Why We're Not Emergent. Chicago: Moody.

Diamond, Billy. (1991). Issues That Can't Wait. Faith Today, 9 (July–August), 27–28.

Diamond, Sara. (1989). Spiritual Warfare. Boston: South End Press.

Divino, Claudio. (2003). Why Don't They Look Like Us. Christian Standard, 138 (January 5), 13–14.

Dixon, Herti. (2009). Christians in West Papua Seek Autonomy. Charisma, 34 (March), 20.

Dixon, Tomas. (1997). The Apology That Took a Thousand Years. Charisma, 28–30 (December), 72–76.

Dixon, Tomas. (1998). Prayer Walk Targets Middle East Strife. Charisma, 24 (December), 20–21.

Dixon, Tomas. (1999a). Apology Crusaders to Enter Israel. Christianity Today, 43 (April 5), 23.

Dixon, Tomas. (1999b). An Apology, 900 Years in the Making. Christianity Today, 43 (September 6), 24.

Dixon, Tomas. (1999c). Prayer Walk from Europe to Middle East Concludes in Jerusalem. Charisma, 25 (October), 28–29.

Dixon, Tomas. (1999d). Texas Missionary Says Evangelism and Muslim Bashing Don't Mix. Charisma, 24 (June), 32–33.

Dixon, Tomas. (2002a). Hate Speech Law Could Chill Sermons. Christianity Today, 46 (August 5), 23.

Dixon, Tomas. (2002b). In the Shadow of the Mosque. Charisma, 28 (August), 56–61.

Dixon, Tomas. (2002c). Missions Expert Calls for Christians to Make Peace with Muslims. Charisma, 28 (October), 26.

Dixon, Tomas. (2005). Twilight of Christian Europe. Charisma, 31 (November), 97–101.

Dixon, Tomas. (2007). Three Christians Martyred in Turkey. Charisma, 32 (July), 28.

Dixon, Tomas. (2010). Charismatics Criticize Swiss Ban on Minarets. Charisma, 35 (February), 21–22.

Dobson, Ed, and Cal Thomas. (1999). Blinded by Might. Grand Rapids, MI: Zondervan.

Dobson, James. (2016). Why I'm Voting for Donald Trump. Christianity Today, 60 (October), 58–60.

Does Islam Have Room for Religious Liberty? (1991). Christianity Today, 35 (August 19), 51–52.

Domigues, Patricia. (1994). Women of the New Christian Right: Ideological Hegemony in Process. PhD diss., Riverside: University of California.

Donaldson, Hal. (1998). Cold Hearts in the Big City. Charisma, 24 (December), 48–54.

Donnally, Ed. (2000). Actor Dean Jones Helps Persecuted Christians via New Relief Efforts. Charisma, 25 (January), 18–20.

Dorsch, Audrey. (1991). The Book of Acts on James Bay. Faith Today, 9 (July–August), 18–22.

Doucet, Daina. (1996). Revival Thaws Frigid Canadian North. Charisma, 22 (December), 14–15.

Douglas, Jim. (2004). Big Faith in Texas. Charisma, 29 (April), 42–51.

Douglas, Jim. (2005). What America Means. *New Man*, 12 (March/April), 38–44.

Doyle, Mary. (1999). Faces of Pesecution. *Faith Today*, 17 (November/December), 24–29.

Doyley, Nicole. (2009). A Plea for Unity. *Charisma*, 34 (March), 63.

Dream vs. Reality. (2008). *World*, 23 (January 26/February 2), 12.

D'Souza, Dinesh. (2007). Cross-Culture Wars. *World*, 22 (January 13), 26–27.

Dugan, Robert. (1985). Discrimination and Public Policy. *United Evangelical Action*, 44 (January–February), 13.

Duin, Julia. (2000). Suffering in Silence. *Charisma*, 25 (January), 50–54.

Duin, Julia. (2002). A Gateway for the Gospel in Jordan. *Charisma*, 27 (January), 48–52.

Duke's Faith Questioned. (1996). *Christianity Today*, 35 (December 16), 63.

Durie, Mark. (2010). Beware Progress. *World*, 25 (February 27), 62–63.

Dyck, Drew. (2008). The Preacher Who Dared to Be President. *Charisma*, 33 (April), 33–41.

Ecumenical News International. (2000). "Christian Nation" Label Rings Hollow. *Christianity Today*, 44 (March 6), 29.

Ecumenical News International and Religious News Service. (2000). Will Shari'a Law Curb Christianity? *Christianity Today*, 44 (October 23), 24.

The Editors. (2008). No Retreat. *World*, 23 (November 15/22), 40–41.

Edwards, Jefferson. (1996). *Purging Racism from Christianity*. Grand Rapids, MI: Zondervan.

Eidsmoe, John. (1992). *Columbus and Cortez: Conquerors for Christ*. Green Forest, AR: New Leaf Press.

Elliott, Barbara, and Marvin Olasky. (2004). Preserving Habitat. *World*, 19 (December 18), 26–29.

Elliott, E. N., and James Henry Hammond. (1968). *Cotton Is King, and Pro-Slavery Arguments: Comprising the Writings of Hammond, Harper, Christy, Stringfellow, Hodge, Bledsoe, and Cartwright, on This Important Subject*. http://www.gutenberg.org/files/28148/28148-h/28148-h.htm.

Ellis, Carl. (1993). What Christians Need to Know about Malcolm X. *Urban Family*, 2 (Winter), 14–18.

Ellis, Carl. (2000). How Islam Is Winning Black America. *Christianity Today*, 44 (April 3), 52–53.

Ellis, Edward. (1989). Out of the Tower of Babel. *World Christian*, 8 (October), 20–23.

Ellis, K. A. (2016). Are US Christians Really "Persecuted"? *Christianity Today*, 60 (September), 36.

Emergent Village. (n.d.). http://www.emergentvillage.com.

Emerson, Michael, and Christian Smith. (2000). *Divided by Faith*. New York: Oxford University Press.

Ensley, Mike. (2008). What to Do When Your Child Is Gay. *Charisma*, 33 (June), 47–50, 79.

Eschliman, Bob. (2016). A Prophetic Political Showdown. *Charisma*, 42 (September), 50–56.

Escobar, Martha. (2008). No One Is Criminal. In CR 10 Publications Collective (ed.), *Abolition Now* (pp. 57–69). Chico, CA: AK Press.

Eskridge, Larry. (2000). When Burkett Speaks, Evangelicals Listen. *Christianity Today*, 44 (June 12), 44–52.

Evans, Elizabeth Eisenstadt. (2016). You Fix This Mess: Post-Election, Evangelicals of Color Disappointed in White Evangelicals. *Religion Dispatches* (December 21). http://religiondispatches.org/you-fix-this-mess-post-election-evangelicals-of-color-disappointed-in-white-evangelicals/.

Evans, Mike. (2007). Persecution in Iraq. *Charisma*, 33 (August), 84.

Evans, Rachel Held. (2011). Mark Driscoll Is a Bully. Stand Up to Him. Blog (July 11). http://rachelheldevans.com/blog/mark-driscoll-bully.

Evans, Rachel Held. (2013). "More Than Serving Tea": A Conversation with Kathy Khang and Nikki Toyama-Szeto (September 6). http://rachelheldevans.com/blog/more-than-serving-tea.

Evans, Rachel Held. (2014a). Comments to White People, White Power, White Platform (August 27). http://www.carisadel.com/3123/white-people-white-power-white-platform/.

Evans, Rachel Held. (2014b). A Kingdom of Rejects. Blog (October 3). http://rachelheldevans.com/blog/lectionary-kingdom-of-rejects?utm_content=buffere4afe&utm_medium=social&utm_source=twitter.com&utm_campaign=buffer.

Evans, Tony. (1990). *America's Only Hope*. Chicago: Moody Press.

Evans, Tony. (1995). *Let's Get to Know Each Other*. Nashville: Thomas Nelson Publishers.

Fan, Daniel. (2013). Revenge of the Rickshaw Rally (December 10). https://ethnicspace.wordpress.com/2013/12/10/revenge-of-the-rickshaw-rally-by-daniel-fan/.

Farnsley, Arthur, II. (2006). Flea Market Believers. *Christianity Today, 50* (October), 114–21.

Farrell, Elisabeth. (1997). Mosques on Main Street. *Charisma, 23* (October), 56–58, 66.

Farrell, Elisabeth. (1999a). Please Don't Forget Us. *Charisma, 25* (November), 42–54.

Farrell, Elisabeth. (1999b). Women in the Danger Zone. *Charisma, 24* (June), 56–64.

Farrell, Elisabeth. (2000a). Journey to the Secret Kingdom. *Charisma, 26* (October), 52–67.

Farrell, Elisabeth. (2000b). Married to Muhammed. *Charisma, 25* (June), 88–93.

Fausset, Richard, and Alan Blinder. (2016). Evangelicals Ignore G.O.P. by Embracing Syrian Refugees. *New York Times* (September 6). http://www.nytimes.com/2016/09/07/us/syrian-refugees-christian-conservatives.html?_r=0.

Fawzy, Samy. (2000). Christian-Muslim Dialogue in Egypt. *Transformation, 17* (January–March), 34–36.

Feedback. (2005). *Charisma, 31* (January), 8–10, 90.

Feedback. (2006). *Charisma, 32* (October), 14–16, 94.

Feedback. (2007a). *Charisma, 32* (May), 10, 74.

Feedback. (2007b). *Charisma, 32* (June), 10–12, 131.

Feedback. (2007c). *Charisma, 33* (October), 10–12, 126.

Feedback. (2008a). *Charisma, 33* (January), 8–10.

Feedback. (2008b). *Charisma, 33* (April), 10.

Feedback. (2008c). *Charisma, 33* (June), 8–10.

Feedback. (2008d). *Charisma, 34* (November), 8–10.

Feedback. (2008e). *Charisma, 34* (December), 8–10.

Feedback. (2009a). *Charisma, 34* (January), 8–10.

Feedback. (2009b). *Charisma, 34* (March), 8–10, 62.

Feedback. (2009c). *Charisma, 34* (April), 8–10.

Feedback. (2009d). God Has Pushed "Reset." *Charisma, 34* (June), 8–10.

Ferguson, Roderick. (2003). *Aberrations in Black*. Minneapolis: University of Minnesota Press.

Fernando, Ajith. (1999). Bombs Away. *Christianity Today, 43* (June 14), 76–77.

Fidler, Brian. (2005). Infiltrating the Darkness. In *Voice of the Martyrs* (p. 4). Caney, KS, Voice of the Martyrs.

Fieguth, Debra. (2004). Persecuted but Not Defeated. *Faith Today, 22* (September/October), 18–21.

Field. (1996). *Family Voice, 8* (August), 22.

Finch, Laura. (2016). Rethinking the Restroom. *World, 31* (August 20), 30–35.

Fiorenza, Elisabeth Schüssler. (1985). *In Memory of Her*. New York: Crossroad.

Firebombed Churches Thank Rebuilding Donors. (1997). *Christian American, 8* (January/February), 12.

Fischer, Michael. (1999). The Fiery Rise of Hindu Fundamentalism. *Christianity Today, 43* (March 1), 46–49.

Fischer, Michael. (2000). Enemies of the State. *Christianity Today, 44* (June 12), 26.

Fish, Stanley. (2005). *Is There a Text in This Class?* Cambridge: Harvard University Press.

Fisher, Cameron, and Adrienne Gaines. (2004). Christians Traveled to Israel Recently to Show Support. Foster Tourism. *Charisma, 29* (February), 18.

Fletcher, Elaine Ruth. (1999). Christians March across Middle East to Apologize for Crusades. *Baptist Standard* (August 4). http://www.baptist standard.com/1999/1998_1994/pages/crusades.html.

Fletcher, Elaine Ruth. (2000). Between the Temple Mount and a Hard Place. *Christianity Today, 44* (December 4), 66–68.

Fletcher, Elaine Ruth. (2001). Holy Land Roadblocks. *Christianity Today, 45* (April 23), 22.

Fletcher, Jim. (2012). Zionism's New Face. *Charisma, 37* (July), 83–86.

Flinchbaugh, C. Hope. (1999a). Arrested Christians Face Deportation. *Christianity Today, 43* (December 6), 31.

Flinchbaugh, C. Hope. (1999b). Christians in the Line of Fire. *Charisma, 25* (October), 72–78.

Flinchbaugh, C. Hope. (2000). Rapes of Christians Put Pakistani Justice on Trial. *Christianity Today, 44* (October 2), 28.

Flinchbaugh, C. Hope. (2001). Christian Workers from United States Remain Jailed in Afghanistan. *Charisma, 27* (December), 28–29.

Flinchbaugh, C. Hope. (2002). Pakistani Christians Unite in Response to Bloody Attacks. *Charisma, 28* (November), 19–20.

Flinchbaugh, C. Hope. (2006). The Muslim Who Heard God's Voice. *Charisma, 32* (August), 66–72, 99.

Flinchbaugh, C. Hope. (2007). Pastor Champions Plight of North Koreans. *Charisma, 32* (January), 24.

Foreman, Dawn. (1999). World Relief. *Charisma, 24* (May), 35–36.

For Koreans in America—Grown and Growing Pains. (1989). *Christianity Today, 33* (March 3), 56.

Forum Examines Immigration. (1986). *United Evangelical Action, 45* (January–February), 12.

Foucault, Michel. (1980). *History of Sexuality* (Vol. 1). New York: Vintage Books.

Foucault, Michel. (1997). *"Society Must Be Defended": Lectures at the College de France, 1975–1976*. New York: Picador.

Fowlds, Sean. (2002). A Watchman on the Wall. *New Man, 9* (May/June), 16–19.

Frame, Randy. (1985). Church Leaders Challenge the Notion That America Is a Melting Pot. *Christianity Today, 25* (May 17), 40–42.

Frame, Randy. (1987). Churches Band Together to Help Register Undocumented Aliens. *Christianity Today, 31* (July 10), 34–35.

Frame, Randy. (1988). Race and the

Church: A Progress Report. *Christianity Today*, 32 (March 4), 16–17.

Frame, Randy. (1990). Dues-Paying Time for Black Christians. *Christianity Today*, 34 (August 20), 51.

Frame, Randy. (1997). Helping the Poor Help Themselves. *Christianity Today*, 41 (February 3), 70–73.

Frame, Randy, and Edgar Tharpe. (1996). *How Right Is the Right?* Grand Rapids, MI: Zondervan.

Francis, Robert. (2007). Colonization: Weapons, Gifts, Diseases and Medicines. *NAIITS Journal*, 5, 45–59.

Franzen, Aaron. (2011). A Left Leaning Text. *Christianity Today*, 55 (October), 32–33.

Freedom House. (1996). *In the Lion's Den: A Primer on Mounting Christian Persecution around the World and How American Christians Can Respond*. Washington, DC: Freedom House.

Freedom Ride for Life. (2010). *Charisma*, 35 (June), 26.

Freeman, Jo. (1972–1973). The Tyranny of Structurelessness. *Berkeley Journal of Sociology*, 17, 151–64.

Friesen, Dwight J. (2007). Orthoparadoxy. In Doug Pagitt and Tony Jones (eds.), *An Emergent Manifesto of Hope* (pp. 202–12). Grand Rapids, MI: Baker Books.

Gabriel, Mark. (2002). Kidnapped! *New Man*, 9 (July/August), 30–33.

Gabriel, Mark. (2004). Empty Prayers to Allah. *Charisma*, 29 (April), 18.

Gage, Carolyn. (1996). Getting Down to Business. *Christian American*, 7 (January/February), 23.

Gaines, Adrienne. (1997). Confederate Flag Divides Christians. *Charisma*, 23 (September), 16–17.

Gaines, Adrienne. (1998). Hunger in a Land of Abundance. *Charisma*, 24 (December), 53.

Gaines, Adrienne. (1999). Black Farmers Crusade for Justice as U.S. Government Agrees to Restitution. *Charisma*, 24 (May), 28–32.

Gaines, Adrienne. (2000). U.S. House Member Renews Call for Apology for Slavery. *Charisma*, 26 (September), 40–41.

Gaines, Adrienne. (2002a). McKinney Starts Urban Ministry Center. *Charisma*, 27 (June), 16–17.

Gaines, Adrienne. (2002b). Nation under God? *New Man*, 9 (September/October), 62–63.

Gaines, Adrienne. (2003). America's Islamic Capital. *Charisma*, 28 (January), 39.

Gaines, Adrienne. (2004). China Launches New Crackdown on Underground-Church Movement. *Charisma*, 29 (April), 22.

Gaines, Adrienne. (2005a). Keith Butler Declares Candidacy for 2006 Senate Race. *Charisma*, 30 (June), 21.

Gaines, Adrienne. (2005b). Michigan Pastor Considers Senate Run. *Charisma*, 30 (March), 18–19.

Gaines, Adrienne. (2006a). A Call to Israel. *Charisma*, 32 (September), 21.

Gaines, Adrienne. (2006b). The Political Power of Pentecostals. *Charisma*, 31 (February), 33–34.

Gaines, Adrienne. (2006c). President of Christian Coalition. *Charisma*, 32 (December), 19.

Gaines, Adrienne. (2007). Ministry Seeks to Mobilize African-Americans in Missions. *Charisma*, 32 (July), 23.

Gaines, Adrienne. (2008a). Atlanta Minister Faces Criminal Investigation. *Charisma*, 33 (January), 24.

Gaines, Adrienne. (2008b). McCain Running Mate Energizes Evangelicals. *Charisma*, 34 (October), 28.

Gaines, Adrienne. (2008c). Pastor Rallies Marriage Amendment Support. *Charisma*, 34 (October), 24.

Gaines, Adrienne. (2009a). Black, White

Believers Break Racial Divide. *Charisma, 34* (June), 22.

Gaines, Adrienne. (2009b). Pro-Israel Group Makes Inroads on Campuses. *Charisma, 34* (July), 24.

Gaines, Adrienne. (2010). Minister Leads Jewish Evangelism Campaign. *Charisma, 35* (April), 21.

Gaines, Adrienne, and Vanessa Chandler. (2008). Pentecostal University Studies Women's Issues. *Charisma, 34* (November), 24.

Gaines, Adrienne, Felicia Mann, and Paul Steven Ghiringhelli. (2009). Christians Urge Prayer for President-Elect. *Charisma, 34* (January), 14–15.

Gaines, Jack. (2000). Let Forgiveness Come First. *Charisma, 26* (November), 70.

Galli, Mark. (1997). Sometimes Persecution Purifies, Unites, and Grows the Church. Sometimes It Doesn't. *Christianity Today, 41* (May 19), 16–19.

Galli, Mark. (2004). The Chinese Church's Delicate Dance. *Christianity Today, 48* (November), 68–73.

Galli, Mark. (2007). A New Day in Vietnam. *Christianity Today, 51* (May), 26–32.

Galli, Mark. (2008). Our Geopolitical Moment. *Christianity Today, 52* (March), 44–50.

Galli, Mark. (2009a). In the Beginning, Grace. *Christianity Today, 53* (October), 22–27.

Galli, Mark. (2009b). Is the Gay Marriage Debate Over? *Christianity Today, 11* (July), 30–33.

Galli, Mark. (2009c). Reasoning Together. *Christianity Today, 53* (August), 7.

Galli, Mark. (2011a). Do Muslims and Christians Worship the Same God? *Christianity Today, 55* (April), 27–30.

Galli, Mark. (2011b). Free at First. *Christianity Today, 55* (October), 50–53.

Galli, Mark. (2011c). Loving Muslims One at a Time. *Christianity Today, 55* (September), 38–39.

Galli, Mark. (2012). A Most Personal Touch. *Christianity Today, 56* (February), 20–22.

Galli, Mark. (2015a). Breaking News: 2 Billion Christians Believe in Traditional Marriage (June 9). http://www.christianitytoday.com/ct/2015/june-web-only/breaking-news-2-billion-christian-believe-in-traditional-ma.html.

Galli, Mark. (2015b). Hope in the Face of Intractable Racism. *Christianity Today, 59* (July/August), 25–26.

Galli, Mark. (2016). This Is a "God Moment" on Race. *Christianity Today, 60* (September), 31–32.

Gardner, Christine. (1998). Congress Approves Modified Religious Persecution Bill. *Christianity Today, 42* (November 16), 32–33.

Gardner, Christine. (1999). Slave Redemption. *Christianity Today, 43* (August 9), 28–33.

Garrett, Brandon. (2011). *Convicting the Innocent.* Cambridge, MA: Harvard University Press.

Garrison, Becky. (2007). Messianic Ministry Evangelizes in Tel Aviv. *Charisma, 32* (May), 24–25.

Gavlak, Dale. (2005a). Evangelical Collective. *Christianity Today, 49* (June), 25.

Gavlak, Dale. (2005b). Longing to Be Heard. *Christianity Today, 49* (April), 87–88.

Gavlak, Dale. (2011). "Religicide" in Iraq. *Christianity Today, 55* (February), 13–16.

Gbonigi, Emmanuel. (2000). Christians Facing Muslim Authorities in Nigeria. *Transformation, 17* (January–March), 19–20.

Geisler, Dave. (1994). Healing America's Wounds. *Charisma, 19* (October), 33–37.

Geisler, Dave. (1995). Taking It to the Streets. *Charisma*, 20 (June), 46–49.

Gentry, Weston. (2012). Exodus from Exodus. *Christianity Today*, 56 (December), 17.

George, Chloe. (2001). The Holy Spirit Melts Divisions. *Charisma*, 26 (January), 58–60, 64.

George, Timothy. (2002a). Is the God of Muhammad the Father of Jesus? *Christianity Today*, 46 (February 4), 28–31.

George, Timothy. (2002b). No Easy Victory. *Christianity Today*, 46 (March 11), 50–57.

George, Timothy. (2007). The Jerry I Remember. *Christianity Today*, 54 (July), 48–49.

Gerson, Michael, and Peter Wehner. (2015). The Power of Our Weakness. *Christianity Today*, 59 (November), 40–46.

Ghezzi, Bert. (2003). One Friendship at a Time. *Christianity Today*, 47 (August), 46–49.

Ghiringhelli, Paul Steven. (2007a). Event to Mark Anniversary of Settlers' Landing in America. *Charisma*, 32 (March), 23.

Ghiringhelli, Paul Steven. (2007b). "Night to Honor Israel" Events Spread across the U.S. *Charisma*, 32 (January), 17.

Gibbs, Eddie, and Ryan K. Bolger. (2005). *Emerging Churches*. Grand Rapids, MI: Baker.

Gilbreath, Edward. (1998a). Catching Up with a Dream. *Christianity Today*, 42 (March 2), 21–29.

Gilbreath, Edward. (1998b). The Jackie Robinson of Evangelism. *Christianity Today*, 42 (February 9), 40–50.

Gilbreath, Edward. (1999). Redeeming Fire. *Christianity Today*, 43 (December 6), 38–47.

Gilbreath, Edward, and Mark Galli. (2005). Harder Than Anyone Can Imagine. *Christianity Today*, 49 (April), 36–43.

Gill, Tom. (2000). Is Israel Holy? *Charisma*, 25 (May), 116.

Gilliard, Dominique. (2015). The Unbearable Whiteness of Being. *Sojourners*, 44 (April), 36–39.

Gilliard, Dominique. (2018). *Rethinking Incarceration: Advocating for Justice that Restores*. Westmont, IL: InterVarsity Press.

Gilmore, Ruth Wilson. (2007). *Golden Gulag: Prisons, Surplus, Crisis, and Opposition in Globalizing California*. Berkeley: University of California Press.

Gilmore, Ruth Wilson. (2017). In the Shadow of the Shadow State. In Incite (ed.), *The Revolution Will Not Be Funded: Beyond the Nonprofit Industrial Complex* (pp. 41–52). Durham, NC: Duke University Press.

Gleanings. (2010). *Christianity Today*, 54 (July), 8–9.

Gleanings. (2013). *Christianity Today*, 57 (December), 18–19.

Gleanings. (2014). *Christianity Today*, 58 (January–February), 14.

Gleanings. (2015a). *Christianity Today*, 59 (July–August), 17.

Gleanings. (2015b). *Christianity Today*, 59 (November), 22–23.

Gleanings. (2016a). *Christianity Today*, 60 (January–February), 18–19.

Gleanings. (2016b). *Christianity Today*, 60 (September), 19.

Global Slavery Is Growing. (2014). *Relevant* (January/February), 28.

Gospel Independence. (2008). *Christianity Today*, 52 (July), 20–21.

Grady, J. Lee. (1994). Pentecostals Renounce Racism. *Christianity Today*, 38 (December 12), 58.

Grady, J. Lee. (1996). Pentecostals Urged to End Bias against Women Ministers. *Charisma*, 11 (December), 15.

Grady, J. Lee. (1998). Pastors Strategize to

Reach Millions of Asians Living in the United States. *Charisma, 24* (August), 35–36.

Grady, J. Lee. (2002). Africa's Islamic Challenge. *Charisma, 27* (May), 45.

Grady, J. Lee. (2003). Invading the Darkness. *Charisma, 28* (January), 35.

Grady, J. Lee. (2005a). Katrina's Silver Lining. *Charisma, 31* (November), 10.

Grady, J. Lee. (2005b). Prophetic Minister Paul Cain Issues Public Apology for Immoral Lifestyle. *Charisma, 30* (March), 20.

Grady, J. Lee. (2005c). Secret Agent Man. *Charisma, 30* (March), 36–42.

Grady, J. Lee. (2006a). A Holy Ghost Haircut. *Charisma, 31* (February), 6.

Grady, J. Lee. (2006b). Jesus and the Immigrants. *Charisma, 32* (August), 8.

Grady, J. Lee. (2007a). Dancing on Division. *Charisma, 33* (November), 8.

Grady, J. Lee. (2007b). Golden Calf Religion. *Charisma, 32* (February), 6.

Grady, J. Lee. (2007c). No More Macho Religion. *Charisma, 32* (June), 8.

Grady, J. Lee. (2008). God Loves Arabs, Too. *World, 33* (May), 8.

Grady, J. Lee. (2009a). Apocalypse Now? *Charisma, 35* (October), 66.

Grady, J. Lee. (2009b). God Has Pushed "Reset." *Charisma, 34* (June), 6.

Grady, J. Lee. (2009c). God's Moment for India. *Charisma, 34* (February), 26–33, 58–59.

Grady, J. Lee. (2009d). They Burn Bibles in India. *Charisma, 34* (February), 6.

Grady, J. Lee. (2012). Mi Casa Es Tu Casa. *Charisma, 37* (May), 96.

Grady, J. Lee. (2015). Why Abortion Is Definitely Not "Women's Heath." *Charisma, 41* (October), 74.

Grady, J. Lee. (2016). What Would Jesus Say to the Transgender Person? *Charisma, 42* (August), 70.

Grady, Lee. (1991). Is the Future Safe for Our Children? *Charisma, 16* (January), 61–68.

Graham, Ruth. (2015). Southern Baptists Grapple with Racist History. *Al Jazeera American*, (April 1). http://america.aljazeera.com/articles/2015/4/1/in-wake-of-ferguson-southern-baptists-grapple-with-racist-history.html.

Graham, Tim. (2001a). Hail to the Fox. *World, 16* (September 15), 21–23.

Graham, Tim. (2001b). True Love Waits, and Waits. *World, 16* (July 7–14), 34–35.

Graham, Tim. (2002). First Comes Reform, Then Comes Marriage. *World, 17* (March 16), 20–22.

Grant, Tobin. (2010). Strange Bedfellows on Immigration, Cocaine, and Campaign Finance (July 30). http://www.christianitytoday.com/ct/2010/julyweb-only/40.52.0.html?start=2.

Gray, John W., III. (2015). We Must Bridge the Racial Divide. *Relevant* (May/June), 46.

Green, Amy. (2004). Southern Baptist Surprise. *Christianity Today, 48* (September), 54–56.

Green, Amy. (2008). 2008 Election Splits Evangelical Vote. *Charisma, 33* (January), 22–23.

Green, Derryck. (2016). Sorry, Jen Hatmaker: Christians Aren't Complicit in Orlando (June 16). https://juicyecumenism.com/2016/06/16/sorry-jen-hatmaker-christians-arent-complicit-happened-orlando/.

Green, Emma. (2017). Russell Moore and the Fight for the Soul of the Southern Baptist Convention. *Atlantic* (March 14). https://www.theatlantic.com/politics/archive/2017/03/russell-moore-southern-baptist-convention/519540/.

Green, Jocelyn. (2007). Voting Values. *Christianity Today, 51* (December), 16–17.

Green, Matthew. (2005). Walking by Faith. *Charisma, 31* (August), 22.

Green, Matthew. (2006). Standing with Israel. *Charisma, 31* (May), 44.

Green, Tanya. (2002). Mina's Story. *Family Voice* (Winter), 14–17; 20–21.

Greene, Bonnie. (1973). These Christians Show the Way. *Eternity, 24* (September), 16–21.

Greenway, Roger. (1989). A Shift in the Global Center of Christianity. *United Evangelical Action, 48* (November/December), 4–7.

Gremore, Graham. (2016). Antigay Evangelicals Have Temper Tantrums over Trump's Gay Marriage Flip Flop. *LGBTQ Nation* (November 16). https://www.lgbtqnation.com/2016/11/antigay-evangelicals-temper-tantrums-trumps-gay-marriage-flip-flop/.

Grenz, Stanley J. (2000). *Renewing the Center.* Grand Rapids, MI: Baker.

Grenz, Stanley J., and John Franke. (2000). *Beyond Foundationalism.* Louisville, KY: Westminster John Knox Press.

Gribben, D. J. (1996). Christian Coalition Goes Global. *Christian American, 7* (June), 35.

Groothuis, Rebecca Merrill, and Douglas Groothuis. (1999). Integrating Mars and Venus. *Christianity Today, 43* (July 12), 47–48.

Grudem, Wayne. (2016). Why Voting for Trump Is a Morally Good Choice. *Townhall* (July 8). http://townhall.com/columnists/waynegrudem/2016/07/28/why-voting-for-donald-trump-is-a-morally-good-choice-n2199564.

Guider, Margaret Eletta. (2004). "Oh, deep in my heart, I do believe . . ." Elements of a Missionary Spirituality for Redressing Racism. *Missiology, 32* (January), 5–13.

Guilherme, George. (2002). Evangelicals Grow as Political Force. *Christianity Today, 46* (December 9), 22.

Gushee, David. (2006). What's Right about Patriotism. *Christianity Today, 50* (July), 48.

Gushee, David. (2015). Disputable Matters. *Sojourners, 44* (January), 22–25.

Guth, James. (1996a). The Bully Pulpit. In John Green, James Guth, Corwin Smidt, and Lyman Kellstedt (eds.), *Religion and the Culture Wars: Dispatches from the Front* (pp. 146–71). London: Rowman & Littlefield.

Guth, James. (1996b). The Politics of the Christian Right. In John Green, James Guth, Corwin Smidt, and Lyman Kellstedt (eds.), *Religion and the Culture Wars: Dispatches from the Front* (pp. 7–29). London: Rowman & Littlefield.

Guthrie, Stan. (1991). A Crescent for a Cross: Islam Prospers in America. *Christianity Today, 35* (October 27), 40.

Guthrie, Stan. (1993). Muslim Mission Breakthrough. *Christianity Today, 37* (December 13), 20–26.

Guthrie, Stan. (2001a). Christians Fear Muslim Backlash. *Christianity Today, 45* (November 12), 30.

Guthrie, Stan. (2001b). Christians Massacred. *Christianity Today, 45* (December 3), 26.

Guthrie, Stan. (2001c). Kidnapped Missionaries Reported Safe. *Christianity Today, 45* (August 6), 28.

Guthrie, Stan. (2001d). Palestine's Christians Persist Despite Pressures. *Christianity Today, 45* (October 1), 30.

Guthrie, Stan. (2002a). Crackdown Hits Churches. *Christianity Today, 46* (May 21), 30–31.

Guthrie, Stan. (2002b). Door to Islam. *Christianity Today, 46* (September 9), 35–45.

Guthrie, Stan. (2002c). Keeping Their Heads Low. *Christianity Today, 46* (November 18), 34–35.

Guthrie, Stan. (2003). Return to Kabul. *Christianity Today, 47* (January), 52–54.

Guthrie, Stan. (2004a). Deconstructing Gulags. *Christianity Today, 48* (December), 19.

Guthrie, Stan. (2004b). A False Cry of Peace. *Christianity Today, 48* (September), 70–71.

Guthrie, Stan. (2004c). Q&A. *Christianity Today, 48* (October), 23.

Guthrie, Stan. (2005). Q&A. *Christianity Today, 49* (July), 17.

Guthrie, Stan. (2006). Islam's Uncertain Future. *Christianity Today, 50* (February), 62–66.

Guthrie, Stan. (2008a). All Monotheisms Are Not Alike. *Christianity Today, 52* (November), 71.

Guthrie, Stan. (2008b). We're Not Finished. *Christianity Today, 52* (May), 66.

Guthrie, Stan. (2008c). Why Evangelize the Jews? *Christianity Today, 52* (March), 76.

Guthrie, Stan. (2009). The Other Side of Church Growth. *Christianity Today, 53* (March), 52–54.

Guthrie, Stan, and Wendy Murray Zoba. (2002). Double Jeopardy. *Christianity Today, 46* (July 8), 26–32.

Hackett, Erna. (2017). Why I Stopped Talking about Racial Reconciliation and Started Talking about White Supremacy (August 23). http://feistythoughts.com/2017/08/23/why-i-stopped-talking-about-racial-reconciliation-and-started-talking-about-white-supremacy/.

Hagee, Diana. (2007). Christians United for Israel Washington, DC, Israel Summit 2007. *Torch, 1* (October), 10–22.

Hagee, John. (2005). The Lord Has Chosen Zion. *Charisma, 31* (October), 68–71.

Hagee, John. (2007a). CUFI and the Peace Process. *Torch, 1* (October), 6–7.

Hagee, John. (2007b). Israel's Holy Covenant. *Charisma Israel, 32* (June), 10.

Haggard, Ted. (1999). Penetrating the Darkness of Islam. *Charisma, 24* (May), 52.

Hall, Stuart. 1988. *The Hard Road to Renewal*. London: Verso.

Hall of Shame. (2010). *World, 25* (January 30), 10.

Hamilton, Michael. (2016). The Past and Its Sins. *World, 36–37* (May 14), 35.

Han, Sora. (2002). *Veiled Threats*. Houston, TX: American Studies Association Conference.

Hansen, Collin. (2005). Bush Comes to Calvin. *Christianity Today, 49* (July), 13.

Hansen, Collin. (2007a). Pastor Provocateur. *Christianity Today, 51* (September), 44–49.

Hansen, Collin. (2007b). Tethered to the Center. *Christianity Today, 51* (October), 70–71.

Hansen, Collin. (2008a). The Elusive Middle. *Christianity Today, 52* (April), 71.

Hansen, Collin. (2008b). Fire and Nice. *Christianity Today, 52* (October), 60–65.

Hansen, Collin. (2008c). Not Easy to Command. *Christianity Today, 52* (March), 19.

Hardage, Jeanette. (2004). Witnesses amid War. *Christianity Today, 48* (July), 67–68.

Harlan, Mark. (2003). A Middle Way in the Middle East. *Christianity Today, 47* (April), 84–85.

Harmon, Cedric. (2000). Deliver from Voodoo's Spell. *Charisma, 26* (October), 78–82.

Harper, Lisa Sharon. (2014). The Other Lie (September 9). http://rachelheldevans.com/blog/the-other-lie-lisa-sharon-harper-ferguson.

Harper, Lisa Sharon. (2015). A History of (Non)Violence (December 1). https://sojo.net/tags/bus-boycott.

Harper, Lisa Sharon. (2016). Open Letter to the Leadership of #Urbana15 and

InterVarsity Christian Fellowship (January 5). https://sojo.net/articles/open-letter-leadership-urbana15-and-InterVarsity-christian-fellowship.

Harris, Alisa. (2007a). Mile-High Hope. *World, 22* (September 1/8), 48–49.

Harris, Alisa. (2007b). This Big Light of Mine. *World, 22* (September 1/8), 22–23.

Harris, Alisa. (2008a). A Black Man's Dilemma. *World, 23* (October 4/11), 58–59.

Harris, Alisa. (2008b). Role Model in Chief. *World, 23* (November 29/December 6), 49.

Harris, Alisa. (2008c). Stealth Treaty. *World, 23* (February 23/March 1), 68–69.

Harris, Alisa. (2008d). Talking Is Cheap. *World, 23* (November 29/December 6), 55.

Harris, Alisa. (2009a). Hitting Home. *World, 24* (February 28), 34–39.

Harris, Alisa. (2009b). Show Me the Money. *World, 24* (February 28), 48.

Harris, Alisha. (2010). Homecoming. *World, 25* (February 13), 38–39.

Harris, Alisa. (2011a). Restricted Areas. *World, 26* (February 12), 54–56.

Harris, Alisa. (2011b). Trafficking Cops. *World, 26* (January 29), 46–48.

Harris, Cheryl. (2011). Critical Ethnic Studies Conference. Plenary Address. University of California, Riverside.

Harris, Paula, and Doug Schaupp. (2004). *Being White*. Downer's Grove, IL: InterVarsity Press.

Hartman, Saidiya. (1997). *Scenes of Subjection*. New York: Oxford University Press.

Hartsock, Nancy. (1990). Foucault on Power: A Theory for Women? In Linda Nicholson (ed.), *Feminism and Postmodernism* (pp. 157–75). New York: Routledge.

Hartwig, Mark. (2001). Portrait of a Terrorist. *Focus on the Family Citizen, 15* (November), 24–25.

Hartwig, Mark. (2002). Spread by the Sword? *Focus on the Family Citizen, 16* (February), 26–29.

Haugen, Gary. (2005). *Terrify No More*. Nashville: W Publishing Group.

Haugen, Gary. (2007). On a Justice Mission. *Christianity Today, 51* (March), 40–43.

Hawkins, B. Denise. (1995). Shoutin' from the Housetops. *Charisma, 20* (June), 23–29.

Hayford, Jack. (2013). Israel in Target. *Charisma, 39* (October), 20–26.

Hedrick, Gary. (2001). The Truth about the Palestinian Problem. *Message of the Christian Jew* (May–June), 1–3, 11.

Heltzel, Peter Goodwin. (2009). *Jesus and Justice: Evangelicals, Race, and American Politics*. New Haven: Yale University Press.

Hemingway, Mollie Ziegler. (2009). California's Temper Tantrum. *Christianity Today, 53* (February), 52.

Henry, Carl F. H. (1987). Lost Momentum. *Christianity Today, 31* (September 4), 30–32.

Henry, Carl F. H., and Richard Mouw. (1991). Preaching Christ or Packaging Jesus. *Christianity Today, 35* (February 11), 29–40.

Hermann, Andrew. (1995). Anti-Welfare Stance Makes Her "Star of Right." *American Family Association Journal, 19* (June), 18.

Herndon, Ernest. (2005a). Healing in the Delta. *Charisma, 30* (July), 62–66.

Herndon, Ernest. (2005b). Mississippi Reporter Draws Inspiration from Faith. *Charisma, 31* (October), 32–34.

Hertzke, Allen. (2004). *Freeing God's Children*. Oxford: Rowman & Littlefield.

Hewitt, Hugh. (2005a). Bush and the Borders. *World, 20* (March 26), 9.

Hewitt, Hugh. (2005b). New McCarthyism. *World, 17* (April 30), 9.

Hewitt, Hugh. (2006). Dressing Up Hate. *World, 21* (May 20), 9.

Hickey, Marilyn. (1997). A Journey Underground. *Charisma, 22* (January), 39–41.

Hickey, Marilyn. (2007). My Israel Adventure. *Charisma Israel, 32* (June), 18.

Hinn, Benny. (2009). The Fig Tree Is in Bloom. *Charisma, 35* (October), 40–44.

Hoang, Bethany Hanke, and Kristen Deede Johnson. (2016). Hope in a World of Rape for Profit. *Christianity Today, 60* (January–February), 67.

Hoffman, Derek. (2005). The Risks of Regime Change. *Christianity Today, 49* (April), 84–86.

Hoffmann, Stephen. (2004). Civilizations and World Order. *Fides et Historia, 36* (Summer/Fall), 116–19.

Hollywood's Race Problem. (2014). *Relevant* (September/October), 20.

Horner, S. Sue. (2002). Trying to Be God in the World: The Story of the Evangelical Women's Caucus and the Crisis over Homosexuality. In Rosemary Radford Ruether (ed.), *Gender, Ethnicity and Religion* (pp. 99–124). Minneapolis: Augsburg Fortress.

Horowitz, Michael, and T. Jeremy Gunn. (2003a). Breaking Chains. *Christianity Today, 47* (March), 46–54.

Horowitz, Michael, and T. Jeremy Gunn. (2003b). Breaking Chains II. *Christianity Today, 47* (April), 88–89.

Horrobin, Peter. (2008). Beware of Strange Fire. *Charisma, 34* (October), 55–58.

Hotel Sudan Isn't a Film—Yet. (2005). *Christianity Today, 49* (May), 26–27.

Hot Sauce for Haiti. (2010). *Charisma, 36* (September), 18.

House Divided. (2007). *World, 22* (November 24), 7.

How America Decides. (2008). *Time, 172* (August 18), 44.

How Can North Americans Help Evangelize Mexico? (1986). *Christianity Today, 30* (September 5), 45.

How Far Is Too Far? (2002). *World, 17* (March 2), B1.

How the Liberals Are Rewriting History. (1995). *Phyllis Schlafly Report, 28* (March), 4.

Hubers, John. (2004). Christian Zionism and Ecumenical Relations. *Perspectives, 19* (August/September), 13–16.

Hughes, Paul. (2008). Continental Divide. *Christianity Today, 52* (February), 14–15.

Hull, Chris. (1997). Diversity Quest. *Journal of Christian Camping, 29* (January–February), 10–16.

Hulsman, Cornelis. (2004). Bad Cops. *Christianity Today, 48* (September), 28.

Hulsman, Cornelis. (2008). The Peacebuilding Prince. *Christianity Today, 52* (February), 64–65.

Hulsman, Kees. (2000). 20 Coptic Christians Die as Village Tensions Flare. *Christianity Today, 44* (February 7), 31–33.

Hulsman, Kees. (2001). Religious Freedom Delegation Gets Cold Shoulder. *Christianity Today, 45* (May 21), 28–29.

Human Race. (2009). *World, 24* (July 18), 11.

Human Rights Watch. (1998). *Shielded From Justice.* New York: Human Rights Watch.

Hunter, Joel. (2004). The New Gender Wars. *New Man, 11* (May/June), 28–35.

Huntington, Samuel P. (2000). The Clash of Civilizations? In L. Crothers and C. Lockhart (eds.), *Culture and Politics* (pp. 99–118). New York: Palgrave Macmillan.

Hutchens, Trudy. (1995). Is the Church Ready for Welfare Reform? *Family Voice, 17* (October), 4–13.

Hutchins, Derrick. (2008). Why I Support Barack Obama. *Charisma*, 34 (October), 37.

Hutchinson, Mark. (1998). It's a Small Church after All. *Christianity Today*, 42 (November 16), 46–49.

Hutchinson, Mary. (2010). Groups Plan Long-Term Relief for Haiti. *Charisma*, 35 (March), 18.

Hutchinson, Mary. (2011). A Home for Stella. *Charisma*, 36 (February), 30–34.

Hyeok, Kang [pseud.]. (2004). The Nightmare of North Korea. *Christianity Today*, 48 (October), 38–42.

Hymowitz, Craig. (1995). Civil Rights Endgame. *Rutherford*, 4 (May), 17.

Imprisoned Chinese House-Church Leader Admits Guilt. (2007). *Charisma*, 33 (October), 37.

In Box. (2002). *New Man*, 9 (March/April), 8–11.

Incite (ed.) (2007). *The Revolution Will Not Be Funded: Beyond the Non-Profit Industrial Complex*. Cambridge, MA: South End Press.

Iraq Church Attacks. (2008). *World*, 24 (August 1), 10.

Isais, Juan. (1998). Mexico: Out of the Salt Shaker. *Christianity Today*, 42 (November 16), 72–73.

Israeli, Albert. (2001). Can We Speed Up the Second Coming? *Message of the Christian Jew* (May–June), 4–7, 14.

Is There Anything Wrong with Voting for a Mormon for President? (2012). *Christianity Today*, 56 (September), 74–75.

I Was a Stranger. (2007). *Christianity Today*, 51 (September), 96.

Jackson, Harry. (2004). A Cultural Exchange. *Charisma*, 29 (June), 94.

Jackson, Harry, Jr. (2005a). Farrakhan's Crusade. *Charisma*, 31 (September), 14.

Jackson, Harry, Jr. (2005b). The New American Dream. *Charisma*, 30 (February), 14.

Jackson, Harry, Jr. (2006). A New Movement for Justice. *Charisma*, 31 (March), 79.

Jackson., Harry, Jr. (2008a). The Changing Black Vote. *Charisma*, 34 (October), 18.

Jackson, Harry, Jr. (2008b). Why I Am for John McCain. *Charisma*, 34 (October), 36.

Jackson, Harry, Jr. (2016). Is Donald Trump Really a Racist? *Charisma*, 42 (September), 72.

Jackson, Harry, Jr., and Tony Perkins. (2008). *Personal Faith, Public Policy*. Lake Mary, FL: FrontLine.

Jackson, Zakiya. (n.d.). Love Is Not Colorblind, It Keeps Us Reckoning with Wrongs. http://thesaltcollective.org/love-is-not-colorblind-it-keeps-us-reckoning-with-wrongs/.

Jacobs, Adrian. (1998). *Aboriginal Christianity: The Way It Was Meant to Be*. Rapid City, SD: Self-published.

Jacobs, Adrian. (1999). *Pagan Prophets and Heathen Believers*. Rapid City, SD: Self-published.

Jamal, Amaney A., and Nadine Naber, eds. (2008). *Race and Arab Americans before and after 9/11: From Invisible Citizens to Visible Subjects*. Syracuse, NY: Syracuse University Press.

James, Kay. (1987). Enlisting Blacks in the Battle against Abortion. *Christianity Today*, 31 (October 2), 65–66.

James, Kay Cole. (1992). *Never Forget*. Grand Rapids, MI: Zondervan.

Jankowski, Jonathan. (1999). Reconciliation—Walking the Walk. *Faith Today*, 17 (March/April), 32–33.

Jefferson, Rich. (2001). The War for Reparations. *Focus on the Family Citizen*, 15 (February), 25.

Jenkins, Jack. (2016). A List of Faith Leaders Calling Out the Religious Right for Failing to Abandon Trump. *ThinkProgress* (October 9). https://thinkprogress.org/a-list-of-faith-leaders-calling-out-the-religious

-right-for-failing-to-abandon-trump-7a2ee8fb26e6#.9woop3528.

Jenkins, Philip. (2014). On the Edge of Extinction. *Christianity Today, 58* (November), 36–42.

Jennings, Willie James. (2015). The Fuller Difference: To Be a Christian Intellectual. *Fuller Magazine* (4), 50–51.

Jesus Freak. (2002). *Christianity Today, 46* (November 18), 58–60.

Jewell, Dawn Herzog. (2007). Red Light Rescue. *Christianity Today, 51* (January), 28–37.

A Jewish Awakening? (2010). *Charisma, 36* (October), 50–54.

John, Kaleem. (2000). Christians and the Blasphemy Laws in Pakistan. *Transformation, 17* (January–March), 20–23.

Johnson, Jan. (1992). L.A. Grace. *Christianity Today, 36* (June 22), 35.

Johnson, J. Carter. (2006a). Deliver Us from Kony. *Christianity Today, 50* (January), 30–37.

Johnson, J. Carter. (2006b). Gridlock on Genocide. *Christianity Today, 50* (May), 22–23.

Johnson, Peter. (1998). Forty on the Street Years. *Charisma, 23* (February), 39–44, 96.

Johnson, Peter. (2002a). How One Woman Challenged Oppression. *Charisma, 27* (April), 77–85.

Johnson, Peter. (2002b). New York's Homeless Pastor. *Charisma, 28* (December), 60–65.

Johnson, Peter. (2003a). The Latinos Are Coming. *Charisma, 28* (March), 58–64.

Johnson, Peter. (2003b). Ministry Reaches Growing Homeless Population in New York City. *Charisma, 28* (June), 22.

Johnson, Peter. (2004). British Evangelist Treks across United States Repenting for Slavery. *Charisma, 29* (April), 39.

Johnson, Peter. (2006a). Coming to America. *Charisma, 31* (April), 98–112.

Johnson, Peter. (2006b). Foreign Workers Flock to Worship Services in China. *Charisma, 31* (April), 40–41.

Johnson, Peter. (2008). David Wilerson's Amazing Challenge. *Charisma, 33* (July), 40–46.

Johnson, Steve. (1989). Rushdie Furor Highlights the Nature of Islamic Faith. *Christianity Today, 33* (April 7), 38.

Johnson, Sylvester. (2004). *The Myth of Ham in Nineteenth-Century American Christianity: Race, Heathens, and the People of God.* New York: Palgrave Macmillan.

Jones, Bob, III. (2003a). Truth or CAIR. *World, 18* (March 22), 16–19.

Jones, Bob, III. (2003b). The War That Never Ends. *World, 18* (May 31), 16–19.

Jones, Bob, III. (2004a). Man of Faith, Man of the Hour. *Christianity Today, 19* (November 13), 18–23.

Jones, Bob, III. (2004b). Minority Report. *World, 19* (August 21), 20–21.

Jones, Bob, III. (2004c). Stolen Base. *World, 19*, 20–21.

Jones, Bob, IV. (1996a). New Curtain. *World, 12* (October 18), 12–15.

Jones, Bob, IV. (1996b). Time to Retool the "Race Industry." *World, 11* (September 14), 16–17.

Jones, Bob, IV. (1998a). Mrs. Taylor's Neighborhood. *World, 13* (May 16), 12–14.

Jones, Bob, IV. (1998b). Shouting Down Christians. *World, 13* (December 19), 14–17.

Jones, Bob, IV. (1998c). True Colors. *World, 13* (October 31), 14–17.

Jones, Melanie. (1999). Messianic Jews in Alabama Take Bold Stand for Christ amid Opposition. *Charisma, 24* (May), 17–18.

Jones, Robert P. (2016). *The End of White Christian America.* New York: Simon & Schuster.

Jones, Robert P. (2018). The End of White Christian America: Understanding America's Identity Crisis. PRRI

(September 14). https://www.prri.org/end-white-christian-america/.
Jones, Tony. (2007). A Hopeful Faith. In Doug Pagitt and Tony Jones (eds.), *An Emergent Manifesto of Hope* (pp. 129–30). Grand Rapids, MI: Baker Books.
Jones, William. (1973). *Is God a White Racist?* Garden City: Anchor Books.
Joseph, Miranda. (2004). *Against the Romance of Community*. Minneapolis: University of Minnesota Press.
June, Lee N. (1996). *Men to Men*. Grand Rapids: Zondervan.
Juster, Daniel. (2008). Why Israel Still Matters. *World, 33* (May), 64–67, 137.
Justice, Jessilyn. (2015). As ISIS Targets Christianity, Godly Warriors Arise. *Charisma, 40* (May), 15.
Justice, Jessilyn. (2016). Setting the Sex-Trafficked Captives Free. *Charisma, 41* (June), 38–46.
Kaba, Mariame. (2014). Indicting a System, Not a Man (November 16). http://www.usprisonculture.com/blog/2014/11/16/indicting-a-system-not-a-man/.
Kanafani, Nancy. (2016). Transformed. *Charisma, 42* (November), 36–46.
Kantzer, Kenneth. (1989). Has the Melting Pot Stopped Melting? *Christianity Today, 33* (March 3), 40–42.
Karha, Kristian. (2002). Death-Row Christian May Hang for "Blasphemy." *Christianity Today, 46* (June 10), 24–25.
Karwur, Samuel. (2009). Post-Election Persecution? *Charisma, 34* (July), 19.
Katz, Robert, and June Cheng. (2016). Struck Down, Standing Fast. *World, 31* (June 11), 46–49.
Kauffman, Richard. (1997). Apostle to the City. *Christianity Today, 41* (March 3), 36–40.
Kazanjian, David. (2003). *The Colonizing Trick*. Minneapolis: University of Minnesota Press.
Keefauver, Larry. (2000). A Season in Miracles. *Charisma, 25* (January), 68–70, 106.
Keefauver, Larry. (2005). Pastor Builds 12,000-Seat "Holy Stadium" in Muslim Stronghold. *Charisma, 30* (April), 23.
Keener, Craig. (2003). Some New Testament Invitations to Ethnic Reconciliation. *Evangelical Quarterly, 75* (July), 195–213.
Keener, Craig. (2004). Mutual Mayhem. *Christianity Today, 48* (November), 60–64.
Kehnemui Liss, Sharon. (2007). Christian Group Warns U.S. against Pressuring Israel on Peace Deal. Fox News (July 30). https://www.foxnews.com/printer_friendly_story/0,3566,291330,00.html.
Kempadoo, Kamala. (2005). Victims and Agents of Crime: The New Crusade against Trafficking. In Julia Sudbury (ed.), *Global Lockdown* (pp. 35–56). New York: Routledge.
Kennedy, D. James. (1996). *The Gates of Hell Shall Not Prevail*. Nashville: Thomas Nelson Publishers.
Kennedy, John. (1996). NAE Issues "Evangelical Manifesto." *Christianity Today, 40* (April 8), 101.
Kennedy, John. (1998). Cuba's Next Revolution. *Christianity Today, 42* (January 12), 18–25.
Kennedy, John. (2002). NAE Rethinks Mission. *Christianity Today, 46* (April 22), 18.
Kennedy, John. (2004). Quake Opens Door to Gospel. *Christianity Today, 48* (March), 19.
Kennedy, John. (2005). Big Dream in Little Rock. *Christianity Today, 49* (April), 42–43.
Kennedy, John. (2008). Preach and Reach. *Christianity Today, 52* (October), 26–30.
Kennedy, John. (2009). The Ultimate Kibitzer. *Christianity Today, 53* (February), 32–35.

Kennedy, John W. (1994). Deeper Than a Handshake. *Christianity Today, 38* (December 12), 62–63.

Khang, Kathy. (2014). #Ferguson Is More Than a Hashtag. Blog (August 21). http://www.kathykhang.com/2014/08/21/ferguson-is-more-than-a-hashtag/.

Khang, Kathy. (2015). In Times of Dire Distress (January 20). https://sojo.net/articles/faith-action/times-dire-distress.

Khang, Kathy. (2016). Mental Health, AAPI Awareness Month, and Being All of Me (May 19). http://www.kathykhang.com/2016/05/19/mental-health-aapi-awareness-month/.

Khang, Kathy. (2018). *Raise Your Voice*. Downer's Grove, IL: InterVarsity Press.

Killing Christians. (2008). *World, 23* (November 1/8), 10.

Killjoy Prophets. (2014a). Killjoy Prophets: Shalom, Palestine and Our Uncle CUFI (December 26). http://www.patheos.com/blogs/emergentvillage/2014/12/killjoy-prophets-shalom-palestine-and-our-uncle-cufi/.

Killjoy Prophets. (2014b). Killjoy Prophets: Troubling and Broadening Our Visions of Liberation (September 26). http://www.patheos.com/blogs/emergentvillage/2014/09/killjoy-prophets-troubling-and-broadening-our-visions-of-liberation/ (no longer available).

Kilpatrick, Joel. (1999). Breaking through America's Bamboo Curtain. *Charisma, 24* (June), 46–54.

Kilpatrick, Joel. (2002). The Spirit's Wind Blows in Hawaii. *Charisma, 27* (January), 60–64.

Kilpatrick, Joel. (2007). A Church of Many Colors. *Charisma, 33* (August), 35–39, 78.

Kilpatrick, Joel. (2008). A Martyr's Cry. *Charisma, 33* (June), 40–44, 77.

Kilpatrick, Kate. (2014). U.S.-Mexico Border Wreaks Havoc on Lives of an Indigenous Desert Tribe. *Al Jazeera* (May 25). http://america.aljazeera.com/articles/2014/5/25/us-mexico-borderwreakshavocwithlivesofanindigenousdesertpeople.html.

Kim, Jodi. (2010). *The Ends of Empire*. Minneapolis: University of Minnesota Press.

King, Jeff. (1998). Global March for Jesus in May Focused on the Persecuted Church. *Charisma, 24* (August), 18–22.

King, Jeff. (2000). The Exodus Continues. *Charisma, 26* (November), 77–83.

King, Sheldon. (1997). We Must Come Together. *New Man, 4* (January/February), 24.

King, Thomas. (2013). Growth Spurth. *World, 28* (June 15), 82.

Kintz, Linda. (1997). *Between Jesus and the Market*. Durham, NC: Duke University Press.

Kisuke, Connie. (1998). Sudanese Christians Bloody, but Unbowed. *Christianity Today, 42* (August 10), 24–25.

Klinghoffer, David. (2006). *Why the Jews Rejected Jesus: The Turning Point in Western History*. New York: Harmony.

Knippers, Diane. (1997). A Global Scandal. *Christianity Today, 41* (September 1), 58–59.

Knippers, Diane. (1998–1999). Violence, Ideology and Policy. *Faith and Freedom, 18* (Winter), 8.

Kondo, Dorinne. (1997). *About Face*. New York: Routledge.

Kraft, Charles. (1991). Receptor-Oriented Ethics in Cross-Cultural Intervention. *Transformation, 8* (January/March), 20–25.

Kremida, Damaris. (2009). Martyrs Killed by Conspiracy. *Christianity Today, 53* (July), 14.

Kuo, David. (2006). *Tempting Faith: An Inside Story of Political Seduction*. New York: Simon and Schuster.

Kuo, David. (2007). Q&A. *Christianity Today, 51* (January), 23.

Kure, Maikudi, and Josiah Idowu-Fearon. (2000). Evangelism among Muslims. *Transformation, 17* (January–March), 17–19.

Labberton, Mark. (2015). Love Matters. *Fuller Magazine* (4), 6–9.

Lakshmanan, Indira. (2008). Obama Wins Young Evangelical Voters in Battleground-State Push (July 28). http://www.bloomberg.com/apps/news?pid =newsarchive&sid=a2ZeHlUH_N7A (no longer available).

Lamer, Timothy. (2005a). Gulf Lore. *World, 20* (September 24), 35.

Lamer, Timothy. (2005b). Operation Offset. *World, 20* (October 1), 18–19.

Lamer, Timothy. (2006). Cruel to Be Kind. *World, 21* (August 12), 29.

Land, Richard. (2001). Rising from the Ashes of Racism. *World, 32* (August 25), 31–34.

Land, Richard. (2007). *The Divided States of America*. Nashville: Thomas Nelson Publishers.

Landers, McBride. (1999). Cuban Catholics Make Gains but Protestant Rights Limited. *Christianity Today, 43* (February 8), 18.

Lane, Gary. (2005). Walking with Christ in Laos. *Voice of the Martyrs* (June), 3–8.

LaPlante, Matthew. (2011). Ethiopia's River of Death. *Christianity Today, 55* (August), 40–44.

Larson, Bob. (1989). *Larson's New Book of Cults*. Wheaton, IL: Tyndale Press.

Latter-Day Politics. (2007). *Christianity Today, 51* (September), 74–77.

Lawrence, Bonita, and Enakshi Dua. (2005). Decolonizing Antiracism. *Social Justice, 32* (4), 121–43.

Lawson, Steven. (1999). Racism against Asians Was Focus of September Prayer Event in California. *Charisma, 25* (December), 26.

Lawton, Kim. (1989). An Elusive Peace. *Christianity Today, 33* (April 21), 34–37.

Lawton, Kim. (1991). Churches Enlist in the War on Drugs. *Christianity Today, 35* (February 11), 44–49.

Lawton, Kim. (1995). Killed in the Line of Duty. *Charisma, 21* (October), 54–58.

Lawton, Kim. (1996). The Persecuted Church Stands Faithful. *Christianity Today, 40* (July 15), 3, 54–64.

Lawton, Kim. (1997). Faith without Borders. *Christianity Today, 41* (May 19), 38–49.

Lawton, Kim. (1998). Saying No: One Church's War on Drugs. *Christianity Today, 32* (October 7), 46.

Leaders Wrestle with Faith and War. (1991). *Christianity Today, 35* (February 11), 50.

LeBlanc, Jeanine. (2005). Walking "The Good Red Road": NAIITS, the Obstacles It Faces and How They Are Being Overcome. *NAIITS Journal, 6*, 5–20.

LeBlanc, Terry. (2000). Compassionate Community—or Unchecked Greed? *Mission Frontiers, 22* (September), 21.

LeClaire, Jennifer. (2010). Pat Robertson Gives Nod to Marijuana Legalization. *Charisma Online* (December 10). http://www.charismamag.com/index .php/news/29827-pat-robertson-gives -nod-to-marijuana-legalization (no longer available).

LeClaire, Jennifer. (2016a). Waging Spiritual Warfare over Israel. *Charisma, 42* (September), 46–48.

LeClaire, Jennifer. (2016b). Will We Make the Right Decision? *Charisma, 42* (September), 44–48.

Lee, Audrey. (2011). When Muslims See Jesus. *Charisma, 37* (September), 34–38.

Lee, Helen. (1995). Racial Reconciliation Tops NAE's Agenda. *Christianity Today, 39* (April 3), 97.

Lee, Helen. (1996). Silent Exodus. *Christianity Today, 40* (August 12), 50–53.

Lee, Helen. (2014). Silent No More. *Christianity Today, 58* (October), 38–47.

Lee, Morgan. (2016a). Life after Prison. *Christianity Today, 60* (September), 38–47.

Lee, Morgan. (2016b). Wheaton Faculty Council Unanimously Asks College to Keep Larycia Hawkins (January 21). http://www.christianitytoday.com/gleanings/2016/january/wheaton-faculty-council-asks-college-keep-larycia-hawkins.html.

Lee, Ron. (1986). Training the World's Evangelists. *Christianity Today, 30* (September 5), 43.

Lee, Sophia. (2014). A Nation at Risk. *World, 29* (December 27), 44–48.

Lee, Sophia. (2015a). Friends and Strangers. *World, 30* (August 22), 38–43.

Lee, Sophia. (2015b). Mosque for the "Unmosqued." *World, 30* (May 30), 65–66.

Lee, Sophia. (2016a). Straight Outta El Barrio. *World, 31* (April 19), 50–53.

Lee, Sophia. (2016b). Way Up North. *World, 41* (31), 48–53.

Leggett, Marshall. (2003). Christianity on the Shelf. *Christian Standard, 138* (March 9), 8–10.

Lehman, Mel. (2000). Death by Sanctions. *Christianity Today, 44* (October 2), 29.

Lehmann, Christine. (1991). Few Gains for Minorities. *Christianity Today, 35* (November 11), 54.

Leonard, Thomas. (n.d.). A Not-So-"Petit" Story of Colonialism and Capitalism. http://www.valuesandcapitalism.com/petit-story-colonialism-capitalism/ (no longer available).

Leslie, R., Jr. (1996). Keeping Their Promises: African American Men and the Promise Keepers. American Academy of Religion Conference. Lecture.

Let's Talk—Seriously. (2009). *Christianity Today, 53* (February), 18–19.

Letters. (1985a). *Christianity Today, 29* (November 22), 7.

Letters. (1985b). *Christianity Today, 29* (December 13), 10–11.

Letters. (1992). *Christianity Today, 36* (December), 5.

Letters. (1997). *Charisma, 22* (July), 8–12.

Letters. (1999). *Charisma, 24* (February), 8–10.

Letters. (2000). *Christianity Today, 44* (November 13), 12–21.

Letters. (2001a). *Charisma, 26* (January), 10–12.

Letters. (2001b). *Christianity Today, 45* (December 3), 7–13.

Letters. (2002a). *Christianity Today, 46* (April 22), 8–10.

Letters. (2002b). *Christianity Today, 46* (June 10), 10–12.

Letters. (2004a). *Charisma, 29* (April), 8–11.

Letters. (2004b). *Charisma, 29* (June), 8–12.

Letters. (2004c). *Charisma, 30* (November), 8–9, 90.

Letters. (2004d). *Charisma, 30* (December), 10–11, 74.

Letters. (2005). *Charisma, 30* (February), 8–9, 74.

Letters. (n.d.). *Cornerstone, 25* (108), 4, 12.

Letters to the Editor. (1998). *Christianity Today, 42* (January 12), 8.

Leveling the Investment Fund. (2006). *Christianity Today, 50* (August), 15.

Lewis, Christopher. (2008). Looking for Home. *Christianity Today, 52* (September), 68–73.

Lewis, Greg. (1995). *The Power of a Promise Kept*. Dallas: Word Books.

Lewis, James. (2002). Does God Hear Muslim Prayers? *Christianity Today, 46* (February 4), 30–31.

Liberating Evangelicalism. (2019). Liberating Evangelicalism: Decentering Whiteness. http://www.liberatingevangelicalism.org.

Lienesch, Michael. (1993). *Redeeming*

America. Chapel Hill: University of North Carolina Press.

Liew, Vicky. (2003). For the Love of Chinatown. *Charisma, 29* (December), 23–26.

LifeWay Church Resources (ed.). (2004). *Far-Out Far East Rickshaw Rally (Racing to the Son)*. Nashville: Lifeway.

Lightbody, C. Stuart. (1992). Canada's Multicultural Mosaic. *Alliance Witness, 127*, 10–11.

Lindner, John. (1997a). Muslims Target Indonesian Churches. *Charisma, 22* (June), 24–26.

Lindner, John. (1997b). "Sparkling" Women Challenge India's Demonic Darkness. *Charisma, 22* (February), 32–33.

Lindner, John. (2000). Reaching Hidden People. *Charisma, 25* (January), 62–66.

Lindner, John. (2008a). Christians Face New Wave of Violent Attacks in India. *Charisma, 34* (November), 19.

Lindner, John. (2008b). Christians Targeted in Violent Clashes in India. *Charisma, 33* (March), 27–28.

Listening to America's Ethnic Churches. (1989). *Christianity Today, 33* (March 3), 25–41.

Little, Stephen. (1997). Black Pastor Bridges Racial Chasm by Reaching North Carolina's Hispanics. *Charisma, 23* (September), 24–25.

Littleton, Samuel. (1999). Hmong Believers Suffer at Hands of Communist Regime in Vietnam. *Charisma, 24* (February), 30–32.

Lockett, Matt. (2014). How to End the Greatest Massacre in History. *Charisma, 39* (March), 32–33.

Loconte, Joseph. (1998). The Bully and the Pulpit. *Policy Review, 92* (November–December), 28–37.

Loconte, Joseph. (2007). The United Nations' Disarray. *Christianity Today, 51* (February), 40–42, 120.

Lombardo, Michele. (2005). Christians in Sri Lanka Face Attacks, Threats of Anti-Conversion Bills. *Charisma, 31* (August), 28–30.

Long, Carolyn. (2000). *Religious Freedom and Indian Rights: The Case of Oregon v. Smith*. Topeka: University of Kansas Press.

The Longest Hatred. (2004). *Christianity Today, 48* (April), 30–31.

Loren, Julia. (2007). African-American Pastor Breaks Tradition in Japan. *Charisma, 32* (June), 31–32.

Lotte, Bill. (1989). How to Meet the Needs of Immigrants, with a Bonus. *Evangelical Missions Quarterly, 25* (July), 256–60.

Loving People Who Are Different. (1986). *Alliance Witness, 121* (February 12), 31.

Lowe, Lisa. (1996). *Immigrant Acts*. Durham, NC: Duke University Press.

Lowe, Valerie. (2000). The History America Chose to Forget. *Charisma, 26* (November), 64–75.

Lowe, Valerie. (2001). Virginia Pastor Takes Bold Stance against Divorce, Racism in Richmond. *Charisma, 27* (November).

Lowe, Valerie. (2005). Transitional Home Offers "Refuge" to Downtrodden in Central Florida. *Charisma, 30* (February), 14.

Lowe, Valerie. (2006a). The Bishop's Campaign. *Charisma, 31* (February), 30–35.

Lowe, Valerie. (2006b). Grace So Amazing. *Charisma, 32* (October), 36–44.

Lowe, Valerie. (2008). Minister Starts "Post–Civil Rights Movement." *Charisma, 33* (June), 20–21.

Lowe, Valerie. (2009a). How to Plan Your Ultimate Israel Pilgrimage. *Charisma, 34* (June), 46–47.

Lowe, Valerie. (2009b). Voice for the Voiceless. *Charisma, 35* (August), 21–25.

Lu, Angela. (2010). Drawn by Grace. *World, 25* (December 18), 58–60.

Lu, Angela. (2011). Jeremy's Call. *World, 26* (February 12), 70.

Lu, Angela. (2013). Grand New Party? *World, 28* (November 2), 42–44.

Lu, Angela, and Brittany Smith. (2011). A Dream Deferred. *World, 26* (October 8), 54–58.

Lucado, Max. (2016). Decency for President (February 26). https://maxlucado.com/decency-for-president/.

Luck, Kenny. (2014). Sexual Atheism and the Christian Single. *Charisma, 39* (June), 44–46.

Luke, George. (2007). Legal Group Lobbies on Behalf of Christians in Pakistan. *Charisma, 32* (February), 21.

Lukins, Julian. (2003). Invading the Danger Zone. *Charisma, 29* (December), 56–59.

Lukins, Julian. (2004a). Behind the Black Veil. *Charisma, 29* (June), 62–66, 100.

Lukins, Julian. (2004b). When a Nation Is Shaken. *Charisma, 29* (June), 66.

Lukins, Julian. (2009). The Faith of Sarah Palin. *Charisma, 34* (January), 26–32.

Lupton, Bob. (1989). How To Create a Ghetto. *World Vision, 33* (October/November), 11.

Lutes, Chris. (1988). Everybody Always Stares: The Personal Side of Prejudice. *Campus Life, 46* (March), 62–66.

Lyons, Julie. (2007). My Secret Struggle. *Charisma, 32* (May), 62–66, 81.

MacHarg, Kenneth. (1999). Twenty-Five Pastors Killed This Year. *Christianity Today, 43* (October 4), 23.

MacHarg, Kenneth. (2000a). Death in the Night. *Christianity Today, 44* (June 12), 30–31.

MacHarg, Kenneth. (2000b). Healing the Violence. *Christianity Today, 44* (August 7), 30.

Maclean, Iain. (2004). Dangerous Memories, Daring Documents, and the Demands of Discipleship: The Christian Church, Racism and Racial Justice. *Missiology, 32* (January), 15–35.

Madison, Terry. (2001). September 11: Real Security in Jesus Christ. *Open Doors Newsbrief, 16* (December), 1.

Mahmood, Saba. (2011). *Politics of Piety*. Princeton, NJ: Princeton University Press.

Mailbag. (2005). *World, 20* (December 3), 50–52.

Mailbag. (2007a). *World, 22* (August 4), 48–49.

Mailbag. (2007b). *World, 22* (November 24), 39–41.

Mailbag. (2007c). *World, 22* (December 1), 39–40.

Mailbox. (2002). *World, 17* (March 30), 30–32.

Mains, Karen. (1994). Finally Listening. *Moody Monthly, 94* (May), 28.

Malachy, Yona. (1978). *American Fundamentalism and Israel: The Relation of Fundamentalist Churches to Zionism and the State of Israel*. Jerusalem: Institute of Contemporary Jewry, Hebrew University of Jerusalem.

Man Bites Dog. (1990). *Christianity Today, 34* (April 23), 42.

The Mandela Moment. (1990). *Christianity Today, 34* (April 23), 12.

Maol, Dan. (1989). Refugees Find Little Refuge. *Christianity Today, 33* (April 21), 40–41.

Maracle, Ross. (1991). Passing By on the Other Side. *Faith Today, 9* (July–August), 29.

Marino, Gordon. (1998). Me? Apologize for Slavery? *Christianity Today, 42* (October 5), 82–83.

Markovic, John Jovan. (2004). The Huntington Thesis. *Fides et Historia, 36* (Summer/Fall), 97–98.

Markovitz, Jonathan. (2015). "A Spectacle of Slavery Unwilling to Die": Curbing Reliance on Racial Stereotyping in Self-Defense Cases. *UC Irvine Law Review, 5* (873), 873–934.

Marsden, George. (1980). *Fundamentalism and American Culture*. Oxford: Oxford University Press.

Marshall, Paul. (1995). World Council Racism Stand Gives New Weapon to Rights Abusers. *Faith and Freedom, 15* (Summer), 11.

Marshall, Paul. (1997). *Their Blood Cries Out*. Nashville: Thomas Nelson.

Marshall, Paul. (2000). Correcting the Secular Vision. *Faith and Freedom, 19* (2), 10–11.

Marshall, Paul. (2006). The Problem with Prophets. *Christianity Today, 50* (September), 90–94.

Martey, Emmanuel. (1994). *African Theology*. Maryknoll, NY: Orbis.

Martin, William. (1996). *With God on Our Side*. New York: Pantheon Books.

Massey, Douglas, and Nancy Denton. (1993). *American Apartheid*. Cambridge, MA: Harvard University Press.

Mathewes-Green, Frederica. (1995). Sweet Mystery of Daisy. *World, 10* (November 4), 24.

Mathewes-Green, Frederica. (1999). Could We Survive Persecution? *Christianity Today, 43* (March 1), 68.

Matthews, Greg. (2003). Pablo's Prayer. *Decision, 44* (December), 32–33.

Maudlin, Michael. (1992). Now, That's Multicultural! *Christianity Today, 36* (January 13), 15.

Maust, John. (1985). The Land Where Spirits Thrive. *Christianity Today, 29* (December 13), 48–50.

Maust, John. (1992). Keeping the Faithful. *Christianity Today, 38* (April 6), 38.

Maust, John. (1993). Hispanics Eye Mission Role. *Christianity Today, 37* (October 25), 92.

Maxwell, Joe. (1991). Getting Out, Staying Out. *Christianity Today, 38* (July 22), 34–36.

Maxwell, Joe. (1993a). The Alien in Our Midst. *Christianity Today, 37* (December 13), 48–51.

Maxwell, Joe. (1993b). Educating Minorities at Christian Colleges: What Schools Are Doing Right. *Urban Family, 2* (Fall), 31–33.

Maxwell, Joe. (1994). Racial Healing in the Land of Lynching. *Christianity Today, 39* (January 10), 24–26.

Maxwell, Joe. (1995). We Must Do Better. *World, 10* (October 28), 12–16.

Maxwell, Joe. (1997). More Than Partners. *Christianity Today, 41* (May 19), 50, 57.

Maxwell, Joe, and Andrés Tapia. (1995). Guns and Bibles. *Christianity Today, 39* (June 19), 34–36, 45.

Mayfield, D. L. (2016). Tales of a Claiborne Again Christian. *Christianity Today, 60* (March), 40–44.

Maynard, Roy. (1994). Leaving the Fold. *World, 10* (October 15), 10–13.

Maynard, Roy. (1998). Jesus, King of the Jews. *World, 13* (June 27), 24.

Maynard, Roy. (1999). And How to Fight Back. *World, 14* (April 10), 20–21.

McAdam, Doug. (1982). *Political Process and the Development of Black Insurgency, 1930–1970* (2nd ed.). Chicago: University of Chicago Press.

McAdam, Lynn. (2004). Lessons from 9/11. *Evangelical Missions Quarterly, 40* (October), 418–19.

McCallum, Dennis. (1996). *The Death of Truth*. Minneapolis: Bethany House Publishers.

McClintock, Anne. (1995). *Imperial Leather*. New York: Routledge.

McDermott, Gerald. (2003). The Land. *Books and Culture, 9* (March/April), 8–9, 40–42.

McDermott, Gerald, and Ross McDermott. (2010). On the Jesus Trail. *Christianity Today, 54* (April), 30–35.

McDonald, Robin. (1992). Stretch Your Racial Comfort Zone. *Christianity Today, 36* (June 22), 14.

McKissic, William Dwight. (2008). Embracing the Spirit's Power. *Charisma, 33* (February), 20.

McKnight, Scot. (2007). Five Streams of the Emerging Church. *Christianity Today, 51* (February), 35–39.

McKnight, Scot. (2008). McLaren Emerging. *Christianity Today, 52* (September), 58–66.

McKnight, Scot. (2010). Rebuilding the Faith from Scratch. *Christianity Today, 54* (March), 59–61, 66.

McLaren, Brian. (2007a). *Everything Must Change.* Nashville: Thomas Nelson Publishers.

McLaren, Brian. (2007b). *A Generous Orthodoxy.* Grand Rapids, MI: Zondervan.

McLaren, Brian, and Duane Litfin. (2004). Emergent Evangelism. *Christianity Today, 48* (November), 42–43.

McNeil, Brenda Salter. (2013). Plenary Address: Justice Conference. Philadelphia, February 22, 2013.

McNeil, Brenda Salter, and Rick Richardson. (2004). *The Heart of Racial Justice.* Downer's Grove, IL: InterVarsity Press.

Mearsheimer, John, and Stephen Walt. (2007). *The Israel Lobby.* New York: Farrar, Straus & Giroux.

Medved, Michael. (2005). Turning Right? *World, 20* (June 25), 30–32.

Mei, Xu. (2006). The Price of Protest. *Christianity Today, 50* (October), 23.

Meral, Ziya. (2008). Bearing the Silence of God. *Christianity Today, 52* (March), 40–43.

Merdian, Wendy. (2016). Where Were You on 9/11? *World, 26* (September 10), 62–69.

Merrill, Dean. (1997). The Education of Ed Dobson. *Christianity Today, 41* (August 11), 26–30.

Merritt, Jonathan. (2011). A Tea Party Gospel. *Relevant* (January–February 1), 50–52.

Merritt, Jonathan. (2016). Marginalizing Russell Moore Is a Grave Mistake for Southern Baptists. *Religious News Service* (December 20). http://religionnews.com/2016/12/20/marginalizing-russell-moore-is-grave-mistake-for-southern-baptists/.

Metzger, Kedri, Mark Tooley, and Mathew Staver. (2013). How Should Churches and Seminaries Respond to Immigrant Pastors Who Minister in the United States Illegally? *Christianity Today, 57* (July/August), 76–77.

Metzger, Paul. (2012). *Connecting Christ.* Nashville: Thomas Nelson.

Metzger, Paul. (2013). White Theology, Part 1 (July 8). http://www.patheos.com/blogs/uncommongodcommongood/2013/07/white-theology-part-i/.

Mexico. (1994). *Rutherford, 3* (3), 16.

Michel, Jen Pollock. (2016). Death to the Death Penalty? *Christianity Today, 60* (June), 73–75.

Mihesuah, Devon, and Angela Cavender Wilson (eds.). (2004). *Indigenizing the Academy.* Lincoln: University of Nebraska Press.

Miles, Jonathan. (1999). Firebombs Bolster Prayers among Messianic Believers. *Christianity Today, 43* (May 24), 34–36.

Miles, Jonathan. (2008). Reconciling Christians. *Christianity Today, 52* (December), 30–31.

Miller, David. (1995). Revival behind Enemy Lines. *Charisma, 20* (January), 40–47.

Miller, David. (1996). Latin America's Sweeping Revival. *Charisma, 21* (June), 32–37.

Miller, David. (1998). Up from the Ashes? *Christianity Today, 49* (May 18), 40–43.

Miller, David. (2001). Divorcing a Dictator. *Christianity Today, 45* (February 5), 22–23.

Miller, David. (2002a). Christians to Help Investigate Crimes. *Christianity Today, 41* (January 7), 27.

Miller, David. (2002b). Rebels Kill Evangelical Pastors. *Christianity Today, 46* (September 9), 31.

Miller, David. (2003). Missionaries Flee Violence. *Christianity Today, 47* (January), 29.

Miller, Gregory. (2004). Toward Armageddon. *Fides et Historia, 36* (Summer/Fall), 110–15.

Miller, John. (1996). The Naturalizers. *Policy Review, 78* (July/August), 50–53.

Miller, Kevin. (1997a). NAE Rebuffs GOP Pressure. *Christianity Today, 41* (April 28), 77.

Miller, Kevin. (1997b). The Rich Christian. *Christianity Today, 41* (April 28), 68–69.

Miller, Rebecca. (2008). "Yes, We Can!" *World, 23* (April 19/26), 42.

Minchakpu, Obed. (2000a). Islamic Law Raises Tensions. *Christianity Today, 44* (January 10), 26.

Minchakpu, Obed. (2000b). Moving toward War? *Christianity Today, 44* (April 24), 29.

Minchakpu, Obed. (2001). Orphaned and Widowed. *Christianity Today, 45* (September 3), 34.

Minchakpu, Obed. (2002). Chronic Violence Claims 2,000 Lives. *Christianity Today, 46* (January 7), 23.

Minchakpu, Obed. (2004a). Back to the Basics. *Christianity Today, 48* (November), 62–63.

Minchakpu, Obed. (2004b). Eye for an Eye for an Eye. *Christianity Today, 48* (July), 17.

Minchakpu, Obed. (2004c). Human Sacrifice Redux. *Christianity Today, 48* (December), 22–24.

Minchakpu, Obed. (2006). Religious Riots Displace Nearly 5 Million in Nigeria. *Charisma, 32* (August), 28–30.

Minchakpu, Obed. (2008). A Kinder, Gentler Shari'ah? *Christianity Today, 52* (March), 24–25.

Mintle, Linda. (2004). The Gay Marriage Debate. *Charisma, 30* (November), 82.

Mission Mississippi. (n.d.). http://missionmississippi.org.

Misunderstanding Sarah. (2008). *Christianity Today, 52* (November), 23.

Mitri, Tarek. (2000). Who Are the Christians of the Arab World? *International Review of Mission, 59* (January), 12–27.

Moeller, Robert. (2007). Nothing but the Best. *World, 22* (September 1/8), 30–31.

Mohler, R. Albert, Jr. (1999). First for the Jew. *World, 13* (June 13), 21.

Mohler, R. Albert, Jr. (2002). A New Low? *World, 17* (April 6), 26.

Moll, Rob. (2004a). Four Missionaries Murdered. *Christianity Today, 48* (May), 18.

Moll, Rob. (2004b). Taliban II? *Christianity Today, 48* (March), 21.

Moll, Rob. (2005). The New Monasticism. *Christianity Today, 49* (September), 38–46.

Moll, Rob. (2014). The New Puritans. *Christianity Today, 58* (September), 66–70.

Mombo, Esther, and Samson Mwaluda. (2000). Relationship and Challenge in Kenya and East Africa. *Transformation, 17* (January/March), 36–41.

Moon, Ruth. (2011). Warning on Witchcraft. *Christianity Today, 55* (March), 12.

Moon, Ruth. (2014). Segregated Surveys. *Christianity Today, 58* (November), 20.

Moore, Art. (2001). U.S. Ally Jails House-Church Leaders. *Christianity Today, 45* (December 3), 27–28.

Moore, John. (1987). In the Name of Fear and Prejudice. *Moody Monthly, 87* (January), 16–18.

Moore, Russell. (2014). Transcript: Eric Garner and the Case for Justice (December 3). http://erlc.com/resource-library/articles/transcript-eric-garner-and-the-case-for-justice.

Moore, Russell. (2016a). After Orlando, Can We Still Weep Together? (June 12).

http://www.russellmoore.com/2016/06/12/orlando-can-still-weep-together/.

Moore, Russell. (2016b). Defending Our First Freedom. *Light Magazine*, 2 (Summer), 3.

Moore, Russell. (2016c). If Donald Trump Has Done Anything, He Has Snuffed Out the Religious Right. *Washington Post* (October 9). https://www.washingtonpost.com/news/acts-of-faith/wp/2016/10/09/if-donald-trump-has-done-anything-he-has-snuffed-out-the-religious-right/?utm_term=.998cf86d2087.

Moore, Russell. (2016d). A White Church No More. *New York Times* (May 6). https://www.nytimes.com/2016/05/06/opinion/a-white-church-no-more.html.

Morey, Robert A. (1992). *The Islamic Invasion: Confronting the World's Fastest Growing Religion*. Eugene, OR: Harvest House, 1992.

Morgan, Timothy. (1994a). Interracial Gathering Set. *Christianity Today, 39* (April 25), 50–51.

Morgan, Timothy. (1994b). NAE Reinvents Itself. *Christianity Today, 38* (April 4), 87.

Morgan, Timothy. (1995a). From One City to the World. *Christianity Today, 39* (April 24), 36–43.

Morgan, Timothy. (1995b). Southern Baptists: Racist No More? Black Leaders Ask. *Christianity Today, 39* (August 1), 53.

Morgan, Timothy. (1996). Youth Are Key in Moving Past "Feel Good" Reconciliation. *Christianity Today, 40* (November 11), 87–88.

Morgan, Timothy. (1997). Church of the Martyrs. *Christianity Today, 41* (August 11), 44–47, 57.

Morgan, Timothy. (2000). Prepared for Pilgrims? *Christianity Today, 44* (March 6), 26.

Morgan, Timothy. (2002). Theologians Decry "Narrow" Boundaries. *Christianity Today, 46* (June 10), 18.

Morgan, Timothy. (2008). After the Aloha Shirts. *Christianity Today, 52* (October), 42–45.

Morgan, Timothy. (2010). From Informant to Informer. *Christianity Today, 54* (June 13), 55.

Morgan, Timothy C. (2014). Why We're Losing the War on Poverty. *Christianity Today, 58* (January/February), 56–59.

Morgan, Timothy, and David Neff. (2004). The Vulnerable. *Christianity Today, 48* (April), 87–89.

Moring, Mark. (2011). A Black & White Production. *Christianity Today, 55* (October), 54–57.

Moring, Mark. (2012a). Class Activist. *Christianity Today, 56* (September), 31.

Moring, Mark. (2012b). Mercy-Full Nurse. *Christianity Today, 56* (September), 30.

Morley, Patrick. (2000). The Next Christian Men's Movement. *Christianity Today, 44* (September 4), 84–86.

Morrison, George. (2007). Obadiah's Warning: A Message for Today. *Torch, 1* (October), 36–38.

Morse, Anne. (2002). View from the Axis. *World, 17* (March 9), 20–25.

Mortimer, Curt. (n.d.). It's Not Easy Being Male. *Cornerstone, 25* (108), 17.

Morton, Jeff. (2011). But Is Islam a Religion of Peace? *Charisma, 37* (September), 44.

Morton, Tom. (1991). The Wages of War. *Christianity Today, 35* (March 11), 54–56, 59.

Mosques in Middle America. (2010). *Christianity Today, 54* (October), 53.

Mouw, Richard. (1997). To the Jew First. *Christianity Today, 41* (August 11), 12–13.

Mouw, Richard. (2001). The Chosen People Puzzle. *Christianity Today, 45* (March 5), 70–78.

Moya, Paula M. L. (1997). Postmodernism, "Realism," and the Politics of Idenity: Cherrie Moraga and Chicana Feminism. In Jacqui M. Alexander and Chandra Talpade Mohanty (eds.), *Feminist Genealogies Colonial Legacies, Democratic Futures* (pp. 125–50). New York: Routledge.

Mugyenzi, Solomon. (2000). Seeking Understanding in Uganda. *Transformation, 17* (January–March), 41–44.

Muller, Alfred. (2000). Messianic Ethiopians Face Discrimination. *Christianity Today, 44* (December 4), 29.

Mumper, Sharon. (1985). Resettlement Program Could Pave the Way for Outreach among Indonesian Muslims. *Christianity Today, 29* (Marcy 15), 37, 39.

Mumper, Sharon. (1986a). The Missionary That Needs No Visa. *Christianity Today, 30* (February 21), 24–26.

Mumper, Sharon. (1986b). Where in the World Is the Church Growing. *Christianity Today, 30* (July 11), 17–21.

Mundy, David Lee. (2004a). Christians Fear Violence in Ambon May Spur Another Religious Conflict. *Charisma, 29* (July), 32.

Mundy, David Lee. (2004b). Muslim-Christian Conflict in Nigeria Claims Thousands of Lives. *Charisma, 30* (October), 19.

Mundy, David Lee. (2005a). Chinese Christian Describes Torture, Coerced Testimony in Labor Camps. *Charisma, 30* (June), 26–27.

Mundy, David Lee. (2005b). Secret Government Report Reveals China's Plan to Oppose Christianity. *Charisma, 30* (February), 19.

Mundy, David Lee. (2006). Christian Leaders Urge U.S. to Support Israel. *Charisma, 32* (October), 26.

Mundy, David Lee, and Adrienne Gaines. (2004). Christians in Pakistan Face Increased Threat of Attacks. *Charisma, 29* (April), 22.

Mundy, David Lee. (2007). Who Will Cry for Justice? *Charisma, 32* (February), 50–54.

Muñoz, José Esteban. (1999). *Disidentifications*. Minneapolis: University of Minnesota Press.

Muslim Phobic No More. (2002). *Christianity Today, 46* (December 9), 28–29.

My People International. (2000). *Vacation Bible School Curriculum, Year 1, Book 1*. Evansburg, Alberta: My People International.

Myra, Harold, and Marshall Shelley. (2005). Jesus and Justice. *Christianity Today, 49* (August), 58–59.

NAE NBEA Groups Join to Condemn Racism. (1990). *Christianity Today, 34* (March 5), 35.

NAE Ouster. (2009). *World, 23* (December 27–January 3), 12.

Nash, Ronald. (1996). *Why the Left Is Not Right*. Grand Rapids, MI: Zondervan.

National Association of Evangelicals Denounces Church's Quran Burning Event. (2010). CNN *Belief Blog* (July 30). http://religion.blogs.cnn.com/2010/07/30/national-association-of-evangelicals-denounces-churchs-quran-burning-event/.

Neff, David. (1990a). God's Latino Revolution. *Christianity Today, 34* (May 14), 15.

Neff, David. (1990b). Love Thy (Arab) Neighbor. *Christianity Today, 34* (October 22), 22.

Neff, David. (1991). The Politics of Remembering. *Christianity Today, 35* (October 7), 28–29.

Neff, David. (1996). Our Extended, Persecuted Family. *Christianity Today, 40* (April 29), 14–15.

Neff, David. (1997a). Dare We Be Colorblind? *Christianity Today, 41* (February 3), 14–15.

Neff, David. (1997b). Progress for the Persecuted. *Christianity Today, 41* (October 6), 19.

Neff, David. (1999). A Call To Evangelical Unity. *Christianity Today, 43* (June 14), 49–56.

Neff, David. (2002). Visible Man. *Christianity Today, 46* (December 9), 54–55.

Neff, David. (2003). Thugs in Jesus' Hometown. *Christianity Today, 47* (December), 60–61.

Neff, David. (2004a). One Lord, One Faith, Many Ethnicities. *Christianity Today, 48* (January), 52–54.

Neff, David. (2004b). Operation Human Rights. *Christianity Today, 48* (October), 106–7.

Neff, David. (2010). Stride toward Peace. *Christianity Today, 54* (July 10), 49.

Neff, David. (2011). Signs of the End Times. *Christianity Today, 55* (August), 46–49.

Neff, David. (2014). Executing Justice? *Christianity Today, 58* (March), 26.

Nelson, Dean. (2006). Someone's Knocking at the Door. *Christianity Today, 50* (September), 84–85.

Nelson, Jill. (2005). Unsettling Gaza. *World, 20* (September 24), 24–25.

Nelson, Jill. (2006a). Medium and Message. *World, 21* (March 25), 22–23.

Nelson, Jill. (2006b). Under Siege. *World, 21* (March 25), 29.

Nelson, Jill. (2006c). War and Peace. *World, 21* (November 11), 18–22.

Nelson, Jill. (2007a). Arrests and Accusation. *World, 22* (August 25), 23.

Nelson, Jill. (2007b). Making or Breaking Peace. *World, 22* (October 13), 16–20.

Nelson, Jill. (2007c). No Turning Back. *World, 22* (May 5), 24.

Nelson, Jill. (2007d). Spreading Conflict. *Charisma, 22* (January), 30–31.

Nelson, Jill. (2008a). Men in Black. *World, 23* (April 5/12), 44–45.

Nelson, Jill. (2008b). The "Sheer Scale" of Anti-Christian Violence. *World, 23* (November 1/8), 58.

Nelson, Jill. (2009a). Black Day. *World, 24* (August 29), 36–38.

Nelson, Jill. (2009b). Copping the Copts. *World, 24* (August 15), 44–46.

Nelson, Jill. (2009c). Not Settled. *World, 24* (July 18), 52.

Nelson, Jill. (2010). We Will Fight You. *World, 25* (November 20), 64–66.

Nettleton, Todd. (2004). My Grace Is Sufficient. *Voice of the Martyrs* (Special Issue), 5.

Nettleton, Todd. (2005a). Dare to Witness. *Voice of the Martyrs* (Special Issue), 6–8.

Nettleton, Todd. (2005b). Having Nothing: Yet Having It All. *Voice of the Martyrs* (June), 3–8.

New Bytes. (1996). *Family Voice, 18* (August), 20.

Newman, Josie. (2004a). Egyptian Christian Escapes Death, Seeks to Aid Persecuted Church. *Charisma, 29* (July), 22.

Newman, Josie. (2004b). Shariah Law under Review in Ontario after Outcry by Human-Rights Groups. *Charisma, 30* (December), 19.

Newman, Josie. (2005). Once-Tortured Christian Is Now an Advocate for the Persecuted Church. *Charisma, 30* (July), 26.

New Republic. (2008). Obama's Evangelical Appeal. *New Republic* (June 15). https://newrepublic.com/article/42421/obamas-evangelical-appeal.

News. (2012). *World, 27* (June 16), 11–18.

News. (2013). *World, 28* (December 28), 6–13.

News Briefs. (1997). *Christianity Today, 41* (April 28), 85.

News Briefs. (1999). *Charisma, 24* (February), 34.

News Briefs. (2004a). *Charisma, 30* (October), 32.

News Briefs. (2004b). *Charisma, 30* (December), 29.

News Briefs. (2005). *Charisma, 31* (August), 42.

News Briefs. (2006a). *Charisma, 31* (April), 44.

News Briefs. (2006b). *Charisma, 32* (September), 36.

News Briefs. (2007a). *Charisma, 32* (January), 30.

News Briefs. (2007b). *Charisma, 32* (April), 36.

News Briefs. (2007c). *Charisma, 32* (May), 36.

News Briefs. (2007d). *Charisma, 32* (June), 46.

News Briefs. (2008a). *Charisma, 33* (April), 30.

News Briefs. (2008b). *Charisma, 33* (June), 29.

News Briefs. (2008c). *Charisma, 33* (July), 25.

News Briefs. (2008d). *Charisma, 34* (October), 31.

News Briefs. (2008e). *Charisma, 34* (October), 29.

News Briefs. (2008f). *Charisma, 34* (August), 25.

News Briefs. (2010). *Charisma, 35* (March), 22.

News of the Year. (2004). *World, 18* (December 27–January 3), 25–37.

News Service Briefs. (2002). *Charisma, 27* (June), 34.

Newton, Bill. (2016). Less Unfit for Power. *World, 31* (November 12), 12.

Newton, Joshua. (2003a). Blockbuster Evangelism. *Christianity Today, 47* (December), 28–30.

Newton, Joshua. (2003b). Fending Off Hindutva. *Christianity Today, 47* (June), 26–27.

Newton, Joshua. (2003c). Machete Attack on American Alarms Local Christians. *Christianity Today, 47* (March), 30–31.

Newton, Joshua. (2004a). Hindu Extremes. *Christianity Today, 48* (March), 23.

Newton, Joshua. (2004b). She Chose to Forgive. *Charisma, 30* (September), 56–61.

Newton, Joshua. (2005). Dalit Christians Fight for Equal Rights in India. *Charisma, 31* (November), 31.

New York Post. (2003). Islamization Agenda. *Jerusalem Connection* (April–May), 8.

Nguku, Kyalo. (2008). Algerian Authorities Crack Down on Evangelicals. *Charisma, 34* (October), 26.

Nickles, Beverly. (2000a). A Precarious Step Forward. *Christianity Today, 44* (March 6), 32–33.

Nickles, Beverly. (2000b). Saving Bodies, Rescuing Souls. *Christianity Today, 44* (April 24), 28.

No-Comment Zone. (1999). *World, 14* (June 5), 12.

Noll, Mark. (2008). Early Returns Are Mixed. *Christianity Today, 52* (June), 53–54.

Norfolk, Marshall. (1975). The Search for Gary. *Moody Monthly, 76*, 114–16.

North Korea: Hopeful for a Better Tomorrow. (2004). *Link* (3rd Quarter), 1–8.

Nyberg, Richard. (1994). Evangelicals Await a Time of Testing. *Christianity Today, 38* (March 7), 50.

Nyberg, Richard. (1999). Missionaries in Congo Flee. *Christianity Today, 43* (February 8), 24–25.

Nyberg, Richard. (2004). Ethnic Cleansing. *Christianity Today, 48* (May), 17.

O'Brien, Brandon. (2008). A Jesus for Real Men. *Christianity Today, 52* (April), 48–52.

O'Brien, Brandon. (2009a). Emergent's Divergence. *Christianity Today, 53* (January), 13–14.

O'Brien, Brandon. (2009b). Emerging vs. Traditional. *Christianity Today, 53* (December), 63.

Oden, Thomas. (1995). So What Happens after Modernity? A Postmodern Agenda for Evangelical Theology. In

David Dockery (ed.), *Challenge of Postmodernism* (pp. 392–406). Wheaton, IL: BridgePoint Books.

Oevering, Margie. (1989). CPJ Assists Native Land Negotiations. *Faith Today, 7* (May/June), 58.

Ogle, Barry. (1995). Churches Helping Children with Incarcerated Parents. *Social Work and Christianity, 22*, 115–24.

Oke, Janette. (1996). *Drums of Change*. Minneapolis: Bethany House Publishers.

Okite, Odhiambo. (1999a). Missionaries or Mercenaries. *Christianity Today, 43* (May 24), 28.

Okite, Odhiambo. (1999b). Truth-Telling on Trial. *Christianity Today, 43* (July 12), 17.

Okite, Odhiambo. (2001). Muslim-Christian Riots Rock Nairobi. *Christianity Today, 45* (January 8), 33.

Okite, Odhiambo. (2002). Returning a Tabor. *Christianity Today, 46* (April 22), 22.

Olasky, Daniel. (2010). The Lowest Place. *World, 12* (June 19), 79–81.

Olasky, Marvin. (1998a). As I Was Saying. *World, 13* (November 14), 34.

Olasky, Marvin. (1998b). Jewish Evangelism. *World, 13* (April 11), 30.

Olasky, Marvin. (1999). Fake Contrasts. *World, 14* (February 20), 34.

Olasky, Marvin. (2001a). A Cold War for the 21st Century. *World, 16* (October 27), 10–52.

Olasky, Marvin. (2001b). Hurrah for Franklin Graham. *World, 16* (December 1), 7.

Olasky, Marvin. (2001c). My House Divided. *World, 32* (August 13), 66.

Olasky, Marvin. (2001d). We Cannot Walk Alone. *World, 32* (August 25), 8–9.

Olasky, Marvin. (2002a). All in the Family. *World, 17* (March 2), 8–55.

Olasky, Marvin. (2002b). The Greatest Spin Ever Told. *World, 17* (April 27), 8–30.

Olasky, Marvin. (2004a). Beyond Wishful Thinking. *World, 19* (December 11), 56.

Olasky, Marvin. (2004b). No Es Facil. *World, 19* (May 1), 36–49.

Olasky, Marvin. (2004c). Snake Eyes. *World, 19* (June 12), 40–48.

Olasky, Marvin. (2004d). Touching, Teaching. *World, 19* (May 29), 48.

Olasky, Marvin. (2005a). American Individuals. *World, 20* (September 24), 44.

Olasky, Marvin. (2005b). Before the Next Crisis. *World, 20* (October 1), 44.

Olasky, Marvin. (2005c). Disasters R Us. *World, 20* (November 26), 19.

Olasky, Marvin. (2005d). Fatal Flaws. *World, 20* (December 17), 44.

Olasky, Marvin. (2005e). Jews and Jesus. *World, 20* (March 26), 48.

Olasky, Marvin. (2005f). Katrina and Christmas. *World, 20* (December 24), 3.

Olasky, Marvin. (2005g). Mexifornia. *World, 20* (April 2), 30–32.

Olasky, Marvin. (2005h). Saying Sorry. *World, 20* (February 5), 30–31.

Olasky, Marvin. (2005i). A Tough Test of Citizenship. *World, 20* (February 19), 44.

Olasky, Marvin. (2006a). Catching a Wave. *World, 21* (November 4), 36–37.

Olasky, Marvin. (2006b). Compassionate Conservatism's Long Tail. *World, 21* (September 2–9), 72.

Olasky, Marvin. (2006c). Hot Issue, Hot Ad. *World, 21* (May 27), 40.

Olasky, Marvin. (2006d). A Marriage Proposal. *World, 21* (February 25), 48.

Olasky, Marvin. (2006e). Temptations of the Rich. *World, 21* (August 12), 36.

Olasky, Marvin. (2006f). Wildfire. *World, 21* (June 24), 16–21.

Olasky, Marvin. (2007a). Appeasement

vs. Firmness. *World*, 22 (September 15), 56.

Olasky, Marvin. (2007b). The Carnegie Way. *World*, 22 (September 1/8), 41–43.

Olasky, Marvin. (2007c). Falwell's Mountains. *World*, 22 (May 26), 12–15.

Olasky, Marvin. (2007d). Fighting the Good Poverty Fight. *World*, 22 (September 1/8), 20–21.

Olasky, Marvin. (2007e). Huckabee Season. *World*, 22 (November 17), 11.

Olasky, Marvin. (2007f). Master to a Slave. *World*, 22 (March 3), 21.

Olasky, Marvin. (2007g). The Pastor Populist. *World*, 22 (February 17), 16–19.

Olasky, Marvin. (2007h). Personal and Political. *World*, 22 (April 14), 40.

Olasky, Marvin. (2007i). A Question of Linkage. *World*, 22 (January 13), 28.

Olasky, Marvin. (2007j). Romney's Problem. *World*, 22 (December 15), 7.

Olasky, Marvin. (2007k). Startling Standards. *World*, 22 (September 29), 40.

Olasky, Marvin. (2007l). Taking It to the Streets. *World*, 22 (July 14), 30–31.

Olasky, Marvin. (2008a). The Death and Life of Compassionate Conservativism. *World*, 23 (August 23–30), 44–45.

Olasky, Marvin. (2008b). Facing Islam. *World*, 23 (December 13/20), 52–56.

Olasky, Marvin. (2008c). Is Mike Huckabee Conservative? *World*, 23 (January 26/February 2), 43.

Olasky, Marvin. (2008d). Minding our p's and c's. *World*, 23 (November 15/22), 84.

Olasky, Marvin. (2008e). Nothing to Fear. *World*, 23 (December 13/20), 27–28.

Olasky, Marvin. (2008f). The Republican Future. *World*, 23 (November 15/22), 24–25.

Olasky, Marvin. (2008g). Tarnished Eloquence. *World*, 23 (May 3/10), 80.

Olasky, Marvin. (2008h). Turning Back the Clock. *World*, 23 (June 14/21), 43–45.

Olasky, Marvin. (2009a). A Faith Too Saturated. *World*, 24 (January 31), 20.

Olasky, Marvin. (2009b). Homeless in Charleston. *World*, 24 (February 28), 27–28.

Olasky, Marvin. (2009c). The Jews of Our Time. *World*, 24 (April 11), 25–26.

Olasky, Marvin. (2009d). On the Road Again. *World*, 24 (May 9), 32–38.

Olasky, Marvin. (2009e). Power Politics. *World*, 24 (January 31, 2009), 76.

Olasky, Marvin. (2009f). Ready to Compete. *World*, 24 (June 20), 31–33.

Olasky, Marvin. (2009g). The Sixth Wind. *World*, 24 (June 20), 40–43.

Olasky, Marvin. (2010a). A Better Path. *World*, 25 (March 13), 80.

Olasky, Marvin. (2010b). Beyond Therapy. *World*, 25 (March 27), 24–25.

Olasky, Marvin. (2010c). The Life of a Slave. *World*, 25 (February 13), 25–27.

Olasky, Marvin. (2010d). Must Israel Die? *World*, 25 (July 3), 9–10.

Olasky, Marvin. (2011a). Reactions to the Occupation. *World*, 26 (November 5), 48–50.

Olasky, Marvin. (2011b). Take a Stand against Rand. *World*, 26 (July 16), 72.

Olasky, Marvin. (2012a). Cashed Out. *World*, 27 (August 11), 38–41.

Olasky, Marvin. (2012b). Innocence ID'd. *World*, 27 (July 28), 26.

Olasky, Marvin. (2012c). The Lamb's Agenda. *World*, 27 (December 1), 28–29.

Olasky, Marvin. (2012d). Liske's Lessons. *World*, 27 (June 16), 35–36.

Olasky, Marvin. (2012e). Remembering Black History. *World*, 27 (February 11), 42–45.

Olasky, Marvin. (2013a). The Cavalry Is Not Coming. *World*, 28 (February 23), 30–31.

Olasky, Marvin. (2013b). Dead Seriousness. *World*, 28 (October 19), 34–41.

Olasky, Marvin. (2013c). Making Tracks. *World*, 28 (June 29), 40–49.

Olasky, Marvin. (2013d). Under Conviction. *World*, 28 (November 2), 28–29.

Olasky, Marvin. (2014a). From Gay to Joyous. *World*, 29 (February 8), 28–29.

Olasky, Marvin. (2014b). Radiating Truth. *World*, 29 (January 25), 26–27.

Olasky, Marvin. (2015a). Blindsided. *World*, 30 (July 11), 32–38.

Olasky, Marvin. (2015b). Hannah and Her Brothers. *World*, 30 (January 24), 28–29.

Olasky, Marvin. (2015c). No Foolish Romance. *World*, 30 (August 22), 84.

Olasky, Marvin. (2015d). Tiny, Powerful Heartbeats. *World*, 30 (August 8), 46–48.

Olasky, Marvin. (2016a). Back to the Future. *World*, 31 (September 3), 6–7.

Olasky, Marvin. (2016b). Beastly Analysis. *World*, 31 (July 9), 5–7.

Olasky, Marvin. (2016c). The Great Reversal. *World*, 31 (November 26), 4–7.

Olasky, Marvin. (2016d). Mascots and Manipulators. *World*, 31 (June 11), 5–7.

Olasky, Marvin. (2016e). A Rare Window. *World*, 31 (December 10), 6–7.

Olasky, Marvin. (2016f). Reckless or Ruthless? *World*, 31 (August 20), 6–7.

Olasky, Marvin. (2016g). The TOP Gospel. *World*, 31 (March 19), 68.

Olasky, Marvin. (2016h). Unfit for Power. *World*, 31 (October 29), 4–7.

Olasky, Susan. (2010). A Woman's Turn. *World*, 25 (February 27), 66.

Olasky, Susan, and Becky Perry. (2005). Helping Hands. *World*, 20 (December 24), 14–18.

Olford, Stephen. (1982). Nation or Ruination. *United Evangelical Action*, 41 (Fall), 8.

Olsen, Ted. (1996). Lutheran, Catholic, and Black Churches Join Graham Effort. *Christianity Today*, 40 (July 15), 67.

Olsen, Ted. (1997a). Mission Leaders Seek to "De-Westernize" Gospel. *Christianity Today*, 41 (February 3), 86.

Olsen, Ted. (1997b), Racial Reconciliation Emphasis Intensified. *Christianity Today*, 41 (January 6), 67.

Olsen, Ted. (2002). GOP Seeks Black Clergy Affiliations. *Christianity Today*, 46 (May 21), 15.

Olsen, Ted. (2003a). Go Figure. *Christianity Today*, 47 (June), 13.

Olsen, Ted. (2003b). The Positive Prophet. *Christianity Today*, 47 (January), 32–42.

Olsen, Ted. (2003c). Under the Sun. *Christianity Today*, 47 (June), 15.

Olsen, Ted. (2004a). Go Figure. *Christianity Today*, 48 (December), 20.

Olsen, Ted. (2004b). Grave Images. *Christianity Today*, 48 (July), 60.

Olsen, Ted. (2005a). Dirty Qur'ans, Dusty Bibles. *Christianity Today*, 49 (July), 50.

Olsen, Ted. (2005b). Go Figure. *Christianity Today*, 49 (February), 24.

Olsen, Ted. (2005c). Go Figure. *Christianity Today*, 49 (March), 22.

Olsen, Ted. (2005d). The Katrina Quandary. *Christianity Today*, 49 (November), 94.

Olsen, Ted. (2005e). Quotation Marks. *Christianity Today*, 49 (April), 23.

Olsen, Ted. (2005f). Rights Brained. *Christianity Today*, 49 (May), 56.

Olsen, Ted. (2007). Jingo Jangle. *Christianity Today*, 51 (May), 20.

Olsen, Ted. (2008). Where Jim Wallis Stands. *Christianity Today*, 52 (May), 52–59.

Olsen, Ted. (2009a). Go Figure. *Christianity Today*, 53 (February), 14.

Olsen, Ted. (2009b). Quotation Marks. *Christianity Today*, 53 (July), 15.

Olsen, Ted. (2010). The Abolitionists' Scandal. *Christianity Today*, 54 (October), 46–49.

Olson, Roger, Charles Pinnock, Thomas Oden, and Timothy George. (1998). The Future of Evangelical Theology. *Christianity Today*, 42 (February 9), 40–50.

Orteza, Arsenio. (2010). Not So Cute. *World*, 25 (July 3), 32.

Osanjo, Tom. (2013). Wolves in Sheep's Clothing. *Christianity Today*, 57 (January/February), 16.

Ostling, Richard. (2008). Can We Talk? *World*, 23 (March 8/15), 58–59.

Otis, George. (1997). Invasion from the Dark Side. *Charisma*, 22 (March), 50–58.

Outpaced by Islam? (2002). *Christianity Today*, 46 (February 4), 26–27.

Owens, Chandler. (1998). Risky Living among Atlanta's Drug Lords. *Charisma*, 24 (August), 48.

Owens, Estelle. (2003). "Maxiumum Christianity: Applied as Well as Advocated": One Good Man vs. Racism. *Baptist History and Heritage*, 38 (Summer/Fall), 35–40.

Owens, Tiffany. (2013). Serving the Sparrows. *World*, 28 (June 15), 56–59.

Padilla, Rene. (1991). Come Holy Spirit—Renew the Whole Creation. *Transformation*, 8 (October), 1–6.

Pagitt, Doug, and Tony Jones (eds.). (2007). *An Emergent Manifesto of Hope*. Grand Rapids, MI: Baker Books.

Palau, Luis. (1998). What Part of the Great Commission Don't You Understand? *Christianity Today*, 42 (November 16), 74–76.

Palmer, Adam. (2005). Supersized Faith. *New Man*, 12 (November/December), 18–19.

Pannell, William. (1993). *The Coming Race Wars*. Grand Rapids, MI: Zondervan.

Parajon, Gustavo. (1989). One Nicaraguan Christian's Perspective. *Christianity Today*, 33 (March 3), 48.

Park, Suey. (2014). This Work Injures Me; This Work Heals Me. http://sueypark.com (no longer available).

Park, Suey, Emily Rice, and Mihee Kim-Kort. (2014). Killjoy Prophets, Asian Americans, and Racial Reconciliation. http://sueypark.com/2014/07/06/killjoy-prophets-asian-americans-and-racial-reconciliation-part-1/ (no longer available).

Parker, Star. (2003). *Uncle Sam's Plantation*. Nashville: Nelson Current Books.

Parshall, Phil, and Julie Parshall. (2002). *Lifting the Veil*. Waynesboro, GA: Authentic Media.

Passages. (2007). *Christianity Today*, 51 (June), 18.

Passages. (2009). *Christianity Today*, 53 (May), 14–15.

Passantino, Gretchen. (1991). Surviving in the City. *Moody*, 92 (September), 36–38.

Patterson, Ben. (1990). South Africa's Ambiguous Hero. *Christianity Today*, 34 (August 20), 15.

Paulson, Bob. (2002). Encouraging Racial Harmony. *Decision*, 43 (February), 31.

Pearson, Catherine. (2011). Mandatory Mayhem. *World*, 26 (June 4), 56–58.

Pearson-Wong, Pamela. (2000). What Money Can't Buy. *Family Voice* (May–June), 14–19.

Pease, Richard. (1985). The Mission Field around Us. *Alliance Witness*, 120 (February 27), 20–22.

Pelt, Leslie. (1989). Wanted: Black Missionaries, but How? *Evangelical Missions Quarterly*, 25 (January), 28–37.

Penemaker, Wesley. (2005). How to Win the War on Terror. *New Man*, 12 (November–December), 50–53, 69.

Perkins, John. (1995a). Love Can Build a Bridge. *Charisma*, 29 (June), 39–42.

Perkins, John. (1995b). *Restoring At-Risk Communities*. Grand Rapids, MI: Baker.

Perry, Becky, and Marvin Olasky. (2007). Circuses and Bread. *World*, 22 (March 17), 28–29.

Persaud, Trevor. (2011). Sweat Lodge Prayers. *Christianity Today*, 55 (April), 13.

Persecution Is a Holy Word. (2003). *Christianity Today, 47* (December), 32–34.
Persecution Panel Appointed. (1997). *Christianity Today, 41* (January 6), 59.
Persecution Watch. (2004a). *Charisma, 29* (January), 16.
Persecution Watch. (2004b). *Charisma, 29* (March), 26.
Persecution Watch. (2004c). *Charisma, 29* (April), 26.
Persecution Watch. (2004d). *Charisma, 29* (July), 36.
Persecution Watch. (2004e). *Charisma, 30* (November), 28.
Persecution Watch. (2004f). *Charisma, 30* (December), 26.
Persecution Watch. (2005a). *Charisma, 30* (January), 22.
Persecution Watch. (2005b). *Charisma, 30* (February), 26.
Persecution Watch. (2005c). *Charisma, 30* (April), 24.
Persecution Watch. (2005d). *Charisma, 30* (June), 34.
Persecution Watch. (2005e). *Charisma, 31* (August), 30.
Persecution Watch. (2005f). *Charisma, 31* (September), 27.
Persecution Watch. (2005g). *Charisma, 31* (October), 34.
Persecution Watch. (2005h). *Charisma, 31* (December), 26.
Persecution Watch. (2006a). *Charisma, 31* (May), 29.
Persecution Watch. (2006b). *Charisma, 31* (June), 30.
Persecution Watch. (2006c). *Charisma, 31* (July), 32.
Persecution Watch. (2006d). *Charisma, 32* (August), 30.
Persecution Watch. (2006e). *Charisma, 32* (September), 26.
Persecution Watch. (2006f). *Charisma, 32* (November), 30.
Persecution Watch. (2007a). *Charisma, 32* (January), 29.
Persecution Watch. (2007b). *Charisma, 32* (March), 29.
Persecution Watch. (2007c). *Charisma, 32* (May), 32.
Persecution Watch. (2007d). Ministry Impacts Chicago's "Little India." *Charisma, 32* (June), 38.
Persecution Watch. (2007e). *Charisma, 33* (November), 36.
Persecution Watch. (2007f). *Charisma, 33* (December), 32.
Persecution Watch. (2008). *Charisma, 33* (June), 27.
Persecution Watch. (2010). *Charisma, 35* (April), 23.
Phiri, Isaac. (1992). The Dawning of African Evangelical Politics. *Christianity Today, 36* (November 9), 40.
Phiri, Isaac. (2006). Hope in the Heart of Darkness. *Christianity Today, 50* (July), 23–31.
Phiri, Isaac. (2009). Building a Peace beyond Understanding. *Christianity Today, 53* (January), 56–61.
Piecuch, Kevin. (1986). Chicago Activists Protest Trial. *United Evangelical Action, 45* (January–February), 7.
Piper, John. (2002). Land Divine? *World, 17* (May 11), 51.
Piper, John. (2006). Being Mocked. *World, 21* (February 18), 43.
Piper, John. (2007). Combat and Cowardice. *World, 22* (November), 43.
Pitts, Edward Lee. (2009a). A Voice on the Inside. *World, 24* (February 28), 8.
Pitts, Edward Lee. (2009b). Out of the Wilderness. *World, 24* (June 20), 51–53.
Pitts, Edward Lee. (2010a). Tea and Trumpets. *World, 25* (February 27), 38–40.
Pitts, Edward Lee. (2010b). Tea Party Transit. *World, 25* (November 20), 46–50.
Pitts, Edward Lee. (2012a). Latin Persuasion. *World, 27* (May 19), 34–39.
Pitts, Edward Lee. (2012b). Tea Party Star. *World, 27* (April 21), 44–46.

Pitts, Edward Lee. (2013). Against the Tide. *World*, 28 (September 21), 40–43.

Plowman, Edward. (1996). Hispanic Christians in the United States. *Christianity Today*, 38 (January 17), 44–45.

Plowman, Edward. (2002). One-Man Truth Squad. *World*, 17 (February 2), 32–33.

Plowman, Edward. (2004a). Motivated by Money. *World*, 19 (March 20), 27.

Plowman, Edward. (2004b). Taking Stock. *Christianity Today*, 19 (November 13), 33.

Plowman, Edward. (2006). I Should Have Been Better Prepared. *World*, 21 (December 16), 28.

Plowman, Edward. (2007). Border Showdown. *World*, 22 (April 14), 32.

Plummer, Glenn. (2008). Black Pastor Marshals Support for Israel. *Charisma*, 33 (July), 16–17.

Plummer, Wy. (2001). Garden-Variety Racial Barriers. *World*, 32 (August 25), 36–39.

Pollard, Mark. (2000). A Prophetic Perspective. *Charisma*, 26 (November), 69.

Ponniah, Moses. (2000). The Situation in Malaysia. *Transformation*, 17 (January–March), 31–34.

Porter, Phillip. (1996). Take My Hand and Walk with Me. *Charisma*, 22 (August), 42–44.

Post, Suzie. (1990). Jesus Is for Jews. *Charisma*, 15 (January), 42–50.

Potter, Ronald. (2000). Was Slavery God's Will? *Christianity Today*, 44 (May 22), 80.

Povinelli, Elizabeth. (2002). *The Cunning of Recognition*. Durham, NC: Duke University Press.

Powell, Charles. (2009). America's Ugliest Crime. *Charisma*, 35 (November), 40–41.

Powell, Pamela Baker. (2000). The Lord in Black Skin. *Christianity Today*, 44 (October 2), 50–55.

Price, Clive. (1997). Just Call Her Saint Caroline. *Charisma*, 23 (August), 68–73.

Price, Clive. (2004a). It's God's Hour for Iran. *Charisma*, 29 (June), 65.

Price, Clive. (2004b). Persecuted Church Takes Spotlight at Human-Rights Gathering in London. *Charisma*, 29 (February), 24.

Price, Clive. (2007a). The Day Slavery Ended. *Charisma*, 32 (February), 40–44.

Price, Clive. (2007b). Marchers Apologize for "African Holocaust." *Charisma*, 32 (March), 22–23.

Promise Keepers. (2009). Honoring Our Spiritual Fathers. *Charisma*, 34 (May), 76.

Provan, Charles. (1987). *The Church Is Israel Now*. Vallecito, CA: Ross House.

Puar, Jasbir. (2007). *Terrorist Assemblages*. Durham, NC: Duke University Press.

Pulliam, Russ. (2004). A Wonderful Life. *World*, 19 (December 25), 18–21.

Pulliam, Russ. (2005). God's Muckraker. *Christianity Today*, 49 (November), 80–81.

Pulliam, Sarah. (2006). Alien Proposals. *Christianity Today*, 50 (June), 15.

Pulliam, Sarah. (2007a). Costly Commitment. *Christianity Today*, 51 (September), 22–23.

Pulliam, Sarah. (2007b). Solution Stalemate. *Christianity Today*, 51 (June), 20–21.

Pulliam, Sarah. (2008a). Election Honeymoon. *Christianity Today*, 52 (December), 15.

Pulliam, Sarah. (2008b). Evangelical Moderates. *Christianity Today*, 52 (November), 16–17.

Pulliam, Sarah. (2008c). Hazy Faith-Based Future. *Christianity Today*, 52 (April), 16–17.

Pulliam, Sarah. (2008d). The Megachurch Primaries. *Christianity Today*, 52 (February), 66–69.

Pulliam, Sarah. (2008e). The Party of Faith. *Christianity Today, 52* (September), 17.

Pulliam, Sarah. (2008f). Q&A. *Christianity Today, 52* (January), 19.

Pulliam, Sarah. (2008g). Q&A. *Christianity Today, 52* (December), 19.

Pulliam, Sarah. (2009a). A Costly Shift. *Christianity Today, 53* (February), 11.

Pulliam, Sarah. (2009b). No "Poster Boy." *Christianity Today, 53*, 14–15.

Pulliam, Sarah. (2009c). The Perfect Hybrid. *Christianity Today, 53* (May), 46–50.

Quaicoo, Shirley. (2011). Magic Words. *Christianity Today, 55* (May), 20.

Quotables. (2009). *World, 24* (May 9), 16.

Qureshi, Nabeel, Roy Oksnevad, and Mark Pfeiffer. (2012). Should Christians Read the Qur'an? *Christianity Today, 57* (November), 32–33.

Rabey, Steve. (1996). Where Is the Christian Men's Movement Headed? *Christianity Today, 40* (April 29), 46–49, 60.

Rabey, Steve. (1998). Conversation or Competition? *Christianity Today, 42* (September 7), 22–23.

Rabey, Steve. (2010). Groups Say Marriage Debate Is Not Over. *Charisma, 35* (February), 12.

Race in America: A Historical Timeline. (2001). *World, 32* (August 25), 10–24.

Rah, Soong-Chan. (2009). *The Next Evangelicalism*. Downer's Grove, IL: InterVarsity Press.

Rah, Soong-Chan. (2015a). *Prophetic Lament*. Downer's Grove, IL: InterVarsity Press. Kindle.

Rah, Soong-Chan. (2015b). Soong-Chan Rah Says Black Lives Matter Because of What Experienced (November 28). http://www.the-nbea.org/articles/soong-chan-rah-says-black-lives-matter-because-of-what-experienced/.

Rah, Soong-Chan. (2016). In Whose Image: The Emergence, Development, and Challenge of African-American Evangelicalism. Dissertation, Duke Divinity School, Durham, NC.

Rainey, Clint. (2006a). Breakout Republicans. *World, 21* (March 11), 25–26.

Rainey, Clint. (2006b). Easy Money. *World, 21* (July 22), 23.

Rainey, Clint. (2007a). Marked Targets. *Charisma, 22* (July 28), 26–27.

Rainey, Clint. (2007b). Open Season. *World, 22* (December 22), 17.

Rainey, Clint. (2007c). The Other Side. *World, 22* (April 21), 18–21.

Rainey, Clint. (2008). The Bloc to Watch. *World, 23* (February 23/March 1), 8–9.

Ramstad, Mans. (2004). Persecution: A Biblical and Personal Reflection. *Evangelical Missions Quarterly, 40* (October), 468–75.

Rana, Junaid. (2011). *Terrifying Muslims*. Durham, NC: Duke University Press. Kindle.

Rapp, Marlene. (1988). World Relief Registers 14,000 in Amnesty Program. *United Evangelical Action, 47* (July–August), 11.

Rausch, David. (1988). Chosen People. *Christianity Today, 32* (October 7), 53–59.

Rayfield, Jillian. (2010). Latest Right-Wing Freak-Out: Obama Wants to Give Manhattan Back to Native Americans (December 28). http://tpmmuckraker.talkingpointsmemo.com/2010/12/latest_right-wing_freak-out_obama_wants_to_give_ma.php.

Reaching Out to Muslims. (2004). *Voice of the Martyrs* (Special Issue), 6–7.

Readers Write. (2004). *Christianity Today, 48* (August), 12–18.

Readers Write. (2005). *Christianity Today, 49* (August), 12–17.

Readers Write. (2007). *Christianity Today, 51* (June), 10–14.

Readers Write. (2008). *Christianity Today, 52* (December), 8–12.

Reapsome, James. (1988). Great Commission Deadline. *Christianity Today, 32* (January 25), 26–29.

Reapsome, James. (1989). What's Holding Up World Evangelization? *Evangelical Missions Quarterly, 25* (January), 18–24.

Rearing Its Ugly Head. (1999). *World, 14* (February 6), 12–13.

The Reconciliation Walk. (2000). http://www.soon.org.uk/page15.htm (no longer available).

Reconciling Race. (2015). *Fuller Magazine* (4), 42–43.

Reed, Eric. (1999). Southern Baptists Take Aim at Urban America. *Christianity Today, 43* (July 12), 24–25.

Reed, Ralph. (1990). *After the Revolution.* Dallas: Word.

Reed, Ralph. (1996). *Active Faith.* New York: Free Press.

Reese, Abigail. (2005). Chicago Pastor Seeks to Develop Minority Entrepreneurs. *Charisma, 30* (April), 29–30.

Religious News Service. (1999). Priest Killed for "Illegal" Conversions. *Christianity Today, 43* (October 25), 25.

Religious News Service. (2000). 2,000 Die in Muslim-Christian Conflict. *Christianity Today, 44* (February 7), 32.

Religious News Service. (2003). Three Killed in Christmas Attack on Church. *Christianity Today, 47* (February), 28.

Reporter at the Border. (1986). *United Evangelical Action, 45* (January–February), 11–12.

Reynolds, Barbara. (1988). Ronald Reagan's Albatross. *Christianity Today, 32* (October 21), 21.

Rice, Chris. (2002). Theology Should Interrogate Our Lives. *Christianity Today, 46* (December 9), 55.

Rice, Chris. (2010). Born Again . . . Again. *Christianity Today, 54* (March), 34–37.

Richardson, Suzy. (2004). Faith-Based Prison Ministries Leave Legacies of Transformation. *Charisma, 29* (March), 27–28.

Richardson, Suzy. (2005). Christian Journalist Targeted for Murder for Exposing Terrorist Web Site. *Charisma, 30* (May), 26–27.

Richardson, Suzy. (2006). Hispanic Christians Tackle Immigration Reform. *Charisma, 31* (July), 24–26.

Richardson, Suzy. (2007). Igniting Prayer for Reconciliation. *Charisma, 32* (May), 42.

Rieger, Megan. (2007a). Recipe for Success. *World, 22* (September 1–8), 50–51.

Rieger, Megan. (2007b). Second-Chance Ranch. *World, 22* (September 1–8), 27–28.

Ritchie, Andrea. (2006). Law Enforcement Violence against Women of Color. In Incite (ed.), *The Color of Violence: Violence against Women of Color* (pp. 138–56). Cambridge, MA: South End Press.

Road Blocks and Voting Blocs. (2003). *Christianity Today, 47* (August), 32–33.

Robertson, Pat. (1994). *The Collected Works of Pat Robertson.* New York: Inspirational Press.

Robinson, Vanessa. (2007). Former Lesbian Says Change Is Possible. *Charisma, 32* (July), 32.

Roddy, Dennis. (2000). Why Holocaust Deniers Turned on One of Their Own. *Action Report Online* (March 4). http://www.fpp.co.uk/online/01/03/PittsburghProvan.html.

Rodriguez, Dylan. (2009a). The Political Logic of the Non-Profit Industrial Complex. In Incite (ed.), *The Revolution Will Not Be Funded: Beyond the Non-Profit Industrial Complex.* (pp. 22–40). Cambridge, MA: South End Press.

Rodriguez, Dylan. (2009b). *Suspended Apocalypse: White Supremacy, Genocide, and the Filipino Condition.* Minneapolis: University of Minnesota Press.

Rodriguez, Samuel. (2012). God's Latino Explosion. *Charisma*, 37 (May), 46–53.

Rodriguez, Samuel. (2013). *The Lamb's Agenda: Why Jesus is Calling You to a Life of Righteousness and Justice*. Nashville: Thomas Nelson.

Rogers, Benedict. (2004). Burma's Almost Forgotten. *Christianity Today*, 48 (March), 52–56.

Roley, Scott. (2004). *God's Neighborhood*. Downer's Grove, IL: InterVarsity Press.

Rolnick, Addie. (2011). The Promise of Mancari: Political Rights as Racial Remedy. *New York University Law Review*, 86, 958–1045.

Rosenberg, Ellen. (1984). *Southern Baptists: A Subculture in Transition*. Knoxville: University of Tennessee Press.

Ross, Bobby, Jr. (2009). Prosperity Gospel on Skid Row. *Christianity Today*, 53 (February), 12–13.

Roth, Sid. (2015). Israel and the World Set Ablaze for Jesus. *Charisma*, 41 (October), 28–34.

Royal, Robert. (1996). Over the Muticultural Rainbow. *Faith and Freedom*, 16 (Summer), 13.

Rudolph, Betsy. (1986). Sanctuary's Shaky Foundations. *United Evangelical Action*, 45 (January–February), 6–7.

Rushton, Christine. (2017). More Than 75 Evangelicals Leaders Call Trump Out on Bigotry, Racism. *Los Angeles Times* (October 7). http://www.latimes.com/nation/politics/trailguide/la-na-live-updates-trailguide-more-than-75-evangelicals-call-trump-1475849049-htmlstory.html.

Russell, Courtney. (2004). Marabout Face. *World Magazine*, 19 (August 7), 28–29.

Rutland, Mark. (2015). Friends of Zion. *Charisma*, 41 (October), 22–26.

Rutledge, Fleming. (2008). When God Disturbs the Peace. *Christianity Today*, 52 (June), 30–33.

Rutledge, Kathleen. (2004). Assault on the Jewish People. *Christianity Today*, 48 (December), 18.

Rutledge, Kathleen. (2005). Dobson on the Gay Marriage Ban. *Christianity Today*, 49 (January), 60.

Safety of Christian Workers Cannot Be Compromised. (1996). NAE *Leadership Alert* (December 15), 1.

Said, Edward. 1994. *Orientalism*. New York: Vintage.

Sailiata, Kirisitina. (2015). Decolonization. In Stephanie Nohelani Teves, Andrea Smith, and Michelle Raheja (eds.), *Native Studies Keywords* (pp. 301–8). Tucson: University of Arizona Press.

Saint, Steve. (1998). The Unfinished Mission to the Aucas. *Christianity Today*, 42 (March 2), 42–45.

Sale, Kirkpatrick. (1990). *The Conquest of Paradise*. New York: Plume.

Salguero, Gabriel. (2015). It's Too Wrapped Up in Privilege. *Christianity Today*, 59 (November), 47–48.

Salvatierra, Alexia, and Peter Heltzel. (2014). *Faith-Rooted Organizing*. Downers Grove, IL: IVP Press.

Salvation Army. (n.d.). An Inspiring Role Model. http://www.salvationarmy.ca/blog/2014/05/20/an-inspiring-role-model/ (no longer available).

Sampson, Sandy. (2002). Indigenous Peoples Issues: A Warning about the "World Christian Gathering on Indigenous People" (June). http://www.deceptioninthechurch.com/lehmann2.html.

Sandvig, Zoe. (2008a). Defining Evangelical. *World*, 23 (May 17/24), 8.

Sandvig, Zoe. (2008b). High-Minded and High-Heeled. *World*, 23 (October 4/11), 53.

Scharold, Kristen. (2007). Campus Capitalism. *Christianity Today*, 51 (October), 19.

Schartel, Stefanie. (2011). "Chrislam" Rising. *Charisma, 37* (September), 23.

Schatzline, Pat. (2013). God Is Not Mad at You. *Charisma, 38* (March), 36–40.

Scheller, Christine. (2006). A Delicate Hospitality. *Christianity Today, 50* (March), 48–50.

Schiavi, Nicole. (2008a). Attack Puts Israel's Messianic Community in the Spotlight. *Charisma, 33* (June), 21.

Schiavi, Nicole. (2008b). Christmas in Bethlehem. *Charisma, 34* (December), 28–32, 62.

Schiavi, Nicole. (2009). 10 Ways to Bless Israel. *Charisma, 34* (May), 48–50, 88–91.

Schiavi, Nicole. (2010). Suspect Charged in Attack against Messianic Family. *Charisma, 35* (January), 21.

Schipper, Gary. (1988). Non-Western Missionaries: Our Newest Challenge. *Evangelical Missions Quarterly, 24* (July), 198–202.

Schweikert, Anahid. (2004). Crossing the Color Line in Memphis. *Charisma, 29* (February), 64–69.

Schweikert, Anahid. (2010). A Voice for Immigrants. *Charisma, 36* (October), 32–37, 72.

Scimone, Diana. (2007). Journey of a Lifetime. *Charisma Israel, 32* (June), 12–36.

Scimone, Diana. (2008). The Pilgrimage of a Lifetime. *Charisma, 34* (October), 1–13.

Scimone, Diana. (2009). Stop Child Slavery Now. *Charisma, 35* (November), 34–38.

Scimone, Diana. (2015). The Journalist Who Became a Modern-Day Mordecai. *Charisma, 40* (March), 44–47.

Sechrest, Love L. (2015). Race Relations in the Church in the Age of Obama. *Fuller Magazine* (4), 64–67.

A Secularist Jihad. (2002). *Christianity Today, 46* (January 7), 30–31.

Seeking Peace but Finding War in the City of Jesus' Birth. (2001). *Open Doors Newsbrief, 16* (December), 5–6.

Seidl, Jonathan. (2009). Freedom Fighter. *World, 24* (April 25), 60.

Seiple, Robert. (2001). Religious Liberty: How Are We Doing? *Christianity Today, 45* (October 22), 98–101.

Sellers, Jeff. (2001a). Forgotten Gulag. *Christianity Today, 45* (August 6), 62.

Sellers, Jeff. (2001b). High Court Injustice. *Christianity Today, 45* (November 12), 95.

Sellers, Jeff. (2001c). How to Spell Debt Relief. *Christianity Today, 45* (May 21), 64–67.

Sellers, Jeff. (2001d). No Greater Tragedy. *Christianity Today, 45* (June 11), 95.

Sellers, Jeff. (2001e). The Violent Face of Jihad. *Christianity Today, 45* (April 23), 100.

Sellers, Jeff. (2002a). Big, Soft Targets. *Christianity Today, 46* (February 4), 50–53.

Sellers, Jeff. (2002b). Crushed by a Soviet Relic. *Christianity Today, 46* (August 5), 54.

Sellers, Jeff. (2002c). Empty Legal Rights. *Christianity Today, 41* (January 7), 50.

Sellers, Jeff. (2002d). Flogged and Deported. *Christianity Today, 46* (April 22), 82.

Sellers, Jeff. (2002e). Heightened Hostilities. *Christianity Today, 46* (December 9), 58.

Sellers, Jeff. (2002f). Hiding from Religion Police. *Christianity Today, 46* (March 11), 70.

Sellers, Jeff. (2002g). Hounded, Beaten, Shot. *Christianity Today, 46* (June 10), 48.

Sellers, Jeff. (2002h). To Confront a Theocracy. *Christianity Today, 46* (July 8), 34–40.

Sellers, Jeff. (2003a). Criminal Faith. *Christianity Today, 47* (July), 61.

Sellers, Jeff. (2003b). Religious Cleansing. *Christianity Today, 47* (April), 98.

Sellers, Jeff. (2004a). Crushing House Churches. *Christianity Today, 48* (January), 63.

Sellers, Jeff. (2004b). Lip Service. *Christianity Today, 48* (April), 95.

Sellers, Jeff. (2004c). Ordinary Terrorists. *Christianity Today, 48* (October), 102.

Sellers, Jeff. (2005a). Deliver Us from Wal-Mart? *Christianity Today, 49* (May), 40–45.

Sellers, Jeff. (2005b). Dumped into Drums. *Christianity Today, 49* (July), 56.

Sellers, Jeff. (2005c). Terrorizing Ally. *Christianity Today, 49* (January), 66.

Seu, Andrée. (2001). True Perspectives. *World, 16* (October 20), 41.

Seu, Andrée. (2004). Light Switch. *World Magazine, 19* (August 14), 47.

Seu, Andrée. (2005a). Fine Distinctions. *World, 20* (February 5), 47.

Seu, Andrée. (2005b). Stepping into the Story. *World, 20* (September 10), 59.

Seu, Andrée. (2008). High-Cost Failure. *World, 24* (August 1), 75.

Seu, Andrée. (2009). Be Shrill. *World, 24* (July 4), 87.

Sexton, Jared. (2008). *Amalgamation Schemes*. Minneapolis: University of Minnesota Press.

Sexton, Jared. (2010). People-of-Color-Blindness. *Social Text, 28* (2), 31–56.

Shaking Hands with Thugs. (2001). *Christianity Today, 45* (December 3), 30–31.

Shaw, R. Daniel. (1990). Culture and Evangelism: A Model for Missiological Strategy. *Missiology, 18* (July), 291–304.

Shea, Nina. (1997). *In the Lion's Den: Persecuted Christians and What the Western Church Can Do about It*. Nashville: Broadman & Holman Publishers.

Sheets, Dutch. (2016). 7 Issues to Consider before You Vote. *Charisma, 42* (September), 72.

Sheldon, Louis B. (2011). The Plan for a Gay (Domi)Nation. *Charisma, 36* (July), 32–35.

Shellnutt, Kate. (2016a). Is It Too Late for Russell Moore to Say Sorry? *Christianity Today* (December 21). http://www.christianitytoday.com/ct/2016/december-web-only/is-it-too-late-to-say-sorry-russell-moore-erlc-sbc-trump.html.

Shellnutt, Kate. (2016b). LifeWay Stops Selling Jen Hatmaker Books over LGBT Beliefs. *Christianity Today* (October 27). http://www.christianitytoday.com/gleanings/2016/october/lifeway-stops-selling-jen-hatmaker-books-lgbt-beliefs-chris.html.

Shellnutt, Kate. (2016c). Trump Elected President, Thanks to 4 in 5 White Evangelicals (November 9). http://www.christianitytoday.com/gleanings/2016/november/trump-elected-president-thanks-to-4-in-5-white-evangelicals.html.

Shenk, Calvin. (1998). Jerusalem as Jesus Views It. *Christianity Today, 42* (October 5), 44–46.

Shenk, Gerald. (2000). Anonymous Are the Peacemakers. *Christianity Today, 44* (December 4), 34–40, 81.

Shepard, Carol. (2002). Indianapolis' Inner-City Innovator. *Charisma, 28* (December), 45–48.

Sherman, Amy. (1994). One "Village" at a Time. *World, 9* (November 19), 10–13.

Sherman, Amy. (1995a). Phoenix Rising. *World, 10* (March 25), 12–14.

Sherman, Amy. (1995b). A Young Life Is Spared. *World, 10* (March 25), 15.

Sherman, Amy. (1996). STEP-ing Out on Faith—and Off Welfare. *Christianity Today, 40* (June 17), 35–36.

Sherman, Amy. (1997). A Call for Church Welfare Reform. *Christianity Today, 41* (October 6), 46–50.

Sherman, Amy. (1999). How Sharon Baptist Discovered Ministry. *Christianity Today, 43* (June 14), 78–80.

Shibley, David. (2009). Is Jesus Really the

Only Way? *Charisma, 35* (October), 28–31, 65.
Shoebat, Walid. (2009). What Every Christian Needs to Know. *Charisma, 34* (May), 74.
Shuler, Clarence. (1998). *Winning the Race to Unity.* Chicago: Moody.
Sider, Ronald. (1988). The Biblical Teaching on Sin. *World Christian, 7* (September/October), 12.
Sider, Ronald. (1998). What Do We Do with Poor, Hungry People? *Charisma, 24* (December), 56–60, 122.
Sider, Ronald. (2016). Why I'm Voting for Hillary Clinton. *Christianity Today, 60* (October), 54–56.
Sidey, Ken. (1990a). Open Season on Christians? *Christianity Today, 34* (April 23), 34–36.
Sidey, Ken. (1990b). What's in a Word? *Christianity Today, 34* (February 5), 40–43.
Sidey, Ken. (1993). Faces of Reconciliation. *World Vision, 36* (August/September), 2–5.
Sieczkowski, Cavan. (2013). Pat Robertson on Transgender Community: "I Don't Think There's Any Sin Associated with That" (July 29). http://www.huffingtonpost.com/2013/07/29/pat-robertson-transgender_n_3672244.html.
A Silent Holocaust. (1999). *Christianity Today, 43* (February 8), 28–29.
Sillars, Lee. (1999). Unaffirmative Action. *World, 14* (June 26), 23.
Sillars, Les, and Lynn Vincent. (1999). Pro-Life? Then Be Quiet. *World, 14* (May 29), 22.
Silva, Denise Ferreira da. (2007). *Toward a Global Idea of Race.* Minneapolis: University of Minnesota Press.
Singh, David Emmanuel. (2005). Christian Relations with Muslims: Review of Selected Issues and Approaches. *Transformation, 22* (January), 48–62.
Singh, Manpreet. (2000a). Christians Scorn "China Model." *Christianity Today, 44* (December 4), 28.
Singh, Manpreet. (2000b). Justice Delayed for Dalits. *Christianity Today, 44* (November 13), 34–35.
Singh, Manpreet. (2001a). Militant Hindus Assault Christians. *Christianity Today, 45* (February 5), 24.
Singh, Manpreet. (2001b). Relief Abuses Rampant. *Christianity Today, 45* (April 2), 32.
Singh, Manpreet. (2002a). 50,000 Dalits Renounce Hinduism. *Christianity Today, 46* (January 7), 25–26.
Singh, Manpreet. (2002b). Harassed Kashmir Christians Reach Out to Discreet Muslims. *Christianity Today, 46* (September 9), 26–27.
Singh, Manpreet. (2002c). Quitting Hinduism. *Christianity Today, 46* (December 9), 18.
Singh, Manpreet. (2002d). Radicals Attack Two Christian Institutions. *Christianity Today, 46* (September 9), 26.
Singh, Manpreet. (2003). Power in Punjab. *Christianity Today, 47* (July), 24–25.
Singh, Manpreet. (2004a). Anti-Conversion Conspiracy. *Christianity Today, 48* (May), 20.
Singh, Manpreet. (2004b). Shock and Awesome. *Christianity Today, 48* (July), 15.
Singh, Manpreet. (2005). Hindu Radical Redux. *Christianity Today, 49* (May), 19.
Singh, Manpreet. (2006). Under Siege. *Christianity Today, 50* (May), 21–22.
Sizer, Stephen. (2005). *Christian Zionism: Road-Map to Armaggedon?* Westmont, IL: InterVarsity Press.
Skeel, David. (2011). Beyond a Knee-Jerk "No." *World, 26* (November 5), 50.
Skeel, David. (2016). Payday Pitfalls. *World, 31* (August 6), 59.
Skinner, Tom. (1989). Black and Free

in Christ. *New Man, 6* (January/February), 64–65.

Slices. (2011). *Relevant* (July/August), 10.

Slices. (2015). *Relevant* (January/February), 10.

Slices. (2016). *Relevant* (January/February), 14.

Smietana, Bob. (2004). Mega Shepherd. *Christianity Today, 48* (February), 28–35.

Smith, Andrea. (1999). The American Way and the Good Red Road. American Indians, the Christian Right, and the (De)Construction of American Religion. In Vincent Wimbush (ed.), *The Bible and the American Myth* (pp. 13–52). Macon, GA: Mercer University Press.

Smith, Andrea. (2005a). Beyond "Pro-Choice versus Pro-Life": Women of Color and Reproductive Justice. *NWSA Journal, 17* (Spring), 117–40.

Smith, Andrea. (2005b). *Conquest: Sexual Violence and American Indian Genocide.* Cambridge, MA: South End Press.

Smith, Andrea. (2008). *Native Americans and the Christian Right: The Gendered Politics of Unlikely Alliances.* Durham, NC: Duke University Press.

Smith, Andrea. (2013). Unsetting the Privilege of Self-Reflexivity. In F. W. Twine and B. Gardener (eds.), *Geographies of Privilege* (pp. 263–80). Hoboken, NJ: Taylor and Francis.

Smith, Andrea. (2014). Native Studies at the Horizon of Death. In Audra Simpson and Andrea Smith (eds.), *Theorizing Native Studies* (pp. 207–34). Durham, NC: Duke University Press.

Smith, Andrea, and J. Kehaulani Kauanui. (2008). Native Feminisms without Apology Symposium. *American Quarterly, 60* (2), 241–315.

Smith, Craig. (1997). *Whiteman's Gospel.* Winnipeg, Canada: Indian Life Books.

Smith, Efrem, and Phil Jackson. (2005). *The Hip-Hop Church.* Downer's Grove, IL: InterVarsity Press.

Smith, J. Alfred, and Ross Maracle. (1989). Listening to America's Ethnic Churches. *Christianity Today, 33* (March 3), 25–41.

Smith, Jay. (2002). Deconstructing Islam. *Christianity Today, 46* (September 9), 37.

Smith, Linda Tuhiwai. (1999). *Decolonizing Methodologies.* London: Zed.

Smith, Michael. (2002). Holy Land Tourism. *Christianity Today, 46* (April 1), 34.

Smith, Rhonda. (2005). Church Seeks to Help Revitalize Detroit. *Charisma, 31* (August), 24–25.

Smith, Robert. (2004). Between Restoration and Liberation: Theopolitical Contributions and Responses to U.S. Foreign Policy in Israel/Palestine. *Journal of Church and State, 46* (Autumn), 833–60.

Smith, Samuel. (2016). Hillary Clinton Wins Wheaton College Student Poll. *Christian Post* (November 8). http://www.christianpost.com/news/hillary-clinton-wins-wheaton-college-student-poll-171390/.

Smith, Warren Cole. (2007a). Growing Up Schaeffer. *World, 22* (October 13), 32–33.

Smith, Warren Cole. (2007b). Home Again. *World, 22* (October 13), 22.

Smith, Warren Cole. (2007c). Numbers Racket. *World, 22* (December 1), 26–27.

Smith, Warren Cole. (2007d). A Shot across the Bow. *World, 22* (October 13), 26.

Smith, Warren Cole. (2008). Divided We Stand. *World, 23* (April 5/12), 34–36.

Smith, Warren Cole, and Rusty Leonard. (2009). "One Heart" Solution. *World, 24* (July 4), 76.

Smith, William. (2005). Moving Goalposts. *World, 20* (September 24), 29.

Soaries, DeForest "Buster." (1986). Putting First Things First. *Christianity Today, 30* (September 19), 24–26.

Soles, Henry. (1985). Confronting Change. *United Evangelical Action, 44* (January–February), 4–6.

The Soul of the Border Crisis. (2009). *Christianity Today, 53* (June), 18.

South Africa: Can the Church Mend the Anguish of a Nation? (1986). *Christianity Today, 30* (November 21), 2/I–19/I.

South African Churches Win at Polls. (1994). *Charisma, 19* (July), 58–59.

South Asia: Into the Heart of Darkness. (1993). *Charisma, 18* (January), 27–31.

Spade, Dean. (2010). *Normal Life*. New York: South End Press.

Spector, Stephen. (2009). *Evangelicals and Israel*. Oxford: Oxford University Press.

Spickard, Paul. (1986). Why I Believe in Affirmative Action. *Christianity Today, 30* (October 3), 12.

Spotlight: Getting Obama's Faith Wrong. (2010). *Christianity Today, 54* (October), 7.

Sprenkle, Sue. (2002). Christians Flee Rioting. *Christianity Today, 46* (February 4), 25.

Spring, Beth. (1985a). Falwell Raises a Stir by Opposing Sanctions against South Africa. *Christianity Today, 29* (October 4), 52–59.

Spring, Beth. (1985b). The Rationalization of Racism. *Christianity Today, 29* (October 4), 18–19.

Spring, Beth. (1986). Billy Graham's Washington Crusade Gains the Support of Black Church Leaders. *Christianity Today, 30* (June 13), 10–11.

Sreeprasad, Vidyadar. (2007). Dalits Join Church amid Persecution. *Charisma, 32* (May), 26.

Stackhouse, John. (1992). PC: Almost Correct? *Christianity Today, 36* (November 23), 17.

Stackhouse, John. (2008). A Variety of Evangelical Politics. *Christianity Today, 52* (November), 52–57.

Stafford, Tim. (1992). Campus Christians and the New Thought Police. *Christianity Today, 36* (February 19), 15–20.

Stafford, Tim. (1996). Robertson R Us. *Christianity Today, 40* (August 12), 26–33.

Stafford, Tim. (2000). Culture Clash. *Christianity Today, 44* (July 19), 42–43.

Stafford, Tim. (2004). India Undaunted. *Christianity Today, 48* (May), 28–35.

Stafford, Tim. (2006). The Call of Samuel. *Christianity Today, 50* (September), 82–85.

Stalcup, Elizabeth Moll. (1999). Swiss Human Rights Group Buys Sudanese Slaves to Free Them. *Charisma, 24* (32–33).

Stamp, Geoff. (2001). The Church Braves Persecution in Indonesia. *Charisma, 26* (January), 72–78.

Stannard, David. (1992). *American Holocaust*. Oxford: Oxford University Press.

Stanton, Glenn. (2009). Up for Debate. *Christianity Today, 53* (January), 38–41.

Stark, Rodney. (2014). Why the World Is Becoming More Violent. *Christianity Today, 58* (April), 60–64.

Stegall, Sarah. (2011). Changed by the Great Transformer. *Charisma, 36* (February), 40–41.

Steinfeld, Peter. (1996). Evangelicals Lobby for Oppressed Christians. *New York Times* (November 15), 26.

Stephen, Anil. (2001). Muslim Leader Appeals to Evangelicals. *Christianity Today, 45* (June 11), 24–25.

Stephen, Anil. (2002). Missionary Couple Remains in Limbo. *Christianity Today, 46* (February 4), 24.

Stertzer, Carol Chapman. (2001). When God Came to the Barrio. *Charisma, 27* (August), 46–56.

Stertzer, Carol Chapman. (2004). They Found His Mercy. *Charisma, 30* (October), 62–68.

Stetson, Nancy. (1997). She Has a Dream, Too. *Christianity Today, 41* (June 16), 34–36.

Stewart, Jimmy. (1999). Christians Still Being Enslaved by Muslims in War-Ravaged Sudan. *Charisma, 24* (May), 37–38.

Stewart, Keith. (2015). *We Were Wrong*. Addison, TX: HIS Publishing. Kindle.

Stichers, Mark. (2006). No Compromise. *Christianity Today, 50* (May), 19.

Stiffler, Matthew. (2010). Authentic Arabs, Authentic Christians: Antiochian Orthodox and the Mobilization of Cultural Identity. Dissertation, University of Michigan.

Stimson, Eva. (1986). White Supremacists Take on Trappings of Religion. *Christianity Today, 30* (August 8), 30–31.

Stone, Perry. (2009). The Secret of the Jews. *Charisma, 34* (May), 53–54.

Stone, Perry. (2011). Black Tide Rising. *Charisma, 37* (August), 44–47.

Stone, Perry. (2016). Could the Antichrist Arise from the 8th Kingdom? *Charisma, 41* (September), 54–57.

Strang, Cameron. (2011). What to Do When We Don't Agree. *Relevant* (May/June), 10.

Strang, Stephen. (1995). Unity of Purpose. *Charisma, 20* (January), 110.

Strang, Stephen. (1998a). A Crisis In Israel. *Charisma, 23* (March), 114.

Strang, Stephen. (1998b). The Season for Giving. *Charisma, 24* (December), 130.

Strang, Stephen. (1998c). Time for Respect. *Charisma, 23* (February), 102.

Strang, Stephen. (2004). Faith under Fire. *Charisma, 30* (August), 50–58.

Strang, Stephen. (2005a). Compassion for Israel. *Charisma, 31* (October), 122.

Strang, Stephen. (2005b). Secret Agent Man. *Charisma, 30* (March), 90.

Strang, Stephen. (2006a). Christians, Unite for Israel. *Charisma, 31* (June), 98.

Strang, Stephen. (2006b). Keith Butler for U.S. Senate. *Charisma, 31* (February), 82.

Strang, Stephen. (2007a). The Case for Huckabee. *Charisma, 33* (August), 90.

Strang, Stephen. (2007b). Feast of Tabernacles Draws Record Crowds. *Charisma, 33* (December), 27.

Strang, Stephen. (2007c). Warring for Our Nation. *Charisma, 32* (March), 82.

Strang, Stephen. (2007d). Why I Support Huckabee. *Charisma, 33* (December), 98.

Strang, Stephen. (2008a). Bomb Shelters for Israel. *Charisma, 33* (March), 98.

Strang, Stephen. (2008b). Intercede for Our Nation. *Charisma, 33* (April), 82.

Strang, Stephen. (2008c). John McCain Speaks Out. *Charisma, 34* (October), 34.

Strang, Stephen. (2008d). My Meeting with Obama. *Charisma, 34* (August), 74.

Strang, Stephen. (2008e). Obama's "Off-the-Record" Meeting with Christian Leaders. *Strang Report* (2010).

Strang, Stephen. (2008f). Terror-Free Investing. *Charisma, 34* (October), 82.

Strang, Stephen. (2008g). We Endorse John McCain. *Charisma, 34* (October), 82.

Strang, Stephen. (2009a). Be a Friend to Israel. *Charisma, 34* (May), 98.

Strang, Stephen. (2009b). A Call to Christian Leaders. *Charisma, 34* (January), 70.

Strang, Stephen. (2009c). Let's Work to End Racism. *Charisma, 34* (February), 66.

Strang, Stephen. (2013a). After Trayvon Martin Tragedy, Pastors Vow to Drive Reconciliation (August 5). http://www.charismamag.com/blogs/the-strang-report/18391-after-trayvon

-martin-tragedy-pastors-vow-to-drive-reconciliation.

Strang, Stephen. (2013b). A Mandate for Injustice. *Charisma, 38* (July), 11.

Strang, Stephen. (2014). Christians Must Get Off the Fence Concerning Israel. *Charisma, 40* (October), 8.

Strang, Stephen. (2015). Bridge-Building in the Body of Christ. *Charisma, 40* (March), 10.

Strang, Stephen. (2016a). Charisma Founder Steve Strang Endorses Ted Cruz for President (January 20). http://www.charismanews.com/opinion/54606-charisma-founder-steve-strang-endorses-ted-cruz-for-president.

Strang, Stephen. (2016b). Mr. Trump, I Have a Few Questions. *Charisma, 42* (September), 20–22.

Strang, Stephen. (2016c). Why Donald Trump Is America's Best Choice. *Charisma, 42* (September), 8.

Strang, Stephen, Harry Jackson Jr., and Samuel Rodriguez. (2012). The Church's Response to Racism. *Charisma, 37* (June), 40–53.

Stricherz, Mark. (2003). Evangelicals Advise on Muslim Dialogue. *Christianity Today, 47* (July), 21.

Stricherz, Mark. (2004). Land of Warlords. *Christianity Today, 48* (October), 22.

Stricherz, Mark. (2005). Better Late Than Never. *Christianity Today, 49* (December), 19.

Stricherz, Mark. (2006). Budget Battle. *Christianity Today, 50* (April), 22.

Strohmer, Charles. (2007). The Christian Message in Lebanon. *Christianity Today, 51* (August), 42–44.

Sutherland, James. (2004). Time for African American Missionaries. *Evangelical Missions Quarterly, 40* (October), 500–511.

Svanoe, Todd. (2001). When Business Aims for Miracles. *Christianity Today, 45* (May 21), 58–61.

Swerdlow, Deborah. (2012). Caught between the Spouse and the Spirit. *Christianity Today, 56* (September), 60–63.

Taber, Charles. (1991). Freedom to Evangelize v. Freedom to Seek Justice. *Transformation, 8* (April–June), 1–5.

Taliban Targets Christian Worker. (2008). *World, 23* (November 1–8), 12.

Tapia, Andrés. (1991). Viva Los Evangelicos! *Christianity Today, 35* (October 28), 16–22.

Tapia, Andrés. (1992). Why Is Latin America Turning Protestant? *Christianity Today, 36* (April 6), 28–39.

Tapia, Andrés. (1993). The Myth of Racial Progress. *Christianity Today, 37* (October 4), 16–27.

Tapia, Andrés. (1994). Churches Wary of Inner-City Islamic Inroads. *Christianity Today, 39* (January 19), 36–38.

Tapia, Andrés. (1997a). After the Hugs, What? *Christianity Today, 41* (February 3), 54–55.

Tapia, Andrés. (1997b). Candor, Repentance Mark PK Latino Summit. *Christianity Today, 41* (June 16), 58–59.

Taulbert, Clifton. (2001). America Listened. *World, 32* (August 25), 26–28.

Taylor, Daniel, and Mark McCloskey. (2008). How to Pick a President. *Christianity Today, 52* (June), 22–28.

Taylor, Greg. (2000). Under Suspicion. *Christianity Today, 44* (May 22), 36.

Taylor, Jeff. (2001). Christians in Detention for Prayer. *Christianity Today, 45* (April 23).

Taylor, LaTonya. (2002). Bloody Sunday. *Christianity Today, 46* (April 22), 23.

Teen Sex: Black Youth Leaders for a Solution. (1990). *Christianity Today, 34* (September 10), 55.

Teeter, David. (1990). Dynamic Equivalent Conversion for Tentative Believers. *Missiology, 18* (July), 305–13.

Teixeira, Brenda. (2001). A Cry from

South of the Border. *Charisma, 26* (January), 93–95.

Tennant, Agnieszka. (2002). The Ultimate Language Lesson. *Christianity Today, 46* (December 9), 32–38.

Tennant, Agnieszka. (2006). The God Who Lives and Works and Plays in Russia. *Christianity Today, 50* (November), 33–41.

Terry, Randall. (1988). *Operation Rescue.* Springdale, PA: Whitaker House.

Thomas, Cal. (1995). The Man, the Message. *World, 10* (October 28), 17.

Thomas, Cal. (1999). Running on Religion. *World, 26* (July 3–10), 35.

Thomas, Cal. (2007). Surrender Syndrome. *World, 22* (April 14), 4.

Thomas, Cal. (2008). Obama's Audacity. *World, 23* (May 3/10), 11.

Thomas, David. (2005). Changing Attitudes of Arab Christians toward Islam. *Transformation, 22* (January), 10–19.

Thomas, Gary. (1998). The Return of the Jewish Church. *Christianity Today, 42* (September 7), 62–69.

Thomas More Society. (2015). Obama Now Officially Forcing Girls to Share Showers with Boys. *Charisma News* (October 22). https://www.charismanews.com/us/52773-obama-now-officially-forcing-girls-to-share-showers-with-boys.

Thompson, Lisa. (2015). What We Get Wrong about Sex Trafficking. *Relevant* (January/February), 44.

Tiansay, Eric. (2002). National Religious Broadcasters' New President Resigns over Remarks. *Charisma, 27* (May), 24–25.

Tiansay, Eric. (2003). Hollywood's Religion of Choice. *Charisma, 28* (January), 44.

Tiansay, Eric. (2004a). U.S.-Based Evangelists Report Thousands of Conversions in Iran. *Charisma, 30* (September), 26.

Tiansay, Eric. (2004b). Winning at Marriage. *New Man, 11* (May/June), 20–23.

Tiansay, Eric. (2005a). Evangelists Use the Quran as a Tool to Preach Jesus among Muslims. *Charisma, 30* (January), 17–18.

Tiansay, Eric. (2005b). Storm Troopers. *Charisma, 31* (November), 51–54.

Tiénou, Tite. (2005). Indigenous Theologizing from the Margins to the Center. *NAIITS Journal, 3,* 5–17.

Tinker, George. (1993). *Missionary Conquest.* Minneapolis: Fortress.

Tise, Larry. (1987). *Proslavery.* Athens: University of Georgia Press.

Tivassoli, Sassan, and Toby Howarth. (2005). Shi'i Muslim Encounter with Christian Thought. *Transformation, 22* (January), 28–48.

Toalston, Art. (1989). AD 2000: Eleven Years to Reach the World. *Christianity Today, 37* (March 3), 48, 50.

Tolchin, Susan. (1996). *The Angry American.* Boulder, CO: Westview Press.

Tooley, Mark. (1996). NCC Turns Alleged Arson Epidemic to Political and Financial Advantage. *Faith and Freedom, 16* (Fall), 4–5.

Tooley, Mark. (2016). James Dobson and Christian Pessimism (September 17). https://juicyecumenism.com/2016/09/17/james-dobson-christian-pessimism/.

Top News Stories of 2008. (2009). *Christianity Today, 53* (January), 12.

Top Ten News Stories of 2003. (2003). *Christianity Today, 47* (January), 22.

Top Ten Stories of 2006. (2007). *Christianity Today, 51* (January), 20.

Toyama-Szeto, Nikki. (2017). Insights from "Silence"—The Embrace of Despisement (January 13). http://www.missioalliance.org/insights-silence-embrace-despisement/.

Tracking the Rise of U.S. Slave Traffic. (2011). *Reject Apathy* (1), 8.

Tracy, Amy. (2007). Q&A. *Christianity Today, 51* (May), 19.

Tracy, Kate. (2014). Native Approach. *Christianity Today, 58* (March), 16.

Turner, Kevin. (2005). Why Isn't the American Church Growing? *Charisma, 30* (January), 52–59.

U.S. Advisory Committee Cites Church's Role in South African Reconciliation. (1987). *Christianity Today, 31* (March 20), 63–64.

Usry, Glen, and Craig Keener. (1996). *Black Man's Religion*. Downer's Grove, IL: InterVarsity Press.

Valentine, Tom. (2000). "Dispensationalism" Impacting U.S. Policy (February 2). http://www.preteristarchive.com/dEmEnTiA/2000_valentine_dispensationalism.html.

Van Biema, David. (2008). The Global Ambition of Rick Warren. *Time, 172* (August 18), 37–41.

Van Leeuwen, Mary Stewart. (1989). Sticking a Needle in Apartheid. *Christianity Today, 33* (March 17), 13.

Van Loon, Michelle. (2008). Willow Creek Pastor Admits "Mistake." *Charisma, 33* (January), 26.

Van Opstal, Sandra Marie. (2016a). Does Your Church's Worship Need a Multicultural Makeover? *Christianity Today, 60* (January/February), 68–70.

Van Opstal, Sandra Marie. (2016b). *The Next Worship: Glorifying God in a Diverse World*. Downer's Grove, IL: InterVarsity Press.

Veenker, Jody. (1999). Called to Hate? *Christianity Today, 43* (October 25), 88–91.

Veenker, Jody. (2000). Sanctions Missing the Mark. *Christianity Today, 44* (June 12), 28.

Veith, Gene Edward. (1998). Morality, Prosperity. *World, 13* (October 31), 29–30.

Veith, Gene Edward. (2001a). Business Unusual. *World, 16* (September 1), 17.

Veith, Gene Edward. (2001b). Freedom versus Legalism. *World, 16* (December 1), 16.

Veith, Gene Edward. (2001c). Memory Loss. *World, 16* (November 17), 14.

Veith, Gene Edward. (2002). Camping Out. *World, 17* (April 20), 14.

Veith, Gene Edward. (2004a). Diversity of Life. *World, 19* (November 6), 33.

Veith, Gene Edward. (2004b). The Image War. *World, 19* (May 22), 30–35.

Veith, Gene Edward. (2005a). Blessings and Curses. *World, 20* (July 23), 22.

Veith, Gene Edward. (2005b). Free to Agree. *World, 20* (September 10), 32.

Veith, Gene Edward. (2005c). Murder, She Wrote. *World, 17* (April 30), 29.

Veith, Gene Edward. (2005d). Praying for Persecution. *World, 20* (October 1), 24.

Veith, Gene Edward. (2005e). Resisting Labels. *World, 20* (May 14), 34–35.

Veith, Gene Edward. (2005f). Riots in the Welfare State. *World, 20* (November 26), 28.

Veith, Gene Edward. (2005g). Structural Problems. *World, 20* (February 12), 26.

Veith, Gene Edward. (2005h). To: Our Chinese Monitor. *World, 20* (July 2–9), 44.

Veith, Gene Edward. (2005i). Whose Politics? *World, 20* (March 19), 30.

Veith, Gene Edward. (2006a). The Bible and Black History. *World, 21* (February 25), 30.

Veith, Gene Edward. (2006b). Cartoon Violence. *World, 21* (February 18), 28.

Veith, Gene Edward. (2006c). Radical Tactic. *World, 21* (January 21), 36.

Veith, Gene Edward. (2007a). Sex and the Evangelical Teen. *World, 22* (August 11), 9.

Veith, Gene Edward. (2007b). Single-Issue Politics. *World, 22* (March 10), 26.

Veith, Gene Edward. (2008a). Beyond Partners. *World, 23* (March 22/29), 35.

Veith, Gene Edward. (2008b). Suicide

Ideology. *World, 23* (February 23/March 1), 33.
Veith, Gene Edward. (2009). A Kinder, Gentler Marxism. *World, 24* (May 9), 56.
Veith, Gene Edward, and Lynn Vincent. (2005). Out of the Ghetto. *World, 20* (July 2–9), 38–41.
Velasco-Sanchez, AnaYelsi. (2016). Brown Girl Worshipping (May 3). https://browneyedamazon.com/2016/05/03/brown-girl-worshipping/.
Vercher, Amy. (2007a). The Divide at El Camino Real. *World, 22* (September 1/8), 52.
Vercher, Amy. (2007b). Vision Quest. *World, 22* (September 1/8), 32.
Vicari, Chelsen. (2015). How the Christian Left Is Twisting the Gospel. *Charisma, 40* (March), 54–58.
Vincent, Lynn. (1999a). Good News for Weary Marchers. *World, 14* (January 30), 19.
Vincent, Lynn. (1999b). How Homosexuals Fight. *World, 14* (April 10), 17–19.
Vincent, Lynn. (1999c). Whose Standards? *World, 14* (November 20), 28–29.
Vincent, Lynn. (1999d). Women's Right to Choose. *World, 14* (July 24), 16–18.
Vincent, Lynn. (2001a). A Run for the Border. *World, 16* (December 15), 10.
Vincent, Lynn. (2001b). Watts, Rising. *World, 16* (June 9), 22–25.
Vincent, Lynn. (2005a). The Last Shall Be First. *World, 40* (October 15), 28–29.
Vincent, Lynn. (2005b). The Philly Five. *World, 20* (January 29), 33.
Vincent, Lynn. (2006a). All Politics Is Local. *World, 21* (April 22), 26–27.
Vincent, Lynn. (2006b). Counterculture Clash. *World, 21* (January 21), 27–28.
Vincent, Lynn. (2006c). Free at Last. *World, 21* (November 11), 22–23.
Vincent, Lynn. (2006d). Purpose Driven AIDS Plan. *World, 21* (December 16), 27–29.
Vincent, Lynn. (2006e). Speaking Her Mind. *World, 21* (September 16), 28–29.
Vincent, Lynn. (2006f). Still in Service. *World, 21* (December 23), 26–29.
Vincent, Lynn. (2007a). California Scheming. *World, 22* (September 29), 24–25.
Vincent, Lynn. (2007b). One-Man Offensive. *World, 22* (August 25), 19.
Vincent, Lynn. (2007c). Silent Witnesses. *Charisma, 22* (July 28), 19–20.
Vincent, Lynn. (2007d). States' Rights. *World, 22* (October 27), 14–17.
Vincent, Lynn. (2008a). Brad Pitt vs. Joe the Plumber. *World, 23* (November 15/22), 44–46.
Vincent, Lynn. (2008b). Realities on the Ground. *World, 23* (November 15/22), 59–62.
Vincent, Lynn. (2008c). Shoot First, Ask Questions (Much) Later. *World, 23* (December 13/20), 13.
Vincent, Lynn. (2009). Illegal Procedures. *World, 24* (May 23), 57–59.
Vincent, Lynn, and John Dawson. (2006). Money-Go-Round. *World, 21* (February 11), 16–19.
Voice of the Martyrs. (2000). Faces of Persecution. *Voice of the Martyrs*, 1–15.
Voice of the Martyrs. (2006). *No Time to Lose.* Caney, KS: n.p.
VOM Staff. (2005). China's Barbaric Christians. *Voice of the Martyrs* (May), 2–7.
Vuoto, Loredana. (2000). Christian Groups Face Wave of Discrimination on U.S. Campus. *Charisma, 26* (September), 36–40.
Waalkes, Scott. (2004). Prescience and Paradigms. *Fides et Historia, 36* (Summer/Fall), 104–9.
Wadsworth, Nancy D. (2014). *Ambivalent Miracles: Evangelicals and the Politics of Racial Healing.* Charlottesville: University of Virginia Press. Kindle.
Wagner, Clarence. (2001). Between a

Rock and a Holy Site. *Christianity Today, 45* (February 5), 62–63.
Wagner, Clarence. (2003). The Error of Replacement Theology. *Jerusalem Connection* (April–May), 7, 20.
Walker, Ken. (1998a). Across U.S., Arson Fires Sparked Unity among Black and White Churches. *Charisma, 23* (February), 23–24.
Walker, Ken. (1998b). China's Leaders Critical of "Clandestine Missions." *Christianity Today, 42* (January 12), 64–65.
Walker, Ken. (1998c). So Many Good Memories. *Charisma, 23* (February), 54–60.
Walker, Ken. (2002). Detroit's Soul-Winner. *Charisma, 28* (December), 54–55.
Walker, Ken. (2004a). Pentecostal Leaders Support Formation of New Church Network. *Charisma, 30* (September), 21–22.
Walker, Ken. (2004b). Vacation Bible School Wars. *Christianity Today, 48* (March), 26.
Walker, Ken. (2005a). Christians Find Ally in Civil Liberties Group. *Charisma, 31* (November), 38.
Walker, Ken. (2005b). To the Bahamas and Beyond. *New Man, 12* (July–August), 44–50.
Walker, Ken. (2007). Stewards of the Earth. *Charisma, 33* (November), 82.
Walker, Ken. (2008a). Bynum and Weeks. *Charisma, 34* (August), 15.
Walker, Ken. (2008b). Pastors Work to Bring Racial Reconciliation. *Charisma, 33* (April), 16–17.
Walker, Ken. (2008c). When Muslims Find Jesus. *Charisma, 34* (December), 34–39, 71.
Walker, Ken. (2009a). Counting Controversy. *Christianity Today, 53* (September), 17.
Walker, Ken. (2009b). Pentecostal Gives Voice to Human Trafficking Victims. *Charisma, 35* (December), 13.
Walker, Ken. (2010a). Christians Oppose U.N. Defamation Resolution. *Charisma, 35* (January), 17.
Walker, Ken. (2010b). Finding a Path to Reform. *Charisma, 35* (May), 29–30.
Walker, Ken. (2010c). Out of Context. *Christianity Today, 54* (April), 14.
Walker, Ken. (2010d). Saving a Son of Hamas. *Charisma, 35* (May), 28.
Walker, Ken. (2013). Inside the New Insider Movement. *Charisma, 39* (September), 42–49.
Walker, Ken. (2015). Why Christians Are the New Targets of Discrimination? *Charisma, 40* (February), 20–26.
Walker, Ken. (2016). Faces of the Persecuted Church. *Charisma, 42* (September), 20–30.
Walker-Barnes, Chanequa. (2015). For Women of Color Who Have Considered Quitting When the Isolation Is Enuf. https://www.ccda.org/blog/12-blog/508-for-women-of-color-who-have-considered-quitting-when-the-isolation-is-enuf (no longer available).
Walker-Barnes, Chanequa. (2016). What You Don't Know about the Cosby Allegations (January 9). https://drchanequa.wordpress.com/2016/01/09/cosby-allegations/.
Walker-Barnes, Chanequa. (2019). *I Bring the Voice of My People: A Womanist Vision for Racial Reconciliation*. Grand Rapids, MI: Eerdmans.
Wallanau, Lance. (2016). Why I Believe Trump Is the Prophesied President. *Charisma, 42* (September), 26–38.
Wallis, Jim. (2014). Stand Your Ground Has No Moral Ground (February 18). https://sojo.net/articles/stand-your-ground-has-no-moral-ground.
Wallis, Jim. (2015). *God's Politics: Why the Right Gets It Wrong and the Left Doesn't Get It*. Grand Rapids, MI: Zondervan.

Wallis, Jim, and John Dilulio. (1997). With Unconditional Love. *Sojourners*, 26 (September–October), 16–22.

Walton, Jonathan. (2009). *Watch This!* New York: New York University Press.

Washington, Raleigh, and Glen Kehrein. (1993). *Breaking Down Walls*. Chicago: Moody Press.

Washington, Shae, and AnaYelsi Velasco-Sanchez. Interlocked and Intersected (February 15). https://www.youtube.com/watch?v=ptxhcf5v-RA.

Waters, Ken. (1992). Healing Our Urban Wounds. *World Vision*, 36 (August/September), 2–7.

Watson, Laura. (2005). Katrina the Sequel. *World*, 20 (September 24), 16–23.

Wax, Trevin. (2014). Ferguson Is Ripping the Bandages Off Our Racial Wounds (August 14). https://blogs.thegospelcoalition.org/trevinwax/2014/08/14/ferguson-is-ripping-the-bandages-off-our-racial-wounds/.

Weary, Dolphus. (1993). The Gift of Race. *Christianity Today*, 37 (April 26), 90.

Weber, Jeremy. (2008). My Heart Is in Gaza. *Christianity Today*, 52 (April), 14–15.

Weber, Jeremy. (2009a). Desert Deaths. *Christianity Today*, 53 (August), 13.

Weber, Jeremy. (2009b). God in Gaza. *Christianity Today*, 53 (March), 13.

Weber, Jeremy. (2016a). God at Work along the Refugee Highway. *Christianity Today*, 60 (March), 26–33.

Weber, Jeremy. (2016b). Outpacing Persecution. *Christianity Today*, 60 (November), 38–47.

Weber, Peter. (2016). Jerry Falwell Jr. Endorses Donald Trump with "Yo Mamma" Joke *Week*, (July 21). http://theweek.com/speedreads/637908/jerry-falwell-jr-endorses-donald-trump-yo-mamma-joke.

Weber, Timothy. (1998). How Evangelicals Became Israel's Best Friend. *Christianity Today*, 42 (October 5), 38–49.

Weber, Timothy. (2004). *On the Road to Armageddon: How Evangelicals Became Israel's Best Friend*. Grand Rapids, MI: Baker Books.

Weheliye, Alexander G. (2015). Plenary Address: NAIITS Conference. Wheaton College. June 6, 2015.

Weheliye, Alexander G. (2005). *Phonographies*. Durham, NC: Duke University Press.

Weheliye, Alexander G. (2008). After Man. *American Literary History*, 20 (Spring/Summer), 321–36.

Weheliye, Alexander G. (2014). *Habeas Viscus*. Durham: NC: Duke University Press.

Whalin, Terry. (1997). Murdered but Not Defeated. *Charisma*, 22 (May), 79–82.

Whalin, W. Terry. (1987). Into the Unknown. *World*, 6 (March/April), 46.

Whalin, W. Terry. (1997). Promise Keepers Gathers Black Leaders. *Christianity Today*, 41 (April 28), 84.

What Defines "Real" Persecution? (2001). *Open Doors Newsbrief*, 16 (December), 4.

What Does "Reached" Mean? An EMQ Survey. (1990). *Evangelical Missions Quarterly*, 26 (July), 316–23.

What Should Churches Do about Illegal Immigrants in Their State? (2011). *Christianity Today*, 55 (February), 52–53.

What's So Important about the Dakota Pipeline? (2017). *Relevant* (January/February), 20–21.

What's the Best Way to Reform U.S. Immigration Now? (2010). *Christianity Today*, 54 (March), 54–55.

What We Really Want. (2008). *Christianity Today*, 52 (January), 23.

White, Canon Andrew. (2003). Dampening the Fuse in Iraq. *Christianity Today*, 47 (July), 38–40.

White, Gayle. (1996). Clergy Conference

Stirs Historic Show of Unity. *Christianity Today, 40* (April 8), 88.

White, Joshua. (2007). Living with Islamists. *Christianity Today, 51* (April), 34–38.

White, Tom. (2004). The Muslim World. *Voice of the Martyrs* (December), 4–5.

White, Tom. (2005). Dare to Be Faithful. *Voice of the Martyrs* (Special Issue), 9–11.

The White Flag. (1998). *World, 13* (April 11), 10.

Whitehead, John. (1995). To Be Left Outside... *Rutherford, 4* (May), 11.

Who's Bashing Whom? (1998). *World, 13* (October 24), 9.

Wiens, Leanne. (1988). Just Who Am I? *Campus Life, 46* (March), 69–70.

Wilderson, Frank. (2010). *Red, White and Black*. Durham, NC: Duke University Press. Kindle.

Williams, Charles. (1996). New Era for Blacks—and Whites. *Alliance Witness, 121* (January 1), 25–26.

Williams, Juan. (2007). Descent into Destruction. *World, 22* (February 3), 32–37.

Williams, Kristian. (2007). *Our Enemies in Blue*. Cambridge, MA: South End Press.

Williams, Reggie. (2015). Empathic and Incarnational: A Better Christian Ethic at Fuller. *Fuller Magazine* (4), 54–59.

Williford, Stanley. (1998). Corporate Success Principles Are Taught to Urban Youth in Los Angeles. *Charisma, 24* (December), 42.

Willimon, William H. (1990). Stag Spirituality. *Christianity Today, 34* (April 23), 26–27.

Wilson, Bill. (1996). Why I Chose To Live in Hell. *Charisma, 22* (October), 55–62.

Wilson, John. (1993). Evil Whites or Bad Families? *Christianity Today, 37* (August 16), 61–62.

Wilson, John. (1999). Mr. Wallis Goes to Washington. *Christianity Today, 43* (June 14), 41–43.

Wilson, Jonathan R. (1998). *Living Faithfully in a Fragmented World: Lessons for the Church from MacIntyre's "After Virtue."* New York: Bloomsbury Publishing.

Wilson, Waziyatawin Angela, and Michael Yellow Bird. (2005). *For Indigenous Eyes Only*. Santa Fe: SAR.

Winner, Lauren. (2000). Book Report: Suffer the Children. *Christianity Today, 44* (June). https://www.christianitytoday.com/ct/2000/june12/39.94.html.

Winter, Ralph. (1991). Response. *Transformation, 8* (January/March), 6–8.

Wisdom, Alan. (2003). Guidelines for Christian-Muslim Dialogue (May 7). http://www.ird-renew.org/muslimdialogue (no longer available).

Witt, Marcos. (1996). What We Can Learn from the Latin American Revival. *Charisma, 21* (June), 40–44.

Witte, John, Jr. (2012). Shari'ah's Uphill Climb. *Christianity Today, 56* (November), 30–35.

Woehr, Chris. (1992). The Horror of Being a Mexican Evangelical. *Christianity Today, 36* (October 26), 68–69.

Wolf, Frank. (2000). Inexcusable Silence. *Christianity Today, 44* (September 4), 104–5.

Wood, Gail. (2001). Vietnamese Churches Growing under Indigenous Leaders. *Charisma, 27* (August), 34–35.

Wood, Gail. (2003). Former Football Pro Has Taken the Gospel into Hundreds of U.S. Prisons. *Charisma, 29* (October), 42–44.

Woodberry, J. Dudley. (2007). Can We Dialogue with Islam? *Christianity Today, 51* (February), 108–9.

Woodberry, J. Dudley. (2011). Flames of Love. *Christianity Today, 55* (September), 32–35.

Woodberry, J. Dudley, Russell Shubin,

and G. Marks. (2007). Why Muslims Follow Jesus. *Christianity Today*, 51 (October), 80–84.

Wooding, Dan. (1994). God's Wake-Up Call. *Charisma*, 19 (July), 29.

Wooding, Dan. (1998). Egypt's Christians Suffer at Hands of Muslim Persecutors. *Charisma*, 23 (March), 36–38.

Woodiwiss, Ashley. (2005). What Is Radical Orthodoxy? *Christianity Today*, 49 (August), 54–55.

Woodlief, Tony. (2009). Pause for Reflection. *World*, 24 (February 14), 50.

World. (2007). Marriage Matters. *World*, 22 (August 4), 34–36.

Worries over Rights in Afghanistan, Iraq. (2004). *Christianity Today*, 48 (January), 32.

Worthen, Molly. (2009). The Controversialist. *Christianity Today*, 53 (April), 42–49.

Wright, Bradley. (2011). They Like You. *Christianity Today*, 55 (August), 20–25.

Wright, Bradley. (2014). Your Faith Might Cost You Your Next Job. *Christianity Today*, 58 (June), 56–59.

Wright, Bradley. (2015). Dear Pastor, Can I Come to Your Church? *Christianity Today*, 59 (July/August), 32–42.

Wunderink, Susan. (2008a). Case by Case. *Christianity Today*, 52 (November), 15–16.

Wunderink, Susan. (2008b). Taliban Targets. *Christianity Today*, 52 (March), 21–22.

Wunderink, Susan. (2009). You've Got Jail. *Christianity Today*, 53 (March), 16–17.

Wydick, Bruce. (2012). Cost-Effective Compassion. *Christianity Today*, 56 (February), 24–29.

Wydick, Bruce. (2016). Married with Benefits. *Christianity Today*, 60 (July–August), 72–75.

Yakos, Marvin. (1990). *Jesus vs. Jihad: A Penetrating Biblical Account of Islam and the Mideast Crisis*. N.p.: Accord Books, 1990.

Yakos, Marvin. (2002). Islam: What You Need to Know. *New Man*, 9 (January–February), 19–20.

Yancey, George. (1996). *Beyond Black and White*. Grand Rapids, MI: Baker.

Yancey, George. (2006). *Beyond Racial Gridlock*. Downer's Grove, IL: InterVarsity Press.

Yancey, Philip. (2001). Letters from a Muslim Seeker. *Christianity Today*, 45 (December 3), 80.

Yancey, Philip. (2002). Why Do They Hate Us? *Christianity Today*, 46 (April 1), 80.

Yancey, Philip. (2006). The Lure of Theocracy. *Christianity Today*, 50 (July), 64.

Yancey, Philip. (2009). A Dream That Won't Die. *Christianity Today*, 53 (March), 96.

Yancey, Philip. (2010). A Living Stream in the Desert. *Christianity Today*, 54 (November), 30–35.

Yang, Jenny, and Matthew Soerens. (2009). *Welcoming the Stranger: Justice, Compassion and Truth in the Immigration Debate*. Downer's Grove, IL: InterVarsity Press.

Yarhouse, Mark. (2015). Understanding Gender Dysphoria. *Christianity Today*, 59 (July/August), 44–50.

The Year in Review. (1996/1997). *World*, 11 (December 18/January 4), 14.

Ye'or, Bay. (2005). *Eurabia*. Plainsboro, NJ: Associated University Press.

Yes: Nominal Evangelicals Exist. (2008). *Christianity Today*, 52 (April), 21.

Yoars, Marcus. (2010). We Will Never Forget. *Charisma*, 36 (October), 60–63.

Yoars, Marcus. (2012). Why Can't We All Just Move On? *Charisma*, 37 (June), 6–7.

Yoars, Marcus. (2013). Our Call for Persecution. *Charisma*, 39 (August), 6.

Yong, Amos. (2015). What False Teachings Are Evangelical Christians Most Tempted to Believe In? That Racism Is Gone. *Christianity Today, 59* (April), 27.

Yung, Bishop Hwa. (2011). A Fresh Call for U.S. Missionaries. *Christianity Today, 55* (November), 42–46.

Zoba, Wendy Murray. (1996). Separate and Equal. *Christianity Today, 40* (February 6), 14–24.

Zoba, Wendy Murray. (1997). Through Bombs and Bullets. *Christianity Today, 41* (September 1), 50–52.

Zoba, Wendy Murray. (1998). "Smuggling" Jesus into Muslim Hearts. *Christianity Today, 42* (October 5), 50–56.

Zoba, Wendy Murray. (1999). Good News for the Lost, Imprisoned, Abducted and Enslaved. *Christianity Today, 43* (August 9), 34–39.

Zoba, Wendy Murray. (2000a). Islam, U.S.A. *Christianity Today, 44* (April 3), 40–50.

Zoba, Wendy Murray. (2000b). A Woman's Place. *Christianity Today, 44* (August 7), 40–48.

Zurowski, Tom. (2004). Camel Boy "Crucified." *Voice of the Martyrs* (Special Issue), 4.

Zylstra, Sarah Eekhoff. (2007). Faith Talk Surprise. *Christianity Today, 51* (November), 16.

Zylstra, Sarah Eekhoff. (2008). Values Clash. *Christianity Today, 52* (January), 20.

Zylstra, Sarah Eekhoff. (2012). How Not to Care for Widows. *Christianity Today, 56* (October), 17–19.

Zylstra, Sarah Eekhoff. (2013a). Counting the Cost (Accurately). *Christianity Today, 57* (September), 15.

Zylstra, Sarah Eekhoff. (2013b). Missing Missionaries. *Christianity Today, 57* (April), 74.

Zylstra, Sarah Eekhoff. (2015a). Christians Debate State Bans on Syrian Refugees after Paris Attacks. *The Galli Report (Christianity Today)* (November 17). https://www.christianitytoday.com/news/2015/november/christians-debate-state-bans-syrian-refugees-paris-attacks.html.

Zylstra, Sarah Eekhoff. (2015b). Crisis Averted. *Christianity Today, 59* (November), 24.

INDEX

abortion, 223, 232; and eugenics, 236, 237, 301n23; and race, 235–40; as slavery, 67
Abramoff, Jack, 212
Abu-Lughod, Lila, 258
Abu Saada, Tass, 170
academic industrial complex, 194; decolonization of, 206–7; and ethnic studies, 7
Acts 29 Network, 51
affirmative action, 66
African American/Black studies, 11
African Americans: belongingness of, 94, 97–98; police murders of, 1
African religions, 95–96
agency: and genocide, 118
Aglow International, 298n13
Aikman, David, 298n20
AIM (American Indian Movement), 204
AIPAC (American Israel Public Affairs Committee), 184
Aldred, Ray, 30, 32, 205; on sovereignty, 208–9
Alexander, Jacqui, 263
Alexander, Michelle, 242
Alfred, Taiaiake, 195
Allen, Paul, 158
Amendment 2 (Colorado antigay proposition), 58
American Jewish Committee, 184
Americanness: and Christianity, 33
Americans for a Safe Israel, 258
American studies, 12
Amjad-Ali, Charles, 196
Anderson, Bill, 16–17
Anderson, Leith, 107, 151, 284
Andrescik, Robert, 217
Ahn, Che, 109

anti-Blackness: and Southern Baptist Convention, 2; and white evangelicalism, 26
anticolonialism, 198. *See also* colonialism; decolonization
Anti-Defamation League, 184
antigay politics: and evangelicals of color, 240
anti-Semitism: and anti-Zionism, 173
antitrafficking movement, 254
antiviolence movement, 252–53, 302n2; feminist of color critiques of, 254–55
apartheid, 15–16, 96–97, 291n3
Arab Americans, 99–103; as objects of mission, 99–100; as threats, 103
Arab American studies, 11
Arabs: racialization of, 27; as threats, 257
Arab World Ministries, 298n9
Argue, Don, 56, 120, 263, 288n6
Armstrong, William, 62–63
Ashcroft, John, 116
Asian Americans: and Asian religions, 104; Christian, 109
Asian American studies, 11
Asuza Street Revival, 14

backlash politics, 211–12
Backlin, Jim, 245–46
Bakke, Raymond, 63–64, 107
Bakker, Jay, 231, 301n19
Baraka, Sho, 277–78
Barber, Donna, 114
Barber, Leroy, 114
Barna, George, 262
Barton, David, 96
Bauer, Gary, 163, 178, 218, 260–61
Bear, Cheryl, 2, 265–66

Beck, Glenn, 255
Begin, Menachem, 160
Bell, Derrick, 53, 54
Bell, L. Nelson, 14
Belz, Joel, 24
Benally, Klee, 198
Benedict XVI (pope), 297n6
Ben-Gurion, David, 159
Bentley, William, 288n6
Berlant, Lauren, 67
Bernard, A. R., 58, 65
Bernis, Jonathan, 145, 296n2
biopolitics, 116–17
biopower: and evangelical Christianity, 117–18; and immigration, 106
Black evangelicals: presumed progressiveness of, 8; and racial reconciliation project, 92–93
Black Lives Matter, 28, 79, 99, 270–71, 274; and Asian Americans, 265; InterVarsity support for, 23; Latinx support for, 114; and racial reconciliation, 272; and white supremacy, 266, 283
Black Nationalism, 99
blackness: and hypervisibility, 90; as property, 99; and white evangelism, 99
Black theology, 224
Bob Jones University, 15; interracial dating at, 287n5
Bolger, Ryan, 45–46
Boone, Wellington, 18, 53, 261–62
Botros, Zakaria, 148
Bowers, Veronica, 125
Boycott, Divestment, and Sanctions (BDS) campaign, 178–79, 298n18
Bradley, Anthony, 66, 74, 77
Brock, Rita Nakashima, 117
Brother Andrew, 119, 137, 153
Brown v. Board of Education, 14
Brown, Austin Channing, 2, 75, 267
Brown, Harold, 33
Brown, Judy, 303n8
Brown, Michael, 84, 272
Burge, Gary, 171, 176–77
Bush, George W., 69, 135, 178, 294n7; Black support for, 232, 301n20; evangelical discontent with, 212; faith-based agenda of, 213–14, 300n1; feminist rhetoric, use of, 255–56; Hispanic support for, 244
Bynum, Juanita, 228, 263

Caldwell, Kirbyjon, 215, 221
Calver, Clive, 62
Camacho, Daniel J., 11
Camden House, 49
Campolo, Tony, 49, 97, 217
Cannon, Mae, 79, 158, 172
capitalism: and critical ethnic studies, 3; Native nationalist critique of, 205–6; and Protestantism, 105; and white supremacy, 31–32
Carrasco, Rudy, 66
Carroll, M. Daniel, 245
Carter, Earl, 94
Carter, Jimmy: on Black Lives Matter, 273; and racial justice, 273
Carter, Stephen, 261
Castelli, Elizabeth, 121–22
Castile, Philando, 273
Cati, W. L., 256, 257–58
Center for Inclusivity, 268
Chambers, Alan, 232
Channing, Austin. *See* Brown, Austin Channing
Chapman, Colin, 153, 175–76
Charisma (magazine), 36, 37, 94; anti-immigrant content in, 105–6; on Asian religions, 292n6; on Christian persecution, 122, 124, 131, 295n9; on Christian Zionism, 187; on class, 61; on gay rights, 68; gender justice in, 263–64; on immigration, 245–46, 247, 248; on Islam, 146, 152; on Israel, 164; on Israel-Palestine conflict, 168, 169–70, 298n17; on Nation of Islam, 98; on Obama, 219; on race, 272; racial justice in, 263–64; and racial reconciliation, 164, 224, 228; and racial uplift, 289n8; on racism, 55, 56; Republican party support of, 213–14; on Trump, 275–76; on Zionism, 164, 166, 224
Cheney, Dick, 214

Chester Fatherhood Initiative, 261
Chicano/Latino studies, 11
CHIEF (Christian Hope Indian Eskimo Fellowship), 11
Chilton, David, 96
Cho, Eugene, 240, 283
Cho Seung-Hui, 104
Chow, Rey, 31–32
Christian Aid Mission, 37
Christian Coalition, 4, 220; class politics of, 59; electoral politics, focus on, 91–92; and racial justice, 57; and racial reconciliation, 55–58, 72; on racism, 71; and social justice, 58
Christian Community Development Association (CCDA), 76, 114, 250, 283
Christian Identity movement, 17–18, 287n1
Christianity Today (magazine): on African religions, 291n2; and anti-Asian racism, 90–91; on apartheid, 291n3; on Arabs and Muslims, 100, 145; on Christian persecution, 124, 127, 130, 132–33, 138, 293n4, 294nn7–8; on Christian Zionism, 171, 172; on George W. Bush, 212; on homosexuality, 69–70; on immigration, 106–8, 247–48, 249; on implicit bias, 93; Institute on Racism, 93; on Islam, 151, 153, 296n3; on Israel-Palestine conflict, 169, 171; and multiculturalism, 34, 38; on New Reformed Movement, 51; on Obama, 219; on poverty, 64; and racial reconciliation, 17, 18, 19, 20, 228; on racism, 54; restitution, call for, 94–95; on same-sex marriage, 239; on Tea Party, 226; on Third World debt, 290n15
Christian Jew Foundation, 299n24
Christian persecution movement, 26–27, 118, 183, 84, 250; and Christian exceptionalism, 121–24, 130, 293n6; critiques of, 138–41; and empire building, 128; evangelical critiques of, 128–35; and human rights, 132–34; history of, 119–21; and Islam, 144, 151, 297n6; Jewish support for, 293n2; necropolitics of, 138; triumphalism, narrative of, 139, 141; and U.S. exceptionalism, 124–28, 129, 133–34, 137–38; and U.S. foreign policy, 295n17; and War on Terror, 135–37
Christian Right, 5; affirmative action critique of, 66; anti-Catholic sentiment of, 104; antiracist organizing in, 13; apartheid, support for, 96–97; and capitalism, 284; and Christian persecution, 125–26; and immigration, 246–47; on Islam, 234; Islamophobia within, 27; "oppression" of, 67–72; politics, rearticulation of, 211–20, 220; and race, 227, 287n4; and racial justice, 6; racial politics of, 14; and racial reconciliation movement, 4; and U.S. exceptionalism, 34; and whiteness, 227–28
Christians for Biblical Equality, 264
Christians United for Israel (CUFI), 142, 162–64, 187; on Israel-Palestine conflict, 166, 179, 298n10
churches, Indigenous, 47
Churches Uniting in Christ (CUIC), 21
Christian Zionism, 9, 27, 29, 103, 143; and biopower, 122; and European racism, 165; evangelical critiques of, 165–79; and Islamophobia, 155, 162, 179; Israel, support for, 159–64; and Jewish evangelism, 158; and racialization of Judaism, 179. *See also* dispensationalism; Zionism
civil disobedience, 55
civil rights movement: and white evangelicalism, 4
civil unions, 231, 301n18. *See also* same-sex marriage
Cizik, Richard, 215, 216, 222, 300n7, 300n9; on immigration, 244
Claiborne, Shane, 48–50
Claydon, David, 146–47
Cleveland, Christena, 2, 250, 266, 274–75
Clinton, Bill, 160, 272, 277, 279
Clinton, Hillary, 121, 216, 277–78
Coe, Douglas, 178
Cohen, Cathy, 61

colonialism: and Christianity, 95, 198, 202; and Christian persecution, 131; and critical ethnic studies, 3; and ethnic studies, 3; and Indigenous peoples, 123; and U.S. exceptionalism, 126

colonization: and Christianity, 202–4; as violence, 192

color blindness, 9, 67, 280; and racial reconciliation, 28; and white evangelicals, 28

Colson, Charles, 125, 223, 241, 290n15, 300n6; on same-sex marriage, 259; on Tea Party, 225–26

Columbus, Christopher, 111–12, 293n17

Combs, Roberta, 181

Concerned Women for America, 55, 60; on Islam, 145; and racial reconciliation, 55–56

Conde-Frazier, Elizabeth, 2

Cone, James, 280

Cooke, Phil, 300n9

Cooper, Rodney, 261

Copeland, Kenneth, 112

Cothran, Charlene, 232

Coulthard, Glen, 83

Cowen, Jamie, 185–86

Cox, Caroline, 296n3

Criswell, W. A., 15

critical ethnic studies, 206, 285; and decolonization, 194; and evangelicalism, 2–4, 11–13, 90; and genocide, 140; and heteropatriarchy, 3; multiculturalism, critique of, 32, 90; and racial justice, 2; racial reconciliation, critique of, 25, 285–86. See also ethnic studies

critical theory: people of color, erasure of, 41

Crosby, Alicia, 268

Crouch, Andy, 19

Cruz, Ted, 275–76

Cryderman, Lyn, 55

cultural nationalism, 109

Curry, Dean, 126

Dalits, 127, 294n7

Daniels, Matt, 247

Darby, John N., 156

Dawson, John, 112

DeBorst, Ruth Padilla, 295n12

Deception in the Church (anti-Indigenous organization), 113

De Jesus, Wilfredo, 246

decolonization, 88; of the academy, 206–7; and anticolonialism, 198; of Christianity, 10–11, 201, 210; defined, 192; and intellectual purity, 197–98; in Native studies, 27; of theology, 207, 210

Deloria, Philip, 193–94

Deloria, Vine, Jr., 5

Diamond, Billy, 112–13

Dilulio, John, 65–66

disidentification, 198–99

dispensationalism, 155, 159, 175–76, 183; and American exceptionalism, 177; and anti-Semitism, 173; and Jewish conversion, 179, 180. See also Christian Zionism

Dobson, Ed, 70, 83

Dobson, James, 217, 218–19, 300n7, 300n9, 301n18; politics of, 220–23; Trump endorsement, 277–78, 279

Dobson, Ryan, 300n7

Driscoll, Mark, 47, 50–52, 73–74

D'Souza, Dinesh, 234

DuBois, Joshua, 214–15

Eckstein, Yechiel, 162, 184

Eckstrom, Kevin, 297n6

Edwards, Jefferson, 94

Eidsmoe, John, 16

Ellis, Carl, 98

Ellis, Edward, 35,

Elon, Binyamin "Benny," 160

Emergent (Emerging) Church model, 43–48, 207–8; and antiracism, 46; and racial reconciliation, 47, 49; and whiteness, 46

Emerson, Michael, 20–21, 27–29, 78–79, 288n9

essentialism, 32

ethnic studies: and identity politics, 3; and multiculturalism, 32, 118; Senate Bill 1070 (Arizona), 206. See also critical ethnic studies

Evangelical Immigration Roundtable, 113
evangelicalism: and anti-Asian racism, 72–73, 90–91; and anti-Black racism, 90–91; biopolitics of, 26; and "Black-white" paradigm, 92; and capitalism, 62–63, 64–67; Christian Zionism, critiques of, 165–67; and class, 289n11; and colonialism, 5, 10, 198; and critical ethnic studies, 2–4, 11–13; definition of, 287n1; and empire building, 128; ex-Muslim narratives of, 256; and fundamentalism, 287n1; and genocide, 110; and globalization, 35; and hypermasculinity, 262; and imperialism, 5, 131; and multiculturalism, 144; and Palestine, 167; people of color, incorporation of, 8–9; presumed whiteness of, 8–9, 11; and race, 13–16, 211; and racialization, 26, 140–41; and racial justice, 6, 12, 78; and racial reconciliation movement, 25, 26, 28, 41, 75–76; and social justice, 2; and structural racism, 55–56; and trans politics, 230, 301n15; and whiteness, 12, 29, 39, 40–42, 72–75, 80, 122–23, 227–28; and white supremacy, 5, 9–10, 274; women-of-color consciousness within, 28
evangelicals: and class, 59–67; on homosexuality, 68–69, 229–30; Israel, support for, 159–64; presumed conservatism of, 5; and prison reform, 242–49; and refugee policy, 293n15; as victims, 67–72
evangelicals of color, 11; and gay rights, 229; and inclusion, 32; Native American, 27; and politics of rearticulation, 8
Evans, Rachel Held, 51–52, 73–75
Evans, Tony, 5, 18, 98

Faith in Action (National Network), 64
Faith Today (magazine), 112–13
Falwell, Jerry, 14, 132, 277; apartheid, support for, 16; on Islam, 150; racism of, 15; support for Israel, 160, 163, 174
Falwell, Jerry, Jr., 269; Trump endorsement, 275, 276–77, 280
Family Research Council, 232, 246

Fan, Daniel, 72, 73
Fanon, Frantz, 206
Farley, Alan, 96
Farrakhan, Louis, 97–98
Farrell, Elisabeth, 256
Feder, Donald, 181
Fellowship of Israel and Black America, 164
feminism, evangelical, 28, 231; and Arab and Muslim women, 255–58; and racial reconciliation, 252; as threat, 303n8
feminists, Native, 209
Ferguson, Roderick, 40
Ferguson protests, 59, 74–76, 114, 265–66, 272–74
Fernando, Ajith, 136
Fiorenza, Elisabeth Schüssler, 81
Fischer, Brian, 225
Fish, Stanley, 44
Focus on the Family (magazine), 33
Focus on the Family (organization), 76, 300n7
Foucault, Michel, 285; on racism, 116–17
Frame, Randy, 34
Francis, Robert, 192, 193, 199–201
Franke, John, 43
Freedman, Helen, 258
Freedom Road, 266
Freeman, Jo, 82
French, David, 280
Fujimori, Alberto, 127–28, 132–33

Galatis, George, 290n15
Galli, Mark, 81, 128
Gao Zhan, 294n7
Gardner, Day, 236–37
Garner, Eric, 272, 303n1
Garrett, Brandon, 302n26
gay rights: and evangelicals of color, 229
gender reconciliation, 23
genocide: and agency, 118; and blackness, 140; and Christianity, 18, 80, 196; Christian Right support for, 128; and colonization, 192; and evangelicalism, 110; of Native peoples, 13, 18, 94–95, 110–12, 202; and whiteness, 140; and white supremacy, 110

Gerson, Michael, 226
Gibbs, Eddie, 45–46
Gilliard, Dominique, 75, 114–15, 302n27
Gilmore, Ruth Wilson: on nonprofit industrial complex, 5; on racism and premature death, 39, 180
Giuliani, Rudy, 220
globalization: and forced migration, 107
Gong Shengliang, 130–31
González, Justo, 35
gospel, civil, 33
Gospel Coalition, 51, 52, 273; on Trump, 278
Grady, J. Lee, 123, 169, 263, 299n27, 302n2; on immigration, 245
Graham, Billy, 14–15, 154
Graham, Franklin, 108–9, 150, 216
Green, Lynn, 103
Grenz, Stanley, 43–45
Grudem, Wayne, 272
Gunn, T. Jeremy, 129–30, 295n11
Gushee, David, 33, 222, 226, 231
Guth, James, 33

Hackett, Erna Kim, 2, 75, 114, 250, 267, 274
Hagee, John, 161, 162–63, 164, 178; on Jewish evangelism, 182–83; support for Israel, 166
Haggard, Ted, 51, 145, 230
Hall, Stuart, 7, 52, 63; on class and ideology, 9
Hammouda, Fisal, 146
Han, Sora, 257
Hanson, Jane, 160
Hanson, Victor Davis, 244
Harambe Center, 66
Hardage, Jeanette, 132
Harlan, Mark, 168–69
Harmon, Bill, 276
Harper, Lisa Sharon, 2, 78–79, 266, 274
Harris, Angela, 92
Harris, Cheryl, 92
Harris, David, 184
Hartman, Saidiya, 92
Hartsock, Nancy, 40, 46
Hartwig, Mark, 148, 153

Hatmaker, Jen, 233–34
Haugen, Gary, 254–55
Hawkins, Larycia, 154–55
Hayford, Jack, 163
Healing for the Native Ministry, 202–3
Hedding, Malcolm, 169
Heimlich, Phil, 55
Heltzel, Peter, 7, 14, 41, 87, 99
Henry, Carl, 70, 291n3
Herndon, Ernest, 288n1 (chap. 1)
Hertzke, Allen, 119, 120
heteronormativity: and evangelicals of color, 232–35; and feminism, 259; and Islam, 234–35
heteropatriarchy: and critical ethnic studies, 3
Hiebert, Paul, 44
Higgins, Michelle, 274
Hilliard, Clarence, 98
Hinduism, 126–27
Hindus, 104
Hinn, Benny, 161, 163, 166
hip-hop church, 47
homeschooling: and desegregation, 14
Horowitz, Michael, 128–29, 295n11
Houston Baptist University, 103
Howse, Brannon, 220–21
Hubers, John, 177–78
Huckabee, Mike, 216, 219, 220–21, 301n25
human rights: in Israel, 165–66, 172
Hunter, Joel, 58, 215, 217
Huntington, Samuel, 152–53
Hurricane Katrina: Bush response to, 212; white evangelical response to, 56
Hussein, Saddam, 136, 144, 213
Hutchins, Derrick, 228
Hybels, Bill, 42, 146, 297n6

identity politics, 3; as conservative project, 32
immigration, 105–9; and biopower, 106; and ethnic studies, 3; and missionary work, 243
immigration reform, 211; and evangelicalism, 242–49
imperialism, U.S.: and Christian

382 INDEX

evangelicalism, 38; and U.S. exceptionalism, 126
Indians for Life, 236
Indigenous peoples: and Christian persecution, 166; and colonialism, 123; and genocide, 110, 111–12
Indigenous studies: and decolonization, 194
Institute of Religion and Democracy, 34, 71, 124–25, 297n7, 303n4 (conc.); on Islam, 144
Interfaith Alliance on Zionism, 258
International Christian Embassy, 184–85
International Fellowship of Jews and Christians, 184
International Justice Mission (IJM), 254–55
International Religious Freedom Act (1998), 120–21
InterVarsity Christian Fellowship, 23, 265, 267
Islam, 27; and blackness, 98; civilization thesis, 152–53; demonization of, 148, 152–53, 176, 297n6; as inherently violent, 146–47, 150; racialization of, 143; represented as evil, 144–49; as threat, 144–45
Islamophobia, 142; and Christian Zionism, 155, 179; critiques of, 149–55; post-9/11, 149, 150–51, 154; and Trump, 155
Ivens, Evelmyn, 2

Jackson, Earl Walker, 54, 57, 236, 237
Jackson, Harry, Jr., 92, 227, 232, 241–42, 246, 272; on Trump, 276
Jackson, Phil, 47
Jackson, Zakiya, 2, 250, 267
Jacob, Charles, 258–59
Jacobs, Adrian, 202, 208, 209
Jakes, T. D., 216
Jamal, Amaney, 142–43
James, Kay Cole, 18, 283
Jarjour, Riad, 177
Jefferson, Mildred, 61
Jenkins, Philip, 138
Jennings, Willie James, 79–80

Jesus for Muslims Network, 109
Jewish evangelism, 158, 160, 179–85, 185, 299n30
Jews for Jesus, 109, 186
Johnson, Nelson, 83, 84
Johnson, Steve, 144
Johnson, Sylvester, 94
Johnston, Patrick, 35
Jones, Bob, III, 152, 170–71
Jones, Bob, IV, 292n9
Jones, Howard, 15
Jones, Micky ScottBey, 2
Jones, Robert P., 287n2, 288n7
Jones, Tony, 45, 47
Jones, William, 118
Justice Conference, 23–24

Kaba, Mariame, 84
Keener, Craig, 98
Keith, Anita, 197
Keyes, Alan, 232
Khang, Kathy, 2, 114, 265, 284
Khoury, Habib, 170
Killjoy Prophets, 80, 90, 115, 142, 179, 267
Kimball, Dan, 47
King, Alveda, 236, 237
King, Martin Luther, Jr., 15, 19; as "Black Zionist," 164; evangelical appropriations of, 55, 70–71
Kjaer-Hansen, Kai, 179
Klinghofer, David, 180
Knippers, Diane, 252–53, 297n7
Kondo, Dorinne, 37
Kuo, David, 213
Kuramitsu, Kenji, 268

Land, Richard, 24, 37–38, 101, 171–72, 218; on Christian persecution, 121; on immigration, 246–47, 248; on Islam, 148
Lane McCoo, Marcia, 236
Lantis, Mick, 291n3
Latinos: evangelizing of, 104–5, 106, 292n12; and immigration, 105
Lawton, Kim, 126
LeBlanc, Janine, 195
LeBlanc, Terry, 194, 205, 208

INDEX | 383

Lee, Sophia, 110
Lee, Trip, 274
Leslie, R., Jr., 17
Lewis, Davis, 160
Lewis, James, 297n5
liberation theology, 295n12
Lieberman, Joe, 163
Lieberman, Paul, 187
LifeWay, 22, 72–73, 90
Lightbody, C. Stuart, 36
Lindsey, Hal, 150, 157, 159
Long, Eddie, 230
Lorde, Audre, 210
Loritts, Bryan, 280
Los Angeles uprising (1992): and racial reconciliation, 17
Loury, Glenn, 76
Lucado, Max, 278
Lucero, Art, 245
Lula da Silva, Luiz Inácio, 133
Lundgren, Jim, 23
Lyons, Charles, 20–21
Lyons, Scott, 194

MacDonald, Gordon, 23
Macedo-Nolan, Mayra, 2, 250
Malachy, Yona, 159
Malcolm X, 76
Mandela, Nelson, 96, 292n3
Manuel, David, 111
Maracle, Ross, 112–13
Markham, Myles, 268
Marocco, James, 110
Marshall, Paul, 111, 119, 153
Martey, Emmanuel, 210
Martin, Andrew, 229
Martin, Trayvon, 272; evangelical response to, 85
Marty, Martin, 226
Maxwell, Joe, 18
Mbembe, Achille, 138
McAdam, Doug, 35–36
McCain, John, 163, 164, 182–83; evangelical engagement of, 216–19
McCallum, Dennis, 34
McCartney, Bill, 16, 58, 186; and racial reconciliation, 23

McClintock, Anne, 148, 193
McClurkin, Donnie, 228
McDermott, Gerald, 168
McKinney, George, 60
McKissick, Drew, 220
McKnight, Scot, 47
McLaren, Brian, 45–46, 208
McNeil, Brenda Salter, 2, 78, 141, 274, 283
Mearsheimer, John, 162
Medved, Michael, 181
Meeks, James, 238
megachurches: seeker model of, 42–43
Merdian, Wendy, 152
Merritt, Jonathan, 226, 279
Messianic Jews, 149, 182, 185–88; racialization of, 186, 188–91
Metzger, Paul, 44, 140
militia groups, 17–18
Miller, Yvonne, 239
Minuteman Civil Defense Corps, 105
Missiology (journal), 36
missionaries, evangelical: as intelligence sources, 125; and non-Black people of color, 92–93; and U.S. foreign policy, 136–37; and U.S. imperialism, 139; and Westernization, 35
missionizaton: of Native peoples, 193, 195–97
Mission Mississippi, 30–31
missions, evangelical: to Africa, 93–94; and the Global South, 35–37
Mitchell, Ben, 22
Mlay, Wilfred, 135
Mohamad, Mahathir bin, 150
Mohler, Albert, 24, 277
Montt, Efraín Ríos, 129, 132
Moore, Russell, 1, 2, 71, 108, 155, 269; response to Pulse shooting, 233; on Trump, 278–80
Moral Majority, 15–16, 220; and feminism, 14; support for Israel, 160
Morey, Robert, 147
Morrison, Cheryl, 161
Morrison, George, 162
Moten, Frederick, 12, 80–81
Mouw, Richard, 173, 174, 178, 181–82
MoveOn.org, 58

Moya, Paula, 40, 46
Moynihan, Daniel Patrick, 260
Moynihan Report, 260, 274
multiculturalism: and antiracism, 32, 82; and Christian Zionism, 144; critiques of, 31; and evangelicalism, 33, 52; and Islamophobia, 144; and Mission Mississippi, 31; and Native Americans, 196; and neoliberalism, 39; and racial justice, 39; and racial reconciliation, 17, 25–26; resistance to, 33; and white supremacy, 39
Munayer, Salim, 170
Muñoz, José Esteban, 198–99
Muriu, Oscar, 38
"muscular Christianity," 262
Muslims, 99–103; evangelizing of, 148; as inherently violent, 153; as objects of mission, 99–100, 103; racialization of, 27, 162, 179; as threats, 103, 144
My People International, 201–2, 205

Naber, Nadine, 142–43
NARAL (National Abortion and Reproductive Rights League), 237
National Association of Evangelicals (NAE), 18, 64, 178; on Christian persecution, 121; on immigration, 248; on Islam, 144, 151; on Latinos, 105; Obama engagement of, 215; political agenda of, 222; racial reconciliation efforts of, 288n6; relationship with NBEA, 18, 288n6; undocumented immigrants in, 106
National Black Evangelical Association (NBEA), 11, 16, 19; relationship with NAE, 18, 288n6
National Hispanic Leadership Conference, 11, 243
nationalism, Native: critique of capitalism, 203–6
National Latino Evangelical Coalition, 64
National Network (Faith in Action), 64
Nation of Islam, 97–98; and masculinity, 262
Native American studies, 11

Native evangelicals, 193, 210
Native Hawaiians, 110
Native studies: decolonization in, 27, 192, 195–98
Neff, David, 104, 112, 178, 297n6, 299n27; on Christian persecution, 132; on death penalty, 301n26; support for same-sex marriage, 231
Netanyahu, Benjamin, 160
New Hope for Youth, 61
New Man (journal), 16, 149, 217; on feminism, 260; on Islam, 235
New Monasticism, 48–50; and racial reconciliation, 49
New Reformed Movement, 50–52; misogyny of, 51–52
Nikkel, Ronald, 178
9/11 attacks: and evangelicals of color, 71–72; and Islamophobia, 27
Nobles, Cathy, 292n4
NoDAPL, 113, 265
Noll, Mark, 91
nonprofit industrial complex (NPIC), 5–6, 63; radical critiques of, 50
North, Gary, 60–61
North American Institute for Indigenous Theological Studies (NAIITS), 27, 192, 193, 195–208; alternative ministry, creation of, 207; decolonization, engagement with, 194; and Emergent Movement, 207–8
Northern Baptists, 2
North Star Christian Academy, 61
Ntlha, Moss, 79

Obama, Barack, 167, 275; backlash against, 39, 155; Christian conservative critiques of, 61–62, 298n10; evangelical engagement of, 214–20; evangelical of color support for, 9, 216, 227; faith-based policies of, 215, 300n11; LGBT politics of, 225; and race, 39, 224–27; racialization of, 162; and racial reconciliation, 211
Oden, Thomas, 67–68
Olasky, Marvin, 101, 126–27, 180, 300n1, 301n15; on death penalty, 241, 301n26

INDEX | 385

Open Doors Ministry, 119, 122, 131–32, 153
Ortberg, John, 178
Osteen, Joel, 275, 277

Page, Frank, 215
Pagitt, Doug, 45, 51
Palau, Luis, 61, 132
Palin, Sarah, 151, 218, 219, 300n4
Pannell, William, 17, 56
Paquin, Andrew, 62–63, 289n12
Parajon, Gustavo, 128
Parham, Charles, 14
Parker, Angela, 2
Parker, Star, 18, 63
Parshall, Janet, 160, 256
Parshall, Phil, 256
Parsley, Rod, 242, 248
Pease, Richard, 107
Pederson, Wayne, 300n9
Pence, Mike, 269
Pentecostal/Charismatic Churches of North America (PCCNA), 18, 21
Pentecostal Fellowship of North America, 18, 21
Pentecostalism, 14, 287n1
Perkins, John, 18, 76, 97, 178
Perkins, Tony, 218, 246; on prison reform, 241–42
Perlmutter, Nathan, 184
Pew, J. Howard, 14
Phelps, Fred, 69
Phillips, Randy, 188–89
PICO (Peoples Improving Communities through Organizing), 64
Pierce, Clifford, 72
Piper, John, 51, 168, 301n9; on Jewish evangelism, 181
Planned Parenthood, 236–37, 272, 275, 287n2, 301n23
Pollard, Mark, 94, 95
Porter, Brandon, 21–22
postmodernism: evangelical, 43–44, 45; Marxist critiques of, 39–40; and truth claims, 43–44; women of color critiques of, 39–40
Pott, David, 112

Potter, Ronald, 19
Povinelli, Elizabeth, 3, 31
premillenialism, 156
Price, Frederick K., 21, 272
prison abolitionist movement, 84, 206
Prison Fellowship, 241
prison industrial complex (PIC), 5–6; Black evangelical critique of, 241
prison reform, 211, 224, 302n26; and Black evangelicals, 241–42
Progressive National Baptist Convention, 25
Project Joseph, 98
pro-life movement: as antiracist, 235–36
Promise Keepers, 58–59, 91; and masculinity, 262–63; and Messianic Judaism, 186, 188–91; and Native peoples, 112; and racialization of religion, 188–91; and racial reconciliation, 16–17, 18, 20–21, 22–23, 188–91
Proposition 187 (California), 106
Proposition 8 (California), 229, 301n13
prosperity gospel, 43
Protocols of the Elders of Zion, 181
Provan, Charles, 173
Puar, Jasbir, 72, 106, 257
Pulse Nightclub shooting, 233

queer theory: whiteness of, 40
Qu'ran: evangelical readings of, 149, 151

race: and sin, 26, 80–81
raciality, 3
racialization: of Arabs and Arab Americans, 142–43, 155, 176; of class, 59; of Islam, 179; of Jews, 155; of Judaism, 143, 179; of Messianic Jews, 186, 188–91; of Palestinians, 169; of religion, 138, 142–43, 211
racial justice, 82, 140; and class, 66; and the Christian Right, 4; and critical ethnic studies, 2; and gender justice, 239–40, 250–51; and heteronormativity, 211; and LGBT justice, 233
racial reconciliation, 4–5, 8, 14, 22–25; African Americans, focus on, 91–92;

biopolitics of, 285; and Black Lives Matter, 272; and the Christian Right, 4; critiques of, 19, 25, 79–80; emergence of, 16–19; failure of, 20; and gender, 263; identity-based approach of, 32; impact of, 29; and multiculturalism, 17, 25–26, 31; and Native peoples, 110–13, 195; and new evangelicalisms, 40–52; and party politics, 227–29; and racial inclusion, 39, 52; and racialization, 9, 72; and racial justice, 29, 32, 75–80; and racism, 203, 260, 272, 285; and sexism, 260; and social action, 54–55, 95; and white Christian American triumphalism, 35, 111; and whiteness, 29, 52, 91, 267; and white supremacy, 17, 25–26, 54, 77, 113, 267

racism: and Ashkenazi Jews, 165; and ethnic studies, 3; and individualism, 20, 288n7; within progressive groups, 6; and racial prejudice, 54

radical antiviolence movement, 87–89

Rah, Soong-Chan, 16, 22, 42, 77–78, 116–18, 140, 228; on "all lives matter" rhetoric, 270–71; campaign against LifeWay, 72–73; on Christian persecution, 139–40; Emergent Church, critique of, 46–47; seeker church model, critique of, 48; on social justice, 78; on urban missions, 283

Rainer, Thom, 73

Rana, Junaid, 143

Reagan, Ronald, 15; and apartheid, 16

Reaganism: and class, 7

rearticulation: politics of, 6–9

recognition: politics of, 31

Reconciliation Walk, 102–3

Reed, Ralph, 34–35, 70, 160; and Abramoff scandal, 212; class politics of, 59; and Israel, 162; oppression rhetoric of, 68; on racial justice, 57; and racial reconciliation movement, 4, 14

Reformation Project, 268

Relevant (magazine), 44, 70, 278; on trafficking, 254

reproductive justice: as "white," 237

Republican Party: white evangelical support for, 287n2

Rice, Chris, 49

Rice, Emily, 2, 80, 113, 250, 267

Richardson, Rick, 78

Rios, Sandy, 149

Rivers, Eugene, 21, 99, 178, 239

Robeck, Cecil, 292n8

Robertson, Pat, 16, 68, 99, 112, 132, 144; electoral politics of, 220; on Islam, 148, 149; on marijuana, 242

Rodgers, Leonard, 298n20

Rodriguez, Dylan, 140, 226; on multiculturalism, 32, 118; on nonprofit industrial complex, 5

Rodriguez, Samuel, 243–44, 246, 248, 272

Roe v. Wade, 14

Roley, Scott, 79, 111

Rolnick, Addie, 92

Romney, Mitt, 220, 276, 300n6

Rosenberg, Ellen, 287n4

Roth, Gary, 303n7

Rove, Karl, 212

Rushdoony, R. J., 60

Russell, Shari, 2, 206, 265

Rutba House, 49

Said, Edward, 80, 258

Sailiata, Kirisitina, 197

Sale, Kirkpatrick, 123

Salguero, Gabriel, 239

Salomon, Gershon, 164

Salvatierra, Alexia, 2, 87–88, 115, 264–65

same-sex marriage, 68–69, 223, 229–31, 239, 299n26, 301nn13–14, 303n7; and evangelicals of color, 238–39

Sanford, Mark, 213

Sanger, Margaret, 236

SB 1070 (Arizona), 247–48, 302n34

Schaeffer, Francis, 215

Schaeffer, Frank, 215

school prayer, 14

Scofield, C. I., 156

Seabrook, Eric, 239

Sechrest, Love L., 79
secularism: and colonialism, 5; presumed whiteness of, 12; and white supremacy, 5
seeker church model, 42–43
segregation, racial, 14–15; evangelical complicity in, 13; within evangelicalism, 16
Seiple, Robert, 133
Sekulow, Jay, 220
Serving in Mission (SIM), 36–37
settler colonialism, 193
Seu, Andrée, 167–68
Sexton, Jared, 92
sex workers: as "trafficked," 254
Sharon, Ariel, 160, 161
Shea, Nina, 119, 120
Sheldon, Louis, 68
Shepard, Matthew, 68, 69–70
Shohat, Ella, 165
Shorrosh, Anis, 299n24
Shuler, Clarence, 76
Sider, Ron, 62, 144–45, 216, 222, 277
Siebeling, John, 22
Silva, Denise Ferreira da, 3, 39, 80–81; on whiteness, 12
Simmons, Bennie, 19
Simple Way, A, 48, 49
Sizer, Stephen, 155–56, 176, 184
Skinner, Tom, 16
slavery: and anti-Blackness, 253; and ethnic studies, 3; evangelical complicity in, 13; as providential, 94–96; and Southern Baptist Convention, 2; and white supremacy, 253
Smart, Ted, 303n8
Smith, Bailey, 180, 184
Smith, Christian, 20–21, 27–28, 29, 78, 79, 288n9
Smith, Chuck, 161, 172
Smith, Craig, 195
Smith, Efrem, 47
social change, 211; and Israel, 168; and NPIC, 6; pessimism toward, 54
Soerens, Matthew, 245
Soles, Henry, 55

Soulforce, 230
Southern Baptist Convention (SBC): and anti-Blackness, 2; and immigration, 247; on Judaism, 180; missionaries, 131, 137, 294n7; organization of, 2; and racism, 274; racism, apology for, 18; and refugees, 108; Rickshaw Rally, 22, 72–73; and slavery, 2; slavery, apology for, 18, 25; and white supremacy, 2, 9
sovereignty, 208–9
Spade, Dean, 82–83, 86
Spector, Stephen, 159, 182
spiritual optimism, 54
Spotlight (website), 174
Spring, Beth, 291n3
Stackhouse, John, 230
Stand in the Gap rally, 17, 22, 58, 188–89
Stassen, Glen, 178
Stearns, Richard, 215
Stern, David, 169
Stetzer, Ed, 73, 284
Stewart, Keith, 64–65
Stiffler, Matthew, 31–32
Stone, Perry, 147
Stott, John, 297n6
Strait Gate Ministries, 174
Strandberg, Todd, 298n12
Strang, Cameron, 44, 216–17
Strang, Stephen, 85–86, 163–64, 187, 216, 259–60, 272–73, 298n20; Cruz endorsement, 275–76; on Obama, 219, 224, 228–29; Trump endorsement, 276
Stringfellow, Thornton, 1
Sullivan, Andrew, 301n14
Sullivan, Kenneth, 61
Sultan, Wafa, 297n4
supercession theory, 172–75
Swaggart, Jimmy, 16

Taber, Charles, 132
Tapia, Andrés, 18
Tarrants, Tom, 55
Tea Party: and racial backlash, 9, 212; rise of, 215–26
Teeter, David, 109
Terry, Randall, 67

Tharpe, Edgar, 34
Thatcherism: and class, 7
theologians, Indigenous, 2–3
Third World Christians, 26
Three Stars, Lenore, 2, 265
Tiénou, Tite, 3–4, 196–97
Tooley, Mark, 249, 303n4 (conc.)
Toyama-Szeto, Nikki, 2, 71, 255
trafficking, 253–55; and anti-Black racism, 253
triumphalism: white Christian, 35, 111, 118
Trump, Donald, 28; evangelical support for, 9–10, 223, 227, 269, 272, 275–84, 285, 287n2, 303nn4–5 (conc.); and Islamophobia, 155; Muslim ban of, 240
Twiss, Richard, 54, 194, 204

United Evangelical Action (journal), 93; on immigration, 105
United Nations Declaration on the Rights of Indigenous Peoples, 265
United Nations Permanent Forum on Indigenous Issues, 210
Urban Family Council, 261
Usry, Glenn, 98

Vacation Bible School, 22, 201
Vanderslice, Mara, 215
Van Opstal, Sandra Marie, 2, 265
Vasquez, Michael, 268
Vaughn, Judy, 82
Veas, Gabe, 235
veiling, 256–57
Velasco-Sanchez, AnaYelsi, 2, 80, 114, 234, 264
Vines, Jerry, 150
Voice of the Martyrs, 119, 122, 125–26, 134, 135–36
Voices Project, 114
Voices United, 160
Volf, Miroslav, 151–52

Wadsworth, Nancy, 288n7, 288n9
Wagner, C. Peter, 276
Wagner, Donald, 176
Waldman, Marty, 189

Walker-Barnes, Chanequa, 2, 11, 114, 250, 251, 266–67
Wallis, Jim, 76, 215, 217, 222
Walt, Stephen, 162
Walton, Jonathan, 8, 263
Warren, Rick, 90, 214, 218; politics of, 220–23, 300n8
Washington, Raleigh, 190
Washington, Shae, 268
Weary, Dolphus, 30–31
Weber, Timothy, 157, 176, 179, 180–81, 183; on Messianic Judaism, 187
Weheliye, Alexander G., 2, 39, 80, 97; on blackness, 140; on poststructuralism, 41; on whiteness, 12
Weiss, Doug, 261
Westboro Baptist Church, 69
Weyrich, Paul, 221
White, Paula, 275
whiteness: and Christianity, 8; and racial reconciliation, 26
white supremacy: and anti-Blackness, 92; and Christianity, 94, 140; and critical ethnic studies, 3; and evangelicalism, 5, 13; and evangelicals of color, 283; and liberal democracy, 5; Orientalist logics of, 99; and racial reconciliation, 83–84, 86; and religion, 91; and Southern Baptist Convention, 2; and subjectivity, 80–81; as sin, 82
Wilderson, Frank, 140
Williams, Juan, 63
Williams, Reggie, 80
Wilson, Darren, 84
Wilson, Jonathan R., 49
Wilson, Waziyatawin Angela, 192–93
women of color: as in need of saving, 252–58; as threats, 258–64
women of color, evangelical, 252–58; intersectional analysis of, 264–68; marginalization of, 250–51; and racial reconciliation, 250; and social justice, 250
Women of Color Institute, 250, 264
Woodberry, J. Dudley, 150
Woodley, Randy, 38, 194, 203, 205

Working Group on Indigenous Affairs, 210

World (magazine), 38, 71; on abortion, 223; on aid programs, 290n14; on anti-Black racism, 86; anti-poverty efforts, 65; on Asian religions, 292n7; on Christian persecution, 123, 126, 130, 294n7, 296n3; and class, 59, 60, 62, 64, 289n6, 289n14; on homosexuality, 68, 69; on human rights, 295n10; on Hurricane Katrina, 36; on immigration, 105, 243–45, 247, 292nn9–10, 302nn29–30, 302n32; on Islam, 100–101, 144, 147–48, 152, 256, 296n1; on Israel-Palestine conflict, 168; on Judaism, 181; Katrina coverage, 56–57, 288n5; on multiculturalism, 34, 100; on Muslims, 162, 296n3; on nonprofit industry, 290n14; on Obama, 219; oppression rhetoric of, 68; on Palestine, 167, 259; on race, 303n1; on racism, 273; on Tea Party, 225–26; on Trump, 276–77; on women in the military, 303n6

World Christian Gathering of Indigenous Peoples (WCGIP), 113

World Indigenous Conference, 114

World Social Forum, 210

World Vision, 64, 135, 172, 299n26

Wright, Bradley, 93

Wurmbrand, Richard, 119

Wynter, Sylvia, 39, 80

Wytsma, Ken, 23–24

Yakos, Marvin, 149–50, 297n8

Yancey, George, 78

Yancey, Philip, 137, 178, 224–25, 295n9, 297n4; on Islam, 153, 235

Yang, Jenny, 2, 264–65

Yellow Bird, Michael, 192–93

Ye'or, Bat, 101

Yep, Jeanette, 23

Yong, Amos, 79

Young, G. Douglas, 185

Youngblood, Gene, 142, 143

Youth-Reach, 65

Zacharias, Ravi, 295n1

Zennah Ministries, 256, 257

Zimmerman, George, 85, 86, 272

Zionism: Protestant liberal support for, 158–59. *See also* Christian Zionism

www.ingramcontent.com/pod-product-compliance
Lightning Source LLC
Chambersburg PA
CBHW032011300426
44117CB00008B/992